A Garland Series

OUTSTANDING
DISSERTATIONS
IN THE

FINE
ARTS

Critical Corpus of the Mosaic Pavements on the Greek Mainland, Fourth/Sixth Centuries
with Architectural Surveys

Marie Spiro

In two volumes
Vol. I

Garland Publishing Inc., New York and London

1978

All volumes in this series are printed
on acid-free, 250-year-life paper.

Library of Congress Cataloging in Publication Data

Spiro, Marie.
    Critical corpus of the mosaic pavements on the Greek
mainland, fourth/sixth centuries, with architectural
surveys.

    (Outstanding dissertations in the fine arts)
    Originally presented as the author's thesis, New
York University, 1975.
    Bibliography: v.   , p.
    Includes index.
    1. Pavements, Mosaic--Greece. 2. Mosaics, Greek.
3. Greece--Antiquities. I. Title. II. Series.
NA3765.S65   1978   738.5   77-94716
ISBN 0-8240-3250-0

Printed in the United States of America

Critical Corpus of the Mosaic Pavements on
the Greek Mainland, Fourth/Sixth Centuries
with
Architectural Surveys

Marie Spiro
February, 1975

A dissertation in the Department of Fine Arts
submitted to the faculty of the Graduate School of
Arts and Science in partial fulfillment of the
requirements for the degree of Doctor of
Philosophy at New York University

Approved

(SIGNED)_____
                Research Adviser

TABLE OF CONTENTS

LIST OF SITES

PREFACE

The purpose of this dissertation is to present a comprehensive regional corpus of the secular and Christian tessellated pavements on the Greek mainland which date between the late fourth and the late sixth centuries and to place them within their architectural contexts. No comparable study has been undertaken and the main sources consist of excavation reports which by their very nature present limited information and few photographs.

Although mosaic pavements abound in every country of the Roman Empire, it is only in recent years that scholars began to recognize their importance in regard to the development of painting during the late antique and the early medieval periods. As a result, regional corpora have appeared on the mosaics of Gaul, Germany, and Switzerland,[1] and an international association was founded in 1963, AIEMA (Association International pour l'Etude de la Mosaïque Antique), which through its publications[2] and colloquia serves as a significant force and influence in this field. At its first colloquium in 1963, guidelines were established

[1] H. Stern, Recueil général des mosaïques de la Gaule. 2 vols., Paris, 1957-67; K. Parlasca, Die römischen Mosaiken in Deutschland, Berlin, 1959; V. von Gonzenbach, Die römischen Mosaiken der Schweiz, Basel, 1961.

[2] Bulletin d'information de l'association internationale pour l'étude de la mosaïque antique, fascicules 1-5 (1968-73).

for the investigation and presentation of mosaic pavements[3]
which influenced in varying degrees the form and content of
subsequent corpora. The effects can be seen in the first
publications to appear under the aegis of AIEMA in 1967,
1970, and 1971 which form three fascicules in A Corpus of
the Ancient Mosaics of Italy,[4] in two fascicules of A Corpus
of the Mosaics of Tunisia,[5] and in the present Corpus of
Greek Pavements.

The project for a Greek corpus was initiated by
Professor Irving Lavin who spent two years on research and
field investigations. When, at his suggestion, I assumed
the responsibility of completing the project, he generously
shared his archival, descriptive, and photographic material
and was a constant source of knowledge, advice, and encouragement. His invaluable records, now in the possession of
the Dumbarton Oaks Center for Byzantine Studies in Washing-
ton, facilitated the task of collecting the published and
unpublished data on the pavements and, moreover, furnished

---

[3]T. Kraus, "Autour d'un corpus international des
mosaiques Greco-Romaines," La mosaique Greco-Romaine, Paris,
1965.

[4]M. L. Marricone Matini, Mosaici Antichi in Italia.
Regione prima. Roma: Reg. X Palatium, Rome, 1967; G. Becatti
et al., Mosaici Antichi in Italia. Regione settima. Baccano:
Villa Romana, Rome, 1970; M. L. Marricone Matini, Mosaici
Antichi in Italia. Studi Monografico (1). Pavimenti di
signino repubblicani di Roma e dintorni, Rome, 1971.

[5]M. A. Alexander, M. Ennaifer et al., Corpus des
mosaïques de Tunisie. Utique: Fascicule 1, Insulae I-II-III,
Tunis, 1973; C. Dulière, Corpus des mosaïques de Tunisie.
Utique: Fascicule 2, Les mosaïques in situ en dehors des
Insulae I-II-III, Tunis, 1974.

important documentation for many pavements which were
destroyed or inaccessible to me (14-20, pls. 35-57; 21, pls.
59-61; 23, pls. 65-68; 29-33, pls. 77-80, 82; 34, pl. 85; 35,
pl. 88; 59-60, pls. 159, 161-163; 62, pl. 171; 66, pls. 182-
188; 72, pls. 220-221; 102-104; 116-122, pls. 403-404, 408,
410-411). Another contribution to the corpus came from
Jean-Pierre Sodini's catalogue of Greek pavements[6] which was
published during the last phase of my research. Although it
is limited to mosaics in ecclesiastical structures, and lacks
archaeological, architectural, and epigraphical data, his
catalogue contains very useful reference material and was a
means to verify the amount and accuracy of many of my
entries. It is my hope that the corpus does justice to the
work of my two predecessors, but especially to the scholarly
and personal contributions of Professor Lavin which cannot
be overestimated.

The Corpus of Greek Pavements synthesizes and analyzes
all the available factual, descriptive, and pictorial material on two hundred and twenty-eight published and unpublished
pavements from over ninety sites in Greece. There are
archaeological and architectural summaries, ground plans,
when available, many showing the distribution of the mosaics
(pls. 76, 103, 114, 118, 146, 157, 189, 198, 237, 295, 315,
452, 568, 613, 618, 628, 633, 647, 676, 677), and

[6]"Mosaïques paléochrétiennes de Grèce," _BCH_, 94 (1970),
pp. 699-753; idem, "Mosaïques paléochrétiennes de Grèce:
compléments," _BCH_, 95 (1971), pp. 581-584.

photographic and bibliographical references. In the mosaic
entries, data such as the overall and individual dimensions
of the designs, and the size, color, and material of the
tesserae (if known) are presented along with precise descriptions and comments on the mosaics and their relationship to
their architectural environment. In addition, internal and
external evidence is used to date most of the pavements. As
a regional study, therefore, it will be useful to all scholars working in this field. Equally important, however, is
that it will help to fill a major lacuna in the area of
early medieval pavement decoration. Unlike other corpora so
far, which deal primarily with Roman mosaics, the majority
of the material comes from a Christian context (one hundred
and fifty pavements can be definitely assigned to ecclesiastical structures). While it is not within the scope of
this corpus to examine in detail the problems of the specific
function of each area of a church or chapel as it is reflected in the mosaics, their disposition and orientation supply
important information on the formal arrangement and internal
divisions of these architectural units, and on the form and
position of such ecclesiastical furnishings as the clergy
bench, ambon, chancel barrier, and synthronon. All these
features have been incorporated into the section on architecture which forms a fundamental part of this study.

The corpus serves as a foundation for subsequent research
in other fields as well. It provides important data for the
art historian on stylistic developments and iconography

during a period from which little is preserved in other media. To the architectural historian, it offers for the first time an analysis of many secular and religious buildings and their various paving materials. The historian benefits from such a study because it can be used to determine certain political, social, and economic currents and cross currents by examining the rise, distribution, and size of secular and Christian communities and the quality of their buildings and decoration. For the epigraphist, there are transcriptions and emendations, and for the general reader, translations of all the preserved inscriptions which, for the most part, are dedicatory.

In the future, it my intention to focus on certain monuments and problems. I have been granted permission by Professor Vladimir Milojčić of the University of Heidelberg to publish the purely ornamental pavements of a basilica which he recently excavated at Demetrias (130-138, pls. 420-444). Another investigation will center on the figural mosaics belonging to a basilica at Delphi (82-83, pls. 240-286). I plan to use the pavements in these two churches as a nucleus for a comprehensive study of all the geometric and figural pavements in this corpus. In undertaking these studies, it will be possible to evaluate more decisively the indigenous and foreign characteristics of the mosaics, and to determine their specific relationship to the overall development of pavements in the Greek East.

A significant contribution to the study of pavements in

the Greek East was made by Professor Ernst Kitzinger who
established a chronological framework for pavements between
the ages of Constantine and Justinian.[7] This framework
served as the main basis for dating the Greek pavements and,
in fact, its viability and accuracy are substantiated by
many of the findings in this study.

The chronological scope of the corpus, fourth through
sixth centuries, is represented by such pavements as those
belonging to PERIOD I in Basilica Alpha at Demetrias (130-
132) and those in a Villa at Hermione (67-68). Although the
Demetrias mosaics are aniconic and somber, and those in the
Villa have polychromatic figural representations, this does
not mean that they reflect a consistent, evolutionary pattern. Rather, this development is only part of the picture.
Nor is the different function of each building an important
consideration. On the contrary, there is sufficient evidence that pavement decoration in both secular and religious
buildings developed along parallel, if not identical, lines.
The similar stylistic and iconographic programs at Demetrias
Alpha (130-135) and the Tetraconch at Athens (6-9), Tegea
(69-70), Corinth (42) and Argos (55), and at Amphipolis Alpha
(213) and Hermione (67) clearly establish the fluidity with
which they passed from one context to another.

The earliest pavements in the corpus date to around the

---

[7]Mosaic Pavements in the Greek East, pp. 209-223; idem,
Mosaics in the Greek East, pp. 341-352.

late fourth or early fifth century. They are distributed
all over Greece: Athens (1; 2-3; 6-9; 21); Epidauros (44-
49); Arkitsa (88-92); Demetrias (130-135); Nikopolis (168);
Dion (178-179); Tsiphliki (196), and clearly reflect a
stylistic and iconographic trend which is distinguished by
"unified geometric designs over large open spaces" containing few if any organic filling motifs.[8] They are simple in
design and contain homogeneous decorative schemes consisting,
for the most part, of various combinations of interlocking,
intersecting, or juxtaposed octagons,[9] circles, squares, and
rectangles which are articulated by simple bands or fillets.
They clothe the surface with close-knit, two-dimensional,
textural patterns which are inscribed with simple geometric
or geometricized floral motifs. The geometricity of the
pavements is heightened by simple color schemes which in two,
perhaps three,[10] buildings are monochromatic in their general effect and emphasis, with color serving primarily as
highlights (88-92; 130-135).

Although aniconic pavements continue to be popular in
the fifth and sixth centuries, they are transformed into
colorful and frequently complex carpets articulated by decorative bands, not simple, flat ones, and enclosed by borders
which are very often wide (see, for example, 77-78; 117-118;

---

[8]Kitzinger, Mosaics in the Greek East, pp. 343-344.

[9]Only one pavement contains an interlace (6, pls. 14-16).

[10]Dion Alpha, vide infra, p. 525, n. 880.

157-158; 220). Along with the more traditional interlocking, intersecting and juxtaposed designs, interlaces appear at Nikopolis Beta (157) and Amphipolis Beta (220) to spread their pulsating curvilinear patterns across the surface.

The embellishment of the geometric carpet is also marked by an increase in the size of the individual units of the designs which create large insets for the abstract filling motifs (compare, for example, 15, pls. 44-46 and 44, pls. 104, 106; 16, pl. 108 and 118, pls. 406-407) and for organic ones which begin to appear around the middle of the fifth century.[11] Their introduction represents the second trend in the development of Greek pavements in the fifth and sixth centuries. At first, the repertory consists only of land and sea animals, and plants which are rigidly contained with the insets created by the geometric configurations like those in the Ilissos Basilica (10-13), the villa at Epidauros (50-51) and Anchialos Gamma (105, 108). Later, toward the end of the fifth century, they also occupy large, independent panels (189-190; 191; 224) surrounded by rinceaux or geo-metric borders. The popularity of these organic forms, whether in small insets (95a, 97, 99b; 115; 150, 152a, 153, 156; 206, 207, 213a,c) or large panels (95b, 98, 99a, 100a; 152b, 153d, 154-155; 211a, 213b) continues into the sixth century.

---

[11]Unlike some floors, the basic geometric design is never replaced by "organic motifs such as florets and rinceaux." Kitzinger, ibid., pp. 347-348.

This figural repertory is enriched by the appearance around the turn of the century of representations of the months and the seasons (42; 69-70; 55b; 75a; 83) and hunters and fishermen (57; 75b; 154-155; 211b). The plethora of figural pavements in such churches as those at Klapsi, Nikopolis (Alpha), and Amphipolis (Alpha) clearly reflects the scope of the mosaicists' imagery in the sixth century and also the progress of the stylistic development. For, by this period, the three-dimensional, modeled forms of the earliest fauna at Epidauros (pl. 115), Ilissos (pl. 32) and Anchialos Gamma (pls. 363-365, 368-374), have been changed into forms which are arranged across the surface and made to respect and reflect its solidity. Thus, whether the figures occupy geometric insets or large panels, any illusion of pictorial space is contradicted by their weightless, unmodeled shapes which project them onto the same plane as the surrounding borders. A comparison of a familiar scene composed of confronting stags on either side of a fountain at Akrini (189-190, pl. 620), Longos (197, pls. 638-640), Amphipolis Alpha (213b, pl. 667), and Hermione (67, pls. 190, 195-196) illustrates the stylistic progression from the second half of the fifth to the late sixth centuries. The Akrini scene represents the first preserved stage. The flora and fauna are naturalistic in movement, pose, and articulation while those at Longos and Amphipolis are more rigid and abstract. The panel at Hermione, the latest in the series, reflects the final stage. All the objects have

become a means of filling the scene with attenuated patterns
and silhouettes of great linearity and variety creating,
thereby, a kind of intricate and delicate polychromatic network across the surface.

Although a somewhat clear picture of the iconographic
and stylistic development of Greek mosaic pavements emerges
from this study, I realize that there are still many problems and conflicts. It is my hope that the Greek Corpus
will encourage mosaic specialists to produce regional
corpora for other areas in the Greek East so that these
matters will be resolved.

* * * * *

A work of this scope could never have been produced
without the extensive training in architecture and mosaics I
received at the Institute of Fine Arts and in Tunisia while
a research associate for the Corpus of the Mosaics of
Tunisia. I would like to express my gratitude, therefore, to
four professors whose teaching provided me with the means to
complete successfully this project. I single out in a very
special way Professor Irving Lavin of the Institute for
Advanced Study, my Research Adviser and the initiator of the
project,[12] whose brilliant seminar on mosaic pavements stim-
ulated my interest in this relatively new field of concen-
tration. He convinced his students that significant pictorial documents were to be found not only at eye level or in

---

[12]Vide supra, pp. lvii-lviii.

the upper regions of buildings, but, also, on floors which
served "the ignominious function of being walked on."[13]

I would also like to express my gratitude to Professors
Hugo H. Buchthal and Richard Krautheimer for their stimulat-
ing courses and seminars and for their guidance and
encouragement during my attendance at the Institute of Fine
Arts. I also owe a debt of gratitude to Professor Margaret
A. Alexander, Co-Director of the Tunisian project, who
taught me how to organize all the data on mosaic pavements
and to present them with clarity and brevity.

The research for this corpus was conducted in Greece
with the aid of a Fulbright-Hays Fellowship and one from the
Greek government. I am indebted to Professor Henry S.
Robinson, the former Director of the American School of
Classical Studies, for the use of its excellent facilities
and to Professor A. K. Orlandos, Secretary of the Greek
Archaeological Service, for his advice and help. Finally, I
would like to thank Dumbarton Oaks for granting me two
fellowships which enabled me to benefit from its superb
library and photographic archives. The interest and support
of each member of the faculty and staff facilitated the
progress of the corpus.

Among those who have helped in putting together this
work, Georgine Szalay Reed deserves a special note of thanks.

_____

[13] I. Lavin, "The Hunting Mosaics of Antioch and their
Sources," DOP, 17 (1963), p. 181.

^ ^ ^

She saved me from innumerable days of frustration,
particularly by organizing the list of illustrations,
arranging and mounting the photographs, and writing in the
Greek inscriptions.

ORGANIZATION OF THE CORPUS

The corpus is divided into general geographic regions from Attica and the Peloponnesus to Thrace, and subdivided into cities and towns. The information on each site is also divided into two sections which, by and large, follow the format of the first two fascicules of A Corpus of the Mosaics of Tunisia.[14]

The first part consists of an archaeological and architectural survey of the building (if preserved), its chronology,[15] and a bibliography which includes not only major reports but notices in To Ergon, the Bulletin de Correspondance Hellénique, the Journal of Hellenic Studies, and the Archäologischer Anzeiger. Although notices of excavations are usually included in every journal devoted to archaeological activities in Greece, I have selected these four because they are accurate and more detailed than the others. The bibliographical list is followed by one in which relevant architectural illustrations with captions are cited. When published illustrations are reproduced in the corpus, their page and/or figure numbers are followed by "=" signs.

The second part contains an introduction in which the

---

[14]Vide supra, p. lvii, n. 5.

[15]Many summaries include the phrase "no datable archaeological finds were unearthed or reported." I use it whenever the excavator does not state that no datable finds were unearthed.

pavements are analyzed, compared to other Greek mosaics, and
dated. Some entries, however, have little comparative
material because either archaeological, architectural, or
epigraphical data provide substantial chronological evidence,
or I agree with the stylistic analysis and dating of the
mosaics presented by the excavator or a mosaic specialist.[16]
This introduction is followed by an abbreviated bibliography
which cites the page and catalogue numbers of a check list
of Greek pavements published in 1970,[17] and by a reference to
the ground plan of the building. The last section comprises
the actual inventory of the mosaics on the site with consecu-
tive numeration for each pavement. Each entry begins with
the catalogue and room numbers,[18] immediately followed by the
size of the room, if known,[19] and a brief notation of certain architectural features which affect the pavement.
Then all the factual data are given which include the overall
and individual dimensions of the pavement and the design
(starting with the north-south axis), and the size, material,
and spacing of the tesserae. This is followed by a general

---

[16]For the first, see 6-9; 130-138; for the second, see
44-49; 88-92.

[17]Vide supra, p. lxiii, n. 6.

[18]Mosaics for which no architectural context survives
are simply listed as fragments or pavements.

[19]Sometimes, reports on buildings which were destroyed
or overgrown omit individual measurements and contain plans
with no keys (see, for example, 4-5, pl. 6). When this
occurs the phrase "no dimensions published" is used.

description of the pavement which precedes a detailed analysis of its parts: surround, if visible; framing; field. If all the colors could not be included in the analysis, then a separate heading, "additional colors," is inserted at the end.[20] The date of the pavement is then noted along with bibliographical and pictorial sources.

Most of the entries lack in varying degrees certain factual or descriptive data. This is because the archaeological reports contain, for the most part, few dimensions, incomplete descriptions and color notations, and bad photographs of pavements which were destroyed or inaccessible to me during my research in Greece. It is hoped that publications such as the Tunisian fascicules will serve to educate the archaeologist in the proper methods of recording and presenting the mosaic data.

---

[20]Since white is commonly employed in surrounds and the grounds of the design, it is omitted from the color notations.

PART I. ATTICA

ATHENS

Metroon

The clearing of the Metroon and other adjacent buildings
on the west side of the Agora was begun in 1896-97 and
resumed in 1907 and 1908, with supplementary clearing in
1934 and 1935.[1]

During its lifetime, between the second half of the
second century B. C. and 267 A. D., the Hellenistic Metroon
functioned both as a depository for the public records and
as a sanctuary for the Mother of the Gods. The complex was
erected over the foundations of the Old Bouleterion[2] and
consisted of four juxtaposed rooms (pl. 3) which were united
along the east side by a wide colonnaded porch, I. The
large room to the north, II, served as the sanctuary proper
while to the south the first and third rooms, III, V, contained the archives. These rooms were separated by a

---

[1]H. A. Thompson, Hesperia, 6 (1937), pp. 172-217; hereafter cited as Thompson.

[2]When the Bouleterion was moved to its present position
on the west side between 411 and 405 B. C., the old building
was converted into a cult place for the Mother of the Gods.
The extent and plan of the first phase of the Metroon are
not clearly defined (Thompson, pp. 192-195, 209-212, 215-
217, pls. VI-VIII).

passageway, IV, which led from the front of the building to
the New Bouleterion to the west.

In 267 A. D. the Metroon was severely damaged by the
Herulians and fell into disuse. In the early fifth century
the building underwent limited repairs and alterations among
which was the installation of a mosaic pavement in Room III.[3]
Although the function of the building during this period is
problematic, it is possible that it served as a private
residence.[4] In a later building phase, Room III was subdivided into three compartments by walls which rested directly on the pavement and an olive press with a rectangular
basin was installed.[5] Subsequently, the building was again
abandoned and was covered by Byzantine and Turkish
structures.

On the basis of a coin hoard found under the mosaic
floor in Room III, the repair of the Metroon is datable to

---

[3]Below the mosaic toward the south side of the room,
Thompson found two long rectangular trenches with traces of
fire which may have belonged to a tavern or eating place of
some kind (pp. 198-199). The chronology of this level is
not discussed.

[4]Thompson, pp. 211-212. In a recent study of this and
other buildings in the Agora, Room III is reconstructed with
an apse on its west side. Since the excavation reports and
plans omit this feature, its addition is curious. (See
H. A. Thompson and R. E. Wycherly, The Athenian Agora. 14.
The Agora of Athens [Princeton, 1972], pp. 210-211, pl. 9.)

[5]Thompson, pp. 201-202, fig. 123.

the early fifth century.[6]

Bibliography. AA, 49 (1934), p. 127; H. A. Thompson, Hesperia, 6 (1937), pp. 172-217; idem, JRS, 49 (1959), pp. 66-67; J. Travlos, Poleodomikē exelixis tōn Athēnōn, Athens, 1960, p. 130; A. Frantz, DOP, 19 (1965), p. 196; H. A. Thompson and R. E. Wycherly, The Athenian Agora, 14. The Agora of Athens, Princeton, 1972, pp. 210-211.

Illustrations. H. A. Thompson, Hesperia, 6 (1937), p. 116, fig. 61 (view from east), p. 201, fig. 123 (Room II), p. 219, fig. 126 (west side of Agora: restored), pl. VI = our pl. 3, pl. VIII (New Bouleterion, Propylon, Hellenistic Metroon: restored).

No. 1

1   Room III (7.95 x 15.65). The pavement was laid up to a

stairway to the east and a long feature, probably a

stone bench, toward the south; covered later by internal

walls and an olive press with a rectangular basin. Pls. 4-5.

Framing, to north and west only: between 2.00 and 2.40.

Field, including fillet: 3.00 x 12.60. Marble and limestone

tesserae (average, 0.025 sq) set 2-4mm apart. Setting bed-

nucleus: "crumbly lime mortar containing much pounded

brick."[7]

Off-centered panel decorated with a simple geometric design

which is enclosed at least to north and west by a double

---

[6]Thompson, p. 200. Among the identifiable coins the earliest bore the name of Constantius II (326-361) and the latest that of Arcadius (395-408).

[7]Thompson, pp. 199-200, n. 1.

border. On the east side it meets a threshold panel in front of the entrance.[8]

Surround: blue tesserae in rows parallel to the walls.

Framing: bluish black fillet; outer border, row of medallions (0.45 diam) set 60 centimeters apart and joined by single bluish black bars (two fillets). The medallions alternate in color (blue and pink) and are outlined in bluish black; bluish black fillet; blue band; bluish black fillet; inner border, undulating bluish black rinceau (two fillets) composed of rigidly arranged scrolls filled alternately with single blue and pink ivy leaves, outlined in bluish black. Springing from each stem is a small curving tendril; bluish black fillet; blue band.

Field, framed by a bluish black fillet: blue and pink intersecting circles forming white concave-sided squares which are inscribed with pink serrate-edged squares. The design is bisected along the margins. Along the south side of the field there are traces of a white surround with parallel rows of tesserae which may well indicate that this side of the pavement was covered by a feature, perhaps a free-standing stone bench.[9]

Threshold panel to east, "between the central panel, the stairway and the east end of the hypothetical bench:"

[8]Since its discovery, additional descruction has occurred to the east side. Judging from the plan (pl. 3), the double border did not turn south but terminated at the east wall. On the west side it probably continued up to the south wall.

[9]Thompson, p. 199.

oblique grid forming squares which are inscribed with small
squares.[10]

Early fifth century; on the basis of coins found under the
pavement.

Illustrations. H. A. Thompson, Hesperia, 6 (1937), p.
198, fig. 121 = our pl. 4, p. 199, fig. 122 = our pl. 5,
pl. VI = our pl. 3.

Private House

On the south side of the Acropolis, midway between the
Odeion of Herodus Atticus and the Theatre of Dionysos, the
north part of a building was discovered during the construction of the new Saint Dionysos the Areopagite Avenue (pl.
2). Since the building lay in the path of the proposed
avenue, it was destroyed.[11]

At least five levels of habitation were exposed, the
earliest represented by a fifth century B. C. house of which
traces survive of a polygonal wall (P, pl. 6). Its east
side was covered in the fourth century B. C. by another
house consisting of a central court with a cistern and
flanking rooms (Ω, pl. 6). This building was destroyed by
fire in the first century B. C., possibly during the invasion

---

[10]Ibid.

[11]J. Meliades, Praktika, 1955, pp. 46-50, p. 39, fig. 1
(A on plan); hereafter cited as Meliades.

of Sulla.[12] The subsequent building history of the site was concentrated along the south side and consisted of long periods of desolation followed by renewed activity. Over three centuries passed before the next building, a long rectangular hall (5.40 x 10.40 max), was erected ($\Sigma \top$, pl. 6). This structure, oriented east-west, was terminated by an inscribed, semi-circular apse (2.60 long) to the west. Since it was unfinished at the time of its destruction in the third century A. D., its function could not be determined.[13] Another period of desolation followed which lasted until the fourth building was installed more than a century later. This building (32.00 wide), oriented north-south, is by far the largest and most richly furnished (X, pl. 6).[14] The exposed north side contains a central hall, I (6.40 max x 9.60), which is terminated by a semi-circular apse, II (4.40 diam), and flanked by rooms and corridors, III-VI. The apse is raised above the rectangular hall[15] and is

---

[12]Meliades, p. 46.

[13]Meliades, p. 47.

[14]Traces of the south side of the building were found in the courtyards of some modern houses south of the avenue. If the shaded area in the plan of the site is intended to show the southern extension of the building, then its over-all length was around 60 meters (pl. 2; Meliades, p. 39, fig. 1).

[15]Although not noted by Meliades, it appears that the apse was "partially closed by orthostates." This was first noted by A. K. Orlandos (To Ergon, 1955, p. 8) and then picked up by other journals (BCH, 80 [1956], p. 232; JHS, 76 [1956], Supplement, p. 6).

decorated with three semi-circular and four semi-hexagonal
niches on its upper surface and marble revetment below (pl.
8). Single niches also decorate the center of each wall in
the rectangular exedra to the north of the apse, III, and
another is built into the west wall of a small shrine room,
VII (2.00 x 3.00), on the east side of the building. In the
shrine room were found a reused marble table or bench for
offerings[16] and a relief of the godess Cybele on the wall
above it. One entrance to the building was located on the
northeast side but it was subsequently blocked by a later
structure (Σ , pl. 6; see following entry, 4-5).

The building has been tentatively identified as a private house which, as evidenced by the large apsidal hall,
probably had a public function as well. H. A. Thompson
excavated two other buildings in the vicinity with the same
plan and suggests that the apsidal rooms may have served as
classrooms or lecture halls.[17] Since Marinos describes the
official residence of Proclus, head of the Neoplatonic
Academy, as being in the vicinity of the Asklepeion, near the
Theatre of Dionysos and visible from the Acropolis, it has
been suggested that this building was his residence and that

---

[16]Its front was carved with a classical grave relief of
Dexiōxis (Meliades, pls. 6b and 7a).

[17]Hesperia, 28 (1959), pp. 104-105; idem JRS, 49 (1959),
p. 68. See also, J. Travlos, Poleodomikē exelixis tōn
Athēnōn, Athens, 1960, pp. 130-134, p. 133 figs. 83-84; A.
Frantz, DOP, 19 (1963), pp. 193-195; idem, Hesperia, 35
(1966), p. 379.

of his predecessors Plutarch and Syrianus.[18] Indeed, the
chronology of this building which, on archaeological evidence, is datable to around 400[19] coincides with the
beginning of Plutarch's tenure as head of the Academy[20]
and its abandonment in the sixth century with the closing of
the schools of philosophy in 529.[21]

Bibliography. J. Meliades, Praktika, 1955, pp. 46-50;
H. A. Thompson, Hesperia, 28 (1959), pp. 104-105; idem, JRS,
49 (1959), p. 68; J. Travlos, Poleodomike exelixis tōn
Athenōn, Athens, 1960, pp. 130-134; A. Frantz, DOP, 19
(1965), pp. 193-195; idem, Hesperia, 35 (1966), p. 379.

Illustrations. J. Meliades, Praktika, 1955, p. 39, fig. 1
(topographical plan of site), pl. 3b = our pl. 6, pl. 4b =
our pl. 7, pl. 5 = our pl. 8.

Nos. 2-3

Aniconic geometric mosaics pave the large apsidal hall,
I-II, filling it with shimmering, curvilinear designs in
various combinations of reds, blues, yellow and white.
Except for a few unpublished drawings[22] and two distant

---

[18]Meliades, pp. 48-49; Frantz, DOP, 19 (1963), p. 193.
Marinos, Vita Procli, ed. J. Boissonade, Leipzig, 1814, pp.
74-75, reprint ed., Amsterdam: Hakkert, 1966.

[19]Meliades, p. 48.

[20]Late fourth century to around 431 to 432 (A. Frantz,
Acts of the VIIth International Congress of Christian
Archaeology, Trier, 1965, p. 528.

[21]The site was uninhabited until the eleventh or
twelfth century when a building was erected on the east side
(Meliades, pp. 47-48).

[22]I would like to take this opportunity to thank Mr.
John Travlos for permitting me to study his drawings of the

views of the mosaics (pls. 7-8), no information is available.
On the basis of stratigraphic and other archaeological evidence, the building and its mosaic program can be assigned to
around 400.[23] It is at this time that Athens began to be
rebuilt after centuries of desolation.[24] Other early
buildings associated with this program also contain purely
geometric carpets (1; 4-5; 6-9; 21; 22).

Pavements destroyed.

2 Room I (6.40 max x 9.60). Hall; south side unexcavated.
   Pl. 8.
   No published information on dimensions and material.

Polychrome pavement comprising a curvilinear design with
geometric filling motifs.[25]

Framing: wide white band; black double fillet; outer
border, wide band decorated with an imbrication pattern composed of alternating light blue/white and pink/white scales,
outlined in black; black double fillet; inner border, black
crowstep pattern.

Field, framed by a black double fillet: two-strand

---

pavements which will be published in his forthcoming book on
the Early Christian and Byzantine monuments of Athens.

[23]Meliades, p. 48.

[24]H. A. Thompson, JRS, 49 (1959), p. 66.

[25]My descriptions of this pavement and the succeeding
one are based primarily on the drawings of J. Travlos (vide
supra, pp. 8-9, n. 22.)

interlace (light blue/l white; yellow/l white, outlined in
black) on a yellow ground forming circles and ellipses which
are inscribed with geometric motifs (for a similar design,
see 6, pls. 14-16). Filling the yellow interstices are
light blue squares set on edge inscribed with red, blue, and
white crosses which follow no chromatic sequence.

Early fifth century.

   Illustration. J. Meliades, *Praktika*, 1955, pl. 5 = our
pl. 8.

3   Room II (4.40 diam). Apse. Pl. 8.
   No published information on dimensions and material.

Polychrome pavement decorated with scales and bordered by an
interlace.
   Framing: black fillet; border, two-strand interlace
(light blue; pink, outlined in black) forming circles which
are inscribed with small light blue circles.
   Field: imbrication pattern composed of scales which are
chromatically identical to those in the border of the hall
to the south (2).

Early fifth century.

   Illustration. J. Meliades, *Praktika*, 1955, pl. 5 = our
pl. 8.

Building

During the clearing of part of a large private house on the south side of the Acropolis (2-3, pl. 2),[26] traces were found of a second building, which overlay its northeast corner (Σ , pl. 6), and two mosaic pavements. Both buildings were destroyed when Saint Dionysos the Areopagite Avenue was completed.

The south side of the building (pl. 9) contains a rectangular room, I, with a well on its northwest side which was surmounted by a reused marble arch. A passageway to the north leads to another sector, II, which was only partially cleared. Both areas are decorated with polychrome geometric pavements which are laid up to a mosaic threshold panel. Although the archaeological report terms this structure an addition to the private house,[27] the evidence contradicts this attribution. The plan and photographs show no communicating door between the two buildings and there appears to be over a 1.50 meter difference in their levels (pls. 7, 9). The isolation of the higher, north structure and its curious orientation suggest that it may have been part of an independent building which continued northward.

Although no datable archaeological finds were unearthed or reported, the secure chronology of around 400 for the

---

[26]J. Meliades, pp. 48-49.

[27]J. Meliades, p. 48.

south building provides a <u>terminus post quem</u> and the sixth century abandonment of the site an <u>ante quem</u>.[28] Given the differences in their levels, it is probable that some time elapsed between the completion of the south building and the erection of the second building.

Bibliography. J. Meliades, <u>Praktika</u>, 1955, pp. 48-49; A. K. Orlandos, <u>To Ergon</u>, 1955, pp. 9-10; <u>BCH</u>, 80 (1956), pp. 232-234.

Illustrations. J. Meliades, <u>Praktika</u>, 1955, pl. 3b = our pl. 6, pl. 4b = our pl. 7, pl. 7b = our pl. 9.

Nos. 4-5

The floors of Rooms I and II were paved with complex polychrome mosaics composed of curvilinear geometric designs in combinations of blues, reds, yellow and white. Except for a photograph (pl. 9) and a schematic drawing,[29] no description of the pavements exists. They can be assigned to a period no later than the sixth century and no earlier than around the middle or second half of the fifth century.

Pavements destroyed.

4 Room I (no dimensions published). Separated from Room II (5) by a wall with a central doorway across which the pavement continues. Pl. 9.

No published information on dimensions and material.

[28]<u>Vide supra</u>, p. 8.

[29]<u>Vide supra</u>, pp. 8-9, nn. 22, 25.

Purely geometric pavement decorated with a polychrome curvilinear design.

Framing: black fillet; narrow white band; black fillet; border, row of tangent lozenges inscribed with geometric motifs; narrow white fillet.

Field, framed by a black double fillet: two-strand chain forming squares set on edge which appear to enclose single concave-sided squares.

Threshold between Rooms I and II: imbrication pattern composed of scales fanning northward.

Between the middle or second half of the fifth century and the sixth century.

Illustration. J. Meliades, *Praktika*, 1955, pl. 7b = our pl. 9.

5   Room II (no dimensions published). Separated from Room I
    (4) by a wall with a central doorway across which the pavement continues. Pl. 9.

No published information on dimensions and material.

Purely geometric pavement decorated with a polychrome curvilinear design.

Surround, preserved only to west: tesserae in rows parallel to the walls.

Framing: black fillet; narrow white band; black fillet; border, two rows of intersecting circles forming concavesided squares; black fillet; narrow white band.

Field, framed by a black fillet: three-strand interlace of alternating circles and squares, outlined in black, which are inscribed with Solomon's knots, zig-zags, checkerboards, stylized rosettes with agitated leaves, and other motifs.[30]

Between the middle or second half of the fifth century and the sixth century.

Illustration. J. Meliades, *Praktika*, 1955, pl. 7b = our pl. 9.

Tetraconch

The large tetraconch, situated between Ares and Aiolou Streets (pl. 2), was partially excavated in 1885 and re-excavated in 1950.[31] In 1970 the site was cleared of debris which had accumulated since the second excavation bringing to light for the first time the southwest sector.[32]

The building (pl. 12) overlays the eastern half of an elongated rectangular pool (ca. 55.00 long), with semicircular termini which decorated the central courtyard of a Library built by the Emperor Hadrian (117-138) and destroyed

---

[30]This description is based solely on the drawing by Mr. John Travlos (*vide supra*, pp. 8-9, nn. 22, 25).

[31]For a summary of the earlier bibliography and excavations, see M. A. Sisson *BSR*, 11 (1929), pp. 50-53; hereafter cited as Sisson; J. Travlos, *Praktika*, 1950, pp. 41-42; hereafter cited as Travlos.

[32]G. Dontas, *AAA*, 3, 2 (1970), pp. 169-170, figs. 6-7.

by the Herulians in 267. Axially oriented, the tetraconch
(pl. 11) comprises a central square, I (15.42), with four
radiating exedrae, a-d, of which the east one, d, forms a
semi-circular apse (8.63 diam). The exedrae on the north,
south, and west sides, however, are larger (11.24 diam) and
articulated by trabeated colonnades, each with four columns
resting on a very low stylobate, and by ambulatories which
create a continuous free-flowing space around the three
sides of the central square. The main entrance to this
section is through a triple doorway on the west side which
leads from the vestibule, II (25.12 x 5.42), flanked by
three rooms to the north, III-V, and probably to the south,
VI-VIII.[33]

The paving of the central section probably consisted of
thin marble plaques[34] while in the ambulatory, and the small
rooms flanking the north side of the vestibule mosaics are
employed.[35]

On the basis of internal and external evidence, the
tetraconch can be dated to the first decade of the fifth
century and associated with a general restoration of the
library complex which had lain deserted since the Herulian

---

[33]Since I have not seen the recently excavated southwest side (vide supra, p. 14, n. 32), Travlos' reconstruction
of that sector must remain hypothetical (see pl. 12).

[34]Traces were found on the south side, in front of the
colonnade (Praktika, 1885, p. 19). The type of paving in
the vestibule, II, is not noted.

[35]Praktika, 1885, pp. 19-20; Sisson, pp. 66, passim.
Travlos, p. 52.

destruction.[36] Although ignored or rejected by some, it is
clear that the inscription (IG, 4224) on the left side of
the entrance porch is related to the rehabilitation of the
entire site.[37] It records the erection of a large statue of
Herculius, Prefect of Illyricum, by Plutarch, Director of the
Neo-Platonic Academy at Athens. Since his tenure as Prefect
(408-412) coincides with that of the building program, there
is little reason to doubt that Herculius was the benefactor.
Why else would a statue have been placed at the entrance to
the complex, if not to honor a man whose generosity and
patronage caused the restoration of the Library, and the
embellishment of its courtyard with an imposing structure?
The statue with its dedicatory inscription, therefore, cannot
be divorced from its context and, indeed, from a consideration of the function of the tetraconch. Although an eccle-

---

[36]On external evidence it is dated no later than ca.
400 (Sisson, p. 70 and nn. 4-7). A terminus post quem is
provided by late fourth century sherds found in the fill
between the pool and the foundations (Travlos, p. 49 and
n. 1). This substantiates the latter's dating of the wall
construction and the mosaics (p. 52, and nn. 3-4). The reconstruction of the library itself has also been attributed
to the same period (Travlos, pp. 54-55; A. Frantz, Acts of
the VIIth International Congress of Christian Archaeology,
Trier, 1965, pp. 379-380).

[37]Although the inscription was noted by Sisson (p. 64),
its importance was not recognized until Travlos' study (pp.
44, 54-56). In a review of the latter, P. Lemerle rejected
this relationship (Revue des études byzantines, 13 [1955],
p. 224). More recently, others have supported Travlos with
convincing arguments (see especially Frantz, op. cit., pp.
528-529; idem, DOP, 19 [1965], pp. 192 and n. 30, 196 and
nn. 53-54; idem, Hesperia, 35 [1966], pp. 379-380, pl. 91a,d;
Krautheimer, Architecture, p. 92).

siastical function has been proposed by some,[38] in the light
of the inscription, it is not likely that a pagan would have
dedicated a statue to a man who had subsidized the building
of a church. It is quite probable, therefore, that the
tetraconch was a secular structure and associated with the
restored Library, functioning as a reading room or a lecture
hall.[39]

Toward the end of the fifth or the beginning of the sixth
century, the tetraconch was destroyed, probably by fire, and
rebuilt as a Christian basilica.[40] Smaller in scale than its
predecessor, the church was incorporated into the central
square, I, which was subdivided into a nave and two aisles
by trabeated colonnades resting on stylobates (0.85 high)
extending from the apse wall to the west piers (pl. 12). A
synthronon was installed in the curve of the east apse, d,
and stylobates with double columns in front of the semi-
circular colonnades to the north, south, and possibly to the
east. In addition, more extensive adjustments were made to

---

[38]Sisson (p. 50, passim) followed by Soteriou (Palaiochristianikai basilikai, pp. 173-174) and Lemerle (loc. cit.).
Travlos, who was the first to regard it as a secular structure (pp. 42-44, 54-56) subsequently termed it a church,
omitting reference to the inscription (Poleodomikē exelixis
tōn Athēnōn, Athens, 1960, p. 139; idem, "Christianikai
Athēnai," Thrēskevtikē kai ethikē enkyklopaideia, col. 727).

[39]Travlos, pp. 42-44, 54-56; Frantz, DOP, 19 (1965), p.
196; idem, Acts of the VIIth International Congress of
Christian Archaeology, Trier, 1964, p. 529; Krautheimer,
Architecture, p. 92. Cf. Sodini, Catalogue, p. 700 and n. 2
who erroneously cites Travlos as having termed the building
a "library."

[40]Travlos, pp. 56-60.

the north and south exedrae, a, c, by the walling up of the
colonnades and the elimination of the ambulatories. Except
for the retention of two of its inner rooms, III, VI, and
its east portal, the vestibule was also eliminated from the
plan. The west ambulatory, b, therefore, was converted into
a narthex and two rooms or recesses were created in its
northwest and southwest corners.

Between the middle of the ninth and the middle or end of
the eleventh century the narthex was used as the burial site
for women, suggesting that the church was affiliated with a
convent.[41] These graves destroyed the mosaics in the west
ambulatory while those in the other sectors lay beneath the
debris from the destruction of the first building. A second
remodeling of the building occurred at the end of the
eleventh or the beginning of the twelfth when a small
Byzantine church was installed on the east side (pl. 12).[42]

Bibliography. Praktika, 1885, pp. 13-25; G. Nikolaides,
ArchEph, 3 (1888), pp. 58-66; M. A. Sisson, BSR, 11 (1929),
pp. 50-72; G. A. Soteriou, Palaiochristianikai basilikai,
pp. 173-174; J. Travlos, Praktika, 1950, pp. 41-63; I. C.
Threpsiades, Polemōn, 5, part 3 (1954), p. 135, n. 8, pp.
137-138; P. Lermerle, Revue des études byzantines, 13 (1955),
pp. 224-225; J. Travlos, Poleodomikē exelixis tōn Athēnōn,
Athens, 1960; idem, "Christianikai Athēnai," Thrēskevtikē
kai ēthikē enkyklopaideia, cols. 714-718; Krautheimer,
Architecture, p. 92 and n. 43; A. Frantz, Acts of the VIIth
International Congress of Christian Archaeology, Trier,
1965, pp. 528-529; idem, DOP, 19 (1965), pp. 192, 196; idem,
Hesperia, 34 (1966), pp. 379-380; G. Dontas, AAA, 3, 2
(1970), pp. 169-170; idem, Deltion, 25 (1970), B1: Chronika,

---

[41]Ibid., p. 60.

[42]Ibid., pp. 60-63, figs. 15-16. No record was made at
the time of its demolition before the excavation of 1885.

pp. 28-29.

Illustrations. M. A. Sisson, BSR, 9 (1929), pl. 17 = our
pls. 10, 13, pl. 25 (reconstruction); J. Travlos, Praktika,
1950, p. 43, fig. 1 (reconstruction of the Library and the
tetraconch), p. 44, fig. 2 (view from east), p. 45, fig. 3 =
our pl. 12, pl. 47, fig. 4 = our pl. 11; G. Dontas, AAA, 3,
2 (1970), p. 169, figs. 6-7 (view of site from east, after
clearing).

Nos. 6-9

Polychrome geometric mosaics with floral borders

originally paved the trilobate ambulatory, Ia-c, and Rooms

III-V on the north side of the vestibule, II (pls. 14-23).

The pavements have deteriorated extensively since the first

excavation and only the decorative program of the ambulatory

can, for the most part, be reconstituted from the published

material.[43]

First decade of the fifth century; on the basis of sherds

found in the fill between the pool and the foundations of the

tetraconch, and the inscription on the entrance porch record-

ing the erection of a statue of Herculius, Prefect of

Illyricum (408-412).

Additional bibliography. Sodini, Catalogue, No. 1,

---

[43]Praktika, 1885, pp. 19-20; Sisson, p. 68. The fragments in the east corner of the south ambulatory, Ic, (pls.
17-18) and Room V (pl. 23) were not discovered until 1950
(cf. our pl. 13 and Travlos, p. 50, fig. 8). Since at the
time of his excavation most of the southwest section had not
been cleared, Travlos' restoration of mosaic pavements in
Rooms VI-VIII is hypothetical (cf. our plans, pls. 11 and
12).

pp. 700-702.

Illustration. M. A. Sisson, BSR, 9 (1929), pl. 17 = our
pl. 13.

6 Room Ia-c (ca. 15.42 long, but to west, 24.50; 3.75 diam).

Ambulatories; in second building period, northwest corner,
a, covered by a wall which rests directly on the pavement
and west side, b, disturbed by graves which destroyed the
pavement. Pls. 13-19.

Scattered fragments: largest to north, a: 3.20 x 7.50.
Framing: a, 0.70; b, 0.95; c, 1.05. Field, to north, a:
2.50 max x 7.50 max. Marble (white, light blue) and limestone (pink, yellow, black) tesserae (0.01 sq) set 2-4 mm
apart. Setting bed-nucleus: "mortar composed of pound
brick and lime."[44]

Trilobate ambulatory with polychrome geometric pavements
originally composed of a single panel along the north side,
a, and radiating panels along the south and, possibly, the
west sides, b-c. The panels were united by a common floral
border which is preserved along the base of the outer walls.
The west and south compartments (b-c) were set within a
guilloche framework which on the south side flanked an inner
border of black and white stepped triangles.

Surround: in rows parallel to the walls.

Framing (pls. 14-16): black fillet, narrow white band;

---

[44]Sisson, p. 68, with identification of material.

black fillet; border, undulating black rinceau (two fillets)
forming rigidly arranged, widely spaced scrolls filled with
single blue heart-shaped ivy leaves which alternate with pink
and yellow ones, in an a-b-a-c sequence. The pointed tips of
the black-outlined leaves touch the margins; black fillet;
narrow white band.

Field, framed by a single or double (b) black fillet.

Ia, north ambulatory (pls. 14-16): two-strand interlace of
circles (0.50 diam) forming concave-sided octagons. The
octagons have been bisected along the margins. Inscribed in
the preserved circles are a two-strand Solomon's knot, a
looped square set on edge, a motif of two interlaced squares,
white spirals on a black ground, and rosettes composed of
alternating light blue and yellow lanceolate leaves.[45]
These floral motifs are placed on white disks, outlined in
black, which are decorated at intervals along the margins
with small black stepped triangles.[46] Each octagon is
filled with a light blue concave-sided octagon set on edge
which contains a similarly-shaped white square in the center;
both are outlined in black.

Ib, west ambulatory: destroyed, except for a small fragment. Although the program was never described, one plan
(pls. 10, 13) shows that the south side of the pavement was

---

[45]Contrary to Sodini, Catalogue, p. 702, the only
floral motifs were rosettes.

[46]For a similar design in which the stepped triangles
have migrated to the strands themselves, see pls. 53-54.

decorated with tangent panels set within a guilloche border.
Whether this compartmentalization extended across the entire
surface cannot be determined. It is clear, however, that
unlike the similar program in the south ambulatory, c, the
panels were not separated by vases.[47] The extant fragment
contains traces of a two-strand guilloche border (yellow/l
white; light blue/l white, outlined in black) on a black
ground. The guilloche, flanked by narrow white bands,
borders a field design of which part of an interlaced circle
survives (same colors as guilloche) which differs from those
in the north ambulatory, a.

Ic, south ambulatory (pls. 17-19): originally, a series
of five "radiating" panels set within a double border and
separated by at least four wedge-shaped compartments enclosed
by a single border. The large panels are bordered by a two-
strand guilloche (same colors as that in Ib) and, in
addition, by an inner band of black and white stepped triangles. They enclose alternating designs of intersecting
circles and imbrication patterns, all outlined in black.[48]
The circles form interlocking patterns of white lanceolate
quatrefoils on a light blue ground which are separated by

_____

[47]It is obvious that the "radiating" panels could not
have incorporated the angular northwest and southwest
recesses as well. Traces of a second ivy rinceau border in
the east corner of the south compartment would indicate that
some other decorative theme was employed (pl. 13).

[48]Both the Praktika (1885, pp. 19-20) and Sisson (p. 68)
have summary descriptions; Travlos (p. 52), none.

serrate-edged yellow squares set on edge. The scales, white
with alternating light blue, yellow, and pink tips, fan
northward and are chromatically arranged in diagonal rows.
According to earlier descriptions, a small compartment, which
was located at each column, separated the panels. It contained a single "cantharus-shaped" vase with leaves which
spread toward the center of the room.[49] The one preserved
fragment (pl. 19) contains a single border of black and white
triangles, and the lower half of a yellow vase striped and
outlined in black, with white highlights and a black rectangular base supporting a circular foot.

Additional color. Ia: interlace design, Solomon's knot,
interlaced and looped squares have strands which are 2 light
blue/2 pink and outlined in black.

First decade of the fifth century.

Illustrations. J. Travlos, Praktika, 1950, p. 48, fig. 5
(Ia), p. 50, fig. 7 = our pl. 14, p. 50, fig. 8 = our pl.
17, p. 51, fig. 10 = our pl. 16.

7 Room III (ca. 4.80 x ca. 3.70). Pavement laid up to
staircase in northeast corner and perhaps retained in
second building phase. Pl. 20.

No published information on dimensions and material.

---

[49]Ibid. Sodini, Catalogue, p. 702, incorrectly
ascribes vases to the north and west ambulatories also.

In a published photograph (pl. 20) there are traces of two
panels separated by a narrow band of tangent reels and bordered along the wall by large zig-zags. The panels, technically inferior to the other mosaics (6, 8-9), are decorated
with schematic imbrication patterns with different
orientations.

Destroyed.

Probably contemporary with the other pavements and, therefore, first decade of the fifth century.

Illustration. J. Travlos, *Praktika*, 1950, p. 50, fig. 9 =
our pl. 20.

8 Room IV (5.20 x 4.80). Pavement laid up to west threshold
   block. Pls. 21-22a, top.

Fragments along north, south, and west sides: in front of
west entrance, 1.10 x 0.50. Materials identical to those in
Ia-c (6).

Traces of a threshold panel and multiple borders.[50]

Framework: outer border, white-centered interlacing
circles[51] (blue/pink/white) on a black ground; inner borders,
indistinguishable (pl. 22a, top).

Threshold panel, framed by a black fillet: pattern composed

---

[50]A large fragment on the northeast side was recently
uncovered (pl. 22a, top).

[51]Cf. Sodini, *Catalogue*, p. 701, who describes them as
tangent.

of a yellow and a pink bead which are separated from each
other and from two flanking pink reels by short black bars.
The motifs are outlined by black/white/black single fillets.

First decade of the fifth century.

   Illustration. G. Dontas, Deltion, 25 (1970), B1: Chronika,
pl. 41a (top) = our pl. 22a (top).

9 Room V (5.20 x 5.90). Pls. 21, 22a (bottom), 23.

   Fragment: 1.90 x 1.50. Framing: ca. 0.64. Field:
0.10 max x 0.70 max. Materials and dimensions identical to
those in Ia-c and IV (6, 8).

In a recently published photograph (pl. 22a, bottom) there
are traces of a central panel enclosed by six borders.[52]
   Surround: light blue tesserae in rows parallel to the
walls.
   Framing: black fillet; first border, undulating black
rinceau (two fillets) composed of rigidly arranged scrolls
filled with single blue heart-shaped leaves which alternate
with pink and yellow ones, in an a-b-a-c sequence. Two
spiral tendrils spring from the rinceau to frame the tip of
each black-outlined leaf, while a third one decorates its
stem; second border, black and white wave crests; third
border, black and white triangles; fourth border, three-strand

_____

   [52]Since the pavement was barely visible in 1969, I
recorded only three of the six borders.

braid; fifth border, light and dark triangles; sixth border, light and dark wave crests.

Field: not visible in the photograph.

First decade of the fifth century.

Illustrations. J. Travlos, Praktika, 1950, p. 51, fig. 11 = our pl. 23; G. Dontas, Deltion, 25 (1970), Bl: Chronika, pl. 41a = our pl. 22a (bottom).

Ilissos Basilica

On the Island of Ilissos, southeast of the Olympeion (pl. 2), excavations in 1916 and 1917 exposed the major part of an Early Christian basilica (overall, 77.75 x 33.65).[53] In 1948, the church was cleared of debris which had accumulated since the second excavation bringing to light for the first time the northeast corner of the building.[54] At the present time, the site is largely overgrown and the south side of the transept covered by a street. During the course of the excavations, traces of tessellated pavements were found in front of the narthex, I, in the south annex, IV, and

---

[53]G. A. Soteriou, ArchEph, 1919, p. 3, fig. 3; hereafter cited as ArchEph, 1919. In earlier and later reports by the same author the dimensions are cited as 57.50 x 23.40 and 57.00 x 29.00 (ArchEph, 1917, p. 106 and Evreterion, pp. 53, 55, respectively). The sector to the west of the narthex was never cleared.

[54]This was occasioned by the demolition of a late nineteenth century theatre (E. Chatzidakis, Praktika, 1948, p. 69; idem, CA, 5 [1951], pp. 61-62; hereafter cited as Praktika, 1948 and CA, 5, respectively.)

in the sectors flanking the bema, X, XI.[55] Eleven fragments
of the pavements from Room X were lifted, consolidated, and
installed in the stoa of the Byzantine Museum at Athens.

Preceded by an atrium or exonarthex, I,[56] and by a
narthex with north and south wings, II-IV (31.90 x 7.15), the
church proper (pls. 24-25) comprises a long nave, V (10.30 x
39.50), flanked by single lateral aisles, VI-VII (ca. 5.70 x
ca. 50.00), and a cross transept with projecting wings and a
raised semi-circular apse, VIII-XI.[57] The nave is separated
from the aisles by stylobates running from the west pier of
the bema to the west wall[58] and from the central bay or bema
by a triumphal arch. Contrary to the earlier archaeological
findings, the excavations in 1948 uncovered evidence that

---

[55]The location and extent of the mosaics are indicated
by the solid lines and the letter "M" or "ΜΩϹΑΪΚΟΝ" in our
plan (pl. 25). The type of paving in the other areas is not
reported.

[56]Since the west side was never completely excavated,
the shape and function of this annex remain uncertain.

[57]CA, 5 (1951), pp. 73-74, with earlier references.
For comments on the roofing of the bema, see Krautheimer,
Tripartite Transept, p. 419, n. 227.

[58]No trace of the internal supports was found. About
six meters from the northeast pier, the north stylobate is
interrupted by a staircase which leads to a vaulted subterranean chamber. It has been identified by some scholars as
the fourth century arcosolium of Leonidas, an archbishop of
Athens, who was martyred in Corinth in 250 and, according to
legend, entombed in Athens (ArchEph, 1919, pp. 8-13, with
earlier references; Evretērion, pp. 52-53, fig. 39 [plan and
section of tomb]). For other early sources see CA, 5 (1951),
p. 61; idem, Praktika, 1958, p. 63 with reference to a sixth
century church with a tessellated inscription citing the
name of this saint (324).

the aisles continued into the transepts,[59] and that the bema
was enclosed by an independent "⊔-shaped" chancel screen
which had a doorway in the center of its west side. Traces
of other important liturgical furnishings, altar, synthronon,
and ambon have not survived. Shortly after the completion
of the church a small annex was built against the north
wall[60] and in the nineteenth and twentieth centuries parts
of the building were covered by constructions which were removed during the course of the excavations.[61]

Although no datable archaeological finds were unearthed
or reported, on the basis of the style of the mosaics the
basilica has been attributed to around the middle of the
fifth century.

Bibliography. A. N. Skias, Praktika, 1893, pp. 124-125;
G. A. Soteriou, ArchEph, 1917, p. 106; idem, ArchEph, 1919,
pp. 1-31; idem, Evreterion, pp. 51-55; AA, 37 (1922), p.
256 ; M. A. Sisson, BSR, 11 (1929), p. 70; Soteriou, Palaiochristianikai basilikai, pp. 208-210; E. Chatzidakis,
Praktika, 1948, pp. 69-80; idem, CA, 5 (1951), pp. 61-74;
idem, CA, 6 (1952), p. 192; J. Travlos, "Christianikai
Athenai," Threskevtike kai ethike enkyklopaideia, Col. 136;
A. Frantz, DOP, 6 (1965), p. 204; Krautheimer, Architecture,
p. 92, n. 42.

Illustrations. A. N. Skias, Praktika, 1893, pl. A (plan
of site); G. A. Soteriou, ArchEph, 1919, p. 3, fig. 3 =

---

[59]Compare, for example, our plans, pls. 24 and 25. The
type of internal supports and divisions between the bema and
the wings was not determined (CA, 5 [1951], pp. 66-68). In
a later note, E. Chatzidakis corrects his plan (our pl. 24)
by removing the short pillars flanking the apse (CA, 6
[1952], p. 192).

[60]For a funerary function, see Praktika, 1948, pp.
70-71.

[61]For the modern building history of the site, see
Evreterion, p. 53; CA, 5 (1951), pp. 61-62.

our pl. 25; idem, Evretērion, p. 52, fig. 39 (plan and section of martyrion), p. 38, fig. 55 (plan); E. Chatzidakis, Praktika, 1948, p. 71, fig. 2 (northeast corner), p. 73, fig. 5 (northeast pier), pl. 5 after p. 76 (plan of foundations of east side); idem, CA, 5 (1951), p. 65, fig. 5 = our pl. 24, p. 69, fig. 6 (reconstruction of transept: second solution), p. 70, fig. 7 (reconstruction of transept: third solution).

Nos. 10-13

Polychrome geometric pavements decorate the west and east sectors of the complex (I, IV, X, XI). They contain simple and complex grids which, with the exception of three bird insets in the transepts, X, XI, are inscribed with geometric motifs or stylized floral ones. The pavements have been attributed to the first half of the fifth century[62] and this appears to be justified by the figures in the transept and by the latter's borders which are decorated with wide, free-flowing rinceaux (pls. 27-29, 32). Since, however, these organic forms are totally absent from other Athenian pavements belonging to the first or second decade of the fifth century (1; 2-3; 6-9; 21; 22) and from contemporary examples elsewhere (44-49; 88-92; 130-138; 178-179; 196), a date closer to the middle of the century is more probable. A terminus ante quem of the second half of the century is

[62]Among others, see G. A. Soteriou, ArchEph, 1919, pp. 14, 17 (fifth century); idem, Evretērion, p. 53 (middle of the fifth century); idem, Palaiochristianikai basilikai, p. 210 ("probably early fifth century"). Nowhere does Soteriou suggest a late fifth century date (cf. Sodini, Catalogue, p. 702). See also CA, 5 (1951), p. 71 (early fifth century).

supplied by the pavements in the two villas at Athens which are highlighted by a profusion of organic detail (14-20; 23).

The pavement in Room X was lifted, consolidated, and installed in eleven sections in a stoa of the Byzantine Museum at Athens; the condition and location of the others is not known.

Additional bibliography. Sodini, Catalogue, No. 2, p. 702.

Illustration. G. A. Soteriou, ArchEph, 1919, p. 3, fig. 3 = pl. 25.

10 Room I (no dimensions published). Exonarthex or atrium.[63] Pls. 25a-26.

Two fragments: to north, ca. 3.00 x 1.50; to south, ca. 3.50 x 4.50.[64] Stone and glass (dark green, blues, turquoise, reds) tesserae (average, 0.012 sq; 0.005 for some details) set 2-4 mm apart.[65]
Two fragments with different aniconic geometric field designs.

Ia, north fragment (pl. 25a).

Surround: white tesserae.

Framing: black band; border, white and black triangles; white triple fillet.

_____

[63]Vide supra, p. 27, n. 56.

[64]These measurements and all the subsequent ones of the fragments in situ are taken from the plan (pl. 25).

[65]Although I only saw the fragments from Room X which are now in the museum, it is reported that the same material was used throughout the church (ArchEph, 1919, p. 21, n. 1).

Field, framed by a black fillet: traces of the "beginning
of a large circle."[66]

1b, south fragment (pl. 26).

Field, framed by a white double fillet: complex straight
grid composed of juxtaposed squares joined by lateral rectangles to form equilateral crosses. The squares are
bisected along the margins. The elements of the design are
articulated by a two-strand guilloche (with a tessera at
each loop) which is outlined by black/white/black fillets
and set on a black ground (for an identical design, see pl.
93). The squares are decorated with smaller concentric
squares enclosing rosettes, and the crosses with alternating
circles and squares set on edge which are inscribed with
quatrefoils and overlapping scales, respectively. The arms
of the crosses with the circles are articulated by spiral
tendrils flanking a small bud.

Toward the middle of the fifth century.

Illustrations. G. A. Soteriou, ArchEph, 1919, p. 22, fig.
25= our pl. 26, p. 23, fig. 26 = our pl. 25a.

11 Room IV (5.15 x 6.28). Southwest annex. Pl. 26a.

Fragment: ca. 2.00 x 6.28. Materials and dimensions
identical to those in Room I (10).

_____

[66]Ibid., p. 23. This fragment was not recorded by
Sodini, Catalogue, p. 702.

Brief mention of a simple geometric design. In a published
photograph (pl. 26a) there are traces of an oblique grid and
two straight squares which are articulated by a black fillet.

Toward the middle of the fifth century.

Illustration. G. A. Soteriou, ArchEph, 1919, p. 21, fig.
24 = our pl. 26a.

12 Room X (5.00 x ca. 9.00). North transept wing. Pls.
    26-34.

Fragment: no dimensions published. Materials and
dimensions identical to those in Room I (10).

Fragment of a polychrome geometric pavement decorated with a
complex grid and geometric and organic filling motifs. An
identical design was found in the south wing (13).

Framing: white band; black fillet; border (pls 27-29),
undulating green/beige/yellow vine rinceau forming loosely
arranged and widely spaced scrolls filled with single sinuous
shoots bearing one or two green and beige grape leaves and a
cluster of grapes, outlined in red. Sometimes at the dark
green curling tip of each shoot there are slightly curved,
dark green strokes, possibly vestigial leaves or tendrils;
black fillet.

Field, framed by a white triple fillet which forms, at the
same time, part of the design: complex grid design of
juxtaposed circles joined by lateral rectangles to form

octagons. The circles are bisected along the margins (pl.
27). The elements of the design are articulated by a two-
strand guilloche (yellow/l white; greyish green/blue/l white;
red/pink/l white, outlined in black, with a white tessera at
each loop) on a black ground. The circles are decorated with
simple wheel motifs with curving white spokes tipped in red
and with stylized red rosettes which contain white centers
and greyish green crosses and which are outlined by a narrow
black and white checkerboard band. The octagons, on the
other hand, contain more complex geometric and organic
motifs which, judging from a photograph of a fragment in situ
(pl. 30), were placed in an alternating sequence. What
probably obtained was that geometric motifs such as umbrella
patterns (pl. 33) and interlaced squares (pl. 34) were
inscribed in circles and alternated with floral and figural
elements which were set against the ground of the octagons
(pls. 31-32).[67] Of the preserved fragments in the Byzantine
Museum, there are three with the border (pls. 28-29), two
with laurel wreaths (pl. 31), one with a floral pattern, two
with pecking birds (pl. 32), one with an umbrella motif (pl.
33), and two with interlaced squares (pl. 34). The laurel
wreaths are bound by a dark green knot and contain flat light
blue and light grey leaves. In one panel (pl. 31; 0.89 x

---

[67]The only visible exception to this sequence is a
rosette in a circle (pl. 27, upper right). Since, however,
it is so geometricized, it differs to a considerable extent
from the other floral patterns.

0.90)[68] the leaves are outlined in dark green while in the
other (0.77 x 0.67) the outlines are omitted and some of the
leaves are dark green. Only one of the bird insets is intact (pl. 32). It shows a long-legged pale blue and grey
bird with white highlights pecking at a red snake at its
feet. The snake, its tail coiled and its mouth agape, is
surrounded by tall curving stalks of green grass and two red
flowers. In the other figural panel traces are preserved of
two confronting birds, one with black outlines, which peck
at red and pink flowers issuing from a single greyish green
stalk between them.[69] The last preserved panel with an
organic motif (1.11 x 0.67) shows part of a delicate bluish
green and dark green foliate pattern forming circles and
spirals which are ornamented with similarly colored ivy
leaves and a yellow lotus blossom. The geometric motifs are
inscribed in a narrow white circle, outlined in black, which
is set on red and blue arcs. The umbrella pattern (pl. 33),
outlined and articulated in black, contains webbing with
alternating blue and red tips fading to white toward the
center. The other preserved panels (pl. 34; 0.89 x 0.87)[70]
are decorated with identical interlaces composed of a

----

[68]The dimensions are of the entire fragment, not the
octagon which measures approximately 0.77 square.

[69]It probably resembled the symmetrical floral pattern
(see pl. 30, right). In 1970 this panel and the succeeding
one could not be photographed.

[70]The other panel measures 0.90 x 1.07.

straight square (1 white/1 yellow/ochre, outlined in black)
laced by a concave-sided square set on edge (dark green/light
blue/white, outlined in black). Black florets accent the
angles of the motif and a stepped square set on edge its
center.

Additional color. Octagon with one bird: outlined and
delineated in light and dark green. Octagon with two birds:
red legs. Interlace: inscribed with a pink/red stepped
square with a white center and black outline.

Toward the middle of the fifth century.

Illustrations. G. A. Soteriou, ArchEph, 1919, p. 19, fig.
20 (bird pecking at snake, in situ), p. 20, fig. 21 (confronting birds, in situ); idem, Evreterion, p. 54, fig. 40
(laurel wreath, in situ), p. 54, fig. 41 = our pl. 27.

13 Room XI (5.20 x 9.00). South transept wing. Pls.
    34a-b.

Fragment: 5.20 x ca. 4.90. Materials and dimensions
identical to those in Room I (10).

Border and field identical to those in the north wing (12).[71]

In two published photographs there are fragments of the
border and field. The former (pl. 34a) contains a cluster
of grapes and a spiral tendril and the latter (pl. 34b) an
octagonal panel with birds flying or perching on the branches
of a tree.

---

[71]ArchEph, 1919, p. 31.

Toward the middle of the fifth century.

Illustrations. G. A. Soteriou, ArchEph, 1919, p. 21, fig. 22 = our pl. 34a.

Villa

The building is located in the National Garden at Athens, near the exit of Queen Sophia Avenue (pl. 2). Although partially excavated in 1846 and noted in subsequent plans of the city, except for minor references to the mosaics, it remains unpublished.[72]

Oriented east-west (pl. 35), the exposed segment contains two long rooms, I and II, which measure 28.38 max meters and 22.72 max x 4.04 meters, respectively. Room II (pl. 36), which is perpendicular to I, runs north-south and is flanked to the east by three juxtaposed rooms, II-V (pl. 37). At the east end of Room I are two stairway platforms which descend into an hypaethral court, VI, which contains a niched fountain inlaid with marble (pls. 38-39). Projecting from the east side of the court and from the facade itself is an onion-shaped apse, VII, which is separated from the

[72]Although the only announcement of its discovery refers to a fountain in a rectangular room, probably VI, and some mosaics (L. Ussing, Archäologische institut des deutschen Reichs, 1846, p. 178), it is clear that at least by 1875 its present shape had been known because it is shown on a map of the city of Athens (see L. and R. Matton, Athènes et ses monuments, Athens, 1963, fig. 22, opposite p. 224 [plan by Kaupert, 1875]). An earlier plan (1862) may also show this building but the outline is rather sketchy (L. and R. Matton, op. cit., fig. 21, opposite p. 217 [plan by von Stranz]).

court by a threshold and a gate. Rooms I and II are on the
same level while III, IV, and V are approximately 11 centimeters higher than II. In Room IV a staircase (1.04 wide
and 0.75 high) leads to an upper level whose threshold shows
traces of a partition of some kind (pl. 49). To the southeast, the forecourt and apse, VI-VII, are 53 centimeters
below the level of Room II. In a later period transverse
walls were installed along the west ends of I (pl. 40) and
the north side of II (pl. 41) which rest on the pavements.

In its present state the plan contains features of a
secular building and probably one which was domestic in
function. A comparison with villa architecture at Piazza
Armerina in Sicily and Nea Paphos on Cyprus[73] reveals certain similarities. In both buildings one finds extended
porticoes on at least three sides of a central courtyard and
the major room or rooms of the complex strung along the corridor opposite the main entrance. At Athens, the corridors
are also long and, although only two have been uncovered and
these truncated by later walls, one additional corridor must
have existed in the original plan, presumably adjoining II on
the east-west axis since this would have produced a more

[73]A. Boëthius and J. B. Ward Perkins, Etruscan and
Roman Architecture, England, 1970, p. 530, fig. 202
(Armerina); hereafter cited as Boëthius and Ward Perkins;
V. Karageorghis, "Chronique des fouilles à Chypre en 1970,"
BCH, 95 (1971), p. 411, fig. 121 (Nea Paphos); hereafter
cited as Karageorghis.

symmetrical plan.[74] The arrangement of rooms at the end of
an axial progression is another feature the three buildings
share. A third analogy can perhaps be suggested. This involves the function and character of some of the rooms
opposite the main entrance. At both Cyprus and Piazza
Armerina, public reception rooms are located on this side,
toward the center of the transverse porticoes, and by virtue
of their size and shape they are the most important rooms if
not of the villas then of their respective sectors.[75] It is
possible that this arrangement obtained for the Athens villa
as well. On the north side of the transverse east corridor,
Room IV occupies an important position in the exposed segment
of the complex. A staircase, located in the center of its
east wall, leads to an area approximately 80 centimeters
above the corridor and the flanking rooms.[76] This room,
therefore, serves as a passageway or vestibule between Room
II and the upper level. Some kind of major room must have
occupied this upper level and in my judgment this is confirmed by the exceptional type of paving, polychrome pebbles,
and the orientation of its design toward the staircase (17,

---

[74]It is obvious that Rooms I and II must have had openings or doorways leading into a courtyard of some kind. At
the present time the walls are covered by thick stucco so
that the original means of communication cannot be determined.

[75]See Boëthius and Ward Perkins, p. 530, fig. 202 (IIA);
Karageorghis, p. 411, fig. 212 (39,40).

[76]For a similar difference in levels, see Boëthius and
Ward Perkins, loc. cit.

pl. 50). It would not be impossible, therefore, to reconstruct a large, formally prominent room in this area and one
which served a public function. Although the thresholds of
the flanking rooms, II and V, must be re-examined more carefully, there does not appear to be any evidence of doorways
which are common features of rooms in the private quarters of
a villa. Moreover, Rooms III-V have very narrow partitions
(0.30 wide) between them. It is probable that these rooms
were also used for the more public activities of a large
villa. Certainly the fountain court unit, VI-VII, belongs to
this category.[77]

On the basis of the similarities with the villas at
Piazza Armerina and Nea Paphos where one finds extended corridors or porticoes around a central court, units opening
off long avenues of which some are opposite the entrance and
distinguished by their size and public function, the Athens
structure belongs to a villa. Although the rooms and especially the corridors are not on a scale with those at Piazza Armerina and Nea Paphos, its original plan and its
decorative pavements must have been rather impressive.

No external evidence was recorded in the brief announcement of its discovery but the style and iconography of the
mosaics which decorate every room, clearly establish a fifth
century date. At this time in Athens there was an outburst

---

[77]The complex has been identified as a nymphaeum (I. C.
Threpsiades, Polemōn, 5, Part 3 [1954], pp. 127-128 , and
n. 5, pp. 139-140).

of building activity which saw the restoration and erection
of innumerable structures between around 400 A. D. and the
beginning of the sixth century.[78] Some of these buildings
were also decorated with mosaics (1; 2-3; 4-5; 6-9; 10-13;
21; 22; 23) and an analysis of them provides a date in the
second half of the fifth century for the building and decorative program of the villa.

Bibliography. L. Ussing, Archäologische institut des
Deutschen Reichs, 1846, p. 178; A. S. Rousopoulos, ArchEph,
2 (1862), col. 150.

Illustration. S. H. Barnsley, The Architectural Association Sketchbook, n.s., 9, 5 (1889), pl. 72 = our pl. 50.

Nos. 14-20

Complex curvilinear and rectilinear designs, many with
flora and fauna insets, spread across the floors of the
rooms and clothe them with polychrome splendor. The decorative program can be assigned to the second half of the fifth
century when large scale, open designs with or without
organic filling elements begin to appear in Athens and elsewhere. Earlier pavements datable to the late fourth and
early fifth centuries contain small scale, aniconic designs
which give a close-knit, textural quality to the surface. A
comparison of the interlace designs in Rooms I and V (pls.

---

[78]H. A. Thompson, "Athenian Twilight: A. D. 267-600,"
JRS, 49 (1959), pp. 61-72; A. Frantz, "From Paganism to
Christianity in the Temples of Athens," DOP, 19 (1965), pp.
187-205. It is curious that neither author mentions this
building.

37, 39, 42, 51) with a similar one in the tetraconch near
the Acropolis (6, pls. 15-16) reveals stages in the development and embellishment of this kind of design. Both contain
curvilinear configurations but those in the villa are defined
by wide, decorative bands which create large insets for
organic and geometric motifs. The pavement in the tetraconch, on the other hand, and a contemporary mosaic near the
Theatre of Dionysos (2, pl. 8) show small scale interlaces
articulated by narrow, undecorated bands and filled with
geometric or geometricized floral motifs. These pavements
are dated to the early fifth century and provide a terminus
post quem for the villa pavements. A similar terminus can
be established for the rectilinear star patterns in Rooms II
and III (pls. 44-47). Although one is aniconic (pls. 44-46)
and the other contains only a few figures (pls. 47-48), both
pavements reflect a tendency to expand the size of the
lozenged and square insets. Earlier examples of this design
(pls. 104, 106, 429, 433) are small in scale, close knit, and,
moreover, lack complex and sophisticated filling motifs, be
they birds or purely geometric ones. Most of the pavements
in the villa, therefore, represent a progressive approach to
geometric carpet decoration which replaces the aniconic,
sober type of the late fourth and early fifth centuries. It
is not until around the middle of the fifth century that geometric carpets began to be embellished by complex designs
with organic and complex geometric motifs. The pavements in
the Ilissos Basilica at Athens represent an early phase in

the progression toward a more decorative pavement (pls. 26-
34) and those at Theotokou (pls. 413-417), Nea Anchialos
(pls. 382-397) and Amphipolis (pls. 648-674, 675-705) a later
one. Since there are only scattered organic fillers in the
Ilissos Basilica, and they are more three-dimensional,
modeled forms, it is probable that the villa decoration
belongs to a later phase. A terminus ante quem is provided
by the pavements in two other villas which contain large
figural panels. These mosaics (pls. 94-98, 118-156) and
similar ones in ecclesiastical structures (pls. 199-216,
240-286) do not appear until the end of the fifth century
and reflect a trend in which figure compositions become the
conveyors of cosmographic and topographic themes. Thus the
pavements in the villa occupy a midpoint in the development
of fifth century Greek pavements. They have discarded the
somber and sober appearance of the early pavements but have
not reached the stage of the later ones. They can, therefore, be assigned to the second half of the fifth century
and probably to the third quarter of that century.[79]

Additional Bibliography. I. Lavin, "Field Notes: Late
Roman Villa at Athens," Dumbarton Oaks, Center for Byzantine
Studies.

Illustration. S. H. Barnsley, The Architectural Association Sketchbook, n.s., 9, 5 (1889), pl. 72 = our pl. 50.

---

[79]For a discussion on the stylistic development of
Greek pavements, vide supra, Preface.

14 Room I (4.00 x 28.40 max). Corridor; shortened at west
    end by a wall with a doorway and steps set directly on the
pavement. Pls. 40, 42-43.
    Framing: 0.33; to east, 0.40. Field: 3.34 x 22.00 max.
Marble and limestone tesserae (ca. 0.015 sq) set 1-3mm apart.

Complex polychrome interlace design bordered by an overlapping
lyre pattern.
    Surround: to north and south, in narrow rows parallel to
the walls; to east, one row of superimposed scales (alternately red, white, yellow, and light and dark blue, outlined
in black) framed by a black fillet along the west side.[80]
    Framing: black double fillet; border, schematic over-
lapping lyre pattern interrupted at six meter intervals by a
black-outlined, white medallion filled with a hexafoil of
alternating red, yellow, blue lanceolate leaves springing
from a black circle. At each medallion the lyre pattern
reverses direction and changes color. In sections containing
red triangular centers, the strands are either grey/pink/
white, grey/light blue/white, or grey/yellow/white. Those
with yellow centers are flanked by red/light blue/rose/white
strands; black fillet; white triple fillet.
    Field, framed by a black fillet (pls. 40, 42-43): inter-
lace of large (0.43 diam) and small circles forming large

---

[80]The scales are not visible in the plates.

concave-sided octagons (ca. 1.00 sq).[81] The three strands
of the interlace are wide and articulated by black/white/
black double fillets. Two of the strands are decorated with
a ribbon motif (white undulating fillet dividing the strand
into pink and red halves with white bars or stepped squares
in the intervals) and a rainbow cord (red/pink/white/light
blue/grey with a white serrate-edged center). Both patterns
are placed on a black ground as is the third type of
decorative band, located along the margin of the design,
which is decorated with a two-strand guilloche (grey/pink/
white; grey/light blue/white, with a white tessera at each
loop). The octagonal and circular compartments formed by
the interlacing elements are filled with various motifs set
on the longitudinal axis of the room. The large octagons
contain alternating fruit trees (primarily with pears and
apples), rosettes with slightly agitated leaves inscribed on
disks, and black-outlined ribbed vases with double looped

---

[81]The same design decorates Rooms V and VI in this
building (18, 19, pls. 51-53). In these pavements and in
another one in the tetraconch near the Agora (6, pls. 14-16),
the circles and the octagonal compartments are the same size.
Here, the octagons predominate and their expansion, with the
concomitant reduction of the size of the circular units,
creates an optical effect in which the basic unit and structure of the design appears to be the octagons. In fact, the
alternating large and small circles determine the octagons.
The decorative system of the cords contributes to this ambiguity because it is organized around the octagons, not the
circles. Thus, the overall effect is one of interlacing
octagons decorated alternately with rainbow and ribbon cords,
joined by a guilloche band along the margins. For a
diagrammatic analysis of this design, see A. K. Orlandos,
"Duo palaiochristianikai basilikai tēs Kō," ArchEph, 1966,
p. 85, fig. 84, a-d.

handles. Water spills from the mouths of some of the vases
in stylized light blue sheets which are crossed by single
black fillets. Although the trees face eastward, the vases
alternate direction and color (red with yellow highlights;
light blue). All the filling motifs in the octagons are
flanked by four small, white-centered, blue disks which are
crossed and outlined in black. The circles, on the other
hand, are inscribed with freely disposed, fruit-bearing
branches which alternate with checkerboard patterns, rosettes,
and stepped squares. Red and yellow serrate-edged zig-zags
decorate the interstices along the margins of the field.

Second half of the fifth century.

15 Room II (22.75 max x 4.04). Corridor; shortened at
     north end by a wall set directly on the pavement. Pls.
41, 44-46.
   Framing: 0.40. Field: 3.24 x 22.35 max. Materials
identical to those in Room I (14).

Polychrome design of interlocking geometric patterns bordered
by ivy leaves.
   Surround: in rows parallel to the walls.
   Framing (pl. 45): black fillet; border, undulating black
rinceau (two fillets) composed of rigidly arranged scrolls
filled alternately with single graduated blue, yellow, red
heart-shaped ivy leaves in an a-b-c sequence. The long

tapered tips of the black-outlined leaves touch the margin;
black fillet; narrow white band.

Field, framed by a black fillet: interlocking geometric
design, articulated by black/2 white/black fillets, composed
of crosses of four lozenges separated by single squares.
The lozenges are bisected along the margins. An alternating
chromatic scheme unifies the lozenges and the interstices
surrounding them. In the former, those on the east-west axis
have red/pink interiors and light blue centers, while their
counterparts on the north-south axis have light blue interiors with pink centers. These color units are complemented
by yellow and red/pink interstices. In contrast to the
simple disks decorating the lozenges, the squares are
inscribed with geometric patterns which follow an a-b-a compositional sequence across the east-west axis. In this way,
a variety of interlacing, intersecting, tangent, and superimposed patterns are arranged in a coherent and organized
manner. Among the preserved motifs are imbrications, braids,
indented squares with inscribed central squares, squares
with corner peltae, foliate cruciform patterns, checkerboards, interlaced squares set on edge, intersecting circles,
interlaced circles, rosettes, stars of eight lozenges,
rosettes, and Solomon's knots.

Second half of the fifth century.

16 Room III (4.10 x 4.69). Pls. 47-48.

Framing: ca. 0.54. Field: 3.02 x 3.61. Materials
identical to those in Room I (14) but the tesserae are more
irregularly-cut (ca. 0.015 x 0.017) and set 2-5 mm apart.

Polychrome design of interlocking geometric patterns, some
with figural insets, bordered by ivy leaves.

Surround except to north: light blue tesserae in rows
parallel to the walls; north side, narrow white scale pattern, outlined in black, decorated with light blue concave-
sided triangles with red and black centers.[82]

Framing (pl. 47): black fillet; border, undulating black
rinceau (one fillet) composed of wide, rigidly arranged
scrolls filled with single, broad heart-shaped ivy leaves,
outlined in black. The leaves alternate blue, yellow, red in
an a-b-c sequence, and their tips touch the margin; black
fillet; narrow white band.

Field, framed by a black fillet (pl. 47): interlocking
geometric design, articulated by black/2 white/black fillets, composed of crosses of four lozenges separated by
single squares. The lozenges are cut along the margins.
Although identical in design, compositional sequence (a-b-a),
and color to the paving in Room II (15, pls. 44-46), the
filling elements differ. White serrate-edged "eye motifs"
with red centers decorate the lozenges while in the squares
and arranged in rows of three along the east-west axis,

---

[82]They are not visible in the plates.

waterfowl alternate with interlaced circles and Solomon's
knots. Four grey birds (pl. 48) and four white and grey
ones, oriented toward the perimeter of the room, are shown in
profile view with their heads pointed downward standing on
or near the inner black frame. They are generalized and
rather two-dimensional representations and, for the most
part, their bodies are disproportionately larger than their
heads and necks. Each grey bird is outlined and delineated
in black and white. Since the white and grey birds, probably swans, are compressed into the small space of the
panels, their legs are forced forward, as if they were
seated, and their necks are pushed downward in ungraceful
and unnatural arcs (pl. 47).

Additional color. Grey birds: orange bills, legs and
feet. Swans: red bills, legs and feet.

Second half of the fifth century.

Additional Bibliography. I. C. Threpsiades, _Polemōn_, 5,
Part 3 (1954), pp. 133 and 137-138, n. 13.

17 Room IV (4.50 x 4.25). The pavement was laid around a
staircase leading to an upper level. Pls. 49-50.

Fragment: 1.13 x 2.30. Pebbles (average 0.015 sq; 0.01
thick) set on edge, 6-10 mm apart.

Fragment of a pebble mosaic originally composed of a large
polychrome foliate pattern (3.00 x 2.60) set on a white

ground and oriented toward the steps.[83]

Field: two black "S-curve" rinceaux with curling tendrils, leaves and branches, rise symmetrically from opposite sides of a heart-shaped base. The latter, inscribed with a red palmette set on a yellow stem, is flanked by black half-palmettes and spirals. Above, radiating inward from each rinceau is a large, curving black branch terminated by a cusp from which emanate additional spiral tendrils and a large medallion. The latter encloses a green-centered palmette-rosette composed of alternating black and yellow lanceolate leaves flanked by red leaves with curled tips. The pattern is bisected by a torch-like motif with a black palmetto head and a green shaft which rises from a black-centered yellow star abutting the heart-shaped base.

Second half of the fifth century.[84]

Additional bibliography. C. Smith, BSA, 3 (1896-7), p. 184; D. M. Robinson, Excavations at Olynthus, II (1930), p. 81; M. E. Blake, MAAR, 8 (1930), p. 70; R. P. Hinks, Catalogue of the Greek, Etruscan and Roman Paintings in the British Museum, London, 1933, p. xlvi.

Illustration. S. H. Barnsley, The Architectural Association Sketchbook, n.s., 9, 5 (1889), pl. 72 = our pl. 50.

18 Room V (4.00 x 4.00). Pls. 37, 51-52.

Framing: ca. 0.54; to east, 0.40. Field: 2.95 x 3.06.

---

[83]The measurements and color descriptions are taken from the drawing (pl. 50).

[84]At one time the pavement was attributed to the Roman period (C. Smith, BSA, 3 [1896-97], p. 184; M. E. Blake,

Materials identical to those in Room I (14).

Polychrome interlace design set within a floral border.

Framing (pl. 37): black fillet; border, undulating black
rinceau (one fillet) composed of wide, rigidly arranged
scrolls filled with single, broad heart-shaped ivy leaves,
outlined in black. The leaves alternate light blue, pink,
pink/yellow in an a-b-c sequence; black fillet; narrow white
band.

Field, framed by a black fillet (pls. 51-52): interlace of
large and small circles forming octagons. The wide strands
of the interlace are articulated by black/3 white/black
fillets and are decorated with a two-strand guilloche (light
blue; pink, outlined in black) on a black ground. Inscribed
in the preserved circles and octagons are light blue and
pink interlaces, braids, and cruciform patterns and, in the
northeast and southeast corners, two land birds. The birds
face each other as well as the interior of the room and are
schematically drawn with short parallel black strokes articu-
lating the breasts and tail feathers of their blue bodies.
In comparison with a similar design in Room I (14, pls. 40,
42-43), the design is flatter, less decorative, and somewhat
crude in execution.

MAAR, 8 [1930], p. 70 and n. 6; B. R. Brown, Ptolemaic Paintings and Mosaics and the Alexandrian Style, Massachusetts,
1957, p. 80 and n. 250). To my knowledge, this is the latest
example of a polychrome pebble mosaic.

Additional color. Birds: red beaks, legs, feet.

Second half of the fifth century.

19 Room VI (9.85 x 10.10). Fountain court. Pls. 53-55.

Framing: 0.40. Field, including triple fillet: north
and south panels, 1.71 x 9.30; east and west panels, 4.80 x
1.80. Marble, limestone, and glass tesserae (0.01 x 0.013;
0.015 sq) set 2-3mm apart.

Fountain (4.83 x 4.50) originally surrounded by four juxtaposed polychrome mosaic panels alternately decorated with
interlaces (a,b) and star designs (c,d) set within a geometric border.[85]

Surround: in two to three rows parallel to the walls.

Framing (pls. 53, 55): black triple fillet; border along
walls and fountain, crude overlapping lyre pattern (red
strands with one white fillet and yellow triangles, outlined
in black).

Field: four panels framed by a black triple fillet.

VIa,b, north and south panels (pl. 53): small scale interlace of circles forming concave-sided octagons (for larger
versions of this design in the building, see 14, pls. 40, 42-
43; 18, pls. 38, 51-52). The simple white cords of the

---

[85]The descriptions in this entry are based on the notes
and photographs of Professor Irving Lavin which are presently
in his possession and in the archives at Dumbarton Oaks. By
1969 the pavement was in very bad condition and covered with
debris.

interlace are outlined in black and decorated at intervals
with black stepped triangles. In contrast to the more decorative filling motifs in the octagons, the circles contain
simple ones: the white-centered circles have one-strand
Solomon's knots; those with dark centers have rosettes. In
the octagons, on the other hand, red triple fillets frame
long-stemmed chalices, unidentifiable land birds, fish, and
human heads (pl. 54) which are primarily oriented toward the
east. Crudely executed, schematic, and two-dimensional, these
filling elements appear as flat patterns clinging to the surface of the floor. An oval and chinless head is shown rising
from a truncated neck which rests on the red fillet of the
frame. Clinging to its pointed skull like a tight cap, its
hair falls in two waves on its forehead which is marked by
some light and dark tesserae. Details such as features and
modeling are executed with flat, juxtaposed strokes which
are fused at the lips and possibly the brows. The visage is
enlivened by flat, black eyes which peer to the right beneath
slightly curving black brows.

VIc, d, east and west panels (pl. 55), separated from the
preceding panels by a black triple fillet: geometric carpet
composed of stars of eight lozenges and squares articulated
by single or double black fillets (for a similar design in
the building, see 20, pls. 56-57). The lozenges are cut
along the margins. Each star pattern comprises four pairs of
lozenges terminated by squares set on edge which alternate

with a large straight square. Surrounded by alternating white, red, and yellow lozenges, the white squares are decorated with figures and foliate motifs arranged in alternating rows along the north-south axis. The squares set on edge contain small rosettes set on disks while the straight squares are filled with various types of white highlighted rosettes and birds. Represented in profile, the birds are arranged in rows of single confronting pairs oriented southward. These figures as well as those in the north and south panels are executed with a profusion of red, blue, and green glass tesserae.

Additional color. Lozenges: white, outlined in red; red, outlined in yellow; yellow, outlined in red.

Second half of the fifth century.

20 Room VII (6.70 diam). Apse; separated from the fountain
    court by a gate with two columnar supports resting on a
raised threshold. Pls. 56-57.

Framing: 0.40. Field: 5.90 diameter. Marble and limestone tesserae (0.015 sq) set 1-2mm apart.

Polychrome design of interlocking geometric motifs bordered
by an ivy rinceau.[86]

Framing: black fillet; border, undulating black rinceau

---

[86]The rinceau is not visible in the plates.

(one fillet) composed of rigidly arranged scrolls filled
alternately with single light blue, yellow, pink heart-shaped
ivy leaves in an a-b-c sequence, outlined in black, with long
tapered tips; black fillet.

Field, framed by a white triple fillet which forms, at the
same time, part of the design: geometric carpet composed of
stars of eight lozenges and squares articulated by black/2
white/black fillets. The design has been cut along the
margins. Each star pattern is composed of four pairs of
lozenges terminated by squares set on edge which alternate
with a large straight square. Alternating rose, yellow, and
blue lozenges surround the white squares which contain
serrate-edged blue squares set on edge with white/black
centers.

Second half of the fifth century.

Villa or Gymnaseion

A second building was partially excavated in the National
Garden at Athens in 1888 (pl. 2).[87] During this campaign

___

[87]For another map of the city, see Judeich, Topographie,
plan I, H, 6. This plan, at K, 5, also notes another tessellated pavement which is still visible on the southeast side
of the Garden. It is decorated with a white surround and the
corners of two wide black frames separated by a similarly wide
white band. The size of the tesserae (0.008 sq) would suggest
an earlier period, perhaps the second century when this section of the city was being developed (J. Travlos, Poleodomikē
exelixis tōn Athēnōn, Athens, 1960, pp. 112-116).

a peristyle courtyard surrounded by porticoes and rooms was
cleared (pls. 58-59). The south portico led to a large semi-
circular nymphaeum with rectangular basins near the cord of
the apse. Since subsequent excavations were never undertaken
and the site is now overgrown, the limits and function of the
complex cannot be determined.[88]

The history of the site is sketchily drawn and no date
is advanced for the construction of the building. It would
appear that there was evidence of its destruction before the
third century and of its subsequent rebuilding.[89] On the
basis of an inscription on a reused block near the north entrance to the nymphaeum, V, the excavator suggests a third
century or a fourth century reconstruction of the building.[90]
This is highly unlikely since there is no evidence of substantial rebuilding in this area and in Athens, generally,
between the Herulian raids in 267 and the beginning of the
fifth century.[91] Indeed, it is certain that at least the
nymphaeum was restored early in the fifth century since its

---

[88]In the original reports the excavators were undecided
about its function (J. A. Koumanoudes, ArchEph, 1888, col.
200; P. Kavvadias, Praktika, 1889, pp. 11-12, and n.3).
Later, it was identified as a villa (M. A. Sisson, BSR, 9
[1929], p. 70 and n. 1; I. C. Threpsiades, Polemon, 5, Part 3
[1954], p. 135, n. 5). It is identified on our plan (pl. 2)
as a gymnasion.

[89]Koumanoudes, op. cit., p. 200.

[90]Kavvadias, op. cit., p. 16. The block contained the
name of the niece of Trajan and the sister-in-law of
Hadrian, "Matidia Augusta."

[91]For a discussion on the destruction and rebuilding of
Athens, vide supra, p. 1 passim.

pavement is very similar to one in the tetraconch near the
Agora (6). Although other tessellated pavements were found
in Rooms Ia, II, III, and VI, (aa on plan, pl. 58), they are
not described and it is impossible to determine to which
building phase they belong. Given the paucity of the data and
the dearth of photographic material, only the pavement in the
nymphaeum will be considered.

Bibliography. J. A. Koumanoudes, ArchEph, 1888, cols. 199-200; P. Kavvadias, Praktika, 1889, pp. 9-10; Judeich, Topographie, p. 38; I. C. Threpsiades, Polemōn, 5, Part 3 (1954), p. 139; M. A. Sisson, BSR, 9 (1929), p. 70.

Illustration. P. Kavvadias, Praktika, 1889, plate after p.
71 = our pl. 58.

No. 21

A polychrome mosaic paves the peristyle on the south
side of the complex (Room V, pl. 58). On the basis of an
early description of the pavement and the preserved fragment
in situ, the design can be, for the most part, reconstituted.
The field, which was enclosed by an undulating ivy rinceau
(pl. 60) and other leaves, contained panels with scales (pl.
61), intersecting circles, and other similar patterns. These
compositional and decorative features are also exhibited in
the south ambulatory, Ic, of the tetraconch near the Agora
(16, pls. 17-18) and, in fact, the excavator makes this comparison.[92] In this light, it is probable that the

---

[92]Vide infra, p. 57, and nn. 94-95.

refurbishing of the nymphaeum occurred at approximately the
same time as the construction of the tetraconch, that is, in
the first decade of the fifth century. It was during this
period that a massive building program was begun in Athens
which lasted over a century.[93]

21 Room V (ca. 15.00 diam). Nymphaeum. Peristyle (3.80
    diam); restored in antiquity with a mosaic pavement.
Pls. 59-61.
  Fragment: ca. 3.80 x 5.00. Framing: 0.40. Field, including fillet: 3.00 x 4.20. Marble tesserae (ca. 0.01 sq) set
1-3mm apart.

Polychrome pavement composed of geometric designs bordered by
rinceaux. According to an early description there were ivy
leaves and other leaves in the various borders and [in the
fields] scales, intersecting circles, and the like. Only the
vases and figural panels in the large pavements in the
palace[94] and in the semi-circles of the tetraconch of Hadrian
were missing.[95] In the preserved fragment (pls. 60-61),

_____

[93]H. A. Thompson, "Athenian Twilight: A.D. 267-600,"
JRS, 49 (1959), p. 66. Other buildings associated with this
program are the Metroon (1), a private house (2-3), the
Ilissos Basilica (10-13), and two villas (14-20; 23).

[94]Presumably he is referring to the villa in the same
Garden (14-20).

[95]Kavvadias, Praktika, 1889, pp. 9-10. Although no distinction is made between the borders and the field, the preserved fragment shows that the scales decorated the field (pl.

58

there is an imbrication pattern and a rinceau.

Framing: black fillet; border, undulating black rinceau
(two fillets) composed of rigidly arranged scrolls filled
alternately with single light blue and pink heart-shaped ivy
leaves, outlined in black. The long tapered tips of the
leaves touch the margins; black fillet; narrow white band
(pl. 60).

Field, framed by a black fillet: red/white, light blue/
white, pink/white, and white scales, outlined in black, which
are set in alternating diagonal rows along the east-west axis
of the room.

First decade of the fifth century.

Thermae

A chance find in 1862 brought to light traces of a
building (26.60 x 12.80) with a mosaic pavement between the
National Garden and the Olympeion.[96] When the site was
systematically excavated in 1873, it was determined that the
building was a bathing establishment and that the mosaic belonged to a large room, II, in the left wing of the complex

61). In my judgment, the intersecting circles also belong to
the field since they were never used as border patterns at
this time.

[96]A. S. Rousopoulos, ArchEph, 2 (1862), col. 150, 5.
It was situated in front of the Zappeion (see Judeich,
Topographie, Plan I, I/6).

(pl. 62).[97] No trace of the building survives.

Although the complex was assigned to a period no earlier
than the end of the Antonine period,[98] the pavement was compared to one in a villa in the National Garden which has been
assigned to the second half of the fifth century (14-20).
Given this comparison, therefore, it is possible that the
Baths were erected during the "outburst of building activity"
in the fifth century when other structures with mosaic pavements were restored or built (1; 2-3; 4-5; 10-13; 21; 23).[99]

Bibliography. A. S. Rousopoulos, ArchEph, 2 (1862), col.
150, 5; J. A. Koumanoudes, Praktika, 1873-74, pp. 33-34; RA,
2 (1873), pp. 50-52; Judeich, Topographie, p. 38.

Illustration. RA, 2 (1873), fig. on p. 51 = our pl. 62.

No. 22

22 Room II (26.60 x 12.80).

No published information on dimensions and material.

"Mosaic pavement similar to the one in the King's Garden[100]
but inferior in technique and design."[101] It was bordered by

---

[97]J. A. Koumanoudes, Praktika, 1873-74, pp. 33-34; RA,
2 (1873), pp. 50-52.

[98]RA, 2 (1873), p. 51.

[99]H. A. Thompson, "Athenian Twilight," JRS, 49 (1959),
p. 66.

[100]It is now called the National Garden.

[101]A. S. Rousopoulos, ArchEph, 2 (1862), col. 150, 5;
RA, 2 (1873), p. 50.

ivy leaves which were regularly disposed.

Possibly fifth century.

Villa

Traces of a villa with a mosaic pavement were found in
1952 at the corner of Nikē and Apollo Streets (pl. 2).
During one brief campaign, it was only possible to clear part
of the south side of the building because the east and north
sides were covered by modern constructions.[102] The exposed
sector was subsequently destroyed by the foundations of an
apartment house but the mosaic pavement was lifted, consolidated, and placed in the Fetiye Djami near the Agora.

During the course of the excavation, a large, semi-
circular nymphaeum with niches, II (6.35 diam), was brought
to light and segments of two rooms, I, III (pls. 63-64).
Although two building phases were identified, the second
belonging to the fifth century, only minor changes occurred
to the original building.[103] The nymphaeum was closed off

------

[102]I. C. Threpsiades, Polemōn, 5, Part 3 (1954), pp. 126,
135; hereafter cited as Threpsiades. He suggests (pp. 135-
136, 137 and n. 10) that part of a mosaic pavement and a
fountain found by chance in 1921 on Metropolis Street to the
north may belong to this villa. This would mean that, like
the private house south of the Acropolis (2-3), the villa was
over sixty meters long.

[103]Threpsiades (p. 136) suggests that the first building
was damaged by the Herulians in 267. Like the Metroon (1),
therefore, over one hundred and twenty-five years elapsed
before the site and its building were refurbished.

from the north room by parapets, its pavement was raised and waterproofed,[104] and Room I was repaved with a mosaic. At a later period a granary was installed in the nymphaeum[105] and this side of the building, at least, became a commercial establishment.

Although no datable archaeological finds were unearthed or reported, on the basis of the mosaics, the second phase of the villa can be assigned to the second half of the fifth century.[106]

Bibliography. I. C. Threpsiades, Polemōn, 5, Part 3 (1954), pp. 126-141.

Illustrations. I. C. Threpsiades, Polemōn, 5, Part 3 (1954), p. 128, fig. 1 = our pl. 63, p. 130, fig. 3 = our pl. 64.

No. 23

In Room I, part of a polychrome pavement was uncovered which contains an interlace design with flora and fauna insets (pls. 65-68). Field designs with organic filling elements do not appear in Greek pavements until the middle of the fifth century. It is at this time that the individual units of both curvilinear and rectilinear designs are

---

[104]Threpsiades, pp. 127-128, 135-136.

[105]Threpsiades, p. 137.

[106]Threpsiades attributes it to the very beginning of the fifth century on the basis of inconclusive comparisons with the pavements in the tetraconch (6-9), the villa in the National Garden (14-20), and the basilica at Epidauros (44-49).

enlarged and begin to become receptacles for floral patterns and denizens of the land and sea.[107] Since only a small portion of the pavement was uncovered, it is difficult to determine whether it is stylistically closer to the mosaics in the Ilissos Basilica (12), dated to the middle of the fifth century, or to the later pavements in a villa in the National Garden (14-20). The rather flat, two-dimensional treatment of the forms argues for the later date, that is to say, for one in the second half of the fifth century.

Fragment lifted, consolidated, and stored in the Fetiye Djami near the Agora.

Illustration. I. C. Threpsiades, Polemōn, 5, Part 3 (1954), p. 130, fig. 3 = our pl. 64.

23   Room I (1.20 max x 3.40 max). Pls. 64-68.

Fragment: 1.20 x 3.40. Framing: south, 0.30; east, 0.80. Field: 0.90 x 2.60. Stone tesserae (0.01 sq) set 1-3mm apart. Setting bed-nucleus: 7cm of "hard red mortar with large and small tile bits."[108]

Fragment of a polychrome interlace design with organic filling motifs set within geometric borders.

Framing (pls. 65-66): outer border preserved to east only, alternating diagonal rows of blue, yellow, and red scales with white bases fanning eastward; black fillet; narrow white

---

[107]For this trend, vide supra, pp. 36-37.

[108]Threpsiades, p. 134.

band; inner border, three-strand guilloche (1 white/pink/red;
1 white/light blue; 1 white/yellow, outlined in black, with
a white tessera at each loop) on a black ground.

Field (pls. 66-68): three-strand interlace (red/pink/white;
light blue/white; yellow/white, outlined in black) of alternating squares (ca. 0.35) and circles (ca. 0.35 diam). They
enclose white panels, outlined in black, which are inscribed
with birds and other motifs oriented southward. Starting at
the southeast corner and moving westward, the sequence of the
five preserved panels is as follows: bird; still life; two
panels with floral motifs; destroyed, except for traces of
the tail feathers of a bird. The first panel is occupied by
a red-crested, light blue aquatic bird with red wings and
white and red tail feathers accented by short black strokes.
Four black branches with lanceolate leaves sprout from a
slightly curving tree behind the bird. The still life comprises a small black and white wicker basket with two yellow
pears rising vertically from its tilted mouth. The third and
fourth panels are decorated with a quatrefoil and hexafoil,
respectively, composed of red, blue, pink, and yellow lanceolate leaves. Of the last panel, only the black-outlined,
red and white tail feathers of a bird are preserved. The
spandrels beyond the circles are decorated with white/blue/
pink/red rectangular triangles[109] with black serrated edges.

[109]For the nomenclature, see H. Stein et al., Répertoire
graphique du décor géométrique dans la mosaïque antique.
Bulletin de l'association internationale pour l'etude de la
mosaique antique, 4th fascicule, Paris, 1973, p. 19, 4.

Additional color. First bird: red beak and legs. Pears:
red and black outlines.

Probably second half of the fifth century.

Mosaic Fragment

Part of a mosaic pavement was discovered by chance in
1930 near Euripides Street, opposite the church of St. John
of the Column. It was lifted, consolidated, and placed in
the courtyard of the Byzantine Museum at Athens. In 1966
additional repairs were made and it was set on a new
foundation.[110]

No. 24

A fragment of a polychrome geometric pavement is decorated with an interlace field design and geometric and floral
borders (pls. 69-70). On the basis of its resemblance to the
pavements in a private villa (2-3, pls. 7-8) and the tetraconch (6, pls. 14-16) near the Acropolis, the pavement can be
attributed to the first half of the fifth century when purely
geometric interlaces with or without geometric or floral
borders reflected an early, aniconic phase in the development
of Greek pavements.

---

[110]E. Chatzidakis, _Deltion_, 22 (1967), B1: _Chronika_,
p. 18.

Bibliography. E. Chatzidakis, <u>Deltion</u>, 22 (1967), Bl:
<u>Chronika</u>, p. 18; Sodini, <u>Catalogue</u>, p. 705, n. 5, p. 749.

Illustration. E. Chatzidakis, <u>Deltion</u>, 22 (1967), Bl:
<u>Chronika</u>, pl. 18b (pavement before consolidation).

24 Mosaic fragment (2.85 sq). Pls. 69-70.

Framing: to south, 0.80 max; to east, 0.35 max. Field:
2.05 max x 2.50 max.[111]

Fragment of a polychrome interlace design, on a yellow ground,
enclosed at least on one side by a double border.

Framing (pl. 69): outer border preserved to south, undulating black rinceau (two fillets) composed of rigidly
arranged, widely spaced scrolls which are filled with single
pink, light blue, and yellow heart-shaped ivy leaves in an
a-b-c sequence. The pointed tips of the black-outlined
leaves touch the margins (for similar borders in Athens, see
1; 6; 15; 16; 18; 20); black fillet; narrow white band; inner
border preserved along south and east sides, three-strand
braid (pink/1 white; light blue/1 white; yellow/1 white, outlined in black with a white tessera at each loop) on a black
ground.

Field, framed by a black fillet (pls. 69-70): two-strand
interlace (light blue/1 white; pink/1 red, outlined in
black) forming circles (ca. 0.45 diam) and ellipses and, in

[111]The directions are based on the position of the
pavement in the courtyard.

the interstitial rows, concave-sided octagons. The circles
enclose various motifs which are set on light or dark grounds
depending on their values. Thus a black hexafoil and two
white and red wheel designs are placed on a white ground, and
a light-colored cruciform interlace and a Solomon's knot
(both, .red/pink/white; yellow/l white) are set on a black
ground. The ellipses and the smaller circles are accented
by pink/red motifs and the octagonal interstitial units with
single, serrate-edged straight squares or squares set on edge
which follow no ostensible color sequence. Their chromatic
scheme, blue and red/pink with black outlines, is repeated
in the serrated triangles along the margins which, however,
alternate color.

First half of the fifth century.

Mosaic Fragments

Nos. 25-26

Fragments of two mosaic panels, found in the vicinity of
the Kerameikos cemetary, are now in different storerooms of
the field house of the German Archaeological Institute. Although no record of their discovery is preserved, and their
archaeological and architectural contexts are not known, they
are so similar in style, technique, and iconography that they
probably belonged to the same building.

Each fragment contains a crude geometric design which is

interrupted in the center by an inset with a single bird
facing to the right and surrounded by abstract foliage (pls.
71-72). The field designs and the figures are flat and
two-dimensional, and the tesserae are irregular in size and
placement. Their dark color schemes are also similar with
red, black, and grey predominating. These fragments differ
greatly from the other tessellated pavements in Athens,
datable to the fifth century (1-20, 23), which are well
executed, have lighter color schemes, and more three-
dimensional, organic forms. It is probable, therefore, that
the Kerameikos fragments belong to a later phase, that is, to
the sixth century.

25 Mosaic fragment (1.20 x 1.17). Provenance unknown.
     Pl. 71.
   Field, including double fillet: ca. 1.08 max x 1.14).
Stone tesserae (0.015 sq; 0.008 for figures) set 2-4mm apart.

Polychrome geometric design with a small figural inset.
   Framing: wide black band; white double fillet.
   Field, framed by a black double fillet: red intersecting
circles forming white concave-sided squares which are inscribed by red stepped squares with light blue centers. The
design is bisected by the margins which are accented at regular intervals with small red florets rising from triple crowstep motifs. A floret and crowstep pattern also borders the
inset panel (0.34 x 0.37), framed by a white/black double

fillet, which contains a light blue and purple land bird
standing on a leaf-bearing branch. Two other branches, one
in front of the bird and the other hovering diagonally above
it, fleck the white surface with brown and green highlights.

Additional color. Bird: red legs.

Probably sixth century.

Illustration. German Archaeological Institute: Ker 1534,
Storeroom 1 = our pl. 71.

26 Mosaic fragment (1.77 x 1.40). Provenance unknown.

Pl. 72.

Field, including double fillet: 1.70 x 1.29. Material
identical to that in the preceding entry (25).

Polychrome grid with a small figure inset.

Framing: wide grey band; white double fillet.

Field, framed by a black double fillet which forms, at the
same time, part of the design: grid composed of dark grey
stepped squares set on edge on a white ground and bisected
along the margins. They are inscribed with concentric red/
white/black stepped squares set on edge containing alternating light blue and white centers. Filling the interstices
are black-centered, red squares which are identical in form
to the other squares. The center of the design is interrupted by a black-framed panel (0.37 sq) decorated with a
grey land bird amid spreading brown branches with green
leaves.

Additional color. Bird: black striations.

Probably sixth century.

   Illustration. German Archaeological Institute: Ker 1535,
Storeroom 2 = our pl. 72.

                          No. 27

     A third mosaic fragment which was at one time in the
possession of the German Archaeological Institute at Athens,
resembles the two preceding entries (pl. 73). Although it
has disappeared and its provenance is not known, it probably
was found in the same vicinity as the others since its nega-
tive number immediately precedes those of the others.

27 Mosaic fragment (dimensions indeterminable). Provenance
    and present location not known. Pl. 73.

Fragment containing a figure inset enclosed by a geometric
border.
   Framing: wide dark band; border, dark indented triangles;
white double fillet.
   Field, framed by a two-tone double fillet: originally a
peacock turned to the left of which traces survive of a
diagonal train with ocellate spots and a spray of leaf-
bearing branches.

Sixth century; probably contemporary with the two fragments found at Kerameikos (25, 26).

Illustration. German Archaeological Institute: Ker 1533 = our pl. 73.

AIXONE

Hall

In 1919, the ruins of a hall were discovered at Aixone, near Glyphada which contained two, possibly three, levels of habitation, the second one belonging to the Early Christian period (pl. 74). This middle level contained a mosaic pavement which was over four meters long. Since the specific location of the site was not noted in the report, the condition of the building and its decoration could not be determined.

At the lowest recorded level, forty centimeters below the mosaic pavement and on the north side of the site, traces were found of a tile and cement floor, and a fountain. Given the brief duration of the excavation, it was not determined if this level belonged to the first phase of the hall or to an earlier building which it replaced. On the basis of the sherds, this level was attributed to the early part of the Roman Empire.[112] The second and possibly the first phase of the building is represented by a rectangular hall, I, which

---

[112]A. D. Keramopoulos, Praktika, 1919, p. 41; hereafter cited as Keramopoulos.

was entered from the west (pl. 74). On its south side were
two small rooms which contained basins of some kind, II-III.
They were paved with marble or ceramic slabs surrounded by
small marble pieces in opus sectile,[113] and the hall with
mosaic. During the last phase, the hall was divided by a
wall running east-west which destroyed a section of the
mosaic, and the small south rooms were compartmentalized.

Although no archaeological finds for the second and
third levels were unearthed or reported, they were assigned
to the Roman or Early Christian period.[114] An Early Christian
date for the second level is indicated by the design of the
mosaic pavement which is datable to the fifth century.

Bibliography. A. D. Keramopoulos, Praktika, 1919, pp. 32-
46; AA, 37 (1923), p. 250.

Illustration. A. D. Keramopoulos, Praktika, 1919, p. 38,
fig. 2 = our pl. 74.

No. 28

A purely geometric design composed of interlocking
lozenges and squares decorates the central part of Room I
(pl. 75). The design is articulated by simple bands and
contains decorative filling motifs which enrich the overall
appearance of the pavement. A terminus post quem of the late

[113]Keramopoulos, p. 37.

[114]At first Keramopoulos states Early Christian (p. 41)
and then Roman or Early Christian (p. 43).

fourth or early fifth century is provided by similar pavements at Epidauros (44, pls. 104, 106) and Demetrias (130;
133, pls. 429, 433) which are more austere and contain simple
fillers. Since, however, the Aixone pavement is aniconic and
its filling elements are not as complex as those belonging
to the second half of the fifth century (15; 16, pls. 44-47),
it can be assigned to the middle of the century.

Illustration. A. D. Keramopoulos, Praktika, 1919, p. 38,
fig. 2 = our pl. 74.

28 Room I (width, 4.80; length indeterminable). Pl. 75.

Fragment: 4.80 x 3.85.[115] No published information on
dimensions and material.

Polychrome design of interlocking geometric motifs bordered
by scales.

Framing: dark fillet; light band; dark fillet; border,
imbrication pattern composed of rows of light scales with
colored tips; dark fillet; light band.

Field, framed by a dark fillet: interlocking geometric
design comprising crosses of four lozenges separated by
squares.[116] The lozenges are bisected along the margins.
The units are articulated by dark/light/dark fillets and are

---

[115]The measurements are taken from the plan (pl. 74).

[116]The reason for the narrowing of the field on the
northwest side is not given. Presumably, it was altered to
accomodate an architectural feature.

set on a dark ground. With the exception of three panels with two heart-shaped ivy leaves placed back-to-back, the lozenges are inscribed with light "eye motifs" with dark centers. The squares are filled with curvilinear and rectilinear motifs which follow no consistent compositional sequence: two-strand Solomon's knots; ovals forming diagonal quatrefoils; checkerboard patterns; grid of rectangular triangles; zig-zags.

Around the middle of the fifth century.

Illustration. A. D. Keramopoulos, *Praktika*, 1919, p. 42, fig. 3 = our pl. 75.

AIGOSTHENA

Basilica

At ancient Aigosthena on the east coast of the Gulf of Corinth a large, five-aisled basilica (pl. 76; overall, 20.38 x 25.15) was brought to light in 1951. Fragments of mosaic pavements were discovered in the narthex, nave, and bema, and in the baptistery unit to the south. At the present time, the pavements are in very poor condition with lacunae and loose tesserae throughout.

Because of the limited scope of the excavation and the ruinous condition of the building, only its general plan was determined. It comprises a narrow narthex, I (20.38 x 3.72), a nave, II (5.90 x 16.43), with two flanking aisles on each

side, IV-VII (average width, 2.80), a bema, III (5.90 x
5.00),[117] and a semi-circular apse with an inscribed stone
synthronon. The nave is separated from the aisles and the
aisles from each other by elevated stylobates running from
the east to the west walls while a chancel screen separates
the bema from the nave.[118] In the complex of rooms on the
south side of the church proper, only the baptistry unit,
VIII-IX, has been identified.

Although no datable archaeological finds were unearthed
or reported, on the basis of the style of the mosaics, the
church is attributed by the excavator to the late fifth or
early sixth century.[119] It will be shown below that the
pavements contain certain stylistic and compositional features which belong to the sixth century.

Sometime during the seventh century the basilica was
destroyed and the site remained uninhabited until the
eleventh century when a monastery with a small triconch
church was built over its ruins.[120] Subsequently, the monastery was destroyed but the church survived and served as a
funerary chapel for a cemetary which was laid out toward the

---

[117]The dimensions of the nave and bema are taken from
the plan (pl. 76).

[118]One base of a column was found on the stylobate between the two north aisles (A. K. Orlandos, Praktika, 1954,
pp. 131-132; hereafter cited as Orlandos). Although it is
not discussed in the reports, traces of the foundations of
the screen are still visible along the east side of the
mosaic pavement.

[119]Orlandos, pp. 13, 138; idem, To Ergon, 1954, p. 17.

[120]Orlandos, p. 140, p. 141, fig. 13 (plan).

west. Many segments of the pavements in the nave and narthex were destroyed by graves.[121] The triconch, now dedicated to the Virgin Mary, still functions as a chapel for the local inhabitants.

Bibliography. A. K. Orlandos, Praktika, 1954, pp. 129-142; idem, To Ergon, 1954, pp. 16-18; E. Stassinopoulos, RAC, 32 (1956), p. 101; A. K. Orlandos, Actes du Ve congrès d'archéologie chrétienne, Aix-en-Provence, 1954 (Vatican, 1957), pp. 110-111.

Illustrations. A. K. Orlandos, Praktika, 1954, p. 130, fig. 2 = our pl. 76, p. 134, fig. 5 (font in baptistery), p. 141, fig. 13 (plan with traces of later monastery).

Nos. 29-33

Crude polychrome geometric mosaics originally paved the most prominent zones--narthex, nave, bema--and the baptistery to the south. With the exception of a figural inset at the entrance to the nave (pl. 80), the mosaics are aniconic and contain homogeneous decorative schemes consisting, for the most part, of various combinations of interlocking, intersecting or juxtaposed lozenges, circles and squares (pls. 77, 82).

Although the pavements have been assigned to the late fifth or early sixth century,[122] certain features argue for a sixth century date. In this period the figures are executed as flat, two-dimensional forms with strong black or dark

[121]Orlandos, p. 138.

[122]Vide supra, p. 74, n. 119.

outlines and appear suspended in the opaque space of their panels. This figure style is employed in the inset panel in the narthex (pl. 80) where birds and plants are scattered across the surface, and in the basilicas at Klapsi (95, pls. 316-332), Nea Anchialos (115, pls. 382-393), Theotokou (123-127, pls. 413-417), and Nikopolis (150-156, pls. 460-532) which are securely dated to the sixth century. In addition, another feature which suggests a later date is the unusual tripartite division of the nave pavement on its longitudinal axis which does not appear in the fifth century. Rather, the scheme usually involves one large panel (pls. 157, 420) or two to three panels (pls. 257-258, 295) which are arranged along the width of the room. Although the more traditional scheme continues into the sixth century (pls. 315, 676), it is at this time that the longitudinal division appears at Nikopolis Alpha (153, pl. 476) and in the basilica at Theotokou (127, pl. 417). On the basis of style and composition, therefore, the Aigosthena pavements can be assigned to the sixth century.

Additional bibliography. Sodini, Catalogue, No. 3, pp. 702-703.

Illustration. A. K. Orlandos, Praktika, 1954, p. 103, fig. 2 = our pl. 76.

29 Room I (20.38 x 3.72). Narthex; partially destroyed by
     later graves. Pls. 77-80.

     Fragment: ca. 7.00 x 3.72. Framing: 0.50. Field: 7.00
max x 2.20. Panel: 0.40 max x 1.00. Irregularly-cut stone

tesserae (average, 0.015 sq; others 0.005 x 0.01) set 2-4mm apart.

Originally, probably three rectangular geometric panels, of which two survive, set within a guilloche framework and bordered by intersecting circles.

Surround: rows of grey tesserae parallel to the walls.

Framing (pl. 78): white double fillet; black fillet; border, white intersecting circles, outlined in black, forming dark grey concave-sided squares set on edge. The latter are inscribed with irregularly-shaped crosslets composed of five white tesserae; black fillet; white double fillet.

Field, framed by a black fillet (pl. 77): traces of two panels set within a guilloche border (grey/1 white; yellow/1 white, outlined in black, with a white tessera at each loop) on a black ground.

Ia, north panel (pl. 79): interlocking design, articulated by black/white/black single fillets, comprising crosses of four lozenges separated by single squares. The design, which is set on a dark grey ground, is cut along the margins. Each lozenge is decorated with a rudimentary "eye motif" composed of a white-centered blue circle, outlined in black, flanked by two yellow stepped triangles. The yellow squares contain concentric dark grey/white squares set on edge and small white central crosslets of five tesserae.

Ib, middle panel (pl. 77): pairs of dark grey and yellow

opposed peltae, outlined in black, arranged in alternating
horizontal and vertical units (for a similar design, see 62,
pls. 170-171). At the entrance to the nave, the design is
interrupted by a grey inset (pl. 80) containing on its preserved south side three stylized white birds and grey flowers
which are oriented westward and set in superimposed registers.
The figures and the panels are outlined by black single and
double fillets, respectively.

Sixth century.

Illustrations. A. K. Orlandos, Praktika, 1954, p. 136,
fig. 8 (Ia), p. 137, fig. 9 (Ib), p. 138 (Ib, inset: drawing).

30 Room II (5.90 x 14.00). Nave; pavement laid up to chancel
    screen and stylobates; sections destroyed by later tri-
conch chapel to east and graves to west. Pls. 81-82.
    Two fragments; larger one to southeast, 4.11 x 1.90.
Border: 0.45. Field: 5.00 x 3.05 max. Panels: 1.00 sq.
Material identical to that in Room I (29).

Traces to the east of a straight grid bordered by an ivy
rinceau.
    Framing (pl. 81): white double fillet; black double fil-
let; border, undulating black rinceau (two fillets) composed
of rigidly arranged, widely spaced scrolls filled with single
red and yellow heart-shaped ivy leaves in an a-b sequence.
The pointed tips of the black-outlined leaves touch the

margins; black fillet.

Field, framed by a white triple fillet (pls. 76, 82):
traces of a straight grid composed of a two-strand guilloche
(same colors as in narthex, 29) forming multiple rows of
three squares each. The three preserved squares[123] are
framed by identical white triple fillets and black and white
stepped pyramids, but contain different patterns. Starting
at the east side, the sequence of filling elements is as
follows: umbrella pattern; octagon and square forming
elongated hexagons; checkerboard pattern composed of three
small squares each which contain alternating black and white
hour glass motifs.[124]

Sixth century.

Illustration. A. K. Orlandos, Praktika, 1954, p. 139,
fig. 11 (octagon and square pattern).

31 Room III (ca. 5.90 x 5.00). Bema
No published information on dimensions and material.

Brief mention of a mosaic pavement which was destroyed by the

---

[123]The west square is not indicated on the plan (pl. 76)
nor is it noted in the report (Orlandos, p. 138). Sodini,
Catalogue, p. 703, notes only two rows of squares. Although
omitted from the plan, pl. 76, traces of the border of triangles encompassing the central row of squares were visible
in 1969.

[124]The photograph for this entry was taken by Professor
Lavin prior to my visit in 1969. The panels are in such
ruinous condition that no color notes could be taken.

foundations of a triconch chapel.[125]

Probably contemporary with the preserved mosaics and, there-fore, sixth century.

32 Room VII (1.62 x 3.41). Vestibule; pavement replaced by
    a layer of rectangular brick slabs.

Brief mention of a mosaic pavement of which traces survive along the north door leading into the south aisle.[126] De-scribed as being a rectangular panel decorated with some kind of volute.[127]

Sixth century.

33 Room IX (3.50 x 3.41). Baptistery; pavement replaced
    by a layer of rectangular brick slabs.
    No published information on dimensions and material.

Brief mention of a mosaic pavement which was subsequently covered by brick slabs.[128]

---

[125]Orlandos, p. 138. This pavement is not noted by Sodini, loc. cit.

[126]Orlandos, p. 135.

[127]Sodini, Catalogue, p. 703.

[128]Orlandos, p. 135; omitted by Sodini (ibid.)

Probably sixth century.

LAVREOTIC OLYMPUS

Basilica

At Lavreotic Olympus, north of the acropolis of
Aigileias, the east side of an Early Christian basilica (pl.
83) was brought to light in 1929. The excavation was resumed
in 1952 at which time the entire structure was cleared (overall, 17.50 x 34.80) and mosaic pavements were discovered in
the bema and apse. At the present time the site is overgrown
and few traces of the pavements are preserved.

Preceded by two narthexes, I-II, the inner one with a
projecting annex, III,[129] the church proper consists of a
nave, V, flanked by two aisles, VIII-IX, and terminated by a
bema with a semi-circular apse, VI-VII. The nave is separated from the aisles by trabeated colonnades resting on
bases set on elevated stylobates and from the bema by a low
chancel screen which abuts two long piers projecting from
the east wall. On the chord of the apse traces were found of
a "Tau-shaped" enkainion beneath an altar which was protected
by a canopy resting on four columns. Behind it rises a marble
synthronon with two lateral steps. On the north side of the
nave, approximately two meters from the screen, lies the ambon
which comprises a circular podium flanked by stairs on the

---

[129]It is identified as a baptistery and Room IV as a

main axis of the building. The bema and apse are paved with
mosaics and the other sections with marble and stone slabs.

Although no significant archaeological finds were unearthed, on the basis of the style of the decorative sculpture, the shape of the ambon, and the typology of the
inscription in the apse, the church has been assigned to the
middle of the fifth century.[130] Although the descriptive and
photographic material on the mosaic pavements is meager,
their iconography appears to substantiate this chronology.

In a later period the north and south colonnades in the
nave were walled up (pl. 84) and the side aisles fell into
disuse. Additional walls were installed between the piers
and columns at the west entrance to the nave and in many
sections of the narthexes and the south wing. In the latter
sector, an olive press and other machinery were installed for
the manufacture of oil.[131]

Bibliography. Soteriou, Palaiochristianikai basilikai, pp.
184-185; N. Ch. Kotzia, Praktika, 1952, pp. 92-128; BCH, 77
(1953), p. 205.

Illustrations. N. Ch. Kotzia, Praktika, 1952, p. 93, fig.
1 (apse with "Tau-shaped" enkainion), p. 96, fig. 1 = our pl.
83, p. 97, fig. 2 = our pl. 84, p. 98, fig. 3 (foundations
of ambon), pp. 105-111 (fragments of decorative sculpture).

---

storage room (N. Ch. Kotzia, Praktika, 1952, p. 114; hereafter cited as Kotzia).

[130]Kotzia, pp. 126-127. He also cites numismatic evidence but since the stratigraphy of the coin is not given and
its attribution is not definite, its chronological usefulness
is doubtful.

[131]Kotzia, pp. 113-118, 127-128.

Nos. 34-35

Glass and stone polychrome mosaics decorate the bema
and the apse and reflect the internal divisions of these
sectors. The bema contains a " ⊔ -shaped" geometric design
with organic and geometric filling motifs which is laid up
to the chord of the apse and framed by an ivy leaf border
(pls. 85-87). Two small sectors between the north and south
piers and the projecting corners of the synthronon are filled
with a smaller version of the design, while the apse is
decorated with scales fanning eastward (pl. 89). Along the
base of the synthronon is a tessellated inscription invoking
the blessing of God for the anonymous donor of the mosaics.

The paucity of adequate photographs of the pavements
precludes a systematic stylistic analysis. Since, however,
organic motifs decorate most of the large octagonal compartments in the bema (pl. 87), the pavement is more advanced
than similar but aniconic designs in the churches at Arkitsa
and Demetrias (89-92; 130-138) which are securely datable to
the late fourth or early fifth century. To a degree this
chronology is substantiated by the style of the scales in
the apse (pl. 89) which show pronounced black/white/black
outlines. This kind of delineation does not appear until
the middle and second half of the century (188, pl. 617; 205,
pl. 645). For these reasons the mosaics are contemporaneous
with the church which has been attributed to the middle of
the fifth century.

Additional bibliography. Sodini, Catalogue, No. 4, p. 703.

Illustration. N. Ch. Kotzia, Praktika, 1952, p. 97, fig.
2 = our pl. 84.

34 Room VI (8.00 x 2.70).[132] Bema. Pls. 85-87.

No published information on dimensions. Marble (white,
black, dark blue, red, yellow) and glass (greens) tesserae.[133]

Polychrome " ⊔ -shaped" pavement decorated with a geometric
network inscribed with geometric and organic motifs.

Framing (pl. 85): border, undulating black rinceau (one
fillet) composed of rigidly arranged, widely spaced scrolls
filled with single red and pink ivy leaves in an a-b sequence.

Field (pls. 86-87): black and white grid of alternating
octagons[134] and equilateral crosses forming elongated hexagons. The octagons are filled with ducks, green ivy leaves,
interlaces forming looped isosceles crosses (pl. 86) and, in
front of the steps of the synthronon, with green trees with
large red fruit (pl. 87).[135] The filling motifs and the
ground of the crosses and hexagons are, for the most part,
light blue and red. A smaller version of this grid design
decorates the sectors between the north and south piers and
the corners of the synthronon.

-----

[132]The measurement is taken from the plan (pl. 83).

[133]Kotzia, p. 112.

[134]Kotzia repeatedly refers to them as hexagons (p. 113).

[135]Kotzia, pp. 112-113.

Middle of the fifth century.

35 Room VII (3.60 diam). Apse. Pls. 88-89.

No published information on dimensions. Materials identical to those in the bema (34).

Polychrome imbrication pattern framed along the east side by an inscription.

Framing: inscription in black letters (0.11-0.13 high) installed by the anonymous donor of the pavement: ΥΠΕΡΕ ΥΧΗΟΟΕΟΟΕΙΔΕΝΤΑΚΑΙΤΟΝΑΡΙΦΝΟΝΕΚΑΛΙΕΡΓΗΟΕΝ (pl. 88).[136]

Field: imbrication pattern composed of light blue and pink scales, fanning eastward, outlined by black/2white/black fillets.[137]

Middle of the fifth century.

Illustrations. Soteriou, Palaiochristianikai basilikai, p. 185, fig. 16 (plan of east side with inscription; N. Ch. Kotzia, Praktika, 1952, p. 112, fig. 2 = our pl. 86, p. 113, fig. 13 = our pl. 87, p. 114, fig. 14 = our pl. 89.

---

[136]The following emendation is by Kotzia, p. 119: ΥΠΕΡΕΥΧΗΟΟ[ΓΟΘ]ΕΟΟΕΙΔΕΝΤ[ΟΟΝΟΜ]ΑΚΑΙΤΟΝΑΡΙΦΝΟΝΕΚΑΛΙΕΡΓΗΟΕΝ. The inscription is visible in Soteriou's plan, Palaiochristianikai basilikai, p. 185, fig. 16.

[137]This design is omitted by Sodini, Catalogue, p. 703.

PART II. PELOPPONESUS

PATRAS

Mosaic Fragment

No. 36

36 Mosaic fragment (no dimensions published).
No published information on dimensions and material.

In 1969 a chance find in Patras brought to light a Christian
mosaic pavement with an inscription citing the name of a
deaconess, Appiana.[138]

Date and present location indeterminable.
Bibliography. Sodini, Catalogue, No. 13, p. 708.

MBOZIKA

Basilica

Beneath the modern church of St. George in Mbozika, near

---

[138]Published in the Greek newspaper, To Vema, March 16,
1969. I would like to thank Professor Eugene Vanderpool of
the American School of Classical Studies at Athens for this
reference.

the ancient city of Titane, traces of an Early Christian
basilica and a mosaic pavement were discovered in 1957. No
systematic excavation was undertaken and the evidence has disappeared.

It was dated to the second half of the sixth century on
the basis of a coin of Justinian II and Sophia which, however, was found at a distance from the site. The style of
the pavement points to a date no earlier than the late fifth
century.

Bibliography. D. I. Pallas, RAC, 35 (1959), pp. 214-215;
BCH, 82 (1958), p. 702.

No. 37

37 Mosaic fragment (no dimensions published). Pls. 89a-b.
No published information on dimensions and material.

Originally, probably a vase from which issued an ivy vine
(see 100, pl. 350; 137, pl. 437; 152, pls. 469-470). All
that remain are traces of a schematized ribbed vase and one
heart-shaped ivy leaf with a curling tendril (pls. 89 a-b).
This part is flanked on one side by a second panel, framed
by five fillets, which contains traces of an intersecting
circle pattern forming concave-sided squares.

Probably sixth century; on the basis of the flat, two-
dimensional style of the vase.

Additional bibliography. Sodini, Catalogue, No. 6, p. 704.

Illustrations. D. I. Pallas, RAC, 35 (1959), p. 215, fig. 30a = our pl. 89a; BCH, 82 (1958), p. 701, fig. 16 = our pl. 89b.

KENCHREAE

Building

At Kenchreae, the port of Ancient Corinth situated on the west bank of the Saronic Gulf, three excavations between 1963 and 1966 brought to light some of the foundations of a complex comprising an apsidal building with flanking halls (overall, 22.50 x 21.50)[139] and additional rooms to the west (pls. 90-91). Traces of mosaic pavements were found in Rooms I, II, III, IX, and marble slabs with decorative strips in VIII.[140] At the present time, the pavements are covered and the site is partially overgrown.

The precise plan of the complex (pl. 91) is difficult to determine because it underwent several periods of reconstruction between the fourth and the sixth centuries, and the archaeological reports are oftentimes obtuse and devoid

---

[139]All the dimensions are taken from the plan (pl. 91). The buildings were constructed over the ruins of "warehouses" belonging primarily to the Roman period (R. L. Scranton and E. S. Ramage, Hesperia, 33 [1964], pp. 138-140; hereafter cited as Hesperia, 1964); idem, Hesperia, 36 (1967), pp. 152-158; hereafter cited as Hesperia, 1967.

[140]Room VI had a paving of packed earth and two unidentified rooms on the west side of the site were paved with marble slabs and ceramic tiles (Hesperia, 1964, p. 193; Hesperia, 1967, p. 156).

of substantive illustrative material. It is clear that the
east side of the complex is dominated by a rectangular structure, II-IV (6.25 x 21.50), with a semi-circular apse to the
east and a small room to the west.[141] Flanking its north and
south sides are pairs of narrow halls, V-VI and VII-VIII
(average width, 3.10) which communicate with each other but
not with the central room.[142] Thus the long transverse unit,
I (22.50 x ca. 3.00), extending the length of the west facade
serves as the sole means of communication between the apsidal
room and its lateral units. The excavations also uncovered
parts of several rooms on the west side of Room I, one with
a tessellated pavement (IX), but it is uncertain if they are
contemporaneous with, or predate, the east buildings.[143]
Since no trace of tessellated pavements were found among the
ruins of the earlier buildings below,[144] it is quite possible
that at least Room IX belongs to the same period as the
apsidal structure and its dependencies to the east. For this
reason, it will be included in the corpus with the understanding that this is subject to change upon the completion

[141]Although the building is oriented northwest, for
purposes of clarity the cardinal points will be used.

[142]A colonnade set on a stylobate separated Rooms VII
and VIII and a "sill" of some kind Rooms V and VI (Hesperia,
1967, pp. 154-155).

[143]Their problematic relationship is based on a difference in their masonry (Hesperia, 1964, p. 139).

[144]Indeed, one would not expect to find mosaics in a
"warehouse," (vide supra, p. 88, n. 139).

of the excavation of this sector.

Although the excavators ascribe an ecclesiastical
function to the apsidal building this is by no means substantiated by the published data. There are vague references
to "Early Christian" furnishings and architectural sculptural
but since they were found in the debris covering the building[145] their usefulness is questionable. In addition, the
plan differs to a considerable extent from any preserved
church in Greece. Its isolation from the flanking halls,
V-VI and VII-VIII is curious as is the division of the west
side into a "narthex" (II) and "nave" (III). Although it is
quite possible that the former room was a vestibule, its
location within the body of the building precludes its
identification as a "narthex." Narthexes in churches in the
Greek East are always external units attached to, not incorporated into, the church proper.[146] Thus, it is doubtful
that this building was a church. On the other hand, it could
have served as a chapel of some kind, as a pistikon for the
catachumens, or as a depository for the offerings or sacred
utensils and vestments. It could even have served as an
audience or reception hall. Similar one-aisled structures
abound in Christian complexes,[147] but its chronology mitigates

---

[145]Hesperia, 1964, p. 139; see also, Hesperia, 1967, pp.
152-157.

[146]See our plans, pl. 24, passim and Orlandos,
Xylostegos basilikē, pp. 94-110, 130-151, and pp. 100-101,
pls. A-B, p. 131, fig. 84, passim.

[147]See, for example, pls. 457, 548.

against this attribution. Pottery finds in the walls of the
building and elsewhere predate the middle of the fourth
century.[148] No other Christian building has been found in
Greece which belongs to this period. Rather, the earliest
ones seem to be clustered around the turn of the century,
that is, the late fourth and early fifth centuries (44-49;
88-92; 130-138; 178-179). For these reasons, the Christian
attribution must be seriously questioned.[149] This is not to
say that in a subsequent phase the building did not serve some
Christian function. Indeed, there is evidence to support
this hypothesis. Before its destruction at the end of the
sixth century,[150] along with the shortening of Room III by
the addition of a second apse to the west of the original
one, benches were installed in Room I and a basin with a
canopy in Room IX (baptismal font?) which destroyed segments
of the tessellated pavements.[151] Similar features are found
in many Greek church complexes so that it is not unlikely
that this one was converted by the Christians.

Bibliography. R. L. Scranton and E. S. Ramage, Hesperia,
33 (1964), pp. 137-140; E. S. Ramage, AJA, 68 (1964), pp.
198-199; BCH, 99 (1964), pp. 710-719; JHS, 84 (1964),

---

[148]Hesperia, 1964, p. 139; Hesperia, 1967, p. 158.

[149]Although the date of the building places it beyond
the chronological scope of this corpus, its purported
Christian function necessitated its inclusion.

[150]No reasons are given for the date and destruction of
the building (see Hesperia, 1967, p. 158).

[151]Hesperia, 1967, p. 156. In an earlier report, the
basin is incorrectly placed in another room (Hesperia, 1964,
p. 139).

Supplement, p. 5; J. Hawthorne, Archaeology, 18 (1965), pp.
191-200; E. S. Ramage, AJA, 69 (1965), pp. 173-174; BCH, 100
(1965), pp. 697-700; JHS, 85 (1965), Supplement, pp. 7-8;
R. L. Scranton and E. S. Ramage, Hesperia, 36 (1967), pp.
152-158.

Illustrations. R. L. Scranton and E. S. Ramage, Hesperia,
36 (1967), p. 128, fig. 2 = our pl. 90; p. 131, fig. 3 =
our pl. 91.

Nos. 38-41

Traces of purely geometric pavements were discovered in
four rooms, I, II, III, IX. The designs consist of various
combinations of interlocking, intersecting or tangent circles
and squares which are inscribed with simple motifs (pls. 92-
93). On the basis of external evidence, the mosaics can be
assigned to the first half of the fourth century.

Additional bibliography. Sodini, Catalogue, No. 11, pp.
707-708.

Illustration. R. L. Scranton and E. S. Ramage, Hesperia,
36 (1967), p. 131, fig. 3 = our pl. 91.

38 Room I (22.50 x 3.00). Corridor; repaired with reused
    marble slabs and large ceramic tiles;[152] along the north-
east and southwest walls, later masonry benches destroyed
segments of the pavement. Pl. 92.

No published information on dimensions and material.

Fragments of a simple geometric mosaic decorated with three

---

[152]Hesperia, 1964, p. 139.

types of grids and an intersecting circle design. The
diversity of patterns and their curious juxtaposition suggest
restoration of some parts of the pavement. Given the paucity
of photographic and descriptive data, the original part of
the pavement cannot be identified.

Ia, section in front of west entrance to Room II (pl. 92
left):[153]

Field: intersecting circles forming concave-sided squares
which are inscribed with small squares set on edge.

Ib, section to west of preceding one (pl. 92, right).

Framing: white band; border to west only, fillet decorated
at regular intervals with small ovals.

Field: simple straight grid composed of juxtaposed circles
joined by short single bars and forming squares with concave
corners. The filling motifs consist of small stepped squares
set on edge.

Ic, section contiguous to Ia and b and separated from them
by a simple fillet (pl. 92, center): straight grid composed
of juxtaposed rows of alternating short bars and circles[154]
which is superimposed by a diagonal grid. The mosaic continues up to the entrance to the south hall (VII).[155]

_____

[153]It is not illustrated in the plan (pl. 91).

[154]An exceptional feature of the design is the omission
of the connecting bars between the circles on the east-west
axis.

[155]This is not indicated in the plan (pl. 91).

Id, section to south of Ic: all that is discernible in the
published photograph (pl. 92, top) is a straight grid composed
of small squares set on edge which are joined by single bars.

First half of the fourth century.

Illustrations. R. L. Scranton, Hesperia, 33 (1964), pl.
23c = our pl. 92.

39 Room II (6.25 x 3.50). Vestibule? Pl. 92.

No published information on dimensions and material.

Brief mention of a mosaic pavement.[156] In a plan and photograph (pls. 91-92), there are traces of a lozenge inscribed
with a circle.

First half of the fourth century.

Illustrations. R. L. Scranton and E. S. Ramage, Hesperia,
33 (1964), pl. 23c = our pl. 92; idem, Hesperia, 36 (1967),
p. 131, fig. 3 = our pl. 91.

40 Room III (6.25; length indeterminable). Pl. 91.

No published information on dimensions and material.

Brief mention of a mosaic pavement.[157] In the plan (pl. 91)
there are traces of two juxtaposed squares of which one

---

[156]Omitted by Sodini (Catalogue, p. 708) because he did
not read the final report (see Hesperia, 1967, p. 153).

[157]Hesperia, 1964, p. 139; Hesperia, 1967, p. 153.

contains a diagonal quatrefoil of lanceolate leaves.

First half of the fourth century.

Illustration. R. L. Scranton and E. S. Ramage, Hesperia, 36 (1967), p. 131, fig. 3 = our pl. 91.

41 Room IX (dimensions indeterminable). Possibly converted
into a baptistry when a basin installed which destroyed
part of the pavement. Pl. 93.

Brief mention of a mosaic pavement.[158] In a published photograph (pl. 93) there is an aniconic grid inscribed with
Solomon's knots.

Surround: in rows parallel to the walls.

Field: complex straight grid of juxtaposed squares joined
by small lateral rectangles to form equilateral crosses.[159]
The squares are bisected along the edges of the field.[160]
The elements of the design are articulated by a two-strand
guilloche (with a white tessera at each loop), set on a dark
ground, which is outlined by dark/2 light/dark fillets. The
squares are inscribed with concentric squares and the crosses
with single squares set on edge containing Solomon's knots.

---

[158]Ibid.

[159]The design is barely visible in the plan (pl. 91).

[160]Since no framing device is used, the ground of the
surround merges with the ground of the half squares. For a
similar design with, however, marginal borders, see pl. 26.
An incorrect caption identifies this pavement as belonging to
the second century A. D. (see J. Hawthorne, Archaeology, 18
[1965], fig. on p. 196).

First half of the fourth century.

Illustration. R. L. Scranton and E. S. Ramage, Hesperia,
33 (1964), pl. 23d = our pl. 93.

OLD CORINTH

Building

A chance find in 1966, southwest of the ancient theatre
of Old Corinth, brought to light a room paved with a mosaic
(pl. 94). Traces of the rest of the building were exposed
but the excavation was halted after three days because the
property was privately owned. At the present time the pavement is in good condition and protected by plastic sheets
and sand.[161]

Since only the general outlines of the room were exposed,
the function and plan of the building were not determined.
Judging from the shape of the pavement and the few preserved
foundations, the room was cruciform in plan with the east-
west arms longer than the north-south ones. The major entrance
was probably located on the south side since this is the
orientation of the central tessellated panel containing an
inscription " ΚΑΛΟΙΚΑΙΡΟΙ " which accompanies a scene with
three figures (pl. 95). Another panel with figures survives

---

[161] I am indebted to Mr. C. K. Williams, Director of the
Corinth Excavations, for clearing the central panel for me
and for giving me a copy of the field notes of the excavator,
Professor H. S. Robinson (Notebook 346: 22-23 August, 1966,
pp. 165-167; 26 August, 1966, pp. 178-179); hereafter cited
as Robinson.

in the east arm (pl. 98) but it faces westward; probably a
third panel occupied the west arm and was oriented, like its
counterpart to the east, toward the center of the room.

No datable archaeological finds were recorded in the
field notes and in the published reports vague references
are made to the fourth century[162] and to an "Early Christian"
building.[163] On the basis of the style and iconography of
the pavement, a date in the second half of the fifth century
is probable.

Bibliography. H. S. Robinson, "Notebook 346: 22-23 August,
1966, pp. 165-167 and 26 August, 1966, pp. 178-179," Archives
of the Corinth Excavations, Corinth, Greece; C. K. Williams,
Deltion, 22 (1967), Bl: Chronika, p. 185; Ph. A. Drosoyianni,
Deltion, 22 (1967), Bl: Chronika, p. 222; BCH, 91 (1967),
p. 635.

Illustration. C. K. Williams, Deltion, 22 (1967), Bl:
Chronika, pl. 135b (general view).

No. 42

The room was probably originally decorated with three
figural panels set within a cruciform design. The main
panel (pl. 95) contains two winged representations of the
Beautiful Seasons (ΚΑΛΟΙΚΑΙΡΟΙ) crowning a third one. It is
flanked to the east by a panel filled with a different species
of birds (pl. 98) which was probably accompanied by a

---

[162]Robinson; C. K. Williams, Deltion, 22 (1967), Bl:
Chronika, p. 185.

[163]Ph. A. Drosoyianni, Deltion, 22 (1967), Bl:
Chronika, p. 222.

similarly disposed scene, now lost, on the west side of the
room. On the basis of the theme of the central panel, the
pavement can be assigned to the second half of the fifth
century when allegorial representations reappear in secular
and religious buildings. They reflect a trend toward the
enrichment of mosaic pavements by means of color, complex
geometric designs, and figures from the land and sea. The
theme of the "ΚΑΛΟΙΚΑΙΡΟΙ" is found in two other pavements
which, however, are derived from a completely different
iconographic model. One pavement at Tegea (70), now lost,
also contained a central figure receiving offerings from two
rushing figures. Unlike the coronation scene in the Corinth
pavement, the flanking figures at Tegea offered baskets of
fruit and were wingless. A later and somewhat expanded version of the Tegea scene decorates the nave of a basilica at
Delphi where the Seasons occupy separate panels (83, pls.
265-268).[164] Despite the iconographic differences, the
thematic similarity is obvious and argues for a date in the
second half of the fifth century.[165]

Additional bibliography. Sodini, Catalogue, p. 709, n. 17.

Illustrations. C. K. Williams, Deltion, 22 (1967), Bl:
Chronika, pl. 135b (general view).

_____

[164]For similar figures with baskets, see the representations of April, May, July, and February at Thebes (75,
pls. 225, 227-230).

[165]The representations of the months and the seasons in
Greek pavements will be the subject of a study in the
immediate future.

42 Room I (no dimensions published). Pls. 94-98.

Guilloche border: 0.40. Central panel: 0.78 x 1.00 max.
East panel: 59.00 x 0.86. Stone and ceramic tesserae (average, 0.01 sq; for features, 0.003-0.005 sq) set 1-4mm apart.

Polychrome pavement decorated with delicate geometric pat-
terms, and figural panels with representations of the
"Beautiful Seasons" and six birds.[166]

Surround: in rows parallel to the walls.

Framing: dark double fillet; border, intersecting grey and
red circles forming white concave-sided squares which are
inscribed with small yellow rectangles.

Field, framed by a dark double fillet (pl. 94): large
cruciform panel composed of pairs of white scales with grey
and pink/red tips arranged in alternating horizontal and
vertical units. The black-outlined scales are cut along the
margins and are interrupted in the middle of the central
and west arms by two rectangular panels with figures.

Ia central panel (pls. 95-97).

Framing: white double fillet; border (0.50), two-strand
guilloche (dark grey/light grey/white; red/pink/white, outlined in black) on a black ground; white double fillet; dark
red double fillet.

---

[166]Since I only saw the central panel, the data on the
other preserved panel are based on Robinson's field notes
which contain few measurements and no color notes for the
east panel.

Field: fragment of a panel, oriented southward, with representations of three Seasons who were originally flanked by
two large cypress trees, outlined in black.[167] The panel is
decorated along the bottom with black bushes with red and
white buds and along the top with an inscription " ΚΑΛΟΙ
ΚΑΙΡΟΙ " in black letters (0.07 to 0.095 high). The scene
shows a figure who is about to be crowned with a wreath of
red and pink flowers held above his head by two flanking figures who rush forward with fluttering wings and tunics.
Their movement is contrasted by the position of their heads
which are turned away from the center. Although little remains of the central figure, it is clear that he faced the
right figure while holding the right hand of the other one,
whose arm is bent at the elbow and folded across his waist
(pls. 96-97).[168] An overall chromatic harmony is obtained
by the use of pale green for the wings, tunics, and hair of
the lateral figures with black (wings and hair), and greyish
green (tunics) for the outlines. In addition, the short,
sleeveless tunics contain dark green fluting and are decorated
with clavi and segmenta of the same color. The flesh tones
of the limbs are represented with little uniformity or agreement in regard to the placement of the white highlights. The
right arm of the figure on the left side contains two rows of

---

[167]Traces of the tip of the right cypress tree were
noted by Robinson (p. 178).

[168]This is not very apparent in the photographs because
their hands are not well defined.

pink and one row of white tesserae while his left arm contains one or two rows of white, one row of light pink and one row of dark pink. Both arms, however, show a similar dark red contour line along the outside. The right arm of the right figure is the same as the left arm of his counterpart but a second row of white tesserae replaces the dark pink row. Unlike the large tesserae which define the limbs, the facial contours and features are executed with smaller tesserae. Their curly-haired heads are round with red outlines and pink moving to white flesh tones. They are distinguished by small eyes, straight or slightly curving eyebrows and lips which are executed with irregularly-cut black tesserae. Their noses are small and angular, and framed on one side by a row of red tesserae.

Generally, the figures are somewhat flat and two-dimensional, and poorly executed. The tesserae are irregularly placed, the limbs are distorted, and the hands and feet summarily rendered. Attempts at foreshortening are unsuccessful as is shown by the flat physiognomies of the lateral figures. The plants at the bottom of the scene, the brief costumes of the figures, and the floral wreath identify the "Beautiful Seasons" as the summer months of May, June, and July.[169]

---

[169]See, for example, the months at Argos (55, pls. 136-145), Tegea (69, pls. 208-214) and Thebes (75, pls. 225, 227-230) where the garments change with the time of the year.

Ib, east panel (pl. 98), framed by a black fillet: three
superimposed registers decorated with pairs of identical confronting birds separated by a sinuous, bud-bearing bush
which rises from the bottom of the panel. The birds, which
become progressively larger and more decorative toward the
bottom of the scene, are depicted standing on one leg and
pecking at the bush in front of them. Their bodies are
outlined by a dark fillet and appear to be modeled, especially in the area of their wings.[170]

Second half of the fifth century.

  Illustration. C. K. Williams, *Deltion*, 22 (1967), B1:
Chronika, pl. 135a = our pl. 98.

ELIS

Mosaic Pavement

    In 1964, during the excavation of an ancient theatre at
Elis, near Olympia, a segment of a mosaic pavement was found
incorporated into the interior of its portico. The pavement
was lifted, consolidated and at the present time is *in situ*
and covered.[171]

    The pavement, which lies at a considerably higher level

---

    [170]*Vide supra*, p. 96, n. 161.

    [171]A. K. Orlandos, *To Ergon*, 1967, pp. 17-18, p. 16,
figs. 11-12.

than the original floor of the portico,[172] covers an area
over twenty-two meters by eight meters and has been attributed to a Christian basilica. Since the only stated reason
for this attribution is the so-called west-east orientation
of the purely geometric designs (pls. 99-102), the function
of the building is problematic[173] but its chronology is not.
Although no datable archaeological finds were unearthed, on
the basis of the style of the mosaics, the building can be
assigned to the second half of the fifth century.

Bibliography. N. Ph. Yialouris, Praktika, 1964, pp. 136-
139; A. K. Orlandos, To Ergon, 1964, pp. 116-117; N. Ph.
Yialouris, Deltion, 20 (1965), B2: Chronika, p. 211; BCH, 89
(1965), p. 749; V. Leon, JOAI, 47 (1964-1965), Beiblatt, pp.
74-102; N. Ph. Yialouris, Praktika, 1967, pp. 20-21; A. K.
Orlandos, To Ergon, 1967, pp. 17-18.

Illustrations. N. Ph. Yialouris, Praktika, 1964, p. 136,
fig. 1 (plan of portico), pl. 133a-b (general views); V.
Leon, JOAI, 47 (1964-65), Beiblatt, p. 77, fig. 41 (plan),
p. 78, fig. 42 (view from west); N. Ph. Yialouris, Deltion,
20 (1965), B2: Chronika, pl. 239a-b (general views).

No. 43

In the published photographs there appear to be many
juxtaposed geometric designs which follow no systematic
orientation (pls. 99-102). There are tangent, interlocking,

[172]The level is not specified (N. Ph. Yialouris,
Deltion, 20 [1965], B2: Chronika, p. 211).

[173]Yialouris, ibid. In my judgement, the types of
designs which are visible in the photographs, admit of no
specific orientation (see especially, pl. 99). Sodini goes
so far as to attribute the pavement to the "nave" of a
basilica (Catalogue, pp. 704, 751).

intersecting, and interlacing elements which are, for the
most part, sharply defined either by emphatic dark/light/dark
outlines or by a superimposition of dark on light or light on
dark motifs. Although no date was suggested by the excavator, on the basis of the decoration of the cruciform patterns
(pls. 101-102) which are very similar to those in a basilica
at Knossos, Crete, the pavement has been ascribed to the
second half of the fifth century.[174]

    Additional bibliography. Sodini, Catalogue, No. 7, pp.
704-705, 751.

43 Mosaic fragment (over 22.00 x 8.00). Pls. 99-102.
    No published information on dimensions and material.

Purely geometric carpet comprising different designs. Visible
in the published photographs are intersecting circles forming
concave-sided squares, imbrication patterns, juxtaposed
circles containing scales, small braids which alternate with
small squares with Solomon's knots, and cruciform patterns
composed of four lozenges, inscribed with complex "eye
motifs," which are set on a chevron covered ground.

    Illustrations. N. Ph. Yialouris, Praktika, 1964, pl. 134b
(general view), pl. 135a (imbrication panel); A. K. Orlandos,
To Ergon, 1964, p. 119, fig. 143 (plan), p. 121, fig. 147 =
our pl. 99; N. Ph. Yialouris, Deltion, 20 (1965), B2:
Chronika, pl. 240a = our pl. 101, pl. 240b = our pl. 102, pl.
240 gamma = our pl. 100; A. K. Orlandos, To Ergon, 1967, p.
16, fig. 12 (after restoration); Sodini, Catalogue, p. 748,
fig. 18.

---

    [174]Sodini, Catalogue, pp. 704-705, 751 and n. 99. He
correctly ascribes both pavements to the same workshop.

EPIDAUROS

Basilica

At Epidauros a large church complex (overall, 45.00 x
60.00) was cleared between 1916 and 1920.[175] Mosaic pavements were discovered in the narthex, III, its north and south
wings, IV, VII, the north annex, V-VI and in the nave, IX.
At the present time the pavements are covered and the site
overgrown.

Since this basilica has been the subject of extensive
investigation and analysis by others, only a brief description of its plan will follow.[176] The major entrance to the
church (pl. 103) is distinguished by a propylon, I, on the
west side which is flanked by either corridors or porticoes[177] ending in two small rooms. Beyond the propylon is a
large atrium, II (ca. 18.00 x 17.90),[178] enclosed by a
colonnaded portico, a-c, resting on narrow stylobates and
flanked to the north and south by rooms and two

---

[175]For a plan of the site, see P. Kavvadias, ArchEph,
1918, p. 172, fig. 12; hereafter cited as Kavvadias.

[176]Soteriou, Palaiochristianikai basilikai, pp. 199-201,
figs. 31-32; Orlandos, Xylostegos basilike, p. 50, p. 51,
fig. 26, and passim; Krautheimer, Tripartite Transept, p.
421; idem, Architecture, pp. 91-92, fig. 34.

[177]For corridors, see Kavvadias, p. 176; for porticoes,
Soteriou, op. cit., p. 199 and Orlandos, op. cit., pp. 98-99,
p. 101, pl. B (upper left corner).

[178]These measurements are taken from the plan, pl. 103.

entrances.[179] Preceded by a narrow narthex, III (22.25 x
3.55), with projecting wings, IV, VII, the main body of the
church (22.00 x 23.70, including transept) consists of a
nave, IX, flanked on either side by two aisles, X-XIII, and
a quinquepartite transept, XIV-XVIII, which is raised one
step above the rest of the church.[180] The nave is separated
from the inner aisles by columns resting on stylobates which
in some places are closed by parapets. The aisles were probably separated from each other by pillars or columns which
supported arcades and were set on stylobates.[181] They communicate with the inner and outer bays of the transept
through single arches[182] and small doors, respectively, while
passage from the nave to the bema is through a narrow opening
in the chancel screen which is built against the piers supporting a triumphal arch. The type of division of the bays
of the transept is problematic and requires further investigation.[183] Except for the chancel screen, no liturgical

---

[179]Since the rooms opening onto the peristyle do not
directly concern this study, they have not been given
individual numbers.

[180]Kavvadias, p. 179.

[181]Kavvadias, p. 178-179.

[182]Krautheimer, Studies, p. 62. Earlier, he suggests
that the inner bays were closed off from the aisles by chancel railings (Tripartite Transept, p. 421).

[183]In the original reports, the stylobates between the
bema and inner bays were said to have supported transverse
clergy benches which, presumably, extended from the shoulder
of the apse up to somewhere in front of the piers where there
were two small passages. The inner and outer aisles were

furnishings were found. The annex, XIX, flanking the north
aisle and comprising four rooms partitioned by projecting
piers may have been the place to which the catachumens re-
tired before the Mass of the Faithful,[184] while the complex
to the northwest, V-VIII, may have been the baptistery with
Room V serving as the vestibule.[185] The narthex, its wings,
two rooms in the baptistery, and the nave are decorated with
tessellated pavements, the porticoes of the propylon, the
atrium, and the aisles have brick surfaces while large and
small stone slabs pave the three entrances to the atrium,
the transept, and the apse.

Although no datable archaeological finds were unearthed
or reported, on the basis of the style of the architecture

---

described as being divided by arcades with three arches (Soteriou, Palaiochristianikai basilikai, pp. 199-201; idem,
PraktAkAth, 4 [1929], pp. 92-94). Krautheimer offers a
somewhat different reconstruction. In an early study he
accepts the triple arcade but restores a double arcade between the bema and the inner bays (Tripartite Transept, p.
421). Later, he suggests that the latter were separated
from the bema by "low walls each of which supported a single
column" (Studies, p. 62) and in his most recent study he
supplied "short column screens" for all the divisions in the
transept (Architecture, p. 91). The columns which were
found between the inner and outer bays, and between the
inner bays and the bema are omitted from our plan (see
Kavvadias, p. 175, fig. 15; Soteriou, Palaiochristianikai
basilikai, p. 200, fig. 31).

[184]It is curious that no door was found leading to the
outside or even into the north wing of the narthex.

[185]Soteriou, Palaiochristianikai basilikai, p. 199;
idem, PraktAkAth, 4 (1929), p. 94. In the center of Room
VI, traces were found of a stone and a small brick feature
(K on our plan, pl. 103). Since it was covered with lime and
a small clay pipe was laid up to it, it may have been the
base of a baptismal font (Kavvadias, p. 199).

and the mosaics, the church has been attributed to the period
between the end of the fourth and the beginning of the fifth
century.[186] In the Byzantine period a small chapel dedicated
to St. John was built into the east end of the basilica in-
corporating the apse into its plan and extending for a short
distance into the nave.[187] Two columns were installed at
the chord of the apse, perhaps for an iconostasis, and tombs
were dug into the nave pavement which destroyed sections of
the mosaic. Subsequently, the walls of the chapel were reinforced and the floor was raised forty centimeters to coincide
with the level outside the chapel. In this phase an altar
was installed in the apse, a screen wall replaced the two
columns, and the building was paved with small, irregular
marble slabs.[188] The chapel continued in use until its
destruction during the course of the excavations.[189]

Bibliography. P. Kavvadias, Praktika, 1916, pp. 39-41;
idem, ArchEph, 1918, pp. 172-195; AA, 37 (1923), pp. 305-306;
G. A. Soteriou, PraktAkAth, 4 (1929), pp. 91-95; idem,
Palaiochristianikai basilikai, pp. 198-201; Kautzsch,
Kapitellstudien, p. 166; Krautheimer, Tripartite Transept,
p. 421; idem, Studies, pp. 61-62; idem, Architecture, p. 91;
Orlandos, Xylostegos basilikē, pp. 50, 51, passim.

---

[186]Soteriou, Palaiochristianikai basilikai, p. 201;
idem, PraktAkAth, 4 (1929), pp. 94-95; Kautzsch, Kapitellstudien, p. 166; Krautheimer, Studies, p. 61; idem, Architecture,
p. 91.

[187]It is not clear if the pavement of the basilica
served as the floor of the chapel (see Kavvadias, p. 190,
and n. 3).

[188]Kavvadias, pp. 177, 179, 183-191; Soteriou,
Palaiochristianikai basilikai, p. 201.

[189]Kavvadias, p. 190.

Illustrations. P. Kavvadias, <u>ArchEph</u>, 1918, p. 172, fig.
12 (plan of site), p. 173, fig. 13 = our pl. 103, p. 176,
fig. 16 (nave, from west); Krautheimer, <u>Architecture</u>, p.
91, fig. 34 (plan).

Nos. 44-49

Simple in design, the aniconic geometric mosaics in the
narthex and its wings, the north annex, and the nave contain
homogeneous decorative schemes consisting primarily of various combinations of interlocking, intersecting or juxtaposed
octagons, circles, squares and lozenges enclosed by simple
borders (pls. 103-113). The clarity and precision with
which the two-dimensional, ornamental patterns are arranged
across the surface of each compartment result from light and
dark color contrasts and from uncomplicated geometric filling
motifs which are carefully and neatly inserted into each
unit. The austere geometricity of the pavements is somewhat
relieved by a polychromatic scheme in which black, white and
light and dark reds predominate with yellow and grey used
sparingly.[190] The pavements are ascribed to the late fourth
or early fifth century and are, therefore, contemporaneous
with the basilica.[191]

Additional bibliography. Ch. I. Makaronas, <u>Makedonika</u>, 1

---

[190]Kavvadias, p. 191. Since there are no specific color
descriptions, only black and white will be noted.

[191]Kitzinger, <u>Mosaics in the Greek East</u>, p. 344 and n.
10; idem,"A Survey of the Christian Town of Stobi," <u>DOP</u>, 3
(1946), pp. 125-127. For other pavements reflecting this
trend, see 6-9; 88-92; 130-138; 178-179; 196.

(1940), p. 231; M. A. Sisson, BSR, 11 (1929), p. 70 and n.
6; E. Kitzinger, DOP, 3 (1946), pp. 125-127; idem, Mosaics
in the Greek East, p. 344 and n. 10; Sodini, Catalogue, No.
8, p. 705.

Illustration. P. Kavvadias, ArchEph, 1918, p. 173, fig.
13 = our pl. 103.

44 Room III (22.25 x 3.55). Narthex. Pls. 104-106.

Panels, including framing: north, a, 8.70 x 3.68; central,
b, 4.35 x 3.65; south, c, 9.20 x 3.55.[192] Marble (black,
white, greenish grey) and ceramic (red, yellow) tesserae.[193]

Three purely geometric panels framed by simple bands.

Framing: wide white band; narrow black band; white band;
wide black band; white band.[194]

Field.

IIIa, north panel (pl. 104), framed by a narrow black band:
interlocking geometric design, articulated by black/white/
black fillets, composed of crosses of two lozenges and two
diamonds separated by single circles. The lozenges and diamonds are cut along the margins. Simple hour glass motifs
decorate the units, including the circles in the diamonds.
The shading of the ground of the field suggests that, like

[192]The measurements of all the pavements are recorded
in the captions of the illustrations in the excavation report
(Kavvadias, passim).

[193]Kavvadias, p. 191 and n. 1.

[194]Since the drawings of the pavements do not indicate
the individual rows of tesserae, bands instead of fillets
will be used.

similar pavements in Athens (15-16, pls. 44-47), an alternating chromatic scheme was used between the arms of the
crosses.

IIIb, central panel (pl. 105), framed by a narrow black
band: .quincunxial design bordered by an outer row of light
and dark stepped triangles and, to the north and south, by an
inner row of overlapping scales fanning eastward. The
quincunx comprises a large central medallion and four disks
in the spandrels. The former, decorated with a shield pattern
of small squares, is bordered by a black undulating ribbon
pattern with a single lotiform flower at each wave, set on a
black ground.

IIIc, south panel (pl. 106), framed by a narrow black band:
identical to the north panel, IIIa, except for the omission
of the hour glass filling motifs.

Late fourth or early fifth century.

Illustrations. P. Kavvadias, ArchEph, 1918, p. 179, fig.
19 = our pl. 105, p. 180, fig. 20 = our pl. 104, p. 180,
fig. 21 = our pl. 106.

45 Room IV (3.45 x 3.65). North narthex wing. Pl. 107.
Materials identical to those in the narthex (44).

Simple polychrome carpet similar to the pavement in the south
wing (48).

Framing: broad white band.

Field, framed by a narrow black band: white intersecting circles, outlined in black, forming concave-sided squares set on edge. The design is cut along the margins.

Late fourth or early fifth century.

Illustration. P. Kavvadias, ArchEph, 1918, p. 181, fig. 23 = our pl. 107.

46 Room V (10.95 x 3.80). Vestibule? Pl. 108.

Materials identical to those in narthex (44).

Straight polychrome grid enclosed by two narrow borders. A decorative panel is set in the south threshold.

Framing: white band; narrow black fillet; outer border, continuous bead-and-reel pattern composed of units of two beads separated by single reels (for a similar border, see 132, pl. 430); narrow black fillet; inner border, black and white stepped triangles.

Field, framed by a narrow white band: straight grid composed of a two-strand guilloche (outlined in black) on a black ground forming eight rows of two squares each. In the center of each loop of the guilloche and flanking each twist is a white tessera. Each square is outlined in white and bordered by white stepped triangles, on a black ground, which expand in the four corners. Eight types of geometric motifs are arranged chiastically in alternate rows. Starting

with the two squares on the northeast side and moving southward, the sequence of motifs is as follows. First row:
diagonal four-pointed star; multiple rows of chevrons.
Third row: imbrication pattern fanning northward; braid.
Fifth row: intersecting circles forming concave-sided
squares; pairs of opposed peltae disposed in alternating
horizontal and vertical units. Seventh row: braid; diagonal
quatrefoil inscribed on a concave-sided square set on edge.
All the motifs appear to be outlined in black or white, or a
combination of the two.

Threshold to south, framed by a narrow black band: undulating black rinceau forming three loosely arranged and widely
spaced scrolls which are filled with single buds and
tendrils.

Late fourth or early fifth century.

Illustration. P. Kavvadias, _ArchEph_, 1918, p. 185, fig.
27 = our pl. 108.

47 Room VI (5.10 x 10.90). Baptistery (?); pavement laid
    around a stone and brick feature, perhaps originally a
baptismal font.[195] Pl. 109.

Materials identical to those in the narthex (44).

Three polychrome geometric panels set within a braid framework

---

[195]_Vide supra_, p. 107 and n. 185.

and enclosed by two narrow borders.

Framing: white band; narrow black fillet; outer border,
undulating black rinceau (one or two fillets) forming rigidly
arranged narrow scrolls filled with single heart-shaped ivy
leaves which appear to be arranged in an a-b chromatic
sequence; inner border, black and white wave crests; narrow
black band.

Framework: three-strand braid.

Field, framed by a narrow white band: three white-outlined
panels bordered by black and white stepped triangles (for a
similar framework and border, see Room V, 46). The border of
the central panel is laid up to stone and brick foundations,
possibly belonging to a baptismal font. The lateral panels
to the east and west are filled, respectively, with overlapping scales, fanning eastward, and a wide braid.

Late fourth or early fifth century.

Illustration. P. Kavvadias, ArchEph, 1918, p. 185,
fig. 28 = our pl. 109.

48 Room VII (4.00 x 3.45). South narthex wing. Pl. 110.
Materials identical to those in narthex (44).

Simple polychrome carpet similar to the pavement in the north
wing (45).

Framing: broad white band.

Field, framed by a narrow black band: white intersecting

circles, outlined in black, forming concave-sided squares
set on edge.

Late fourth or early fifth century.

   Illustration. P. Kavvadias, ArchEph, 1918, p. 181, fig.
22 = our pl. 110.

49 Room IX (6.85 x 23.70). Nave; east side covered by west
    walls of the chapel of St. John and sections further west
destroyed by graves; later, east side of pavement covered
by small marble slabs. Pls. 111-113.
   West panel, a: 6.95 x 7.95, including framing. Central
panel, b: 6.95 x 7.85, including framing. East panel:
6.75 x 7.90, including framing. Materials identical to
those in narthex (44).

Polychrome pavement composed of three geometric panels surrounded by identical inner and outer borders.
   Framing: wide white band; narrow black fillet; white band;
outer border, row of alternating squares and rectangles, outlined in black, filled primarily with geometric motifs. The
squares contain two-strand Solomon's knots and the lozenges
quincunxial patterns composed of central lozenges and
rectangular triangles in the corners. The lozenges in the
west and central panels, a-b, are inscribed with small rectangles and circles which are generally flanked or surrounded
by decorative motifs giving them the appearance of

rudimentary "eye" patterns; the lozenges in the east panel, c, have hour glass motifs on colored grounds; narrow black band; white band; narrow black band; inner border, black undulating ribbon pattern with a single lotiform flower at each wave; narrow black band.

IXa, west panel (pl. 111), framed by single white/black bands: white intersecting circles, outlined in black, forming concave-sided squares. The design is bisected along the margins.

IXb, central panel (pl. 112), framed by a white band which forms, at the same time, part of the design: rectilinear design, articulated by black/white/black fillets, of intersecting octagons forming squares and elongated hexagons (for a similar design, see 90, pls. 311-312). The squares are inscribed with a series of smaller squares.

IXc, east panel (pl. 113), framed by a single white/black band: white intersecting circles, outlined in black, forming concave-sided squares which are inscribed with small colored disks. The design is bisected along the east margin.

Late fourth or early fifth century.

Illustrations. P. Kavvadias, ArchEph, 1918, p. 182, fig. 24 = our pl. 111, p. 183, fig. 25 = our pl. 112, p. 184, fig. 26 = our pl. 113.

Secular Building

Over thirty meters to the south of the large basilica at
Epidauros (44-49) part of a secular building (ca. 34.00 x
19.50) was excavated in 1916 and 1918[196] which contained two
mosaic pavements.[197] At the present time, the mosaics are
covered and the site overgrown.

Since the report is brief and the north part of the
building was in ruinous condition at the time of its discovery (pl. 114), only the south side will be described.
The irregularly-shaped building, oriented east-west, is
divided into two groups of rooms by a corridor, I, which communicates with the south side of the building through three
doors leading into Rooms II, IV, and VI. The central and
largest doorway opens onto a two-room unit, IV, VIII, which,
because of its size, location, and decoration, clearly domi-
nates the south side. It is probable that this part of the
building was used for public functions with Rooms IV (4.90
x 4.08) and VIII (6.00 x 6.68) serving as a vestibule and
reception hall, respectively. This kind of arrangement is
used in a villa at Phtelia, near Nikopolis (172-175, pl.
590) where a similar division by means of a corridor serves

---

[196]For a plan of the site, see P. Kavvadias, ArchEph,
1918, p. 172, fig. 12; hereafter cited as Kavvadias. All the
measurements for this entry are taken from the plan, pl. 114.

[197]The type of paving in the other rooms is not described.

to separate the public and private sections. Still, not
enough survives of the building at Epidauros to identify it
as a villa.

Although no datable archaeological finds were unearthed
or reported, on the basis of the iconography of the pavement
in Room IV, the building can be dated to around the middle
of the fifth century.[198]

Bibliography. P. Kavvadias, Praktika, 1916, p. 40; idem,
ArchEph, 1918, pp. 172, 191; AA, 37 (1923), pp. 306-307.

Illustration. P. Kavvadias, Praktika, 1918, p. 187,
fig. 32 = our pl. 114.

Nos. 50-51

Polychrome mosaics decorate the vestibule, IV, and a
large hall, VIII. With the exception of the organic filling
motifs in Room IV (pl. 115), the overall style, iconography
and, presumably, the color scheme[199] of the pavements closely
resemble those in the basilica to the north (44-49). The
same types of borders are used (ivy rinceaux, stepped triangles, wave crests, bead-and-reel, guilloche, squares
alternating with triangles) and the same clarity and precision distinguish the two-dimensional ornamental designs and

[198]On the basis of their similar rubble and lime wall
construction, Kavvadias assigns the basilica (44-49) and the
secular building to the same period (p. 191). This kind of
construction is so common in Greece in the fifth and sixth
centuries that, in my judgment, it cannot be used as a
chronological tool.

[199]Kavvadias implies that they are identical (p. 191).
Vide supra, p. 109, and n. 190.

filling motifs. For these reasons, the pavements can be
assigned to the same workshop. Whether, however, they belong
to the same phase, that is, to the end of the fourth or the
beginning of the fifth century, is difficult to determine.
The presence of bird insets in Room IV argues for a somewhat
later date. All the early Greek pavements in secular and
religious buildings (1; 2-3; 6-9; 38-41; 88-92; 130-138;
178-179; 196) are completely aniconic, even those which contain the same design (137, pl. 437; 179, pl. 602). It is
probable, therefore, that the pavements in the secular building postdate those in the church, but by only a few years
since the birds appear to be quite naturalistic and three-
dimensional.[200] Later fifth century fauna like those in two
villas at Athens (16, pls. 47-48; 18, pl. 52; 19, pl. 55;
23, pl. 68) begin to lose their plasticity and become more
abstract.

Additional bibliography. I. C. Threpsiades, Polemōn, 5,
Part 3 (1954), pp. 133 and 137, n. 10; Sodini, Catalogue,
p. 705, n. 8.

Illustration. P. Kavvadias, ArchEph, 1918, p. 187, fig.
32 = our pl. 114.

50 Room IV (4.08 x 4.90). Vestibule; pavement laid up to
    stone threshold blocks to north and south. Pl. 115.
    No published information on dimensions. Materials

---

[200]Although this judgment is based on limited photographic material (pls. 115-116), the birds are more modeled
and organic than later ones.

identical to those in the adjacent basilica (44-49).[201]

Polychrome geometric carpet with small figural panels bordered by six narrow decorative bands.[202]

Framing: white double fillet;[203] first border to north
and south only, undulating black rinceau (two fillets) forming rigidly arranged narrow scrolls filled with single heart-
shaped ivy leaves which appear to be arranged in an a-b
chromatic sequence (see also pl. 109); black fillet; white
double fillet; black fillet; second border, bead-and-reel
pattern composed of units of two beads separated by single
reels, outlined in black (see also, pl. 108); third border,
black and white wave crests; black double fillet; fourth
border, black and white stepped triangles; white double
fillet; fifth border, three-strand braid (outlined in black)
on a black ground which is accented by a white tessera in
each loop and at each twist; white double fillet; sixth
border, black and white stepped triangles.

Field, framed by a black fillet: an octagon surrounded
by alternating lozenges and squares. The lozenges, which
are cut along the margins, are inscribed with dark lozenges
with small white disks while the squares are filled with

---

[201]P. Kavvadias, p. 191.

[202]For the colors, vide supra, p. 109 and n. 190.

[203]Unlike the drawings of the pavements in the basilica
(pls. 104-113), these show the number of fillets.

aquatic and land birds which are placed along the cardinal
points of the room and face in the same direction. These
bird panels radiate from an octagon which contains a water
fowl oriented toward the entrance. It is enclosed by a
medallion with a tight two-strand interlace border (same
technique as the braid in the border) on a black ground
which is framed by triple fillets.

Around the middle of the fifth century.

    Illustrations. P. Kavvadias, ArchEph, 1918, p. 187, fig.
33 (pavement, inverted), p. 188, fig. 34 = our pl. 115.

51 Room VIII (6.00 x 6.68). Reception hall? Pavement laid
    up to stone panel near north threshold. Pl. 116.

    No published information on dimensions. Material identical
to those in vestibule (50) and in the adjacent basilica (44-
49).

Polychrome interlace carpet inscribed with abstract motifs
and bordered by two to three narrow decorative bands.

    Framing: wide white band; border to north only, single row
of light and dark hour glass motifs; white double fillet;
middle border, row of alternating squares and rectangles,
outlined in black, filled with geometric motifs. The former
contain two-strand Solomon's knots, sometimes a quatrefoil
or a perspectivized dentil. The rectangles have quincunxial
patterns composed of central lozenges and rectangular

triangles in the corners. Like the east panel in the nave of
the basilica (49, pl. 113), the lozenges contain light and
dark hour glass motifs on colored grounds; inner border,
black and white wave crests; white double fillet.

Field, framed by a black fillet: interlace forming alternating squares and circles which are inscribed with a plethora
of geometric motifs or geometricized floral ones. Among
them are flat quatrefoils and polyfoils, intersecting circles, checkerboard patterns, knots forming squares, chevrons,
spirals, and wheels of triangles which follow no consistent
compositional scheme.

Around the middle of the fifth century.

Illustration. P. Kavvadias, ArchEph, 1918, p. 189, fig.
35 = our pl. 116.

PALEOPYRGA

Building

At Paleopyrga, around one and one half kilometers from
the ancient theatre of Argos, part of a building was excavated in 1963 and 1968 bringing to light three mosaic pavements. At the present time they are covered with sand and
the site is overgrown.

The plan and function of the building were never determined and the reports are vague about the location of the
four rooms, I-IV, which were exposed. Two of them were long

and parallel to each other, I-II, with the more southerly
one, I, ending in an apse; two other smaller rooms III-IV,
were located somewhere to the east and west, respectively.
Except for the latter room, they were decorated with mosaic
pavements.[204]

Although no archaeological finds were unearthed or reported, on the basis of the mosaic pavements, the building
was correctly ascribed to the "Early Christian" period.[205]
Their style suggests a date in the late fifth and the sixth
centuries.

Bibliography. E. Protonotariou-Deïlakē, Deltion, 19
(1964), B1: Chronika, pp. 126-127; E. Kounoupiotou, Deltion,
24 (1969), B1: Chronika, pp. 164-165.

Nos. 52-54

Polychrome geometric and figural pavements decorate
three rooms of indeterminate function and form. Although the
photographic and descriptive material is inadequate and the
pavement in the room to the east, III, is not published, it
is possible to discern certain stylistic and technical differences between the pavements in the other rooms, I and II
(pls. 117, 117a-b). In the former (pl. 117, bottom) the

---

[204]E. Protonotariou-Deïlakē, Deltion, 19 (1964), B1:
Chronika, pp. 126-127; E. Kounoupiotou, Deltion, 24 (1969),
B1: Chronika, pp. 164-165; hereafter cited as Deltion, 19
and Deltion, 24, respectively.

[205]Deltion, 19, p. 127.

tesserae are irregular in size and disposition, and the
amphora and the flora and fauna decorating the apse appear
to be highly stylized and two-dimensional.[206] These pavements resemble the mosaics in the basilica at Klapsi (95,
pls. 315-331; 100, pls. 350-352) which belong to the middle
of the sixth century. In contrast, the pavement in Room II
(pl. 117, top; pl. 117a) is more carefully executed and may
well represent an earlier phase. Its border and field contain patterns which first appear in the late fifth century
(64, pl. 179; 83, pl. 256; 165, pl. 581) and continue into
the sixth century (29, pl. 77; 150, pl. 461). On the other
hand, the only counterpart to the complex interlace in the
central panel (pl. 117a) is one belonging to the early sixth
century (69, pl. 150). Although both pavements belong to a
relatively late period, these stylistic and technical differences are strong enough to warrant their placement in
separate decorative phases. The third mosaic in Room III
cannot be ascribed to either phase until a photograph of it
is published.

   Additional bibliography. Sodini, Catalogue, No. 5, pp.
703-704.

PERIOD I, PHASE 1

52 Room II (18.50 x 3.80). North room. Pls. 117, top, 117a.

---

[206]For a detail of the organic motifs in the tangent
circles, see Deltion, 19, pl. 124gamma = our pl. 117b.

No published information on dimensions and material.

In published photographs there is an aniconic geometric
carpet, bordered by an undulating ribbon, comprising identical panels with peltae and interlaces which are separated by
a complex interlace.[207]
Framing: border, undulating ribbon pattern with single
lotiform flowers at each wave; dark fillet; white triple
fillet.

Ib, central panel framed by a dark fillet (pl. 117a):
quincunxial design composed of a circle and four ivy leaves
in the spandrels. The former is decorated with a complex
circular interlace of alternating large and small circles
joined to a looped, straight square.

Ia,c, lateral panels, framed by a black fillet.
Framing: border, chain of interlaced circles (pl. 117,
top, right); dark fillet; light double fillet.

Field, framed by a dark fillet: pairs of opposed peltae
arranged in alternating horizontal and vertical units.[208]

Late fifth or early sixth century.
Illustration. E. Protonotariou-Deïlakē, Deltion, 19

---

[207]No colors were recorded for this pavement.

[208]Although Sodini studied this pavement in situ, his
description is, for the most part, incorrect (Catalogue,
p. 704, and n. 6).

(1964), Bl: <u>Chronika</u>, pl. 124d = our pl. 117a; E.
Kounoupiotou, <u>Deltion</u>, 24 (1969), Bl: <u>Chronika</u>, pl. 166a-b =
our pl. 117 (top).

PERIOD I, PHASE 2

53 Room I (no dimensions published). Apsidal room to the
    south of Room II (52). Pls. 117, bottom, 117b.

No published information on dimensions and material.
Irregularly-cut tesserae (0.01 x 0.02).[209]

Rectangular room, Ia, with a semi-circular apse, Ib, decorated with crude white, black, yellow, and red geometric and
figural designs.

Ia: three panels separated by a triple border.

Framing (pl. 117, lower right): outer border, black
intersecting circles forming white concave-sided squares set
on edge; middle border, two-strand guilloche on a black
ground with a white tessera at each loop; white double fillet; inner border, three-strand braid on a dark ground with
a white tessera at each loop; white band.[210]

Field: central panel with "circular patterns" flanked by
panels with identical designs of eight-pointed lozenge stars
and squares set on edge (pl. 117, lower right).

---

[209]<u>Deltion</u>, 19, p. 126.

[210]The report does not state if the borders went all
around the field (<u>Deltion</u>, 24, p. 164).

Ib, semi-circular panel in apse (pl. 117, lower left):
ribbed vase with a wide mouth and curved handles from which
issue two vines with leaves and clusters of grapes. Surrounding this central scene is a row of tangent circles
inscribed with rosettes, land birds, water fowl, and fish
(pl. 117b).

Probably around the middle of the sixth century.

Illustrations. E. Protonotariou-Deïlakē, Deltion, 19
(1964), Bl: Chronika, pl. 124gamma = our pl. 117b; E.
Kounoupiotou, Deltion, 24 (1969), Bl: Chronika, pl. 166gamma
and delta = our pl. 117 (bottom).

54 Room III. Room of indeterminable size situated to the
    east of Rooms I and II (52, 53).

No published information on dimensions and material.

Brief mention of a pavement with intersecting circles.[211]

Possibly belonging to phase 1 or 2.[212]

ARGOS

Villa

In the course of three excavations between 1929 and 1955

---

[211]Deltion, 24, p. 164.
[212]Vide supra, p. 124.

the west side of a large villa (pl. 118) in Argos was cleared.
Since the rest of the complex continued into sectors covered
by modern buildings, work on the site was discontinued in
1955. Mosaic pavements were found in three of the five rooms,
Ia-b, II, V, and brick (III-IV) and stone (I) paving in the
others. The tessellated pavements were lifted, consolidated,
and reset in their original disposition in the Argos Museum.

The exposed sector of the building comprises a peristyle
court, I, flanked on the west and south sides by porticoes,
a-b,[213] which lead to a triclinium and kitchens, III-IV, on
the west side and another room at the east end of the south
portico, V.[214]

Although no datable archaeological finds were unearthed,
on the basis of the style and iconography of the mosaics, the
building was attributed to the end of the fifth or the
beginning of the sixth century. It will be shown below that
the pavements belong to the sixth century and reflect a trend
in Greek mosaics which is characterized by abstract, two-
dimensional organic forms.

Bibliography. BCH, 54 (1930), p. 481; W. Volgraff,

---

[213]Since traces of a wall along the north side are indicated in the plan (pl. 118), it appears that there was no
portico on that side of the court.

[214]No plan was published of the excavations in 1955 when
the east side of the south portico and the east room were
cleared. An unpublished photograph in the archives of the
French School at Athens shows the relationship between these
sectors (pl. 133, top). I would like to thank Mr. George
Daux, formerly director of the School, for permission to
reproduce the photograph.

Mededelingen der Koninklijke Akademie van Wetenschappen, 72,
B, 3 (1931), pp. 84ff; BCH, 78 (1954), pp. 168-170; R.
Ginouvès, BCH, 80 (1956), pp. 396-398.

Illustrations. BCH, 78 (1954), fig. 1 opposite p. 158
(plan of 1953 excavations), p. 168, fig. 20 = our pl. 118;
R. Ginouvès, BCH, 80 (1956), fig. 1 opposite p. 360 (plan
of 1955 excavations.)

Nos. 55-57

Polychrome mosaics with multiple figural compositions
decorate two porticoes (Ia-b) and two rooms (II, V). The
pavements are concentrated in the most prominent zones of
the building and clearly accentuate the formal arrangement
of these areas. Surrounded by wide decorative borders, each
pavement extends the length and width of its respective area
and reflects its orientation. Thus, in the triclinium, II,
the Dionysiac panel to the east faces the interior of the
room where, as the design of the pavement informs us, the
diners sat around a small sigma-shaped table (pls. 118, 146).
In this manner, they had an unobstructed view before them of
other revelers led by the god of wine (pls. 146-153). In
the porticoes, Ia-b, as well, the figures in the panels are
arranged to be viewed in the context of a progression from
north to south (pls. 119-132) and then eastward (pl. 133)
toward another room, V, which has a mosaic oriented toward
the entrance from the south portico. Even the masks, rep-
tiles, birds, and animal and human protomes in the rinceaux
in these three sectors are made to obey the orientation of

the panels by facing in the same direction as the figures
(pls. 119-120, 134, 136).[215]

Scenes of the hunt and representations of the months
form the main decorative themes of the porticoes and the
southeast room. In the west portico (pls. 119-120, 125-132),
falconry scenes are presented, beginning with the preparation
in the first two panels,[216] followed by the hunt which occupied at least two of the succeeding four panels,[217] and
ending with the return from the hunt in the seventh panel
(pl. 132). Although these falconry scenes are unique, they
belong to a traditional repertory of villa decoration involving the depiction of all aspects of country life of which
the hunt formed an integral part.[218] A second hunting scene
in the southeast room shows a large lion attacking and being
attacked by hunters (pls. 155-156). Representations of the
months and the seasons, also common themes in villa

[215]Along the short sides, however, the objects turn
inward in order to mark the limits of the field (pls. 122-
123, 135).

[216]Since this theme is clearly established in the second
panel where a hunter is adjusting his leggings (pls. 126-
127), the first panel must have had a similar theme.

[217]Although the fifth and sixth panels are lost, it is
probable that they, also, contained hunting scenes because
they are followed by the return from the hunt in the seventh
and last panel (pl. 132).

[218]See, for example, I. Lavin, "The Hunting Mosaics of
Antioch and their Sources," _DOP_, 17 (1963), pp. 181ff.

decoration,[219] decorate the south portico (pls. 133-134).
The sequence begins with the personifications of January and
February (pl. 136) in the second panel and ends with the
months of November and December (pl. 145) to the east.
Although only the border of the first panel which begins the
series is preserved, it is possible to suggest a reconstruction of this scene. In an ecclesiastical building at Tegea
(69-70), similar representations of the twelve months were
accompanied by a scene, now lost, showing the Beautiful
Seasons (KAΛOI KAIPOI). Since it paved the apse and, therefore, the more important sector of the building, it can be
said to have begun the program which unfolded in the nave to
the west. For iconographic and formal reasons, it is not
impossible that here, also, the program of the months was
inaugurated by the "KAΛOI KAIPOI."

In a study of the south portico, the pavements were
attributed to the end of the fifth or the beginning of the
sixth century.[220] In my judgment, stylistic considerations
clearly substantiate a sixth century attribution. A pervasive
feature of the decorative program is the two-dimensionality
of all the objects. The floral and animate forms are arranged
across the surface and, like an extended geometric carpet, are

[219]D. Levi, "The Allegories of the Months in Classical
Art," AB, 23 (1941), p. 278, and n. 64; J. C. Webster, The
Labours of the Months in Antique and Medieval Art, Princeton,
1938; H. Stern, Le Calendrier de 354, Paris, 1953.

[220]R. Ginouvés, BCH, 81 (1957), p. 250.

made to respect and reflect its solidity. Thus, although
the figures are placed in separate, clearly articulated compartments, any illusion of pictorial space is contradicted
by their weightless, unmodeled, and two-dimensional shapes
which project them onto the same plane as the surrounding
borders and the geometricized rinceaux. Even the continuous
undulating ground lines which the months stand on while
earnestly displaying their attributes serve more as decorative devices than terrestrial markers (pls. 139, 141).
These figures float within the two-dimensional space of the
panel as much as the ecstatic members of the Thiasos in
Room II for whom no ground lines exist (pls. 146, 150, 152).
In this manner, the ambiguous relationship between a three-
dimensional, plastic figure and a two-dimensional picture
space which obtains in the fifth century pavements at Tegea
(pls. 207-216) and elsewhere (pls. 242-252, 261-268, 363-365,
368-369, 620) has been resolved by creating a common plane
for all the objects. For stylistic reasons, therefore, the
Argos pavements belong to around the second quarter of the
sixth century and represent the latest preserved pavements
with the representations of the months and the seasons.[221]

   Illustration. BCH, 78 (1954), fig. 20 opposite p. 168 -
our pl. 118.

55 Room I (13.00 x 14.60; width, a, 2.90; b, 3.18). West and

---

[221]See 42, 69-70, 75, 83.

south porticoes a,b; wide diagonal lacuna running from the northwest to the southeast; ancient repair in many sections of the south portico, b. Pls. 119-145.

West portico, a. Surround to east and west: 0.22. Framing: 0.78. Panels, including fillets: 1.09 x 1.27. South portico, b: Surround to northeast and east: 0.49. Framing: 0.71. Panels, including borders: 1.27 x 1.09. Stone and ceramic (red) tesserae (0.01 sq) set 2-4 mm apart.

L-shaped peristyle comprising two porticoes, each decorated with seven figural panels set within an acanthus framework and enclosed by multiple borders. The panels are oriented away from the court and are to be read from north to south (Ia) and from west to east (Ib).

Ia. Originally probably seven hunting scenes, of which five are preserved, set within an acanthus rinceau.

Surround to east and west: narrow black undulating rinceau (one fillet) forming loosely arranged widely spaced scrolls filled with single red (ceramic)[222] and red/black leaves, outlined in black, in an a-b sequence (pl. 121).

Framing: border (0.32), crude chain (pl. 121) composed of squares set on edge (1 grey/1 white; 1 pink/1 ochre; 1 red [ceramic]/1 ochre, outlined in black) on a white and black ground. Single white tesserae decorate the loops and sides

[222]Since there are red stone tesserae also, only the ceramic ones will be noted.

of the pattern.

Field.

Acanthus framework (0.46): undulating inhabited rinceau,
on a black ground (pls. 119-120, 122-124), of stylized spiral
acanthus leaves emerging from ochre cornucopian ocreae to
form circles (for a similar pattern, see 115, 189). The flat
ochre leaves enclose animate and inanimate objects which,
like the panels, are oriented westward. Among the filling
motifs are animal and human protomes, birds, buds, tendrils,
flowers, fruit, and vases which have the same ochre, brown,
red (ceramic), white color scheme of the leaves. At the
corners of each panel single pink masks of bearded and beard-
less men peer out from foliate hoods, their contrasting
visages highlighted by black brows, eyes and upper lids and
by red pursed lips.

First panel to north (pl. 125).

Field: destroyed, except for traces of the lower part of
a man, turned toward the right, wearing dark brown leggins
with a black tie and short red (ceramic) boots. Between
him and the gnarled trunk of a brown tree on the right side
of the scene, stands a tethered falcon[223] which turns its
head toward the man.

Second panel. The preparation for the hunt (pls. 126-127).

Framing: double white fillet; black fillet.

Field: two unshaven hunters prepare to depart for the hunt.

---

[223]The plumage of the bird is destroyed.

One of them, a falconer, carries a dark brown eagle with an
orange and ochre speckled breast on the dark brown gauntlet
covering his left arm, and holds the leash of a leaping red
(ceramic) dog in his right hand. He turns to the left and
looks at his companion who has placed his right leg on a
high grey rock to tighten the red (ceramic) strap of his
grey and white boot while a white dog, as eager as the first
one for the hunt to begin, yaps impatiently below. This
hunter wears a dark brown hat, outlined in black, which falls
below his ears, and white knee breeches, outlined in grey.
The falconer is hatless and wears long, dark brown leggins
which cover most of his pink boots. Both men are clad in
long-sleeve tunics which fall to the knee and short capes
fringed with tassels.

Ancient repair between the arms of the falconer.

Third panel. Duck hunt. Pls. 128-129.

Field: in a grey brush a defenseless grey and white duck
is felled by a large brown eagle which clings with its sharp
brown talons to its back.[224] Two other grey and ochre ducks
which have escaped the onslaught of the eagle fly above,
their grey and red (ceramic) wings flapping in the air. To
the left of the scene, the falconer with a drawn knife in
his right hand, extends his gauntleted left arm and commands

---

[224]Since the talons of the eagle and the wings of the
duck are the same brown color, it is difficult to distinguish
between them. One claw, near the tailfeathers of the duck,
is discernible in pl. 128.

the eagle to return to him. He is clad in a long sleeve
white tunic which falls to the knee, long dark brown leggins
with ochre patches and dark brown boots. His shoulders are
covered by an ivory-colored cape, outlined in dark brown,
with red (ceramic) tassels and red (ceramic) and ochre
folds and stripes. Except for some differences in the color
of the cape, the man bears a striking resemblance to the
falconer in the second and seventh panels.

Fourth panel. Rabbit hunt. Pls. 130-131.

Field: in a scene marked by a brown fruit tree and a
floating branch, a hunter with a brown staff in his left
hand runs toward the right where the dogs have flushed two
rabbits. In the lower register, a dark grey dog, outlined
in black, with a red (ceramic) collar lands on the back of a
grey rabbit whose legs buckle from the attack. The dog
turns his head to look at his red (ceramic) counterpart who
leaps toward an escaping rabbit in the upper register. With
its powerful hind legs propelling it toward the edge of the
field, the rabbit turns to check the progress of the attacking dog. The hunter wears a long sleeve pale orange tunic,
outlined and delineated in brown, and a grey cape with black
tassels. His muscular legs are covered with white knee
breeches, and short grey boots, outlined in dark grey and
black, which are bound by white laces.

Fifth panel. Destroyed.

Sixth panel. Destroyed.

Seventh panel. Return from the hunt. Pl. 132.

Field: a falconer with an eagle on his left arm turns to
look at the second hunter who follows closely behind, his
right hand holding the leashes of two dogs. He carries over
his left shoulder a rabbit tied to a brown staff. The
colors of the garments and the animals are identical to those
in the second and third panels.[225]

It is clear that the scenes belong to one series devoted
to falconry. Except for minor changes in their attire, the
same hunters appear throughout. The falconer is always shown
with rather long brown and black hair which falls over his
forehead, a cape with tassels, a long sleeve white tunic and
long dark brown leggins which cover the greater part of his
boots (panels 2, 3, 7). The second hunter wears a long
sleeve pale orange tunic, white knee breeches, short boots,
and a short cape with tassels (panels 2, 4, 7). Since his
head is destroyed in two of the three panels, it cannot be
determined if he continued to wear the tight-fitting hat
which appears in the second panel. The style and coloring
of the attire of the two men, therefore, is a consistent
feature in the preserved scenes.[226] This similitude obtains
as well for their skin coloration, pink with dark red outlines and ochre highlights, and for their physiognomies.

_____

[225]The cape of the falconer resembles more closely that
worn in the third panel.

[226]Not enough is preserved of the man in the first panel
to identify him (pl. 125). The warm clothing which the men
wear suggests that the hunt took place during the winter
months.

Both men have pronounced dark red and black brows, and black
eyes which are emphasized by straight black upper lids and
dark red semi-circular lower lids. The faces are strong and
masculine and covered by grey stubble. The figures are
spread across the surface of the panels and sometimes even
interrupt the black fillets along the margins (second and
third panels, pls. 126-127). There is little overlapping of
the figures, no ground lines to stabilize them, and little
modeling. They are weightless, abstract forms wedded to the
spaceless, two-dimensional space of the panels.

Additional color. Acanthus rinceau. Ocreae: red mouth.
Leaves: red (ceramic) and brown veins, with white highlights. Masks: outlined in dark brown, dark pink, or red;
red lower lids. First panel: ochre highlights on tree
trunk. Third panel. Left hunter: pale orange tunic, outlined and delineated in brown; dark grey cape with black
folds and tassels. Falconer: white tunic, outlined and
delineated in grey; dark brown cape with red and black striations, red folds, ochre highlights, and red tassels. Right
dog: ochre along ventral side, outlined in black, and black
and white eye. Third panel. Eagle: dark grey and red
(ceramic) outline and highlights. Falconer: tunic outlined
and delineated in grey. Fifth panel. Tree: grey and black
outlines; black leaves and fruit. Rabbits: dark grey and
brown markings along the dorsal side and ivory along the
ventral side; dark grey outlines. Leaping dog: ivory markings along the neck, belly and legs.

Ib. Originally seven panels, of which six are preserved,
with de face representations of the months. The panels are
framed by 2 white/1 black fillets.[227]

Surround to northeast and east (pl. 135): rows of juxtaposed, knotted white circles which are laced along the
margins by similar, dark grey semi-circles; black fillet.

Framing (Pls. 134-136): white triple fillet; black fillet;
border, overlapping lyre pattern (0.31) with black centers
flanked by alternating red/1 white and pink/1 white cords
which are outlined in black and set on a yellow ground; white
triple fillet.

Field.

Acanthus framework (0.49): undulating inhabited rinceau,
on a black ground (pls. 134-136, 139), of stylized spiral
acanthus leaves emerging from cornucopian ocreae to form
circles. The flat leaves enclose animate and inanimate
objects which, like the figural panels and the masks accenting their corners, are oriented southward. The rinceau is
identical in style, technique, iconography, and color to the
one in the west portico (Ia).

First panel to west. Destroyed, except for traces of a
border.

Border: white bead-and-reel pattern on a red ground.

----

[227]In 1957 a detailed study of this pavement appeared
with complete color descriptions (R. Ginouvés, BCH, 81 [1957],
pp. 216-268). For this reason, only a summary of the decoration and iconography will be presented. For other information, the reader is referred to this excellent article, hereafter cited as Ginouvés.

Field: originally, possibly the "Beautiful Seasons"
(ΚΑΛΟΙ ΚΑΙΡΟΙ).[228]

Second panel. Figures identified by inscriptions at the
top as January (ΙΑΝΟΥ/ΑΡΙΟC) and February (ΦΕΒΡΟΥ/ΑΡΙ/ΟC).
Pl. 136.

Border: red and white wave crests.

Field, framed by a black fillet: January is represented
as a Consul distributing largesse. He holds in his upraised
right hand a *mappa circensis* from which a shower of gold coins
cascades onto the *sella curulis* below.[229] In contrast to the
important rank given to January, February is shown as a
heavily shrouded peasant who displays in his folded arms
two ducks (for similar personifications, see 69, pl. 208;
75, pl. 228).

Third panel. Figures identified by inscriptions at the top
as March (ΜΑΡ/ΤΙ/ΟC) and April (ΑΠΡΙΛΙ/ΟC). Pls. 137-138.

Border: red and white stepped triangles.

Field, framed by a black fillet: March is represented as
the god, Mars, and is shown fully armed with a helmet, breast
plate, a skirt covered with metal and leather plates, and a
long spear with a banner. He points to a bird in the upper
left corner and at his left foot is a cauldron with white
liquid which has been identified as milk.[230] His counterpart

[228]Vide supra, p. 131.

[229]The original model for this figure held an object in
his left hand which has been omitted from this copy.

[230]Ginouvès, p. 259.

to the right, April (pl. 138), is a shepherd who displays a lamb in his arms (for a similar personification, see 75, pl. 230).

Fourth panel. Figures identified by inscriptions near the top as May (MA/IOC) and June (IOYNI/OC). Pls. 139-140.

Border: zig-zag pattern, on a red ground, composed of alternating black and white ellipses. The interstices are decorated with small black and white crosslets.

Field, framed by a black fillet: both figures are shown with attributes associated with the months they personify. May, his head crowned with a wreath of flowers, carries a second one in his right hand, and a wicker basket filled with the same kind of flowers in the palm of his left hand (pl. 140). An isolated rose bush adds a colorful note to the plain ground between May and June. The latter carries in the crook of his left arm a sheaf of wheat which he has harvested with the scythe so prominently displayed in his right hand (for a personification of July with similar attributes, see 69, pl. 210).

Fifth panel. Figures identified by inscriptions at the top as July (IOY/ΛI/OC) and August (A[Y]Γ/OY/CTO/C). Pls. 141-142.

Border: white bead-and-reel pattern on a red ground.

Field, framed by a black fillet: July carries a shovel in the crook of his right arm and a chest in the palm of his left hand[231] while August displays a watermelon in the palm of his right hand and a fan in his left (for a similar personification, see 69, pl. 211).

Sixth panel. Figures identified by inscriptions at the top as September (CΕΠΤΕ/ΜΒΡΙ/ΟϹ) and October (ΟΚΤѠΒΡΙΟ[Ϲ]). Pls. 143-144.

Border: red and white wave crests.

Field, framed by a black fillet: both months display their attributes. September originally held an object in his raised left hand which is now lost.[232] Near his left leg is a vat-like object and near his right, a large wicker basket filled with grapes. October holds a cup of red wine in his right hand which he has poured from the bottle in his left (for a similar representation of October, see 69, pl. 213). Signs of damage and ancient repair, especially on the right side of the panel (pl. 144).

Seventh panel. Figures identified by inscriptions at the top as November (ΝΟΕΝ/ΒΡΙ/ΟϹ) and December (ΔΕΚΕΜ/ΒΡΙ/ΟϹ). Pl. 145.

Border: red and white stepped triangles.

Field, framed by a black fillet: November carries a plow in his right hand and an axe in his left, the tools of his

---

[231]The top is sprinkled with white, green, and yellow tesserae, but its contents cannot be identified.

[232]Ginouvés identifies the object in his left hand as a double cluster of grapes (p. 243) but this section is too damaged to accept this identification.

labor, while the last month, December, is represented as a grey-haired, old man with a cane. Unlike most of his counterparts,[233] he is not displaying the tools of produce of a specific month but, rather, a small sack which dangles from his right hand.

Signs of damage and ancient repair, especially on the right side of the panels.

Around the second quarter of the sixth century.

Additional bibliography. BCH, 54 (1930), p. 481; J. C. Webster, The Labors of the Months in Antique and Medieval Art, Princeton, 1938, pp. 28, 124, no. 13; D. Levi, AB, 23 (1941), pp. 253-254; idem, Antioch Mosaic Pavements, I, Princeton, 1947, p. 37; H. Stern, Le Calendrier de 354, Paris, 1953, pp. 222-223; BCH, 78 (1954), pp. 168-170; R. Ginouvès, BCH, 80 (1956), pp. 396-398; idem, BCH, 81 (1957), pp. 216-268; E. Goffinet, BCH, 86 (1962), p. 250, nn. 7-8, p. 252; R. Bianchi Bandinelli, Rome: The Late Empire, New York, 1971, pp. 328-329.

Illustrations. BCH, 54 (1930), p. 481, fig. 20 (Ia, third panel, drawing); BCH, 78 (1954), fig. 20 opposite p. 168 = our pl. 118; R. Ginouvès, BCH, 80 (1956), p. 397, fig. 58 (Ib, rinceau with bird), p. 397, fig. 59 (Ib, rinceau, mask), p. 398, fig. 60 (Ib, August); idem, BCH, 81 (1957), p. 217, fig. 1 = our pl. 134, p. 221, figs. 2-3 (Ib, rinceau), p. 223, figs. 5-6 (Ia,b masks), p. 225, fig. 7 = our pl. 136, p. 225, fig. 8 (Ib, March and April), p. 227, fig. 9 = our pl. 139, p. 227, fig. 10 = our pl. 141, p. 229, fig. 11 (Ib, September and October), p. 229, fig. 12 (Ib, November and December), pp. 231-232, figs. 13-20 (Ib, rinceau with filling motifs), p. 257, figs. 33-38 (Ib, footwear of June, February, March, November, May and October); R. Bianchi Bandinelli, Rome: The Late Empire, New York, 1971, p. 331, fig. 313 (Ib, July and August [colored reproduction]).

---

[233]The months of January and March are the exceptions.

56   Room II (6.00 sq). Triclinium; pavement destroyed along
     northeast side. Pls. 146-154.

   Framing: to north and south, 0.63; to west, 0.90. East
panel, a, including border: 3.59 max x 1.71 max. West panel,
b: 3.76 x 1.90. Apsidal panel: 1.23 diam. Stone, glass
(green, blue) and ceramic (red)[234] tesserae (ca. 0.01 sq;
ca. 0.005 for features) set 2-4mm apart.

Two rectangular panels, one with a Dionysiac scene, a, and
the other with placements for couches and a sigma table, b,
set within a wide geometric framework.

   Framework: dark blue and red intersecting circles forming
white concave-sided squares set on edge which are inscribed
with similar squares.

   IIa, east panel (pls. 146-147), framed by a narrow black/
white/black band.

   Framing: border, row of white juxtaposed stepped diamonds
with dark blue centers, set on a red ground; white triple
fillet.

   Field, framed by a black double fillet: large fragment
showing Dionysos flanked by dancers[235] and other members of
the Thiasos. A brown cloak partially covers the effeminate
body of Dionysos (pl. 148) who holds a long green (glass)

---

[234]Since there are green, blue, and red stone tesserae
as well, only the glass and ceramic ones will be noted.

[235]On the north side the leg of a dancer is discernible
in the drawing (pl. 146).

staff in his left hand. He rests his left elbow on a short,
light grey column which is entwined with a vine laden with
clusters of red and orange grapes and large green (glass
and stone) leaves. His pose is very casual, with his booted
right leg behind his left, and it appears that he, too, is
responding to the music by dancing on his toes. At his feet
is a snarling grey panther (pl. 149) with blue (glass) spots
which turns its head away from a man leaning on a brown staff
of whom only the lower part of his body survives showing blue
leggins, with light grey highlights, and part of a short blue
tunic. Beyond this man there are traces of the foot and
flowing garment of a dancing figure (pl. 146). The barefoot
members of the Thiasos to the right of the scene include a
merry Bacchante with clappers (pls. 150-151) and white and
brown arm bracelets who wears a diaphanous grey and white
gown with red and green (glass) folds which undulate to the
rhythm of her lively dance. She turns toward a nude dancing
man behind her who carries a pedum (pl. 152) while ahead of
her two other members of the procession stand and gaze
intently at the red wine flowing from a cornucopian object
near Dionysos (pl. 153).[236] A winged eros holds a bowl to
capture the wine while a satyr in a grey and white kilt fills
the air with music from a brown curving horn. The pink skin
of the figures is outlined in dark brown and red and contains

---

[236]The exact nature and disposition of the wine source
cannot be determined.

white highlights. A general physiognomic similitude is
visible in their black brows, eyes, and upper lids which are
accentuated by dark brown shading.

IIb, west panel (pls. 146, 154), framed by a black/white/
black band.

Field: rectantular panel inscribed with a semi-circle
which is divided into seven wedge-shaped strips by a two-
strand guilloche (red [ceramic]/1 ochre; white/1 ochre, with
a white tessera at each loop) on a black ground. The strips,
which are covered with plain panels, mark the position of the
couches as the apsidal panel in front of them marks the
position of the sigma table. Rimmed in grey and with a pink
field, the panel contains a white platter with two brown,
red, and ochre fish which are outlined in brown and dark
bluish grey on their dorsal and ventral sides, respectively.
In each of the west spandrels between the semi-circle and
the edge of the rectangle stands an ochre vase with a heart-
shaped body and a circular foot set on a rectangular base.[237]
Single undulating blue and grey vines issue from the wide
red (ceramic) mouth of the vase and fill the surface with
clusters of red (ceramic) grapes, ochre or red (ceramic)
leaves, outlined in black, ochre or white ones with green

[237]A curious feature of the vase is the placement of
the spiral handles on the front and back, rather than on the
sides, which is their usual position (see, for example, pls.
324, 350, 437, 470).

outlines, and ochre spiral tendrils. Two confronting bluish
grey and white herons with red (ceramic) crests, beaks, and
legs stare at each other across the top of the vase.

Additional color. Panel IIa. Framing: red and blue small
squares with white centers. Dionysos: robe outlined and
fluted in dark blue and white; boots, brown and white.
Column: outlined in dark blue. Panther: dark blue outlines
and tail, and white highlights; scattered orange and ochre
tesserae around head and ventral side of body. Pedum and
horn: black outline. Satyr: kilt outlined and spotted in
black; ribs articulated by red (ceramic) tesserae. Panel
IIb. Platter: outlined in dark bluish grey and red. Vase:
outlined in dark bluish grey.

Sixth century, around the second quarter.

Additional bibliography. BCH, 78 (1954), pp. 168-170;
R. Ginouvès, BCH, 81 (1957), p. 216.

Illustrations. BCH, 78 (1954), fig. 210 opposite p.
168 = our pl. 118, pl. VII = our pl. 146.

57 Room V (3.30 x 4.50). Southeast room. Pls. 155-156.

Framing: 0.90. Field: 1.80 x 1.27. Stone and ceramic
(red) tesserae identical in size to the ones in the preceding
entries (55-56).

Fragment of a hunting scene comprising a lion attacking a man
and being attacked by a man with a spear.

Framing (pl. 156): outer border (0.34), dark grey and red

(ceramic) intersecting circles forming white concave-sided squares set on edge;[238] narrow white band; middle border (0.44), an inhabited rinceau which is identical to those in the porticoes, Ia-b (55, pls. 119-120, 122-124, 133-135); white triple fillet; inner border (0.12), two-strand guilloche (red [ceramic]/1 pink; brown/1 white; sometimes ochre/1 white, with a white tessera at each loop) on a black ground.

Field, framed by a white fillet: to the left (pl. 155) a hunter in a long sleeve, black-belted white tunic, with a short paneled skirt, is felled by an attacking ochre and red lion. Behind the beast, a second hunter in a light brown tunic lunges forward with spear in hand. The figures stand on an undulating dark brown ground line which serves as a dividing marker between the pink ground behind them and the ivory ground beneath them.

Additional color. Both hunters wear short black and white boots with white cuffs and have pink skin, outlined in dark reddish brown with white highlights. Fallen hunter: tunic outlined in brown with ochre striations. Second hunter: tunic outlined in brown with white highlights.

Sixth century, around the second quarter.

Additional bibliography. R. Ginouvés, BCH, 80 (1956), p. 396; idem, BCH, 81 (1957), p. 216.

---

[238]The framing is barely visible in pl. 156 (right side).

ASTROS

Christian Chapel

The presence of mosaic fragments was noted along the
south side of the convent church of the monastery of St.
Luke, near Astros. On the basis of the architectural pieces
scattered around the site, the mosaics have been attributed
to a Christian chapel.[239]

Bibliography. Sodini, Compléments, pp. 581-582.

No. 58

58 Mosaic fragments (no dimensions published). Pl. 156a.

No published information on dimensions and material.

Traces of at least two fragments decorated with different
patterns: ivy rinceau; two-strand guilloche bordering a
field of octagons set on edge.[240] Whether the fragments
belong to one or two pavements is not noted.

Probably fifth century.

Illustration. Sodini, Compléments, p. 583, fig. 1 = our
pl. 156a.

---

[239]I was unaware of the existence of these mosaics when
I was in Greece and have, consequently, used Sodini's data
(Compléments, p. 582).

[240]The design is similar to those at Nea Anchialos
Gamma (pls. 392-393) and Demetrias (pl. 430).

HERMIONE

Basilica

In the courtyard of the Gymnasion at Hermione, a large
Early Christian complex was cleared in 1955 and 1956, bringing to light a basilica (overall, 17.60 x 40.00) with multiple annices and seven mosaic pavements (Rooms I, II, Vb,
VI, VII, IX, XII).[241] At the present time, some of the pavements have been destroyed, some have deteriorated extensively, and others are choked with weeds or covered by debris.

For such a large complex (pl. 157), there is surprisingly
little published information.[242] Preceded by a large
hypaethral atrium, V, with its main entrance on the southwest
side, I-II, the basilica (17.60 x 27.35) comprises a narrow
narthex, VI (17.60 x 3.00), with projecting wings, VII-VIII,
and a nave flanked by two aisles, IX-XI, and terminated by a
semi-circular apse (3.50 radius). The nave is separated
from the aisles by colonnades resting on bases set on elevated
stylobates and from the bema by a chancel screen.[243] A long

---

[241]Part of the tessellated pavement in Room VI was visible in 1950 (V. B. and M. H. Jameson, "An Archaeological and
Topographical Survey of the Hermionid," Papers of the American School of Classical Studies at Athens, June, 1950, pp.
40-41).

[242]For the reports, see E. G. Stikas, Praktika, 1955,
pp. 236-239; idem, Praktika, 1956, pp. 180-181; hereafter
cited as Stikas, 1955 and Stikas, 1956, respectively.

[243]Stikas, 1956, pp. 179-180. The chancel screen is
omitted from the plan. The present rectangular prothuron on
the east side (pl. 157) is obviously a later addition since

bench abuts the north wall of the north aisle and another
one is inscribed in the rectilinear exedra in the center of
the west wall of the narthex.[244] Traces of the liturgical
furnishings--ambon, synthronon, altar--have not survived.[245]
The northwest and south sides of the complex contain rooms
but, except for I and II, their function was not determined.

Although no datable archaeological finds were unearthed
or reported, on the basis of the style of the mosaics on the
east side, the basilica can be assigned to the second half of
the fifth century.

In the sixth century, the west side of the complex was
restored by an unknown bishop, Epiphanios, who sponsored the
repaving of Rooms I, II, VI, VII, and possibly Room V. In a
subsequent period, Room VII became a passageway between the
basilica and a new complex which was erected along the north
side. Because of the physical relationship between the two
buildings, it is suggested that the addition served as the
residence of the Archbishop or as a combined baptistery and
residence.[246]

---

it rests on the pavement. It was probably installed at the
same time as the ambon.

[244]Stikas, 1955, pp. 238-239.

[245]For the present ambon and prothuron, vide supra,
p. 150, n. 243.

[246]For the first, see Stikas, 1956, pp. 180-181; for the
second, A. K. Orlandos, To Ergon, 1956, p. 79, p. 78, fig. 78
(plan of the north complex). The reports do not explain the
hatched areas in the plan (pl. 157) which appear along the
northeast wall of the basilica, the apse, and in some sections
of the south side.

Bibliography. E. G. Stikas, Praktika, 1955, pp. 236-239;
A. K. Orlandos, To Ergon, 1955, pp. 76-82; E. G. Stikas,
Praktika, 1956, pp. 179-181; A. K. Orlandos, To Ergon, 1956,
pp. 76-80; BCH, 80 (1956), pp. 271-272; JHS, 76 (1956),
Supplement, pp. 13-14; BCH, 81 (1957), pp. 545-546; E.
Stassinopoulos, RAC, 32 (1956), pp. 97-98; D. I. Pallas, RAC,
35 (1959), pp. 216-217.

Illustrations. E. G. Stikas, Praktika, 1955, p. 237, fig.
1 = our pl. 157; idem, Praktika, 1956, p. 180, fig. 1 (north
complex: plan).

Nos. 59-65

Polychrome geometric pavements, some with figural
insets, decorate seven rooms in the complex (I, II, V, VI,
VII, IX, XII). Since the plan of the building and the
archaeological finds offer no clue to the chronology of the
basilica, the excavator and others have relied on the style
of the pavements with conflicting results. At issue is an
important tessellated inscription in Room II which states
that the work was restored by an unknown bishop named
Epiphanios: ". . . ΑΝΑΝΕѠΘ(Η)ΤΟϹΡΓΟΝ." Until recently,
it was assumed that only the room with the inscription was
redecorated and that it occurred in the seventh century.[247]
A careful examination, however, of the animal panels in Room
II (pls. 164-165) and the horse in the narthex (pl. 171)
reveals that both are products of a common workshop and are
contemporaneous. This is quite evident not only in the rigid

[247]A. K. Orlandos, To Ergon, 1955, p. 81. The excavator,
Stikas, ignores the inscription and dates all the pavements
to the sixth century (1955, p. 239).

pose and the abstract style of the animals but in the curious
lanceolate stripes which descend from their backs to their
bellies. To some extent, the body of the leaping stag in
the narthex (pl. 176) is also treated in this manner.
Another similarity between the pavements in the two rooms is
the way in which the animals are surrounded by thick, sharply
defined trees and bushes which fill the white ground with
spreading and undulating trunks, branches, and leaves.[248]
It is quite probable, therefore, that Epiphanios sponsored
the restoration of the pavements in both rooms with figural
panels which, on the basis of their style, can be assigned
to the early sixth century.[249] The pronounced contour lines
and patternization of the fauna and flora, and the overall
reduction of plasticity and three-dimensionality are consistent features of the sixth century pavements at Longos
(197, pls. 638-640) and Amphipolis (213, pl. 667). The aniconic pavements in Room I may also belong to this period,
although this is by no means certain. This attribution is
based solely on a comparison with the geometric carpet in
the nave which is probably contemporary with the erection of
the building because its designs and patterns (pls. 157, 179,
181) are rectilinear and uncomplicated and contain simple

---

[248]Similar flora are represented in the north panels,
now destroyed, which are illustrated in the plan (pl. 157).

[249]In this, I concur with Sodini who, however, does not
justify his chronology (Catalogue, p. 707). He notes traces
of the original mosaics in the two rooms. I was only able to
find definite traces in Room II (vide supra, pp. 153-154).

filling motifs. Room I, on the other hand, is paved with
curvilinear as well as rectilinear designs which undulate
and spread across the surface and carry with them intricate
rainbow and other rich filling motifs (pls. 158-161). The
complexity and variety of the designs, as exemplified by a
panel with an interlace in the south compartment (pls. 159-
160), reflect a later stage in the development of geometric
carpets and it is not improbable that, given its advanced
date and its physical proximity to the pavement containing
Epiphanios' inscription, it also formed part of his program
of restoration. It is difficult to ascribe the pavement in
the north wing of the narthex to the first or second decorative phase because it is so different from the others (pl.
178), but similar textural, close-knit designs only appear
in sixth century pavements (122, pl. 411; 151, pl. 465).
One other pavement, Room XII, remains to be discussed. Its
design and color scheme are very similar to the original
sections of the pavement in Room II which was restored along
its east side with the figural insets and an identical design.
Thus, the pavement in Room XII is probably contemporaneous
with the mosaic in the nave.

Two well defined decorative phases emerge from an
analysis of the pavements. The first, represented by the
mosaics east of the narthex and on the south side of Room II,
comprises aniconic geometric pavements with a limited and subdued vocabulary. The second is buoyant, richer, and more
complex and contains figural as well as aniconic panels. To

this phase belong all the pavements on the west side of the complex which, on the basis of style, can be assigned to the early part of the sixth century.[250] Although only the pavements in Rooms II and VI can be attributed with certitude to the sponsorship of Epiphanios, it is not unlikely that he was responsible for the others as well. With the terminus provided by the mosaics of this phase, the original pavements can be placed in the fifth century and probably belong to the second half of the century.

Additional bibliography. Sodini, Catalogue, No. 9, pp. 705-707.

Illustration. E. G. Stikas, Praktika, 1955, p. 237, fig. 1 = our pl. 157.

59   Room I (2.10 x 12.45). Porch; pavement laid up to an off-centered staircase at the southwest entrance to Room II.   Pls. 158-161.

No published information on dimensions. Stone and ceramic (red) tesserae (0.01-0.013 sq) set 3-5mm apart.

Two rectangular compartments, a-b, separated by a staircase, decorated with complex rectilinear and curvilinear designs.[251]

---

[250]Since a tessellated pavement was found beneath the present stone paving on the south side of Room V (61), it is probable this section was restored at the same time.

[251]Except for a segment of the east panel (pl. 158), the pavements were covered with weeds at the time of my visit. For this reason, the color notations and the descriptions of the designs are derived from the field notes of Professor I. Lavin and from the published drawings. For the former, see "Field Notes: Hermione," Dumbarton Oaks, Center for Byzantine Studies.

Surround: pale grey fillets in rows parallel to the walls.

Framing (pl. 159): black fillet; border, single row of
alternating white/red and grey perspectivized dentils set at
a distance from each other on a black ground; black fillet.

Field.

Ia, east compartment (pls. 157-158), decorated with three
purely geometric panels, 1-3, set within a double grey fillet.

North and south panels, 1,3 (pl. 158): two strand interlace (grey/light grey; red/grey, outlined in black) of small
and large circles forming curvilinear octagons. The circles
and octagons enclose, respectively, small red circles and
irregular, light grey octagons, outlined in red.

Central panel, 2: wide close knit braid.

Ib, west compartment (pls. 159-161), decorated with three
purely geometric panels, 1-3, set within a grey double fillet
which in the north and south panels forms part of the design.

North and south panels, 1,3 (pls. 159, 161): octagon
inscribed with a small central square and surrounded by an
alternating series of straight squares and squares set on
edge. The former are decorated with rainbow motifs and the
latter with Solomon's knots. The square in the octagon contains a grey isosceles cross with alternating red and grey
trilobate termini, set on a black ground.[252] White lozenges
fill the corners of the octagons and rainbow motifs the

---

[252]This is not visible in the illustration.

angles between the octagons and squares. The predominent colors are dark grey, red, black and white.

Central panel, 2 (pls. 159-160).

Framing: border, black and grey stepped triangles.

Field: complex quincunxial pattern comprising an eight-pointed star and four rectangular triangles in the corners. The star is laced to a central chain motif forming a square by curvilinear triangles which create an intricate pattern of interconnected and interlacing elements articulated by 1 white/grey; 1 white/red strands, outlined by black double fillets.

Early sixth century, probably restored by Epiphanios.

Illustration. E. G. Stikas, *Praktika*, 1955, pl. 84b = our pl. 160.

60   Room II (5.26 x 4.50). South entrance to atrium; raised two steps above Room I; pavement laid up to a stone threshold to north. Pls. 162-165.

Framing: 0.40; to south, 0.60. Field: ca. 3.66 x 3.70. Stone and ceramic (red) tesserae (0.01-0.013 sq) set 3-5mm apart.

Polychrome geometric mosaic restored with two figural insets to east and an inscription in the north border.

Framing (pl. 162): outer border except to south, flat black bead-and-reel composed of two juxtaposed beads joined

by a short bar and flanked by single, tangent reels; black
double fillet; inner border except to south, red and white
wave crests which are interrupted on the north side by a
black tabula ansata containing a two-line inscription in black
letters (ca. 0.05-0.06 high). Oriented southward, it cites
the name of an unknown bishop, Epiphanios, who was responsible for the restoration (ΑΝΑΝΕѠϹΙϹ) of parts of the
basilica (pl. 162): "ΕΠΙΤΟΥΘΕΟΦΙΛΕΠΙϹΚΟΗΜѠΝ/
ΕΠΙΦΑΝΙΟΥΑΝΑΝΕѠΘΤΟΕΡΓΟΝ ";[253] border to south only,
three-strand braid (yellow/1 white; red/1 white; grey/1 white,
outlined in black) on a black ground.[254]

Field, framed by a white/black double fillet (pls. 162-
163): interlocking geometric design, set on a yellow ground
and articulated by white/black double fillets, comprising
crosses of four lozenges separated by single squares. The
lozenges are bisected along the margins. The chromatic
sequence consists of an alternation of red and yellow lozenges with the former inscribed with long white crosslets and
the latter with long black ones. The red squares, on the
other hand, contain white stepped squares. Two octagonal
figural insets, set over one meter apart and oriented southward, interrupt the original geometric design on the east side

---

[253]Stikas, 1955, p. 237, pl. 84a. For an emendation, see
E. Stassinopoulos, RAC, 32 (1956), p. 97: ΕΠΙ ΤΟΥ ΘΕΟΦΙΛ(ΕϹΤΑΤΟΥ)
ΕΠΙϹΚΟ(ΠΟΥ) ΗΜѠΝ/ ΕΠΙΦΑΝΙΟΥ ΑΝΑΝΕѠΘ(Η) ΤΟ ΕΡΓΟΝ.

[254]This border and part of the south side of the field
belong to the original pavement.

of the room. The north panel contains a grey and blue heraldic eagle with outspread wings grasping a similarly colored
partridge in its red talons (pl. 164). In comparison with
this theme of bird and prey, the south octagon (pl. 165)
contains a placid and idyllic scene in which a doe or lamb
calmly nibbles on a leaf from a bush in front of it while a
second bush rises on its flank. It accents the surface with
flat black and yellow leaves and with one terminal red and
white bud. The bud sways to touch the undulating, flame-
like crest of a tree whose trunk is bisected by the light
grey and yellow lanceolate-striped body of the animal. The
figures move and stand within the frontal plane of the octagons and are rendered with a modicum of modeling and with
strong black outlines which emphasize their two-dimensionality.

Additional color. North panel. Birds: yellow breasts
and black eyes. South panel: bushes outlined in dark green.

Early sixth century, restored by Epiphanios.

Illustrations. E. G. Stikas, Praktika, 1955, pl. 84a
(inscription), pl. 85a (eagle and partridge), pl. 85b (doe
or lamb).

61 Room Vb (ca. 4.00 x 9.65).[255] South side of atrium;
repaired with irregularly-cut marble slabs.

---

[255]The north-south dimension was taken from the plan
(pl. 157).

No published information on dimensions and material.

Traces of a border decorated with a "meander in perspective"
were noted by Sodini on the east side.[256]

Possibly contemporary with the original pavements to the east
(64, 65); second half of the fifth century.

62 Room VI (17.60 x 3.00). Narthex. Pls. 166-177.

Framing: 0.50. Field: North compartment, a: ca. 4.50 x
ca. 2.30. Second compartment, b: 6.00 x ca. 2.30. Third
compartment, c: 2.65 x ca. 2.30.[257] South compartment, d:
2.00 x ca. 2.30. Stone and ceramic (red) tesserae (0.01 -
0.012 sq) set 2-4mm apart.

Four compartments, a-d, of varying dimensions, filled with
geometric and figural panels and set within a wide framework.[258]

Surround: in rows of dark grey tesserae parallel to the
walls.

Framing: black fillet; border, three-strand braid (pls.

---

[256]He is the only person to have seen this panel
(Catalogue, p. 706).

[257]Because of the bad condition of this pavement, the
individual measurements are taken from the plan (pl. 157).

[258]Although the two south compartments are clearly
separated by the braid pattern, Sodini considers them to be
one unit (Catalogue, p. 706).

168-169) (red/1 white; yellow; 1 white; dark grey/1 white,
outlined in black, with a white tessera at each loop).

Field, framed by a white double fillet.

VIa, north compartment (pls. 166-168): two panels set
within a double border.

Framing: black fillet; outer border (0.32), eight-pointed
lozenge star and square pattern forming small squares set on
edge. The large and small squares are filled with concave-
sided or rectilinear squares, both set on edge, which repeat
the yellow color scheme of the lozenges and are set on black
or red grounds; black fillet; white double fillet; inner
border, complex interlace, set on a dark ground, forming
irregular, elongated loops which are pierced by two continuous horizontal red bars; both outlined in black with an inner
row of white.[259] (For a similar pattern, see pls. 225, 256).

Field: both panels are destroyed, except for traces of the
trunks of two trees (pl. 167). At the time of the excavation,
traces were still visible of one or two animals, oriented
westward.[260]

VIb, second compartment (pls. 168-169).

Framing: border, two-strand guilloche (red/1 white; light

[259]The published drawings erroneously show a more regu-
larized and symmetrical interlace (Stikas, 1955, pl. 89a,
with an incorrect caption ascribing it to the nave = our pl.
168; Sodini, Catalogue, p. 712, fig. 2g).

[260]Stikas, 1955, p. 238. The sections are visible in
the plan (pl. 157).

grey/1 white, outlined in black) on a black ground.

Field: destroyed. Originally, a geometric network of alternating octagons and small squares inscribed with floral and geometric motifs.

VIc, third compartment (pls. 170-171).

Framing: black double fillet; border, pairs of black and light grey opposed peltae, outlined in black, arranged in alternating horizontal and vertical units; black double fillet.

Field: extensive deterioration throughout. Originally, a scene, oriented eastward, comprising a tethered horse[261] pawing at the ground with its right foreleg, amid luxuriant, undulating trees and bushes. Its body was decorated with lanceolate stripes which are similar to those on the hide of the animal in Room II (pl. 165). All that is preserved is a fragment of the left side of the panel containing some blue and black branches and traces of the front of the animal.[262]

VId, south compartment (pls. 170, 172-176): two rows of two figural panels each, one-four, oriented northward.

Framework: two-strand guilloche (light grey/1 white; lost/ 1 white, outlined in black, with a white tessera at each loop)

---

[261]It is clearly not a lamb (cf. Stikas, 1955, p. 238).

[262]The photograph (pl. 171) was taken in 1964 by Professor I. Lavin.

on a black ground.[263]

Field: beginning at the southeast side and moving westward
the sequence of panels is as follows.

Panel one (pl. 173): opposed, long-legged, grey land birds
stretch their thin rubbery necks to drink from the crater
behind them. The broad grey vase, outlined in white/grey,
rests precariously on a small circular foot set on a triangular base.

Panel two (pl. 174): grey amphora with spiral handles
flanked by two pairs of confronting grey birds set in superimposed registers. In the lower zone, ducks stand facing
each other while above them two land birds move forward to
drink from a vase from which issue two stunted grey branches.
In contrast to the gentle action of this feathered menagerie,
the lower panels, three-four, contain wild animals running
amid trees and bushes.

Panel three (pl. 175): black spotted panther with extended
black claws cuts across a rigid light and dark grey tree
which rises in the center of the scene.

Panel four (pl. 176): amid more sinuous and plentiful
flora than those in the preceding panel, a grey stag, whose
hide is reminiscent of that of the horse in the preceding
compartment, c (pl. 171), leaps over an ivy plant composed
of two large flat leaves.

---

[263]All the tesserae have disappeared from one strand
of the guilloche (pls. 173-174).

Throughout the pavement, there are signs of crude, ancient repair with irregularly-cut tesserae averaging 2 to $2\frac{1}{2}$ centimeters in length. This is especially apparent along the north side where the original design is replaced by an imbrication pattern (pl. 177). Elsewhere (pl. 176), the pavement has been patched with the same material (for similar crude repairs in the nave, see pl. 180).

Early sixth century; restored by Epiphanios.

Additional bibliography. V. B. and M. H. Jameson, "An Archaeological and Topographical Survey of the Hermionid," Papers of the American School of Classical Studies at Athens, June, 1950, pp. 40-41; I. Lavin, "Field Notes: Hermione," Dumbarton Oaks, Center for Byzantine Studies.

Illustrations. E. G. Stikas, Praktika, 1955, pl. 87a (VId, general view), pl. 87b (VId, panel three), pl. 88a (VId, panel two), pl. 88b (VId, panel one), pl. 89a = our pl. 168.

63 Room VII (2.50 x 3.60). North wing of narthex; north wall replaced and threshold installed on northeast side, destroying the pavement. Pl. 178.

Surround: 0.10; to north, 0.40. Field: ca. 2.00 x 3.40. Materials identical to those in Room VI (62).

Wide braid enclosed by a plain band.

Surround: in rows of light grey tesserae parallel to the walls.

Field: wide, close-knit braid (yellow/1 white; red/1 white; light grey/1 white, outlined in black, with a white tessera at each loop) on a black ground.

Probably early sixth century; contemporary with the restoration by Epiphanios.

64 Room IX (7.60 x 27.35). Nave; northeast and east sides
    covered by a later ambon and prothuron which rest direct-
ly on the pavement. Pls. 179-181.

West compartment, a: ca. 7.20 x 16.80. East compartment,
b: two fragments of a border, 0.30.[264] Stone and ceramic
(red) tesserae (0.01-0.012 sq) set 2-3mm apart.

Originally two compartments, a-b, of which the west one
survives. It contains two aniconic panels, one-two, set on
a ground of peltae.

IXa, west compartment.

Surround: in rows parallel to the stylobates and walls.

Field, framed by a black double fillet.

Ground (pl. 179): pairs of black and red opposed peltae
arranged in alternating horizontal and vertical units on a
light grey ground (for a similar pattern in the narthex, see
62, pl. 170).

West panel, one: black on white meander pattern enclosing
red lozenges inscribed with narrow white crosses.[265] In

---

[264]Only the border on the north side is visible in the
plan (pl. 157). In a later plan, more of the north border is
indicated (Stikas, 1956), p. 180, fig. 1). Presumably, no
trace of the field was found (see A. K. Orlandos, To Ergon,
1955, p. 81).

[265]This pavement is not illustrated in the reports and
its present ruinous condition precludes a satisfactory
reproduction.

antiquity the east side of the panel was restored with a
crude panel (1.15 x 0.97) composed of irregularly-cut tesserae (0.01-0.02 x 0.01-0.03) set 3-7mm apart. The scene,
oriented eastward (pl. 180), contains two small confronting
birds standing on opposite edges of a fountain containing
purplish water (for a similar scene, see narthex 62, pl. 174).
Flanking the base of the fountain are two pin wheel motifs
inscribed in concentric circles. The forms are articulated
solely by means of single dark grey fillets. Whether or not
the panel was executed at the same time as the crude repairs
in the narthex cannot be determined (pl. 177).[266]

East panel, two (pl. 181): straight grid composed of a two-
strand guilloche (dark grey/1 white; red/1 white, outlined in
black, with a white tessera at each loop) on a black ground,
forming ten rows of fourteen small squares each. On the east-
west axis each row contains identical filling motifs, on a
black ground. Starting on the northeast side and moving
southward, the sequence of filling elements is as follows:
black and white checkerboard patterns; two-strand Solomon's
knots (same colors as guilloche border); grey and white peltae, outlined in black; white perspectivized dentils; two
rows of identical circles inscribed with concave-sided
squares; Solomon's knots (same as first set); perspectivized

---

[266]There is no reference to this repair and it is omitted
from the plan (pl. 157). There is no evidence to support
Sodini's attribution of the repairs to the late sixth century
(Catalogue, p. 707).

dentils; peltae; Solomon's knots (same as first set).

IXb, east compartment: destroyed, except for traces of a
floral border on the north and south sides.[267]

Framing: border, undulating black rinceau (two fillets)
forming loosely arranged scrolls filled with single black
agitated ivy leaves.

Second half of the fifth century.

Illustration. E. G. Stikas, Praktika, 1955, pl. 89b = our
pl. 181.

65 Room XII (dimensions indeterminable). South annex;[268]

   wall built on north side covering the pavement. Pl. 157.

Stone and ceramic (red) tesserae (0.01-0.012 sq).

Polychrome geometric pavement comprising interlocking patterns of lozenges and diamonds bordered by a braid.

Framing: border, three-strand braid (yellow/1 white; red/
1 white; light grey/1 white, outlined in black) on a black
ground; white double fillet; black double fillet.

Field: interlocking geometric design comprising crosses of
two lozenges and two diamonds separated by single squares set
on edge. The units are articulated by black/white single

267Vide supra, p. 165, n. 264 and pl. 157.

268This room is not discussed in the reports. Since it
is overgrown, the color notations are derived from the field
notes of Professor Irving Lavin.

fillets and placed on a yellow ground. Each cruciform pattern has an alternating a-b chromatic sequence with the vertical lozenges containing a red ground inscribed with a narrow light grey crosslet and the horizontal diamonds a light grey ground with a red crosslet. The squares, on the other hand, contain a consistent chromatic scheme of red crosses on a light grey ground (for a similar design in Room II, see 60, pl. 162).

Second half of the fifth century.

Mosaic Fragment

A fragment of a mosaic pavement (pls. 182-188) is visible in front of the pharmacy at Hermione. Originally ascribed to a Christian basilica because of traces of an apse on the east side of the pavement,[269] it has since been established that the apse was installed at a later time and cuts into the pavement.[270] No serious investigation of the site has been conducted and its use as a parking lot prevented me from examining the remains. The pictorial and descriptive data in this entry, therefore, are provided by Professor Irving Lavin

---

[269] J. Basiliou, Hermionis (Athens, 1907), p. 77, cited by Sodini, Catalogue, p. 707 and n. 11.

[270] I. Lavin, "Field Notes: Hermione," Dumbarton Oaks, Center for Byzantine Studies. Although Sodini also noted that the apse is later, he attributes the pavement to a pre-existent basilica without corroborative evidence (op. cit., p. 707, n. 12).

who visited the site in 1964.[271]

Bibliography. I. Lavin, "Field Notes: Hermione," Dumbarton Oaks, Center for Byzantine Studies; Sodini, Catalogue, p. 707.

No. 66

Fragment of an aniconic geometric pavement containing bichrome patterns to the west and polychrome ones to the east separated by a plain grey panel. In the center of the pavement is a long seam (pl. 184) which reveals an antique restoration of the pavement. Its original section is represented by the black and grey patterns to the west (pls. 182-183) because they are much simpler and the tesserae are smaller. Bichrome pavements articulated by plain bands and containing flat, uncomplicated motifs belong to an austere, sober trend in Greek pavements which is datable to the end of the fourth or the beginning of the fifth century.[272] In comparison, the restored section is filled with complex patterns and borders (pls. 185-188) and the chromatic scheme includes blue, yellow, red, and purple. These features are also found in the pavements decorating a nearby villa (67-68), and it is probable that the same workshop was responsible for both decorative programs. Thus, the restored section of the pavement can be attributed to the second half of the sixth

---

[271]Vide supra, p. 168, n. 270.

[272]See, for example, 88-92, 130-138, 196.

century.

Additional bibliography. V. B. and M. H. Jameson, "An Archaeological and Topographical Survey of the Hermionid," Papers of the American School of Classical Studies at Athens, June, 1950, pp. 40-41.

66 Mosaic fragment (6.67 x 6.50).[273] Destroyed to east by

later apse. Pls. 182-188.

No published information on dimensions and material.

Tesserae in east section (0.015-0.02 sq).

Fragment of a bichrome pavement decorated with four long tangent panels (pls. 182-184). The east side was restored with a grid inscribed with complex polychrome motifs (pls. 185-188).

Panel a, original sector to west (pls. 182-184): imbrication pattern composed of black and grey scales oriented southward; narrower band containing a row of alternating black lozenges and circles on a grey ground; black double fillet; wide grey panel with a seam running down its center (pl. 184).

Panel b, restored sector to east: traces of a straight grid framed along the west and south sides by a wide decorative border.[274]

------

[273] In 1950, its size was around 8 meters (V. B. and M. H. Jameson, "An Archaeological and Topographical Survey of the Hermionid," Papers of the American School of Classical Studies at Athens, June, 1950, p. 41).

[274] It is difficult to accept Sodini's description that the border "surrounds" the field since it is destroyed to the north and east (op. cit., p. 707).

Framing (pl. 185): black fillet; light double fillet;
border, triple overlapping lyre pattern containing, for the
most part, light blue, yellow, and purple/dark red triangles
edged in white.[275] These are flanked by strands of the same
color which, set on a dark ground, are outlined in black and
contain an inner row of white tesserae; light double fillet.

Field: traces of a straight grid composed of a two-strand
guilloche (dark red/1 white; yellow/1 white alternating with
light blue/1 white, outlined in black, with a white tessera
at each loop) on a black ground. The squares formed by the
grid are filled with geometric patterns which, beginning at
the north side, are as follows. First square (pl. 186):
diagonal rows of alternating light blue, yellow, and purple
scales with white stems and black outlines. Second square
(pl. 187): intersecting circles forming light blue concave-
sided squares set on edge which are filled with white/black
stepped squares. Short dark bars spring from the sides of
the stepped squares to form cruciform motifs. Third square:
destroyed, except for traces of an undulating ribbon motif.[276]
Fourth square: wide braid (light blue/1 white; dark red/1
white; bright red/1 white; yellow/1 white outlined in black,
with a white tessera at each loop) on a dark ground.

Additional colors. Grid: quatrefoils in second square
have bright red, purple, and light blue centers.

---

[275]The blue and yellow triangles are also tipped in red.
[276]Only noted by Sodini (loc. cit.)

Late fourth or early fifth century, with a restoration in the second half of the sixth century.

Villa

At Hermione, two brief excavations were undertaken to determine the extent of a mosaic pavement which had lain exposed in the courtyard of a house belonging to the Meïntani family. During the course of clearing the site, the northeast sector of a secular building (pl. 189; overall, 15.00 max x 12.00 max) and two mosaic pavements were brought to light.[277]

Since the excavations were limited to this small sector, only four rooms were cleared, I-IV, along with what appears to be the corner of a corridor, V. Because a clay drainage system was found in "two small rooms" somewhere in this sector, the excavator concluded that one room was a bath and the other a toilet. For this reason, he determined that the building was a private house or villa.[278]

Although no datable archaeological finds were unearthed, on the basis of the style of the mosaics, the building can be

---

[277]The pavements were noted in 1950 by V. B. and M. H. Jameson ("An Archaeological and Topographical Survey of the Hermionid," Papers of the American School of Classical Studies, June, 1950, pp. 36-40, p. 38, figs. 16-18). The owner of the house informed me that one part of the mosaic was exposed when the house was built in the early part of this century.

[278]E. G. Stikas, Praktika, 1956, p. 184.

attributed to the late sixth century.

Bibliography. V. B. and M. H. Jameson, "An Archaeological and Topographical Survey of the Hermionid," Papers of the American School of Classical Studies at Athens, June, 1950, pp. 36-40; E. G. Stikas, Praktika, 1955, p. 239; A. K. Orlandos, To Ergon, 1955, pp. 82-83; E. G. Stikas, Praktika, 1956, p. 184; A. K. Orlandos, To Ergon, 1956, pp. 79-80; BCH, 80 (1956), p. 273; E. Stassinopoulos, RAC, 32 (1956), p. 98; BCH, 81 (1957), pp. 546-547.

Illustration. E. G. Stikas, Praktika, 1956, p. 182 fig. 2 = our pl. 189.

Nos. 67-68

Polychrome figural and geometric mosaics pave Room I and the east side of Room II.[279] In the figural panels (pls. 190-193, 195-196), heraldic birds and animals strut, prance, or walk across a vine and flower strewn ground and cover it with two-dimensional surface patterns and silhouettes. The linearity of these flat, attenuated, abstract shapes, the total absence of modeling, proportion, anatomical detail, and depth, and the schematic treatment of the flora are stylistic characteristics which can be assigned to the late sixth century.[280] A comparison of the large panel (pls. 193, 195-196) with similar ones at Akrini (189, pl. 620) and Longos (197, pls. 638-640), which are dated to the end of

---

[279] I was only able to study the three figural panels in Room I. The rest of the mosaics are covered with debris.

[280] E. G. Stikas, Praktika, 1955, p. 240. For another pavement executed by the same workshop, see Sodini, Catalogue, pp. 751-753, and nn. 100-101.

the fifth century and the early sixth century, respectively, reveal successive stages in the progression toward purely abstract, weightless, and inorganic patterns which find their most developed expression at Hermione.

Additional bibliography. Sodini, Catalogue, pp. 705-707, n. 9, pp. 751-753 and nn. 100-101.

Illustration. E. G. Stikas, Praktika, 1956, p. 182, fig. 2 = our pl. 189.

67 Room I (5.60 x 11.00). Large hall; pavement laid up to a stone threshold block to east; divided by a modern wall.[281] Pls. 190-196.

Framing: 1.00; to west, 1.20. Field: ca. 4.00 x 8.40. East compartment, a: ca. 4.00 x 1.50. Central compartment, b: ca. 4.00 x 2.30. Central strip, c: ca. 4.00 x 1.00. West compartment, d: ca. 4.00 x 3.50. Stone and ceramic (red) tesserae (ca. 0.015 sq) set 2-5mm apart.

Polychrome mosaics composed of heraldic animals and birds to the east and complex geometric designs to the west, enclosed by a wide framing.

Surround to west only: in rows parallel to the walls.

Framing: outer fillets destroyed or covered; outer border, a row of dark grey intersecting semi-circles forming ogive arches; dark grey fillet; inner border, two-strand guilloche

---

[281]Most of the measurements for this and the succeeding entry (68) are taken from the plan (pl. 189).

(red; light grey, outlined in black) on a black ground.[282]

Field (pls. 190-196): three compartments (a-b,d),
separated by a central strip, c, comprising figural scenes
to the east, oriented eastward, and geometric designs to the
west.

Ia, east compartment, framed by dark grey/white fillets
and separated by an overlapping lyre pattern (0.70 wide),
outlined by white/dark grey fillets and set on a dark
ground.[283] It has alternating red/tan and red/dark grey triangular centers flanked, respectively, by 1 dark grey/red
and 1 dark grey/tan strands.

South panel. Pls. 190-191.

Framing: border, narrow red and white checkerboard pattern set on a dark grey ground.

Field: two confronting dark grey peacocks with red and
white striated wings and trailing tail coverts, accented by
red and white occeli. They face each other beneath the
curving branches of a dark grey palm (?) tree and peck at
two isolated red leaves which spring from the narrow tree
trunk above them. Abstract and graceless vines with dark
grey leaves, tendrils, and checkerboard-patterned clusters
of grapes emerge from the side and bottom of the scene.

North panel. Pls. 190, 192.

_____

[282]On the plan (pl. 189), this border is only represented
on the west side. The framing is not visible in the plates.

[283]The ground on the east and west sides is white (see
E. G. Stikas, _Praktika_, 1956, pl. 79b).

Framing: border, narrow red and white checkerboard pattern
set on a dark grey ground.

Field: all-over figural design composed of strutting and
walking birds which is dominated by an elongated peacock
with red and white striated wings and trailing tail coverts,
accented by red and white occeli. Above it and facing in
the opposite direction is a second but smaller peacock which
turns its head away from a small dark grey bird to snift at
a checkerboard-patterned flower. Along the bottom of the
scene, two dark grey chickens (one not visible in the plate)
follow the trail of a large light grey goose which is honking
at a speckled snake. A small bird walks above the head of
the snake, oblivious to the imminent danger below. Completing the composition are large, graceless, dark grey ivy
leaves, tendrils, and speckled flowers which spring from the
four sides of the panel.

Additional color. Birds: dark grey or white eyes. South
panel: dark grey and white grapes. North panel. Chickens:
red and white striations. Goose: red wing, outlined in
white/dark grey with dark grey outlines. Snake: dark grey
and white.

Ib, central compartment (pls. 190, 193-196), framed by a
series of dark grey/white/dark grey/white/dark grey double and
triple fillets.

Field: two attenuated, confronting deer strut majestically
toward a large vase-like fountain from which issue two long

dark grey vines. Running water in the form of alternating
red and dark grey diagonal lines fills the mouth of the long-
necked vase which rests precariously on a small, dark grey
circular foot supported by a red triangular base, outlined
in dark grey. Its body (pl. 194) and neck, joined by two
spiral handles, are striated with curving rows of dark grey,
red, white, and light purplish brown tesserae which emphasize
its two-dimensional shape. The two deer (pls. 195-196)
advance on spindly legs and appear like weightless, patterned
silhouettes floating amid a thicket of curving vines, tendrils, and ivy leaves which almost camouflage their dark
grey antlers. Like the vase, the hide of the stag to the
right (pl. 195) is also striated (ochre and red) while the
hide of the brown roe deer (?)[284] to the left is speckled
with red and light purplish brown tesserae (pl. 196).

Additional color. Vase: red center in neck and light
purplish brown center in body; dark grey handles and outlines. Vine: dark grey, with light grey ivy leaves which
are outlined by one or two rows of dark grey, sometimes by
light purplish brown/dark grey.

Ic, central strip (pl. 189):[285] a row of five small tangent panels comprising an overlapping lyre pattern in the

---

[284]This is suggested by the curving antlers.

[285]Since this side of the pavement was covered, only a
brief description will follow.

center, flanked by imbrication patterns and followed by interlacing squares forming eight-pointed stars which are inscribed with lanceolate hexafoils.

Id, west compartment: four squares separated by a wide imbrication pattern composed of scales, oriented westward. The first register appears to be decorated with intersecting circles forming concave-sided squares and the second with intersecting designs forming diagonal, four-pointed stars.

Late sixth century.

Illustrations. V. B. and M. H. Jameson, "An Archaeological and Topographical Survey of the Hermionid," Papers of the American School of Classical Studies, June, 1950, p. 38, fig. 16 (Ib, right side), p. 38, fig. 18 (Ia, north panel); E. G. Stikas, Praktika, 1955, pl. 90a = our pl. 192, pl. 90b = our pl. 190; idem, Praktika, 1956, pl. 79b (Ia, central border).

68   Room II (ca. 3.60 x ca. 6.80). Pl. 189.

No published information on dimensions and material.[286]

Fragment of a pavement decorated with scales fanning south-ward and part of a floral border. The latter contains traces of a rinceau forming loosely arranged and widely spaced scrolls filled with single agitated ivy leaves.[287]

---

[286]The measurement is taken from the plan (pl. 189).

[287]No border exists on the south and southeast sides of the room and the purpose and material of the juxtaposed rectangular panels along the north and west sides is not explained in the reports.

Late sixth century.

TEGEA

Christian Building

Excavations in 1891 and 1934, northeast of the Temple
of Athena Alea at Tegea (pl. 197), brought to light an
oriented, one-aisled apsidal building (pl. 198; 5.13 x 13.00,
without apse) with mosaic pavements.[288] At the present time,
all traces of the wall foundations and the apse with its
mosaic pavement have disappeared. The mosaic in the rectangular hall was lifted, consolidated and reset in situ
where it is protected by a concrete and wooden enclosure.

Except for two brief announcements of its discovery and
clearing and three illustrations, no information on the
archaeological and architectural history of the building has
been published.[289] As a result, its function as well as its
chronology remain problematic. A tessellated inscription at
the west entrance which cites the name of an unknown bishop,
Thyrsos, confirms the Christian character and sponsorship of
the building.[290] Its function, on the other hand, could not

---

[288]Traces of a Byzantine church were found to the south
of the building (V. Bérard, BCH, 16 [1892], p. 12 and our
plan [pl. 197]).

[289]A monograph is being prepared by A. K. Orlandos.

[290]I would like to thank Professor Ihor Sevcenko of
Harvard University for the translation of this inscription
which, at one time, was identified as belonging to a Jewish

have been liturgical because its plan militates against it
(pl. 198). Single-aisled buildings, especially those with
rich, decorative tessellated carpets, never served as churches
in Greece during this period. Rather, they fulfilled non-
liturgical functions within the Christian community such as
chapels and episcopal audience halls and were always adjuncts
to basilicas.[291] At Nikopolis, for example, Basilicas Alpha
(Room V, pl. 457) and Beta (Room XV, pl. 548) contain on
their south sides single-aisled rectangular structures with
apses which are richly adorned with mosaic carpets. Although
their specific function is still uncertain, it is generally
conceded that the ones physically related to the narthex
were chapels of some kind, perhaps for the reception and
consecration of the offerings.[292] They varied in size
(Alpha, 11.93 x 4.50, with apse; Beta, 4.00 x 9.50) but never
in their one-aisled plan. The precise form and function of
another building at Beta, I (pls. 548-549), to the east of
the apsidal structure, cannot be determined since it was not
completely cleared. Its larger size (6.30 x 12.75 max) and
location, however, suggest a reception hall, perhaps for
Archbishop Alkison whose name is contained in the tessellated

synogogue (see G. A. Soteriou, Atti del IV congresso internazionale di archeologia Christiana, 1, 1938 [Vatican, 1940],
p. 365)., Vide infra, p. 186, n. 301.

[291]See, for example, pls. 103, 157, 356, 362, 424, 647,
676.

[292]Orlandos, Xylostegos basilikē, p. 130-206; idem, Hē
metakinēsis tou diakonikou, pp. 353ff, pl. 74.

pavement. This is not improbable since no other church in
Greece has two chapels on the same side.

As far as the building at Tegea is concerned, therefore,
its plan and inscription establish its relationship to an
ecclesiastical complex. Indeed, the inscription speaks of a
"sacred precinct" and of the buildings with "delicate tesserae" which were sponsored by this unknown priest and
bishop. Whether it was a chapel or reception hall will remain problematic until the entire site is cleared, but two
factors suggest the more secular function. It is larger than
most chapels in Greece[293] (5.13 x 13.00, without apse), and
its inscription is not dedicatory or supplicatory as at
Nikopolis[294] and elsewhere.[295] Rather, it is a eulogy for
Thyrsos who "eclipsed" his eighteen predecessors and who
sponsored ". . . all kinds of noble things. . ." It is the
kind of inscription one would expect to find in the more
secularized atmosphere of an audience hall in which "the most
holy Thyrsos" held court. Unfortunately, the date of his
episcopacy cannot be determined and no external evidence was
unearthed or reported during the excavations. The mosaics,

---

[293]The average size is around 10.00 x 4.00.

[294]See 152, 153, 161. The inscription in the north wing
of Nikopolis Alpha (154) belongs to a separate category be-
cause of its descriptive character (Kitzinger, Mosaics at
Nikopolis, pp. 95ff; idem, "World Map and Fortune's Wheel: A
Medieval Mosaic Floor in Turin," Proceedings of the American
Philosophical Society, 117, no. 5 [1973], pp. 369-370).

[295]See 88; 95; 98; 115; 142.

however, can be placed well into the fifth century and it is
during this period that Thyrsos occupied the episcopal throne.
Ostensibly, therefore, the see at Tegea was established as
early as the fourth century since Thyrsos was the nineteenth
occupant of the throne.

Bibliography. V. Bérard, BCH, 16 (1892), pp. 528-549;
idem, BCH, 17 (1893), pp. 1-24; AA, 49 (1934), col. 156; AA,
52 (1937), col. 139; G. A. Soteriou, Atti del IV congresso
internazionale di archeologia Cristiana, 1, 1938 (Vatican,
1940), p. 365; CIG, V, 2, 169.

Illustrations. V. Bérard, BCH, 16 (1892), pl. 13 = our pl.
197; S. Bettini, La pittura bizantina, Parte, II: I mosaici,
Florence, 1939, fig. on p. 9 (general view, looking east);
G. A. Soteriou, Atti del IV congresso internazionale de
archeologia Cristiana, 1, 1938 (Vatican, 1940), p. 366, fig.
12 = our pl. 198.

Nos. 69-70

Two polychrome pavements with allegorical representations of the months and the seasons and organic and geometric
borders decorate the hall, I, and apse, II (pl. 198). The
latter is decorated with a scene, now lost, composed of a
handsome man flanked by two young men who run toward him
carrying baskets of fruit and vegetables. The figures are
identified by an inscription as the Beautiful Seasons (ΚΑΛΟΙ
ΚΑΙΡΟΙ)[296] and it is this seasonal theme which is continued
in the preserved rectangular pavement to the west. It contains busts of the twelve months of the year which are set in

[296]For other pavements with the "ΚΑΛΟΙ ΚΑΙΡΟΙ," see
42, pl. 95; 83, pls. 265, 267.

a straight grid and flanked to the east and west by the Four
Rivers of Paradise.

The pavement is remarkable for its cosmographic and
geographic iconography, its delicate chromatic scheme--pink,
red, orange, yellow, light blue, grey--and for its classicistic figures which are rendered with a fluidity of line and
movement absent from the majority of the pavements in Greece.
For these reasons, it has been ascribed to the first half of
the fifth century.[297] In the light of recent discoveries,
however, which have increased our knowledge of the development of Greek pavements between the fourth and the seventh
centuries, it can be assigned to the second half of the century. It is in this period that aniconic and austere geometric pavements in Churches and villas are replaced by ones
which are either more complex or are filled with lively
representations of the land and sea. One particular aspect
of the latter trend is the appearance in both secular and
ecclesiastical structures of the late fifth and early sixth
centuries of representations of the months and the seasons
(42; 55; 75; 83). This type of decorative program contrasts
sharply with earlier programs belonging to a period between
the late fourth and the middle of the fifth centuries. At
Athens (1; 2-3; 6-9; 21; 22) and Epidauros (44-49), for
example, the late fourth or early fifth century pavements are

[297]AA, 49 (1934), col. 156; H. Stern, Le Calendrier de
354, Paris (1953), p. 224. An early fifth century date was
suggested by Soteriou (vide supra, p. 179, n. 290).

purely geometric and have small scale designs and narrow
borders to contain them. Even somewhat later pavements at
Athens, datable to around the middle of the century, show a
remarkable aversion to multiple figure compositions (4-5;
10-13). It is for iconographic reasons, therefore, that the
chronology of the pavements at Tegea should be reconsidered
and advanced to the second half of the fifth century. In my
judgment, the beautiful workmanship of most of the panels,
the classicistic figures and their delicate coloration reflect the hand of a superior artisan who was better equipped
than many of his contemporaries to translate the painted
images in the pattern books into tessellated ones.

Additional bibliography. Kitzinger, Mosaic Pavements in
the Greek East, p. 218, n. 5; H. Stern, Le Calendrier de
354, Paris, 1953, pp. 223-224; G. M. A. Hanfmann, The Seasons
Sarcophagus at Dumbarton Oaks, Cambridge, Mass., 1957, p.
265, n. 31; Sodini, Catalogue, No. 15, p. 709; R. Bianchi
Bandinelli, Rome: The Late Empire, New York, 1970, p. 329.

Illustrations. G. A. Soteriou, Atti del IV congresso
internazionale di archeologia cristiana, 1, 1938 (Vatican,
1940), p. 366, fig. 12 = our pl. 198.

69 Room I (5.13 x 13.00). Hall. Pls. 198-216.

Framing: 0.95. Field: 3.24 x 11.00. Panels, including
borders: 0.95. Tabula ansata: 1.67 x 0.61. Stone tesserae
(0.01 sq; for features, 0.005-0.01 sq) set 1-3mm apart.

Straight grid with sixteen large figural insets set within a
meander framework and enclosed by a wide border. At the west
entrance, the border is interrupted by a long inscription.

Framing (pls. 198, 201-202): border, grid, articulated by

black/2 white/black fillets, composed of alternating rows of
one and two juxtaposed straight octagons forming small
squares. The latter are simply decorated with small white/
pink/red disks which are crossed by two diagonal black fillets
with white centers.[298] In contrast, the larger (0.53) and
more elaborate octagons contain decorative borders, among them
stepped triangles, undulating ribbons, semi-circles, rainbow
cables, and checkerboard and bead-and-reel patterns, which
follow no particular arrangement or sequence. They are set
on grey or white grounds depending on the color scheme of
the patterns which are generally rose, pink, red, orange,
yellow, and grey.[299] The octagons are inscribed with geometric motifs, vases, and marine creatures, oriented toward
the field (pl. 201),[300] which are chromatically similar to
the borders. Various types of interlaced cruciform patterns,
sometimes inscribed in, or enlaced by, squares and circles,
radiating disks, and juxtaposed, serrated rainbow cables
serve as abstract, static counterparts for the lively representations of fish, octopi, dolphins, and lobsters. In the
octagons cut by the margins, on the other hand, there are

---

[298]The outer interlace border noted by V. Bérard (BCH,
17 [1893], p. 13) is not visible at the present time nor in
the photograph and plan after the second excavation (S.
Bettini, La Pittura bizantina, Parte II: I mosaici,
Florence, 1939, fig. on p. 9; see also our pl. 198)

[299]Because of unexpected difficulties at the site, my
color descriptions are incomplete.

[300]Only the two creatures on the northwest side of the
tabula ansata face westward (pl. 204).

arrayed geometricized floral motifs composed of pairs of
crossed ivy leaves, and trefoils of lanceolate leaves flanked
by palmettos or ivy leaves. The border is interrupted at the
west entrance by a large tabula ansata (pls. 203, 205, 206)
which is held by two putti and contains a five-line inscription in black letters (ca. 0.07 high). Oriented westward,
it cites the name of a priest and bishop, Thyrsos, who
sponsored the erection and decoration of buildings in the
"sacred precinct."

    ΤΟΥϹΕΠΤΟΥΤΟΥΤΟΥΤΕΜΕΝΟΥϹ⁚ ΕΝΪΕΡΕΥϹΕΙΝ/
ΕΝΝΕΑΚΑΙΔΕΚΑΤΟϹ⁚ΘΥΡϹΟϹΟΟϹΙωϹΗΓΗϹΑΜΕΝΟϹ/
ΑΜΦΟΤΕΡωΝΕΚΡΥΨΕΝΠΡΟϹΗΓΟΡΙΑϹΠΑϹΙΝΕϹΘΛΟΙϹ/
ΚΑΙΜΑΡΤΥΡΙΤΑΚΤΙϹΜΑΤΑΚΑΙΛΙΘΟΥΛΕΠΤΑΛΕΗϹ/
ΕΥϹΥΝΘΕΤΟϹΚΟ [ϲ] Μ [Οϲ]   301

Two chubby, neckless putti in three-quarter view (pls. 203,
205) walk toward the tabula holding its ansae in their hands.
They wear short, black and white boots and white tunics
which are belted at the waist and adorned with orange borders and folds. Wreaths of pink flowers decorate their curly
black hair which frames their pink and orange faces. The
emphatic red contours of their figures and heads is repeated
in their facial features which show a general similitude in
regard to arched eyebrows, pronounced eyelids, short aquiline

---

301ΤΟΥ ϹΕΠΤΟΥ ΤΟΥΤΟΥ ΤΕΜΕΝΟΥϹ⁚ ΕΝ ΪΕΡΕΥϹΕΙΝ/
ΕΝΝΕΑΚΑΙΔΕΚΑΤΟϹ⁚ΘΥΡϹΟϹ Ο ΟϹΙωϹ ΗΓΗϹΑΜΕΝΟϹ/
ΑΜΦΟΤΕΡωΝ ΕΚΡΥΨΕΝ ΠΡΟϹΗΓΟΡΙΑϹ ΠΑϹΙΝ ΕϹΘΛΟΙϹ/ΚΑΙ
ΜΑΡΤΥΡΙ ΤΑ ΚΤΙϹΜΑΤΑ ΚΑΙ ΛΙΘΟΥ ΛΕΠΤΑΛΕΗϹ/ΕΥϹΥΝΘΕΤΟϹ ΚΟϹΜΟϹ

Transcription and emendation by Professor Ihor Ševčenko of
Harvard University.

noses, and small pursed lips. In comparison with most of the figures in the field, certain deficiencies in modeling and anatomy are evident in the putti. Their flesh tones lack subtle transitions, their limbs and faces are bloated, and their neckless bodies appear squat and awkward. The elegance and grace of such figures as the Tigris and Euphrates Rivers (pls. 215-216) and the months of May and August (pls. 209, 211) in the field are absent from this side of the border. It is clear, therefore, that an inferior craftsman executed the putti and, perhaps the figures of July (pl. 210), September (pl. 212), and October (pl. 213) which are also marked by the same kind of technical and anatomical weaknesses.

Field (pls. 199-200): straight grid comprising de face busts of the twelve months and the four Rivers of Paradise[302] disposed in eight rows of two panels each which are set within a geometric framework.

Framework (pls. 200-201): meander forming swastikas and squares. The latter are decorated with black squares inscribed with small white, grey, pink, and yellow quatrefoils, radial disks, checkerboard motifs, lozenges, and triangles. Beginning at the northeast side and moving southward, the sequence of panels is as follows.

First panel. River Geon.

Destroyed.

Second panel. Figure identified by an inscription in the

---

[302]At the present time, the River Geon and the months of January, March, June, and December are lost.

upper left corner as the River Phison (ϕΙⲤⲱ/Ν). Pl. 207.

Border: white undulating ribbon on a red ground.

Field: traces of a figure who carries in his right hand a cornucopia and in his left a long undulating lily stalk with ivy-shaped leaves and small tendrils. His hair is decorated with a wreath and traces of his garment are visible on his left shoulder and arm (for a similar representation to the west, see pl. 216).[303]

Third panel. January.[304]

Destroyed.

Fourth panel. Figure identified by an inscription on either side of his head as February ([ϕⲉ]ΒΡΟΥΑ/ΡΙ0Ⲥ). Pl. 208.[305]

Border: tangent white disks, on a black ground, inscribed with concave-sided squares set on edge.

Field: fragment of the left side of a shrouded figure who, originally, probably carried ducks in his hands (for a similar personification, see 55, pl. 136; 75, pl. 228).[306]

Fifth panel. March.

Destroyed; described as containing a figure wearing a red

---

[303]Only the stalk is reproduced in the plan (pl. 198).

[304]At the time of its discovery, only the inscription was preserved (V. Bérard, BCH, 17 [1893], p. 13).

[305]H. Stern incorrectly recorded the inscription ([ϕⲉ] ΒΡΟΥ[ΑΡ]Ι0Ⲥ) in Le Calendrier de 354, Paris, 1953, p. 223.

[306]The plate does not do justice to his delicate features and subtle modeling.

helmet and a cuirass and carrying a spear in his right hand and a red shield in his left[307] (for a similar representation, see 55, pl. 137).

Sixth panel. April.

Destroyed; noted in 1891.[308]

Seventh panel. Figure identified by an inscription on either side of his head as May (ΜΑΙΟϹ), the Beautiful Season (ΚΑΛΟϹ ΚΑΙΡΟϹ).[309] Pl. 209.

Border: light and dark wave crests.

Field: traces of a figure wearing a floral crown and a long sleeve, belted yellow tunic and holding in front of him a basket of flowers which is tipped forward (for a similar representation, see 55, pls. 139-140).

Eighth panel. June.

Destroyed, except for traces of a cable border.[310]

Ninth panel. Identified by an inscription on either side of his head as July (ΙΟΥΛΙΟϹ). Pl. 210.

Border: floral band composed of single clusters of flat laurel leaves which emanate from hollow, right angled containers in the corners. In the center of each side of the panel, the leaves are bound by an undulating ribbon.

---

[307]V. Bérard, BCH, 17 (1893), p. 14; see also D. Levi, AB, 23 (1941), p. 282; H. Stern, op. cit., p. 223.

[308]V. Bérard, BCH, 17 (1893), p. 14.

[309]Ibid.

[310]It is absent from the plan (pl. 198).

Field: young man with a spray of wheat in his hair, carrying a scythe in his right hand and a sheaf of wheat in his left. He appears to be dressed in some kind of garment, perhaps an _exomis_, and possibly a sheer undergarment.[311] The exaggerated and awkward position of the arms, the crude musculature, and the abstract highlighting reveal the hand of an inferior craftsman who probably also worked on the figures of September and October (pls. 212-213). The other figures who hold objects in front of them, especially May and November (pls. 209, 214), are much better executed in regard to anatomy and foreshortening.

Tenth panel. Figure identified by an inscription on either side of his head as August (ΑΥΓΟΥϹΤΟϹ). Pl. 211.

Border: two-strand guilloche (outlined in black, with a white tessera at each loop and along the margins).

Field: a handsome man wearing a yellow garment fastened at the left shoulder and a crown of leaves on his luxuriant black hair proudly displays the produce of the month. He holds with the fingertips of his right hand a large curving eggplant while a round, striated watermelon is nestled in the palm of his left hand. His strong chest and shoulders strain

---

[311]Initially, it appears that the diagonal band formed the only protection for his torso, since there is no evidence of sleeves. This is contradicted, however, by the collar at the base of his neck. In other representations of this month in Greece, July is protected by a sleeveless tunic (75, pl. 227; 83, pl. 267) or a long sleeve one (55, pl. 141). In the Tegea panel, either the mosaicist forgot to articulate the sleeves or the collar is a mistake and he was supposed to be partially nude.

against the diaphanous robe which is decorated with vertical
red striations and two sleeve panels (for a similar representation, see 55, pls. 141-142).

Eleventh panel. Figure identified by an inscription on
either side of his head as September (CЄΠΤЄΜΒ[ΡΙΟϹ]). Pl.
212.

Border: two-strand guilloche (similar to the preceding
panel).

Field: right side of a fully clad figure with a crown of
blue lanceolate leaves holding a basket of apples in the
palm of his hand. His arm, crudely executed like the limbs
of July and October (pls. 210, 213), is covered to the elbow
by the sleeve of his white tunic which has a blue skirt and
belt, outlined in black.

Twelfth panel. Figure identified by an inscription on
either side of his head as October (ΟΚΤѠΒΡΙ/ΟϹ). Pl. 213.

Border: cruder version of the border of the July panel
(pl. 210).

Field: figure with a vine leaf crown on his black hair
wearing a loose fitting red and orange, belted tunic with
three-quarter sleeves. He pours red wine from a ribbed
oinochoë into a round bowl which he holds against his chest
with his right hand. The entire right side of his body is
crudely executed and the arm appears to show a particular
ineptitude in regard to foreshortening (for a similar representation, see 55, pls. 143-144).

Thirteenth panel. Figure identified by an inscription,

the first half of which is lost, as November ([ΝΟΕΜ]ΒΡΙΟC).
Pl. 214.

Border: undulating ribbon pattern decorated with a light
trefoil at each wave.

Field: figure wearing a wreath of blue leaves and a yellow
tunic with three-quarter sleeves. A red cape, fastened at
the left shoulder, curves diagonally across his chest and
covers his right arm. He cradles part of the cape in front
of him, perhaps to hold the contents of the horn which floats
in space near his right shoulder. Unlike the other personifications, his specific attributes are not clearly defined
and identifiable.[312]

Fourteenth panel. December.

Destroyed, except for traces of a checkerboard border which
is identical to the one in the Tigris panel.

Fifteenth panel. Figure identified by an inscription on
either side of his head as the River Tigris (ΤΙΓΡΙC).
Pl. 215.

Border: checkerboard pattern of red and white squares composed of four tesserae each.

Field: bearded, semi-nude figure whose hair is decorated
with two branches of leaves which are joined in the center of
his forehead by a circular clasp. He holds in the crook of
his drapery-covered left arm a stalk of corn which is a

---

[312]H. Stern suggests that he is carrying a tray (Le
Calendrier de 354, Paris, 1953, p. 223).

curious attribute for a river personification. The two other personifications of the Rivers of Paradise (pls. 207,216) carry sinuous stalks with heart-shaped lily leaves. Despite this floral confusion, he carries the traditional attribute of a river god comprising a fountain with flowing water which spills over into a rectangular receptacle. Unlike his counterparts, his head is turned to the left and his pose is more informal.

Sixteenth panel. Figure identified by the last three letters of an inscription (ΤΗϹ) in the upper left corner as the River Euphrates ([ΕΥΦΡΑ]ΤΗϹ).[313]

Border: identical to the undulating ribbon patterns framing the November panel.

Field: a semi-nude figure carries a cornucopia overflowing with water in his right hand and an undulating lily stalk with ivy-shaped leaves in his left. His hair is decorated with blue leaves and a yellow cloak covers his left shoulder and arm.

The preserved panels contain many similar features. They are framed by single white/orange fillets and are inscribed with busts of well-modeled male personifications[314]

---

[313]H. Stern (loc. cit.) misspells the last part of the name (ΕΥΦΡΑΘΕΙϹ).

[314]Only the figure of July (pl. 210) lacks this subtle modeling. The broad flat areas of highlights on his chest and arms reduce the plastic effect created by the curving contour lines. For similar highlighting, see the figures of July and August at Delphi (pls. 265- 267).

who are, with one exception (Tigris) presented de face displaying their individual attributes in their hands. Pronounced curvilinear contour lines, generally red for the areas of the skin and red, black, orange, for the garments and symbols, serve to separate the objects from the neutral ground of the panels and, at the same time, to augment their corporeality. Most of them have broad torsos and shoulders and rather strong, virile faces which are defined by thin, arched eyebrows, elliptical lids, and deep set eyes. Their noses are straight and bridgeless with slightly flared nostrils and their mouths are formed by a single row of tesserae, with an extra row below the lower lip. Except for the heavily shrouded figure of February, their heads are decorated with wreaths of flowers, leaves, or wheat which rest on the curly grey and black hair framing their faces. Their hands are poorly executed and some of the figures (July, September, October) are clearly inferior. This probably reveals the hand of a second craftsman who may also have executed the squat putti in the border to the west (pls. 203, 205).

Second half of the fifth century.

Illustration. G. A. Soteriou, Atti del IV congresso internazionale de archeologia Cristiana, 1, 1938 (Vatican, 1940), p. 366, fig. 13 = our pl. 206.

70 Room II (2.35 radius). Apse.

First border: 0.80. No other published information on

dimensions and material.

Polychrome panel, now lost, containing three figures which are identified by an inscription as the Beautiful Seasons (ΚΑΛΟΙ ΚΑΙΡΟΙ).[315]

Framing: brief mention of a wide interlace[316] and three smaller inner borders.

Field: two young men with windblown capes rush forward to offer their baskets of fruit to a "beautiful man" standing between them. He is clad in a short, sleeveless tunic and knee-length, red boots and supports in the palm of his right hand a deep basket filled with fruit while his left hand, which rests on his hip, carries a branch with leaves.[317] From the description of this lost panel, there can be no doubt that the figures represent the warm months, May, June, and July or, perhaps, June, July, and August. The sleeveless garment of the central figure, and the kinds of fruit in the baskets held by the flanking figures--white melons, black eggplants, "red apples and pears"[318] are features which are

---

[315]This description is based on that of V. Bérard (BCH, 17 [1893], p. 13) who is the only one who recorded it.

[316]In the plan (pl. 198), it appears to be a double row of interced squares set on edge. A more simplified version of this chain pattern is used at Delphi (83, pl. 256).

[317]Although his attributes are different, his pose is probably very close to that of the month of July at Argos (55, pl. 141).

[318]One wonders if the apples were not, in fact, peaches. The attribute of September in the nave is the apple.

encountered in other representations of the spring and summer months.[319] It should be noted that the two predominent iconographic types for the months and seasons in Greek pavements are united in this pavement. One type is found in the nave and elsewhere (55, pls. 136-145) where the personifications passively display their symbols, as the central figure does. Another type, represented by the flanking figures, is the rushing, active month with or without a windblown cloak who eagerly offers his produce in his outstretched arms or hands (75, pls. 225, 227-230; 83, pls. 265, 267).[320]

Second half of the fifth century.

Basin

A few meters to the east of the apsidal building at Tegea (69-70) another mosaic was noted in 1891 (pl. 197). It surrounded a marble basin which was one and a half meters in diameter.[321] At the present time, the site is completely overgrown and the condition of the pavement is unknown.

---

[319]See for example, July and May at Thebes (75, pls. 227, 229) and the seasons at Corinth and Delphi (42, pl. 95; 83, pls. 265, 267). For the symbols, especially a combination of eggplants and melons, see August (pl. 211) and a similar personification at Delphi (85, pl. 265).

[320]Vide infra, p. 210, n. 342.

[321]The basin appears to be rectangular and quite small (see pl. 197).

Since the basin is so close to the apsidal building, it
is possible that it was also erected by Thyrsos and belonged
to the "sacred precinct" cited in the inscription on the
west side of the building.[322] The basin can be tentatively
assigned to the second half of the fifth century until such
time as the excavations are resumed and its chronology veri-
fied.

Bibliography. V. Bérard, BCH, 17 (1893), p. 14.

Illustration. V. Bérard, BCH, 16 (1892), pl. 13 = our pl.
197.

No. 71

71 Mosaic pavement (no dimensions published).

No published information on dimensions and material.

Brief mention of a mosaic pavement which surrounded a marble
basin.

Possibly second half of the fifth century; on the basis of
its proximity to the building erected by Thyrsos to the
west (69-70).

[322]Vide supra, pp. 179-181, 186 and n. 301.

PALLANDION

Basilica

At Pallandion in Arcadia, approximately three to four
kilometers south of the Tripolis-Megalopolis highway, the
foundations of the central part of an occidented, Early
Christian basilica (overall, 18.00 x 35.30) was brought to
light in 1940 (pl. 217).[323] A mosaic pavement was discovered
in the nave and marble pavements in the bema and narthex. At
the present time the site is completely overgrown.

Because of the brevity of the excavation, only the
narrow narthex, I (18.00 x 3.85), the nave, II (ca. 24.00
long; width indeterminable), and the apse (5.50 diam) were
cleared (pl. 217). In the apse were found an enkainion and
the foundations of a semi-circular synthronon with an episcopal throne in the center. No other ecclesiastical furnishings survive. Different types of pavements differentiate
and accentuate the formal arrangement and internal divisions
of the building. The narthex is paved with marble slabs in
opus sectile which are arranged in the form of a large
rosette at the west entrance to the nave. Beyond the narrow
doorway lies a long polychrome pavement in opus tessellatum

---

[323]G. Libertini, Actes du IXe congrès international
d'études byzantines, 1953, Hellenika, 9 (1955), pp. 250-254;
hereafter cited as Libertini, Actes. Hopefully, the exceptional westward direction of the church will be explained in
the forth coming book on the Italian excavations of this
region by A. De Franciscus (see Sodini, Catalogue, p. 708,
n. 15).

which is succeeded by large marble slabs in the bema and
apse.[324]

Although no datable archaeological finds were unearthed,
on the basis of the style of the pavings in the narthex and
nave, the church was attributed to the fifth or the sixth
century.[325] It will be shown below that the tessellated
pavement belongs to a period no earlier than the middle of
the sixth century. In a subsequent period a wall and a doorway were installed along the chord of the apse and the bema,
respectively.

Bibliography. G. Libertini, Annuario della scuola di
Atene, n.s., 1-2 (1939-40), p. 228; AA, 57 (1942), pp. 147-
148; G. Libertini, Actes du IXe congrès international
d'études byzantines, 1953, Hellenika, 9 (1955), pp. 250-254.

Illustrations. G. Libertini, Actes du IXe congrès international d'études byzantines, 1953, p. 253, fig. 1 = our pl.
217, pl. 48, 1 (apse and nave, from west), pl. 49, 3 (narthex
and nave, from northwest).

No. 72

The paucity of illustrative and descriptive material on
the pavement decorating the nave precludes an adequate analysis of its style and iconography. From the meager data,
however, part of the decoration can be reconstructed. The

---

[324]The marble paving is omitted from the plan but it is
visible in a photograph (Libertini, Actes, pl. 48, 2).

[325]Libertini, Actes, pp. 253-254. In an earlier article,
he proposed a third or fourth century date (Annuario della
scuola di Atene, n.s., 1-2 [1939-40], p. 228; hereafter cited
as Libertini, Annuario.

field, bordered by rectangles, is divided into several panels
which contain two large juxtaposed animals[326] and geometric
designs, some with animal insets.[327] Although the geometric
designs (pls. 220-221) cannot be dated without additional information, the large animal panels (pls. 218-219) can be
assigned to a period no earlier than the middle of the sixth
century. Despite their crude execution, which obtains as
well for the other panels, the schematic, two-dimensional
treatment of the animals and the flora surrounding them reflect a late trend in Greek pavements. It is probable that
the pavement belongs somewhere between the figural pavements
in a basilica (60, pls. 165-166, 62, pls. 171-176) and a villa
(67, pls. 191-196) at Hermione which have been assigned to
the early and late sixth centuries, respectively.

Additional bibliography. Sodini, Catalogue, No. 12, p. 708;
I. Lavin, "Field Notes: Pallandion," Dumbarton Oaks, Center
for Byzantine Studies.

Illustration. G. Libertini, Acts du IXe Congrès International d'etudes byzantines, 1953 [1955], pl. 49 = our pl.
217.

72 Room II (ca. 24.00 long; width indeterminable). Nave.

Pls. 218-221.

No published information on dimensions and material.

---

[326]Although they are assigned to the border, it is
clear that they occupy the field (see Libertini, Actes,
p. 252).

[327]Libertini, Annuario, p. 228. The reference to the
animals insets is omitted from his later description (Actes,
p. 252).

Red and black geometric and figural designs enclosed by a
wide geometric border.

Border (pl. 218): tangent rectangles inscribed with lozenges which are decorated with single crosses set on disks.

Field: toward the east all that is visible are two
rectangular panels, separated by a dark double fillet ending
in an ivy leaf (pls. 218-219), inscribed with two animals
facing in opposite directions. One animal appears to be a
running stag which turns its head to gaze at an unidentifiable animal above it. The latter is shown with stationary
hind legs and moving forelegs. Both animals are surrounded
by curious disk-like flowers which rise from rigid, vertical
stems. Somewhere toward the west side of the room, segments
of two panels were studied and photographed by Professor I.
Lavin in 1964.[328] One panel (pl. 220) is decorated with a
two-strand interlace (both red, outlined by white/black
single fillets) forming concave-sided octagons set on edge.
The circles are inscribed with red stepped squares and the
octagons with black or red disks. A second panel (pl. 221)
has an oblique grid pattern composed of a single black fillet
forming small squares which are inscribed with red or black
squares.[329]

---

[328]"Field Notes: Pallandion," Dumbarton Oaks, Center for
Byzantine Studies.

[329]Libertini also notes a panel with disks inscribed
with stars (Actes, p. 252).

No earlier than the middle of the sixth century.

Illustrations. G. Libertini, *Actes du IXe congrès inter-national d'etudes byzantines*, 1953, pl. 49, 1 = our pl. 218, pl. 49, 2 = our pl. 219.

PHILIATRA

Basilica

In the region of Haghia Kyriake, near Philiatra, a short campaign in 1960 brought to light the general plan of a five-aisled Early Christian basilica (overall, 20.80 x 28.60) and a fragment of a tessellated pavement in the bema, IV.[330] At the present time, the site is completely overgrown and the condition of the pavement is not known.

Preceded by an atrium or narthex, I,[331] the church proper (pl. 222) consists of a nave, III, flanked on either side by two aisles, V-VIII, and a raised bema terminated by a semi-circular apse, IV. The nave is separated from the aisles by arcuated colonnades resting on elevated stylobates[332] and from the bema by a chancel screen which abuts the shoulder of

---

[330]The nave is paved with white, black, and porphyry schist slabs. The other pavements are not described (D. I. Pallas, *Praktika*, 1960, p. 184; hereafter cited as *Praktika*, 1960).

[331]The function and form of this room were not deter-mined because the excavation stopped about two meters from the west wall of the church proper (*Praktika*, 1960, p. 178; D. I. Pallas, *Deltion*, 16 [1960], B: *Chronika*, p. 123, here-after cited as *Deltion*, 16; A. K. Orlandos, *To Ergon*, 1960, p. 142, hereafter cited as *To Ergon*, 1960).

[332]The type of divisions between the aisles was not noted.

the apse and contains an entrance in the middle of its west
side. In the bema traces were found of an altar and two of
the four bases of a canopy which surmounted it, and the nave
contains a stepped octagonal ambon with a set of steps on the
main axis of the church.

On the basis of the style of the architecture and the
decorative sculpture, the church has been dated to the end of
the fifth or the first half of the sixth century.[333] The
church was destroyed, probably by an earthquake, and the nave
rebuilt before the end of the sixth century.[334] At this time,
a room to the south of the bema was created which probably
served as a prothesis or diakonikon.[335] In the Byzantine
period, a small one-aisled basilica was built over the ruins
of the second church and vestiges of it were still visible at
the time of the excavation.

Bibliography. D. I. Pallas, Praktika, 1960, pp. 177-194;
idem, Deltion, 16 (1960), B: Chronika, pp. 122-125; A. K.
Orlandos, To Ergon, 1960, pp. 141-144; BCH, 85 (1961), pp.
718-719.

Illustrations. D. I. Pallas, Praktika, 1960, p. 178, fig.
1 = our pl. 222, pl. 145a (apse, from south), pl. 145b
(ambon).

---

[333]Praktika, 1960, pp. 188-189; Deltion, 1960, p. 125;
To Ergon, 1960, p. 144. Sodini (Catalogue, p. 709) only
cites the second date.

[334]A treasure of approximately three hundred and forty
coils was found in the nave (Praktika, 1960, p. 191; Deltion,
1960, p. 124; To Ergon, 1960, p. 144).

[335]Praktika, 1960, pp. 189-190; Deltion, 1960, p. 123;
To Ergon, 1960, p. 144.

No. 73

Fragment of a polychrome pavement composed of three
panels bordered by floral and geometric motifs. The absence
of adequate descriptive and illustrative material precludes
a stylistic analysis of the pavement. Since it appears to be
contemporaneous with the basilica, it can tentatively be
ascribed to the late fifth or the first half of the sixth
century.

Additional bibliography. Sodini, Catalogue, No. 14, pp.
708-709.

Illustration. D. I. Pallas, Praktika, 1960, p. 178, fig.
1 = our pl. 222.

73 Room IV (ca. 6.00 x 2.20). Bema; pavement laid up to the
    chord of the apse. Pl. 223.

No published information on dimensions. Marble (black and
white), ceramic (red), and glass tesserae.[336]

Fragment of a polychrome pavement comprising a central panel
flanked by two others with similar patterns.[337]

IVa,c, flanking panels.

Framing: border, large squares subdivided by checkerboards

---

[336]Praktika, 1960, p. 184.

[337]Sodini's description is at variance with the descriptive and illustrative material in the report (cf. Catalogue,
p. 709 and Praktika, 1960, p. 184).

of light and dark triangles forming squares set on edge. The four spandrels of each square are alternately filled with white and red triangles. At right angles to this pattern is another border containing a straight grid composed of a checkerboard of light and dark squares superimposed by a narrow oblique grid, which is accented at regular intervals by white disks with two opposed dark peltae.

Field: juxtaposed circles enclosing two opposed peltae. Along one side, the circles are bisected by the margin.

IVb, central panel.

Destroyed, except for traces of a border decorated with an undulating vine rinceau with leaves and possibly grapes in its scrolls.

Late fifth or first half of the sixth century.

Illustration. D. I. Pallas, _Praktika_, 1960, pl. 150a = our pl. 223.

PART III. CENTRAL GREECE

TANAGRA

Basilica

A Christian basilica (40.00 x 20.00) was discovered in
the early part of the twentieth century near the ancient city
of Tanagra. It was decorated with mosaic pavements which
were assigned to the "fourth century."[338] The precise location and condition of the pavements could not be determined.
   Bibliography. N. Platon, ArchEph, 2 (1937), p. 667.

No. 74

74 Mosaic pavements (no dimensions published).
   No published information on dimensions and material.

Brief mention of mosaic pavements belonging to an Early
Christian basilica.

Fourth century (?)
   Additional bibliography. Sodini, Catalogue, No. 23,
p. 713.

---

   [338]N. Platon, ArchEph, 2 (1937), p. 667.

THEBES

Christian Building

On property belonging to the Stamati family in Classical
Thebes, segments of two rooms with tessellated pavements, I-
II, were discovered by chance in 1964.[339] Since the north,
south, and east sides of the site were covered by modern
buildings (pl. 224), the overall plan and function of the
structure were never determined. The pavements were lifted,
consolidated, and placed in the courtyard of the local
museum.[340]

The rooms communicated with each other through a central
door with a marble threshold which was one of only two
architectural features found in situ (pls. 224-225). Inscriptions to the east and west of the threshold, that is, on
the east side of Room I and the west side of Room II, are
contained within tabulae ansatae and are oriented westward.[341]
They clearly mark the main orientation of the rooms and this

---

[339]P. Lazarides, Deltion, 20 (1965), B2: Chronika, p.
237, pp. 253-255; hereafter cited as Deltion, 20. Although
never recorded, additional clearing of the later buildings
was undertaken before the pavements were lifted bringing to
light a bull in Room II (cf. pls. 225 and 234) and a larger
portion of the two grids in Room II (cf. pl. 224 and an unpublished segment in the Museum at Thebes).

[340]P. Lazarides, Deltion, 24 (1969), B1: Chronika, p.
180; BCH, 95 (1971), p. 920.

[341]When the pavement was lifted, the tabula of the
inscription in Room I was destroyed (cf. pls. 225 [in situ]
and 226 [in museum]).

is substantiated by the similar arrangement of the figural
compositions.

Since Room I is much narrower than II (3.40 max and
7.80 max, respectively), it is possible to suggest that I
served as a corridor or vestibule to the larger room to the
east and that probably another doorway existed to the south
of the four figure insets (pl. 225). Upon entering this side
of the building, therefore, a visitor encountered in the
inscription to the right (pl. 232) the names of the donor
of the pavement, Paul, ". . . the priest and teacher of the
Holy Writ . . .," the designer, Demetrios, and the mosaicist,
Epiphanes. As he left Room I there was another inscription
for him to read, now partially destroyed (pl. 226), which
probably cited the names of other men responsible for the
decoration, and, beyond it, at the entrance to Room II, a
third inscription informed him of the donation of Konstantine,
". . . the revered and wise teacher of the orthodox faith.
. . ." (pl. 235).

The content of the inscriptions is clearly Christian
but whether the building functioned as a church, an Episcopal
palace, or as a school of some kind supervised by the "wise
teacher," Constantine, and Paul, the "teacher of the Holy
Writ," cannot be determined. Although no archaeological
finds were uncovered or reported, on the basis of the style
and iconography of the mosaics, the building can be dated to
the late fifth or early sixth century.

During the last building phase of the site, the present

structures were installed and a well was sunk into the area south of the threshold.

Bibliography. P. Lazarides, Deltion, 20 (1965), B2: Chronika, pp. 237, 253-255; JHS, 85 (1964-65), Supplement, p. 15; JHS, 87 (1966-67), Supplement, p. 13; BCH, 92 (1968), p. 862; BCH, 95 (1971), p. 920; BCH, 96 (1972), pp. 920-921.

Illustrations. P. Lazarides, Deltion, 20 (1965), B2: Chronika, pl. 310a = our pl. 224, pl. 310b = our pl. 225.

Nos. 75-76

Polychrome mosaic pavements with lively figural representations and complex borders decorate Rooms I and II. In the former group, a bull hunt (pls. 225, 233-234) is represented on the south side while to the north two pairs of months (July, February; May, April) rush toward each other with flying drapery holding their attributes in outstretched hands (pls. 225, 227-230). These scenes are accompanied by an unusual inscription (pl. 232) which cites the names of the designer of the pavement, Demetrios, and the mosaicist, Epiphanes. In the second room two long panels decorated with oblique grids inscribed with birds (pls. 224, 235-236) flank a panel of which only a small section is preserved.

These pavements are so similar in style, iconography, and technique to those at Delphi (82, 83, pls. 242-260, 265-268), and Hypati (101, pl. 354) that a common workshop must have produced them. The same kind of oblique grid is employed with the same species of birds inscribed on white disks, and the iconography of the personifications of the months and seasons is identical in regard to a rushing figure with outstretched hands (pls. 225; 265, 267).[342] Moreover, the figures are anatomically and physiognomically alike, are modeled and outlined in the same way, and their tunics have the same kind of plastic definition. Other features which the Theban and Delphi pavements share[343] are a vivid chromatic scheme, and multiple borders composed of complex interlaces. Given these similarities, the pavements are the products of the same workshop and were possibly executed by the same artists, Demetrios and Epiphanes, whose names are cited in the Theban inscription. They belong to a period no earlier than the second half of the fifth century when multiple figural compositions begin to replace the purely geometric and sober carpets of the early decades of the fifth century.[344] Since, however, the figures are more plastic, solid, and three-dimensional than those executed in the first half of the sixth century or later (55-57; 60; 62; 67; 95-98; 100; 115; 123-128;

---

[342]See also the lost apse mosaic at Tegea (70, pp. 182, 195). Elsewhere, the months are represented de face and passively displaying their attributes (55, pls. 136-145; 69, pls. 209-214). The iconography of the rushing figure of a month or season will be the subject of a study in the immediate future. It is to be noted that the Greek examples and those in the top register of the Dominus Julius mosaic from Tabarka, now in the Bardo Museum, are obviously derived from a common model (see B. Bandinelli, Rome: the Late Empire, New York, 1971, pp. 223, 225, pl. 208.

[343]Only a small segment of the Hypati mosaic was exposed (pl. 354).

[344]See, for example, 1; 2-3; 4-5; 6-9; 21; 22; 44-49; 88-92; 130-138.

150-156; 197; 206-214; 217-223), they can be assigned to the
late fifth or early sixth century.[345]

Additional bibliography. Sodini, Catalogue, No. 24, pp.
713, 745 and n. 89.

Pavements lifted, consolidated; installed in seven sections
on the facade of the Museum at Thebes in 1968.[346]

75   Room I (width, 3.40; length not published). Vestibule or
      corridor; to east, pavement laid up to a wall, now
destroyed, and a threshold block. Part of the right side of
the May panel and the east side of the border were destroyed
by a marble plaque and a well, respectively; north side
destroyed and south side covered by modern construction.
Pls. 224-234.

No published information on dimensions. Marble (bluish
grey), limestone, ceramic (red, ochre), and glass (blues,
greens, red) tesserae (0.01 sq; for details, 01005 sq) set
1-3mm apart.

Fragment of a polychrome pavement composed of two figural
compartments, a-b, bordered by complex interlaces.

Framing (pls. 225, 231): black fillet; outer border, complex interlace forming elongated loops (bluish grey/l white,

---

[345]For a summary of the chronology of the Delphi
Basilica, see Sodini, Catalogue, p. 711.

[346]Vide supra, p. 207, n. 340.

outlined in black) which are pierced by two continuous parallel bars (ochre/1 white; red [ceramic]/1 white, outlined in
black). For a similar pattern, see pls. 166-167; 256. At
the entrance to Room II, the border is interrupted by a
tabula ansata containing a four-line inscription in black
letters·(pl. 226).[347] Oriented westward, the preserved portion of the inscription reads as follows: " [ ] ΑΤΟΜΟΡΦ/
[ ] ΜΕΝΟΝΟΥΔΑΓΕΓΕΡΑϹ /[ ] ΧΝΗΠΑΝΤΑΤΕΛΕϹϹΕΝΑΠΕΡ
ΝΟΟϹΕΝΘΕΤΟΧΕΙΡΙ"[348]

Field: two figural compartments, a-b, decorated with
different borders.

Ia, north compartment (pls. 225, 227-230), framed by a white
double fillet: four panels with male representations of the
months of July, February; May, April set within a three-strand
braid (ochre/1 white; red/1 white; bluish grey/1 white, outlined in black, with a white tessera at each loop) on a black
ground. The four panels are arranged in two superimposed
registers, each with two figures of the months who rush
toward each other offering their individual attributes with
outstretched arms. Thus July is paired with February, and
May with April in scenes decorated with dark blue and green
inscriptions and small scale bushes and trees, or stalks of

---

[347]The tabula was destroyed when the mosaic was lifted
(vide supra, p. 207, n. 341).

[348][ ]ΑΤΟ ΜΟΡΦΗΝ/[ ] ΜΕΝΟΝ ΟΥΔ ΑΓΕ ΓΕΡΑϹ/[ ] ΧΝΗ
ΠΑΝΤΑ ΤΕΛΕϹϹΕΝ ΑΠΕΡ ΝΟΟϹ ΕΝΘΕΤΟ ΧΕΙΡΙ.
Emendation cited in Deltion 20, p. 254.

wheat. The dynamic movement of the figures is emphasized by
their flying drapery and their convoluted skirts which fall
in stylized triangular folds. They wear short, belted tunics
which are sleeveless for the warmer months and are shod in
short striped boots or leggins (pl. 228). Single or double
rows of white highlights create patterns on their pink and
beige faces and limbs which are articulated differently.
Unlike the courser, double fillets outlining the limbs,
single rows of smaller tesserae define the facial contours
and features. This enhances their delicate physiognomies
which are quite similar. Structurally, each head is broad at
the forehead and cheeks, diminishing to a narrow chin. Below
arching eyebrows, button eyes peer out from oval lids and a
short aquiline nose tilts toward small pursed lips whose
shadow is defined by a short row of miniscule tesserae on the
chin. Crowning the heads of April, May, and July are short
black curls, sometimes highlighted with red (July) or dark
brown (April).

Top row, east side.

First panel. Figure identified by an inscription in the
upper left corner as July (IOYΛIOC). Pl. 227.

Field: the figure is clothed in a white tunic, outlined
and delineated in black, and a trailing beige cape which is
articulated by broad red (ceramic) outlines. Completing his
ensemble are a webbed ochre cap and black and white boots.
He carries in his outstretched hands a sheaf of wheat composed of ochre, dark purplish brown, and scattered red

tesserae which form a kind of checkerboard pattern in the
center (for similar personifications, see 55, pl. 139; 69,
pl. 210; 83, pl. 267). Rising awkwardly in front of July is
a thick, light and dark green tree which is flecked with
yellow and bluish grey.

Second panel. Figure identified by an inscription in the
upper right corner as February (ΦЄΒΡΟΥΑΡΙΟϹ). Pl. 228.

Field. Unlike his counterparts, this month is warmly
dressed. His head and hands are protected by a red (ceramic)
cape and his arms by the sleeves of a white tunic which is
shaded in dark blue. In addition, his legs are well protected by short black and white boots and ochre leggins which
are secured by black and white ties. As February strides
forward, unaware of the two shafts of unripen wheat which
bend from the force of his movement, one of the two ochre and
white ducks nestled in his arms turns back to gaze at him.

Bottom row, west side.

Third panel. Figure identified by an inscription in the
upper left corner as May (ΜΑΙΟϹ). Pl. 229.

Field: the figure is clothed in a white tunic, outlined
and delineated in black, and a trailing beige cape which is
articulated by broad black and brown outlines. A spray of
ochre and red wheat in his hair[349] and red (ceramic) and
white boots complete his ensemble. It is evident from the
position of his outstretched arms that May was also

---

[349]It is not visible in the photograph; similar to the
spray worn by a season at Delphi (83, pl. 267).

represented as offering his symbol, perhaps, like his counterparts elsewhere, a basket of flowers (55, pl. 139; 69, pl. 209). Two dark green and blue (glass) bushes with red flowers (roses) fill the lower part of the scene.

Fourth panel. Figure identified by an inscription in the upper right corner as April (ΑΠΡΙΛΙΟC). Pl. 230.

Field: the figure is clothed in a white tunic with black and ochre outlines and folds, and a rather voluminous trailing ivory cape which, along the top, is outlined and delineated in ochre. Toward the bottom of the cape the colors become more vibrant with dark green folds and red (ceramic) outlines. Completing his ensemble are dark blue and green boots striped with white. Nestled in April's arms is a wide-eyed white lamb,[350] outlined in black, whose dangling hind leg almost touches the dark green leaf of a slender bluish grey bush below.

Ib, south compartment, framed by a black double fillet and an inner white triple fillet (pls. 231-234): fragment of a panel with a hunting scene framed by a bluish grey band, outlined in black.

Framing (pls. 225, 231): border, to east and west, intricate chain pattern, on a black ground, composed of interlaced

[350]Although it is not visible in the photograph, two kinds of white tesserae are used. The center of the body and the snout are ivory while the rest of the head and body are white.

squares set on edge (alternately red/1 white; bluish grey/1
white, outlined in black) which are laced along the sides by
a continuous zig-zag band (ochre/1 white, outlined in black).
The center of each square is marked by a narrow white diagonal cross and the corners by a white tessera. Along the
inner edges of the border are white truncated crosslets which
change to inverted, serrate-edged triangles in the corners.
The border is interrupted on the north side by a five-line
inscription in black letters on a white ground, oriented
westward (pl. 232).

ΔΗΜΗΤΡΙΟϹ ΕΠΙΦΑΝΗϹΤΕΤΟΜΟΥϹΙΟΝΠΟΕΙ /
ΔΗΜΗΤΡΙΟϹΜΕΝΝΕΝΟΗϹΑϹΤΗΝΓΡΑΦΗΝ /
ΤΑΥΤΗϹΔΥΠΟΥΡΓΟϹΕΠΙΦΑΝΗϹΕΥΝΟΥϹΤΑΤϹ /
ΠΑΥΛΟϹΔΕΠΑΝΤωΝΑΙΤΙΟϹΤωΝΕΥΠΡΕΠϹ /
ΙΕΡΕΥϹΤΕΚΑΙΘΕΙωΝΛΟΓωΝΔΙΔΑϹΚΑΛϹ

351

Field (pls. 225, 233-234): bull hunt in a grey and ochre
mountainous landscape which is marked by black and red
crevices. Accompanied by a yapping grey and black dog with
a pointed snout, a youthful hunter, holding a brown shield in
his left hand and a black spear in his right, lunges forward
to attack a rearing brown bull.[352] He wears a long sleeve

---

[351]The last word "ΔΙΔΑϹΚΑΛϹ" is incorrectly transcribed
as "ΔΙΔΑϹΚΑΛΟϹ" in the report (<u>Deltion</u> 20, p. 254) which
offers the following emendation.
ΔΗΜΗΤΡΙΟϹ ΕΠΙΦΑΝΗϹ ΤΕ ΤΟ ΜΟΥϹΙΟΝ ΠΟΕΙ/ΔΗΜΗΤΡΙΟϹ ΜΕΝ
ΕΝΝΟΗϹΑϹ ΤΗΝ ΓΡΑΦΗΝ/ ΤΑΥΤΗϹ Δ' ΥΠΟΥΡΓΟϹ ΕΠΙΦΑΝΗϹ
ΕΥΝΟΥϹΤΑΤ(Ο)Ϲ /ΠΑΥΛΟϹ ΔΕ ΠΑΝΤωΝ ΑΙΤΙΟϹ ΤωΝ ΕΥΠΡΕΠ(ωΝ)Ϲ/
ΙΕΡΕΥϹ ΤΕ ΚΑΙ ΘΕΙωΝ ΛΟΓωΝ ΔΙΔΑϹΚΑΛ(Ο)Ϲ.

[352]There is no evidence that the bull has been impaled
(cf. Sodini, <u>Catalogue</u>, p. 713). On the contrary, the small
triangular motif in front of the bull is the tip of the spear.

brown garment with beige highlights, which falls in wide triangular pleats on his thighs, and a flying white cape which
is gathered in loose folds across his chest. A domical light
green hat, edged and striped in dark blue, covers his short,
curly yellowish brown hair, delineated in black, and red
(ceramic), white, and dark grey striped boots encase his feet.
Physiognomically, the hunter resembles the months in the
adjacent compartment and the beige flesh tones of his face
are also similar. Since his black-outlined legs are not
flesh-colored but, rather, bluish grey along the edges with
wide paths of white highlights toward the center, it is
probable that the hunter is wearing tight-fitting hosiery of
some kind. In contrast to the lunging movement of the hunter
behind him, a negro identified by an inscription as "Ακκωλος"
calmly sips the brown liquid from a dark brown bowl which he
holds in his hands. He is differentiated from the Caucasians
in this panel and in compartment Ia by his dark brown skin,
flat cheeks and nose, and by his thick brows, eyebrows, and
lips. Even his slanted eyes and large flat feet confirm his
racial identity. He wears a white, sleeveless tunic which is
belted at the waist and falls below his knees in vertical
folds. Tufts of short black hair protrude from beneath a
dark brown skull cap which, originally, extended beyond the
bluish grey frame of the panel (see pl. 225; in situ).

Additional color. Compartment a. Bodies of the months:
red (ceramic) outlines along the back of the legs and the
inner part of the arms; purplish brown outlines along the

front of the legs and the outer part of the arms. Features:
black (April, February); red (May, July). Second panel.
Ducks: dark blue (lower) and pale green (upper) heads with
red (ceramic) beaks and contours, and black eyes, outlined
in black. Compartment b. Dog: red collar. Shield: greyish blue rim and black outline. Bull: beige highlights,
with black outlines and delineations. Hunter's garment: outlined and delineated in dark purple and red (ceramic), with
light green cuffs and shoulder and chest ornaments. Cape:
light grey shading, with black outlines and folds. Features:
black with red lips. Negro: black eyebrows and red lips.

Late fifth or early sixth century.

  Illustrations. P. Lazarides, Deltion, 20 (1965), B2:
Chronika, pl. 310a = our pl. 224, pl. 310b = our pl. 225, pl.
311a-b (July and February), pl. 312a-b (May and April), pl.
313b = our pl. 232; idem, Deltion, 24 (1969), B1: Chronika,
pl. 197b = our pl. 226.

76 Room II (7.80 max x 4.25 max). To west, pavement laid up
    to a wall and a threshold block; part of the southwest
border and the east side destroyed by a well and a building,
respectively; north and south sides covered by modern buildings. Pls. 224, 235-236.

  No published information on dimensions. Materials identical
to those in Room I (75).

Fragment of a polychrome mosaic composed of three tangent
panels framed at least along the west side by two geometric

borders.

Framing: outer border, traces of a wide braid (ochre/1
white; bluish grey/1 white; pink/ 1 white, outlined in black,
with a white tessera at each loop); black double fillet;
white double fillet; inner border, complex chain composed of
interlaced squares set on edge (bluish grey/1 white; ochre/1
white; red [ceramic]/1 white, outlined in black, with a white
tessera at each loop); white double fillet.

Field: fragment of a wide geometric panel, b, enclosed to
the north and south by oblique grids, a,c, and to the west by
a tabula ansata. The latter, framed by red (ceramic) and
black triangles, contains a four-line inscription in white
letters on a black ground. Oriented westward, it cites the
name of   Konstantine, a ". . . teacher of the
orthodox faith . . ."

ΠΟΛΛΗCΠΑΛΑΙΜΕΤΕΙΧΟΝΑΠΡΕΠΟΥCΘΕΑC/
ΑΛΛΑΜΕΟCΕΜΝΟCΚΑΙCΟΦΟCΔΙΔΑCΚΑΛΟC/
ΤΗCΟΡΘΟΔΟΞΟΥΠΙCΤΕωCΚωΝCΤΑΝΤΙΝΟC/
ΕΔΙΞΕΝΟΥΤΟΠΕΡΙΦΑΝωCΗCΚΕΝΟΝ   353

IIa,c, north and south panels.

Field: oblique grid composed of a two-strand guilloche
(red [ceramic]/1 white; bluish gren/1 white, outlined in
black, with a white tessera at each loop) on a black ground

353For the emendation see Deltion, 20, p. 255.
ΠΟΛΛΗC ΠΑΛΑΙ ΜΕΤΕΙΧΟΝ ΑΠΡΕΠΟΥC ΘΕΑC/
ΑΛΛΑ ΜΕ Ο CΕΜΝΟC ΚΑΙ CΟΦΟC ΔΙΔΑCΚΑΛΟC/
ΤΗC ΟΡΘΟΔΟΞΟΥ ΠΙCΤΕωC ΚωΝCΤΑΝΤΙΝΟC/
ΕΔΙΞΕΝ ΟΥΤΟ ΠΕΡΙΦΑΝωC ΗCΚ(ΗΜ)ΕΝΟΝ.

forming squares. The guilloche bifurcates along the edges of the design and forms a continuous outer border which cuts in varying degrees the adjacent squares. The black squares, out-lined in white, are inscribed with ochre-rimmed, white medallions which serve as an opaque ground for lively representations of water fowl and land birds, oriented westward. Shown in profile, the feathered menagerie include light and dark blue and green parrots (pl. 236) and ducks, grey owls, and unidentifiable land birds whose speckled plumage is represented by small black and white checkerboard patterns. For the most part, the birds are naturalistically rendered and three-dimensional and are defined by vivid colors and fluid black outlines. Unlike later examples (95, 98-99, pls. 316-320, 324-331, 339-347; 150-156, pls. 461-542) their feet appear to bear the weight of their solid bodies, and their movement is natural and convincing. The plasticity of these figures is contradicted by the flat disks behind them which constrict the space of the inset panels. This ambiguity be-tween the objects and the insets entends to the decoration in the large truncated squares along the edges of the design which, in the preserved areas, contain shaded ochre and grey palmetto motifs.[354]

IIb, central panel (pl. 235).

Framing: border, white undulating ribbon with red (ceramic)/

---

[354]For clearer photographs of similar birds and flora, see pls. 242-249.

light grey/bluish grey waves alternating with ochre/red ones.

Field: in a published photograph (pl. 235),[355] there are traces of a meander pattern composed of double fillets and a band decorated with small tangent squares set on edge.

Additional color. Panels a,c. Birds. Parrots and ducks: some outlined in black; ochre and red (ceramic) beaks and feet. Owls: bodies outlined and delineated in black, with red (ceramic) beaks and feet; black eyes with black and red outlines. Speckled birds: scattered light blue in bodies and heads; ochre beaks and feet.

Late fifth or early sixth century.

Illustrations. P. Lazarides, Deltion, 20 (1965), B2: Chronika, pl. 310a = our pl. 224, pl. 314a = our pl. 235, pl. 314b = our pl. 236.

ANTHEDON

Basilica

At Anthedon, on the shore of the Euripos Channel near Loukis, part of a long, narrow three-aisled basilica (over-all, 20.00 max x 37.84) was excavated in 1888 and 1889, bringing to light mosaic pavements in the narthex and nave (pl. 237).

Preceded by a narthex, I (20.00 max x 3.87), the main body of the church consists of a nave terminated by a

---

[355]This panel is not on exhibition in the museum.

semi-circular apse, II-III (8.20 x ca. 34.00), and flanked
by two aisles, IV-V (4.20 x ca. 31.00).[356] The nave is
separated from the aisles by colonnades resting on elevated
stylobates and from the bema by two projecting piers of unequal size which may have supported a triumphal arch. Other
divisions may have separated the aisles from the wings but
their form is unclear. No other descriptive or archaeological information is available on the building which has since
disappeared.

Although originally identified as a Roman building, A. K.
Orlandos correctly recognized its ecclesiastical function and
attributed it to the Early Christian period.[357] The style of
the mosaics indicates a fifth century date and one in the
middle or second half of the century.

Bibliography. J. C. Rolfe, AJA, 6 (1890), pp. 101-104;
A. K. Orlandos, ABME, 3 (1937), pp. 172-174.

Illustration. A. K. Orlandos, ABME, 3 (1937), p. 173,
fig. 1 = our pl. 237.

Nos. 77-78

Fragments of aniconic geometric pavements were discovered
in the narthex and nave of a basilica (pls. 237-238). On the
basis of their style and iconography, they can be assigned

---

[356]All the measurements are taken from the plan by J. C.
Rolfe, AJA, 6 (1890), pl. XIV; hereafter cited as AJA, 6.
For different measurements, see A. K. Orlandos, ABME, 3
(1937), p. 173, fig. 1 = our pl. 237; hereafter cited as
ABME, 3.

[357]Cf. AJA, 6, p. 96 and ABME, 3, p. 172.

to the middle or second half of the fifth century. The field design in the narthex is very similar to those at Nea Anchialos and Trikkala (117, pl. 403; 142, pl. 447) and the design in the nave is similar to an early one at Demetrias (137, pl. 437). Since, however, the nave design has filling motifs which are clearly more complex than those at Demetrias, it is probable that the Anthedon pavements are somewhat later and, therefore, closer in date to the Anchialos and Trikkala mosaics which belong to the middle or second half of the fifth century.

Additional bibliography. Sodini, Catalogue, No. 16, p. 710.

Illustration. A. K. Orlandos, ABME, 3 (1937), p. 173, fig. 1 = our pl. 237.

77 Room I (20.00 max x 3.87). Narthex. Pl. 238.

Three fragments: largest, 5.80 x 3.87. Framing: ca. 0.60. Field: 5.80 x 2.67.[358] No published information on dimensions and material.

Fragments of a geometric pavement bordered by an interlace.

Framing: three-strand braid; dark fillet; light fillet.

Field, framed by a dark fillet: rows of three juxtaposed circles joined by diagonal quatrefoils to form horizontal and vertical elongated hexagons with concave sides. Large

---

[358]The measurements for this and the succeeding entry are taken from the plan in the AJA, 6, pl. XIV of which our pl. 238 is a detail.

diagonal quatrefoils inscribed in the circles complete the
design.

Middle or second half of the fifth century.

Illustration. J. C. Rolfe, AJA, 6 (1890), pl. XIV =
our pl. 238 (detail of right side of plate).

78 Room II (8.20 x ca. 31.00) Nave. Pl. 238.

Fragment: 8.00 x 9.80. Framing: ca. 0.60. Field: ca.
7.00 x 9.80.[359] No published information on dimensions and
material.

Fragment of a complex geometric design composed of interlocking patterns bordered by a meander.

Framing: at least four light and dark bands; border,
meander pattern forming swastikas and squares, the latter
inscribed with geometric motifs; multiple light and dark
bands.

Field, framed by a dark fillet: originally, probably a
single row of octagons set around two meters apart and surrounded by an alternating series of lozenges and squares.[360]
The design has been cut along the margin. In the preserved
west section, there is part of an octagon with a shield pattern, bordered by wave crests, which, presumably, enclosed a

---

[359]Vide supra, p. 223, n. 358.

[360]Sodini (Catalogue, p. 710) omits the lozenges.

central medallion, now lost. Only traces survive of the outer
fillets of the second octagon toward the east. The surrounding lozenges and squares contain a variety of geometric and
geometricized floral motifs which are set on a light ground.
Generally, the lozenges are inscribed with smaller lozenges
or with interlaces forming guilloches and Solomon's knots
which are usually accompanied by schematized floral motifs
consisting of S-curves, trilobes, and heart-shaped ivy
leaves. Along the margin, the lozenges are filled with
single ivy leaves and flanking spiral tendrils. The more
commodius squares are decorated with intersecting circles,
eight-pointed lozenge stars and squares, and interlaces of
crosses and alternating circles and squares.

Middle or second half of the fifth century.

Illustration. J. C. Rolfe, AJA, 6 (1890), pl. XIV -
our pl. 238 (detail of right side of plate).

SKRIPOU

Basilica

Traces of an Early Christian church with a mosaic pavement were brought to light in 1895 beneath the present ninth
century church of the Dormition of the Virgin at Skripou-
Orchomenos. No other information is available and the site
was not examined.

Bibliography. A. H. S. Megaw, BSA, 61 (1966), p. 28, n.
126.

79 Fragment of a mosaic pavement (no dimensions published).

No published information on dimensions and material.

Brief mention of traces of a mosaic pavement belonging to an
Early Christian basilica.

Additional bibliography. Sodini, Catalogue, No. 22, p. 713.

MALADRINO

Mosaic Fragment

A small excavation in 1932 near Maladrino brought to
light a large fragment of a mosaic pavement (6.44 x 6.32).
The site was never cleared and the condition of the pavement
is not known. It contained part of an inscription which
stated that the most pious Evtychianos and others, whose
names were destroyed, sponsored the decoration of the
"atrium ([ΥΠΟ]CΤΥΛΟΝ)." Given the Christian content of the
inscription, it is quite probable that the atrium formed part
of the forestructure of a church.

Bibliography. AA, 48 (1933), p. 217; Praktika tēs
Christianikēs archaiologikēs hetaireias, 4(1936-38), pp. 50-
52.

No. 80

80 Fragment (length, 6.44; width, 6.32). Atrium.

No published information on material.

Fragment of a polychrome mosaic containing geometric and floral motifs and traces of two inscriptions.

Framing: border, interlace; border, intersecting circles.[361]

Field: stylized ivy leaves. Of the two inscriptions in the pavement, only the left side of one was legible.

ΟΙΕΥΛΑΒΕССΤ[ ]/ΑΝΑΓΝѠСΤΕ[ ]/ΚΑΙΕΥ
ΤΥΧΙΑΝΟCΑ/ΜΑΤΑΙСΕΥΛΑΒΕС/СΤΑΤΑΙСΑΥΤѠ/
ΟΙΚΟΔΕССΠ[ ]/ΥΠΕΡΕΥΧΗ[ ]ΝΕΚΕΝΤ
ΗС[ ]С/ΤΥΛΟΝ [362]

Early Christian.

Additional bibliography. Sodini, Catalogue, No. 20, p. 712.

DENTRA

Mosaic Fragment

A mosaic fragment (pl. 239) was discovered near the iconostasis of the seventeenth century church of St. Athanasios at Dentra.[363] Whether this fragment was in situ, at a

---

[361]The relative positions of the borders are not noted in the report (C. Karusos, Praktika tēs Christianikēs archaiologikes hetaireias, 4 [1936-38], pp. 50-51), hereafter cited as Karusos.

[362]For the emendation, see Karusos, p. 51.
ΟΙ ΕΥΛΑΒΕССΤ(ΑΤΟΙ)/ΑΝΑΓΝѠСΤΕ[ ]/ΚΑΙ ΕΥΤΥΧΙΑΝΟС Α/
ΜΑ ΤΑΙС ΕΥΛΑΒΕС/СΤΑΤΑΙС ΑΥΤѠ(Ν)/ ΟΙΚΟΔΕССΠ(ΟΙΝΑΙС)/
ΥΠΕΡ ΕΥΧΗ(С ΑΥΤѠ)Ν ΕΚΕΝΤΗС(ΑΝ ΤΟ ΥΠΟ)С/ ΤΥΛΟΝ.
[363]A. K. Orlandos, ABME, 3 (1937), pp. 185-186.

lower level than the present floor, or a reused piece cannot be determined from the report. It was ascribed to the Roman or Early Christian period.[364]

Bibliography. A. K. Orlandos, ABME, 3 (1937), pp. 185-186.

No. 81

81 Fragment (no dimensions published). Pl. 239.

No published information on dimensions and material.

Originally, juxtaposed panels, of which part of one survives, set within an interlace framework.

Framing: dark double fillet; outer border, light and dark stepped triangles; light fillet; dark fillet.

Field.

Framework: tight, two-strand interlace, outlined by a dark fillet, forming small circles.

Preserved panel, framed by a single dark outer fillet and a light inner double fillet:

Framing: border, dark and light stepped triangles.

Field: imbrication pattern composed of dark-tipped scales fanning in the same direction.

Roman or Early Christian.

Additional bibliography. Sodini, Catalogue, p. 713, n. 25.

---

[364]Ibid., p. 186.

Illustration. A. K. Orlandos, ABME, 3 (1937), p. 186, fig. 2 = our pl. 239.

DELPHI

Basilica

A chance find in 1959, north of the Hotel Apollo at Delphi, brought to light the north half of an Early Christian basilica (overall, 7.60 max x 23.05 max) with well preserved mosaics in the narthex and nave (pls. 240, 253). The mosaics and the foundations of the east and west walls of the narthex, and the west side of the north stylobate were lifted, consolidated, and placed in the courtyard of the Museum at Delphi.[365]

Although a detailed archaeological report and plan of the building are still awaited, some tentative conclusions regarding its form and decoration can be drawn from its present disposition in the museum courtyard. In its preserved state, the basilica (7.19 max x 19.10 max) comprises a narthex, I (7.60 max x 3.95), which has two entrances on the

----

[365]Although the Greek Archaeological Service undertook the excavation (P. Lazarides, Deltion, 16 (1960), B: Chronika, p. 167), the more complete report is to be found in the periodical of the French School at Athens (BCH, 84 [1960], pp. 752-756. The building was situated on the south side of the street leading to the church of St. Elias (see Les Guides bleus-Grèce, Paris, 1953, pp. 260-261 [maps of site]). For other churches at Delphi, see E. Dyggve, "Les traditions cultuelles de Delphes et l'église chrétienne: quelques notes sur ," CA, 3 (1948), pp. 9-28, p. 15, fig. 4 (plan); E. Goffinet, "L'église Saint-Georges à Delphes," BCH, 84 (1962), pp. 242-260; our No. 84.

northwest side and an equal number on the northeast side
leading into the church proper, II-III. The latter is subdivided into nave and north aisle by columns or piers[366] set
on an elevated stylobate. A segment of its foundations (0.68
x 3.40 max) survives in the northwest corner (pl. 254) and it
is clear that the pavement was laid up to it and to its
original extension along the north side (pls. 253, 270, 274).
On this side of the nave, approximately 3.54 meters from the
east end of the pavement, there is a stone block (0.80 x 1.16)
with four shallow circular openings for colonettes (pls. 255,
270, 274). Apparently, this is the block which is cited in a
report as belonging to the base of an ambon.[367] Similar
free-standing columnar ambons survive in other Early Christian
churches, but always with steps permitting access to a raised
platform supported by the colonettes on which the priest or
deacon stood during certain parts of the Mass of the Catachumens.[368] In this fragment, there is no trace of a stairway and, indeed, no sign of its existence on the surface of
the pavement. The function of this piece of furniture is

---

[366]Presumably, the columns and capitals set along the
wall of the courtyard belong to the church (pl. 253, top).

[367]BCH, 84 (1960), p. 756.

[368]See, for example, Soteriou, Palaiochristianikai
basilikai, pp. 243-246, figs. 77-79; Orlandos, Xylostegos
basilike, pp. 538-566, especially pp. 541-555, and fig. 503-
504, 506, 513-515. Although the broken ridge on the south
side is identified as a step (BCH, 84 [1960], p. 756), any
type of stairway to the platform would have been, of neces-
sity, diagonal to the vertical body of the ambon (see Orlandos, ibid., p. 548, fig. 13).

problematic but it is contemporaneous with the pavement or
predates it. Although the original juncture between the two
was destroyed and repaired with concrete when they were reset
in the courtyard, it is clear that the design of the pavement
was altered to accommodate the base because the marine repre-
sentatións inscribed in the other elongated hexagons (pl.
274), have been replaced by solid fields in the two hexagons
bisected by the base. This method of eliminating figures in
truncated hexagonal compartments is employed all along the
margins of the field. This stone feature and fragments of a
chancel screen in the bema[369] are the only furnishings found
in situ.

   Although no datable archaeological finds were unearthed
or reported, on the basis of the style and iconography of
the mosaics, the church can be attributed to the late fifth
or early sixth century.

   Bibliography. P. Lazarides, Deltion, 16 (1960), B:
Chronika, p. 167; BCH, 84 (1960), pp. 752-756.

   Illustration. P. Lazarides, Deltion, 16 (1960), Plates,
pl. 149a (narthex mosaic in situ).

                        Nos. 82-83

   Rectilinear and curvilinear geometric designs with multiple figural insets pave the narthex and nave filling these

_____

   369The bema was left in situ (BCH, 84 [1960], p. 756).

---

areas with polychrome splendor.[370] Sharply delineated against a white or colored ground, birds, animals, fish, and humans move freely and actively in opaque square, octagonal, hexagonal, and semi-circular panels. The oblique grid in the narthex (pls. 240, 242-248) is decorated, for the most part, with birds which strut, peck, or turn their heads, while personifications of two warm seasons in the west compartment in the nave (pls. 259, 265-268) rush toward the center of an intricate design which is occupied by an animal combat scene originally surrounded by four strutting peacocks and four flying eagles (pls. 258, 260-264). This image of nature in all her glory is accompanied by an image of the world in the east compartment of the nave where a zoological menagerie of leaping, walking or running animals in the octagonal insets and fish in the hexagons symbolize the earth and the sea (pls. 271, 273-285).

This kind of decorative program does not appear in Greek pavements before the second half of the fifth century when themes pertaining to nature, the world,[371] and to villa and country life began to be represented in pavements. This pictorial outburst and flowering is accompanied by an increase in the size, number, and complexity of the surrounding borders as is evident, also, in the Delphi pavements (pl. 256). These

---

[370]The north aisle was paved with brick slabs and the bema with marble ones (ibid., p. 756).

[371]For a discussion of these programs at Corinth, Argos, and Tegea, see 42; 55-57; 69-70.

pavements and those at Thebes and Hypati (75-76, pls. 224-236; 101, pl. 354) represent the production of one workshop and possibly of two artisans whose names are inscribed in one of the tessellated pavements at Thebes (75, pl. 232) and who, on the basis of the style of the pavements, worked in the late fifth or early sixth century.[372]

  Additional bibliography. E. Kitzinger, Mosaics in the Greek East, p. 347; Sodini, Catalogue, No. 18, pp. 710-711, 745; idem, Complements, p. 582.

82 Room I (7.60 max x 3.95). Narthex; pavement extends beyond the preserved south thresholds on the west (ca. 0.24) and east (0.23) sides.[373] South side destroyed by later foundations. Pls. 240-254.

Framing: to north and east, 0.38; to west, 0.62, including threshold. North panel, a, including double fillet: 5.70 x 2.81. South panel, b, including inner border and double fillet: 1.25 max x 2.81. Medallion, including double borders: 2.13 diam. marble (white), limestone (ochre, black, brown), ceramic (red), and glass (red, greens, blues) tesserae (average, 0.01 sq; for details, glass 0.005 sq) set 1-3mm apart.

---

  [372]For a comparison of these pavements and their chronology, vide supra, pp. 209-210.

  [373]Since most of the mosaics flanking the thresholds still retain their terminal fillets, it is probable that they did not continue across the thresholds but were laid up to stone sills.

North part of a polychrome mosaic composed of two panels, a-b, with figural insets bordered by an imbrication pattern.

Framing (pl. 240): mixed black fillet;[374] border, white scales, outlined in mixed black, with colored tips arranged in alternate chevron rows of dark grey/pink/light grey/reddish brown.[375] At the entrance to the nave, this border is interrupted by a white tabula ansata (pl. 241), outlined in mixed black,[376] containing the first part of a four-line inscription in mixed black letters (0.06-0.09 high). It is oriented westward and preceded by a small mixed black crosslet: "ΑΜΑΡΤ ιω[ ]/ωπρεπιΑ[ ]/ΚΑΘωΟΙΚϹΟΥ[ ]."

Field: two polychrome panels, a-b, decorated with figures and set within narrow white/mixed black bands.

Ia, north panel (pls. 240, 242-251): oblique grid composed of a two-strand guilloche (1 dark mottled grey/1 pale grey/ 1 white; 1 reddish brown/1 pink/1 white, outlined in mixed browns, with a white tessera at each loop) forming squares (ca. 0.67). The guilloche bifurcates along the edges of the design to form a continuous outer border which cuts in varying degrees the adjacent squares.[377] The mixed black squares,

---

[374]This term and mixed brown will be used throughout the entries to denote a combination of black and dark brown, and different shades of dark brown, respectively.

[375]The scales separate in the northwest corner: one section moves southward; the other across the north side and then southward.

[376]The color of the preserved ansa was not recorded.

[377]Only the squares to the northwest and south retain figures. The rest are filled with floral motifs or are left undecorated. Vide infra, p. 236.

outlined in white, are inscribed with white disks which
serve as opaque grounds for lively representations of water
fowl and land birds, oriented southward.[378] A consistent
arrangement of the same species of birds is evident in the
diagonal registers moving from the northwest to the southeast. This, of course, produces an alternation of these
types on the opposite northeast-southwest diagonal axis.
Starting on the northwest side and moving eastward, the
sequence of filling elements in the diagonal rows is as
follows (pl. 240). First row (pls. 242-243: land birds
whose plumage is defined by small grey and ochre checkerboard
patterns (pl. 245). Second row: ducks (pls. 246-247).
Third row: grey birds with striped bodies. Fourth row:
grey and ochre birds with striped wings and tail feathers
(pl. 242). Fifth row: dark blue fowl (pls. 244, 248).
Sixth row: emerald green parrots. Seventh row: white and
blue speckled birds (possibly male counterparts to the grey
speckled birds in the first row). Most of the birds, shown
in lively poses and in profile, move or face toward the
perimeter of the room in an alternating sequence. For the
most part, they are naturalistically rendered and three-
dimensional, and are defined by vivid colors and fluid black
outlines. Unlike later examples (95, 98-99, pls. 316-320,
324-331, 339-347; 150-156, pls. 461-542), their feet appear

---

[378]Exceptions to this orientation are the three birds
along the northwest side, which are oriented westward, and a
vase on the north side which faces in that direction.

to bear the weight of their solid bodies and their movement
is lively and convincing. The plasticity of the figures is
contradicted by the opaque, white disks behind them which
constrict the space of the insets. This ambiguity between
the objects and the panels extends to the decoration in the
large truncated squares along the edges of the design. With
two exceptions, they contain modeled floral motifs of which
nine are palmettos, some with trailing tendrils at their
bases (pl. 249).[379] They are beige, grey or white with
darker tones for shading. The other floral motifs consist of
a white and ochre acanthus pattern (pl. 250) similar to those
decorating the spandrels of the south panel (pl. 251), two
clusters of heart-shaped ivy leaves with pointed tips, one
with three dark grey mottled leaves; the other, with a reddish
brown tubular center with a bulbous top and flanking light
grey leaves (pl. 240, lower right). The value of the ground
in these truncated panels depends on the value of the motifs.
Thus, light motifs are placed on dark grounds and dark motifs
on light ones.

Ib, south panel (pls. 240, 251-252): fragment of the north

[379]On the northwest side is a long-necked, light grey
vase, outlined in dark grey. It has a ridged mouth and a
heart-shaped body with two spiral handles. Its long foot is
attached to a double light and dark grey base. In a smaller
panel in the northwest corner stands a bird whose species and
colors were not recorded. The other triangular sections are
decorated with single or concentric triangles in mixed black,
or mixed grey and black.

part of a large rectangular panel with a figural composition.

Framing: border, three-strand braid (0.34; 1 dark mottled grey/1 pale grey/1 white; 1 reddish brown/1 pink/1 white, outlined in mixed black with a white tessera at each loop and at intervals along the edges).

Field, framed by a white double fillet: large figural medallion, bordered by an outer band of white and mixed black wave crests (0.18) and an inner mixed black and red (ceramic) band, decorated with a laurel wreath with a brown tubular clasp (0.28). From the short sides of the clasp flow successive overlapping groups of dark green laurel leaves, outlined in white, which on one side are accented by brown calices and dark blue bases. In contrast to the two-dimensionality of the laurel leaves, two subtly modeled, ochre acanthus leaves sprout from the mixed black northeast and northwest spandrels of the panel (pl. 251). The preserved section of the medallion (pl. 252) contains traces of a frontal, three-quarter figure who clasps in its brown left hand the base of a long-necked grey vase. Dark blue water spills in an unbroken line from the mouth of the vase and forms a rectangular pool below. Except for a small section of the lower brown arm and a grey and white garment covering the left shoulder and thigh, the rest of the figure is destroyed.

East threshold (pls. 241, 253): undulating ribbon (2.70 max x 0.23) with white highlights (alternately, light pink/ reddish brown; dark grey/pale grey/dark grey; dark grey/pale

grey/pale yellow/pale grey/dark grey, outlined in white) on
a mixed brown ground. At each wave is a small crowstep composed of four to five rows of white tesserae.

  Additional color. Panel a. Birds: red (ceramic) legs and
beaks; black corneas, white retinas, and, usually, black outlines. North and south speckled birds: dark mottled grey
crests, beaks, legs. Ducks: males have light and dark brown
bodies with ochre wings, outlined in dark mottled grey, and
emerald green and dark blue heads; females have light brown
and ochre bodies with dark grey mottled breasts and heads, and
light and dark brown wings, delineated by a row of white tessera on the underside; light grey bodies with dark grey
breasts and heads, and light and dark brown wings delineated
by a row of white tesserae on the underside. Third row:
black and white stripes and brown wings. Fourth row: three
with grey and ochre bodies, wings and tail feathers of which
two are striped in black; colors of fourth bird not recorded.
Fifth row: fowl have red (ceramic) coxes and black wings,
articulated in beige, or beige and light brown wings, delineated by beige and black strokes on underside. Panel b.
Acanthus leaves: various tones of grey with touches of red
(ceramic). Clasp: outlined and delineated in white and red
(glass). Medallion: concentric dark grey, white, and mixed
black fillets. Hand: white highlights and red (ceramic)
knuckles. Vase: light and dark grey with brown mouth and
white highlights; outlined and delineated in mixed browns.

Late fifth or early sixth century.

Illustrations. P. Lazarides, Deltion, 16 (1960), Plates, pl. 149 (pavement in situ), pl. 150 = our pl. 240).

83   Room II (7.19 max x 19.10 max). Nave; pavement laid up
to the north stylobate, of which traces survive on the
west side (pl. 254), and to a stone block on the northeast
side (pl. 255); destroyed to northeast, east, south, and
wouthwest, and in the middle of compartments a and b Pls.
253-286.

Framing: 0.91; to west, 1.35. West compartment, a: 6.08
x 6.13 max. Medallion: 1.56 diam. Rectangles with semi-
circular sides: 1.48 x 0.80. Heptagons: 1.37 x 1.33. Figural squares: 1.07. Meanders: 1.40 sq. East compartment,
b: 10.10 max x 5.85 max. Inscription: 0.60 max x 0.44.
Materials identical to those in Room I (82) with the addition
of yellow glass.

Polychrome mosaic composed of two geometric compartments,
a,b with figures set within a rectilinear interlace framework
and surrounded by interlaced circles.[380]

Framing: black fillet; outer border, complex interlace
composed of a chain of interlacing circles (light grey/l

---

[380]Contrary to Sodini (Catalogue, p. 711), the interlaced circles do not divide the two panels but serve as the
surrounding outer border (see pl. 269). In addition, the
drawing to which he refers (ibid., p. 711, and p. 712, fig.
2e) is not of these interlaced circles but shows the middle
border which exists on the west side only and which he does
not discuss.

white; reddish brown/1 white, outlined in black); black
double fillet; triple white fillet; black double fillet;
middle border to west only (pl. 256), chain of interlaced
squares set on edge (reddish brown/1 white; ochre/1 white,
outlined in black) which are laced along the margins by a
continuous undulating strand (1-2 grey/1 white, outlined in
black). In the center of each square is a diagonal black
crosslet; black double fillet; white triple fillet; black
double fillet.

Field.

Interlace framework (Pls. 256, 260, 271): complex interlace forming an undulating rectilinear strand (grey/1 white,
outlined in black) which is laced by two continuous parallel
bars (both, reddish brown/1 pink/1 white, outlined in black)
(for curvilinear versions of this pattern, see pls. 166-167,
225, 231).

Ia, west compartment, framed by a white double fillet which
forms, at the same time, part of the design (pls. 253, 257-
260): intricate symmetrical design originally composed of a
central cruciform interlace surrounded by four heptagons and
enclosed by squares in each corner.[381] The entire program is

----

[381]Although the pavement contains lacunae along the south
and southwest sides, enough evidence exists to reconstruct the
original design. Of the rectangles with semi-circular short
sides, the north one is intact and those to the east and
south partially preserved. Nothing survives to the west, but
it is clear that a similar panel existed since part of the
interlace which bound it to the central medallion survives
(pl. 259). South of this loop is a five centimeter white
area which is all that survives of the southwest heptagon (pl.

formed by a continuous two-strand guilloche (dark grey/1
light grey/1 white; reddish brown/1 ochre/1 white, outlined
in black, with a white tessera at each loop) on a black
ground. The central composition consists of a medallion and
four rectangles on the cardinal points (pls. 259-260). The
former·is decorated with an animal combat scene (pl. 261),
oriented westward, showing a blue spotted grey panther attacking a brown stag whose lacerated hide drips with blood (ceramic red). As its forelegs collapse from the momentum of the
attack, the running stag thrusts its head backward in an agony
of terror and pain caused by the clinging, clawing panther who

---

260, upper right). It contains, however, part of a curving
row of black tesserae which is identical in size, color, and
shape to those outlining the wings of the eagles in the three
preserved heptagons to the northeast, northwest, and southeast
and permits a restoration of a fourth bird in this section.
Although the southwest angle of the design is destroyed, and
the southeast angle fragmentary, these sectors can also be
reconstituted with certainty. The southeast angle (pls. 260,
upper left; 271, lower right) contains fragments of two
guilloche panels whose decoration and diagonal disposition are
identical to those along the preserved north side which flank
figural panels. It is probable, therefore, that the south
panels bounded on two sides a third one which occupied the
corner and was also figural. This latter reconstruction is
substantiated by epigraphic and iconographic evidence. The
northeast figural panel is inscribed with the letters "KA" and
the northwest one (pl. 267) with "KAI" which form the first
letters of the inscription "KAΛOI KAIPOI" or, the Beautiful
Seasons, a theme which is seen in two other pavements in
Greece (42, pl. 95; 69). In the two south panels, therefore,
there were single figures accompanied by the second part of
the inscription "ΛOI" and "POI" who were also probably rushing
toward the center of the composition with their attributes in
their outstretched hands. Iconographically, therefore, the
relationship between the figures in the north and south panels
would mirror that in the pavement at Thebes which belongs to
the same workshop (75, pl. 225). Vide supra, p. 210, n. 342.

bites into its spinal column. The action of the scene is entirely contained within the medallion whose shape is repeated
by the contrasting curvilinear patterns of the bodies of the
animals which are sharply etched against the stark white
ground. The guilloche border of the medallion bifurcates on
the cardinal points to form interlaced rectangular panels,
each with its semi-circular side toward the center. Of these,
only the north one (pl. 262) is preserved to any degree. Outlined in black, it contains a profile view of an ochre-winged,
dark blue peacock who parades toward the center on grey and
dark blue legs, trailing behind it an emerald green, pink, and
reddish brown striated tail covert. Highlighting the plumage
are two brilliant eyes composed of yellow, blue, and light
green tesserae resting on single white veins.[382] Between the
arms of the central cruciform interlace are large heptagons
(pls. 259, 264) with concave and straight sides filled with
light purplish brown eagles which, although turned away from
the central scene, reflect the theme of hunter and hunted.
This is indicated by their pose which shows them in flight
with outspread wings and grasping talons preparing to descend

---

[382]Part of this panel was restored before it was reset in
its present location, but it is difficult to determine the
extent. It is clear that the beginning of the tail feathers
was reworked with grey and white tesserae which are irregularly placed. In addition, some disturbance is noticeable in
the central part of the tail plumage (it appears as a darker
tone in the plate). Whether this represents a restoration or
the original part cannot be determined. It is possible that
the irregular blue and white striations on the wing represent
a reworking since in the untouched east panel they are set in
an imbrication pattern (pl. 263).

on their prey (see, for example, pl. 164). Each black-
outlined bird is shown with the right side of its head in
profile, the left side of its body and legs in three-quarter
view, and with frontal wings and tail feathers. Three
squares in each angle complete the design: one with a representation of a season; two with meander patterns. The preserved figural panels in the northeast and northwest corners
(pls. 259, 260) show personifications of two warm months who
stride toward the center of the design offering their individual attributes in their outstretched arms. They wear
short, sleeveless tunics which are belted at the waist and
their light brown skin is highlighted by double, sometimes
triple, rows of pink tesserae which create abstract patterns
on their faces, necks and limbs (pls. 265-268). The emphatic
dark reddish brown contours of their limbs and heads contrast
with their more delicate, similarly colored facial features.
Although the structures of their heads differ somewhat, their
features show a general similitude in regard to black button
eyes with pronounced oval lids, aquiline noses and small
pursed lips whose shadows are defined by a short row of miniscule tesserae on the chins.[383] Crowning their heads are
short, reddish brown (east) and grey (west) curls delineated
by short curving strokes of black tesserae.

Northeast panel, framed by a black fillet and inscribed with

---

[383]The head in the northeast panel lacks eyebrows and
the placement of the tesserae shows a certain ineptitude,
especially in the highlighting of the face and neck.

the letters "KA" on the upper left side (pls. 265-266, 269):
the figure probably personifies the month of August since his
brown basket is filled with the produce associated with that
month (for similar attributes, see 55, pls. 141-142; 69, pl.
211). They are shown in vertical perspective with a green
watermelon and red (glass) grapes suspended above the rim of
a basket which partially obscures a black and reddish brown
eggplant and a pink squash (?) and peach (?). Since the
mosaicist omitted the back of the basket, the produce is
shown against the white of the ground. The running barefoot
figure of August is clothed in a thin beige and brown tunic,
outlined and delineated in shades of blue and a row of white,
which clings to his thighs and ends in a triangular white
fold in the back.

Northwest panel, framed by a black fillet and inscribed
with the letters "KAI" on the upper left side: unlike its
counterpart, this season wears grey and blue boots and carries a sheaf of wheat composed of light and dark reddish
brown stalks with single checkerboard shafts. His hair is
decorated with a spray of wheat and he is clothed in a pale
grey and white tunic which is articulated by wide contours
and delineations in blue sprinkled with mauve (glass). Since
the month of July in a pavement in Thebes also carries a
sheaf of wheat (75, pl. 227), it is possible that the Delphi
figure is to be identified as that month or, at least a

somewhat cooler month than August who is barefoot.[384]

In the two squares decorating the angles of the west panel there are meanders composed of intersecting guilloches forming swastikas. The continuous guilloche, therefore, branches out to become a purely geometric pattern while, at the same time, forming a unifying border for all the figural panels in the design (pl. 269).

IIb, east compartment, framed by a white double fillet which forms, at the same time, part of the design (pls. 269-271): black and white network of alternating octagons and equilateral meander crosses forming elongated hexagons.[385] The elements of the design have been changed to irregular tetragons along the margins. On the east side, presumably at the entrance to the bema, is a panel (pls. 272-273) containing the first part of a four-line inscription in black letters (ca. 0.10 high) which is flanked on the north side by a lamb. Framed in black, the inscription is oriented westward and preceded by a small black crosslet: "ΤΙϹΟΤΟΥΚΑ[ ]/ΟΙΚΟΥ ΕΥΡΕΤ[ ]/ΚΑΙΘΕΟΠΡΕΠΙΑ[ ]/ΕΠΟΙΗϹΑΝΤΟΝ[ ]."

Toward the west of the inscription, land and sea animals move

---

[384]One minor problem concerns the difference in headgear. At Thebes, July wears a webbed cap while another month, May, wears a spray of wheat (pl. 229). At Argos, on the other hand, it is June who carries a sheaf of wheat (55, pl. 141). For a discussion on their probable counterparts to the south, vide supra, p. 240, n. 381.

[385]Sodini terms them lozenges (Catalogue, p. 711). For similar designs with geometric or organic motifs, see 95, 136.

freely and oftentimes energetically in their spaceless
octagonal and hexagonal insets and form on the east-west
axis a veritable cosmographic menagerie which is accompanied
on the west side by two vases and a man (pls. 271, 281). In
an alternating sequence of six and seven octagons on the main
axis, wild and domesticated animals leap, strut, turn or walk
within static geometric frames while, to the west, a solitary
human figure strides forward, ostensibly leading the donkey in
the adjacent south octagon (pls. 271, 283).[386] Beginning
with the first octagon to the northeast and moving southward,
the sequence of figures is as follows (pl. 273). First row:
walking white lamb with a wide flat tail. Second row: leaping grey tiger with mixed black and white stripes; leaping
brown deer. Third row: preserved hind legs of a leaping
grey feline. Fourth row: running brown gazelle; preserved
snout and paws of a light and dark brown bear. Fifth row
(pl. 274): leaping and leering yellowish brown lion with
white teeth and a red (ceramic) tongue and nose (pl. 275).
Sixth row (pls. 274, 276): leaping white hound with dark
brown collar and grey shading. Seventh row: prancing zebra
with white/tan/dark brown/dark reddish brown/ and red
(ceramic) stripes and three black ones on its head and neck
(pl. 277). Eighth row: running dark brown boar with white
tusks (pl. 278); running light brown doe with an ochre collar
(pls. 274, 277); running dark brown animal, perhaps a dog

---

[386]Vide infra, p. 248.

(pl. 280).[387] Ninth row: leaping light brown dog with a
reddish brown collar; dark pink water buffalo (pl. 280); forepart of a snarling grey tiger with black stripes. Tenth row:
dark brown walking fox (?) (pl. 274); beige and light purplish
brown fighting cock (pl. 279); preserved body of a white
crane with dark brown wing and red (ceramic) legs; prancing
pink horse with a red (ceramic) saddle and halter (pl. 280).
Eleventh row (pl. 281): seated grey goat; preserved forepart
of a snarling grey tiger with black stripes; grey cat walking
with a black and mauvre rat in its mouth (pl. 282). Twelfth
row: walking white lamb with a wide flat tail; dark pink and
reddish brown vase with a long neck and base; traces of a
similar vase; walking white lamb. Thirteenth row (pls. 269,
283-284): dark purplish brown dromedary; donkey driver with
a red (ceramic) cane; dark brown and purplish brown donkey
with a light brown harness.

All the filling elements in the octagons are sharply
etched against a white ground by means of dark outlines,
usually black or mixed black, which also serve to define the
inner contours. With the exception of the frontal head of
the cat (pl. 282), the animals are presented in profile with
frontal, staring black eyes which are sometimes circular,
sometimes oval. Except for the zebra (pl. 277), crane, horse
(pl. 280), and dromedary (pl. 281), which are rendered with

---

[387]The body is that of a dog while the head approximates
that of the goat in the eleventh row.

bodies of uniform color,[388] the animals show some degree of
modeling but with no gradations between values and colors.
Invariably, the darker area is displayed along the top of the
animal[389] and frequently it extends to the head and the legs
farthest from the viewer. In some bodies, deer, dogs, fox
(pls. 273-274, 277), a third white band is introduced along
the ventral side which sometimes continues to the chest and/
or hind legs. The skin of the solitary male figure to the
west (pl. 284) also shows this same lack of gradation. Dark
pink in color, it is highlighted toward the center by single
or multiple rows of light pink tesserae which create abstract
patterns on his face, neck, and limbs. The strong red
(ceramic) contour lines in these areas are replaced by more
delicate ones for his features which bear a strong resemblance
to those of the seasons in the west compartment (pls. 266,
268). He is represented as striding forward with a cane in
his right hand and a bent left arm which ends in a fist, suggesting that the prototype for this figure held something in
his hand, perhaps the reins of the donkey in the next panel.
His simple attire consists of a short, sleeveless red and
brown tunic, cinched at the waist by a grey and white girdle
with black outlines, thin black sandals, and an ochre and

---

[388]The boar and the cat are somewhat different in that,
although uniform in color, they have strips of pink (boar)
and white (cat) along their bellies.

[389]Most of the fish are rendered this way (vide infra,
p. 250.

yellowish brown, webbed cap which covers most of his short
black hair. In addition to the fauna, two vases, of which one
is intact, decorate the middle octagons in the twelfth row
and are flanked by an equal number of lambs which advance
toward them. The preserved vase (pl. 281) is presented from
two points of view which negate each other. The grey mouth,
upper part of the body, and the three lower rungs of the base
are tilted forward while the neck and the rest of the body,
including the circular foot of the base, are presented
frontally. This conflict results in a curious still-life in
which the body is balanced precariously on a narrow disk while
the neck rises incongrously from the front part of the body.
The modeling of the vase does nothing to correct this dis-
tortion since, like the hides of the animals, it is rendered
by means of flat areas of contrasting colors (reddish brown
and dark pink).

Uniting the octagons are simple equilateral meander
crosses (pl. 281) formed by four white swastikas around a central square. The latter contains a dark, reddish brown disk,
outlined in red (ceramic), which is inscribed with a dark
brown diagonal cross marked by a central white crosslet.
Various species of marine life (pls. 273-274, 280-281, 285-
286), including porpoises, dolphins, eels, cuttle fish, and
squid, fill the elongated hexagons. Although lacking a compositional sequence in regard to species and orientation, a
chiastic chromatic balance is evident. In an alternating
rhythm around the octagons and crosses, dark grey fish (pl.

285) are set on a reddish brown ground and reddish brown
fish (pl. 286) on a dark grey ground. Like the majority of
the animals, the fish are presented in profile view, with
black or mixed black contours and button eyes, and are modeled
in an abstract manner. Thus the dorsal sides of the reddish
brown fish are articulated by bands of reddish brown which
are succeeded by dark pink bands and, then, by white ones on
the ventral sides. This kind of modeling obtains for the
grey fish as well: dark grey; light grey; white. In some
examples, red (ceramic) is employed for additional detail
such as teeth, dorsal fins and eyes. In addition to their
dark contours, the fish are articulated by an outer row of
white tesserae which serves to separate them from their dark
ground and, at the same time, to emphasize their contours.

Additional color. West compartment, a. Northeast panel.
Basket: black outlines. Watermelon: various shades of
green with some yellow highlights. Grapes: outlined in dark
reddish brown with white centers. Squash(?) and peach(?):
red (ceramic) outlines with some black (peach). East compartment, b. Octagons. First row: lamb, light brown
shading. Second row: deer, reddish brown shading and white
highlights. Fourth row: gazelle, reddish brown shading.
Sixth row: hound with red (ceramic) nose and tongue. Eighth
row: boar's hide flecked with black and outlined along belly
by one row of pink tesserae; dog, grey shading with white
highlights and red (ceramic) nose and tongue; dog(?), white
ears and forelegs. Ninth row: dog, grey shading and white

highlights, with red (ceramic) nose and tongue; water buffalo, reddish brown shading and grey hooves. Tenth row:
fox (?), triple row of black tesserae along back and tail and
single and double rows of white along belly and chest,
respectively; grey shading; cock, red (ceramic) cox and dark
grey beak; horse, grey hooves. Twelfth row: lamb, light
brown shading; lamb, ochre shading and grey hooves.

Late fifth or early sixth century.

   Illustrations. P. Lazarides, Deltion, 16 (1960), Plates,
pl. 149d = our pl. 257; BCH, 84 (1960), p. 755, fig. 3
(IIb, donkey driver).

                    Mosaic Fragments

   Some foundations of a building with fragments of a
mosaic pavement are situated two hundred meters to the east
of the Museum at Delphi. The dearth of archaeological,
architectural and descriptive data precludes a determination
of the plan and function of the building.[390]

----

   [390]Since no systematic excavation of the site is recorded, it is probable that the building or part of it lay
exposed at least as early as the nineteenth century. In the
first published reference (M. P. Foucart, Archives des
missions scientifiques, 2, 10 [1865], p. 105ff), the local
designation of the building, "Chapel of St. George," was
used and it has been repeated in subsequent publications (BCH,
81 [1957], p. 707; E. Dyggve, CA, 3 [1948], pp. 15-16, p. 15,
n. 4). See also the most recent article by E. Goffinet (BCH,
86 [1962], pp. 242-260) who questions the dedication but not
the function. His acceptance of an ecclesiastical function
is based on inconclusive evidence. Although the "Christian
finds" to which he refers are datable to the Christian period,

On the basis of the style of the mosaic, the building has been assigned to the sixth or seventh century.

Bibliography. M. P. Foucart, *Archives des missions scientifiques*, 2, 10 (1865), p. 105ff; *BCH*, 81 (1957), p. 707; E. Dyggve, *CA*, 3 (1948), pp. 15-16, p. 15, n. 1; E. Goffinet, *BCH*, 86 (1962), pp. 242-260.

Illustrations. E. Dyggve, *CA*, 3 (1948), p. 15, fig. 4 (plan with location of Christian churches at Delphi, including "St. George"); E. Goffinet, *BCH*, 86 (1962), p. 243, fig. 2 (general view of site).

No. 84

Fragments of a crude polychrome pavement composed of a simple field design with a double border (pls. 287-291). On the basis of the schematization and geometrization of the rinceau and the mask in the borders, the mosaic clearly belongs to a period no earlier than the sixth century. It postdates, therefore, the more three-dimensional pavements which were transferred to the Delphi Museum (82-83).[391]

Additional bibliography. Sodini, *Catalogue*, No. 19, p. 711.

Illustration. E. Goffinet, *BCH*, 86 (1962), p. 249, fig. 8 (northwest side, looking north).

---

they are by no means Christian in iconography and function. Moreover, these objects were not found in the building but, rather, south of it during the construction of a new road. There exists, therefore, no secure archaeological context for the finds and no evidence that the building ever served as a church or chapel.

[391]Goffinet (*BCH*, 86 [1962], pp. 252, 260) attributes the mosaic to the sixth or early seventh century but his reasons are not at all clear. Sodini dates it to the late sixth century (*Catalogue*, No. 19, p. 711).

84 Mosaic fragments (4.70 max x 8.20 max). Pavement covered
    by two stone blocks on the northwest and southwest sides.
    Pls. 287-291.

   Two fragments: larger one, 4.70 max x 5.00 max. Framing:
1.08. Field: 3.70 max x 4.00 max. Irregularly-cut marble
(grey, white, reddish brown, pink) and limestone (grey, white,
dark brown) tesserae (0.01-0.015 sq) set 3-5mm apart.

Fragment of the northwest sector of a crude mosaic pavement
composed of a double border and an imbrication field design.
   Framing: outer border, undulating dark brown rinceau (one
fillet) forming rather loosely arranged and widely spaced
scrolls filled with single white (limestone) heart-shaped ivy
leaves. Dark brown spiral tendrils spring from the rinceau
to form arches for the pointed tips of the leaves (pls. 288-
290);[392] inner border, wide two-strand overlapping lyre pattern composed of reddish brown/pink/white (marble) triangular
centers flanked by light grey (limestone)/light grey (marble)/
white (marble) strands, which alternate with light grey
(limestone)/white (marble) triangular centers flanked by reddish brown/pink/white (marble) strands. The units are

   [392]Goffinet's color notations are at variance with mine.
Compare, for example, one statement in which the leaves are
"black on white" (BCH, 86 [1962], p. 247) and a later one
(ibid., p. 252) in which the black is termed "deep blue."
The drawing accompanying his article and reproduced here
(pl. 287) is also inaccurate in regard to the formation of
the rinceau because it does not comprise individual tangent
"U-shaped" units but a continuous rinceau to which the tendrils have been added.

outlined in dark brown and set on a ground of the same color
which is accented at regular intervals by a white (marble)
tessera. The centers of the loops formed by the undulating
strands are filled with clusters of white (marble) tesserae;
white (marble) double fillet; dark brown double fillet. At
the preserved northwest corner, the border is interrupted by
a white panel (ca. 0.34 max x 0.50) with single black crosslets in the corners and a dark brown disk in the center (pl.
288).[393] Although the contents of the disk are no longer
preserved, in a published drawing (pl. 287) there is visible
a mask with "white, black, and pink" foliated hair.[394]

Field, framed by a white (marble) double fillet (pls. 288,
291): imbrication pattern fanning eastward composed of grey
(limestone)/grey (marble)/ white (marble) scales and reddish
brown/pink/white (marble) scales which are chromatically arranged in alternating diagonal rows. Each scale is outlined
by a dark brown/white (marble)/dark brown triple fillet.

No earlier than the sixth century.

Illustrations. E. Goffinet, BCH, 86 (1962), p. 248, fig.
7 = our pl. 287, p. 250, fig. 10 (mask), p. 250, fig. 11
(rinceau).

[393]Sodini omits the inner lyre pattern border and incorrectly places the mask in the corner of the outer rinceau
border (Catalogue, p. 711).

[394]Goffinet, op. cit., p. 250.

AMPHISSA

Mosaic Fragments

In 1970, a chance find at Amphissa brought to light two
fragments of a mosaic pavement. They were lifted and placed
in the Museum at Delphi.[395] No other information is available and no archaeological finds were noted in the brief
announcement. On the basis of their style and iconography,
the pavement can be assigned to a period no earlier than the
second half of the fifth century.

Bibliography. M. Michaelides, Deltion, 25 (1970), B1:
Chronika, p. 18; BCH, 96 (1972), p. 694.

No. 85

Fragments of a polychrome geometric mosaic comprising a
network of octagons inscribed with a peacock, lamb, and lion
and a meander border (pl. 291a). The organic filling motifs
in this pavement provide a means of establishing its chronology because it is not until the middle of the fifth century
that they begin to appear in Greek pavements. Earlier pavements with similar rectilinear designs (49, pl. 112; 88-89,
pls. 306-307; 132, pl. 430, 137, pl. 440) are completely aniconic and contain geometric filling motifs or geometricized

---

[395]M. Michaelides, Deltion, 25 (1970), B1: Chronika,
p. 18; BCH, 96 (1972), p. 694.

floral ones. Since the fauna show a degree of modeling and
three-dimensionality and their poses are natural, they predate similar designs with organic insets belonging to the
sixth century (99, pls. 345-346; 115, pls. 384-385) which are
decorated with more abstract and schematic land and marine
creatures.

Fragments lifted and placed in the Museum at Delphi.

85 Two fragments (no dimensions published). Pl. 291a.

No published information on dimensions and material.

Fragments of a polychrome geometric mosaic with figural insets
bordered by a meander pattern.

Framing: traces of a border comprising a meander pattern
forming swastikas and squares which are inscribed with a
basket of fruit and a Solomon's knot; narrow light band;
light and dark wave crests; dark fillet.

Field, framed by a narrow light band: network composed of
tangent octagons forming squares set on edge. The design is
cut along the margin. In the three preserved octagons there
are a peacock displaying its occelate feathers which serve as
a decorative mandorla for its slender body; a lamb; a lion
leaping in front of a tree. The small squares contain a
variety of floral motifs.

Second half of the fifth century.

Illustrations. M. Michaelides, _Deltion_, 25 (1970), B1:
Chronika, pl. 16a-b = our pl. 291a.

ANO TITHOREA-VELITSA

Mosaic Fragment

A small excavation in 1960 brought to light the remains
of a mosaic pavement 1.65 meters below the floor of the
modern church of Abbot Zosima in the city of Ano Tithorea-
Velitsa. The pavement is described as belonging to an "Early
Christian" building which, to date, has not been excavated.

Bibliography. P. Lazarides, Deltion, 16 (1960), B:
Chronika, pp. 164-165.

Illustration. P. Lazarides, Deltion, 16 (1960), B2:
Chronika, fig. on p. 165 (site plan).

No. 86

86 Mosaic fragment (no dimensions published).

No published information on dimensions and material.

Brief mention of a mosaic pavement.

Early Christian.

Additional bibliography. Sodini, Catalogue, No. 29, p. 715.

MARIOLATA

Basilica

During two brief campaigns in 1962 and 1963, sections of

an Early Christian basilica with a mosaic pavement (overall,
14.25 x 24.35, without annexes) were cleared in Mariolata, a
small village at the foot of the acropolis of ancient Boion.
Since no subsequent excavations were conducted, the annexes
which flanked the northwest and southwest sides of the church
proper were not completely cleared (pl. 292).[396] At the
present time, the site is overgrown and the condition of the
pavement is not known.

The church proper (14.25 x 18.60) is preceded by a narthex, I (14.25 x 5.75), which is flanked by three rooms: one
on the north side, II; two on the south side, III-IV.[397] The
body of the church consists of a nave, V, separated from the
two side aisles, VI-VII, by columns resting on bases set on
marble slabs, and a transverse tripartite transept with a
semi-circular apse opening off the central bay, VIII.[398] The
nave was decorated with a tessellated pavement, of which two
fragments are preserved on the east side of the north and
south colonnades.[399]

The preliminary nature of the excavations, the dearth of

---

[396]P. Lazarides, Deltion, 18 (1963), B1: Chronika, p.
132; hereafter cited as Deltion, 18; idem, Deltion, 19 (1964),
B2: Chronika, pp. 237-238, hereafter cited as Deltion, 19.

[397]The absence of communicating doors between the two
south rooms and along the west wall of the narthex is not
explained.

[398]Deltion, 19, p. 237.

[399]Deltion, 19, p. 238. The paving in the other sectors
is not noted.

external evidence, and the poor condition of the mosaics preclude a determination of the precise chronology of the
basilica. A terminus post quem of the middle of the fifth
century is provided by the type of interlace border in the
nave (pl. 294) which does not appear in earlier pavements.
The basilica was eventually abandoned and covered with dirt
and fill. Sometime between the seventh and ninth centuries,
a one-room apsed chapel was built one meter above the bema
and the rest of the site was converted into a cemetary. The
funerary chapel was destroyed during the Turkish occupation
and, at an unspecified date, was replaced by the present
chapel of St. Demetrios (pl. 293). It would appear that this
later building also served as a funerary chapel since the
rest of the site continued to function as a cemetary. Many
of the graves, especially those installed during the second
building phase of the site, destroyed sections of the tessellated pavements.[400]

Bibliography. P. Lazarides, Deltion, 18 (1963), B1:
Chronika, p. 132; idem, Deltion, 19 (1964), B2: Chronika, pp.
237-238; JHS, 84 (1964), Supplement, p. 14; BCH, 91 (1967),
pp. 690-691.

Illustrations. P. Lazarides, Deltion, 18 (1963), B1:
Chronika, pl. 169a (general view of site, from west); idem,
Deltion, 19 (1964), B2: Chronika, p. 237, plan 1 = our pl.
292, pl. 282b = our pl. 293.

[400]Ibid.

87 Room V (no dimensions published). Nave; covered by graves
    which destroyed the pavement. Pl. 294.

  Two fragments. No published information on dimensions.
Stone tesserae (0.015-0.02 sq).[401]

In a published photograph (pl. 294) there are traces of a
rather wide border composed of interlaced circles. The
report notes a three-color scheme and the presence of other
geometric motifs.[402]

Around the middle or the second half of the fifth century.
  Additional bibliography. Sodini, Catalogue, No. 21, p. 712.
  Illustration. P. Lazarides, Deltion, 18 (1963), B1:
Chronika, pl. 169gamma = our pl. 294.

ARKITSA

Basilica

  The basilica, visible from the Athens-Thessaloniki
National Highway, is located to the north of Arkitsa, between
the towns of St. Nicholas and St. Constantine, in the former
Deme of Daphnousion. During a short campaign in 1929, at
which time almost the entire structure (overall, 16.60 x

---

[401]Ibid.   [402]Ibid.

23.00, with apse) was cleared (pl. 295), well preserved
mosaic pavements were discovered in the nave and transept.[403]
At the present time, the panels are in poor condition with
lacunae throughout.

Preceded by an atrium or exonarthex, I,[404] and a shallow
esonarthex, II, the main body of the church (16.60 x 18.00)
consists of a nave, III, flanked by two aisles, IV-V, and a
transverse tripartite transept with projecting wings and a
raised, semi-circular apse, VI-IX. The nave is separated
from the aisles by arcuated colonnades,[405] joined by parapets
and resting on bases set on elevated stylobates, and from the
central bay (bema) by a triumphal arch. Triumphal arches may
also have separated the bema, VI, from the north and south
wings, VII-VIII, which are accessible to the aisles through
screen doors or partitions. The bema (pls. 297-298) was enclosed by a low, semi-independent chancel screen with pierced
parapets which projected from two lateral steps abutting the

---

[403]Although never recorded, the fill covering part of
the aisle and narthex, along the south side, was subsequently
removed (cf. A. K. Orlandos, Byzantion, 5 [1929/30], p. 208,
fig. 1; hereafter cited as Byzantion, 5; idem, Xylostegos
basilikē, p. 172, fig. 126).

[404]Since the west side was never completely excavated,
the shape and function of this annex remain uncertain.
Soteriou favored an exonarthex (Palaiochristianikai basilikai,
p. 207) and A. K. Orlandos an atrium (PraktAkAth, 4 [1929],
p. 227; hereafter cited as PraktAkAth, 4; see also Byzantion,
5, p. 210).

[405]Orlandos restored the colonnade with arches because
six impost blocks were found in situ (PraktAkAth, 4, pp.
227ff.; Byzantion, 5, pp. 216-221).

shoulders of the apse.[406] Traces of other important liturgical furnishings, altar, and ambon have not survived.[407]

The mosaic pavements are concentrated in the most prominent liturgical zones of the church--nave, transept, and
apse[408]--and clearly reflect and accentuate the formal
arrangement and internal divisions of these areas (pls. 295-
298). Surrounded by decorative borders or simple bands, each
mosaic panel extends the length and width of its respective
area, but rarely exceeding the limits imposed by the stylobates, arches, doors, chancel screen and thresholds. This
strict delimitation of the mosaic pavements by the architecture is very pronounced in the nave-bema zone. A narrow
mosaic threshold panel (not indicated on plan, pl. 295; see
pl. 296) serves as a transition between the brick pavement in

---

[406]In two illustrations, the reconstruction of the transept and apse is incorrect because they show the chancel
screen abutting the shoulders of the apse (Byzantion, 5, p.
211, fig. 2 = Xylostegos basilikē, p. 499, fig. 458). For
the correct form, see Orlandos, Xylostegos basilikē, p. 526,
fig. 490 and our pl. 295.

[407]The present stone ambon is a later addition (vide
infra, p. 265, and n. 413). There is general agreement that
the main synthronon was located in the semi-circular apse and
that the steps abutting the shoulders of the apse functioned
both as a stairway to the raised apse and as subsidiary
synthrona (Byzantion, 5, p. 212; PraktAkAth, 4, p. 229;
Orlandos, Xylostegos basilikē, pp. 498-499; Soteriou, Palaiochristianikai basilikai, p. 228). Low masonry benches,
possibly later additions, lay along the walls of the south
wing of the transept, VIII, and covered the tessellated band
(Byzantion, 5, p. 209, n. 2, pl. 32; PraktAkAth, 4, p. 229,
fig. 3).

[408]The aisles and the narthex were paved with simple
brick slabs (0.31 sq and 0.06 deep).

the narthex and the tessellated carpet in the nave, while a truncated "Tau-shaped" section bridges the space between the end of the nave panel and the chancel screen in the bema (pl. 308). The unusual shape of this second threshold panel, and of the bema mosaic, as well, is dictated by the stylobates for the columns of the triumphal arch and by the form of the chancel unit enclosing the clergy-altar site. No such transitional panels exist between the north and south wings and the bema, or between the wings and the side aisles.

Conclusive evidence of the contemporaneity of the architectural and decorative programs is supplied by the inscription on the east side of the nave which states that the donors, the most illustrious Eugeneios and his wife Dionyseia filled the church from the foundations " . . . CYMΠANTO ΕΡΓΟΝ ΤΗC . . . ΕΚΛΗCΙΑC ΕΚ ΘΕΜΕΛΙΩΝ ΕΠΛΗΡΩCAN." Although no datable archaeological finds were unearthed or reported, on the basis of the style of the architecture, sculpture, and mosaics, the church has been attributed to the period between the end of the fourth and the beginning of the fifth century.[409]

Bibliography. A. K. Orlandos, PraktAkAth, 4 (1929), pp. 226-231; idem, Byzantion, 5 (1929/30), pp. 207-228; idem, Xylostegos basilikē, pp. 207-208; Kautzsch, Kapitellstudien,

---

[409]Byzantion, 5, pp. 205ff, especially pp. 225, 227; PraktAkAth, 4, p. 162 and nn. 2, 4, 6, and passim (Sodini, Catalogue, p. 710, incorrectly states that Orlandos proposed a date in the first half of the fifth century); Soteriou, Palaiochristianikai basilikai, p. 208; Kautzsch, Kapitell-studien, p. 166; Krautheimer, Tripartite Transept, pp. 418-419; idem, Architecture, p. 328, n. 45.

p. 166; Krautheimer, <u>Tripartite Transept</u>, pp. 418-419; idem, <u>Architecture</u>, p. 328, n. 45.

Illustrations. A. K. Orlandos, <u>Byzantion</u>, 5 (1929/30), p. 208, fig. 1 (ground plan), p. 211, fig. 2 (view of transept and apse: restored), p. 214, fig. 4 (chancel plaque), p. 215, fig. 5 (detail of nave columns: restored), p. 218, fig. 7 (nave capitals with post blocks), p. 220, fig. 8 (longitudinal section of church: restored), p. 222, fig. 8 = our pl. 295, pl. 32 (transept, looking south), pl. 33 (nave, looking east: restored), pl. 34 (nave, looking east); idem, <u>PraktAkAth</u>, 4 (1929), p. 229, fig. 3 (transept, looking north); idem, <u>Xylostegos basilikē</u>, p. 172, fig. 126 (ground plan, p. 524, fig. 490 (chancel barrier: restored).

Nos. 88-92

Simple in design and color, the purely geometric mosaics in the nave, III, transept, VI-VIII, and apse, IX, contain homogeneous decorative schemes consisting of various combinations of interlocking, intersecting or juxtaposed octagons, circles, and squares (pls. 296-314). The clarity and precision with which the two-dimensional, ornamental patterns are arranged across the surface of each compartment result from light and dark color contrasts, and from uncomplicated filling motifs, primarily geometric, which are carefully and neatly inserted into each unit. The austere geometricity of the pavements is heightened by the simple color scheme which is bichrome in its general effect and emphasis (dark bluish grey and white) with red, buff, maroon, and green serving primarily as highlights.

In attributing the mosaics to the late fourth or the early fifth century, A. K. Orlandos notes the simplicity of

the compositions, the "antique" influence and the "Hellenistic themes," the absence of Christian ornamental motifs, and
the character of the letters of the inscription (pls. 300-
302).[410] Citing parallels in other areas of the Greek East,
E. Kitzinger attributes the mosaics to the late fourth century.[411]

Mosaics lifted in 1966, consolidated, and reset.[412]

Additional bibliography. Ch. I. Makaronas, Makedonika, 1
(1940), p. 231; A. K. Orlandos and D. I. Pallas, Praktika,
1959, p. 111, nn. 1-4; Kitzinger, Mosaics in the Greek East,
pp. 343-344; Sodini, Catalogue, No. 17, p. 710.

Illustration. A. K. Orlandos, Byzantion, 5 (1929/30),
p. 222, fig. 9 = our pl. 295.

88 Room III (6.10 x 11.50). Nave; southeast side covered by
a later stone ambon which rests directly on the pavement.[413] Pls. 296, 297, 299-308.

Framing: ca. 0.90. West and central panels, a-b, including
triple fillet: 4.80 x 2.87. East panel, c, including triple
fillet: 4.80 x 3.80. Threshold panel: 0.20 max x 2.10 max.

[410]Byzantion, 5, pp. 225-226; PraktAkAth, 4, pp. 230-231;
Soteriou, Palaiochristianikai, basilikai, p. 208.

[411]Mosaics in the Greek East, pp. 343-344 and nn. 11, 13.
For other pavements reflecting this trend, see 1; 2-3; 4-5;
6-9; 21; 44-49; 130-138; 178-179; 196.

[412]P. Lazarides, Deltion, 21 (1966), B1: Chronika, p.
246, pl. 240a-b (after clearing of site and before the consolidation of the mosaics).

[413]The double-stepped design of the ambon as well as its
placement on top of the mosaic suggest a later addition
(Byzantion, 5, p. 221; PraktAkAth, 4, p. 230).

Marble (dark bluish grey, white, green) and ceramic (red, ochre) tesserae (0.01-0.015 sq) set 2-4mm apart.

Dark bluish grey and white mosaic, with polychrome high-lights, composed of three geometric panels, a-c, set within an overlapping lyre pattern framework and surrounded on three sides by a vine rinceau.

Framing (pls. 299-300): border, except to east, undulating dark grey rinceau (two fillets) forming loosely arranged and widely spaced scrolls filled with single, dark bluish grey, agitated, heart-shaped ivy leaves. Dark grey spiral tendrils spring from the stem of each leaf and from the rinceau itself and form, sometimes, a frame for the curving tips of the leaves. At the tip of each spiral are three to five slightly curved parallel strokes, possibly vestigial leaves or ten-drils; dark bluish grey double fillet; narrow white band.

Field: three panels, set within a lyre framework, deco-rated with simple aniconic geometric designs.

Framework (pls. 299-300): schematic two-strand overlapping lyre pattern with alternating ochre/1 white and red/1 white triangular centers flanked, respectively, by white and red/ochre/1 white strands which are outlined in dark bluish grey and set on a ground of the same color. At the entrance to the bema, it is interrupted by a dark grey and white tabula ansata containing a four-line inscription, in white letters (ca. 0.07 high), terminated by a white ivy leaf (pls. 301-303). Oriented westward, it cites the names of the sponsors of the architectural and decorative programs, Eugeneios and

his wife Dionyseia.

ΕΥΓΕΝ[ΕΙΟCO] ΛΑΜ(ΠΡΟΤΕΡΟ)⁵ [ΚΑΙΔΙΟΝΥC]ΕΙΑ/
[ΥΠΕΡΕΥΧΗCΕΑΥ]ΤΩΝ [ΚΑΙΤΩΝΠΕΔΙ]ΩΝ/
[ΑΥΤΩΝCΥΜΠΑΝΤΟ]ΕΡΓΟΝΤΗC ΑΓΙΑCΤΟΥΘΕΟῩ/
[ΕΚΛΗCΙΑC ΕΚ ΘΕΜΕΛ]ΙΩΝ ΕΠΛΗΡΩCΑΝ   414

IIIa, west panel (pls. 296, 299, 304-305), framed by a
white triple fillet: white intersecting circles (0.27 diam)
forming dark bluish grey concave-sided squares which are
inscribed with small circles. The latter, outlined in red,
contain three crosslets set on an ochre and dark bluish grey
ground. The design is bisected along the margins (for
similar patterns in the same building, see pls. 307-308,
313).415

IIIb, central panel (pls. 296, 306), framed by a white
triple fillet which forms, at the same time, part of the
design: white on dark bluish grey network composed of tangent octagons (0.37 diam) forming squares set on edge (0.24).

414Since its discovery, almost half of the inscription
has been destroyed. The accurate reading of the word God is
"ΘΕΟῩ" not "ΘῩ" (cf. Byzantion, 5, p. 226, fig. 14, p. 227
[top]; PraktAkAth, 4, p. 230). Another error in transcrip-
tion involves "ΑΓΙΑC" which is incorrectly reproduced as
"ΑΠΑC" (Byzantion, 5, p. 226, fig. 14). The title
"ΛΑΜΠΡΟΤΕΡΟC" appears in another early church at
Demetrias (130, 136).

415Sodini (Catalogue, p. 710) makes a distinction between the designs in the west panel of the nave and the south
transept (pls. 304-305, 313) and the east panel of the nave
(pl. 307). The former group he terms quatrefoils, the latter
intersecting circles. I see no difference.

These motifs interlock to form oblique four-armed cross patterns across the surface. The octagons are filled with white swastikas and circles which are, with few exceptions, alternately placed. The circles enclose small squares or circles inscribed with quatrefoils or geometric motifs which follow no consistent compositional or chromatic sequence. The foliate motifs, lanceolate and ivy leaves, and lotiform flowers, are either white and placed on a red ground or red on a white ground, producing a light-dark or dark-light contrast and a clear articulation of the individual motifs. The geometric forms are also sharply defined. Thus, diagonal red squares with white crosslets are set on white straight squares and a Solomon's knot contains strands (white/dark bluish grey/light green; white/dark bluish grey/ochre) which are placed on a red ground. The other components of the composition, the small squares set on edge, are decorated with alternating white, ochre, white, red hour glass motifs.

Beginning with the first medallion to the northwest and moving eastward, the sequence of filling elements is as follows. First row: swastika; quatrefoil with ivy leaves; swastika; quatrefoil with lotiform flowers; swastika; four lotiform flowers separated by diagonal lanceolate leaves. Second row: quatrefoil with lanceolate leaves; swastika; Solomon's knot; swastika; destroyed; swastika. Third row: destroyed; Solomon's knot (?); swastika; quatrefoil with ivy leaves; swastika; quatrefoil with lanceolate leaves. Fourth row: quatrefoil with lanceolate leaves; swastika; concentric

circles; swastika; quatrefoil with lanceolate leaves; swastika. Fifth row: destroyed; square set on edge with central
crosslet; swastika; quatrefoil with lotiform flowers; plain
white medallion (ancient or modern repair); destroyed. Sixth
row: concentric circles (?); swastika; destroyed; swastika;
square set on edge with central crosslet; swastika. Seventh
row: quatrefoil with lanceolate leaves; swastika; hexafoil;
quatrefoil with lanceolate leaves; swastika; square set on
edge with central crosslet. Eighth row: swastika; quatrefoil with ivy leaves; swastika; swastika; square set on edge
with central crosslet; swastika.

IIIc, east panel (pl. 307), framed by a white triple fillet
which forms, at the same time, part of the design: this
third and largest panel is decorated with a dark bluish grey
on white design composed of large intersecting circles (0.77
diam) forming concave-sided squares set on edge (for a similar design, see 100, pl. 353). The design is bisected along
the margins. The concave-sided squares are inscribed in the
center with concentric straight squares and, in each angle,
with a small triangle. Tangent to the angles of each square
are four smaller squares which are accented by flanking
darts. The polychrome highlights are restricted to the filling elements and follow no particular chromatic system.

Threshold panel to west (pl. 296):[416] part of a rectangular

416This is not noted by Orlandos in his plan (Byzantion,
5, p. 222, fig. 9 = our pl. 295), nor by Sodini (loc. cit.).

270

strip, outlined in dark bluish grey, decorated with a single
row of dark bluish grey intersecting circles forming ogive
arches.

Additional color. East panel, c. Triangles: red, ochre,
or grey, outlined in dark bluish grey. Squares: ochre with
red centers, red with ochre centers, or white with red or
ochre centers, all outlined in dark bluish grey; frequently
with a white tessera in the center. Darts: red or dark
bluish grey.

Late fourth or early fifth century.

Illustrations. A. K. Orlandos, Byzantion, 5 (1929/30), p.
226, fig. 13 (drawing of panel c, detail), p. 226, fig. 14
(inscription), pl. 33 (nave, looking east: restored), pl.
34 (nave, looking east), pl. 36 (panel c, detail).

89 Room VI (ca. 6.60 x 5.10). Bema. Pls. 298, 308-310.

Framing: 0.28. Field, including triple fillet: 5.54 x
3.54. Threshold panel, including triple fillet: 5.80 x
1.07. Framing: 0.14. Field: 5.66 x 0.83. Marble (dark
bluish grey, white, green, maroon), limestone (beige), and
ceramic (red, ochre) tesserae (0.01-0.015 sq) set 2-4mm
apart.

Simple black and white geometric designs, with polychrome
highlights, enclosed by decorative borders.

Surround: in rows parallel to the walls.

Framing (pl. 309): dark bluish grey double fillet; narrow

white band; border, two-strand guilloche (1 dark green/beige/
1 white; red/1 maroon/1 white, outlined in dark bluish grey,
with a white tessera at each loop) on a dark bluish grey
ground.

Field, framed by a triple white fillet which forms, at the
same time, part of the design (pls. 309-310): white on dark
bluish grey design composed of tangent octagons (0.29 diam)
set on edge forming four-pointed stars. These motifs interlock to form alternating rows of octagons and stars of which
the latter are bisected along the margins (for a similar
design, see 132, pl. 430). Alternately placed within the
octagons are a red circle and a dark bluish grey square, each
containing an identical white square set on edge. The central filling motifs differ, however. The red circles contain
dark bluish grey lanceolate quatrefoils whose leaves are separated by single dark bluish grey tesserae; the dark grey
squares enclose smaller red squares with crosslets of five
white tesserae. The other component of the composition, the
four-pointed star pattern, is inscribed with a white square
enclosing concentric grey/red squares which sometimes contain
white centers. White highlights are also present in the subsidiary spaces between the major motifs.

Threshold panel (pl. 308) in the form of a truncated "Tau,"
decorated with a geometric design.

Framing: dark bluish y triple fillet: border, dark
bluish grey and white stepped triangles.

Field, framed by a white triple fillet: white intersecting

circles (0.24 diam) forming dark bluish grey concave-sided squares which are inscribed with small circles. The latter, outlined in red, contain white crosslets set on a buff and dark bluish grey ground. The design is bisected along the margins.[417]

Late fourth or early fifth century.

Illustrations. A. K. Orlandos, Byzantion, 5 (1929/30, p. 211, fig. 2 (transept and apse: restored), p. 224, fig. 12, (border between bema and north wing, detail), pl. 32 (transept, looking south), pl. 35 = our pl. 310; idem, PraktAkAth, 4 (1929), p. 229, fig. 3 (transept, looking north).

90   Room VI (5.30 x 4.95). North wing of transept; later bases for columns installed in the southeast and southwest corners covering the pavement.[418] Pls. 311-312.

Framing: 0.45; to south, 0.60. Field, including triple fillet: 4.25 x 4.05. Dark bluish grey and white marble tesserae (0.01-0.015 sq) set 2-4mm apart.

White on dark bluish grey pavement decorated with intersecting octagons and a foliate border.

Framing (pl. 311): white band; border, undulating rinceau (two fillets) forming loosely arranged and widely spaced scrolls filled with a single, agitated, heart-shaped ivy leaves. A spiral tendril springs from the stem of each leaf

---

[417]Contrary to the plan, pl. 295, the mosaic extends the full length and width of this area.

[418]PraktAkAth, 4, p. 227; see also the south wing (91).

and is framed at the tip by four slightly curving parallel
strokes, possibly vestigial leaves or tendrils.[419] (for similar borders in the same building, see pls. 299-300, 314).

Field, framed by a white triple fillet which forms, at the
same time, part of the design: traces of a rectilinear
design composed of intersecting octagons forming squares which
are decorated with crosslets of five white tesserae. Within
the elongated hexagons created by the intersection of the
octagons are small white circles flanked by three white tesserae forming rudimentary "eye motifs."

Late fourth or early fifth century.

Illustrations. A. K. Orlandos, Byzantion, 5 (1929/30), p.
223, fig. 10 = our pl. 312, p. 225, fig. 12 (border between
bema and north wing, detail); idem, PraktAkAth, 4 (1929), p.
229, fig. 3 (looking north).

91 Room VIII (5.40 x 4.92). South wing of transept; bases
    for columns installed in the northeast and northwest
corners and a masonry bench along the walls, covering the
pavement. Pl. 313.

Framing: 0.50-0.60. Field, including triple fillet: ca.
4.30 x 3.92. Marble (dark bluish grey, white) tesserae (0.01-
0.015 sq) set 2-4mm apart.

----

[419]Orlandos notes the presence of this foliate border on
the south side only, the other three sides having a wide undecorated band (Byzantion, 5, pp. 223-224 and our pl. 295).
This error is repeated by Sodini (Catalogue, p. 710).

Black and white geometric design framed by a plain band.

Framing: wide dark bluish grey band.

Field, framed by a white triple fillet (pl. 313): white
intersecting circles (0.24 diam) forming dark bluish grey
concave-sided squares which are inscribed with white crosslets composed of five white tesserae.

Late fourth or early fifth century.

Illustrations. A. K. Orlandos, Byzantion, 5 (1929/30), p.
224, fig. 11 (drawing of field, detail), pl. 32 (transept,
looking south); idem, PraktAkAth, 4 (1929), p. 229, fig. 3
(transept, looking north).

92 Room IX (1.40 diam). Apse. Pl. 314.

Fragment: 0.30 long. Material identical to that in the
preceding entry (91).

Traces of a white on black border.

Described as being bordered by a smaller version of the ivy
rinceau in Room VII (pl. 311) but with "blue flowers."
Destroyed, except for an undulating white double fillet forming small, closely spaced scrolls (pl. 314).[420]

Late fourth or early fifth century.

---

[420]The closely spaced scrolls in this fragment indicate
a rinceau which differs from Orlandos' description and reconstruction (Byzantion, 5, pp. 224-225, p. 211, fig. 2). It
appears that there was evidence of a field design (loc. cit.,
with reference to "Planche I" which does not accompany the
article).

SAINT CONSTANTINE

Basilica

In the village of Saint Constantine, north of Arkitsa, traces of an Early Christian basilica with a mosaic pavement were found in 1966.[421] The pavement was covered until a systematic excavation could be undertaken.

Although no datable finds were unearthed or reported, the iconography of the pavement provides a means of establishing a terminus post quem of the first half of the fifth century.

Bibliography. N. Pharaklas, B. Philippake, and S. Symeonoglou, Deltion, 22 (1967), Bl: Chronika, p. 246; P. Lazarides, Deltion, 22 (1967), Bl: Chronika, pp. 292-293.

No. 93

93 Mosaic pavement (no dimensions published).

No published information on dimensions and material.

Brief mention of a pavement decorated with "circles inscribed with squares, dolphins, etc."[422] Since the pavement contains

---

[421]The pavement is approximately ten meters south of the modern church of St. Constantine where another pavement with an inscription was found at the same time beneath the north aisle. No date was suggested for this second pavement. (N. Pharaklas, B. Philippake, and S. Symeonoglou, Deltion, 22 (1967), Bl: Chronika, p. 246).

[422]Ibid.; P. Lazarides, Deltion, 22 (1967), Bl: Chronika, pp. 292-293.

organic filling motifs, it can be assigned to a period no
earlier than the middle of the fifth century.

KLAPSI

Basilica

In the village of Klapsi, about six kilometers from
Karpenision, an Early Christian triconch basilica (overall,
18.50 x 28.00) was excavated in 1958 and 1959, bringing to
light seven mosaic pavements (pl. 315). At the present time,
the building is protected by a concrete and wooden enclosure.

Preceded by a narthex, I, the main body of the church
consists of a nave flanked by two aisles, II-IV, and a transverse tripartite transept with projecting conches and a raised
semi-circular apse, V-VIII. The nave is separated from the
aisles by pillars set on elevated stylobates[423] and the central bay of the transept is separated from the south wing, at
least, by an arcade of two arches.[424] Evidence of other internal divisions and the major entrances have not survived.[425]

---

[423]The pillars may have supported arcades (E. Chatzidakis,
Praktika, 1958, p. 60; hereafter cited as Praktika, 1958;
idem, Praktika, 1959, p. 35; hereafter cited as Praktika,
1959).

[424]Praktika, 1958, p. 60.

[425]The only preserved passageway is the small opening
(0.60-0.65 wide) on the west side of the south transept
(Praktika, 1958, p. 60). The reconstruction of a similar
opening on the west side of the north transept, as it appears
on a plan after the excavation of 1958 (pl. 315), was

A synthronon and an altar were found in the bema along with the marble foundations of a canopy which was installed sometime after the room was paved.[426] Traces of other liturgical furnishings, ambon and chancel barrier, have not survived.

Although no archaeological finds were unearthed or reported, on the basis of the style of the architecture, the church can be assigned to the sixth century when triconch churches began to appear.[427] In a subsequent period, the colonnades were blocked up and walls were built on the east ends of the aisles and on the south side of the north wing.[428] Whether or not the canopy belongs to this period, or to an earlier or later one, cannot be determined.

---

subsequently eliminated after the 1959 excavation (Praktika, 1959, p. 35). No plan of the results of the latter excavation has appeared.

[426]The foundations clearly cut into the mosaics as do the two blocks on the northwest and southwest corners of the apse.

[427]Two other triconch churches at Dodona and Paramythia have been securely dated to the first half of the sixth century (Soteriou, Palaiochristianikai basilikai, pp. 204-205, fig. 36, [Paramythia], p. 206, fig. 37 [Dodona]; Krautheimer, Tripartite Transept, p. 422, n. 232; Orlandos, Xylostegos basilike, pp. 172-173, figs. 128, 132; D. I. Pallas, RAC, 35 [1959], pp. 195-196, fig. 9; Krautheimer, Architecture, p. 189, and n. 16; Sodini, Catalogue, p. 717 and n. 31).

[428]The walls are omitted from the plan (pl. 315). Except for briefly noting their presence, the excavator is silent on the relationship of these walls to the function and plan of the building (Praktika, 1958, p. 60). In the only published photograph showing them in situ (pl. 333), they have since been removed, it appears that the walls of the south colonnade and the east side of the south aisle met. This suggests that the south aisle, at least, was blocked off from the nave and probably fell into disuse.

Bibliography. BCH, 81 (1957), p. 581; E. Chatzidakis, Praktika, 1958, pp. 58-63; A. K. Orlandos, To Ergon, 1958, pp. 63-68; D. I. Pallas, RAC, 35 (1959), pp. 191-193; E. Chatzidakis, Praktika, 1959, pp. 34-36; A. K. Orlandos, To Ergon, 1959, pp. 31-33; BCH, 83 (1959), pp. 663-664; JHS, 79 (1959), Supplement, p. 11.

Illustrations. E. Chatzidakis, Praktika, 1958, p. 59, fig. 1 = our pl. 315; pl. 47 = our pl. 333; idem, Praktika, 1959, pl. 33a (north conch), pl. 35a (south conch).

Nos. 94-100

Mosaic pavements decorate all the floors of the building.[429] With the possible exception of the mosaic in the north aisle, the pavements are suffused with organic motifs, especially animals, birds and fish (pls. 316-320, 324, 335, 338, 339). These motifs occupy many of the small insets in the geometric designs and are shown, as well, in large scale compositions. This iconographic homogeneity is accompanied by a stylistic and technical similitude in which the figures and the geometric configurations in the borders and fields are rendered in an abstract and stylized manner. Throughout the church the tesserae are irregular in size and placement, and the chromatic scheme is based on various combinations of dark grey, ivory, and red, with greens and yellows serving only as highlights. These factors suggest a common workshop for the pavements and this, to some extent, is substantiated

---

[429]Missing from the plan (pl. 315) are the pavements in the narthex, and the north and south transepts.

by the epigraphical evidence.[430] The name of a reader and
steward, Melissos, is cited in tessellated inscriptions in
the nave, II, and bema, V, so that these pavements, at least,
belong to the same program. Since the remaining pavements
closely resemble those bearing Melissos' name, their contemporaneity is evident. Other donors are cited in the pavements: Polygēros, another reader, and Andromacha, a deaconess, in the bema; Evtychianos and Polykarpos, two priests,
John, a sub-deacon, and other members of the clergy in the
east compartment of the nave; an anonymous deacon in the west
compartment of the nave; Didymos, perhaps a lay person, in
the north conch. The inscriptions, therefore, record the
names of two priests, other members of the clergy, a deacon,
sub-deacon, deaconess and two readers. Although these people
have yet to be identified, it is clear that a rather large
ecclesiastical community existed somewhere in the vicinity of
the church and that, moreover, it belonged to an episcopal
see which at that time was under the jurisdiction of a bishop
Aimelianos whose name is recorded in the east compartment of
the nave. Unfortunately, the bishop cannot be identified so
that the specific location of his seat and his tenure as
bishop cannot be ascertained from the historical sources.[431]

---

[430]For a different opinion, see Praktika, 1958, p. 60.
Sodini also favors a common workshop (Catalogue, p. 717, n.
30).

[431]See P. I. Basileiou, "Aimilianos," Thrēskevtikē kai
ēthikē enkyklopaideia, col. 1052. Nothing is recorded in the
CIG or in published episcopal lists (B. A. Mustakidos,

Since, however, the style of the architecture belongs to the sixth century, it is probable that Aimelianos presided during that century. The eleventh indication (IA'), therefore, which terminates the inscription citing his name corresponds to the eleventh indication of the sixth century which begins with the year 503 and continues for fifteen year intervals until the end of the century.[432]

The style of the pavements substantiates the sixth century date. They resemble the mosaics in Basilica Alpha at Nikopolis (150, 152-155, pls. 460-464, 466-532) which, although technically superior, also contain flat, two-dimensional organic and geometric forms.[433]

Pavements lifted in 1966, consolidated, and reset; protected by an enclosure.[434]

Additional bibliography. Sodini, Catalogue, No. 33, pp. 716-717.

Illustration. E. Chatzidakis, Praktika, 1958, p. 59, fig. 1 = our pl. 315.

"Episkopoi katalogi," EEBS, 12 [1936], pp. 151ff., especially lists for Lamia, Larissa, Nafpactos, Arta, and Nikopolos).

[432]That is, 503, 518, 535, 548, 563, 578, 593 (V. Grumel, Traité d'études byzantines, Vol. 1: La chronologie, Paris, 1958, p. 314). A terminus ante quem of 551 was suggested in one report when an earthquake devastated the region. (Praktika, 1958, p. 63).

[433]See also, Praktika, 1958, p. 63.

[434]E. Chatzidakis, Deltion, 21 (1966), B1: Chronika, p. 19; P. Lazarides, Deltion, 21 (1966), B2: Chronika, pp. 238, 274-275.

94 Room I (original dimensions indeterminable). Narthex.

Fragment: 1.20 x 2.45. Tesserae (average, 0.01 sq) set 1-3mm apart.

Dark grey on ivory geometric design of poor quality and technique.

Fragment with traces of a meander border and a field design of intersecting octagons of which one contains an organic filling motif, probably a bird.[435]

First half of the sixth century.

95 Room II (5.65 x 14.42). Nave; signs of fire in central and east sectors. Pls. 315-331.

West compartment, a: 5.65 x 9.35. Framing: 1.05. West panel, including border: 2.00 max x 2.40. Central panel, including border: 2.10 max x 2.06. East panel: 3.60 max x 2.65. Tabula ansata: 3.20 x 0.43. East compartment, b: 5.58 x 4.60. Framing: 0.89. Field, including double fillet: 3.80 x 2.82. Irregularly-cut tesserae (average, 0.01 sq; 0.005 for some details in west panel), set 1-3mm apart.

Polychrome pavement composed of two large rectangular

---

[435]It is omitted from the plan (pl. 315). A report also notes the inferior quality of the fragment (Praktika, 1959, p. 35). Sodini notes "a pavement decorated with motifs inserted into a geometric network" (Catalogue, p. 716).

compartments, a-b, inscribed with figural and geometric
designs and three inscriptions.

IIa, west compartment: three panels enclosed by a double
border.[436]

Framing: dark grey double fillet; outer border (0.20),
narrow row of single red intersecting circles forming dark
grey ovals (pl. 322); dark grey double fillet; inner border
(pls. 315, 322), chain of interlaced squares set on edge
(ivory; red, outlined by white/black single fillets) which are
laced along the margins by a continuous undulating strand
(grey green, outlined by white/dark grey single fillets).[437]
In the center of each square is a concave-sided red square,
outlined in dark grey; white double fillet.

West panel (pl. 316).

Framing: two-strand guilloche (0.20; red; ivory, outlined
by white/dark grey double fillets); ivory double fillet;
dark grey double fillet.

Field: traces of the profile body and frontal tail covert
of a peacock, outlined in dark grey, standing amid spreading
dark green grape vines.[438] Its grey and white body is flecked

---

[436]Sodini only describes the inner border (loc. cit.).

[437]A similar border was executed at Thebes (75, pls.
225, 231) and Delphi (83, pl. 256).

[438]At the time of its discovery, the peacock's body was
intact along with two clusters of grapes (cf. out pl. 316 and
Praktika, 1958, pl. 49b). E. Chatzidakis restores the composition with two confronting peacocks flanking a vase
(Praktika, 1958, p. 62).

with dark green, blue and red (all glass) while its trailing
ocellate tail covert is decorated with two rows of brilliant
eyes composed of dark red (glass), dark green (glass) and
white tesserae. Portions of two dark grey inscriptions (0.07-
0.08 high) are preserved in the panel. The first, located
along the northeast side and oriented northward, contains the
letters "[ ]ΟCΔΕΚΑΝSΔΕΟΜΕΝ ΑΓS ."[439] The second inscription is inserted on the west side and is oriented in that
direction: "ΕΝΤΗΖ[ ]ΤΑΡΑΜ[ ]."[440]

Central panel (pls. 317-318).

Framing: dark grey double fillet; border, red and white
wave crests; dark grey fillet; ivory double fillet.

Field, framed by a dark grey double fillet: sea creatures
swim across the surface of the panel. Dominating the scene
is the arched body of a large light and dark grey dolphin with
ivory stripes and red fins (pl. 317) which is devouring the
tail fin of an inverted lavender and ivory fish. Beneath
the dolphin (pl. 318) is another fish with a similarly curved
ivory and red body and grey fins. Its segmented tail fin
almost touches the body of an ivory and white squid while its
head is turned toward a dark grey eel which moves sinuously
toward the dolphin above. Scattered around this nucleus are

---

[439]"ΑΓS" is incorrectly transcribed as "ΑΓϨ" in the
Praktika, 1956, p. 62.

[440]Although omitted from the report, it is shown in the
plan (pl. 315) which has a different transcription from mine
(ΠΑΓΑΜΟΝ).

red and light grey worms, another squid (dark grey), eel (dark grey), and fish (grey and white) which, for the most part, are only partially preserved.

East panel (pls. 319-320), framed by an ivory double fillet: dark grey and ivory network of alternating octagons (ca. 0.45 diam) and equilateral crosses (0.50 sq) forming elongated hexagons. The hexagons have been changed to irregular tetragons along the margins (for a purely aniconic version of this design, see 137, pl. 440). The octagons, disposed in alternating rows of two and three on the main axis of the church, are filled with schematic geometric and floral motifs, and with six figures in profile which face in various directions. Beginning with the first octagon to the northeast and moving southward, the sequence of filling elements is as follows.[441] First row: two-strand Solomon's knot (ivory, outlined in dark grey); rosette composed of four heart-shaped ivy leaves set tip-to-tip (two ivory, two grey with white edge, outlined in dark grey); land bird surrounded by diagonal bushes with buds; indeterminable color. Second row: rosette composed of four heart-shaped ivy leaves (same colors as first); fish with curved body surrounded by worms (damaged; some grey and yellow); destroyed, but on plan (pl. 315) a land bird oriented eastward. Third row: ivory and light green pelican (pl. 319)

---

[441]The following errors and omissions are evident in the drawing of this panel (pl. 315). Third row: pelican, not a rosette; traces of a bird in the adjacent blank panel. Fourth row: whorl. Fifth row: add dolphins.

oriented northward, pecking at a large ivory and light grey fish; traces of a bird. Fourth row: two-strand whorl (red/ 1 white; ivory, outlined in dark grey) on a red ground; two-strand Solomon's knot (same colors as first). Fifth row: ivory and white bird with red breast and wing surrounded by three red buds or dolphins (pl. 320); destroyed, but in plan (pl. 315) a bird oriented westward. The crosses separating the octagons are decorated with two-strand red guilloches, outlined in ivory, while the elongated hexagons are filled with stylized floral trilobes composed of single reels flanked either by lanceolate leaves or curling tendrils. A single leaf, usually heart-shaped, accents the truncated panels along the margin. The east side of the panel is occupied by a tabula ansata containing a three-line inscription in dark grey letters (0.09 high). Oriented westward, it cites the names of a bishop, Aimelianos, two priests, Evtychianos and Polycarpos, a reader and steward, Melissos, and the eleventh indication (pl. 321).

ЄΠΙΤΟΥΑΓΙωΤΑΤϹЄΠΙϹΚϹΗΜωΝΑΙΜЄ[ ]ΙΑΝΟΥΚЄΠΡϹ/
ЄΥΤΥΧΙΑΝΟΥΚЄΠΟΛΥΚΡΠΟΥΚЄΜЄ[ ]ΙϹϹΟΥΤΟΥЄΥ
ΛΑΒϹΤϹΑΝΑΓϹΚЄΟΙΚΟ/ΝΟΜΟΥΚЄΠΑΝΤϹΤΟΥΚΛΗ
ΡΟΥЄΓЄΝЄΤΟΗΧΑΜΟΚЄΝΤΗϹΙϹ ΙΝΔ ΙΑʹ ⁴⁴²

---

⁴⁴²The use of the word "ΧΑΜΟΚЄΝΤΗϹΙϹ " for a mosaic pavement appears here for the first time. Previously, the shortened version "ΚЄΝΤΗϹΙϹ " was employed (see 142, pl. 448). This new term is also present in the bema (vide infra, pp. 295-296). For the emendation, see Praktika, 1958, pp. 61-62.

ЄΠΙ ΤΟΥ ΑΓΙωΤ(ΑΤΟΥ) ЄΠΙϹΚ(ΟΠΟΥ) ΗΜωΝ ΑΙΜЄ[Λ]ΙΑΝΟΥ ΚЄ
ΠΡ(Є)Ϲ/(ΒΥΤЄΡωΝ)ЄΥΤΥΧΙΑΝΟΥ ΚЄ ΠΟΛΥΚΑΡΠΟΥ ΚЄ

IIb, east compartment: geometric medallion flanked by two animal friezes.

Framing (pls. 322-323): dark grey double fillet, border, three-strand braid (ivory; grey; red, outlined by white/dark grey single fillets).

Field (pls. 324-331), framed by a dark grey double fillet: in the center, a shield pattern (2.70 diam), outlined in red, composed of concentric rows of dark grey and white triangles radiating from a small central medallion. The latter, outlined in red, contains a light and dark grey land bird, oriented eastward, and an undulating rose bush with a red bud and grey branches. Enframing the north and south sides of the shield are two friezes composed of animals and birds amid spreading vines and plants. Generally, the flora and fauna follow no systematic direction within the compositions and are schematically rendered and irregularly arranged along the curved surface. Except possibly for the two dogs with extended red tongues standing back-to-back (pls. 327-328), the rest of the north frieze is filled with an agglomeration of figures which are compositionally and thematically unrelated to each other. The group in the west corner (pls. 325-327) is composed of a large, ivory-colored bird with a trailing lime tail covert and two small flanking birds which stare

---

ΜΕ[Λ]ΙϹϹΟΥ ΤΟΥ ΕΥΛΑΒ(Ε)ϹΤ [ΑΤΟΥ] ΑΝΑΓ(ΝѠ)Ϲ (ΤΟΥ)
ΚΕ ΟΙΚΟ/ΝΟΜΟΥ ΚΕ ΠΑΝΤ(Ο)Ϲ ΤΟΥ ΚΛΗΡΟΥ ΕΓΕΝΕΤΟ
Η ΧΑΜΟΚΕΝΤΗϹΙϹ ΙΝΔ ΙΑʹ.

at each other. In the opposite corner (pls. 324, 328), the
two birds are turned away from each other: one facing a rose
bush; the other facing a dog. Between the latter group is a
hybrid floral form composed of a green, bell-shaped bud or
blossom, outlined in white/lime (pl. 328), which is decorated
with radiating red lanceolate leaves and a red mouth. The
motif is precariously supported by a dark grey and lime
stalk, with somewhat angular stems, and a triangular red base
situated near the bottom of the scene. The remaining plants,
usually bearing lanceolate leaves, have similar red triangular bases situated near the bottom of the margin so that
there is a uniformity in the disposition and direction of all
the flora. Generally, a uniform color scheme obtains as
well: grey stems; red or dark green leaves. All the
elements in this frieze are flat and two-dimensional and, for
the most part, crudely executed. With the exception of some
polychromy in the small birds, the figures are bichromatic
with the major portions of their bodies rendered in the same
ivory color as the ground. The absence of a sharp contrast
between the bodies and the ground, and between the bodies and
their lime outlines, reduces the clarity of the forms, sometimes to the point of illegibility.

In the south frieze (pls. 324, 329-331), the forms are
much more clearly defined because darker colors are used.
The scene is dominated by two running animals: a dark grey
boar with lime, dark green, ochre, and pink striations; a

greenish grey donkey or dog[443] whose body is delineated by white and orange strokes. Below the hind legs of this curious hybrid, stands a small bird facing westward while the opposite corner to the east is decorated with a large, long-necked vase with pelta-shaped handles and a circular foot set on a curving triangular base.[244] Thick, dark grey vines issue from the tipped mouth of the vase and fill the surrounding area with large bunches of red and grey grapes, grey, trident-shaped leaves, curling tendrils, and one red rose bud. Unlike the similarly colored flora in the north frieze, the plants spring from the top and corners of the scene, not the bottom. Along the west side of the field, is a one-line grey inscription in which a sub-deacon, John, asks St. Leonidas to protect him: " ΑΓΙΕΛΕωΝΔΗΦΥΛΑΞΟΝΤΟΝΔΟΥΛΟΝ COΥΙωΑΝΝΗΝΥΠΟΔΙΑΚ_ς ."[445]

Additional color. IIa, west compartment. Central panel. Marine creatures: generally, ivory/dark grey outlines with ivory details and red gills. East panel. Pelican: outlined in dark green with red legs and beak; fish, outlined in dark

---

[443]The figure has an equine body, head, and ears. Its long curling tail and protruding tongue, however, are similar to the features of the dogs in the north frieze. If this animal is supposed to be a dog, then it is probable that the model for the scenes in both friezes was a boar hunt.

[444]Except for different handles, an identical vase occupies the south conch (pl. 350).

[445]For the transcription and emendation, see Praktika, 1958, p. 61: " ΑΓΙΕ ΛΕωΝΔΗ ΦΥΛΑΞΟΝ ΤοΝ ΔΟΥΛΟΝ COΥ ΙωΑΝΝΗΝ ΥΠΟΔΙΑΚ(ΟΝΟΝ)."

grey with red gills. IIb, east compartment. Medallion.
Bird: body, some pink and green, outlined and delineated in
red. North frieze. Dog facing east: ivory with an ochre
belly, lime outline, grey eye. Large bird and small one in
front of it: outlined and delineated in lime. Small bird in
northwest corner, facing north: light and dark green with
red and white collar rings and wings; lime outline. Small
bird in northeast corner, facing east: green and ochre with
light green in wings; outlined and delineated in lime. Small
bird in northeast corner facing west: grey and ivory checkerboard pattern; outlined and delineated in lime. South
frieze. Boar: dark grey bristles and dark green outline
along forelegs and belly; dark grey eye and white marking on
head. Dog (?): red and white delineations and dark greyish
green outlines. Bird: indeterminable color.

First half of the sixth century.

   Illustrations. E. Chatzidakis, Praktika, 1958, pl. 48a
(IIb, from northwest), pl. 49a = our pl. 321, pl. 49b (IIa,
west panel), pl. 50b, (IIa, central panel); A. K. Orlandos,
To Ergon, 1958, p. 67, fig. 59 = our pl. 324.

96 Room III (2.65 x ca. 12.00). North aisle; to east block-
    ed by a later rubble wall which was set on the pavement;
subsequently removed by the excavator. Pls. 315, 332.
   Two fragments: larger one toward east, 2.65 x 5.40,

including surround.[446]   Framing: ca. 0.57. Field, including
double fillet: ca. 1.51 x 4.90 max. Material identical to
that in Room II (95).

Fragment decorated with a complex interlace design bordered
by small rectangles and squares.

   Surround to south: in rows parallel to the stylobate.[447]

   Framing: dark grey double fillet; ivory double fillet;
border, alternating squares (0.57) and rectangles (0.57 x
0.49), outlined by ivory or black double fillets. The
squares are segmented by red double fillets forming eight
units which alternate white and white with red centers. The
rectangles are filled with various motifs, primarily geometric, which follow no consistent order: scales; Solomon's
knots; concentric circles; schematic rosettes and others
which are rendered in various combinations of dark grey,
ivory, and red; double white fillet.

   Field (pl. 332), framed by a dark grey double fillet: two-
strand interlace (red; grey, outlined by white/dark grey
single fillets) of circles forming concave-sided octagons set
on edge. The design is bisected along the margin. An abrupt
alteration in the size and decoration of the major units

---

   [446]The smaller fragment to the west (1.80 x 1.60) is in
bad condition and is omitted from the plan (pl. 315).

   [447]The undecorated area between the border and the
stylobate (on the plan pl. 315) is occupied by an ivory
surround.

produces a shift in the optical effect and focus of the
design. On the east side the emphasis is on the concave-
sided octagonal units (1.60 diam) with the circles (ca. 0.14-
0.18 diam) serving as subordinate elements (pl. 332, bottom).
This effect is increased by the presence of solid octagonal
filling motifs in the octagons which are inscribed with
circles or checkerboard patterns. The circles, on the other
hand, are not only proportionately very small, but empty.
The predominance of the octagons is maintained for only two
and one half rows at which point, and for the rest of the
pavement (pl. 332, top), the octagons become smaller (1.35-
1.40 diam) and the circles larger (0.45-0.50 diam). In conjunction with this change, the circles receive floral filling
motifs, oriented westward, while the motifs in the octagons
are reduced to red octagonal fillets. As a result, the
octagons and circles become coequal elements of the design.[448]
The reason for the alteration of the design is difficult to
ascertain. There is no evidence of a restoration of the
pavement. The style, technique, and material are identical
in the two sections and there are no seams or sutures at the
juncture between them.[449]

---

[448]The drawing (pl. 315) omits this change. For similar
interlaces with coequal elements, see 2, pl. 8; 6, pls. 14-
16; 18, pls. 38, 51; 19, pls. 53-54; 160, pls. 460-461. For
a pavement in which the octagons predominate, vide supra, p.
44, and n. 81, pls. 40, 42-43.

[449]The two seams visible in the photograph (pl. 332, top
and bottom) represent repairs when the mosaic was reset in
situ.

Additional color. Octagons: red with black circle outlined in white; ivory with red center; red and grey checkerboard; all outlined in dark grey. Circles. Plants: dark
grey leaves; ivory and red buds; rest indeterminable.

First half of the sixth century.

97 Room IV (2.65 x 10.50 max). South aisle; pavement laid up
    to the north stylobate.[450] To east, blocked by a later
rubble wall which was set on the pavement; subsequently removed by the excavator. Pls. 333-335.

Two fragments: larger one toward east: 2.54 x 4.22 max.[451]
Framing: 0.30. Squares: 0.69. Material identical to that
in Room II (95).

Fragment decorated with a straight grid with geometric and
figural filling motifs set within a guilloche framework.

Surround to north: in rows parallel to the stylobate.

Framing: dark grey double fillet; ivory double fillet;
dark grey double fillet.

Field, framed by an ivory double fillet: straight grid composed of a two-strand guilloche (ivory; red, outlined by

---

[450]The undecorated area between the border and the
stylobate on the plan (pl. 315) contains an ivory surround.

[451]The smaller fragment to the west (1.60 x 2.57) is in
bad condition and is omitted from the plan (pl. 315). It
contains parts of two panels and the border.

white/dark grey single fillets, with a white tessera at each loop) forming squares. The guilloche bifurcates along the edges of the design to form a continuous border. The squares are inscribed with geometric and figural elements which maintain the chromatic scheme of the guilloche. Starting at the northeast side, their sequence is as follows (pl. 334). First row: three-strand braid (ivory; red; dark grey, outlined by white/dark grey single fillets, with a white tessera at each loop); cruciform interlace (red; dark grey, outlined by white/dark grey single fillets) composed of a central circle and four loops inscribed with a single white tessera. Dark grey and white hour glass motifs decorate the circle while, beyond, red trefoils spring toward the angles of the squares. Second row: traces of an ivory-colored meander pattern forming swastikas set on a dark grey ground; three-strand braid (same colors as first, but with narrower strands composed of one row of colored tesserae). Third row (pls. 333, 335): traces of a leaping grey dog (pl. 335) flanked by dark grey plants; destroyed, but on the plan (pl. 315) it appears to be a hare. Fourth row (pl. 333): traces of a red and white scale pattern, fanning northward.

First half of the sixth century.

Illustration. E. Chatzidakis, _Praktika_, 1958, pl. 47 = our pl. 333.

98 Room V (5.78 x 5.85). Bema; pavement laid up to the
altar site toward the east and to mosaic and stone
thresholds along the north and south sides, respectively.[452]
North side covered by a later wall with a doorway which
rested directly on the pavement; subsequently removed by the
excavator; destroyed by two bases to northeast and southeast
and by four bases of a canopy for the altar. Pls. 336-338.

Framing: 0.68. Inscription at entrance from nave: 1.75 x
0.50. Field: 4.42 x 4.49. Inscription in front of altar:
1.39 x 1.70. Inscription to north: 0.77 x 0.89. Material
identical to that in Room II (95).

Straight grid forming rectangles of varying dimensions which
are inscribed with geometric and figural filling motifs.

Surround to west only: in rows parallel to the east-west
axis.

Framing: dark grey double fillet; border (pl. 315), row of
juxtaposed dark grey circles (0.47) crossed by red quatrefoils, outlined by white/grey single fillets. The border is
interrupted at the west entrance to the bema by a four-line
inscription in dark grey letters (ca. 0.09-0.010 high) which
at the time of its discovery was damaged extensively:
"[ ]ΟΥΠΡΕCΒΥΤΕΡC/[ ] ΟΥ/[ ] ΑC/[ ]ΤC;"[453] dark grey

---

[452]I found no evidence of stone "threshold slabs" along
the northeast side (see Praktika, 1959, p. 35).

[453]Praktika, 1958, p. 61. In 1969, only some of the
letters in the first row were preserved: "[ ]ΕΒΥΤΕΡ[ ]/
[ ]ΟΥ."

double fillet; ivory fillet.

Field, framed by an ivory double fillet: straight grid
composed of a two-strand guilloche (ivory; red; dark grey,
outlined by white/dark grey single fillets, with a white tessera at each loop) on a dark ground forming rectangles (pls.
336-338). The guilloche bifurcates along the edges of the
design to form a continuous border. The rectangular panels
surrounding the altar site are inscribed with figural and
geometric motifs and with inscriptions citing the names of
the donors. The largest inscription is situated in front of
the altar and contains thirteen lines of dark grey letters
(0.11 high) which are oriented westward. At the time of its
discovery, lacunae existed and, since then, it has suffered
additional damage.

ΕΠ[ ]ΑΝ/ΝΟ[ ]ΝΘΕ/ΟΦΙΛ[ ]ΠΡΕΣ/ΒΥΤΕΡωΝ[ ]ΛΙССΟΥ/
ΤΟΥΘΕΟΦ[ ]СΤΑΤΟΥ/ΑΝΑΓΝΟСΤΟΥΚΑΙΟΙΚΟ/ΝΟΜΟΥΤΗС
ΕΝΘΑΔΕ/ΑΓΙωΤΑΤΗСΕΚΛΗСΙΑС/ΚΕΠΑΝΤΟС[ ]ΘΕΟΦΙΛΗ/
[ ]ΟΥΑ[ ]СΘΗΟΑΓΙ/[ ]ΟΟ[ ]ΝΕΝΔΟΞΟΥ/[ ]ΥΛΕ[ ]
ΔΟΥΚΑΙΕΤΕΝΕ/ΤΟ[ ]СΧΑΜΟΚΕΝΤΗСΕΟСΕΡΓ[ ]   [454]

Since the inscription contains the words priests
(ΠΡΕСΒΥΤΕΡωΝ), and reader and steward (ΑΝΑΓΝΟСΤΟΥΚΑΙΟΚΟ/ΝΟΜΟΥ),
it is clear that the sponsors of the mosaic program in the

_____

[454]I neglected to transcribe and photograph the inscription. This transcription was published in the Praktika for
1958 (p. 61) and differs from the transcription in the plan in
regard to some letters. First line: another letter before
"ΑΝ" which is difficult to read. Fourth line: no "Λ"
before " ΙССΟΥ." Eleventh line: "[ ]οС[ ]ΝΕΝΔΟΞΟΥ,"
instead of "[ ]ΟΟ[ ]ΝΕΝΔΟΞΟΥ." Thirteenth line: "ΤΟ "
omitted.

bema were also members of the ecclesiastical community. In an emendation, these people are identified as the same ones whose names are inscribed in the tabula ansata in the nave (95, pl. 321).[455]

ΕΠ[ΙΕΥΤΥΧΙ]ΑΝ/ΝΟ[Υ ΚΑΙ ΠΟΛΥΚΑΡΠΟΥ Τω]Ν ΘΕ/
ΟΦΙΛ[ΕϹΤΑΤωΝ ΗΜωΝ] ΠΡΕϹ/ΒΥΤΕΡωΝ [ΚΑΙ
ΜΕ]ΛΙϹϹΟΥ/ ΤΟΥ ΘΕΟΦ[ΙΛΕ]ϹΤΑΤΟΥ/ ΑΝΑΓΝωϹΤΟΥ
ΚΑΙ ΟΙΚΟ/ΝΟΜΟΥ ΤΗϹ ΕΝΘΑΔΕ/ ΑΓΙωΤΑΤΗϹ
ΕΚΚΛΗϹΙΑϹ/ ΚΑΙ ΠΑΝΤΟϹ [ΤΟΥ] ΘΕΟΦΙΛΗ/
[ΚΛΗΡ]ΟΥ Α[ΝΕΚΑΙΝΙ]ϹΘΗ Ο ΑΓΙ/[ΟϹ ΝΑΟ]Ϲ
Ο[ΥΤΟϹ ΤΟΥ ΠΑ]ΝΕΝΔΟΞΟΥ/ [ΑΓΙΟ]Υ
ΛΕ[ωΝΙ]ΔΟΥ ΚΑΙ ΕΓΕΝΕ/ΤΟ [ΤΟ ΤΗ]Ϲ
ΧΑΜΟΚΕΝΤΗϹΕΟϹ ΕΡΓ(ΟΝ).

I agree that there is evidence to justify the restoration of the name Melissos in the fourth line ([ ]ΛΙϹϹΟΥ). It is also probable that the name of the saint in the twelfth line should be restored as Leonidas, since his name is also invoked by John, the sub-deacon on the west side of the east compartment of the nave (95), pl. 324. There is no justification, in my judgment, for the restoration of the names "ΕΥΤΥΧΙΑΝΟΥ" and "ΠΟΛΥΚΑΡΠΟΥ" in the first and second lines since only four letters are preserved "ΑΝ/ΝΟ." A third inscription on the north side of the room is better preserved. Oriented westward, it also cites the names of church figures in dark grey letters (0.07-0.08 high): Polygeros, a reader; Andromacha, a deaconess. "ΠΟΛΗΓΗΡΟϹ Ο/ΕΥΛΑΒΕϹΤΑΤϹ/ΑΝΑΓϹΚΕΑΝΔΡΟ/ΜΑΧΑΗΘΕΟΦΙΛϹ/ΤϹΔΙΑΚΥΠΕΡ

---

[455]Ibid.

ƐⲨ/ⲬⲎⳞⲀⲨⲦⲰⲚ҄Ɛ/ⲔⲀⲖⲒⲈⲢⲅⲎⳞⲀⲚ.ⁿ[456]

Although united by a common border and framework, the
panels show a distinct heterogeneity in regard to theme, disposition, and size, suggesting the absence of a programmatic
model. The figural panels contain flat, two-dimensional
birds and fish in profile view. In the panel to the northeast which is oriented northward (pls. 336-337), confronting
grey birds with striped wings walk toward a leaf-bearing dark
green tree. Above and beyond this scene are two smaller grey
birds, facing in opposite directions, and green plants. The
small bird to the west, introduces a second axis to the panel
since it and the adjacent plants are oriented toward the west.
The two other figural panels contain marine scenes which have
livelier figures. In the partially preserved west panel, a
dark grey, red, and white squid with spreading red tentacles
hovers above a red and white speckled eel and fish. Completing the scene and filling the rest of the surface are some
worms and sea urchins. Recalling the marine scene in the
nave (pls. 317-318), the panel on the south side (pl. 338)
contains a large white bellied grey and red dolphin with
curving body. Around it swim red and dark grey or ivory and
dark grey, speckled eels and fish with similarly arched
bodies, which are shown feeding on undulating worms. To the

---

[456]For the emendation, see Praktika, 1958, p. 61.
ⲠⲟⲖⲨⲅⲎⲢⲟⳞ ⲟ/ⲈⲨⲖⲂⲈⳞⲦⲀⲦ(ⲟ)Ⳟ/ ⲀⲚⲀⲅ(ⲚⲱⳞⲦⲎ)Ⳟ Ⲕⲉ
ⲀⲚⲆⲢⲟ/ⲘⲀⲬⲀ Ⲏ ⲐⲈⲟⲪⲒⲖ(Ɛ)Ⳟ/ Ⲧ(ⲀⲦⲎ) ⲆⲒⲀⲔ(ⲟⲚⲒⳞⳞⲀ)
ⲨⲠⲈⲢ ⲈⲨ/ⲬⲎⳞ ⲀⲨⲦⲱⲚ Ɛ/ⲔⲀⲖⲒⲈⲢⲅⲎⳞⲀⲚ.

left, an isolated, dark grey sea urchin feeds alone. Beginning with the first panel to the northwest and moving southward, the sequence of filling elements is as follows. First row: confronting birds; four-pointed stars of two grey lozenges and two red diamonds; alternating rows of ivory, red, dark grey chevrons. Second row: inscription; damaged marine scene. Third row: two-strand interlace (ivory; red, outlined by white/dark grey single fillets) on a dark grey ground forming a diagonal cross; inscription; alternating red and ivory scales, fanning northward. Fourth row: opposed red and ivory peltae; three-strand braid (same colors as interlace); squid panel; intersecting grey octagons.

Additional color. Bird panel: generally, dark grey outlines and dark grey, ivory, and red stripes for wings and bodies with red beaks and legs; large bird to left has light and dark green in lower part of body. Marine and geometric panels: dark grey outlines.

First half of the sixth century.

99 Room VI (5.10 x 7.00, including conch). North transept wing; pavement laid up to a natural rock formation to east; blocked to west and south by a later wall and a doorway, respectively, which rested directly on the pavement; subsequently removed by the excavator. Pls. 339-348.

Conch, a: ca. 2.40 diam. Framing: 0.29-0.33. Field: ca. 1.37 diam. Rectangular panel, b: 3.16 x 4.50, including

south threshold. Framing: 0.43-0.48. Field: 1.65 x 3.70.
Material identical to that in Room II (95).

Figural and geometric panels decorated with birds and fish.
  VIa, conch (pls. 339-343).
  Surround, to north: decorated with dark grey and ivory
triangles.[457]
  Framing: dark grey double fillet; ivory double fillet;
border, (pl. 339), red and ivory wave crests (for a similar
pattern in the nave, see 95, pl. 317).
  Field, framed by a dark grey double fillet (pls. 339-343):
scene with primarily marine creatures swimming across the
surface of the white ground. Dominating the center are two
large light and dark grey confronting dolphins, one devouring
the tail fin of a small fish (for a similar motif in the
nave, see 95, pl. 317). At the apex of the conch and between
their snouts is an inscription in black letters citing the
name of the sponsor of the decoration, Didymos (pl. 342):
"ЄΠΗΤѠΝΚΑΙΡѠΝ/ΔΙΔΥΜΟΥΚΡ/ЄΚЄΝΤΗΘΗ ." Swimming around the
curving ivory striped bodies of the dolphins are other sea
creatures such as large and small ochre and red speckled fish
feeding on grey worms, and a lone dark grey squid which (pl.
340) moves toward an isolated, similarly colored sea urchin.
Amid all these curving, feeding, and swimming marine forms, a

----

[457]The surround corrects the irregular shape of the
conch (see Praktika, 1959, p. 34, and pl. 33a).

large green and white heron with red wings stands stolidly
at the bottom of the scene, its feet resting on the edge of
the border (pls. 339-340) and its long red beak almost touch-
ing the chin of a large fish.[458]

VIb, rectangular panel (pls. 343a-347).

Surround to east only, around the base of a rock (pl.
343a): undulating ribbon alternately dark grey and ivory.[459]

Framing: ivory double fillet; border (pl. 344), three-
strand braid (ivory; red; dark grey, outlined by white/dark
grey single fillets, with a white tessera at each loop);
ivory double fillet.

Field (pls. 344-345), framed by a dark grey double fillet
which forms, at the same time, part of the design: dark grey
and white network of alternating octagons and meanders. The
octagons have been cut along the margin. They are disposed
in alternating rows of one and two along the main axis of the
church and are filled with interlaces and two-dimensional
figures in profile which face in various directions. The
truncated octagons along the south and west sides, on the
other hand, contain white and red trefoils. Beginning with
the first octagon to the northeast and moving southward, the
sequence of filling elements is as follows. First

[458]The grey object between the tail fin of this fish and
the right dolphin is curious. It looks like a vase of some
kind (pl. 343).

[459]Praktika, 1959, p. 35.

row:[460] diagonal Solomon's knot (red; dark grey, outlined by
white/dark grey single fillets, with a white tessera at each
loop). Red trefoils spring from the four sides of the knot;
destroyed. Second row (pl. 344): yellow and grey striped
bird in flight, oriented eastward, flanked by two smaller
standing yellow and grey birds, oriented northward. Third
row (pl. 344): dark grey eel and fish with some red and pink
highlights, oriented southward; diagonal cruciform interlace
(ivory; red, outlined by white/dark grey single fillets, with
a white tessera at each loop) composed of a central circle
and four loops which are separated by red trefoils. Fourth
row (pl. 344): two dark grey and ivory birds (ducks),
oriented southward and accompanied by red buds on sinuous
grey stems. Fifth row (pl. 344): two-strand whorl (red;
ivory, outlined by white/dark grey single fillets); two confronting ochre and grey birds (pl. 346), oriented southward
and separated by red trefoils on sinuous grey stems. Sixth
row (pl. 345): pair of red and ochre speckled fish (pl. 347).
Seventh row (pl. 345): red Solomon's knot (same colors as
first one) decorated on three sides with single trefoils;
oriented southward, a large speckled bird facing a small red
one.

South threshold (0.71 x ca. 6.00): pairs of opposed red
peltae, outlined in dark grey, placed in alternating horizontal and vertical units (pl. 348).

---

[460]It is barely visible (see pl. 344, bottom).

Additional color. VIa, conch. Dolphins and fish: dark
grey outlines; red fins, mouths and gills. Sea urchins: red
centers. Heron: red legs. VIb, rectangular panel: all outlines in dark grey. Fourth row. Birds: wings and neck
striped in red, white, and grey. Fifth row. Birds: red
wings. Seventh row. Birds: large one, speckled with grey,
ivory, yellow; small one, some grey, yellow.

First half of the sixth century.

Illustrations. E. Chatzidakis, Praktika, 1959, pl. 33a
(VIa, general view), pl. 33b = our pl. 342, pl. 34a-b (VIb,
bird and fish insets), pl. 36a (VIb, bird inset), pl. 36gamma
= our pl. 343a.

100 Room VII (5.50 x 6.63, including conch). South transept
       wing; pavement laid up to a stone threshold to north;
blocked to west by a later wall which rested directly on the
pavement; subsequently removed by the excavator. Pls. 349-
353.

Conch, a: ca. 2.50 diam. Framing: 0.54. Field: 1.31
diam. Rectangular panel, b: 2.50 x 6.10. Framing: 0.38.
Field: 1.82 x 5.62.

Geometric and floral panels bordered by curvilinear patterns.
   VIIa, conch (pls. 349-352).
   Surround to south: in irregular rows of tesserae (ca.
0.015 sq).
   Framing (pl. 349): dark grey double fillet, border, red

intersecting circles, outlined in white, forming concave-
sided squares with white or red centers and dark grey outlines; dark grey double fillet; ivory double fillet.

Field (pls. 350-352), framed by a dark grey double fillet:
large vase, oriented southward, from which issue a red lotus
bud and two thick red grape vines, outlined in dark grey.
The long-necked red and green vase is adorned with dark grey
spiral handles and has a wide ribbed body which rests on a
circular foot supported by a triangular base with voluted
ends. The undulating vines spread symmetrically across the
surface, filling it with clusters of red grapes, trident-
shaped spatulate leaves and dark grey curling tendrils.[461]
Amid this schematic floral display, are two pale green birds
(pls. 351-352) which peck at the grapes dangling before them.
One is placed on the lower left side (pl. 351) while the
other, inverted in relation to the orientation of the scene,
is situated in the upper right corner (pl. 352).

VIIb, rectangular panel (pl. 353).

Framing: dark grey double fillet; ivory double fillet;
dark grey double fillet; border, identical to that in the
north transept (99, pl. 344); dark grey double fillet.

Field (pl. 353): ivory intersecting circles (ca. 0.50
diam), outlined by white/black single fillets, forming red

---

[461]The vase and foliage are very similar to those in the
east compartment of the nave (95, pl. 329).

concave-sided squares. The design is cut along the margins.
The concave-sided squares are inscribed with red straight
squares which are accented at their angles by four smaller
squares (for a similar design, see 88, pl. 307).

Additional color. VIIa, conch. Grapes: outlined in dark
grey. Leaves: dark grey. Birds: some red and ivory in
wings; dark grey outlines.

First half of the sixth century.

Illustrations. E. Chatzidakis, Praktika, 1959, pl. 35a
(VIIa, general view), pl. 35b (VIIa, detail of right bird).

HYPATI

Mosaic Fragment

Near the south side of the Byzantine church of St.
Nicholas in Hypati, a section of a mosaic pavement was discovered by chance in 1959. Since further examination of the
site was not possible, the function of the building was not
determined.[462] At the present time the pavement is covered.

Although no datable archaeological finds were unearthed
or reported, on the basis of the style of the mosaic, the
building can be assigned to the late fifth or early sixth

<hr/>

[462]Later structures covered the rest of the floor (P.
Lazarides, Deltion, 16 [1960], B: Chronika, pp. 165-166).
There was no evidence that the building was an "Early
Christian basilica" (cf. Sodini, Catalogue, p. 716, and n.
28).

century. This pavement and those at Thebes and Delphi (75-
76, pls. 224-236; 82-83, pls. 240-291) represent the production of one workshop and possibly of two artisans whose
names are inscribed in one of the tessellated pavements at
Thebes (75, pl. 232) and who worked in the late fifth or
early sixth century.[463]

Bibliography. P. Lazarides, Deltion, 16 (1960), B:
Chronika, pp. 165-166.

No. 101

101 Mosaic fragment (ca. 2.00 x 6.00). The major part of
the pavement is covered by the foundations of the church
of St. Nicholas and a road abutment. Pl. 354.

No published information on dimensions and material.

In a published photograph (pl. 354), there is a fragment of a
polychrome field design comprising a grid with bird insets.[464]

Framing: traces of a light double fillet.

Field: oblique grid composed of a two-strand guilloche
(with a white tessera at each loop) forming squares. The
guilloche bifurcates along the edges of the design and forms
a continuous border which cuts in varying degrees the adjacent

---

[463]For a comparison of these pavements and their chronology, vide supra, pp. 209-210, 232-233.

[464]Although the color scheme was not noted in the
report, the tonal differences in the photograph confirm the
polychromy of the pavement.

squares. The whole squares, outlined by a light double
fillet, are inscribed with light disks which serve as an
opaque ground for profile representations of one water fowl
and two land birds (for similar designs with identical
organic filling motifs, see 76, pls. 235-235; 82, pls. 240-
252).

Late fifth or early sixth century.

   Additional bibliography. Sodini, Catalogue, No. 32, p.
716.

   Illustration. P. Lazarides, Deltion, 16 (1960), Plates,
pl. 148b = our pl. 354.

PART IV. THESSALY

NEA ANCHIALOS

Basilica Alpha

Between 1924 and 1928, systematic excavations brought to
light a large basilica (overall, 32.00 x ca. 58.00 in the city
of Nea Anchialos (Christian Thebes).[465] Crude tessellated
pavements were discovered in Rooms VII and VIII, and in the
north aisle, X. At the present time, except for part of the
pavement in Room X, which has been reset on a new foundation,
the other mosaics have probably disappeared.[466]

Designated Alpha, the church is the first in a series of
four churches discovered in this city (pl. 355).[467] In each
building (pls. 356, 362, 399), the esonarthex is preceded by
a large atrium, frequently with flanking rooms, and is

---

[465]For a summary of the political and ecclesiastical
history of Christian Thebes, see G. A. Soteriou, "Hai
Christianikai Thēvai tēs Thessalias," ArchEph, 1929, pp. 6-9,
hereafter cited as ArchEph, 1929.

[466]N. Nikonanos, Deltion, 25 (1970), Bl: Chronika, p.
286, pl. 243a. The present excavator of the site, P.
Lazarides, refused to grant me permission to view this church
and the two others on this site (105-122). My descriptions
of the architecture and the decorative programs, therefore,
are based on the published reports, the photographs, and on
the field notes of Professor Irving Lavin at Dumbarton Oaks.

[467]For Basilica Beta which has no tessellated floors,
see ArchEph, 1929, pp. 132-247.

distinguished by projecting annexes on its north and south
sides. The nave is separated from the aisles by colonnades
resting on elevated stylobates and from the bema by a large
chancel screen. Distinctive and homogeneous in plan, the
semi-independent "U-shaped" screen projects from two lateral
clergy benches abutting the shoulders of the apse and terminates in a prothuron in the center of its west side. On the
east side of the bema, in front of a stepped, semi-circular
apse, is a rectangular altar which protects an enkainion.
Unlike Basilicas Gamma and Delta, it is probable that Alpha
was originally paved with large stone and ceramic slabs which
were replaced in Rooms VII, VIII, and X by crude tessellated
pavements.

Since Basilica Alpha has been the subject of extensive
investigation and analysis,[468] only a brief description of
its plan will follow. A distinctive feature of the west side
of the complex (pl. 356) is the design of the atrium, I,
which comprises two rectangular porticoes (a,b) which are
joined by a semi-circular portico (c) on the west side. The
north and south porticoes are flanked by two rectangular rooms
with apses[469] which are preceded by vestibules, VII, VIII.

---

[468]ArchEph, 1929, pp. 19-111; Orlandos, Xylostegos
basilike, pp. 93, passim; Krautheimer, Architecture, pp.
94-95.

[469]The north room has been identified as a baptistery
(ArchEph, 1929, p. 45) and the south one as a sacristy
(ibid.), and a consignatorium (Krautheimer, Architecture,
p. 94).

Completing this part of the plan are two small rooms in the
front corners which contain staircases (II, IV).[470] Preceded
by an esonarthex with projecting wings, the church proper
(20.00 x 29.00) consists of a nave, IX, flanked by two
aisles, X, XI (pl. 358), and terminated by a raised semi-
circular apse. The nave is separated from the aisles by
colonnades resting on bases set on elevated stylobates and by
intercolumnar parapets,[471] while the bema is enclosed by a
long chancel screen which projects from two lateral clergy
benches abutting the shoulders of the apse. Traces of an
altar surmounted by a canopy were found immediately in front
of the chord of the apse along with a submerged cruciform
enkainion beneath it.[472] Beyond this sacred compartment, lies
a double-tiered circular ambon which rises from a semi-
circular base.[473] The church was richly decorated with marble
sculpture, wall revetments in opus sectile, and with polychrome mosaics on the upper parts of the walls. Marble and
slate slabs pave Rooms VI, IX-XI, and brick slabs the colonnaded porticoes and the rooms to the north of the north

[470]They have been interpreted as towers (ArchEph, 1929,
pp. 49, 105) and as a prothesis and diaconikon (Orlandos, Hē
metakinēsis tou diakonikou, p. 355).

[471]The north and south colonnades are interrupted at the
fourth intercolumniation from the west by two lateral doors
which correspond to the doors in the outer walls.

[472]For a reconstruction of the bema and its furnishings,
see ArchEph, 1929, pl. E after p. 120.

[473]For a reconstruction, see ArchEph, 1929, pl. D after
p. 96.

aisle.[474] Crude tessellated floors were found in Rooms VII,
VIII, and in sections of the north aisle, X, which probably
belong to a second decorative phase.

On the basis of the brick work, the plan, and the style
of the sculpture, the building has been assigned to around
the middle of the fifth century.[475] In later periods, the
colonnades in the nave and the east side of the aisles were
walled up,[476] and the baptistery was repaved with brick
slabs.[477] The site has been cleared and is in good condition.

Bibliography. AA, 41 (1926), p. 430; AA, 43 (1928), pp.
599-600; G. A. Soteriou, ArchEph, 1929, p. 19-109; AA, 47
(1932), pp. 153-154; G. de Jerphanion, Atti della Pontificia
Accademia Romana di archeologia, serie 3, memorie 3 (1932-
33), pp. 112-122; AA, 54 (1939), p. 255; AA, 55 (1940), pp.
251-252; Orlandos, Xylostegos basilikē, pp. 93 passim;
Krautheimer, Architecture, pp. 94-95; AA, 55 (1940), pp.
251-252.

Illustrations. G. A. Soteriou, ArchEph, 1929, p. 18, fig.
15 (view from east), pl. B after p. 20 = our pl. 356, p. 22,
fig. 17 (plan with later additions), p. 23, fig. 22 (nave,
from west), pp. 53-97, figs. 53-126 (ornamental sculpture),
pl. E after p. 120 (reconstruction of bema); P. Lazarides,
Praktika, 1969, p. 18, fig. 2 = our pl. 355.

---

[474]ArchEph, 1929, pp. 32, 34, 37, 43-44, 46.

[475]ArchEph, 1929, pp. 22, 51, 97. Krautheimer dates it
to around 470 (Architecture, p. 94, and caption to fig. 35,
p. 94) and Kautzsch to between 480 and 500 (Kapitellstudien,
p. 77).

[476]ArchEph, 1929, pp. 9, 28, p. 21, fig. 17 (plan with
additions). Nothing is said about the condition and function
of the west side of the complex during these periods.

[477]ArchEph, 1929, p. 41.

Nos. 102-104

Tessellated pavements decorate the vestibules of Rooms
III and V and parts of the north aisle, X (pls. 357-361).
Simple in design and color (black, white, red), the pavements
contain tangent curvilinear and rectilinear geometric patterns which are crudely executed with large, irregularly-
cut tesserae set at a distance from each other. This type
of pavement is also found in Basilica Beta at Dion (180-183,
pls. 607-610) and in Basilica Alpha at Longos (197-202, pls.
633, 642) which are datable, the latter with certainty, to
the sixth century. It is to this period or later that the
Anchialos pavements belong and they represent, therefore, a
repair or replacement of the original pavements. This is
substantiated by the curious agglomerate or pastiche quality
of the pavement in the north aisle (pl. 358) where two strips
are juxtaposed with the marble paving in a disproportionate
and asymetrical manner. Given the splendid quality of the
sculptural and mural decoration of this building, and the
absence of this kind of floor in other rooms with marble
paving, it is evident that the tessellated pavings were not
part of the original program of the building but were used to
repair the damaged sectors. The repair of the pavement in
the north aisle provides a terminus post quem for the block-
ing up of the colonnades and the east side of the aisles

which caused the aisles to fall into disuse.[478] When this
building phase occurred is not known but it clearly postdates
the sixth century.

Additional bibliography. Sodini, Catalogue, No. 36, p. 718.

Illustration. P. Lazarides, Praktika, 1969, p. 18, fig.
2 = our pl. 355.

102   Room VII (4.40 x 4.40).[479] Vestibule of baptistery.

No published information on dimensions and material.
Irregularly-cut tesserae (0.01-0.04 long).

Brief mention of a mosaic pavement similar to those in the
south vestibule (103, pl. 357) and the north aisle (104, pls.
358-361).[480] Traces at the east entrance of a zig-zag
pattern.[481]

Probably sixth century, or later.

Additional bibliography. I. Lavin, "Field notes: Nea
Anchialos, Alpha," Dumbarton Oaks, Center for Byzantine
Studies.

103. Room VIII (4.40 x 4.40). Vestibule of a sacristy or

---

[478]Vide supra, p. 310, and n. 476. For the probable
relationship between the pavements and ones in opus sectile,
vide infra, p. 534.

[479]The measurements are taken from the plan (pl. 356).

[480]ArchEph, 1929, pp. 44, 46.

[481]I. Lavin, "Field Notes: Nea Anchialos, Basilica
Alpha," Dumbarton Oaks, Center for Byzantine Studies.

consignatorium.[482] Pl. 357.

No published information on dimensions. Irregularly-cut marble tesserae (no dimensions published).

Red, black, and white pavement similar to that in the north vestibule (102).[483]

Framing: narrow white band; border, black and white zig-zag pattern.

Field: in a published photograph (pl. 357), there are six rows of twelve juxtaposed white spindels on a dark ground.

Probably sixth century, or later.

Illustration. G. A. Soteriou, ArchEph, 1929, p. 47, fig. 49 = our pl. 357.

104 Room X (4.65 x 29.00). North aisle; blocked by later walls along east and south sides. Pls. 358-361.

Northeast band, a: 1.25 wide. Northwest band: 1.44 wide. South band: ca. 65 wide. Irregularly-cut tesserae (0.01-0.04 long).

Marble pavement (pl. 358) repaired along the north and south sides by tessellated bands with geometric designs in red,

---

[482]Vide supra, p. 308, n. 469.

[483]ArchEph, 1929, p. 46. Here the type of pavement is erroneously termed opus sectile and for this reason it is omitted by Sodini (Catalogue, p. 718).

black and white. The central marble strip (2.00 wide) bifurcates at the side entrances in the north wall and the north
colonnade to divide the mosaics into two unequal sections.

Xa, north band: to the east (pl. 359), squares or rectangles filled with hour glass motifs formed by two white triangles placed tip-to-tip which alternate with similarly
disposed black or red ones. To the west (pls. 358, 360),
there are alternating large horizontal rectangles and small
vertical ones, the former inscribed with lozenges and geometric motifs; the latter, with flat disks.

Xb, south band (pls. 358, 361), separated from the north
colonnade by a narrow strip of marble slabs: smaller version
of the northwest pattern (pl. 360) of horizontal and vertical
rectangles. The lozenges in the horizontal rectangles are
usually inscribed with plain disks, sometimes containing
simple decorative motifs.

Probably sixth century, or later.

Illustrations. G. A. Soteriou, ArchEph, 1929, p. 23, fig.
23 = our pl. 358, p. 27, fig. 29 = our pl. 361, p. 27, fig.
30 = our pl. 360, p. 32, fig. 35 = our pl. 359, p. 47, fig.
49 = our pl. 357.

Basilica Gamma

During two series of excavations at Nea Anchialos, 1929-
1954, and from 1969 to the present, the major part of an Early
Christian basilica, designated Gamma (overall, 39.00 x

78.00),[484] was brought to light (pls. 355, 362). Mosaic pavements were found at different levels within the church proper
and its annexes. At the present time, most of them have been
lifted and consolidated.

Despite a plethora of archaeological reports, the building history of the site remains obscure. Although as many as
five levels have been discovered in some of the rooms (Ia,
VII, VIII, X, XII, XV-XVI), it is impossible, for the most
part, to determine their physical and chronological relationship. No absolute measurements above or below sea level are
used,[485] and there has been no attempt to correlate the
recent investigations and discoveries with the earlier ones.
For these reasons, only a description of the present plan of
the building will be given. The church proper is preceded by
an atrium and an exonarthex, I, II, which are flanked along
their north and south sides by annexes, III-VIII. At the
time of the initial excavations, G. A. Soteriou found evidence
that these forebuildings belonged to an earlier basilica and
were incorporated into the plan of the present one.[486] Although recent soundings in the nave and bema have uncovered

----

[484]It was subsequently changed to the "Basilica of the
Archbishop Peter" because of an inscription found in the pavement of the south aisle (P. Lazarides, Praktika, 1970, p. 37;
vide infra, p. 349 and n. 565). Vide supra, p. 307, n. 466.

[485]Only ground levels are used which, by their very
nature, are inconsistent. Vide infra, pp. 317-318.

[486]G. A. Soteriou, Praktika, 1933, p. 52; Praktika,
1934, p. 61.

multiple levels of habitation,[487] there is no reason at this time to reject this conclusion. The second building phase is represented by the rooms to the east of the exonarthex which comprise the esonarthex, IX (6.30 x 5.00), the annex along the south side and an adjacent room, XV-XVII,[488] and the main body of the church. The latter contains a wide nave, X (14.75 x ca. 31.00,[489] separated from two lateral aisles, XIII-XIV (average width, 5.00; length, 43.80),[490] by a high stylobate (0.50) which supported an arcuated colonnade, and from the bema, XI, by a long semi-independent "⊔-shaped" chancel screen. The latter, distinguished by a prothuron in the center of its west side, abuts two transverse clergy benches flanking the apse. Within the bema area traces were found of a stepped synthronon along the chord of the apse, an altar surmounted by a canopy resting on four columns, and a cruciform enkainion.[491] Beyond this liturgical site proper, lies an octagonal ambon with a set of steps on the main axis of the

---

[487]Traces of a bath complex were discovered at a depth of 1.05 meters below the present level of the bema, XI (P. Lazarides, Praktika, 1971, p. 39). The relationship between this level and those of the original nave and forebuildings, however, is not discussed.

[488]Room XVII is identified as a mosaic workshop (G. A. Soteriou, Praktika, 1929, p. 69; idem, Praktika, 1954, pp. 145-146).

[489]The length is taken from the plan (pl. 362).

[490]The west side of the south aisle reaches a width of 6.60 meters (P. Lazarides, Praktika, 1970, p. 48).

[491]P. Lazarides, Praktika, 1969, pp. 23-25; idem, Praktika, 1971, pp. 35-39.

church. In subsequent periods, walls were built in the north
and south aisles which constricted their length and width,[492]
and the south colonnade of the atrium was blocked up.[493]

The pavements which can be attributed with certitude to
the present building are the tessellated ones in the north
and south aisles (XIII, XIV) and the marble slabs in the esonarthex, nave, and bema (IX, X, XI). It is also evident that
the lower level pavements decorating the earlier forebuildings
to the west were in use during this building phase (I-VIII).[494]
Thus, a fairly clear picture of the design and the types of
some of the paving has emerged during the recent excavations.
Moreover, the relationship between the basilica and a building
beneath its south side has been clarified. Recent probings
established that the south wall of the south aisle of the
basilica rests on the north wall of an earlier building.
Thus, the tessellated pavement which was described earlier as
lying beneath and outside the south aisle of the basilica,
that is to say, extending to the north part of the south annex

---

[492]P. Lazarides, Praktika, 1971, p. 22.

[493]G. A. Soteriou, Praktika, 1934, p. 59.

[494]Except for the south aisle and the present marble
floor of the exonarthex, the floors in the west half of the
complex are attributed to the lower level or Period I (G. A.
Soteriou, Praktika, 1930, pp. 32-33; idem, Praktika, 1931,
p. 37, n. 1, p. 41; idem, Praktika, 1933, pp. 48, 51).
Since they were not covered by later floors, they must have
been in use during the second building phase, II (for their
stratigraphy, see P. Lazarides, Praktika, 1971, pp. 20-40).

(XV),[495] is, in fact, two pavements which are divided by the
newly discovered north wall.[496] When the present basilica
was built, this part of the building was re-used, its level
raised, and a colonnade installed.[497] Here, however, as elsewhere, the position of these tessellated pavings is obscured
by discrepancies. In an early report, the depth is given as
80 centimeters below the present level of the south aisle.[498]
More recently it is given as 1.20 meters (mosaic below south
aisle) and 1.55 meters (mosaic below north aisle of annex).[499]
These discrepancies exist as well for the other lower level
mosaics on the west side. Any attempt, therefore, to establish precise levels for these early pavements is negated by
the dearth of accurate and consistent data.

In regard to the chronology of the present building,
there is surprisingly little datable external evidence. At
least, none has been reported. Since there are traces of fire
throughout, a _terminus ante quem_ of the end of the seventh
century has been advanced because the entire city of Nea
Anchialos was destroyed by invasions.[500] A restoration of the

---

[495]G. A. Soteriou, _Praktika_, 1930, p. 32; idem, _Praktika_,
1931, p. 37; idem, _Praktika_, 1933, pp. 48-49.

[496]A. K. Orlandos, _To Ergon_, 1971, p. 30. This wall is
not noted in the _Praktika_ for that year.

[497]P. Lazarides, _Praktika_, 1971, pp. 24-25.

[498]Vide supra, p. 318, n. 495.

[499]Vide supra, p. 318, n. 496.

[500]G. A. Soteriou, _Praktika_, 1930, p. 33; idem, _Praktika_,
1933, p. 47; idem, _Praktika_, 1934, p. 59; idem, _Praktika_, 1954,
p. 147; P. Lazarides, _Praktika_, 1969, p. 25.

basilica proper occurred in the sixth century, probably under
the sponsorship of an Archbishop Peter whose name is
inscribed in one of the mosaic panels in the south aisle.[501]
Evidence for the date of this restoration, which involved the
installation of an arcuated colonnade between the nave and
the aisles, is supplied by an inscription on a stone plaque
imbedded in one of the north arches. It refers to the Nika
riots of 532[502] and supplies a concrete terminus ante quem
for the second phase of the building and post quem for its
restoration.[503] A restoration of this type, which obviously
involved a major portion of the superstructure, implies a
partial destruction of the building by means of fire or some
other disaster.[504] Thus, the time between the erection of
the present basilica and its restoration need not have been
protracted. Since the style of many of the lower level
pavements in the forebuildings can be dated to the fifth
century,[505] it is possible to assign the erection of the

[501]Vide infra, p. 349, and n. 565.

[502]P. Lazarides, Praktika, 1969, p. 21.

[503]This find is of major importance and refutes an early
report in which the basilica is attributed to the late sixth
or early seventh century (G. A. Soteriou, Praktika, 1934, pp.
13, 60-61), with a possible restoration in the seventh century (idem, Praktika, 1931, p. 43). In an early publication,
E. Kitzinger correctly attributed the colonnades to the early
Justinianic period on the basis of the style of the capitals
(DOP, 3 [1946], p. 134).

[504]It would appear that the west side was never restored.

[505]G. A. Soteriou, Praktika, 1934, p. 61; E. Kitzinger,
op. cit., pp. 137-138; Sodini, Catalogue, pp. 719-720, and
n. 36.

second basilica and its esonarthex to sometime before the
end of the fifth century or the beginning of the sixth century.

Bibliography. AA, 43 (1928); AA, 45 (1930), p. 123; G. A.
Soteriou, Praktika, 1930, pp. 11-13, 30-35; idem, Praktika,
1931, pp. 7-9, 37-43; AA, 46 (1931), p. 270; G. A. Soteriou,
Praktika, 1933, pp. 46-57; idem, Praktika, 1934, pp. 58-61;
AA, 49 (1934), pp. 165-166; G. A. Soteriou, Praktika, 1935,
p. 65; AA, 50 (1935), pp. 214-215; AA, 51 (1936), pp. 142-
143; AA, 52 (1937), pp. 147-148; G. A. Soteriou, Praktika,
1940, pp. 6-7, 18-22; AA, 57 (1942), pp. 158-159; AA, 58
(1943), p. 321; idem, Praktika, 1954, pp. 14, 143-148; A. K.
Orlandos, To Ergon, 1954, p. 19; BCH, 79 (1955), pp. 269-272;
JHS, 54 (1934), Supplement, p. 159; P. Lazarides, Praktika,
1969, pp. 16-25; A. K. Orlandos, To Ergon, 1969, pp. 11-19;
BCH, 94 (1970), p. 1041; P. Lazarides, Praktika, 1970, pp.
37-49; A. K. Orlandos, To Ergon, 1970, pp. 22-33; BCH, 95
(1971), p. 932; P. Lazarides, Praktika, 1971, pp. 20-42;
A. K. Orlandos, To Ergon, 1971, pp. 27-36; BCH, 96 (1972),
p. 711; A. K. Orlandos, To Ergon, 1972, pp. 13-17.

Illustrations. G. A. Soteriou, Praktika, 1940, p. 19,
fig. 2 (plan); idem, Praktika, 1954, p. 145, fig. 3 (plan);
P. Lazarides, Praktika, 1969, p. 17, fig. 1 = our pl. 355, pl.
24b (south colonnade, from west), pl. 26a (Room IV), pl. 28b
(synthronon), pl. 30a (bema); idem, Praktika, 1970, pl. 54
(marble pavement in bema), pl. 58b (south aisle, looking
west); idem, Praktika, 1971, p. 21, fig. 1 (plan), p. 26, fig.
2 (Room VII, showing earlier foundations), p. 28, fig. 3
(south side showing earlier foundations in Rooms II, VII-
IX), p. 37, fig. 6 (cross section along north stylobate in
Room XIII), pl. 26a (Room XIV, general view), pls. 35-46
(stratigraphic finds); A. K. Orlandos, To Ergon, 1972, p. 14,
fig. 7 = our pl. 362, p. 15, fig. 8 = our pl. 381.

Nos. 105-115

Traces of eleven polychrome mosaic pavements were discovered at various levels in the complex and along its south
side. Given the paucity of descriptive and pictorial data,
their physical relationship is obscure. On the basis of
their style and iconography, however, it is possible to

establish a chronological framework for them which contains
two, possibly three, decorative phases. In considering the
pavements, it is more advantageous and constructive to begin
with those belonging to the last phase for which a terminus
post quem of 532 is established by inscriptional and decorative evidence in the restored north and south colonnades.
Since the pavements in the aisles are laid up to the stylobates supporting these colonnades (pls. 381a-382), it is
certain that they were set during or after the restoration
mentioned in the tessellated inscription in the south
aisle.[506] It is also clear that they were the sole mosaics
installed at this time because they are very different from
the others. A comparison of the south aisle pavement with
the others to the west shows that, although rectilinear
geometric designs continue to be used,[507] their style and
technique differ to a considerable extent. In the figural
insets on the west side (Rooms I, VI-VII, pls. 363-365; 367;
pls. 368-374) the fauna are well modeled and three-dimensional
and are set within two-dimensional rectilinear spaces. In
the south aisle (pls. 383-396), however, although the spatial
treatment is the same, the figures are flat and sharply outlined and defined, and occupy the same plane as the surrounding geometric configurations. Moreover, the number of

_____

[506]Vide supra, p. 319 and n. 501.

[507]Two panels in the south aisle (pls. 389-391), however,
are decorated with interlaces.

borders is increased by two or three bands resulting in a
constriction of the field. There are also technical differences. An overall poverty of execution is evident in the
irregular size and placement of the tesserae, and the crude
figural and geometric configurations (pls. 389-396). Clearly
then, the pavements in the north and south aisles were the
only ones installed during this restoration and represent
the last decorative phase of the basilica which can be
assigned to a period no earlier than around the middle of
the sixth century.

The other pavements belong to an earlier phase and this
corresponds with the archaeological evidence.[508] They lie
below the present level of the basilica, but, except for those
in Rooms Ib, II, VI-VIII, no secure architectural context
has been established. These pavements fall into two general
groups: aniconic geometric carpets (Rooms II, VIII, IX, XIV
[lower level], XV); those with figural insets (Rooms Ib, VI,
VII). Of the six rooms on the west side, three (II, VIII,
IX) are decorated with aniconic designs which have been
attributed to the late fourth or early fifth century on insufficient grounds.[509] The similarities between the pavement
in Room VIII (pls. 375-376) and one in Basilica Delta (pl.
408) are crucial in determining chronology. Both are polychromatic, and their field designs and central shield

---

[508]Vide supra, p. 317, and n. 494, p. 319 and n. 505.

[509]P. Lazarides, Praktika, 1970, pp. 22, 25.

patterns are identical. The filling motifs, quatrefoils and wave crests, especially, and the types of interstitial floral motifs composed of ivy leaves and trefoils resemble each other. The pavement in Delta has been reliably dated to the second half of the fifth century and it is around this time that Gamma's pavement was executed. Both differ to a considerable extent from an earlier mosaic at Demetrias (pls. 437-438) which exhibits a similar field design but which lacks the chromatic and decorative exuberance of the later pavements.[510] Another pavement associated with this phase and, in fact, with this level decorates Room II (pl. 366).[511] Although its overall design is different, once again, the central pattern is a shield composed of the same kind of triangular units, it is polychromatic, and like the pavement in Delta it is enclosed by a two-strand guilloche.[512] A third pavement in this group, IX (pl. 381), cannot be assigned to any specific decorative phase without additional data and photographs. It was covered by two later stone floors as was its presumed counterpart in the nave[513] and may belong to the first basilica or to its rebuilding. Other aniconic pavements were found beneath and outside the south aisle of the

---

[510]It is black, white, and grey with polychrome highlights. For similar bichrome pavements in and around Thessaly, see 88-92; 130-138; 178-179.

[511]G. A. Soteriou, Praktika, 1930, p. 34.

[512]Even G. A. Soteriou noted the resemblance (ibid.).

[513]Vide infra, p. 341 and n. 551.

church, XIV-XV, but, again, there is little useful information on their levels and architectural contexts.[514] On the
basis of their wall construction, they have been assigned to
the late fourth or fifth century (110; 111, pls. 377-380).[515]
Among the six aniconic pavements, therefore, only those in
Rooms II and VIII can be assigned with any degree of certainty
to a specific period, that is to around the middle or the
second half of the fifth century.[516] For the most part, the
more attractive figural pavements in Rooms Ib, VI, VII also
belong to this period. On stylistic grounds, the pavement in
Ib (pls. 363-365) has been correctly assigned to around the
middle of the fifth century[517] and, therefore, it is
probably contemporaneous with the aniconic pavements in Rooms
II and VIII.[518] The combination of aniconic and figural pavements is, after all, a feature of the decorative program at
Delta, as well, where figures are represented in the southwest
annex (pls. 400-401) and in the later pavement in the northwest annex (pls. 409-410). The iconographic similarities

[514]Vide supra, pp. 317-318.

[515]P. Lazarides, Praktika, 1969, p. 22; A. K. Orlandos,
To Ergon, 1969, p. 15. Earlier, they were attributed to the
third and the fifth centuries (G. A. Soteriou, Praktika, 1931,
p. 43 and Praktika, 1934, p. 61, respectively).

[516]For this reason, only two building periods will be
used, I and II.

[517]E. Kitzinger, DOP, 3 (1946), pp. 137-138. The pavements in Rooms VI and VII had not been properly reproduced at
the time of his study.

[518]It is at the same level (G. A. Soteriou, Praktika,
1931, p. 37, n. 1; idem, Praktika, 1933, p. 51; idem, Praktika,
1934, p. 60).

between the pavement in Gamma and those in Delta are so
strong that they must have been products of a common workshop,
perhaps the same one which was discovered on the south side
of Gamma (Room XVI).[519] Some crucial differences between the
pavements in the two basilicas may denote a chronological
disparity. Each pavement in Delta is distinguished by very
pronounced multiple borders which reduce the size of the
fields and, by their complexity, enrich the overall effect.
A comparison of identical grids with figures in Gamma and
Delta (pls. 364 and 400) and their purely geometric pavements (pls. 375-376 and 408)[520] confirms this difference.
This distinction can be used for chronological purposes since
multiple borders characterize many of the pavements belonging
to the second half of the fifth century and later. They are
even present in the securely dated sixth century pavements in
the north and south aisles (114; 115, pls. 382-396). It is
probable that the workshop executed the lower level pavements
at Gamma and, then, decorated Basilica Delta.

The two remaining pavements in Rooms VI (pl. 367) and
VII (pls. 368-374) certainly belong to this general period.
Although Room VII is between thirty-five and forty centi-
meters higher than Rooms Ib, II, and VIII,[521] the composition

---

[519]Vide supra, p. 316, n. 488.

[520]Although not visible in the photograph, there are
four borders in the pavement at Delta.

[521]G. A. Soteriou, Praktika, 1930, p. 33; idem, Praktika,
1931, p. 37, n. 1. The level of Room VII is not recorded.

and iconography of its pavement are so close to those in the
pavement in Room Ib (pls. 363-365) that no more than a few
years, possibly a few decades, separate them. The absence of
multiple borders in VII may well indicate that it, also, predates the pavements at Basilica Delta. The last pavement with
figural insets on the west side of the complex (Room VI, pl.
367) is also decorated with a grid but one which is composed
of an alternating sequence of octagons and meander crosses
bordered by interlaced circles. This kind of field design
and border are also employed at Delphi (83, pls. 256, 270,
273-274) but there are differences which suggest that the
Anchialos pavement may represent an earlier version. First
of all, the pecking strutting and standing birds belong to
the fifth century Anchialos repertory (see pls. 364-365, 368-
375) as do the distinctive floral motifs. Second, the elongated hexagons formed by the juncture of the octagons and
meanders are filled with aniconic motifs, chevrons, not
marine life as they are at Delphi. The Delphi pavement may
well represent the last phase in the evolution of this design
whereby some and then all the compartments become receptacles
for denizens of the land and sea. It can be assigned to the
end of the fifth or the beginning of the sixth century and
the Anchialos pavement probably predates it by a few decades.
It is not improbable, therefore, that the pavement in Room VI
postdates the other pavements on this side of the complex and
that it was laid either immediately before the rebuilding of
the basilica during the second phase or in conjunction with

it. Later versions of this type of octagon design and an interlace border decorate the south aisle (pls. 383-391) but the figures have lost their plasticity and three-dimensionality, and the chain has been misunderstood (pl. 389).

In conclusion, the tessellated pavements belong to at least two decorative phases which are datable on internal and external evidence to the fifth and sixth centuries. Possibly a third and earlier phase is represented by the pavements under the south aisle and in the south annex but this is problematic until the area is completely cleared. The technical and qualitative differences between the fifth and sixth century pavements may very well reflect the decline or disappearance of the mosaic workshop to the south by around 532. The same difference occurs at Basilica Delta where the pavement in the northwest annex is inferior to the rest of the pavements (see pl. 400 and pls. 409-410). The birds and fish are completely two-dimensional and schematic and beg comparison with those in the south aisle at Gamma. Moreover, the field is constricted by a very wide framing device like that at Gamma.[522] Whether the decline or disappearance of the workshop reflects a change in the economic conditions of the city of Nea Anchialos toward the middle of the reign of Justinian or just a trend away from tessellated pavements with a concommitant loss of skilled craftsmen cannot be determined at this time. It is evident, however, that a

---

[522]Vide infra, 121, p. 309.

proper study of the results of the excavations will furnish
important data to the historian as well as the art historian.

Additional bibliography. Sodini, Catalogue, No. 37, pp.
718-720, 745-746; idem, Complements, p. 582.

Illustration. A. K. Orlandos, To Ergon, 1972, p. 14,
fig. 7 = our pl. 362.

PERIOD I

105   Room Ib (7.50 x 13.40). South portico of atrium; later,
      north side walled up, west side partitioned and piers
installed.[523]   Pls. 363-365.

No published information on dimensions and material.

Polychrome rectilinear pavement with fifty-five figural
insets surrounded by two borders.

Framing: outer border, presumably, a narrow undulating
vine rinceau forming scrolls which are filled with ivy
leaves;[524] inner border, wide band decorated with intersecting circles forming concave-sided squares set on edge
which are inscribed with similar but smaller squares.

Field: straight grid composed of a two-strand guilloche
forming on the east-west axis eleven rows of five small

-----

[523]G. A. Soteriou, Praktika, 1934, pp. 12-13, 59. This
compartment was identified as Room IV in the early reports
and its numeration is retained by the present excavator (see
plan, pl. 362).

[524]Ibid. This border is omitted by Sodini, Catalogue,
p. 719.

squares each. The guilloche bifurcates along the edges of
the field to form a continuous border. The squares are
filled with naturalistic fish, animals (deer), pecking birds
(pls. 364-365), and an owl which stand amid branches and
flowers and are executed in green, blue, red, bluish white,
and white.[525]

Middle of the fifth century.

Pavement lifted and consolidated.[526]

Additional bibliography. E. Kitzinger, DOP, 3 (1946), pp.
137-138.

Illustrations. G. A. Soteriou, Praktika, 1933, p. 52, fig.
4 = our pl. 364; idem, Praktika, 1934, p. 58, fig. 2 = our pl.
363, p. 59, fig. 3 = our pl. 365; idem, Praktika, 1940, p. 20,
fig. 3 (general view).

106 Room II (26.20 x 4.70).[527] Exonarthex; pavement laid up
     to north wall.[528] Pl. 366.

No published information on dimensions and material.

Purely geometric carpet composed of large circles enclosed by

_____

[525]G. A. Soteriou, Praktika, 1933, pp. 12, 51, p. 52,
fig. 4 (incorrectly attributed to the left or north side of
the atrium). Sodini only notes the presence of animals
(ibid.).

[526]P. Lazarides, Praktika, 1969, p. 59; idem, Praktika,
1971, p. 34.

[527]This compartment was identified as Room V in the early
reports (G. A. Soteriou, Praktika, 1930, pp. 13, 34) and its
numeration is retained by the present excavator (see plan, pl.
362).

[528]P. Lazarides, Praktika, 1969, p. 20.

two narrow borders.

Framing: outer border, light and dark wave crests;[529] dark fillet; inner border, interlocking pattern composed of alternating pairs of horizontal and vertical peltae with cruciform stems.

Field, framed by a dark single or double fillet which forms, at the same time, part of the design: series of large circles, framed by a two-strand guilloche, inscribed with a shield pattern composed of alternating dark blue and white triangles. In a published photograph (pl. 366), there are traces in two spandrels of simple trilobate forms composed of a reel flanked by single lanceolate leaves and accompanied by small disks along the arc of the circle.[530]

Middle of the fifth century.

Pavement extensively damaged; lifted and consolidated.[531]

Illustration. G. A. Soteriou, Praktika, 1931, pl. A, fig. 1 = our pl. 366.

107 Room VI (5.62-86 x 8.56-60). Southwest annex of atrium.
Pl. 367.

---

[529]This is omitted by Sodini, Catalogue, p. 719.

[530]For the general description, see G. A. Soteriou, Praktika, 1930, pp. 13, 34; idem, Praktika, 1933, pp. 11, 51. Whether the circles were tangent or juxtaposed is not noted, but Sodini is incorrect in ascribing only one "rosace" to this area and one border (Catalogue, p. 719).

[531]P. Lazarides, Praktika, 1971, p. 23.

No published information on dimensions and material.

Rectilinear design composed of octagons, with figural insets, and meanders, enclosed by two interlace borders.[532]

Framing: two-strand chain forming circles which are inscribed with geometric and organic filling motifs. Among the former there are concentric squares set on edge, two-strand Solomon's knots, and three-strand knots with six loops. The organic motifs are represented by fruit-bearing branches, quatrefoils composed of trilobate or curling leaves, and at least three juxtaposed pecking or strutting birds which are located either on the east or west side of the border;[533] inner border, three-strand braid.

Field, framed by a narrow light band: network of alternating octagons and equilateral meander crosses forming elongated hexagons (for similar designs with and without figures, see 83, 95, 137). The octagons are cut along either the north or south margin and the hexagons on all sides of the field. Land and sea animals stand, sit, or swim in the

---

[532]Except for a drawing (pl. 367), no descriptions or photographs have been published. It is highly probable that this is the floor briefly noted by G. A. Soteriou in 1930 as having a "Syriac scroll," a common Greek term for this pattern (Praktika, 1930, p. 33). An error in the report, however, places the pavement to the "north of Room VII which, as he subsequently shows, has a completely different border and field (see 105). The caption accompanying the drawing incorrectly places it in Room VIII (A. K. Orlandos, To Ergon, 1972, p. 132, fig. 123 = our pl. 367).

[533]The orientation of the pavement is not noted in the reports.

constricted spaces of the octagons[534] and serve as animated
foils for the surrounding geometric framework. Among the
identifiable creatures, which reverse direction toward the
center of the room, are dolphins, octapi, crayfish, and
rabbits nibbling at clusters of grapes. In addition, there
is a menagerie of perching, pecking, and strutting land birds
and water fowl usually accompanied by freely disposed branches
with buds and cup-like flowers (for similar birds and flora
in an adjacent room, see pls. 368-370, 372-374). In an
alternating rhythm of six and seven octagons on the longitudinal axis, the sequence of figures is as follows.[535]
First row: dolphin; traces of a bird; ribbed vase with spiral
handles, a wide mouth, and a small base; bird with two bud-
bearing branches. Second row: bird with two bud-bearing
branches; traces of an octopus or crayfish; destroyed. Third
row: octopus; second, third and fourth panels contain a
pecking duck with two cup-like flowers. Fourth row: traces
of a duck (?); traces of a wicker basket with grapes; duck
with two cup-like flowers. Fifth row: traces of a fish;
animal, perhaps a rabbit; pecking duck similar to one in third
row; seated rabbit nibbling on grapes. Starting with the
sixth row, the figures face in the opposite direction. Sixth
row: rooster with bud-bearing branch; hen with three chicks;

---

[534]The exceptions to the fauna are two fruit laden
baskets and a vase.

[535]The sequence starts at the upper left side of the
photograph and moves across the width of the room.

rooster with bud-bearing branch. Seventh row: dolphin; land bird with two bud-bearing and flower-bearing branches; wicker basket with clusters of grapes and other fruit; land bird like the one in the second octagon in this row. Eighth row: destroyed; crayfish; two superimposed pecking birds facing in opposite directions (for a similar composition in Room VII, see pl. 374). Ninth row: octopus; probably a nesting land bird; two confronting birds perched on the rim of a wide-mouthed vase set on a narrow base (for a similar composition in Room VII, see pl. 370); nesting duck. Tenth row: bird with two bud-bearing branches; seated rabbit nibbling grapes; land bird with two cup-like flowers. Eleventh row: traces of a dolphin; two superimposed fish facing in different directions; pecking duck with two cup-like flowers; two superimposed fish facing in different directions. Twelfth row: first two octagons destroyed; pecking bird with two bud-bearing branches.

The majority of the fauna is arranged systematically so that the central octagon in each row is usually flanked by confronting creatures of the same species. This type of symmetrical disposition is employed for the figures in the grid design in Room VII (pls. 368-369) and in the southwest annex of Basilica Delta (pl. 400).

Probably second half of the fifth century.

Pavement lifted and consolidated.[536]

Illustrations. P. Lazarides, Praktika, 1971, pl. 34a (general view); A. K. Orlandos, To Ergon, 1972, p. 132, fig. 123 = our pl. 367.

108 Room VII (ca. 5.75 x 2.95).[537] Southeast annex of

atrium; pavement laid up to south threshold block and

continued into north threshold.[538] Pls. 368-374.

No published information on dimensions and material.

Polychrome rectilinear pavement with ten figural insets and an ivy rinceau border.

Framing: border, undulating vine rinceau forming rigidly arranged scrolls filled with single heart-shaped ivy leaves with trailing tips. In front of the north entrance to the room (pl. 368), stand two small confronting ducks which appear to be pecking at the vine itself or at a tendril; dark fillet.

Field, framed by a narrow light band: straight grid

---

[536]P. Lazarides, Praktika, 1971, p. 27.

[537]This compartment was identified as "Hall 1" and then "Hall 2" (see G. A. Soteriou, Praktika, 1930, p. 33 and idem, Praktika, 1931, p. 37, n. 1 and captions to pls. A-E). Its present designation is "Room II" and it is so identified on the latest plan (pl. 362).

[538]In a report the directions are reversed but this appears to be an error (see P. Lazarides, Praktika, 1971, pl. 31). It is clear that the threshold block on the right side of the photograph (pl. 368) is the east one (see plan, pl. 362). The threshold at the top of the photograph, there-fore, is, in fact, on the north, not the south, side.

composed of a two-strand guilloche forming two rows of five
squares each (0.70). The guilloche bifurcates along the
margins to form a continuous border. The figures in the
squares, oriented eastward, are arranged symmetrically on
either side of the central squares. Thus the top row shows
two confronting deer (male and female) facing a square (pl.
369) with a large ribbed crater with flowing water (pl. 370)
which is flanked by two pairs of superimposed land birds.
At the top, a confronting pair perch on the rim of the crater:
one looking straight ahead; the other leaning forward to
drink. Below them, opposing birds turn toward each other,
their curving bodies repeating the line of the vase. The two
wide-eyed, heraldic stags which face this scene (pls. 368-369,
371) are represented with white bellies and distinctive
checkerboard markings along their dark dorsal sides. The
symmetrical organization of these three panels is repeated in
the bottom row where confronting birds, a peacock (pl. 372)
and a peahen with chicks (pl. 373), flank a large wicker
basket filled with fruit (pl. 369). At its base two small
birds stretch their necks to peck at the clusters of grapes
which fall from the sides of the basket. In contrast to the
heraldic compositions and figures in the center of the pavement, the remaining four squares on the extreme north and
south sides contain mundane scenes of superimposed ducks idly
pecking at bud-bearing branches (pls. 368-369, 374). The
compositional incongruity of these scenes causes them to
appear as insertion motifs, perhaps to fill up the space

allotted to the field.[539] The fauna are three-dimensional
and have supple black outlines but they are contained within
the rigid, spaceless environment of the panels. This obtains
as well for the superimposed ducks and chicks and for the
flora which are liberally spread across the surface of most
of the panels.

Additional color. Birds: blue, green, white details. Red
flowers.

Middle of the fifth century.

Additional bibliography. Ch. I. Makaronas, Makedonika, 1
(1940), p. 231; E. Kitzinger, DOP, 3 (1946), p. 137.

Illustrations. G. A. Soteriou, Praktika, 1931, pl. A, fig.
2 (view looking north) pl. B, fig. 3 = our pl. 372, pl.
Gamma, fig. 3a = our pl. 370, pl. D, fig. 3b = our pl. 374, pl.
E, fig. 3gamma = our pl. 371; BCH, 79 (1955), p. 270, fig.
6 = our pl. 369, p. 270, fig. 7 = our pl. 373; A. K. Orlandos,
To Ergon, 1971, p. 32, fig. 33 = our pl. 368.

109 Room VIII (7.25 x 5.85). South annex of exonarthex.[540]

Pls. 375-376.

No published information on dimensions. Stone tesserae
(0.01 sq) set 1-3mm apart.[541]

---

[539]The original design was probably similar to the one
decorating Room IV (pl. 400) in Basilica Delta.

[540]This compartment was identified in the early reports
as a "Stoa" (G. A. Soteriou, Praktika, 1929, p. 67; idem,
Praktika, 1930, pp. 13, 32-33). Its present designation is
"Room I" and it is so identified on the latest plan (pl. 362).

[541]The size and colors of the tesserae were recorded by
Professor I. Lavin ("Field Notes: Basilica Gamma," Dumbarton
Oaks, Center for Byzantine Studies).

Purely geometric carpet surrounded by a wide grid and, along
the north side, at least, by an outer border of intersecting
circles.[542]

Framing: outer border to north (pl. 375), white intersecting circles forming black concave-sided squares set on edge
which are inscribed with small red disks; white double fillet;
black double fillet, which forms, at the same time, part of

---

[542]The confusion generated by Sodini, regarding the
attribution of the pavement to this room is wholly unwarranted
(see Catalogue, p. 719 and n. 34). A careful reading of the
early reports clearly differentiates between the pavement in
this room (which is at a low level) and the top level one in
the south aisle (Room XIV, 115) (for the first, see G. A.
Soteriou, Praktika, 1930, pp. 13, 32-33; for the second, idem,
Praktika, 1933, pp. 10, 47). While it is true that G. A.
Soteriou published a photograph of this pavement with the
erroneous caption "south aisle," (Praktika, 1954, p. 147, fig.
5 = our pl. 376) the text does not correspond with the photograph but with an earlier description of the top level pavement in the south aisle (cf. Praktika, 1930, pp. 13, 32-33 and
Praktika, 1933, pp. 10 and 47; Praktika, 1954, pp. 144 and
147). Sodini is also confused about the caption and text
accompanying the same photograph in the BCH (79 [1955], p.
250, fig. 5). Since the term "portique" is used, he incorrectly assumes that this refers to the "portique situé au S.
de la basilique," that is, to Room XV. This is nonsense since
the text clearly ascribes the "portique" to the atrium on the
west side of the basilica (p. 272). In fact, the French term
is merely a translation of the Greek word "stoa" which was
the curious designation for this room (vide supra, p. 336, n.
540). After this misinterpretation, Sodini finally accepts
G. A. Soteriou's attribution but, subsequently, changes his
mind and ascribes the pavement "au portique qui longe la
basilique au S," that is, either to Room XV or XVI (Compléments, p. 582). For evidence, he cites a recent excavation
report (P. Lazarides, Praktika, 1969, p. 22) which, however,
contains no data to substantiate his reattribution. It is
possible that he was confused by an erroneous reference to
inscriptions in the pavement, a mistake which is corrected in
a subsequent article (P. Lazarides, Praktika, 1971, p. 31).
In fact, the inscriptions in Room VIII were not tessellated
ones but inscribed on reused impost blocks at the east entrance
and belong to an earlier period (G. A. Soteriou, Praktika,
1930, p. 35, fig. 5; idem, Praktika, 1935, p. 65).

the pattern in the inner border which is decorated with grid
composed of wide bands alternating with narrow ones to form
rectangles and large and small squares. Each rectangle is
decorated with two white hour glass motifs, and a black and
light grey triangle or a bright red and light blue triangle.
The small squares contain concentric white/red/black squares
and the large squares two-strand Solomon's knots on a black
ground, white concave-sided squares set on edge, and white
quatrefoils on a bright red ground; white double fillet.

Field, framed by a black double fillet. In a published
photograph (pl. 376) there is a large octagon surrounded by
an alternating series of single squares and lozenges which
are delineated by black/white/black double fillets. The
octagon is inscribed with a circle containing a light and
dark shield pattern of light and dark triangles which radiate
from a small central circle which was presumably decorated
with a Solomon's knot.[543] The preserved squares contain
quincunxial patterns composed of four small disks or ivy
leaves in the spandrels and a central circle bordered by a
two-strand guilloche or light and dark wave crests. They
enclose a quatrefoil or a Solomon's knot which are probably
chromatically similar to those in the inner border. Floral
motifs decorate the only visible, complete lozenge while the
truncated ones along the margins are filled with trefoils or

---

[543]In a description of this panel, the Solomon's knots
are called crosses (G. A. Soteriou, _Praktika_, 1930, pp. 13,
32-33).

clusters of ivy leaves.

Additional color. Solomon's knots: light blue/white; bright red/white, outlined in black, with a white tessera at each loop. Concave-sided squares: set on a black disk against a bright red ground; light blue centers.

Pavement lifted and consolidated.

Middle of the fifth century.

Illustration. G. A. Soteriou, Praktika, 1954, p. 147, fig. 5 = our pl. 376.

110 Room XIV (dimensions indeterminable). Covered by later
     pavements.

No published information on dimensions and material.

Fragment of a geometric pavement which is probably from the same building as those on the north side of the south annex (XV, III).[544] No other data have been published.

Fourth or fifth century.

111 Room XV (30.50 max; width indeterminable). Pavement

---

[544]P. Lazarides, Praktika, 1971, p. 24 and n. 1. His incorrect reference to a photograph of this pavement in an earlier Praktika (1936), p. 33, fig. 4) repeats the erroneous attribution made by G. A. Soteriou (Praktika, 1954, p. 144). A photograph of this pavement was never reproduced.

laid up to south wall;[545] covered by four pavements.[546]
Pls. 377-380.

No published information on dimensions and material.

Fragments of a purely geometric pavement which is probably
from the same building as the fragment in Room XIV (110).[547]
One segment of the pavement contains three tangent panels
inscribed with curvilinear designs (pls. 377, 379). The
central panel has intersecting circles forming concave-sided
squares set on edge and is flanked on one side by a wide
braid[548] which is bordered on one side by overlapping circles
(pls. 377-378). On the other side of the intersecting
circles is a pattern of pairs of opposed peltae set in
alternating horizontal and vertical units.[549] A fourth panel
whose relationship to the others cannot be ascertained at the
present time contains a simple meander and square design

---

[545]G. A. Soteriou, Praktika, 1933, pp. 47-49; P.
Lazarides, Praktika, 1971, p. 25.

[546]P. Lazarides, Praktika, 1971, pp. 24-25.

[547]Part of this pavement was noted by G. A. Soteriou,
Praktika, 1933, p. 49; idem, Praktika, 1934, p. 60, fig. 58
= our pl. 378.

[548]This was described in an earlier report as a "continuous pattern of crooked crosses" (G. A. Soteriou,
Praktika, 1933, p. 49; idem, Praktika, 1934, p. 60).

[549]The panel is barely visible at the top of our
pl. 378.

articulated by flat light bands on a dark ground (pl.
380).[550] The irregular size and setting of the tesserae and
the style of the design suggest a different phase or, at
least, a different hand.[551]

Fourth or fifth century.

Illustrations. G. A. Soteriou, Praktika, 1934, p. 58,
fig. 1 = our pl. 378; P. Lazarides, Praktika, 1971, pl. 32a
= our pl. 377, pl. 32b = our pl. 380; A. K. Orlandos, To
Ergon, 1971, p. 31, fig. 32 = our pl. 379.

Period I or II

112 Room IX (ca. 26.20 x 5.00). Esonarthex; covered by two
     layers (1.00 thick) of stone paving. Pl. 381.

No published information on dimensions and material.

Traces of an aniconic mosaic pavement, set on a dark ground,
decorated with an interlocking geometric design of crosses
of four truncated lozenges separated by single squares. The
geometric elements are delineated by pronounced light/dark
double and triple fillets which serve to heighten the

---

[550]It was described as "curvilinear meanders" in the
Secretary's report to the Greek Archaeological Society, but
is omitted, oddly enough, from the field report for that
year (cf. G. P. Oikonomou, Praktika, 1933, p. 10 and G. A.
Soteriou, Praktika, 1933, p. 49).

[551]See also P. Lazarides, Praktika, 1971, p. 24. He
refers to traces of destruction and repairs to the pavement
without identifying them.

two-dimensional appearance of the design. The lozenges are
inscribed with concentric lozenges and a central disk while
the squares contain smaller concentric squares set on edge.
The interstices between the lozenges and the squares are
filled with elongated darts.[552]

Probably middle or late fifth century; installed either
during the first or second building phase.

   Illustration. A. K. Orlandos, To Ergon, 1972, p. 15,
fig. 8 = our pl. 381.

113 Room X (dimensions indeterminable). Covered by two
      layers (1.26 thick) of stone paving.[553]

   No published information on dimensions and material.

Two notations of fragments of geometric mosaics lying below
the present paving.[554] Whether they belong to the same pavement or to different ones cannot be determined at the present
time.

Probably middle or late fifth century; installed either during

   [552]On the basis of its technique and design, it is
attributed to the same period as the lower level pavement
(depth, 1.26) in the nave, X (113). See A. K. Orlandos,
To Ergon, 1972, p. 15.

   [553]A. K. Orlandos, To Ergon, 1972, p. 13.

   [554]Ibid.; G. A. Soteriou, Praktika, 1940, p. 49.

the first or second building phase.[555]

Period II

114 Room XIII (4.90 x 43.60). North aisle; pavement laid
up to south stylobate; partitioned by later east and
southeast walls which rest on the pavement.[556] Pl. 381a.
No published information on dimensions and material.

In a bad published photograph (pl. 381a), there is a rectilinear design enclosed by two borders.

Framing: outer border, light and dark wave crests; light/
dark/light bands; inner border, wide row of interlaced
squares set on edge which are inscribed with concave-sided
straight squares.

Field: straight grid composed of a two-strand guilloche
forming squares. Among the visible motifs filling the
squares there are a wide braid, scales, and possibly a
figure (pl. 381a, top).

No earlier than around the middle of the sixth century.

Illustration. P. Lazarides, Praktika, 1971, pl. 26a =
our pl. 381a.

---

[555]On the basis of its technique and design, it is
attributed to the same period as the lower level pavement
(depth, 1.00) in the esonarthex, IX (112). Vide supra,
p. 342, n. 552.

[556]P. Lazarides, Praktika, 1969, p. 20; idem, Praktika,
1970, p. 39; idem, Praktika, 1971, p. 22.

115 Room XIV (5.21-6.62 x 43.63-43.80). South aisle; pavement laid up to north stylobate; partitioned by later
north and east walls which rest on the pavement.[557] Pls.
382-397.

East panel, a: border, 1.21. Second panel, b: border,
1.58. .Third panel, c: border, 1.46. Fourth panel, d:
border, 1.21. Fifth panel, e: border, 1.31. No other
published information on dimensions and material.

Polychrome geometric pavement composed of five panels, a-e,
with different rectilinear and curvilinear designs and
multiple borders, which are enclosed by two decorative outer
borders.[558] One panel, c, contains an inscription citing the
name of an Archbishop Peter who sponsored a major restoration
of the church.

Surround: to west, at least, in rows parallel to the wall.

Framing (pl. 383): dark fillet; outer border, bead and
reel; dark fillet, inner border, light and dark wave crests;
dark fillet; light double fillet.

XIVa, east panel (pls. 382-383): rectilinear design with
figural insets, oriented westward.

---

[557]P. Lazarides, Praktika, 1970, p. 45; idem, Praktika,
1971, p. 22.

[558]Only summary descriptions of the pavements have been
published and their exact relationship cannot be determined
without additional illustrative material (see P. Lazarides,
Praktika, 1969, p. 25; A. K. Orlandos, To Ergon, 1969, p. 19;
P. Lazarides, Praktika, 1970, pp. 44-47; A. K. Orlandos, To
Ergon, 1970, pp. 27-31).

Framing: border, undulating acanthus rinceau (0.67) with
cornucopian ocreae enclosing birds, clusters of grapes, and
other types of fruit. At the mouth of each ocrea are curling
tendrils or small leaves; dark fillet, light double fillet.

Field, framed by a dark fillet: alternate rows of three and
four juxtaposed octagons which form between them small straight
squares. The design is cut along the margins. The octagons,
delineated by dark quadruple fillets, are inscribed with
various denizens of the land and sea, and with vases and other
types of still lifes. Among the land creatures are a leaping
deer, panther, and domesticated dog (pls. 384, 386), a grazing stag (pl. 387), and a long-legged bird pecking at the
ground (pl. 386). The dog wears a collar around its neck and
the panther surges forward trailing a rope with frayed edges
signaling its successful escape from captivity. Land birds
and water fowl are shown in such natural acts as preening and
pecking or are arranged in heraldic opposing pairs either
supporting a garland between them in their beaks or flanking
a vase with a ribbed body, spiral handles, and a mouth so
wide that it dwarfs the cornucopian neck supporting it (pls.
385, 387). The still lifes represented are a catch of fish
dangling from a line attached to the frame, fruit laden
baskets (pl. 384) and platters which are tipped forward to
reveal their contents whether a fish or a turtle (pls. 384,
388). Space filling flora such as branches, leaves, and
flowers are scattered around most of the figures and simple
geometric motifs decorate the small squares, among them

straight and concave-sided squares, and tangent polygons.
Generally, the flora and fauna are two-dimensional and
rather poorly executed. The tesserae are irregularly cut and
set and reveal a technical inferiority which increases in the
three succeeding panels to the west, b-d. The latter (pls.
389-396) are coarse and the designs are marked by distended,
imprecise, and asymmetrical elements and by other irregulari-
ties which reveal the hand of a totally incompetent craftsman.
The east panel, on the other hand, is better executed and the
geometric configurations more precise. Still, like the other
panels, the tesserae are irregular in shape and placement and
the figures poorly executed.[559] By and large, all the panels
in the south aisle are more abstract and less skillful than
those on the west side of the complex which, although belonging to an earlier phase, continued to be used during this
period.

XIVb, second panel (pls. 389-91): curvilinear design with
figural insets enclosed by four interlace and floral borders.
At a later time, one section of the field design was replaced
by a composition containing two confronting stags and birds
on either side of a large fountain.

Framing (pl. 389): first border, row of juxtaposed

---

[559]Whether this difference reflects different decorative
phases, perhaps a restoration by different hands, cannot be
determined without additional photographs, especially of the
junctures of the panels. There is no evidence, however,
either in the reports or the photographs of any kind of
break between each panel.

quatrefoils, with checkerboard centers, composed of ivy
leaves placed back-to-back on small disks which are separated
by trefoils of ivy leaves along the margins; second border,
two-strand guilloche; narrow light band; third border, double
chain of interlaced ellipses and small circles; narrow white
band; fourth border, two-strand guilloche on a dark ground;
narrow white band.

Field (pls. 390-391): interlace of quatrelobes forming
concave-sided octagons. The former are decorated with large,
flat leaves, sometimes nets, inscribed with small squares
which are decorated with birds and fruit. The octagons, on
the other hand, enclose, for the most part, denizens of the
sea, octopi, sepiae, dolphins, and long-legged birds.[560] An
overall crudity of execution distinguishes the design and the
filling motifs. Lacking symmetry and precise definition, the
geometric elements form distended heterogeneous enclosures
for the equally gross motifs. Thus, although the basic design
is exceptional, the mosaicist lacked the skill to execute it
properly.[561] This poverty of execution extends to the section
with a large figural composition containing a double-tiered,
scalloped fountain flanked by two heraldic stags and two
small birds. This scene represents a rather unusual example
of a replacement, not a restoration, of part of the mosaic

---

[560]In one row (pl. 390), these marine creatures are replaced by medallions inscribed with polygons.

[561]This is the only preserved pavement in Greece with
interlacing quatrelobes.

because it is quite evident that the figures were superimposed onto the original design which was intact at the time.
This kind of selective and purposeful destruction and redeco-
ration is curious and it is possible that the scene was
installed immediately after the completion of the geometric
design, perhaps at the instigation of a dissatisfied
sponsor.[562] Indeed, this may account for the apparent
technical and stylistic similarity between the original
design and its replacement.

XIVc, third panel (pls. 392-394): rectilinear geometric
design with figural insets and a long inscription enclosed by
at least two borders.[563]

Framing: outer border, double chain of interlaced circles
articulated by small cruciform motifs in the interstices;
dark double fillet; light double fillet; inner border, two-
strand guilloche; light double fillet.

Field, framed by a dark fillet: rows of tangent octagons
set on edge, forming concave-sided squares set on edge. The
motifs, which are cut along the margin, interlock to form
alternating rows of octagons and squares and are filled with
creatures from the land and sea, and fruit and fruit laden
baskets. In the octagons, these objects are enclosed by

[562]Possibly, he was the same Archbishop Peter whose name
is inscribed in the next panel.

[563]Unlike the other panels the number of the borders is
omitted from the reports (P. Lazarides, *Praktika*, 1970,
pp. 46-47; A. K. Orlandos, *To Ergon*, 1970, p. 31).

medallions with wave crest borders (pl. 393) and in the concave-sided squares by smaller straight squares which are
flanked by geometric and floral motifs (for an aniconic version of this design, see 132, pl. 430). On one side of the
panel[564] is a tabula ansata (1.62 x 1.24) containing an eight-
line inscription in black letters (0.07-0.11 high). Preceded
by a small cross and decorated with single or double red and
black ivy leaves at the ends of the second, third, and seventh
lines, the inscription cites the name of an unknown Archbishop, Peter, who restored the church.

OTHCMEΛICCHC/THCCOΦHCΔIΔACKAΛOC/
THCΠNEYMATIKHC/APXIEPEYCKΛYTOC
ΦANEIC/ΠETPOCTOCEMNON/EPΓONAΞ
IOΠPEΠWC/EΔEIΞEKAITOYTO/ΠPEΠON
EICNAONΘEOY [565]

By virtue of its asymmetrical disposition, the archaeologist
concludes that the inscription is a later addition.[566] A
careful examination of the tabula (pl. 394), however, refutes
this hypothesis because there are no signs of seams or
sutures. On the contrary, the inscription is contemporary

---

[564]Its orientation cannot be determined.

[565]For the following transcription, see P. Lazarides,
Praktika, 1970, p. 46.
O THC MEΛICCHC/THC COΦHC ΔIΔACKAΛOC THC
ΠNEYMATIKHC/ APXIEPEYC KΛYTOC ΦANEIC/
ΠETPOC TO CEMNON/ EPΓON AΞIOΠPEΠWC/
EΔEIΞE KAI TOYTO ΠPEΠON EIC NAON ΘEOY.
[566]P. Lazarides, Praktika, 1970, p. 47.

with the rest of the pavement and its position in relation to
the field is easily explained by the asymmetry of the field
design itself in which the octagons to the left are bisected
by the margin while those to the right are not (pl. 392). If
the inscription had been centralized, then its relationship
to the birds, which face it, would have been destroyed and it
would still have looked asymmetrical because of the truncated
octagons on the left side. The mosaicist, therefore,
elected to place the inscription in relation to the central
octagons which, as a result, serve as a symmetrical framing
device.

XIVd, fourth panel (pls. 395-396). Apparently, a rectilinear design with figural insets enclosed by five borders.[567]

Framing: border, two-strand guilloche on a dark ground;
light double fillet; border, tangent rectangles inscribed with
quincunxial patterns composed of geometric motifs in the
center and dolphins and leaves in the corners (pl. 395). In
the four angles of the border stand single ribbed vases with
long necks and wide mouths from which issue vines laden with
grape leaves, clusters of grapes and spiral tendrils (pl.
396); border, two-strand guilloche on a dark ground; light
double fillet.[568]

Field: large diagonal squares (0.95) alternating with

---

[567]Only a summary description of this pavement is published (P. Lazarides, Praktika, 1970, p. 47).

[568]The two other borders are not described nor are they
visible in the photograph (pl. 395).

meanders which are inscribed with "birds, fish, et al."[569]

XIVe, fifth panel (pl. 397): geometric motifs enclosed by multiple borders.[570]

Early description.

Framing: outer border, braid or guilloche; middle border, wave crests; inner border, rectangles inscribed with lozenges, circles, etc.

Field: large interlacing lozenges inscribed with circles containing vases and fruit.[571]

Recent description.

Framing: four borders and four narrow bands; middle border (0.64), white, black, and red meanders.

Field: geometric design composed of squares and octagons which contain, for the most part, birds.[572]

No earlier than around the middle of the sixth century.

West panel, e, in poor condition.[573]

---

[569]P. Lazarides, _Praktika_, 1970, p. 47.

[570]Only one bad photograph of the pavement has been published and two somewhat different descriptions. Since it was covered with lime at the time of the first description (G. A. Soteriou, _Praktika_, 1929, p. 67; idem, _Praktika_, 1933, pp. 10, 47) and had deteriorated extensively by the time of the second (P. Lazarides, Praktika, 1970, p. 47), these discrepancies will probably never be resolved. For this reason, both descriptions will be presented.

[571]G. A. Soteriou (_vide supra_, p. 351, n. 570).

[572]P. Lazarides (_vide supra_, p. 351, n. 570). In this report he states that this is the pavement excavated by G. A. Soteriou.

[573]P. Lazarides, _Praktika_, 1969, p. 22; idem, _Praktika_, 1970, p. 47.

Illustrations. G. A. Soteriou, Praktika, 1933, p. 49, fig. 2 = our pl. 397; P. Lazarides, Praktika, 1969, pl. 32a = our pl. 385, pl. 32b = our pl. 387, pl. 33a-b = our pl. 386, pl. 34 a-b = our pl. 387; idem, Praktika, 1970, pl. 58b = our pl. 382, pl. 59a = our pl. 383, pl. 59b = our pl. 384, pl. 60a = our pl. 389, pl. 60b = our pl. 391, pl. 61a = our pl. 394, pl. 61b = our pl. 393, pl. 62a = our pl. 395, pl. 62b = our pl. 396; A. K. Orlandos, To Ergon, 1970, p. 28, fig. 25 = our pl. 390.

Basilica Delta

Around three hundred meters beyond the walls of the city of Nea Anchialos (pl. 355) the foundations of a fourth basilica (overall, 29.50 x 44.00 max), designated Delta,[574] were cleared between 1934 and 1936. Mosaic pavements were discovered in the northeast and southeast rooms, III, IV, the north and south aisles, VI, VII, and in the lateral annexes, VIII, IX, X. The pavements in the north and south aisles were lifted, consolidated, and reset in situ; the condition of the others is not known.[575]

Preceded by an atrium with porticoes, Ia-c (4.40 x

---

[574]It is now called the church of St. Demetrios because of a newly discovered inscription in Room III (vide infra, p. 365, n. 600).

[575]For the consolidation, see P. Lazarides, Deltion, 25 (1970), B2: Chronika, p. 286; A. K. Orlandos, To Ergon, 1970, p. 193, figs. 205-206 = our pls. 402, 405. Although I was not permitted to enter the site (vide supra, p. 307, n. 466), Sodini was. He notes the disappearance of the pavement in the southeast annex, X, but does not comment on the condition of the others (Catalogue, p. 721 and n. 39).

7.07),[576] and a narthex, II (17.00 x 4.35), with projecting
wings, III, IV, the church proper (ca. 16.00 x 20.50) comprises a nave flanked by two aisles, V-VII, and terminated
by a semi-circular apse (pls. 398-399). It is separated
from the aisles by colonnades resting on bases set on elevated
stylobates and from the bema by a long, "⊔-shaped" chancel
barrier projecting from two lateral clergy benches which abut
the shoulders of the apse. Traces of other liturgical
furnishings, ambon, episcopal chair, altar, were not found in
situ although fragments reputedly belonging to them were
found in the vicinity.[577] Since the basilica is situated
outside the walls of the city, it served as the cemetary
church for the Christian community. Abundant evidence of
this function is supplied by the vaulted subterranean tombs
which were found beneath Rooms X and XI,[578] and by others
which were found in the vicinity of the building.[579] It
would appear that no tombs were found beneath Rooms IX and
XII or beneath II and IV so that their function is problematic.

---

[576]Except for traces of the exterior walls and the
foundations of the stylobates, the atrium was destroyed (G. A.
Soteriou, Praktika, 1936, p. 60; hereafter cited as Praktika,
1936). A recent clearing of the site in 1971 uncovered
traces of a pool in the center of the west wall of narthex
and additional rooms along the north and south sides (A. K.
Orlandos, To Ergon, 1972, p. 18). Compare our plans, pls.
398 and 399.

[577]G. A. Soteriou, Praktika, 1934, p. 63; hereafter
cited as Praktika, 1934; idem, Praktika, 1935, pp. 56-57;
hereafter cited as Praktika, 1935.

[578]Praktika, 1934, p. 63; Praktika, 1935, p. 60.

[579]Praktika, 1935, p. 58.

G. A. Soteriou reconstructs the two latter rooms as "towers"
with staircases leading to the galleries and suggests that
the room east of the north "tower", VIII, may have been a
later addition.[580]

On the basis of the style of the sculpture and the
mosaics, a seventh century date was proposed for the erection
of the building.[581] This chronology is correctly rejected by
Sodini who suggests a date in the second half of the fifth
century.[582] This is substantiated by the style of most of
the mosaics, with those in Rooms III and VIII probably belonging to a later phase.

Bibliography. G. A. Soteriou, Praktika, 1933, p. 56; idem,
Praktika, 1934, pp. 61-65; AA, 49 (1934), pp. 167-168; G. A.
Soteriou, Praktika, 1935, pp. 52-64; AA, 50 (1935), pp. 214-
215; G. A. Soteriou, Praktika, 1936, pp. 57-67; BCH, 60
(1936), pp. 475-476; AA, 51 (1936), pp. 142-143; AA, 52
(1937), pp. 147-148; AA, 55 (1940), p. 252; A. K. Orlandos,
To Ergon, 1972, pp. 18, 131.

Illustrations. G. A. Soteriou, Praktika, 1934, p. 61, fig.
5 (east side showing chancel screen); idem, Praktika, 1935, p.
52, fig. 1 (nave, from southwest); idem, Praktika, 1936, p.
58, fig. 1 (nave, from west), p. 59, fig. 3 (narthex, from
south, showing north part of pavement in southeast room),
pl. A after p. 64 = our pl. 398; P. Lazarides, Praktika,
1969, p. 18, fig. 2 = our pl. 355; A. K. Orlandos, To Ergon,
1972, p. 16, fig. 10 = our pl. 399.

---

[580]Praktika, 1936, p. 57 and p. 59, respectively.
Orlandos suggests that Rooms III and IV served as a prothesis
and diakonikon, respectively (Hē metakinēsis tou diakonikou,
p. 357, passim).

[581]Praktika, 1936, p. 59.

[582]Catalogue, p. 721 and n. 38.

Nos. 116-122

Polychrome mosaic pavements (pls. 400-411) containing
rectilinear geometric designs with geometric or figural
insets pave the north and south annexes of the narthex and
nave, and the north and south aisles.[583] The rest of the
floors are covered with marble slabs, sometimes forming a
design in opus sectile (narthex, nave, bema).

On the basis of the style of the mosaics, especially of
the figural panels in Room IV (pls. 400-401), the majority of
the pavements can be attributed to the second half of the
fifth century.[584] The organic filling motifs are much more
fluid, plastic, and three-dimensional than ones belonging to
the first half of the sixth century (60, pls. 164-165; 62,
pls. 171-176; 150, pls. 460-464; 152, pls. 466-472; 153, pls.
473-485; 154-155, pls. 486-532) and are closer to fifth century representations, such as those at Athens (16, pls. 47-
48; 18, pl. 52; 19, pl. 55) and Akrini (189, pls. 619-621)
which still retain some naturalistic characteristics. This
chronology is substantiated to a great extent by the increased
width of the borders and the concommitant shrinkage of the
fields. Although no measurements are available, a comparison

[583]Since I was not permitted to study the mosaics in
situ, my descriptions are based on the published material
and the field notes of Professor I. Lavin in the possession
of Dumbarton Oaks.

[584]Vide supra, p. 354, n. 582.

of the south aisle (pls. 406-407) with a similar pavement at
Epidauros (16, pl. 108) reveals a distinct change in the ratio
between the field and the border, with the latter assuming an
important role in regard to the overall decorative scheme.
This obtains as well in the north aisle (pl. 402) where the
field is bordered by a poly-strand braid each side of which
almost equals half the width of the field, and, presumably,
in the northeast annex.[585] In the other pavements, (Rooms
IV, VIII, IX) triple or quadruple borders, not single ones,
produce the same effect. Although it is by no means consistent, there appears to be a general trend from the second
half of the fifth century onward in which the width of the
framing of the pavements increases, becomes more complex, and,
in some examples becomes a receptacle for land and sea
animals (69, pls. 198, 201-202, 204; 83, pl. 256; 156, pls.
470-471; 153, pls. 473-476). Given the paucity of adequate
photographs of the pavement in the northwest annex, III (pls.
409-410), only a tentative proposal regarding its chronology
is possible. The flora and fauna appear to be more two-
dimensional and schematic with a resultant loss of plasticity.
In general terms, although the straight grid pattern is
similar to that in the southwest annex (pl. 400), it only
encloses six figural insets in contrast to the twelve in its

---

[585]Although there is no photograph of the framing, even
the excavator noted that the border was so wide that the field
could only accomodate six panels (Praktika, 1936, p. 64).

counterpart to the south. Since the rooms are approximately the same size, this could only mean that the framing is considerably wider resulting in a narrower path for the field design. In light of these stylistic and formal differences, the pavement in the northwest annex is probably later and should be assigned to the sixth century. Indeed, the pavement resembles those in the securely dated north and south aisles of Basilica Gamma (115, pls. 383-396) which are assigned to a period after 532.[586] To this phase may belong the room adjacent to this annex which, on obscure grounds, is considered to be an addition.[587] Its braid pattern is different in color, design, and technique from that decorating the border of the north aisle (cf. pls. 411 and 412). A more positive attribution of these two pavements to a later phase must, of course, await the results of a re-investigation of the site which is now in progress.[588]

Additional bibliography. Sodini, Catalogue, No. 38, pp. 720-721. I. Lavin, "Field Notes: Nea Anchialos, Basilica Delta," Dumbarton Oaks, Center for Byzantine Studies.

Illustration. G. A. Soteriou, Praktika, 1936, pl. A after p. 64 = our pl. 398.

---

[586]Vide supra, p. 327, and n. 522.

[587]Praktika, 1936, p. 59.

[588]P. Lazarides, Deltion, 25 (1970), B2: Chronika, p. 286; A. K. Orlandos, To Ergon, 1970, p. 193.

PERIOD I, PHASE 1

116 Room IV (5.30 x 4.35). Southwest annex. Pls. 400-401.

Square panels: 0.55. No other published information on
dimensions. Marble (white), glass (reds, greens), and stone
tesserae (0.01 sq).[589]

Polychrome rectilinear mosaic with twelve figural insets
surrounded by three borders of varying widths.

Framing: narrow light/dark/light bands; outer border,
meander forming swastikas; narrow light/dark/light bands;
middle border, two-strand guilloche (with a light tessera at
each loop) on a dark ground; narrow light/dark bands; inner
border, light and dark wave crests; narrow light/dark bands.

Field, framed by a narrow light band: in a published
photograph (pl. 400), there is a straight grid composed of a
two-strand guilloche (same as middle border) forming four
rows of three squares each (for similar designs in Basilica
Gamma, see 105, pls. 363-365; 108, pls. 368-369). The
guilloche bifurcates along the margin to form a continuous
border. Each row comprises a central square flanked by confronting animals or birds which are surrounded by undulating
branches. The extreme north and south rows contain identical
compositions of two deer (pl. 401) facing a vase, while in
the middle rows birds flank squares filled with superimposed

---

[589]Praktika, 1936, p. 62.

fish and a bird. Reds, greens are used throughout to enhance the figures and the flora.[590]

Second half of the fifth century.

Illustrations. G. A. Soteriou, Praktika, 1936, p. 59, fig. 3 (general view of narthex showing north side of pavement), p. 63, fig. 7 = our pl. 401; idem, Praktika, 1954, p. 150, fig. 7 = our pl. 400.

117 Room VI (4.28 x 20.50). North aisle. Pls. 402-404.

No published information on dimensions and material. Irregularly-cut tesserae (0.015-0.02).[591]

Originally, at least two rectangular panels, with geometric designs, bordered by a broad braid.[592]

Framing (pl. 402): border, wide braid (1 white/2 yellow/2 white; 1 white/2 orange/2 white; 1 white/2 purple/2 white; 1 white/2 light blue/2 white, outlined in black, with a white tessera at each loop); black triple fillet; white double fillet; light blue double fillet.

Field (pls. 403-404), framed by a white double fillet whith forms, at the same time, part of the design.

---

[590]Ibid. Except for this general notation, the colors of the individual objects are not specified.

[591]Ibid.

[592]Only one panel is described in the report (ibid.) and by Sodini who saw the pavement in the 1960's. In 1964, Professor Lavin noted the presence of two compartments and the destruction of almost two-thirds of the pavement. Vide infra, p. 360, n. 593.

VIa, west panel (pl. 403): an interlocking design composed
of juxtaposed circles joined by diagonal quatrefoils to form
horizontal and vertical elongated hexagons with concave sides
(for similar designs, see 77, pl. 238; 142, pl. 447). The
design is delineated by white double fillets, outlined in
black, and is cut along the margins. The squares are filled
with diagonal quatrefoils which are set on square or quadru-
lobate grounds and the hexagons are decorated with two juxtaposed circles joined by a "V-shaped" fillet.

VIb, east panel (pl. 404), framed by a light blue double
fillet which forms, at the same time, part of the design:
light blue network of tangent octagons and small squares
which is cut along the margins. The octagons contain
Solomon's knots, checkerboard motifs, diagonal or straight
quatrefoils, and crosses composed of four heart-shaped ivy
leaves placed tip-to-tip; the squares have plain red/white or
light blue/white centers. The overall color scheme of the two
panels is black, white, light blue, red, yellow, and dark
purple.[593]

Second half of the fifth century.

Pavement lifted, reset on new foundations; **visible in situ**.

Illustration. A. K. Orlandos, To Ergon, 1970, p. 193,
fig. 206 = our pl. 402.

---

[593]For the colors, see I. Lavin, "Field Notes: Nea
Anchialos, Basilica Delta," Dumbarton Oaks, Center for
Byzantine Studies.

118 Room VII (4.15 x 20.50). South aisle. Pls. 405-407.

Squares: ca. 0.60. No other published information on dimensions. Material and dimensions identical to those in Room IV (117).

Polychrome rectilinear design forming squares surrounded by a broad, complex interlace.

Framing (pl. 407): single chain of interlaced squares set on edge and enclosing concave-sided straight squares which are inscribed with small dark disks; dark/white/dark double fillets.

Field (pls. 406-407), framed by a white double fillet: straight grid composed of a two-strand guilloche (with a single tessera at each loop) on a dark ground forming squares which enclose geometric and floral motifs. Among the latter are diagonal quatrefoils of heart-shaped ivy leaves placed tip-to-tip, trefoils, and diagonal quatrefoils of lanceolate leaves. The geometric motifs comprise wheel patterns of wave crests around a circle, looped circles, interlaced crosses, scales, braids, and Solomon's knots.[594] These motifs appear to be set on colored squares, outlined by dark/light double fillets. The range of colors is identical to that in the north aisle (117).

[594]Praktika, 1935, p. 54; Praktika, 1936, p. 62. Sodini, Catalogue, p. 721. For similar patterns, see Room IX, pl. 408.

Second half of the fifth century.

Pavement lifted, reset on new foundations; <u>visible in situ.</u>

Illustrations. G. A. Soteriou, <u>Praktika</u>, 1933, p. 53, fig. 2 = our pl. 406, p. 54, fig. 3 (detail of a square), p. 61, fig. 6 = our pl. 407; A. K. Orlandos, <u>To Ergon</u>, 1970, p. 193, fig. 205 = our pl. 405.

119 Room IX (4.35 x 5.00). Northeast annex. Pl. 408.

No published information on dimensions and material.

Polychrome geometric design with geometric filling motifs surrounded by four borders.[595]

Framing: first border, yellow and white triangles; second border, black and white wave crests on a red and yellow ground; third border, overlapping lyre pattern with alternating white/red/white and white/yellow/white triangles flanked, respectively, by yellow/white and red/white strands which are outlined in black and set on a colored ground; white/black double fillet; fourth border, wave crests like those in the second border; black fillet; white/black double fillets.

Field, framed by a white double fillet which forms, at the same time, part of the design: large octagon surrounded by an alternating series of single squares and lozenges which are delineated by white/black/white double fillets and cut along the margins (for a similar design in Basilica Gamma, see 109, pls. 375-376). The octagon is inscribed with a circle, bordered by a two-strand guilloche, containing a shield pattern of light and dark triangles which radiate from a small central circle decorated with a Solomon's knot. The geometric and floral motifs in the squares and lozenges are arranged around the octagon in paris of opposing panels with identical motifs. Similar to those in the south aisle (pl. 407), the motifs in the squares consist of looped circles, wheels of wave crests, diagonal quatrefoils of lanceolate leaves, and heart-shaped ivy leaves placed tip-to-tip. The complete lozenges and the truncated ones along the margin are decorated primarily with trefoils or trefoil-like patterns composed of heart-shaped ivy leaves, and single ivy leaves or buds with trailing tendrils. The range of colors is identical to that in the north and south aisles (117-118).

Second half of the fifth century.

Illustrations. G. A. Soteriou, Praktika, 1936, p. 58, fig. 2 (general view, looking north); F. van der Meer and C. Mohrmann, Atlas of the Early Christian World, London, 1958, p. 100, fig. 285 (general view).

120 Room X (4.35 x 5.00). Southeast annex; pavement almost totally destroyed, possibly when vaulted tombs looted.[596]

Pl. 408a.

No published information on dimensions and material.

---

[596]Praktika, 1935, pp. 61-62.

In a bad photograph (pl. 408a), there appears to be a straight
grid composed of circles united by short bars which form
concave-sided octagons. It is, perhaps, similar to the pavements in Basilicas Beta (160, pl. 563) and Delta (164, pl.
576) at Nikopolis.

Second half of the fifth century.

  Illustration. G. A. Soteriou, Praktika, 1936, p. 60, fig.
4 = our pl. 408a.

PERIOD I, PHASE 2

121 Room III (5.05 x 4.30). Northwest annex. Pls. 409-410.
No published information on dimensions and material.

Polychrome rectilinear design with six figural panels
surrounded by a broad border or borders.[597]
  Framing: wide border, black and white intersecting circles
forming concave-sided squares which are inscribed with small
red circles.
  Field: straight grid composed of a two-strand guilloche
forming three rows of two rectangles each (for a similar
design in Room IV, see 116, pl. 400). The panels are filled

---

[597]This description is primarily based on Sodini's entry
(Catalogue, p. 720) and Professor Lavin's field notes (vide
supra, p. 360, n. 593). In one report, a photograph of this
pavement (our pl. 409) is incorrectly attributed to the southwest annex, Room IV (G. A. Soteriou, Praktika, 1954, p. 152,
fig. 9).

with land birds, water fowl, and fish.[598] In a published
photograph (pl. 409), there are two confronting birds on
either side of a bush. All the elements are schematically
rendered and two-dimensional and differ from similar figures
in the southwest room (pl. 400). This unnaturalistic style
obtains as well for the red and light blue fish in another
panel (pl. 410) which are arranged in an asymmetrical and
unbalanced composition.[599] Somewhere in the room there is an
inscription invoking the name of St. Demetrios: "ΔΗΜΗΤΡΙΕ
ΒΟΗΘΙ ."[600]

Probably sixth century; on the basis of a stylistic and
technical resemblance to the late pavements in Basilica Gamma
(115, pls. 384-394).

   Illustration. G. A. Soteriou, Praktika, 1936, p. 63, fig.
8 = our pl. 409.

122   Room VIII (5.05 x ca. 2.20). Room east of northwest
      annex (121); possibly a later addition.[601] Pl. 411.
   No published information on dimensions and material.

_____

   [598]Sodini, Catalogue, p. 720.

   [599]In the majority of the marine scenes, they are
arranged in superimposed registers (see Room IV, pl. 400 and
Klapsi, pls. 317-318, 338-341).

   [600]A. K. Orlandos, To Ergon, 1972, p. 131; vide supra,
p. 352, n. 574.

   [601]Vide supra, p. 357, n. 587.

Purely geometric carpet surrounded by a triple border.

Framing: outer border, black and white wave crests; white/ dark double fillets; middle border, two-strand interlace (yellow/1 white; light blue/1 white, outlined in black) forming small dark circles, outlined in white; black double fillet; inner border, wave crests.

Field, framed by a white fillet which forms, at the same time, part of the design: wide braid (yellow/1 white; red/ 1 white; light blue/1 white, outlined in black) decorated with small dark squares at each loop which becomes concave-sided triangles along the margin.[602] In comparison with a similar braid in the border of the pavement in the north aisle (pl. 402), this one is more decorative but coarser.

Probably contemporary with, or later than, the sixth century pavement in the adjacent room (121).

THEOTOKOU

Basilica

At a place called Theotokou, on the tip of the Magnesian Peninsula, an Early Christian basilica (overall, 19.00 x 27.00) was excavated in 1907 and re-excavated in 1930,[603]

---

[602]Vide supra, p. 360, n. 593.

[603]A. J. B. Wace and J. P. Droop, BSA, 13 (1906-1907), pp. 315-321; hereafter cited as Wace and Droop; Soteriou, Palaiochristianikai basilikai, pp. 182-183. Except for the

bringing to light tessellated pavements in the majority of the rooms. At the present time traces of the foundations and walls of the narthexes and apse are visible, but the pavements are covered with vines and debris.[604]

Preceded by a porch, I, and two narthexes, II, V, the outer one with north and south annexes, III, IV, the church proper (pl. 412; 13.00 x 13.00) comprises a nave, VI, separated from single flanking aisles, VII-VIII, by elevated stylobates and terminated by a semi-circular apse. The type of internal divisions between the nave and aisles and the nave and bema was not determined nor were any traces found of the original liturgical furnishings.[605] Traces of another building and walls were found in the vicinity, but they have not been excavated.

On the basis of the iconography of the pavements, the church was assigned by the excavators to the fifth century with a terminus ante quem of 570-571 supplied by a follis of Justin II and Sophia which was found somewhere "in the

---

measurements of the nave and ailes, the dimensions are taken from the plan by Wace and Droop (pl. 10). Our plan (pl. 412) comes from Soteriou's study which lacks a key and has few measurements inscribed on the plan.

[604]E. Kourkoutidou, Deltion, 23 (1968), B2: Chronika, p. 275, pl. 215b-d.

[605]Soteriou (Palaiochristianikai basilikai, p. 183) presents convincing arguments for ascribing the altar base in the apse and the chancel screen along its chord to a later period.

church."[606] Since the location of the coin is not specified
and five coins of John Tzimiskes (969-976) were also found
"in the church," the numismatic evidence is inconclusive, as
is the iconographic analysis.[607] It will be shown below,
that the church belongs to a period no earlier than the late
fifth century and probably is to be placed into the first
decades of the sixth century. Upon its destruction, it was
partially restored and served a different function. The
south wall of the porch, I, was extended, the exonarthex was
divided by a later wall, and the doorway between the narthex
and the nave was blocked up.[608] The chronology and the
function of the building in this phase could not be determined.

Bibliography. A. J. B. Wace and J. P. Droop, BSA, 13
(1906-07), pp. 309-327; Soteriou, Palaiochristianikai
basilikai, pp. 182-183; E. Kourkoutidou, Deltion, 23 (1968),
B2: Chronika, p. 275.

Illustrations. A. J. B. Wace and J. P. Droop, BSA, 13
(1906-1907), p. 309, fig. 1 (plan of site), p. 315, fig. 6
(west end of church, from north), pl. X (plan); Soteriou,
Palaiochristianikai basilika, p. 183, fig. 14 = our pl. 412;
E. Kourkoutidou, Deltion, 23 (1968), B2: Chronika, pl. 215b-d
(architectural fragments).

Nos. 123-128

Polychrome geometric pavements containing rectilinear

---

[606]Nowhere is it stated that the coin was found "sur la
mosaïque" (see Sodini, Catalogue, p. 722).

[607]For the dating, see Wace and Droop, pp. 319-320.

[608]Wace and Droop, pp. 320-321 and pl. X (plan).

designs with organic and geometric filling motifs pave most
of the rooms.[609] With one exception,[610] the published illustrative material comprises black and white drawings of the
pavements which, by their very nature, prevent a satisfactory
analysis of their style. The flora and fauna appear to be
quite two-dimensional and schematic and are reminiscent of
figures belonging to the late fifth and the sixth centuries.
This chronology is substantiated by the types of borders,
especially those in Rooms V and VI (pls. 416-417) which do
not antedate that period. Similar interlace borders decorate
the pavements at Delphi (83, pl. 256), Nikopolis (164, pls.
575, 578-579), Akrini (189, pls. 620-621), Longos (197, pls.
635, 637) and Stobi (pl. 641) which belong to around the turn
of the century. Individual filling motifs and patterns such
as the interlace in Room III (pl. 415) composed of rainbow and
guilloche strands and the complex lozenged motifs in Room II
(pl. 414) also belong to this period (52, pl. 117, top; 59,
pl. 160; 213, pls. 663-665; 220, pl. 693). Although the
chromatic scheme of the Theotokou pavements is difficult to
determine, it is clear from the various types of stipled,
hatched, horizontal, and vertical lines inscribed in the
drawings, that they were richly colored (yellows, blues, reds,

---

[609]During the second excavation Room IV was cleared but
its paving was not noted (Soteriou, Palaiochristianikai
basilikai, p. 183).

[610]Vide supra, p. 367, n. 604. The descriptions of the
pavements (123-128) are based on the published material
(Wace and Droop, pp. 315-318, and pl. XI).

reddish brown, green).[611] This polychromy is another reason
for an advanced date since earlier pavements in the vicinity
(130-137) and, in fact, elsewhere in central and northern
Greece (88-92; 178-179), are primarily black and white with
polychrome highlights. Another feature which suggests a
later date is the unusual tripartite division of the nave
pavement on its longitudinal axis (pl. 417). No fifth century pavement is compartmentalized in this manner. Rather,
the scheme involves one large panel (pls. 157; 420) or two to
three panels (pls. 103; 257-258; 295) which are arranged
along the width of the room. Although this traditional
scheme continues into the sixth century (pls. 315; 676), it
is at this time that the longitudinal division makes its
appearance in the securely dated church at Nikopolis (153,
pl. 476) and at Aigosthena (30, pls. 76, 82). Although these
comparisons are based on inadequate illustrations, it is very
probable that the pavements belong to the very late fifth
century or, more likely, to the first decades of the sixth
century.

Additional bibliography. Sodini, Catalogue, No. 39, p. 721.

Illustration. Soteriou, Palaiochristianikai basilikai,
p. 183, fig. 14 = our pl. 412.

---

[611]In the legend in the lower right corner of the plate
containing the drawing of the pavements (pl. 416), each
color is listed with an appropriate lined or stipled box.
Since, however, this is very difficult to read, and it is not
clear if the colors obtain for all the floors or only for the
esonarthex, Room V, the polychromatic scheme is not presented
in the entries.

123   Room I (8.40 x 3.20).   Porch, Pls. 413, 416.

No published information on dimensions and material

Polychrome rectilinear design originally composed of forty-
eight organic and geometric insets of which twenty-seven
survive.

Framing: outer border, simple two-strand interlace (outlined in black) forming small circles which are inscribed
with light and dark hour glass motifs (pl. 416); dark blue
fillet; narrow white band; dark blue fillet.

Field: straight grid composed of a two-strand guilloche
(with a light tessera at each loop)[612] on a dark ground forming two rows of four squares each. The squares are filled
with organic and geometric motifs which are similar to those
inscribed in a similar design in Room V (126, pl. 416).[613]
Beginning at the northeast corner and moving westward, the
sequence of filling elements is as follows. First row:
destroyed; interlaced rectangles; interlaced squares, one set
on edge;[614] destroyed. Second row: checkerboard pattern;
bird (pl. 413, bottom left); undulating rinceau forming rigidly arranged scrolls filled with single heart-shaped ivy leaves
(pl. 416); fruit (pl. 413, top left). Third row: bush (pl.

---

[612]Wace and Droop compare this border to the one in Room
II (pl. 414).

[613]Wace and Droop, p. 316 and n. 2.

[614]For the interlaces, see pl. 416, top.

413, right); rest destroyed. Fourth row: two interlaces
(see first row and pl. 416, top); rest destroyed. Fifth row:
basket (pl. 413); rest destroyed. Sixth row: destroyed;
pinwheel (pl. 413); rest destroyed. Seventh row: bush (pl.
413); destroyed; destroyed; diagonal quatrefoil of lanceolate
leaves (pl. 413). Eighth row: not recorded; two interlaces
like those in the first and fourth rows (pl. 416, top);
imbrication (pl. 416, right); destroyed. Ninth row: completely destroyed. Tenth row: apple tree; plant with lotus
flowers, buds, and two rosettes (pl. 413, top); apple tree;
pear tree (pl. 413). Eleventh row: four squares with birds
(pl. 413, bottom left). Twelfth row: interlaces like those
in first, fourth, and eighth rows (pl. 416, top); "marble"
panel;[615] checkerboard.

Very late fifth century; more likely sixth century.

   Illustration. A. J. B. Wace and J. P. Droop, BSA, 13
(1906-1907), pl. XI, C,F = our pls. 413-416.

124 Room II (8.40 x 3.20). Exonarthex; pavement, presumably,
   laid up to west threshold step; covered by mortar along
north side.[616] Divided by later wall. Pl. 414.

   615Wace and Droop, p. 316.

   616Ibid. The exact relationship between the west
threshold and the mosaic is not clear. Although this block
is visible in the original plan (ibid., pl. X) and the corrected one (our pl. 412), it is omitted from the drawing of
the mosaic (pl. 414). Since the excavators think that the
step and the pavement are contemporaneous, the borders must

Interlocking polychrome design of lozenges and squares
inscribed with flora and geometric motifs and, in the center
of the room, with four birds.

Framing: wide light band; narrow dark band; outer border,
light and dark wave crests; narrow light band; inner border,
two-strand guilloche identical to that in Room I (123).

Field: interlocking geometric design composed of crosses
of four lozenges separated by squares. The lozenges are bisected along the margins (for similar designs, see 15; 44).
Four squares in the center of the room are inscribed with
single birds in profile (pl. 414) flanked by narrow bushes
or branches. The rest of the squares contain a cluster of
grapes and "floral and geometric ornamentation" like the
porch and narthex (pls. 413, 416).[617]

Very late fifth century; more likely sixth century.

Illustration. A. J. B. Wace and J. P. Droop, BSA, 13
(1906-1907), pl. XI,D = our pl. 414.

125 Room III (ca. 3.70 square). North annex; pavement laid
     up to southeast threshold block. Pl. 415.

No published information on dimensions and material.

Square polychrome panel comprising a complex interlace

have been laid up to it as is the case in Rooms III, V, and
VI (pls. 415-417).

[617]Wace and Droop, p. 316.

surrounded by two decorative borders. To the north, a wide
ornamental band flanks a projecting threshold block.

Framing: to north only, checkerboard pattern of light and
dark triangles; dark fillet; light band; dark fillet; outer
border, ostensibly, an overlapping lyre pattern;[618] dark
fillet; narrow light band; dark fillet; inner border, light
and dark crowsteps.

Field, flanked to north and south by a row of three tangent
lozenges: two-strand interlace (serrate-edged rainbow cable
on a white ground; two-strand guilloche, on a dark ground)
forming a square. Toward the center, the interlace bifurcates
to form a circle which is inscribed with an umbrella pattern
containing a central disk, with an hour glass filler, and
radiating ribs and concentric semi-circular termini. Single
lotiform flowers spring from the four spandrels between the
square and the circle.

Very late fifth century; more likely sixth century.

Illustration. A. J. B. Wace and J. P. Droop. BSA, 13
(1906-1907), pl. XI,E = our pl. 415.

126 Room V (ca. 12.30 x 2.30). Esonarthex; pavement laid up
     to threshold blocks on west side. Pl. 416.

No published information on dimensions and material.

---

[618]Although this is not at all clear in the drawing, it
is probably similar to the pattern at Arkitsa (88, pl. 299).

Off-centered polychrome rectilinear pavement with twenty or
twenty-four[619] organic and geometric insets, bordered to the
south by two decorative bands and to the west by a single
band.

Framing: to south, outer border, _semis_ of scales (pl. 416,
bottom, right); inner border, light and dark wave crests (pl.
416, bottom, left); to west, flanking the thresholds, light
rinceau, on a dark ground, forming rigidly arranged and
closely spaced scrolls filled with single light, heart-shaped
ivy leaves with tendrils (pl. 416, center).

Field: straight grid composed of a two-strand interlace
(see also border of Room I, 123) forming small circles which
are inscribed with light and dark hour glass motifs.[620] The
interlace encloses twenty or twenty-four rows of two squares
each which contain figural scenes and geometric motifs similar
to those in Room I (pl. 413). Among the latter are interlaced
rectangles, interlaced straight and curvilinear squares, and
pinwheel motifs (pl. 413, bottom). One panel has a large
flower and six panels are decorated with birds in profile
flanked by narrow bushes or branches (pl. 413, bottom).
Others contain a hen with three chicks, a rooster, a grazing
tailess doe (?) with striations along its back, and a seated

---

[619]There is a discrepancy between the number cited in the
text (Wace and Droop, p. 317) and the number in the ground
plan (24, our pl. 416, lower left).

[620]This is the only preserved example of a grid formed
by an interlace. The others, as in Room I (123) have a
guilloche framework.

buck accompanied by narrow shoots (pl. 413, bottom).[621]

Very late fifth century; more likely sixth century.

Illustration. A. J. B. Wace and J. P. Droop, BSA, 13 (1906-1907), pl. XI,C = our pl. 416.

127 Room VI (6.70 x 13.00). Nave; pavement laid up to west
    threshold step; in a later period, entrance blocked.
Pl. 417.

Fragment on northwest side of room. No published information on dimensions and material.

Originally, probably, a pavement which was divided into three sections on its longitudinal axis. The preserved segment (pl. 417) shows a compartmentalized field design of which only the northwest panel and the dividing border survive.

Framing: outer border, imbrication pattern composed of sharply outlined scales fanning southward; inner border to west, complex chain forming circles which are inscribed with a Solomon's knot, a star-crossed disk, a tree and, toward the center of the doorway, a displaying peacock (see also, 152, pls. 470-471) standing de face in an enlarged circle. At this point the chain bifurcates toward the east to form a second border between the panels of the field. Single triangles along the margins complete the pattern.

---

[621]The sequence of insets is not given (vide supra, p. 375, n. 619).

Field, preserved to north only: originally, probably, a rectilinear design of alternating octagons and meanders which in the preserved part are decorated with disks and a cruciform interlace. The design has been cut along the margin and is decorated with small floral-like shapes.

Very late fifth century; more likely sixth century.

Illustration. A. J. B. Wace and J. P. Droop, BSA, 13 (1906-1907), pl. XI,A = our pl. 417.

128   Room VII (2.50 x 13.00).   North aisle.   Pl. 418.

No published information on dimensions and material.

"Rather carelessly executed" pavement comprising a simple geometric design of light intersecting circles forming dark concave-sided squares set on edge which are inscribed with small light disks. It appears that the dark ground of the field continued into the west threshold and framed the north side of the pavement (pl. 418, bottom).[622]

Perhaps contemporary with the other pavements and, therefore, very late fifth century or, more likely, sixth century.

Illustration. A. J. B. Wace and J. P. Droop, BSA, 13 (1906-1907), pl. XI,B = our pl. 418.

---

[622]Except for the comment on the technique (Wace and Droop, p. 318), no description of this pavement is published.

PLATANIDIA

Christian Building

At Platanidia, on the shore of the Gulf of Volos, an apsidal structure with a mosaic pavement was discovered by chance in 1965. At the present time, the building is covered by rocks and sand carried in by the tide which regularly inundates the site.

Although no systematic excavation can be undertaken until a retaining wall is built to control the tide, a brief examination of the site in 1969 by N. Nikonanos, the Byzantine Epimelete of Thessaly, revealed that, contrary to the initial reports, the exposed segment of the apsidal structure was not the nave of a church[623] but a one-room annex with an entrance on the north side. This entrance led to a larger structure which awaits excavation.[624] It is not impossible, therefore, that, like many Christian complexes with south annexes in Greece, the larger building will prove to be a Christian church (pls. 103; 157; 356; 362; 457; 547; 568; 647; 676). Like some annexes, it was lavishly decorated with marble incrustation, excellent architectural sculpture, and a tessellated pavement which covered a distance of between twelve

---

[623]D. R. Theoharis, Deltion, 21 (1966), B2: Chronika, p. 254; E. Kourkoutidou, Deltion, 22 (1967), B2: Chronika, p. 317. See also Sodini, Catalogue, p. 718.

[624]I would like to thank Mr. Nikonanos for relating this useful piece of information to me.

to fifteen meters.

No other information is available and no plan of the
site is published. The limited scope of the excavation and
the poor condition of the site precluded a study of the
building and its pavement which is attributed to the Early
Christian period.[625]

Bibliography. D. R. Theoharis, Deltion, 21 (1966), B2:
Chronika, pp. 254-255; E. Kourkoutidou, Deltion, 22 (1967),
B2: Chronika, p. 317.

Illustration. E. Kourkoutidou, Deltion, 22 (1967), B2:
Chronika, pl. 225b-gamma = our pl. 419.

No. 129

A "beautiful" polychrome mosaic pavement was found in a
one-room apsidal building. Except for a brief description,
two bad photographs, and an Early Christian attribution,[626]
no other information is available.

Early Christian.

Covered by debris and water.

Additional bibliography. Sodini, Catalogue, No. 35, p. 718.

129 Room I (no dimensions published). Annex? Pl. 419.

---

[625]D. R. Theoharis, Deltion, 21 (1966), B2: Chronika, p.
255; E. Kourkoutidou, Deltion, 22 (1967), B2: Chronika,
p. 317.

[626]Ibid.

Pavement: 12.00 - 15.00. No other published information
on dimensions. Marble (white, black, yellow) and ceramic
(red) tesserae.

In a published photograph (pl. 419), there are traces of a
geometric field design and part of a border.

Framing: border, black and white checkerboard pattern;
border, guilloche (pl. 419, bottom); border, black and
white wave crests; border, chain of circles.[627]

Field (pl. 419, top): part of a large lozenge inscribed
with a wheel pattern set within a medallion.

Early Christian.

Illustration. E. Kourkoutidou, _Deltion_, 22 (1967), B2:
Chronika, pl. 225b-gamma = our pl. 419.

DEMETRIAS

Basilica Alpha

A basilica, Alpha (pl. 420), situated between the citadel
of the ancient city of Demetrias and a large Roman bath,[628]
was discovered by chance in 1912 and partially cleared a

---

[627]E. Kourkoutidou, _Deltion_, 22 (1967), B2: _Chronika_,
p. 317; Sodini, _Catalogue_, p. 718.

[628]_BCH_, 95 (1971), p. 949, fig. 322 (plan of city).

decade or so later.[629] The site was systematically excavated
between 1969 and 1971 and, except for the south and west
sides, has been cleared. In the course of the excavations,
several build-periods have been uncovered but, except for
brief announcements,[630] no detailed study has been published.
A few discussions with the archaeologist, Professor Vladimir
Milojčić of the University of Heidelberg,[631] and my own observations at the site form the basis for the following
architectural survey.

In its present state (pls. 420-422), the church complex
(overall, 28.00 max x 63.00) comprises a large three-aisled
basilica, I-III (20.80 x 29.90),[632] with an apse to the east
and a narthex to the west, IV (21.75 max x 4.10), which is
preceded by an atrium, V, surrounded on three sides, a-c, by
porticoes (pls. 423-424). The main entrance, VI, is located
in the center of the west side of the atrium and is flanked

---

[629]A. Arvanitopoulos, Praktika, 1912, p. 166; idem,
Praktika, 1916, p. 31; Soteriou, Palaiochristianikai basilikai,
pp. 181-182; F. Stählen, E. Meyer, A. Heidner, Pegasai und
Demetrias, Berlin-Leipzig, 1934, pp. 154-155 and fig. 33;
D. R. Theocharis, Deltion, 18 (1963), Bl: Chronika, p. 139.

[630]AJA, 74 (1970), p. 273; AJA, 75 (1971), p. 305; BCH,
95 (1971), pp. 938-941, pp. 947-949, figs. 318-322.

[631]I would like to take this opportunity to thank Professor Milojčić for giving me permission to study and publish
the mosaics.

[632]Because of its east to west architectural evolution,
the numeration of the rooms begins with the church proper.

by rooms of varying sizes (pl. 424). Other rooms lie along
the north side of the atrium while a three-room baptistry unit
borders the north aisle and the narthex. The design of the
complex evolved westward: the first period represented by
the basilica up to the eighth intercolumniation from the east;
the second, by its extension westward by around 6.40 meters;
the third, by the addition of a narthex, atrium with porticoes, and the entrance. Subsequent phases involving the
construction of the annexes flanking the hall and the north
side will not concern us since there is no evidence that they
were paved with mosaics.

PERIOD I

To this period belongs the church proper (21.15 x 23.20)
consisting of a nave flanked by single aisles and terminated
by a semicircular apse. Judging from the off-centered
tessellated threshold panel (pls. 420, 428) on the west side
of the nave, the main entrance to the church was through a
single door. Columns, possibly set on bases (pls. 429-430),
may have divided the nave from the aisles[633] and, as delineated
by the mosaic (pl. 425), a "⊔-shaped" chancel screen enclosed

---

[633]It is evident that the preserved fragments of bases
belong to a reconstruction of the north and south colonnades
in PERIOD II because they interrupt and destroy the borders
in the original part of the building (pls. 425, 429-430). In
the west extension, however, the pavements are clearly laid
up to the bases (pl. 433).

the bema up to the shoulders of the apse. Traces of other important liturgical furnishings, synthronon and ambon,[634] have not survived. Black and white geometric mosaics, with polychrome highlights, pave the nave and aisles of the church and clearly accentuate the formal arrangement and internal divisions of these areas. On the east side of the nave mosaic, in front of the presumed entrance to the bema, an inscription records the name and title of the donor of the church and the mosaics, Damokratia (pls. 425, 427), who also sponsored the addition of the narthex and atrium in Period III. It is quite likely that, to commemorate her beneficence, she was buried in the grave which is located on the south side of the south aisle (pls. 420, 422, 430) near the original west entrance.[635]

PERIOD II

The church proper was extended westward by around 6.40 meters and divided by the present system of colonnades which were set on bases and possibly closed by parapets.[636]

---

[634]The destruction of the stone paving in the bema (pl. 425) removed any trace of the altar which might have existed.

[635]The grave destroyed part of the border and field of the mosaic.

[636]Since the mosaics are terminated by a black fillet along the colonnades, and are separated by a 40 to 45 centimeter caesura (pls. 425, upper left, 430) it would appear that they were laid up to a partition of some kind, or marble paving. The relatively narrow width of the partition would

Pavements were laid in these sectors which are similar in form, style, and technique to those of Period I (cf. pls. 426, 429, 430 and pls. 432-434).

PERIOD III

With its expansion in this period, the design approximates more closely the standard type of ecclesiastical building in Greece.[637] Thus, the approach to the basilica is through a hall and across the north and south porticoes of the atrium into the narthex. This room communicates with the nave and side aisles through triple and single doorways, respectively. As a tessellated inscription in the narthex informs us (pl. 436), the same Damokratia sponsored this architectural and decorative program with the result that the black and white geometric pavements are very similar to those belonging to Periods I and II. Since she sponsored the first and last periods of the building, and probably the second one as well, it is not unlikely that only a few decades separate them. Archaeological evidence securely dates Period I to the late fourth or early fifth century and provides, therefore, a chronological terminus for Periods II and III which should be assigned to the first half of the fifth

preclude a stylobate, which averages between 80 to 90 centimeters in width, but it is narrow enough for parapets.

[637]Krautheimer, Architecture, pp. 91-95.

century.

In subsequent periods, additions and repairs to the church were undertaken but their chronology cannot be determined. It is possible, however, to place them into two categories: those which clearly reflect the continuing existence and function of the ecclesiastical precinct; those which do not. To the first belong a low masonry and rubble bench along the south side of the south aisle,[638] which partially covered the grave ascribed to Damokratia (pl. 430) and, at least, the baptistery unit.[639] In addition, the restoration of the mosaics in the north portico (137, pl. 438-439) and the hall (138, pl. 444) indicate an attempt to preserve the decorative program of the west side of the complex.[640] The second category is represented by three crude mortar and rubble constructions whose function is apparently unrelated to the church: an oven in the northwest corner of the north portico which rests on a restored section of the pavement (pl. 439); a basin for the processing of lime on the north side of the south portico (pl. 441); an unidentified rectangular feature on the southwest side of the south aisle (pl. 422).

Bibliography. Soteriou, Palaiochristianikai basilikai,

---

[638]For a similar bench in this part of the church see pls. 295, 646, 676).

[639]The function of the rooms to the west of the baptistery and flanking the entrance hall, VI, is not known.

[640]For the inset panel in Room VI, vide infra, p. 403.

pp. 181-182; <u>BCH</u>, 95 (1971), pp. 939-941; <u>BCH</u>, 96 (1972), p. 719.

Illustrations. <u>BCH</u>, 95 (1971), p. 947, fig. 318 (plan), p. 948, fig. 13 (baptistery), p. 949, fig. 322 (plan of city).

Nos. 130-138

Simple in design and color, the purely geometric mosaics (pls. 426-443) contain homogeneous decorative schemes consisting of various combinations of interlocking, intersecting, or juxtaposed motifs. The two-dimensional patterns are arranged in single panels across extended surfaces and are executed with clarity and precision produced by light and dark contrasts and by uncomplicated filling elements which are carefully inserted into each unit. The geometricity of the pavements is heightened by the simple color scheme which is bichrome in its general effect and emphasis (black and white) with buff and reddish purple and brown serving primarily as highlights.

Stylistic, iconographic, and chromatic similarities between these pavements and those at Arkitsa (88-92, pls. 295-314) and Dion (178-179, pls. 601-605), datable to the late fourth or early fifth century confirm the chronology established by the archaeological evidence for the pavements in Period I. Since these characteristics continue to be displayed in the later pavements of Periods II and III, there can be no doubt that the same workshop executed them. Thus, toward the middle of the fifth century the workshop continued to execute mosaics in the style and technique of the initial period, even though by this time, purely aniconic, sober, and austere pavements had begun to be replaced by richer, ornamental and figural pavements.[641] Two types of repairs to the mosaics occurred sometime after their installation. In one (137, pl. 439), the repair maintains the general decorative and chromatic scheme of the original. In the other, however (138, pl. 444), a polychromatic emblema is introduced. Although the panel is badly damaged, traces of a tabula ansata and a column denote a scene with a figure or figures. This panel clearly reflects a different decorative phase for which the adjacent mosaics provide a terminus post quem of around the middle of the fifth century.

Additional bibliography. Sodini, Compléments, pp. 583-584.

PERIOD I

130 Room I (10.00 x 23.20). Nave; pavement laid up to a
     chancel barrier. Lengthened 6.35 meters when west wall
razed. Pls. 425-428.

Framing: 0.51 to north and south; to east, 0.36. Field, including double fillet: 8.96 x 17.30 with a north and south extension to the bema wall of 5.10. Threshold panel: 2.31 x 1.10. Central panel: 6.70 x 15.28. Tabula ansata: 1.66 x

[641]See, for example, 10-13; 69-71; 75-76; 82-83, and the pavements at Nea Anchialos to the south (105, 107-108).

0.33. Irregularly-cut marble (black, white), limestone (dark red), and ceramic (buff, reddish purple, reddish brown) tesserae (0.015 sq; 0.015 x 0.02) in major portions of pavement set 3-5mm apart; (0.01-0.012 sq) in inscription set 1-3mm apart.

Black and white geometric pavement, with polychrome highlights, composed of a large panel with a tabula ansata set on a ground of intersecting circles.

Framing: traces of a black fillet; border, on north and most of south sides, black undulating rinceaux (one fillet) composed of scrolls alternately filled with long-stemmed, agitated ivy leaves and curling tendrils;[642] black band; white band.

Field (pls. 425-426).

Ground, framed by a black double fillet: black on white design composed of intersecting circles (0.42 diam) forming white concave-sided squares which are inscribed with small black disks. The design is bisected along the margins at which point the disks are replaced by stepped triangles. To the east, the ground branches off to enclose the north-south sides of a chancel screen (pl. 425) and, to the west, it is interrupted by an off-centered rectangular panel which

---

[642]Absent along the chancel screen and the southeast and east sides; probably destroyed along the west side when the wall was razed. The border is visible on the right side of pl. 430.

marks the location of the original threshold of this period (pl. 428).

Threshold panel (pl. 428).

Framing: black double fillet; white band.

Field, framed by a black triple fillet; black on white quincunxial pattern composed of concentric black/white/black/buff/black lozenges in the center and rectangular triangles in the four corners. The former is inscribed with an "eye motif" composed of a black-centered buff medallion which is articulated by black/white/black inner concentric rings and flanked by two buff beads. Four black rectangular triangles with single white ivy leaves complete the patterns (for a similar pattern in Room V, see 137c, pl. 441).

Central panel.

Framing: black double fillet; white band.

Field, framed by a black double fillet: white on black design composed of large intersecting circles (1.37 diam) forming concave-sided squares. The design is bisected along the margins. The concave-sided squares are inscribed with straight squares (0.50 diam) filled with two-strand Solomon's knots (grey/1 white; reddish brown/1 white, outlined in black) on a black ground. Adjacent to the angles of each of these squares are four black-centered white squares (for a similar design, see 88c, pl. 307; 100, pl. 353). Opposite the west entrance to the bema, the panel design is interrupted by a reddish brown on white tabula ansata (pl. 427) which is bisected by a reddish brown fillet. It contains a two-line

inscription in black letters (0.08-0.095 high), oriented
westward, which cites the name and title of the female donor
of the church: "ΔΑΜΟΚΡΑΤΙΑ/ΗΛΑΜΠΡΟΤΑΤΗ ."[643]

Late fourth or early fifth century.

131 Room II (5.05 x 23.40). North aisle; lengthened 6.35
     meters when west wall razed. Pl. 429.
   Framing: 0.37. Field: 3.78 x 22.68. Irregularly-cut
marble tesserae (0.015 sq; 0.015 x 0.02) set 3-5mm apart.

Design of interlocking white geometric patterns on a black
ground.
   Surround: parallel to the walls and to the colonnade.
   Framing: black and white wave crests.
   Field: carpet composed of an interlocking design of crosses
of four lozenges (0.35 x 0.70) separated by squares (0.35).
Along the south, east, and west margins, the lozenges have
been bisected; along the north side they have been truncated,
creating an asymmetrical composition.[644] The lozenges are
inscribed with small black disks which change to small crosslets or stepped triangles along the margins. The squares, on
the other hand, are filled with white disks, outlined in black

----

[643]Although typographically different, an identical text
is situated in the narthex (136, pl. 436; p. 397, n. 650).

[644]See also, 44, pls. 104-106.

on a grey ground, which are replaced at the sixth intercolumniation from the west wall (ca. 16.00 distance) by black
ones, outlined in white and set on a black ground.[645] For a
symmetrical version of this design in the same sector, see the
west addition, 134, pl. 433.

Late fourth or early fifth century.

132 Room III (4.80 x 23.35). South aisle; lengthened 6.35
     meters when west wall razed. A grave was placed on the
southwest side, destroying the pavement. Subsequently, the
south side of the grave and the pavement were covered by a
low bench (0.37 wide) extending from the east wall up to a
rectangular feature whose function remains unknown. Pl. 430.
   Framing: 0.42. Field, including double fillet: 3.76 x 22.
35. Tesserae identical to those in Room II (131).

White on black geometric design composed of tangent geometric
forms inscribed with schematized floral motifs.
   Surround: in rows parallel to the walls and the colonnade.
   Framing: black double fillet; border, continuous bead-and-
reel pattern composed of two reels separated from each other
and from flanking single beads by long bars; at the two

---

[645]This change coincides with the disappearance of the
small black triangular motifs in the bisected lozenges along
the south margin. Another alteration occurs at a distance of
9.90 meters from the east wall at which point the dark red
outline of each inner lozenge (absent from the first row to
the east) is replaced by a black one.

corners this pattern is terminated by small black and white squares;[646] black double fillet; white double fillet.

Field (pl. 430), framed by a black double fillet: tangent octagons (0.58-0.62 diam) set on edge forming concave-sided squares set on edge (ca. 0.63). The motifs interlock to form alternating rows of octagons and squares of which the latter, inscribed with small white squares with grey centers, are cut along the margins.[647] Filling the octagons are black-centered white quatrefoils on black medallions which relieve the stark geometricity of the surface.

Late fourth or early fifth century.

PERIOD II

133 Room I, extension (10.00 x 6.35). Nave; west extension
      created when wall of Period I was razed. Pls. 428, 431-
432.

Field, including double fillet: 9.05 x 6.15. Irregularly-cut marble tesserae identical in size to those of the earlier mosaic to the east (130).

Black on white geometric pavement decorated with small panels

646They are not visible in the photograph.

647The squares are enlarged in these areas. See also the west addition, 135, pl. 434.

placed at regular intervals on a ground of intersecting circles.

Surround: parallel to the colonnades.

Field (pl. 432), framed by a black double fillet.

Ground: black intersecting circles (0.41 diam) forming white concave-sided squares which are inscribed with small black disks.[648] The design is bisected along the margins and the small circles changed to stepped triangles (pl. 428).

Panels (pls. 428, 432), framed by black double fillets: alternating checkerboard patterns, set 64 centimeters apart, composed of small black and white squares (0.60), and black and white tesserae (0.01 x 0.02). In a panel opposite the original threshold panel to the east, the checkerboard has been replaced by a black diagonal cross whose arms are separated by single "V" motifs (pl. 428, bottom). Unlike the two other additions to the original pavements in the north and south aisles (134-135, pls. 433-434), this mosaic differs to a considerable extent from its predecessor to the east (pl. 426). In the earlier pavement, a large central panel on a ground of intersecting circles serves as a focal point for the decorative composition. In the later one, although the circle design is almost identical, the composition is decentralized and its unity is achieved by the regular repetition of small units or panels over the entire surface. Another difference is the elimination of the ivy rinceaux. The

---

[648]The disks are eliminated along the frames of each panel.

mosaic has been skillfully joined to the east panel and the
technique and materials are similar (pls. 428, 431).

First decades of the fifth century.

134   Room II, extension (5.05 x 6.35).   North aisle; west
      extension created when wall of Period I was razed.
Pls. 431, 433.

  Field, including triple fillet: 4.06 x 5.55. Irregularly-
cut marble tesserae identical to those of the earlier mosaic
to east (131).

Mosaic decorated with a design of interlocking white geometric motifs on a black ground which imitates the earlier
pavement to the east (131, pl. 429).

  Surround: parallel to the walls and the colonnade.

  Field (pl. 433), framed by a black triple fillet: interlocking design of crosses of four lozenges (0.39 x 0.76) separated by squares (0.36). Along the margins, the lozenges
have been bisected and their inner black double fillets
changed to triangles. Small black disks inscribed in the
squares complete the design. Although the technique, materials, and design are similar to those of the earlier panel to
the east (131, pl. 429), some differences are evident. The
border is replaced by a simple wide band, some of the filling
elements have been altered or eliminated, and the lozenges are
tangent, not juxtaposed. This produces a symmetrical

composition which is terminated on four sides by half-
lozenges. Unlike its counterparts in the nave and south
aisle (pls. 428; 434), the juncture between the earlier and
later sections of the paving is jagged and carelessly executed (pl. 433, top).

First decades of the fifth century.

135 Room III, extension (4.80 x 6.44, including extension
      into south threshold). South aisle; west extension
created when wall of Period I was razed. Pl. 434.
   Framing: 0.13. Field, including triple fillet: 3.83 x
5.83. Irregularly-cut marble tesserae identical to those of
the earlier panel to east.
   Surround: parallel to the walls and the colonnade.
   Framing: black band; white band.
   Field, framed by a black triple fillet: tangent octagons
(0.67 diam) set on edge forming four-pointed stars (0.65 sq).
The motifs interlock to form alternating rows of octagons and
stars of which the latter, inscribed with small white squares
with black centers, are cut along the margins.[649]

First decades of the fifth century.

---

[649]The star pattern is enlarged in many places along the
margins.

PERIOD III, PHASE 1

136 Room IV (21.75 max x 4.10). Narthex; unexcavated to
      south. Pls. 435-436.

  Framing: 0.14. Field, including triple fillet: 21.28
max x 3.13. Tabula ansata: 1.69 x 0.45. Irregularly-cut
marble tesserae identical to those belonging to Periods I
and II (130-135).

Pavement decorated with a black and white star pattern and a
tabula ansata.
  Surround: parallel to the walls.
  Framing: black band; white band.
  Field (pl. 436), framed by a triple black fillet. The
design can be read two ways: interlocking stars composed of
four pairs of white lozenges (0.17 x 0.35) forming a central
four-pointed black star which is inscribed with a white
square (ca. 0.16); white tangent octagons set on edge (ca.
0.70 diam) filled with diagonal four-pointed stars inscribed
with black-centered squares set on edge (0.16). For a more
decorative version, see 219, pls. 676, 688. The design is
cut along the margins and interrupted at the entrance to the
nave by a black on white tabula ansata (pl. 436) containing
a two-line inscription in black letters (ca. 0.11 high),
oriented westward. It cites the name and title of the female

donor of the additions: **"ΔΑΜΟΚΡΑΤΙΑ/ΗΛΑΜΠΡΟΤΑΤΗ."**[650]

Toward the middle of the fifth century.

137 Room Va-c (maximum length: 19.80, north-south; 13.40,
    east-west; width a, 3.54; b, 3.05; c, 2.70 max). Atrium
with north, west, and south porticoes; unexcavated along the
south side. An oven and a basin were installed on the pavements in the northwest corner and on the south side, respectively. West half of north portico, a, restored, Pls. 437-
441.

North portico, a. Framing: 0.42-0.47. Field with restorations: 2.65 x 12.55, including double fillet. Original
pavement: to east, 2.65 x 4.10; west strip, 2.65 x 0.78.
West portico, b: Framing: ca. 0.36; to east, 0.55. Field,
including double fillet: 15.91 max x 2.13. South portico,
c: Framing: 0.41. Field, including double fillet: 2.10
max x .22 max. Threshold panel: 1.64 max x 0.81. Irregularly cut marble tesserae in original and restored portions
(0.013 x 0.023; 0.018 x 0.026; 0.02 sq) set 3-6mm apart.

---

[650]For an identical text in the nave, see 130, pl. 427.
This inscription differs from the earlier one. The right
stroke of the squatter and broader Delta continues beyond the
left stroke. The Alpha is marked by a "V-shaped" cross bar
instead of a slightly arched one. The Mu and Lambda are
angular nor curvilinear, and the Omichron circular not tetrag-
onal. In addition, four horizontal white fillets separate
the lines.

United by a common floral border, three interlocking black
and white geometric panels decorated with simple and complex
designs articulated by black or white double fillets.

Surround, along north side of south portico only (pl. 441):
rows of grey tesserae parallel to the wall.

Framing: black fillet; border, undulating black rinceaux
(one fillet), on a grey ground, forming rigidly arranged
narrow scrolls filled with single white heart-shaped ivy
leaves. The pointed tips of the black-outlined leaves touch
the margin; narrow black band; white band, in north portico
only.

Va, north portico: west half of pavement restored.

Field (pls. 437-438), framed by a black double fillet:
originally, a single row of octagons, set 1.05 meters apart,
surrounded by an alternating series of single lozenges (0.57
x 1.05) and squares (0.57). In the preserved east section,
one octagon (1.57 diam) and part of a second (1.30 diam)
survive. The former (pl. 437), bordered by a white wave
crest pattern on a black ground, is inscribed with a long-
necked, ribbed vase, facing westward, with two spiral handles
and a narrow base. The grey and black vase, highlighted in
white, is flanked by two curving black branches with black
lanceolate leaves which issue from its mouth. In the second
octagon (pl. 438), traces remain of a grey octagon, on a white
ground, and a shield pattern of black and white triangles.
The northwest side of the octagon has been restored with a
reel with trailing tendrils. The surrounding lozenges and

squares contain a variety of filling elements which are set
on grey, white or, more frequently, on black grounds in a
light-dark or dark-light combination. Generally, each
lozenge is filled with a schematic floral or floral-like
motif composed of a circle or reel flanked by heart-shaped
ivy or lanceolate leaves, tendrils, stepped triangles, or
beads.[651] In the squares, on the other hand, simple geometric motifs predominate:[652] two-strand Solomon's knots
(both, grey/1 white, outlined in black) on a black ground;
stepped or concave-sided squares; swastikas; various combinations of octagons, circles, semi-circles, checkerboard
patterns. Except for a narrow patch (0.78 wide) of the
original mosaic, the entire northwest side was crudely
restored with tesserae which probably came from the original
pavement (pl. 439). In the border, the original rinceau is
replaced by one with wider undulations and smaller, more
agitated leaves. The field design has been altered by the
replacement of the octagons with additional squares and
lozenges, thereby destroying the harmony and rhythm of the
overall design. Subsequent to this restoration, an oven was

---

[651]An unusual motif decorates the lozenges in the northeast and southeast corners. It comprises a rectangle flanked
on its short sides by triangles and inscribed with a long bar
(northeast) or a white oval (southeast).

[652]The few foliate patterns consist of lanceolate
quatrefoils and hexafoils, and one cruciform pattern composed
of four black heart-shaped ivy leaves set tip-to-tip on a
grey ground. The latter are outlined in white and have
curving white stems.

placed in the northwest corner (pl. 439).

Vb, west portico (pls. 424, 440).

Field, framed by a white double fillet which forms, at the
same time, part of the design: black and white network of
alternating octagons (0.63 diam) and equilateral crosses (ca.
0.63 sq) forming elongated hexagons (for a similar design,
see 95, pls. 319-320). The hexagons have been changed to
irregular tetragons along the margins. Generally, the filling
motifs are arranged in alternating sequences of light on
dark and dark on light. Thus, two-strand guilloches (white)
decorate the black crosses and black superimposed triangles,
around a central square, fill the white crosses. This alternating bichrome contrast is repeated in the octagons and
hexagons. The former are inscribed with a variety of motifs,
primarily geometric: rectilinear swastikas; awning and shield
shapes; triangles; interlaced or tangent circles; multiple
interlaced rectangles forming crosses; schematic floral
rosettes composed of simple flat lanceolate leaves and heart-
shaped leaves either in clusters with trailing tendrils (not
illustrated), or in cruciform patterns of four leaves set
tip-to-tip. The hexagons are filled with floral-like "eye
motifs" composed of circles flanked by beads, reels flanked
by curling tendrils, and with simple geometric motifs such as
multiple chevrons, elongated hexagons with rectangular
centers and stepped termini. Although the motifs in the
cruciform compartments are regularly disposed in an

alternating sequence over the entire surface, the others are inserted at random.

Vc, south portico. Pavement laid up to northeast drain (pl. 441).

Field, framed by a white double fillet which forms, at the same time, part of the design: imbrication design composed of white/black scales fanning eastward.

East threshold: traces of three tangent compartments of which two are inscribed with simple patterns, outlined in black. The central one is filled with a large diagonal quatrefoil composed of white lanceolate leaves which spring from a central square composed of four white tesserae. In the center of each margin is a black stepped triangle. Although the other compartment to the south is only partially excavated, its decoration can be reconstituted. It comprises a quincunxial pattern composed of concentric black/white/ black lozenges in the center and rectangular triangles in the four corners. A grey bead, outlined in black, is visible in the right corner of the grey lozenge, suggesting a filling motif common to this section (pls. 437, 440) which comprises a central medallion or reel flanked by two beads. For a similar threshold in Room I, Period I, see pl. 428.

Toward the middle of the fifth century.

PERIOD III, PHASES 1 and 2

138   Room VI (9.02 x 6.76). Entrance hall. East part of

pavement restored probably when west entrance blocked.[653]

Pls. 442-444.

Framing: 0.91-1.01. Field, with restoration: 4.75 x
8.10. Original west compartment, including fillet: 4.75 x
4.68. Original east compartment, including fillet: 4.75 x
3.64. Restored east panel, including borders: 3.21 x 3.34.
Field, including double fillet: ca. 1.40 sq. Irregularly-
cut black and white marble tesserae in original east compartment and outer border (0.013 x 0.023) set 3-5mm apart; marble
(black, white, grey) limestone (dark purple, ochre) and
ceramic (red) tesserae in restored east panel (ca. 0.015 sq)
set 1-3mm apart.

Originally, probably a black and white mosaic composed of two
compartments enclosed to the north, south, and west by a
geometric border. Restored to east with a polychrome panel,
oriented westward.

Framing (pl. 442): black fillet; wide white band; border,
alternating white squares (0.74) and rectangles (0.75 x 1.43)
on a black ground inscribed with simple black and white

[653]Professor Milojčić did not know the date of the disappearance of the west entrance. It is not impossible,
however, that the panel was installed after the conversion
of the passageway into a room.

geometric motifs. Among the motifs decorating the squares
are clusters of superimposed peltae, concentric circles,
alternating black and white hour glass motifs, and quatrefoils of lanceolate leaves separated by small disks. The
rectangles are inscribed with lozenges decorated with black
and white hour glass motifs or with various types of "eye
motifs" formed by a circle and two flanking beads or bars;
wide white band.

VIa, west compartment (pls. 442-443), framed by a black
fillet: white intersecting circles (0.72 diam) forming
black concave-sided squares which are inscribed with small
black-centered white disks. The design has been bisected
along the margin at which point the disks are replaced by
stepped triangles.

VIb, east compartment (pl. 444): originally, separated
from the north-south borders, from the east threshold, and
from the west panel by a wide white band.

Field, framed by a black fillet: black and white imbrication pattern, oriented east-west, preserved along the north
(0.38 wide) and south (1.16 wide) sides of a later polychrome
panel.[654]

Restored panel: off-centered inset, oriented westward and
separated from the original pavement and from the east
threshold block by a double border.

_____

[654]It cannot be determined whether in its original state
this pattern served as a field design or as a flanking border
to another panel.

Framing: black fillet; outer border (0.28), traces of an undulating ribbon pattern with short white strokes in each undulation: outer undulations, white/grey; inner undulations, alternately grey/red and grey/ochre; black fillet; white band; inner border (ca. 0.38), three-strand braid (grey/1 white; red/1 white; dark purple/1 white, outlined in black, with a white tessera at each loop) on a black ground; narrow white band.

Field, framed by a black fillet. Although only a 40 centimeter strip survives along the north side, it is certain that the scene and its inscription faced the west side of the room. The evidence for this orientation is supplied by the position of a white column with grey spiral flutes whose double base rests on a stylobate which is situated on or near the west margin of the field. This column extends the length of the scene and is terminated by an Ionic capital of which traces are preserved of a black, white, and dark purple volute. Resting on the capital is part of a narrow red and white tabula ansata, on a dark purple ground, which contained a one-line inscription of which the imprint of the first letter, Z (0.06 high), survives.[655] The central part of the scene has been destroyed except for a small patch containing two curving rows of black tesserae set on a white ground.

---

[655]Originally, the central scene must have been placed within a symmetrical architectural setting with a second column supporting the right side of the tabula.

Toward the middle of the fifth century with a later restoration.

To the north and east, pavement crudely repaired with
large stones.

Basilica Beta

Outside the walls of ancient Demetrias, on the south
slope of the Prophet Elias hill, a church, designated Beta,
was discovered in 1962. Partial excavation of the area
established the general plan (overall, 31.20 x 16.10)[656] as
well as the types of paving.

Preceded by a narthex with some kind of annex to the
north, the main body of the basilica consists of a nave
separated from two flanking aisles by colonnades resting on
stylobates. A semi-circular apse with a stepped synthronon
and a narrow entrance opens onto the bema and a second one
pierces the center of the south wall of the south aisle (pl.
445).[657]

On the basis of the numismatic evidence and its style,
the building has been assigned to the end of the fourth
century.[658]

-----

[656]Only the south aisle, bema, and sections of the narthex
were cleared (D. R. Theoharis, Deltion, 18 [1963], Bl:
Chronika, p. 139; hereafter cited as Theoharis).

[657]The second apse is an unusual feature in Greek
basilicas.

[658]Theoharis, p. 140.

Bibliography. D. R. Theoharis, Deltion, 18 (1963), Bl:
Chronika, pp. 139-﹍0; JHS, 84 (1964), Supplement, p. 15;
BCH, 89 (1965), p. 786.

Illustration. D. R. Theoharis, Deltion, 18 (1963), Bl:
Chronika, p. 139, plan 2 = our pl. 445.

Nos. 139-140

139 Room IV (no dimensions published). Bema.

140 Room V (no dimensions published). East apse.

No published information on dimensions and material.

Brief mention of geometric mosaics in the bema and apse of

an Early Christian church.659

End of the fourth century.

Additional bibliography. Sodini, Catalogue, No. 31, pp.
715-716.

659The paving of the narthex is not recorded; those of
the side aisles are brick. Sodini's description of the
"black and white" tessellated floors (Catalogue, p. 715) is
at variance with the archaeological report and it is unclear
if his additional, and sometimes contradictory, information
is an error or was communicated to him by Mr. Theoharis. He
notes mosaics in two other places: south apse, now destroyed;
nave, (quatrefoils) and describes the bema mosaic as comprising an all-over pattern of opposed peltae and an inscription.
Theoharis, on the other hand, states that the floor in the
south apse was completely destroyed at the time of its discovery, inscriptions were inscribed on stele, and the like (p.
140), and omits any reference to a mosaic in the nave.

PHILIA

Basilica

Somewhat north of the village of Philia, on the site of
an ancient theatre dedicated to Athena, a systematic excavation in 1964 brought to light traces of the foundations of
an Early Christian basilica (11.60 x 24.20, with apse) and
evidence of a mosaic pavement in the apse (pl. 446). At the
present time, the mosaic has disappeared and the site is
overgrown.

Because of its ruinous condition, only the general outline of the basilica was determined. Preceded by a narrow
narthex, I (3.30-3.45 x 11.60), it consists of a nave separated from single flanking aisles by stylobates and terminated
by a semi-circular apse. No trace was found of the internal
supports or liturgical furnishings and, unlike many Greek
churches, there were no annexes.[660] The apse was paved with
polychrome mosaics and the nave with brick slabs.

Since no datable archaeological finds were unearthed,
and the style of the architecture is inconclusive, the church
was not assigned to a specific period.

Bibliography. D. R. Theoharis, Deltion, 19 (1964), B2:
Chronika, pp. 244-245.

Illustration. D. R. Theoharis, Deltion, 19 (1964), B2:
Chronika, p. 245, plan 1 = our pl. 446.

---

[660]D. R. Theoharis, Deltion, 19 (1964), B2: Chronika,
pp. 244-245.

No. 141

141   Room III (2.60 diam). Apse.

No published information on dimensions and condition.

Brief mention of the presence of two small fragments of a
polychrome mosaic.[661]

Early Christian.

Pavement destroyed; site overgrown.

Bibliography. Sodini, Catalogue, No. 34, p. 717.

TRIKKALA

Basilica

A chance find in 1956 near the city of Trikkala brought
to light the north section of a room (6.60 max x 3.10 max)
which was paved with mosaics (pl. 447).[662]   At the present
time, the site is overgrown and the condition of the pavement
is not known. A tessellated inscription identifies the room
as the narthex of a church and the sponsor of the decoration
as an archpriest by the name of Pardalas. Except for traces

---

[661]Only one fragment is indicated on the plan (pl. 446).

[662]The site is marked "A" in a plan accompanying the
report (A. K. Orlandos, ABME, 8 [1955-56], p. 117, fig. 1);
hereafter cited as ABME, 8.

of some walls, the rest of the basilica is destroyed.[663]

Although no datable archaeological finds were unearthed or reported, on the basis of the style of the pavement, the building can be attributed to the middle or second half of the fifth century.

Bibliography. A. K. Orlandos, ABME, 8 (1955-56), pp. 117-125; D. R. Theoharis, Praktika, 1958, pp. 70-71; D. I. Pallas, RAC, 35 (1959), p. 194.

Illustration. A. K. Orlandos, ABME, 8 (1955-56), p. 118, fig. 2 = our pl. 447.

No. 142

Of the three panels, only the north and central ones are preserved.[664] The latter (pls. 447-448), with its distinctive triple arcade design enclosing an inscription and organic elements, was probably situated in front of the entrance to the nave.[665] Its polychromatic and naturalistic figural iconography is important for the chronology of the pavement, since early pavements in Thessaly and out-lying districts are aniconic and bichromatic. Basilicas at Arkitsa (88-92, pls. 295-314), Demetrias (130-138, pls. 421-444) and Dion (178-

---

[663]Three Christian graves were found a short distance from the narthex suggesting that the building was a cemetary church (D. R. Theoharis, Praktika, 1958, p. 71).

[664]For a discussion of the original decoration and the dimensions of the narthex, see ABME, 8, p. 120.

[665]For figural panels in similar locations, see pls. 77, 80; 569-571; 620-621.

179, pls. 601-605), which are reliably dated to the late
fourth and the first decades of the fifth century, contain
pavements which show a consistent aversion to figures and
polychromy. The pavement at Trikkala, therefore, is not
earlier than the middle of the fifth century. This is substantiated by the design in the north panel (pl. 447) which,
although based on an intersecting pattern, is totally foreign
to the first half of the century. Pavements at Epidauros,
Arkitsa, and Demetrias (pls. 107, 110; 304-305, 313; 425)
always present the basic pattern not its more decorative
derivative as at Trikkala. Although the earlier type of
design continues into the second half of the century and
into the sixth century (pl. 78), it is in the second half of
the fifth century that the more decorative type appears in
such places as Anthedon (77, pl. 238) and Nea Anchialos (117,
pl. 403).

Additional bibliography. Sodini, Catalogue, No. 40, pp.
722-723.

Illustration. A. K. Orlandos, ABME, 8 (1955-56), p. 118,
fig. 2 = our pl. 447.

142   Room I (6.60 max x 3.15 max). Narthex; pavement laid up
to, or destroyed by, northwest threshold block.[666]

Pls. 447-449.

---

[666]The block is not discussed in the reports. An adequate description of the pavement is given in the ABME, 8,
pp. 120-125. Sodini's entry is incomplete (Catalogue, pp.
722-723).

Framing: 0.43. Field: 6.17 max x 1.29.[667] Slate tesserae (0.01-0.015 sq).

Fragment of a polychrome pavement composed of a geometric and
a figural panel set within a wave crest framework and bordered by a running rinceau.

Surround to east only: in rows parallel to the walls.

Framing: white fillet; black fillet; outer border, undulating dark green rinceau forming widely spaced scrolls
filled with single dark green spiral tendrils; black double
fillet.

Field: framed by a white triple fillet: traces of two
rectangular panels set within a dark green and white wave
crest framework.

Ia, north panel (pl. 447).

Framing: black fillet; border to north only, undulating
dark green rinceau (one fillet) forming rigidly arranged
scrolls filled with single dark green ivy leaves.

Field, framed by a white band which forms, at the same time,
part of the design: interlocking design composed of two rows
of four juxtaposed dark purple circles each (0.55 diam)[668]
joined by diagonal quatrefoils to form horizontal and vertical elongated hexagons with concave sides. The design is
delineated by white double fillets, outlined in black, and

---

[667]This measurement is taken from the drawing (pl. 447).

[668]Vide supra, p. 411, n. 667.

is cut along the margins. Large dark purple quatrefoils fill
the squares decorating the circles and each hexagon is inscribed with two small purple and white trefoils set back-to-
back.[669]

Ib, central panel, framed by a black single fillet.

Field (pls. 448-449): arcade of three arches resting on
capitals supported by fluted columns and pilasters set on
stepped bases. Under the central and larger arch, is a six-
line inscription terminated by a narrow dark green undulating
rinceau with spiral tendrils (pl. 448). Oriented westward,
it cites in dark green letters the function of the room and
the name of the donor of the pavement, the archpriest
Pardalas: "ΥΠΕΡΕΥΧΗCΟΠΡ[ ]/ΤΟΠΡΕCΒΥΤ[ ]/C ΠΑΡ
ΔΑΛΑC[ ]/ΕΚΕΝΤΗCΕ[ ]/ΤΟΝΝΑΡΘΗΚΑΝ ."[670]
Below the inscription swim a dolphin and an unidentifiable
marine creature and above it two confronting land birds with
red breasts drink from a circular fountain resting on a small
triangular base. An ivy vine issues from the mouth of the
fountain and fills the tympanum with leaves and tendrils.
Accompanying this scene were probably two confronting birds
in the spandrels of which the north one is preserved (pl.
477). Symmetrically disposed on either side were narrower

---

[669]Although their color scheme is not noted, it would
appear that the vertical hexagons contain dark purple trefoils
on a white ground and the horizontal ones white trefoils ona
a dark purple ground.

[670]For the following emendation, see Orlandos, pp. 119-
120. "ΥΠΕΡ ΕΥΧΗC Ο ΠΡ[Ω]ΤΟ ΠΡΕCΒΥΤ[ΕΡΟ]/C
ΠΑΡΔΑΛΑC/ ΕΚΕΝΤΗCΕ[Ν] ΤΟΝ ΝΑΡΘΗΚΑΝ."

413

arcades probably enclosing similar scenes with vases, vines
and birds.[671] The preserved north arcade contains a long-
necked vase with a narrow ribbed body resting on a circular
foot set on a triangular base. Its long spiral handles are
almost hidden by two undulating ivy and grape vines which
cascade symmetrically from its mouth and fill the surrounding space with spiral tendrils, ivy leaves, and clusters of
yellow grapes. A third vine with tendrils moves sinuously
up toward the apex of the arch and serves as a perch for two
pairs of confronting land birds. In one register, two white-
throated birds with gracefully curving bodies swoop to drink
from the vase while above them two other birds stand in
heraldic confrontation.[672]

Between the middle and second half of the fifth century.

Illustrations. A. K. Orlandos, ABME, 8 (1955-56), p. 118,
fig. 2 = our pl. 447, p. 119, fig. 3 (inscription), p. 122,
fig. 4 (Ia), p. 123, fig. 5 (Ib, north arcade); D. R.
Theoharis, Praktika, 1958, pl. 51a = our pl. 448, pl. 52a =
our pl. 449.

---

[671]Enough remains of the right side of the south arcade
to accept a restoration of the vase and the cascading vines.
The upper register is, of course, hypothetical.

[672]It is noted that this panel is rich in polychromy.
In addition to the colors in Ia, light purplish brown,
yellow, and red are used (ABME, 8, p. 124).

KALAMBAKA

Basilica

Traces of the foundations of an Early Christian basilica
were discovered in 1926 and 1969 beneath a sixteenth century
church dedicated to the Dormition of the Virgin at Kalambaka.
Fragments of tessellated pavements were found between nine
and twenty-five centimeters below the pavements of the bema
and the north and south aisles of the church. They were
covered over until a systematic study could be undertaken.

Although the overall plan of the earlier church was not
determined, traces were found of the north and south stylobates which separated the nave from the single flanking
aisles. Given the limited scope of the investigation, no
archaeological finds were unearthed or reported and no date
was suggested. On the basis of the style and iconography of
the tessellated fragments, however, the building does not
appear to be earlier than the middle of the fifth century.

Bibliography. G. A. Soteriou, EEBS, 6 (1929), p. 293;
N. Nikonanos, Deltion, 25 (1970), B2: Chronika, pp. 290-291.

Nos. 143-145

Brief mention of the discovery of mosaic pavements
belonging to the Early Christian period. On the basis of
very inadequate descriptive and illustrative (pls. 450-451)
material, a tentative date of the middle of the fifth century

or later is suggested by the peacock panel under the bema (145)[673] and the grid of circles and bars forming octagons under the north aisle (pl. 450).

143 Mosaic fragment under north aisle (no dimensions published). Pl. 450.

No published information on dimensions and material.

In a published photograph (pl. 450), there are traces of a light and dark wave crest border and a field design composed of juxtaposed circles which are united by short bars to form concave-sided octagons (for similar patterns, see 160, pl. 563; 164, pl. 576).[674] In one truncated octagon along the margin, there is a reel flanked by two trailing tendrils with spirals.

No earlier than the middle of the fifth century.

Illustration. N. Nikonanos, Deltion, 25 (1970), B2: Chronika, pl. 246b = our pl. 450.

144 Mosaic fragment under south aisle (no dimensions published). Pl. 451.

---

[673]Only a description of this fragment is published (G. A. Soteriou, EEBS, 6 [1929], p. 293).

[674]This pavement is compared to the one in the bema (145) which, however, appears to be quite different (cf. N. Nikonanos, Deltion, 25 [1970], B2: Chronika, p. 290 and n. 9 and infra, pp. 415-416 and n. 675).

No published information on dimensions and material.

In a published photograph (pl. 451), there are traces of an
overlapping lyre pattern, a two-strand guilloche, and a small
rectangular panel inscribed with two rectangular triangles.

No earlier than the middle of the fifth century.

Illustration. N. Nikonanos, Deltion, 25 (1970), B2:
Chronika, pl. 246gamma = our pl. 451.

145 Mosaic fragment under bema (1.80 x 0.65).

No published information on dimensions and material.

Brief mention of a panel containing a peacock surrounded by
vines and pomegranates and a border with interlace and
geometric patterns.[675]

No earlier than the middle of the fifth century.

---

[675]G. A. Soteriou, EEBS, 6 (1929), p. 293; vide supra,
p. 415, n. 674.

PART V. EPIROS

ISLAND OF KEPHALOS

Basilica Alpha

On the deserted island of Kephalos in the Gulf of Arta,
a series of excavations between 1965 and 1968 brought to
light a Christian basilica (pls. 452-453; overall, ca. 29.00
x ca. 37.00),[676] which was designated Alpha.[677] Fragments
of tessellated pavements were discovered in the nave and
bema.[678]

The excavations uncovered traces of an atrium, I, with
two rooms II-III, along its south side and a long exonarthex,
IV (13.15 x ca. 400), along its east side. The latter opens
onto a south annex, V, and communicates with an esonarthex,
VI, through two doors. This somewhat shorter and wider room
(12.60 x 4.50) is flanked to the north and south by annexes,
VII-VIII, which project beyond the walls of the church
proper. The latter (12.90 x 15.85) comprises a nave, IX,
separated from single flanking aisles, XI, XII, by columns

---

[676]The measurements are taken from the plan (pl. 452).

[677]Basilica Beta was found in 1968 (148).

[678]Since I was unable to visit the site, the condition
of the building and the mosaics was not determined.

resting on bases set on elevated stylobates which extend from
the east to the west walls, and from the bema, X, by a chancel
screen. Except for the screen, no other liturgical furnishing was found in situ although fragments of an ambon and small
columnar supports, possibly belonging to an altar, were discovered elsewhere in the church.[679]

Although only a general attribution to the Early
Christian period is given in the reports,[680] on the basis
of the architectural sculpture and brick stamps, the church
has been ascribed to the sixth century,[681] a date which is
substantiated by the style of the pavement in the bema, X.
The pitiful condition of the mosaics was caused by the installation of a late one-aisled chapel over the ruins of the
east and north sides of the church.[682] The condition and
paving of the other rooms is not noted; presumably the
paving was stone and brick.

Bibliography. Ch. N. Mbarla, Praktika, 1965, pp. 78-84;
A. K. Orlandos, To Ergon, 1965, pp. 47-52; Ch. N. Mbarla,
Praktika, 1966, pp. 95-102; A. K. Orlandos, To Ergon, 1966,
pp. 87-92; BCH, 90 (1966), pp. 840-843; JHS, 86 (1966),
Supplement, p. 13; Ch. N. Mbarla, Praktika, 1967, pp. 28-32;
A. K. Orlandos, To Ergon, 1967, pp. 24-27; BCH, 91 (1967),

---

[679]Ch. N. Mbarla, Praktika, 1968, pp. 20-21; A. K.
Orlandos, To Ergon, 1968, pp. 23-24.

[680]Ch. N. Mbarla, Praktika, 1965, p. 78, hereafter cited
as Praktika, 1965; A. K. Orlandos, To Ergon, 1965, p. 47,
hereafter cited as To Ergon, 1965.

[681]Sodini, Catalogue, p. 724, n. 44.

[682]No evidence was found to date the destruction of the
church or the erection of the chapel (Praktika, 1965, p. 80
and n. 1; To Ergon, 1965, p. 49).

pp. 679-681; JHS, 87 (1967), Supplement, p. 14; Ch. N. Mbarla, Praktika, 1968, pp. 16-21; A. K. Orlandos, To Ergon, 1968, pp. 21-25.

Illustrations. Ch. N. Mbarla, Praktika, 1965, p. 79, fig. 1 (Room X: mosaic in situ); A. K. Orlandos, To Ergon, 1965, p. 50, fig. 59 = our pl. 453; idem, To Ergon, 1966, p. 50, fig. 38 (general view of bema with traces of later chapel); Ch. N. Mbarla, Praktika, 1968, pl. 14a (Room V, from west), pl. 16a-b (chancel slab: front and back); A. K. Orlandos, To Ergon, 1968, p. 22, fig. 23 = our pl. 452.

Nos. 146-147

Mosaic pavements decorate the nave[683] and bema. Sodini has correctly compared the style and iconography of the mosaic in the bema (pls. 453-454) to those in the churches at Nikopolis in neighboring Epiros.[684] The combination of a field design containing a grid with circles and bars forming octagons and an imbrication border with bichrome scales, are features which are encountered at Basilicas Beta (160, pl. 563) and Delta (164, pl. 576). It is quite probable, therefore, that the pavements belong to approximately the same period, that is, to the early sixth century, and reflect the production of Epirotic artisians whose base of operation was Nikopolis.

Additional bibliography. Sodini, Catalogue, No. 42, pp. 723-724.

Illustration. A. K. Orlandos, To Ergon, 1965, p. 48, fig. 56 = our pl. 453.

---

[683]The nave mosaic is not shown in the plan (pl. 453).

[684]Catalogue, p. 741 and n. 86.

146   Room IX (5.80 x 15.18).   Nave; except for small

fragment, pavement destroyed by foundations of later

chapel. Pl. 453a.

Fragment. No published information on dimensions and

material.

In a published photograph (pl. 453a), there are traces of

two borders and a field.[685]

Framing: outer border, indeterminable pattern; dark

fillet; inner border, two-strand guilloche.

Field, framed by a dark fillet: destroyed, except for

traces of a light ground.

Probably contemporary with the church and the bema pavement;

early sixth century.

Illustration. Ch. N. Mbarla, Praktika, 1966, pl. 86a =
our pl. 453a.

147   Room X (4.42 x 5.00).   Bema; pavement partially destroyed

by the foundations of a later chapel. Pls. 453-454.

Two fragments: larger one to west, 1.75 x 2.30. Border:

0.50. Field: 1.25 x 1.80.[686] No published information on

material.

---

[685]This fragment is not illustrated in the plan (pl. 453).

[686]The field measurement is taken from the plan (pl. 453).

Fragment of a polychrome geometric mosaic comprising a grid
design with organic filling motifs and an imbrication border.

Framing:[687] outer border, imbrication pattern composed of
bichrome scales arranged in diagonal rows. At the entrance
to the bema (pl. 453) the border is interrupted by a medallion
inscribed with a pattern composed of twelve rays; dark fillet;
light triple fillet.

Field, framed by a dark fillet: straight grid composed of
juxtaposed circles united by short bars to form concave-
sided octagons. The latter are filled with fish and birds
which appear to be oriented eastward. The circles, which are
cut along the margins, are decorated with stepped squares
set on edge.

Early sixth century.

Illustrations. A. K. Orlandos, To Ergon, 1965, p. 48,
fig. 56 = our pl. 453, p. 50, fig. 59 = our pl. 454.

Basilica Beta

In 1968 and 1970 a second basilica, Beta, was excavated
on the sland of Kephalos in the Gulf of Arta[688] with traces

---

[687]In the plan (pl. 453), there is an inexplicable 20
centimeter caesura between the pavement and the stylobate to
the north and the chancel screen to the west. This is not
substantiated by the photograph which shows that, originally,
the pavement was laid up to these features (pl. 454; see also
To Ergon, 1965, p. 50, fig. 58 [general view of bema]).

[688]It is situated about one hundred and twenty meters
south of Basilica Alpha (147). Vide supra, p. 417 and n. 678.

of a mosaic pavement in the nave.

Only the northeast and extreme southwest foundations of the building are preserved (pl. 455)[689] so that its plan remains, for the most part, problematic. It was a one-aisled basilica with two narthexes to the west and a tripartite transept to the east. The preserved north wing is about fifty centimeters above the floor of the bema and is paved with brick slabs while the bema has a marble floor. Two fragments of tessellated paving were found on the north and east sides of the nave (Ψ, on pl. 445).

Although no datable archaeological finds were unearthed, the tripartite transept supplies a means of dating the structure. In adjacent Nikopolis, a series of churches erected between the end of the fifth century and the middle of the sixth century are all distinguished by tripartite transepts with or without projecting wings (150-156; 157-161; 162-164; 165-167).[690] It is to this period, therefore, that Basilica Beta belongs and it is probable that artisans from Nikopolis were involved in its construction. To some extent, this is substantiated by the style and iconography of the mosaic pavement which, although in ruinous condition, shows Nikopolitan characteristics.

---

[689]See also Ch. N. Mbarla, *Praktika*, 1970, p. 91, fig. 1 (later plan) which shows the progress of the excavations on the west side of the complex, hereafter cited as *Praktika*, 1970.

[690]For similar transepts, but with apses, see the sixth century churches at Klapsi (94-100) and Dodona and Paramythia (*vide supra*, p. 277 and n. 427).

Bibliography. Ch. N. Mbarla, Praktika, 1968, pp. 21-23;
A. K. Orlandos, To Ergon, 1968, pp. 26-27; BCH, 94 (1970),
p. 1017; Ch. N. Mbarla, Praktika, 1970, pp. 90-95; A. K.
Orlandos, To Ergon, 1970, pp. 82-87; BCH, 95 (1971), p. 916.

Illustrations. Ch. N. Mbarla, Praktika, 1968, p. 22, fig.
3 = our pl. 455; idem, Praktika, 1970, p. 91, fig. 1 (plan),
pls. 129-143 (general views of site and building).

No. 148

Two small fragments (pl. 456) of a mosaic border were
discovered on the northeast and east sides of the nave (Ψ,
pl. 455). Although in ruinous condition, Nikopolitan influ-
ences are evident in the flat interlace, the stepped triangles along the margin and the stylized bird in the fragment
on the north side (pl. 456, bottom).[691] These characteristics are found in the pavements at Basilicas Alpha (150, pl.
461; 153, pls. 473-476), Beta (157, pls. 550-554) and
Epsilon (165, pl. 581; 167, pls. 582-583) which have been
assigned to a period between the end of the fifth and the
middle or latter part of the sixth centuries. These similarities reflect a common workshop which was probably located
in Nikopolis and which executed the mosaics in Basilica Alpha
on Kephalos.

Illustration. Ch. N. Mbarla, Praktika, 1968, p. 22, fig. 3
= our pl. 455.

---

[691]The east fragment (pl. 456, top) is barely visible
and legible. It has been described as having flowers and
leaves (Ch. N. Mbarla, Praktika, 1968, p. 22; hereafter cited
as Praktika, 1968).

148   Room I (ca. 5.00 x 6.50).[692]   Nave.   Pl. 456.

Two fragments. No published information on dimensions and material.

Two small fragments of the border of a mosaic pavement are preserved on the northeast and east sides. One border (pl. 456, top) contained "leaves and flowers" and the ohter (pl. 456, bottom) an interlace forming circles which are inscribed with birds and plants.[693]   No other information is available.

Late fifth or sixth century.

SAINT GEORGE

Mosaic Pavement

In the town of Saint George, near Preveza, a chance find in 1964 brought to light a building with a mosaic pavement belonging to the "Roman or Early Christian period." At the present time, the pavement is covered and the site is overgrown. A systematic excavation of the site was planned but, to date, no report has appeared.

Bibliography. S. I. Dakares, _Deltion_, 19 (1964), B3: _Chronika_, p. 309.

---

[692]The measurement is taken from the latest plan (_Praktika_, 1970, p. 91, fig. 1).

[693]_Praktika_, 1968, p. 22; A. K. Orlandos, _To Ergon_, 1968, p. 27; _vide supra_, p. 423, n. 691.

149 Mosaic fragment (no dimensions published).

No published information on dimensions and material.

Brief.mention of a pavement.

Roman or Early Christian.

NIKOPOLIS

Basilica Alpha

In 1915, excavations were begun at a site in the south
sector of the Byzantine city of Nikopolis.[694] In four subsequent campaigns ending in 1926, a large basilica, designated Alpha, was cleared (pls. 457-459) bringing to light
pavements in Rooms I-VI and X-XI, and stone paving in the
others. The pavements have undergone periodic repairs, beginning in 1926, and between 1962-1966 those in the porticoes
of the atrium, in the north annexes of the narthex, and in
the nave were placed on new foundations.[695] At the present

---

[694]The ruins of the church were noted by W. A. Leake in
1805 (Travels in Northern Greece, London, 1835, p. 189).

[695]G. A. Soteriou, Praktika, 1926, p. 126; A. Philadelpheus, Praktika, 1926, p. 130; A. K. Orlandos, Praktika, 1962,
p. 181; idem, To Ergon, 1966, pp. 171-173; idem, Praktika,
1966, p. 196.

time, the mosaics are in good condition and only those in the
west portico, Ic, are covered.

Although an inscription in the atrium states that the
church was dedicated to St. Demetrios, it is more often
referred to as Basilica Alpha by virtue of its being the
first in a series of five basilicas discovered in Nikopolis
and environs (157-161).[696] In each church, the narthex is
preceded by a large atrium and is distinguished by projecting annexes on its north and south sides.[697] The east side
ends in a tripartite transept, usually with projecting wings,
a bema with clergy benches, and a raised, stepped apse. Unlike Basilicas Beta through Epsilon, however, the transepts
and nave in Alpha are decorated with tessellated, not stone,
paving.

Since Alpha has been the subject of extensive investigation and analysis, only a brief description of its plan will
follow.[698] The major entrance to the church complex (pl.
457) is distinguished by a propylon on the west side which

---

[696]For Gamma which does not have tessellated pavements,
see A. K. Orlandos and G. A. Soteriou, Praktika, 1937,
pp. 81-82.

[697]These rooms have been reconstructed as protheses and
diakonika (Orlandos, Hē metakinēsis tou diakonikou, pp. 354,
passim).

[698]See Soteriou, Palaiochristianikai basilikai, pp. 206-
207, fig. 37; Orlandos, Xylostegos basilikē, pp. 98, passim,
p. 101, pl. B, p. 174, fig. 134, p. 206, fig. 166,5; Krautheimer, Tripartite Transept, pp. 418-423, p. 418, fig. 16;
idem, Architecture, pp. 98-99, fig. 37; idem, Studies,
pp. 60-61.

opens onto an atrium, I (17.90 x 14.28), surrounded by a peristyle or colonnade, a-c (pls. 533-535, 544; 4.30 wide).[699]
Preceded by a shallow narthex, II (17.90 x 4.50), with projecting wings, III, IV, V, the main body of the church (16.96
x 26.90, including transept) consists of a nave, VI, flanked
by two aisles, VIII-VIII, and a tripartite transept, IX-XI
(pls. 458-459). The central bay or bema is raised one step
above the wings and the nave and the apse five steps above the
bema. The nave is separated from the aisles by colonnades
resting on bases set on elevated stylobates, and from the
bema by a triumphal arch supported by pillars or columns.[700]
Single arches on pillars divide the area between the aisles
and the wings while projecting pilasters and chancel screens
serve to distinguish and isolate the bema from the wings.[701]

---

[699]The plan of the atrium is not clear. In the original
reports, the court is described as being surrounded by a low
wall (0.50 high and 0.65 wide); see A. Philadelpheus, ArchEph,
1916, p. 122; idem, Praktika, 1916, p. 52; idem, ArchEph,
1917, p. 49, fig. 1 (plan); hereafter cited as ArchEph, 1917;
Soteriou, however, places a colonnade around the court
(Palaiochristianikai basilikai, pp. 206-207, fig. 37). It is
this plan which is reproduced by Krautheimer (Architecture,
p. 98, fig. 37) and by Orlandos (Xylostegos basilike, p. 176,
fig. 134). In a recent plan, however, Orlandos restores the
wall (our pl. 457). Unfortunately, during my field work at
Nikopolis, I neglected to check this detail.

[700]Soteriou, Palaiochristianikai basilikai, p. 206. At
one time, A. K. Orlandos questioned this restoration (PraktAk-
Ath, 1929, p. 231, n. 2 and Byzantion, 5 [1929-30], p. 209,
n. 3). In a recent plan, however, he inserts columns and
bases (our pl. 457) which could only mean that he accepts
Soteriou's reconstruction.

[701]For a discussion of these divisions, see Krautheimer
(vide supra, p. 426, n. 698).

Near the chord of the apse were found an enkainion (0.60
deep) containing some human bones and colored tesserae[702]
and thick marble slabs which may have belonged to the
altar.[703] Flanking the altar site are two clergy benches
which were probably attached to the marble slabs of the
chancel screen as at Beta (pl. 548). Traces of the screen
and its foundations were found abutting the east piers but
none along the west side or between the short sides of the
benches and the east and west surfaces as reconstructed by
Soteriou.[704] Around the base of the elevated apse (1.50
high) is an enclosed corridor which opens onto the north and
south sides of the bema. The north annex, III-IV, may have
served as the baptistery or prothesis of the church.[705] and
the south annex as its chapel. In a subsequent period or

---

[702]The enkainion is described as "Omega-shaped" (A.
Philadelpheus, Praktika, 1915, p. 60; idem, ArchEph, 1916, p.
35), "crossed-shaped" (G. A. Soteriou, Hieros syndesmos,
[Dec. 1-15, 1915], p. 10) and "T-shaped" (idem, Palaiochristianikai basilikai, p. 207). For A. K. Orlandos' reconstruction, see our pl. 457.

[703]A. Philadelpheus, ArchEph, 1916, p. 35ff. In 1929,
Soteriou noted traces of the base of the altar in situ
(Palaiochristianikai basilikai, p. 207) but no published plan
contains this feature.

[704]Palaiochristianikai basilikai, pp. 206-207 and fig.
37; see also Krautheimer, Tripartite Transept, p. 418, fig.
16 and Architecture, p. 98, fig. 37. The early reports and
plans (A. Philadelpheus, ArchEph, 1916, pp. 36ff; ArchEph,
1917, p. 49, fig. 1) and the latest plan (pl. 457) do not
support this reconstruction.

[705]For the first, see Soteriou, Palaiochristianikai
basilikai, p. 207; for the second, see Orlandos, He
metakinesis tou diakonikou, pp. 359-360 and supra, p. 426,
n. 697.

periods, two benches were installed along the northeast and northwest walls of the narthex and it is possible that at this time a large brick base (2.60 x 1.80 was erected in Room IV.[706]

Mosaic pavements decorate the peristyle of the atrium, the narthex and its annexes, the nave, and the north and south transept wings. Marble slabs pave the atrium court, the bema, and the apse, and irregularly-cut marble pieces are scattered across the surface of the north and south aisles.

Although few datable archaeological finds were unearthed or reported, on the basis of the inscriptions in the atrium, nave and the south chapel, the church and the majority of its mosaics have been assigned to the second quarter of the sixth century.[707] In the second half of the century, the porticoes of the atrium were paved with rather crude mosaics.

Bibliography. W. M. Leake, Travels in Northern Greece, London, 1835, p. 189; A. Philadelpheus, Praktika, 1915, pp. 31-33, 59-95; G. A. Soteriou, Hieros syndesmos (Dec. 1-15, 1915), pp. 1-26; AA, 30 (1915), p. 196; A. Philadelpheus, Praktika, 1916, pp. 32-33, 49-54; AA, 31 (1916), pp.148-151; A. Philadelpheus, ArchEph, 1916, pp. 34-54, 65-73, 121-122; idem, ArchEph, 1917, pp. 48-72; F. Grossi-Gondi, Nuovo bullettino di archeologia cristiana, 23 (1917), pp. 121-127; A. Philadelpheus, ArchEph, 1918, pp. 34-41; AA, 37 (1923),

---

[706]A. Philadelpheus, ArchEph, 1916, pp. 40, 122; idem, Praktika, 1916, p. 52; idem, ArchEph, 1918, p. 38. The date of the brick feature, which may have been the foundation of a sarcophagus or tomb, is not discussed. Beneath its base were found coins of the fifth or sixth century (A. Philadelpheus, Praktika, 1916, p. 52).

[707]Kitzinger, Mosaics at Nikopolis, pp. 84ff., with earlier references and chronology.

pp. 248-249; A. Philadelpheus, Praktika, 1924, pp. 108-115;
G. A. Soteriou, Praktika, 1926, pp. 122-127; A. Philadelpheus,
Praktika, 1926, pp. 127-130; AA, 42 (1927), p. 389; AA, 43
(1928), p. 599; G. A. Soteriou and A. K. Orlandos, Praktika,
1929, pp. 22-24, 86; Kautzsch, Kapitellstudien, no. 216, p.
68; Soteriou, Palaiochristianikai basilikai, pp. 206-207; AA,
46 (1931), pp. 264-265; Krautheimer, Tripartite Transept, pp.
418-423; Kitzinger, Mosaics at Nikopolis, pp. 82-122; A. K.
Orlandos, Praktika, 1961, pp. 98-107; BCH, 86 (1962), pp. 763-
766; A. K. Orlandos, Praktika, 1964, pp. 179-183; idem, To
Ergon, 1964, pp. 152-158; BCH, 89 (1965), pp. 761-765; A. K.
Orlandos, Praktika, 1966, pp. 195-196; idem, To Ergon, 1966,
pp. 171-173; BCH, 91 (1967), pp. 672-674; Krautheimer, Architecture, pp. 98-99; G. Tsimas and P. Papahadjidakis, Monuments
de Nikopolis, vol. 1 (Séries: monuments de l'art byzantin en
Grèce) Athens, n.d.

Illustrations. A. Philadelpheus, ArchEph, 1916, p. 34, fig.
1 (apse, from southwest), p. 37, fig. 2 (general view, from
west), p. 39, fig. 4 (narthex, from southwest); idem,
Praktika, 1916, p. 56, fig. 5 (atrium with inscription, from
west); Soteriou, Palaiochristianikai basilikai, p. 206, fig.
37 (plan); A. K. Orlandos, To Ergon, 1964, p. 154, fig. 173 =
our pl. 457.

Nos. 150-156

Polychrome pavements suffused with flora and fauna
decorate the major sectors of the church (pls. 461-545). The
north and south transept wings are paved with large scale
figural compositions set in idyllic landscapes and surrounded
by wide decorative friezes which, for the most part, are filled
with animated denizens of the land and sea and with hunters
and fishermen who struggle to capture them.[708] The remaining

[708]For various interpretations of the iconography of the
pavements, see J. S. Pelekanides, Zeitschrift fur Kirchengeschichte, 3, folge X, vol 59 (1940), pp. 114-124; Kitzinger,
Mosaic Pavements in the Greek East, pp. 209-223; idem, Mosaics
at Nikopolis, pp. 95-122; A. Grabar, CA, 12 (1962), pp. 142-
149; G. C. Tomasevic, Heraclea-3 (1967), pp. 46-62, especially
pp. 61-62; E. Kitzinger, Proceedings of the American Philosophical Society, 117 (1973), pp. 369-370.

pavements in the atrium, Ia-c, the narthex and its annexes,
II-V, and the nave, VI, are decorated with rectilinear and
curvilinear geometric designs forming squares and circles
which, except for the mosaic in Rooms III-IV, enclose flora,
and marine and land creatures. Three tessellated inscriptions in the south annex (152), nave (153) and the north
transept wing (154) cite the name of a bishop at Nikopolis,
Dometios, who erected the church. To this phase belong all
the mosaics with the exception of those in the atrium, which,
according to an inscription in the pavements (156), were
sponsored by a second bishop of the same name who was a pupil
and successor to the first Dometios. The pavements belonging
to this second decorative phase are clearly inferior to the
mosaics executed during the episcopacy of the first Dometios
and have been attributed to the second half of the sixth
century. All the other pavements have been assigned to the
second quarter of the century.[709]

Additional bibliography. G. A. Soteriou, Hieros syndesmos
(Dec. 1-15, 1915), pp. 1-26; St. Pelekanides, Zeitschrift für
Kirchengeschicte, 3, X, 59 (1940), pp. 114-124; Kitzinger,
Mosaic Pavements in the Greek East, pp. 209-223; idem,
Mosaics at Nikopolis, pp. 82-122; A. Grabar, CA, 12 (1962),
pp. 142-149; G. Tomasevic, Heraclea-3 (1967), pp. 46, passim;
Sodini, Catalogue, No. 43, pp. 724-726.

Illustration. A. K. Orlandos, To Ergon, 1964, p. 154,
fig. 173 = our pl. 457.

---

[709]The chronology was established by Kitzinger, Mosaics
at Nikopolis, pp. 88-92.

PERIOD I, PHASE 1

150 Room II (17.90 x 4.50). Narthex; benches installed
along the northeast and northwest walls, covering the
pavements; subsequently, removed by the excavators. Pls.
460-464.

Framing: 0.70; along west side, 0.90. Field: 16.50 x
3.10. Stone, ceramic (red) and glass (green, blue) tesserae
(0.01 sq) set 1-3mm apart.

Polychrome interlace design filled with organic motifs and
bordered by interlaced circles.

Surround: generally, in rows of white tesserae parallel
to the walls; along west side, dark blue and white wave
crests (pl. 460).

Framing (pls. 458, 460): black fillet; white triple fillet;
black fillet; border, complex chain of interlaced circles
(pink/1 white; grey/1 white, outlined in black) with red
centers[710] (for similar borders in the nave, atrium and elsewhere, see pls. 476; 543; 256); black fillet; white triple
fillet; black fillet; triple pink fillet.

Field (pls. 460-462), framed by a black fillet: two-strand
interlace (pink/1 white; greenish grey/1 white, outlined in

---

[710]At regular intervals, the red centers are replaced
by white ones. Whether this represents the original scheme,
or ancient or modern repair could not be determined. For a
different color description, see ArchEph, 1917, p. 58ff.

black) of circles forming concave-sided octagons (for a
similar design in the nave and elsewhere, see 153, pls. 476,
482-483; 12, pls. 40, 42-43; 96, pl. 332).[711] The design is
arranged in twenty-three rows of four circles each and is
accented along the margins by serrate-edged rainbow triangles
in three superimposed rows of red/pink/greenish grey/black.
The circles are inscribed with a variety of land and sea
creatures and vegetables and plants which are all oriented
northward. Brilliant polychromy is evident in the birds
which are remarkable for their grey (stone) and green, blue,
and turquoise (all glass) plumage with white, pink, red,
and black for their sharp outlines and interior details.
Some bird insets contain curving branches with red-tipped
buds, but, generally, the birds are set against a blank
ground and seem to float within the opaque circles. This
effect is heightened by the flat two-dimensional treatment
of their bodies which in many instances (pl. 462) are supported by limp feet which curve downward as if they were tip-
toeing across the surface. The marine creatures (pl. 461),
like the grey and white fish and octopi, and the black plants
with white and red buds, the green and brown beans or cucumbers, and the light brown and reddish brown eggplants are
also unmodeled and sharply etched against a neutral ground.
In this manner, all the filling motifs adhere to the surface
plane articulated by the unfolding interlace and by the simple

---

[711]Vide supra, p. 44 and n. 81, 291 and n. 448.

geometric motifs filling the concave-sided octagons. They
consist of two-strand knots (pink/1 white; greenish grey/1
white, outlined in black) which sometimes succeed in main-
taining a square appearance but which, more frequently,
deteriorate into distended and amorphous forms. Although a
list of the sequence of filling motifs beginning at the
southeast corner is published,[712] it is inaccurate. Beginning at the same corner and moving westward, the sequence is
as follows. First row: water fowl; two eggplants; four
green beans; land bird. Second row: plant with three buds;
water fowl; land bird; sepia. Third row: land bird; plant
with three buds, land bird; land bird. Fourth row: water
fowl; water fowl; plant with three buds; land bird. Fifth
row: plant with three buds; water fowl; land bird standing
on two bud-bearing stalks; sepia. Sixth row: fish; land
bird pecking at a bud-bearing branch; destroyed; land bird.
Seventh row: water fowl; plant with three buds; land bird;
plant with three buds. Eighth row: land bird; fish; water
fowl; land bird. Ninth row: land bird; vine leaf and bunch
of grapes; destroyed; land bird. Tenth row: destroyed;
cock; rabbit; water fowl. Eleventh row: all destroyed.
Twelfth row: land bird; rabbit; water fowl; rabbit.
Thirteenth row (pl. 460): destroyed; destroyed; land bird;
three pears. Fourteenth row: land bird; destroyed; water
fowl; land bird. Fifteenth row: destroyed. Sixteenth row:

---

[712]ArchEph, 1917, p. 59.

destroyed. Seventeenth row: destroyed; destroyed; serrate-
edged square set on edge (four rows of black/pink/greenish
grey/red/black); land bird. Eighteenth row (pl. 461): two
pears; water fowl; two eggplants; sepia. Nineteenth row:
land bird; land bird in front of a bud-bearing vine; plant
with three buds; land bird. Twentieth row: destroyed; land
bird; fish; plant with three buds. Twenty-first row: land
bird (?); plant with three buds; water fowl; land bird.
Twenty-second row: destroyed; destroyed; star-crossed
rosette; cock. Twenty-third row: land bird; land bird;
plant with three buds; land bird.

Additional color. Birds: generally, red beaks and legs
and white eyes with black centers.

Second quarter of the sixth century.

Illustrations. A. Philadelpheus, ArchEph, 1917, p. 58,
fig. 13 (part of field and border), p. 59, fig. 14 (twelfth
row); A. K. Orlandos, To Ergon, 1964, p. 157, fig. 177 (rows
six to nine), p. 158, fig. 178 (rows four to seven).

151 Rooms III-IV (6.25 x 7.00) North annex; possibly a
baptistery unit or prothesis.[713] In Room IV, pavement
laid up to, or destroyed by, a brick foundation.[714] Pl. 465.

Fragment in Room III: 5.80 x 3.05. Stone and ceramic
(red) tesserae (ca. 0.01 sq) set 2-4mm apart.

---

[713]The function and chronology of the features along the
north and west walls are not discussed in the reports (see
pl. 457).

[714]Vide supra, p. 429, n. 706.

Crude, purely geometric design forming a dense curvilinear carpet in Rooms III-IV; fragment preserved in Room III.

Surround: in rows parallel to the walls.

Framing: bluish black fillet, triple white fillet.

Field (pl. 465), framed by a bluish black fillet: close-knit interlace (red/1 white; grey/1 white, outlined in black).

Second quarter of the sixth century.

Illustrations. A. Philadelpheus, Praktika, 1916, p. 51, fig. 2 (general view); A. K. Orlandos, To Ergon, 1966, p. 172, fig. 203 = our pl. 465.

152 Room V (11.93, with apse, x 4.50). South chapel.

Pls. 466-472.

Nave: 9.83 x 4.50. Framing: 1.09. Field: ca. 7.65 x 2.12. Apse: 2.12 diam. Framing: 0.65. Field: 1.47. Materials identical to those in narthex (150).

Polychrome mosaic comprising a figural composition in the apse and a geometric carpet with organic filling motifs in the nave which is enclosed by three borders. Near the west entrance is a dedicatory inscription citing the name of Bishop Dometios.

Va, nave (pls. 466-468).

Framing: bluish black fillet; outer border, bluish black and white wave crests; bluish black fillet; triple white fillet; middle border, close-knit, two-strand interlace (red/ 1 white; light blue/1 white, outlined in bluish black) of

small circles forming concave-sided octagons (for similar
designs, see the narthex (pl. 461) and the atrium (pl. 543);
bluish black fillet; triple white fillet; bluish black
fillet; inner border, undulating bluish black rinceau (two
fillets) forming rigidly arranged and closely spaced scrolls
alternately filled with single light blue and red ivy leaves,
outlined in dark blue; bluish black fillet.

Field (pls. 467-468), framed by a double white fillet:
straight grid formed by wide polychrome bands with a series
of red/white/light blue stripes, outlined in dark blue (for
a similar design, see the atrium [pls. 533-536, 538-542] and
Basilica Beta in the same city [161, pl. 566]). The intersections of the bands are decorated with small dark blue
diagonal crosses, on a light blue ground, which accent the
corners of the squares (0.23) formed by the grid. In the
twenty-one rows of seven squares each, birds, marine creatures, plants, and vegetables, which are oriented northward,
predominate over geometric motifs. Stylistically and
chromatically, these filling elements are very similar to
those in the narthex (150, pls. 461-464) with the main difference being that their rectilinear habitat creates a more
rigid and staccato rhythm across the surface. Beginning
with the first square to the southeast, the sequence of filling elements is as follows.[715] First row (pl. 469): land

---

[715]This sequence is correctly recorded by A. Philadelpheus, _Praktika_, 1917, p. 62.

bird; plant with two buds; bird; two cucumbers or beans;
bird; plant with two buds; water fowl. Second row: grapes;
water fowl; two pears; cock; cock; grapes; land bird. Third
row: land bird; land bird; land bird; cucumbers or beans;
land bird; watermelon. Fourth row: watermelon; plant with
two buds; land bird; rabbit; small leafless branch; rabbit;
land bird. Fifth row: sepia; two pears; grapes; grape leaf;
land bird; two cucumbers or beans; two pears. Sixth row:
lemon; land bird; rabbit; rabbit; crayfish; land bird; plant
with two buds. Seventh row: sepia; prawn; bivalve; land
bird; fish; crayfish; sepia. Eighth row: two cucumbers or
beans; plant with two buds; land bird; gold cup;[716] two
pears; land bird; watermelon. Ninth row (pl. 467): diagonal
quatrefoils of light blue and red lanceolate leaves, outlined
in black, in all squares. Tenth row (pl. 467): two-strand
interlace (red/1 white; light blue/1 white, outlined in bluish
black) forming squares in all seven squares. Eleventh row:
land bird; two cucumbers or beans; water fowl; two pears;
land bird; two cucumbers or beans; diagonal quatrefoil like
those in inth row (pl. 467). Twelfth row: water fowl; fish;
diagonal quatrefoil (see row nine); land bird; interlace (see
row ten); fish; water fowl (pl. 468). Thirteenth row:
diagonal quatrefoil (see row nine); fish; two cucumbers or
beans; land bird; two pears; diagonal quatrefoil (see row

---

[716]An error in a plan incorrectly places this in the
narthex (marked "Ψ"). See A. Philadelpheus, ArchEph, 1917,
p. 65, p. 49, fig. 1.

nine); crayfish. Fourteenth row: land bird; interlace (see row ten); plant with buds; sepia; water fowl; ivy leaf; two pears. Fifteenth row: diagonal quatrefoil (see row nine); two cucumbers or beans; plant with two buds; land bird; two cucumbers or beans; diagonal quatrefoil (see row nine); interlacé (see row ten). Sixteenth row: diagonal quatrefoil (see row nine); water fowl; rabbit; rabbit; plant with two buds; unidentifiable sea creature; two pears. Seventeenth row: land bird; crayfish; bush with narrow branches; sepia; two pears; diagonal quatrefoil (see row nine); water fowl. Eighteenth row (pl. 466): plant with one bud; crayfish; fish; two pears; water fowl; crayfish; two cucumbers or beans. Nineteenth row: two opposed peltae; sepia; water fowl; two land birds; cock; plant with one bud; plant with one bud. Twentieth row: land bird; spiral ornament; water fowl; diagonal quatrefoil (see row nine); land bird; two pears; land bird. Twenty-first row: two cucumbers or beans; water fowl; plant with one bud; land bird; crayfish; fish; sepia.

Dominating the west side of the field is a red tabula ansata (0.49 x 1.92) containing a four-line inscription in red letters (ca. 0.09-0.10 high). Oriented westward and preceded by a cross (pl. 466), it cites the name of a bishop of Nikopolis, Dometios I, who is also mentioned in the inscriptions in the nave, north transept wing, and the atrium (153, 154, 156).

ΟΙΚΟΝΑΠΑΣΤΡΑΠΤΟΝΤΑΘΥΧΑΡΙΝΕΝΘΑΚΕΝΘΑ/
ΔΗΜΑΤΟΚΑΙΚΟΣΜΗΣΕΚΑΙΑΓΛΔΙΗΝΠΟΡΕΠΑΣΑΝ/
ΔΟΥΜΕΤΙΟΣΠΕΡΙΠΥΣΤΟΣΑΜΩΜΗΤΩΝΙΕΡΗΩΝ/
ΑΡΧΙΕΡΕΥΣΠΑΝΑΡΙΣΤΟΣΟΛΗΣΠΑΤΡΗΣΜΕΓΑΦΕΝΓΟ /   717

Vb, apsidal panel, separated from the nave panel by the
outer wave crest border (pls. 469-472).

Framing: bluish black fillet; white triple fillet;
bluish black fillet; outer border, arcade of nine bluish
black arches supported by rectilinear capitals set on light
blue columns with square bases (for similar arcades in
Basilica Beta at Nikopolis, see 158, pl. 555). The arcuated
units are filled with single displaying peacocks (pls. 470-
471) standing de face on curving bluish black, leafless
branches (for a similar peacock, see 127, pl. 417). Their
dark blue, purple, and dark green spread trains, highlighted
by purple or dark green ocelli, create heraldic mandorlas
for their similarly colored heads and heart-shaped bodies
which are supported by black spindly legs and limp feet. In
the spandrels flanking the central arch, toward which the peacocks' heads are turned (pl. 470), stand single confronting
dark blue and grey birds. They are accompanied in the other

717Transcribed in the ArchEph, 1917, pp. 62-63, fig. on
p. 63. For a different transcription of lines 2 and 4, see
A. Ch. Chatzē, ArchEph, 1918, p. 32; G. A. Soteriou, Hieros
syndesmos (Dec. 1-15, 1915), p. 15. The last two letters in
lines 1 and 2, and the last three in line 4 are located beyond
the tabula, on either side of the ansae. A similar inscription decorates the west entrance to the nave (153). For the
following emendation, see ArchEph, 1917, pp. 62-63.
  ΟΙΚΟΝ ΑΠΑΣΤΡΑΠΤΟΝΤΑ Θ(ΕΟ)Υ ΧΑΡΙΝ ΕΝΘΑ Κ(ΑΙ) ΔΗΜΑΤΟ ΚΑΙ
ΚΟΣΜΗΣΕ ΚΑΙ ΑΓΛΑΪΗΝ ΠΟΡΕ ΠΑΣΑΝ/ ΔΟΥΜΕΤΙΟΣ ΠΕΡΙΠΥΣΤΟΣ
ΑΜΩΜΗΤΩΝ ΙΕΡΗΩΝ/ΑΡΧΙΕΡΕΥΣ ΠΑΝΑΡΙΣΤΟΣ ΟΛΗΣ ΠΑΤΡΗΣ ΜΕΓΑ ΦΕΝΓΟ(Σ).

spandrels by single white and red buds on curving black
branches; bluish black fillet; white triple fillet; bluish
black fillet; inner border, bluish black and white wave
crests; white double fillet.

Field (pls. 470, 472), framed by a bluish black fillet:
vase, oriented northward, from which issue two large graceful
grape vines. The bulbous grey ribbed body is adorned with
two bluish black spiral handles which are attached to the
tips of its sagging, protruding lip. Flanking the vases'
circular foot and triangular base are two minute grey birds
in flight which peck at clusters of grapes. The undulating,
convoluted green vines spread symmetrically across the surface and fill it with delicate foliate patterns and clusters
of red grapes, outlined in bluish black, which are highlighted by single white tesserae (for a similar composition,
see 100, pls. 350-352).

Additional color. Peacocks: white webbing and white and
bluish black contour lines.

Second quarter of the sixth century.

Illustrations. A. Philadelpheus, ArchEph, 1917, p. 60,
fig. 15 = our pl. 466, p. 61, fig. 17 = our pl. 469, p.
63, fig. 18 (Vb, detail).

153 Room VI (8.05 x 19.19). Nave; northwest panel partially
     destroyed by later drain (pls. 473, 476, 478). Pls.
473-485.

Fragment to west: 8.05 x 6.96 max. Framing: 0.91.

Field: 6.25 x 6.05 max. North compartment, a: 1.42 x 6.96
max. Border: 0.80 x 2.40 max. Middle compartment, b:
1.10 x 2.30 max. Border: 0.80 x 2.30 max. South compartment, c: 2.40 x 2.70 max. East panel, d: 1.75 x 1.70.
East panel, e: 2.45 x 1.30. Stone and ceramic (red) tesserae. (0.01 sq) set 2-4mm apart.

Polychrome pavement, preserved to the west, composed of figural and geometric compartments, a-c, bordered by a wide
interlace with figures which is interrupted in front of the
west entrance by a long inscription.

   Framing (pls. 473, 476): white band of five to seven rows;
grey triple fillet; black fillet; border, two-strand interlace (2 red/1 white/2 red; 1 grey/1 white/3 grey, outlined in
black) forming alternating circles (0.55 diam) and lozenges
(0.50 x 0.60) which enclose organic motifs similar to those
in the narthex (pls. 460-464) and the chapel (pls. 466-472).
In the preserved northwest section of the border, moving
eastward, there are a ram, vase, camel (pl. 474), a land
bird, three eggplants, a lozenge and circle containing confronting ducks, one standing in front of a bush, a lozenge
and circle with confronting cocks (pl. 475), three cucumbers
or beans, a land bird, and a cock. Although the rest of the
north border has disappeared, traces of it were noted in an
earlier report. Near the northeast corner were a "numidian
guinea fowl" and then an "antelope with black vertical

stripes on its body."[718] In the preserved southwest section
of the border, moving eastward (pl. 476), there are a crane,
vase, land bird, fish, two-strand interlace (same colors as
border), land bird, and a large fish. Again, the earlier
report supplies information on the missing panels. The last
preserved panel was succeeded by two cocks, one with its
head turned, a hen, and a crane. The rest of the border
was in fragmentary condition at the time of its discovery
but it appears that it continued up to the so-called
"solea."[719] Although stylistically identical to the flora
and fauna in the narthex and chapel, the polychromy is restricted to reds, grey, and brown, with black and white for
outlines and details. This conforms to the overall chromatic
scheme of the field toward which all the filling elements are
turned.

At the west entrance, this border is interrupted by a
tabula ansata (1.80 x 0.62), outlined in black, containing a
five-line inscription in black letters (0.10-0.11 high).
Oriented westward and preceded by a cross (pls. 458, 476),
it cites the name of a bishop of Nikopolis, Dometios I, who
is also mentioned in inscriptions in the south chapel, north
transept wing, and the atrium (152, 154, 156). The text
informs us that Dometios was reponsible for the erection of

---

[718]ArchEph, 1917, p. 55.

[719]ArchEph, 1917, p. 53. For a discussion on the decoration of the extreme east side, vide infra, pp. 447-448.

the building "from its foundations" and for the decorative
program.

ΛΙΘΟΝΑΠΑΣΤΡΑΠΤΟΝΤΑΘΥΧΑΡΙΝΕΝΘΑΚΕΝΘΑ/
ΕΚΘΕΜΕΘΛΩΝΤΟ[ ]ΥΠΕΥΣΕΚΑΓΛΑΙΗΝΠΟΡΕΠΑΣΑΝ/
ΔΟΥΜΕΤΙΟΣΠΕΡΙΠΥΣΤΟΣΑΜΩΜΗΤΩΝΙΕΡΗΩΝ/
ΑΡΧΙΕΡΕΥΣΠΑΝΑΡΙΣΤΟΣΟΛΗΣΠΑΤΡΗΣΜΕΓΑΦΕΓ/
ΑΥΤΗΗΠΥΛΗΤΟΥΚΥΔΙΚΑΙΟΙΕΙΣΕΛΘΟΝΤΩΝ/ [720]
Δ

Two dark blue heraldic peacocks (pls. 476-477) flank the
tabula but only the north one is accompanied by plants with
two white and red buds which float above its curving back;[721]
black fillet; triple white fillet; black fillet; grey triple
fillet.

Field (pls. 476, 478-485), framed by a black fillet: to
the west, tripartite design composed of three compartments,

_____

[720]The transcription and following emendation are in the
ArchEph, 1917, pp. 48, 50-51.

ΛΙΘΟΝ ΑΠΑΣΤΡΑΠΤΟΝΤΑ Θ(ΕΟ)Υ ΧΑΡΙΝ ΕΝΘΑ Κ(ΑΙ) ΕΝΘΑ/
ΕΚ ΘΕΜΕΘΛΩΝ ΤΟ[Λ]ΥΠΕΥΣΕ Κ(ΑΙ) ΑΓΛΑΪΗΝ ΠΟΡΕ ΠΑΣΑΝ/
ΔΟΥΜΕΤΙΟΣ ΠΕΡΙΠΥΣΤΟΣ ΑΜΩΜΗΤΩΝ ΙΕΡΗΩΝ/
ΑΡΧΙΕΡΕΥΣ ΠΑΝΑΡΙΣΤΟΣ ΟΛΗΣ ΠΑΤΡΗΣ ΜΕΓΑ ΦΕΓ(ΓΟΣ)/
ΑΥΤΗ Η ΠΥΛΗ ΤΟΥ ΚΥ(ΡΙΟΥ) ΔΙΚΑΙΟΙ ΕΙΣΕΛΘΟΝΤΩΝΔ.

This emendation was accepted by Kitzinger, Mosaics at
Nikopolis, p. 87, but G. A. Soteriou corrected line 5 to read
"ΠΥΛΗ ΚΥΡΙΟΥ ," and in line 6 he read "ΑΦΜ" in the right
corner (Hieros syndesmos (Dec. 1-15, 1915, p. 14).

[721]As the plate shows, most of the tesserae have been
lost or replaced. Except for its head, the south peacock is
destroyed. An early photograph reveals a much longer and
fuller bird than the north one but no plants which is
curious, since the space is greater than that on the north
side. It is possible that this panel was restored in
ancient times (ArchEph, 1917, p. 50, fig. 1a).

a-c, decorated with figural and geometric panels and separated by double borders.[722] To the east, probably at the
entrance to the bema, were two other panels (d-e), now lost
(pls. 484-485).

VIa, north compartment (pls. 473, 476): traces of at least
four superimposed panels, one to four, of which three contain
figural scenes. Beginning at the west side the sequence of
scenes is as follows.

Panel one (pls. 473, 476, 478), preserved only to north:
grazing grey duck, outlined in black. Above it are two
diagonal black plants with three spreading branches adorned
with white and red buds. Originally, the duck probably had a
counterpart to the south, since this symmetrical disposition
of the fauna obtains in the two succeeding panels and in the
north transept (154, pl. 493).

Panel two (pl. 479): two confronting grey ducks, outlined
in black, which float above a narrow black and grey ground
line articulated by short curving blades of grass. Between
and above them are black plants with spreading branches
tipped with leaves and white and red buds.[723]

Panel three (pls. 473, 480-481), separated from panel two
by a two-strand interlace (red/1 white; grey/1 white, outlined

---

[722]Only two other pavements have this type of tripartite
division on the longitudinal axis (33, pl. 76; 127, pl. 417).

[723]These panels are not discussed in the original report
(see ArchEph, 1917, pp. 56-58).

in black) forming small circles: traces of a bird in flight
and some flora (pls. 473, 481). Originally (pl. 480), a
large centralized composition composed of a fruit-bearing
tree flanked by flying, pecking birds above and "grazing
geese (?), ducks, and partridges" below[724] (for a similar
composition in the north transept wing, see 154, pl. 493).

Panel four, separated from the preceding panel by an
undulating black vine rinceau (one fillet) forming rigidly
arranged and widely spaced scrolls alternately filled with
single red and grey ivy leaves, outlined in black, traces of
a grey interlace of indeterminable design.

VIb, middle compartment (pl. 476), separated from the north
and south compartments, a, c, by a double border.[725]

Framing: white double fillet; narrow grey band; red triple
fillet; outer border, complex chain of interlaced circles
(red/1 white; grey/1 white, outlined in black; for a similar
border in the narthex, see pl. 460); white double fillet;
inner border, traces of an undulating ribbon (red/white/grey;
brown/pale green/white/brown; white double fillet.

Field (pl. 482), framed by a double red fillet: two-strand
interlace (red/1 white; grey/1 white, outlined in black) of

_____

[724]A. Philadelphius, ArchEph, 1917, p. 58. He omits the
first, second, and fourth panels and Sodini, the fourth
(Catalogue, p. 725).

[725]This is omitted from the reports and from Sodini's
Catalogue. See the preceding note.

circles (0.45-0.50) forming concave sided octagons (for a similar field in the narthex, see pls. 460-461). The design is arranged in rows of two circles each and is accented along the margins by serrate-edged rainbow triangles (black/red/ grey/white). Most of the filling motifs in the circles have disappeared, but an early report notes apples, eggplants, birds, fish, and grapes.[726] The octagons are filled with concave-sided squares set on edge which have the same rainbow coloration as the marginal triangles.

VIc, south compartment (pls. 476, 483), framed by a grey triple fillet: same type of interlace as in the preceding panel, VIb, but with smaller circles (ca. 0.25) and geometric filling motifs of stepped squares (grey/red/black) with small black-centered white crosslets.

The east side of the nave originally contained two other panels, d-e, with opposed peacocks flanking vases (pls. 484-485). Although their exact location is not specified, it is clear that they were placed beyond the border enclosing the field to the west since it runs along the bottom of each panel (pl. 485).[727] Either the published description is incorrect and the borders did not continue "as far as the solea,"[728] or they bifurcated near the base of the panels and

---

[726]ArchEph, 1917, p. 56.

[727]Only the white band is visible in the north panel (pl. 484).

[728]Vide supra, p. 443 and n. 719.

enclosed them on four sides. It is possible, therefore, to
suggest that these panels were placed somewhere near the
entrance to the bema and not in the northeast and southeast
"corners"[729] which, presumably, would have been occupied by
the borders. Moreover, since the panels are described as
being in opposite "corners," they must have been separated
by a considerable distance. Given this fact, one can reconstruct a decorative band between the panels, possibly the
same one which surrounded them. The east side of the pavement, therefore, would comprise two juxtaposed panels set
within an interlace framework of lozenges and circles.

VId, north panel (pl. 484), framed by a dark fillet:
two "life-size" peacocks flanking a long-necked "dark blue"
vase, with "dark green" fluting, which has spiral handles
and a wide curvilinear mouth.[730] Rising from the center of
its mouth is an oblong feature which may represent a snout of
some kind.[731] Filling the rest of the surface are convoluted
vines with leaves and clusters of grapes and some birds.

VIe, south panel (pl. 485), framed by a dark fillet: two
peacocks flanking a vase from which issue two convoluted
vines which spread across the surface and fill it with leaves
and clusters of grapes. The vase, broader and squatter than

---

[729]ArchEph, 1917, pp. 53, 54-55.

[730]ArchEph, 1917, p. 56.

[731]It is unclear if the vines, like those in the south
panel, issued from the mouth of the vase (cf. ibid.)

that in the north panel, contains alternating "red and blue"
ribs, outlined in white.[732]

Additional color. Southwest panel, c. Birds: black legs,
red beaks, black-centered white eyes.

Second quarter of the sixth century.

Illustrations. A. Philadelpheus, ArchEph, 1917, p. 50,
fig. 1a (peacock on south side of tabula ansata), p. 50,
fig. 2 (bird in southeast border), p. 51, fig. 3 (bird in
south border), p. 51, fig. 4 (cock in south border), p. 52,
fig. 5 (bird in south border), p. 52, fig. 6 = our pl. 485,
p. 53, fig. 7 (confronting ducks in north border), p. 54,
fig. 8 (cocks in north border), p. 54, fig. 9 (bird in north
border), p. 55, fig. 10 = our pl. 484, p. 56, fig. 11 (VIb,
detail), p. 57, fig. 12 = our pl. 480.

154 Room X (7.08 x 6.80). North transept wing. Pls. 486-
     497.

Surround: 0.12. Framing: 2.16. Panel, including single
fillet: 3.01 x 2.35. Stone, ceramic (red) and glass (green,
blue) tesserae (0.01 sq; 0.005 for facial details) set 1-3mm
apart.

Large landscape with water fowl and land birds accompanied by
a long inscription and enclosed by five figural and ornamental borders.[733]

_____

[732]ArchEph, 1917, pp. 53-54.

[733]With some important omissions and errors, both this
wing and the south one (155) have been discussed and analyzed
in extenso (A. Philadelpheus, Praktika, 1915, pp. 68-70;
idem, ArchEph, 1916, pp. 65-72; vide supra, p. 430 and n.
708).

Surround: in rows of grey tesserae parallel to the walls.

Framing (pl. 486): black fillet; first border, black
meander pattern forming swastikas and squares which are inscribed with white/pink/red rosettes crossed by dark green
branches; white triple fillet; second border, marine frieze
(pls. 486-491) inhabited by various species of fish, some
long legged water fowl, long stemmed water plants, and three
partially clad fishermen (pls. 489-491).[734] The figures move
freely and energetically within a deep blue and dark green
ocean accented by short choppy white and dark green waves.
Among the marine creatures, large and small fish numbering
almost one hundred predominate (pls. 487-491). They are
uniformly represented with white contours along their spiney
dorsal sides and tail fins, white along their ventral sides,
and with large mouths and black button eyes rimmed in white.
Their light and dark green, red, brown or blue bodies are
decorated with stylized crescent gills and with white semi-
circular or circular motifs which bear no recognizable organic
function. These fish almost obscure the few white sepia and
octopi, brown conch shells, red crustaceans, white water fowl
and long-stemmed water plants with heart-shaped leaves which
are sprinkled around the frieze. On the north, south, and
west sides of the frieze (pls. 487-488), the water plants
support semi-circular brown and white bowls which are usually

---

[734]See A. Philadelpheus (ArchEph, 1916, p. 66) and,
therefore, Kitzinger (Mosaics at Nikopolis, p. 94) who note
only two fishermen.

filled with nesting green and white ducks. Three methods of
fishing are represented by the actions of the three sole
human beings in the frieze. On the south side (figs. 488-489)
a youth in short trunks lunges with a trident and pierces the
head of a large fish which is idly feeding on a heart-shaped
water plant. The energy of the harpoon thrust is reflected
in the pose of the man who appears to have stepped off into
space from a brown and white feature, perhaps a vestige of a
pier or boat. The lively action of the scene contrasts with
the more passive activities of the two other fishermen. One,
in the north border (pls. 486, 490), is seen fishing with a
pole from the dipping stern of a brown boat.[735] The third
figure in the east border is represented sitting on a brown
and white striated rock formation fishing with a white hand
line (pl. 491). The figures have pink skins, outlined in
black, with white highlights in the center of their limbs and
bodies. Since the only fully preserved head, that of the har-
poonist on the south side, so closely resembles those of the
men in the south wing (155), it will be included in the general discussion below;[736] white triple fillet; black fillet;

---

[735]This figure was not noticed by A. Philadelpheus (see
preceding note). In photographs of two sections of this
north frieze, the captions read "east side" (ArchEph, 1916,
figs. 10, 12, between pp. 72-73). In my notes and photographs, they are identified as belonging to the north side.
Until such time as a return trip to Nikopolis is possible, I
prefer to rely on my own data. Whether the man was nude or
clothed in flesh-colored trunks was impossible to determine.

[736]See pp. 455-456.

third border (pl. 486), two-strand interlace (red; dark
green, outlined in black) forming large and small circles.
Each circle (0.29 diam) is decorated with a small dark
green, yellow or purple bird with a wind-blown pink ribbon
around its neck. Springing from the sides of the small
circles are single, dark grey ivy leaves; wide red band;
fourth border (pl. 486), dark blue and white wave crests;
white triple fillet; fifth border, white bead-and-reel pattern composed of units of two reels separated by single
beads, on a grey ground; white triple fillet.

Field (pls. 492-497), framed by a dark blue fillet: large
panel decorated with a forest of nine trees with water fowl
below and birds in flight above. The stylized trees create
an abstract rhythm across the surface of the panel by means
of the repetition in a single plane of tall, bare brown
trunks and verdant leaves. This rhythm is emphasized by
the symmetrical disposition of the types of trees flanking
a central nucleus composed of a pomegranate tree and four
cypress trees. This core is succeeded by an apple tree on
the left (pl. 494) and a pear tree on the right (pl. 495) and
along the margins by single cypress trees. The red and
yellow colors of the fruit relieve the otherwise somber ton-
ality of the dark green and black foliage. Plants rise from
the bases of the trees and fill the white interstices with
dark green patterns. The strict symmetry of the composition
is reinforced by the presence of two large grey ducks which
confront each other across a wide space in the foreground,

their large bodies partially hiding the trunks of the apple
and pear trees (pls. 493, 496-497). They float above the
dark green grass shoots decorating the ground line and face
a land bird, now lost, which was grazing near the left
duck.[737] The majesty and sobriety of the scene is somewhat
relieved by the eight small green and yellow birds which are
shown flying above, or descending onto, the tops of the
trees. Unlike the flora and fauna below, they are sketchily
rendered with short black strokes for their wings and tail
feathers. Running along the bottom of the scene is a black
tabula ansata (width, 0.58) containing a four-line inscription in white letters (0.11 high). Oriented westward and
preceded by a cross (pls. 492-493), it cites the name of a
bishop of Nikopolis, Dometios I, who is also mentioned in
inscriptions in the south chapel, nave, and atrium (152, 153,
156).

ΩΚΕΑΝΟΝΠΕΡΙΦΑΝΤΟΝΑΠΙΡΙΤΟΝΕΝΘΑΔΕΔΟ
ΡΚΑϹ/ΓΑΙΑΝΜΕϹϹΟΝΕΧΟΝΤΑϹΟΦΟΙϹΙΝΔ
ΑΛΜΑϹΙΤΕΧΝΗϹ/ΠΑΝΤΑΠΕΡΙΞΦΟΡΕΟΥϹ
ΑΝΟϹΑΠΝΙΕΙΤΕΚΑΙΕΡΠΕΙ/ΔΟΥΜΕΤΙΟΥ
ΚΤΕΑΝΟΝΜΕΓΑΘΥΜΟΥΑΡΧΙΕΡΗΟϹ   [738]

---

[737]Another bird may have been located in the right side
of the pomegranate tree (A. Philadelpheus, ArchEph, 1916, p.
67 and fig. 14, between pp. 72 and 73).

[738]Transcription by A. Philadelpheus, Praktika, 1915,
p. 69; idem, ArchEph, 1916, p. 67, fig. 14, between pp. 72-
73. "ΠΕΡΙΦΑΝΤΩΝ" in line 1, "   " in line 3 and "ΜΕΓΑΘΥΜΟΥ"
in line 4 were restored by A. Philadelpheus. His emendation,
which was accepted by Kitzinger (Mosaics at Nikopolis, p.
100), is as follows.

ΩΚΕΑΝΟΝ ΠΕΡΙΦΑΝΤΟΝ ΑΠΙΡΙΤΟΝ ΕΝΘΑ ΔΕΔΟΡΚΑϹ/

Additional color. Water plants: green or brown and white.
North frieze: boat, black outlines and white highlights; man,
pale pink trunks. South frieze: man, blue trunks with
white highlights. Third border: birds, white outlines for
wings. Panel: ducks, dark grey strokes for feathers; black
feet, outlines, and delineations of wings.

Second quarter of the sixth century.

Additional bibliography. E. Kitzinger, Proceedings of the
American Philosophical Society, 117 (1973), pp. 369-370.

Illustrations. A. Philadelpheus, ArchEph, 1916, figures
between pp. 72-73: fig. 6 (borders, west side); fig. 7
(marine frieze, west side); fig. 8 (marine frieze, northwest
corner); fig. 9 (marine frieze, north side); fig. 10
(borders, east side [sic]); fig. 11 (marine frieze with
seated angler, east side); fig. 12 (marine frieze, east side
[sic]); fig. 13 = our pl. 488, fig. 14 = our pl. 492.

155 Room XI (7.08 x 6.80). South transept wing. Pls. 498-
     532.

Surround: ca. 0.05. Framing: ca. 2.29. Panel, including
double fillet: 2.42 x 2.24. Materials identical to those
in north transept wing (X).

Scene comprising two life-size figures and a dog enclosed by

ΓΑΙΑΝ ΜΕССΟΝ ΕΧΟΝΤΑ СΟΦΟΙС ΙΝΔΑΛΜΑСΙ ΤΕΧΝΗС/
ΠΑΝΤΑ ΠΕΡΙΞ ΦΟΡΕΟΥСΑΝ ΟСΑ ΠΝΙΕΙ ΤΕ ΚΑΙ ΕΡΠΕΙ/
ΔΟΥΜΕΤΙΟΥ ΚΤΕΑΝΟΝ ΜΕΓΑΘΥΜΟΥ ΑΡΧΙΕΡΗΟС.

For the interpretation of this inscription, see Kitzinger,
op. cit., pp. 100-103; idem, Proceedings of the American
Philosophical Society, 117 (1973), pp. 369-370.

three figural and decorative borders.[739]

Framing (pl. 498): dark blue fillet; first border, meander
pattern identical to that in the north transept (pl. 486);
white triple fillet; second border, marine frieze similar to
that in the north transept (pls. 486-491) except that four
men are represented and they all are participating in litoral,
shallow water fishing. In the northwest corner of the north
frieze (pl. 499) a man in a blue loin cloth, identified by a
black inscription as "ΟΦΕΛΛΥΡΑϹ ," is shown trying to
capture a white crane or ibis which has nestled its head
under its left wing. Before it, rises a water plant supporting an empty bird's nest. Further east is another man,
identified by an inscription in black letters as "ΕΡΜΗϹ,"
who sits on a cluster of rocks and fishes with a black and
white hand line (pl. 500).[740] This scene is the only one to
have a counterpart in the north transept (pl. 491), the only
difference being that, here, the angler is clad in a white
loin cloth while the other wears trunks or a short skirt.
Whether or not the two other fishermen, one casting a net in
the east frieze (pl. 501) and the other fishing with a brown
pole (pl. 502) wear loin cloths or are nude is difficult to
determine. Surrounding these men are fish (pls. 503-504)

---

[739]For a summary of the bibliography, vide supra, p.
430 and n. 708.

[740]There is no evidence that he is fishing with a net
(see A. Philadelpheus, ArchEph, 1916, p. 68; Kitzinger,
Mosaics at Nikopolis, p. 94).

which are identical in style and technique to those in the
marine scene in the north transept (pls. 487-491); dark blue
fillet; narrow white band; dark blue fillet; third border,
inhabited vine rinceau (reddish brown/light bluish grey)
forming sixteen circles of varying diameters (0.76-0.90)
alternately inscribed with a hunter confronting his prey (pl.
498). With the exception of the chicken hunt (pls. 519-520),
the semi-nude men are shown rushing forward with fluttering
drapery and long black spears which are thrust into the
adjacent circles and, in some cases, into the animals themselves. The anticipated or realized contact between spear
and prey is reflected in the snarling, pawing, and rearing
actions of the half figures of the animals which emerge from
corollas of flat green and reddish brown leaves. The only
full figure is a red and black rooster (pl. 521) whose flapping wings are powerless to carry it beyond the range of the
sword of the advancing hunter (pl. 520). All the hunters are
shod in calf-high yellowish brown and black striped boots
with trailing laces and the majority wear flying garments
which emphasize their forward movement and, with one exception (pl. 509), their nude and sexless bodies. In this transept, as well as in the north one, the small figures show a
general stylistic and technical similitude. Short, single or
double strokes of white highlights create horizontal and vertical patterns on their pink bodies which are usually outlined with an inner and outer row of dark brown and black,

respectively.[741] Each man is distinguished by a rather
broad, flat face and a narrow chin, sometimes bearded, prominent straight black eyebrows which merge with the upper
lids, semi-circular lower lids, and large black eyes. The
nose is straight, outlined in black on the far side, and
highlighted down the center by a row of small white tesserae.
Short or long brown and black hair and, sometimes, crested
helmets (pls. 512, 526) crown their heads which are executed
with small tesserae, frequently oblong and irregularly cut.
The rearing animals are also drawn with sharp, black outlines
and details and with a coloristic exuberance which contrasts
with the flat and simple coloration of the surrounding leaves.

Beginning with the circle in the northwest corner and
moving eastward, the sequence of figures is as follows.
North side. First circle (pls. 505-506): long-haired hunter
in a yellowish green garment, outlined in black; some mauve
shading in legs and right arm. The left side of the circle
and his left leg up to the calf are restored.[742] Second
circle (pls. 505, 507): dark brown stag with yellow highlights and red/black outlines; speared in chest. The leaves
and ground in the center are restored. Third circle (pls.
508-509): black-bearded and long-haired hunter with olive

[741]In the north transept, only a black fillet defines
the contours (pls. 489-491).

[742]All the restorations in this frieze are modern. See
plates 505, 508, 511, 514, 519, 522, 525, which show the
border at the time of its discovery and the other plates which
show their condition in 1969.

green shorts, outlined in dark blue, highlighted in white,
and edged with white and black studs; some olive green shading
along undersides of arms. Fourth circle (pls. 508, 510):
reddish brown bear with dark blue highlights speared through
mouth and head; blood at mouth. East side. Fifth circle
(pls. 511-512): hunter with a green cloak, outlined in
black, and a red-crested, bluish black helmet. Sixth circle
(pls. 511, 513): black and red bull with yellow highlights
and white curving horns, outlined in brown. Seventh circle
(pls. 514-515): long-haired hunter with a bluish black
garment, outlined in black. Part of the circle in front of
him and some stems have been restored. Eighth circle (pls.
514, 516): yellowish brown animal[743] with white highlights
and red tongue; at left, dark grey and white spear tip, outlined in black. South side. Ninth circle (pl. 517): short-
haired hunter with red garment outlined in red glass. Tenth
circle (pl. 518): reddish brown boar (?) with black bristles.
Some of the leaves below its left leg are restored. Eleventh
circle (pls. 519-520): man with drawn sword in raised right
hand and dark blue garment or scabbard, outlined in dark blue
(glass). Twelfth circle (pls. 519, 521): red and black
rooster, highlighted in pink, with dark red comb, and neck,
wing, and tail feathers. Its black legs and the bottom of
the field are restored. West side. Thirteenth circle (pls.

---

[743]It is identified as a hyena by A. Philadelpheus,
ArchEph, 1916, p. 71.

522-523): grey bearded hunter with short hair and olive green garment; some olive green shading in chest and legs. The two upper leaves on the right side are restored. Fourteenth circle (pls. 522,524): yellowish brown and black bear pierced in chest by spear; red teeth and tongue. A vertical strip in the center of the bear is restored. Fifteenth circle (pls. 525-526): hunter in a narrow olive green garment and blue helmet, outlined in black, with red crest. His right foot and the area around it are restored. Sixteenth circle (pls. 525, 527): dark blue and red stag with yellow highlights and red and yellow antlers bleeds from a spear thrust into its neck. The leaf and ground beneath its left leg is restored.

Field (pls. 528-532).

Framing: border, red and white crowsteps; black double fillet.

Field: fragment of a panel with two life-size men in three-quarter view who walk toward a schematized, dark green tree carrying between them a white tabula ansata (1.15 long). Only the last black letters of the first two lines of a four-line inscription are preserved (originally, probably 0.40 wide:[744] "[ ]MONAC[ ]CEONTAC."[745] Both men hold long,

---

[744]The position of the right ansa indicates that the inscription continued for two more lines (pl. 529). Traces of the left ansa are visible in pl. 530. Both were decorated with abstract four-legged animals.

[745]See also, Kitzinger, Mosaics at Nikopolis, pp. 94-95, and 115, n. 142.

dark brown spears with white and grey blades and the man on
the right (pl. 529) carries a shield strapped to his left
arm.[746] He wears a short-sleeved, brown tunic and his
counterpart, an olive green cuirass originally decorated with
some kind of grey and white patterns on the front (pl.
530).[747] Completing their ensemble are short yellowish brown
and black striped boots with flying laces and white highlights. Physiognomically, the men resemble the others in the
borders with the exception that their black eyebrows are independent of the upper lids, resulting in larger and more
intense eyes (pls. 531-532). Both have black hair, beards,
and mustaches and skin tones which appear swarthy in comparison with the others because of the addition of mauve and
browns. The entire scene is framed along the sides and bottom
by dark green, leaf-bearing vines and ground lines, respectively. The latter are articulated by green and red flowers
which rest on a striated white and green bed.

Additional color. Third border: wings of birds outlined
in white. Panel: brown, red, and white shield (?) in front
of man to left.

---

[746]Only its black outline is preserved. His counterpart
to the left may have also carried a shield, since traces of a
curvilinear, striated feature are visible under his right arm
(pl. 530). Since there is no trace of a strap on his upper
arm, it was perhaps suspended from his wrist. His left hand
probably supported the ansa of the tabula. See Kitzinger,
Mosaics at Nikopolis, p. 94 and n. 47.

[747]There is no evidence that both men were cuirassed
(cf. A. Philadelpheus, ArchEph, 1916, p. 72).

Second quarter of the sixth century.

Illustrations. A. Philadelpheus, ArchEph, 1916, figures
between pp. 72-73: fig. 15 (marine frieze, Ophellyras); fig.
16 (marine frieze, man casting net); fig. 17 (marine frieze,
east side); fig. 18 (marine frieze, east side); fig. 19
(marine frieze, man with pole); fig. 20 = our pl. 522; fig.
21 = our pl. 525; fig. 22 = our pl. 505; fig. 23 = our pl.
508; fig. 24 = our pl. 511; fig. 25 = our pl. 514; fig. 26
(ninth and tenth circles), fig. 27 = our pl. 519; fig. 28 =
our pl. 528; pl. I (marine frieze, Ophellyras: colored
drawing), pl. II (thirteenth circle: colored drawing of
hunter's head).

PERIOD I, PHASE 2

156 Room I (17.90 x 14.28). Atrium: north and south porti-

coes, Ia-b, 4.30 x 9.70; west portico, c, 17.90 x 4.30.

North and south pavements laid up to piers on west side.

Pls. 533-545.

Framing: Ia, 0.86; Ib, 0.98.[748] Field: Ia, 3.44 x 8.84;

Ib, 3.32 x 8.72. Stone, ceramic (red), and glass (greens,

blue) tesserae (ca. 0.015 sq; 0.01 sq for glass) set 3-5mm

apart.

Crudely executed polychrome mosaic pavements containing pri-

marily organic filling motifs and, at the west entrance, an

inscription.[749]

---

[748]Since the west portico, Ic, was covered, the mosaic
could not be measured or studied.

[749]The published data on these three porticoes are
obscure and sometimes inaccurate (G. A. Soteriou, Hieros
syndesmos [Dec. 1-15, 1915], pp. 15-16; A. Philadelpheus,
Praktika, 1916, pp. 52ff.; ArchEph, 1917, p. 66). Certain

Ia, b north and south porticoes.

Framing (pls. 533-534): outer border, black and white wave
crests; three to five red fillets; inner border, two-strand
interlace (red/1 white; grey/1 white, outlined in black)
forming circles which are inscribed with red rosettes with
white centers crossed by two black fillets. In the south
portico, each twist is accented by a single red ivy leaf
which rests on the margin (pls. 538, 544).

Field: grid design formed by wide bands which, in the north
portico, Ia (pls. 533, 535-537), are light grey, outlined in
dark grey. In the south portico, Ib (pls. 538-542) the bands
are polychrome (lime, red, grey, white stripes) and outlined
in black.[750] The intersections of the bands in both porticoes are decorated with small black, lime, pink, or red
diagonal crosses, on a white ground, which accent the corners
of the squares (0.29) formed by the grid. These squares are
filled with animals, birds, plants, and fruit (pls. 535-542)
which, although crudely executed in comparison with those in
the rest of the church, are distinguished by a plethora of
green and blue glass tesserae. Generally, red, light and
dark grey, white, and greens are employed in various

errors regarding dimensions and colors in Kitzinger's
descriptions are, therefore, understandable (Mosaics at
Nikopolis, pp. 88-89).

[750]Cf. Kitzinger, Mosaics at Nikopolis, p. 88) who
thought that both grids were monochromatic. A published
photograph of the north portico was incorrectly identified as
the south portico (A. K. Orlandos, To Ergon, 1966, p. 174,
fig. 205 = our pl. 533).

combinations and black is used infrequently. Each grid
extends up to the projecting piers toward the west where, at
least in the south portico, Ib, it is replaced by a threshold
panel decorated with a two-strand interlace enclosing ivy
leaves and rosettes (pl. 544).[751]

Ic, west portico: in two published photographs there is a
compartmentalized field surrounded by a complex interlace
(pls. 543-545).

Framing: complex chain of interlaced circles (for similar
borders in the narthex, nave, and elsewhere, see pls. 460-
461; 476; 256).[752]

Field, framed by a wide dark band: toward the north (pl.
543), a central panel decorated with an interlace of circles
forming concave-sided octagons set on edge is flanked to the
east and west by foliate panels. The latter are decorated
with single undulating rinceaux forming rigidly arranged and
widely spaced scrolls filled with single heart-shaped ivy
leaves.[753] The south side of the field (pl. 544) contains an
interlace of alternating circles and squares filled with
plants, fruit, and animals (for a similar aniconic design in

[751]It is probable that another threshold panel decorated
the northwest side of the north portico.

[752]Sodini incorrectly compares this border to those in
the north and south porticoes (Catalogue, p. 724).

[753]G. A. Soteriou places this section in the north
portico (Hieros syndesmos [Dec. 1-15, 1915], p. 15).

Basilica Beta, see 158, pl. 560). Dominating the center of the field is a broad decorative panel with an imbrication pattern fanning southward (pl. 543). At the west entrance, it is interrupted by a five-line inscription (2.95 x 1.48) in dark grey letters (0.21-0.22 high). Oriented westward (pls. 457, 545), it cites the saint to whom the church is dedicated, Demetrios, and the names of the episcopal sponsors of the first and second decorative phases, Dometios I and his successor, Dometios II.

ΔΟΜΗΤΙΟCΜΕΝΟΠΡШΗΝΤΟΝCΕΒΑCΜΙΟΝ
ΚΑΤΕCΚΕΥΑCΕΝΟΙΚΟΝ/ΔΟΜΗΤΙΟCΔΕΟΝΥΝ
ΓΕΝΠΕШΝΕΚΙΝΟΥΚΑΙΤΗCΙΕΡШCΥΝΗCΔΙΑ
ΔΟΧΟC/ΔΥΝΑΜΙΧΡΤΗΝΠΑCΑΝΕΚΑΛΙΕΡΓΗC
ΕΝΤΡΙCΤШΟΝ/ΕΥΦΡΟCΥΝΟCΜΗΝΕΝΤШΝΕШ
ШCΜΑΘΗΤΗCΤΟΥΠΡΟΤΕΡΟΥΠΗΜΑΙ [ ]/
ΔΗΜΗΤΡΙΟΥΜΑΡΤΥΡΟCΕΚΑΤΕΡΟCΕΥΧ
ΑΡΙCΤШΝΤΗΠΡΟCΤΑCΙΑ   754

Second half of the sixth century.

Illustrations. A. Philadelpheus, Praktika, 1916, p. 58, fig. 6 = our pl. 536; idem, ArchEph, 1917, p. 65, fig. 20 (Ia, detail); A. K. Orlandos, To Ergon, 1966, p. 173, fig. 204 = our pl. 544, p. 174, fig. 205 = our pl. 533, p. 175, fig. 206 = our pl. 545, p. 175, fig. 207 = our pl. 543.

754The transcription and the following emendation are in the ArchEph, 1917, p. 66; see also, Kitzinger, Mosaics at Nikopolis, p. 87.

ΔΟΜΗΤΙΟC ΜΕΝ Ο ΠΡШΗΝ ΤΟΝ CΕΒΑCΜΙΟΝ
ΚΑΤΕCΚΕΥΑCΕΝ ΟΙΚΟΝ/ ΔΟΜΗΤΙΟC ΔΕ Ο ΝΥΝ
ΓΕ ΝΠ(ΝΙΚΟΠΟΛΕШC) ΕШΝ ΕΚΙΝΟΥ ΚΑΙ ΤΗC
ΙΕΡШCΥΝΗC ΔΙΑΔΟΧΟC/ΔΥΝΑΜΙ ΧΡ(ΧΡΙCΤΟΥ)
ΤΗΝ ΠΑCΑΝ ΕΚΑΛΙΕΡΓΗCΕΝ ΤΡΙCΤШΟΝ/

Basilica Beta

In 1921, excavations were begun at a site situated in
the center of the Byzantine city of Nikopolis. In seven subsequent campaigns, ending in 1938, a large basilica, designated Beta, and some buildings on the south side were cleared
(pl. 548). Mosaic pavements were discovered in the atrium,
Ia-c, the narthex, II, and in Rooms XIIIa-b, XV, and I to
the south. At the present time, those in the south portico
of the atrium and the narthex have been consolidated and are
visible. Since the other porticoes are covered and the south
complex choked with weeds, the condition of their pavements
is not known.

The plan of the south complex (pls. 548-549) was never
fully determined so that its overall function and its building
history remain obscure. It is described in early reports as
a Roman house,[755] a secular building,[756] and as a secular
building which was converted in the sixth century into a
bishop's palace or a parochial school.[757] In subsequent

ΕΥΦΡΟCΥΝΟC ΜΗΝ ΕΝ ΤΩ ΝΕΩ ΩC ΜΑΘΗΤΗC
ΤΟΥ ΠΡΟΤΕΡΟΥ ΠΗΜΑΙ [ ]/ΔΗΜΗΤΡΙΟΥ ΜΑΡΤΥΡΟC
ΕΚΑΤΕΡΟC ΕΥΧΑΡΙCΤΩΝ ΤΗ ΠΡΟCΤΑCΙΑ.

[755]A. Philadelpheus, _Praktika_, 1924, pp. 73, 109.

[756]G. A. Soteriou, _Praktika_, 1926, p. 124, and n. 1.

[757]A. Philadelpheus, _Praktika_, 1924, p. 110; idem, _Les
Fouilles de Nicopolis_, 1913-1926, Athens (1933), p. 13; hereafter cited as _Fouilles_.

reports, references to the conversion of the complex are
omitted and its erection is attributed to the early sixth
century and to the episcopacy of Alkison whose name is cited
in a tessellated inscription in a large hall to the east,
I.[758] Since Alkison's tenure as bishop can be assigned to a
period between 491 and 516,[759] it supplies us with some kind
of chronological framework, if not for the entire south
complex then, at least, for Room I and its dependencies.[760]
Because of the paucity of reliable and consistent data on this
sector and the discrepancies between the first plans (pls.
546, 549) and those executed in the 1930's (pls. 547-548),
the basilica and the west part of the south complex, I-XVIII,
will be presented as representative of one architectural and
decorative period. There is sufficient evidence to corrob-
orate this conclusion as there is for ascribint the east part
of the south complex, I-III, to a second period. It is
during this period that Room I with the Alkison inscription

[758]A. Philadelpheus, Praktika, 1922-23, p. 42; idem,
Praktika, 1924, p. 110; idem, DCAH, 4, 2 (1927), p. 57; idem,
Fouilles, p. 16. In one plan (pl. 546), the inscription is
placed in the wrong room.

[759]Soteriou, Palaiochristianikai basilikai, p. 201, n. 1;
Kitzinger, Mosaics at Nikopolis, pp. 88-90 and n. 31, with
earlier references.

[760]Kitzinger (Mosaics at Nikopolis, p. 90, n. 33) notes
that a north-south "break or some kind of dividing line" between Room XV and the Alkison building may represent evidence
of two building periods (see our pl. 549). If he is referring to the serrated lines, these mark the boundaries of the
width of the area and are so marked (12.40). The solid line
to the east represents a row of some kind of slabs, which
continues across the chord of XVIII.

was added to the south wall of the basilica.[761]

PERIOD I

Basilica

The church (pl. 548) was discovered by chance in 1929 during the clearing of the south complex. In three subsequent campaigns, the last in 1938, the entire structure was cleared. Because of its enormous size (overall, 31.60 x 51.05) and its position in the center of the city,[762] it is believed to have been the Metropolitan church of Nikopolis.[763]

Preceded by a large colonnaded atrium, I (22.10 x 20.20),[764] and a shallow narthex, II (29.80 x 4.45), with projecting wings, III-IV,[765] the main body of the church consists of a nave, V, flanked on either side by two aisles,

---

[761]A. Philadelpheus, DCAH, 4, 2 (1924), p. 126; idem, DCAH, 4, 2 (1927), p. 58; Soteriou, Palaiochristianikai basilikai, p. 201, n. 1; Krautheimer, Tripartite Transept, p. 423; Kitzinger, Mosaics at Nikopolis, p. 90 and n. 33.

[762]For the location of Basilicas Alpha, Delta and Epsilon, see pp. 371, 427, 436.

[763]G. A. Soteriou and A. K. Orlandos, Praktika, 1929, p. 86; idem, Praktika, 1930, p. 80.

[764]Most of the measurements for this building are inscribed in two plans (pls. 546, 548). The foundations to the west of the atrium belong to a vaulted portico which may have encircled the entire precinct (G. A. Soteriou, Praktika, 1926, p. 124ff.; idem, Palaiochristianikai basilikai, p. 85).

[765]These rooms have been reconstructed as a prothesis (III) and a diakonikon (IV) by Orlandos, Hē metakinēsis tou diakonikou. pp. 354, passim.

VI-IX, and a transverse tripartite transept, X-XII. The
center bay or bema is raised one step above the wings and
the nave and the apse four steps above the bema.[766] The nave
is separated from the aisles and the aisles from each other
by colonnades resting on bases set on elevated stylobates.
Stylobates are also used in the transept to support the square
pillars which carry single arcades of three arches.[767] The
compartmentalization of the transept into three distinct
units is emphasized by the placement of screens between the
pillars which restrict communication between the bema and
the wings to narrow passageways at the east and west ends.
Pillars and screens also separate the aisles from the north
and south wings while columnar divisions on stylobates are
employed in the atrium and at the entrances to Rooms III and
IV. In the bema traces were found of the supports of an
altar and the foundations of the canopy which surmounted
it.[768] The altar site is surrounded by a semi-independent
chancel barrier which extends from the shoulders of the apse
to the beginning of the first intercolumniation of the nave.
It is interrupted on the north and south sides by clergy
benches and, like Basilica Delta (pl. 568), its west entrance

---

[766]Soteriou, Palaiochristianikai basilikai, p. 203.

[767]Ibid., p. 201; G. A. Soteriou and A. K. Orlandos,
Praktika, 1930, p. 80; Krautheimer, Tripartite Transept,
p. 420.

[768]Soteriou, Palaiochristianikai basilikai, pp. 203,
231; G. A. Soteriou and A. K. Orlandos, Praktika, 1929, p. 86
and fig. 3 (altar: restored).

contains a prothuron.[769] Opposite this entrance, rises the
apse which has an enclosed corridor along its base and a
stepped platform. Beyond this clergy-altar site is an ambon
comprising two sets of steps on the axis of the church and an
upper platform which is decorated with a mosaic frieze.[770]
Mosaic pavements decorate the porticoes of the atrium and the
narthex, marble slabs the atrium court and the north and
south transept wings, polychrome marble in opus sectile the
nave, bema, and apse,[771] and irregular stone pieces the north
and south wings of the narthex and the aisles.

Although no datable archaeological finds were unearthed
or reported, the basilica can be placed within a relatively
secure chronological framework. A terminus ante quem of 491-
516 is established by the datable structure on the east side
of the south complex, Room I,[772] which was an addition to the

[769]The transept wings are partitioned by high screens
which enclose an area approximately 1.15 wide (Soteriou,
Palaiochristianikai basilikai, p. 230). A. K. Orlandos considers these compartments to be improvised vestries and
sacristies (Praktika, 1959, p. 92, n. 1; idem, To Ergon,
1959, p. 69). Krautheimer thinks that they are extensions
of the chancel screen, but is silent on their specific
function (Tripartite Transept, p. 421).

[770]Only two medallion busts are preserved (G. A. Soteriou
and A. K. Orlandos, Praktika, 1937, pp. 78, 80-81, figs.
5-7). For a recent study, see A. Xyngopoulos, who attributes
them to the end of the fifth or the beginning of the sixth
centuries ("Hai duo psēphidōtai prosōpographiae tēs
Nikopoleōs," Deltion, 22 [1967], Meletai, pp. 14-20, with
earlier references, and pls. 16-18).

[771]Soteriou, Palaiochristianikai basilikai, p. 203;
idem, Praktika, 1938, p. 116; Orlandos, Xylostegos basilikē,
p. 260, fig. 210 (drawing).

[772]Vide supra, p. 466, and n. 759.

church. Since the style of the architecture is similar to
that of Basilica Alpha (pl. 457) belonging to the second
quarter of the sixth century, it is clear that Beta cannot
be too far removed in time and, therefore, should be placed
toward·the end of the fifth century.[773] It belongs to a
group of Epirotic churches, Alpha (pl. 457), Gamma,[774] Delta
(pl. 568), and Epsilon (pl. 580) at Nikopolis and two others
at Dodona and Paramythia which contain tripartite transepts.
These churches have been attributed by most scholars to the
late fifth and the sixth centuries and represent a survival
or, perhaps, a revival of tripartite transepts in Greece.[775]

South Complex, West Side (XIII-XVIII)

Excavations were begun in 1921 and continued intermit-
tently until 1929 when the basilica was discovered. Mosaic
pavements were found in Rooms XIIIa-b, and XV, marble and
brick slabs in Room XIII, XVI, and irregular pieces of

---

[773]Soteriou attributes the church to the second half of
the fifth century (Palaiochristianikai basilikai, p. 201 and
n. 1). Both Krautheimer (Tripartite Transept, p. 423) and
Kitzinger (Mosaics at Nikopolis, p. 90) use Alkison's dates
as a terminus ante quem. More recently, the former assigns
the building to around 500 (Architecture, p. 99). D. I.
Pallas suggests the unlikely date of the middle of the sixth
century (RBK, col. 227).

[774]For Gamma which has no tessellated pavings, see A. K.
Orlandos and G. A. Soteriou, Praktika, 1937, pp. 81-82, p.
83, fig. 9 (plan); they attribute it to the post-Justinianic
period.

[775]Vide supra, pp. 277 and n. 427, 422 and n. 690.

polychrome marble in Room XVII.[776]

The plan (pl. 549) is dominated by a large peristyle,
XIII (14.65; width indeterminable), with porticoes along the
west and south sides, a-b, and an apsed room, XV (4.00 x
9.50, including apse), to the northeast. The latter has a
door on the west side which leads to an unexcavated section,
XIV. Another door on its northwest side is noted in a
report[777] as well as in two early plans (pls. 546, 549), but
it is eliminated from the final plan (pl. 548).[778] No reason
for this alteration is given and it is curious that there
would be no communicating doorway between the room and the
narthex as in other Nikopolitan churches. Along the south
side of the peristyle is a large room, XVI, with a doorway
opening onto the portico. In the original plan (pl. 549),
the east side of the peristyle contains a corridor, XVII
(5.28 x 2.40), and a semi-circular exedra, XVII, which is
flanked by two reused Corinthian columns.[779] In later plans
(pls. 546-548), the shape of the exedra is changed and the
corridor is eliminated, again, with no explanation. The relationship between the apsed building, which was probably a
chapel, and the basilica is not really as problematic as

---

[776]A. Philadelpheus, Praktika, 1922-23, p. 41; idem,
DCAH, 4, 2 (1927), pp. 49, 54-55, 58.

[777]Ibid.; A. Philadelpheus, DCAH, 4, 2 (1927), p. 52.

[778]See also, Orlandos, Xylostegos basilikē, p. 101,
pl. B.

[779]A. Philadelpheus, DCAH, 4, 2 (1927), pp. 49-59. The
columns are not noted in the plan (pl. 549).

E. Kitzinger would have us believe.[780] In my judgment, there
is every reason to believe that they were erected at the same
time and I would restore a door on the northwest side of the
chapel as it is clearly represented on the three of the four
plans (pls. 546-547, 549) so that access to this room was
from the narthex as well as from the outside. In all the
churches at Nikopolis and elsewhere, any type of room adjoining the narthex always has a passageway on the north side.[781]

PERIOD II

South Complex, East Side (I-III)

The partially excavated southeast side (pls. 548-549)
is dominated by a large hall, Room I (6.30 x 12.75 max),[782]
which is flanked along the south side by three to four rooms
and along the west side by a corridor, XVII. Other than a
brief description of Rooms I and II, nothing is known of the
building history or function of this sector. Indeed, later
plans omit Rooms II and XVII entirely (pls. 546-548). Since

---

[780]Mosaics at Nikopolis, p. 90, n. 33.

[781]For a representative group, see Orlandos, Xylostegos
basilikē, pp. 199-101, pls. A-B.

[782]In the reports, a length of 12 meters is given (A.
Philadelpheus, Praktika, 1921, p. 43; idem, Praktika, 1922-23,
p. 42) and 12.25 meters (idem, DCAH, 4, 2 [1927], p. 55).
Given the numerous typographical errors in such publications,
I prefer to use the length of 12.75 meters which is inscribed
on a plan (pl. 549).

it was established during the excavations that Room I was added to the south wall of the basilica,[783] it is clear that this part of the complex postdates the basilica and, probably, the west side of the complex. Room I is decorated with a mosaic pavement which contains an inscription citing the name of Bishop Alkison who was archbishop of Nikopolis between 491 and 516. This chronology serves as a terminus for this sector and especially for Room I which, according to the inscription, was "built from the foundations" by Alkison.[784]

Bibliography. A. Philadelpheus, Praktika, 1921, pp. 11-12, 42-44; idem, ArchEph, 1922, pp. 66-79; idem, Praktika, 1922-23, pp. 8, 40-44; BCH, 46 (1922), pp. 515-516; A. Philadelpheus, Praktika, 1924, pp. 72-74, 108-112; idem, DCAH, 4, 2 (1924), pp. 121-127; idem, Praktika, 1926, pp. 127-130; idem, DCAH, 4, 2 (1927), pp. 46-61; Soteriou, Palaiochristianikai basilikai, pp. 201-203, 231; G. A. Soteriou and A. K. Orlandos, Praktika, 1929, pp. 22-24, 83-86; idem, Praktika, 1930, pp. 21-23, 79-80; AA, 45 (1930), pp. 122-123; A. Philadelpheus, Les fouilles de Nicopolis, 1913-1926, Athens, 1933, pp. 22-29; G. A. Soteriou and A. K. Orlandos, Praktika, 1937, pp. 15, 78-81; BCH, 61 (1937), pp. 461-462; G. A. Soteriou, Praktika, 1938, pp. 16-18, 112-117; BCH, 62 (1938), pp. 470-471; AA, 54 (1939), pp. 253-254; Kitzinger, Mosaics at Nikopolis, pp. 88-90; Krautheimer, Tripartite Transept, pp. 420-423; D. I. Pallas, "Epiros," RBK, col. 227; A. K. Orlandos, Praktika, 1962, p. 181; BCH, 86 (1962), p. 760; A. K. Orlandos, To Ergon, 1964, pp. 158-161; BCH, 89 (1965), p. 761; A. K. Orlandos, Deltion, 20 (1965), B2: Chronika, pp. 375-377; idem, Praktika, 1966, p. 196; idem, To Ergon, 1966, pp. 173-176; idem, To Ergon, 1968, p. 148; Krautheimer, Architecture, p. 99 and n. 54.

Illustrations. A. Philadelpheus, DCAH, 4, 2 (1927), p. 48, fig. 1 = our pl. 549, p. 51, fig. 3 (general view of Room SV), p. 55, fig. 7 (Room I, looking east); G. A. Soteriou and A. K. Orlandos, Praktika, 1929, p. 83, fig. 1 (basilica, apse), p. 84, fig. 2 = our pl. 546; Soteriou, Palaiochristianikai basilikai, p. 231, fig. 54 (altar: reconstruction);

---

[783]Vide supra, p. 467, n. 761.

[784]Vide supra, p. 466, n. 759.

idem, Praktika, 1930, p. 79, fig. 1 (transept: plan); G. A.
Soteriou and A. K. Orlandos, Praktika, 1937, pl. opposite
p. 78 = our pl. 547; G. A. Soteriou, Praktika, 1938, p. 113,
fig. 2 (narthex, from south), pl. 10 opposite p. 16 = our
pl. 540; Orlandos, Xylostegos basilikē, p. 447, fig. 405
(altar: restoration); G. Tsimas and P. Papahadjidakis,
Monuments de Nikopolis (Séries: monuments de l'art byzantin
en Grèce, Vol. 2, Athens, n.d., pl. 1 (nave and south aisle),
pl. 3 (transept and apse, from west); ibid., Vol. 3, pl. 2
(basilica: apse from east), pl. 4 (ambon), pl. 21 (nave and
north aisle), pl. 25 (bema), pl. 26 (bema and altar site).

PERIOD I

Nos. 157-160

Polychrome mosaic pavements with complex geometric

designs which, in one room, XV, enclose organic filling

motifs, decorate the west side of the basilica and three

sections on the west side of the south complex (pls. 550-

565). The pavements are contemporaneous with the architec-

ture and, therefore, can be assigned to the end of the fifth

century. This chronology is substantiated by the style of

the pavements which are distinguished by rich, intricate

designs and wide borders.

Additional bibliography. Sodini, Catalogue, No. 44, pp.
726-727.

Illustrations. G. A. Soteriou and A. K. Orlandos,
Praktika, 1937, pl. 1 opp. p. 78 = our pl. 547; A. Philadelpheus, DCAH, 4, 2 (1927), p. 48, fig. 1 = our pl. 549.

Basilica

157 Room Ia-c (maximum length: 22.50, north-south; 18.20,

east-west; width 3.90). Atrium with north, a, south, b, and west, c, porticoes. South portico cut by drain with stone lids in northeast corner;[785] its west side covered by a pier and column which destroyed the pavement. Pls. 550-554.

No published information on dimensions and material in the north, a, and west, c, porticoes. South portico, b. Framing: ca. 100; to east, ca. 1.30. Field: 2.85 x 14.75. Stone tesserae (0.01 sq) set 1-3mm apart.

Intricate geometric interlace enclosed by a wide border in the south portico, b.

Ia, north portico: extensive deterioration. No photographic or descriptive material available.[786]

Ib, south portico (pls. 550-554): interlace design inscribed with complex interlaces and bordered by an imbrication pattern.

---

[785]Since the pavement is destroyed in this sector (pl. 550), it is impossible to determine if it covered the drain or was laid up to it, as is the case in the narthex (pls. 560-561). It is clear that this drain continued a diagonal course under the threshold into the narthex and under the south doorway leading into the south aisle. Although it was impossible to trace its course beyond this point, it could, conceivably, have joined up with the subterranean structure on the northeast side of Room XV, which has been identified as a storage unit for water (G. A. Soteriou, Praktika, 1926, p. 124; see our pl. 549). The role of the cistern on the east side of the atrium in regard to this underground system is not noted. For the cistern, see G. A. Soteriou, Praktika, 1938, pp. 114-116.

[786]Cf. G. A. Soteriou, Praktika, 1938, p. 116.

Surround: in rows parallel to the walls and the stylobate.

Framing: black fillet; border (pl. 551), imbrication pattern composed of alternating diagonal rows of bichrome scales which are half white, and half red, light green, light purplish brown, light bluish grey, outlined in black; black fillet; white triple fillet; border to east only (pl. 550), row of double chevrons alternately red/1 white and light green /light bluish grey/1 white, outlined in black; white triple fillet.

Field (pls. 550-552): two-strand interlace of large circles (ca. 0.90 diam) forming concave-sided octagons (for similar designs in Basilica Alpha in the same city, and elsewhere, see 150, pls. 460-461; 153, pls. 476, 482-483; 12, pls. 40, 42-43; 96, pl. 332). The strands of the interlace (1 white/red; 1 white/1 light green/1 light bluish grey, outlined in black) bifurcate along the edges of the design to form a continuous rectilinear frame (pl. 551). Each circle is filled with a complex two-strand interlace (same colors as design; sometimes with an ochre/1 white strand) which clothes the surface with undulating lines. Although many lacunae exist, it appears that in each row the outer interlaces are identical and the central one repeats a motif found elsewhere in the pavement (pl. 552). Some of the interlaces comprise alternating squares and circles around a circle (pls. 552-553), large and small circles around a square (pl. 551), and looped circles forming an equilateral cross which is decorated with peltae between its arms (pl. 552). Other

patterns are formed by four interlaced ellipses which are
arranged around a circle (pl. 554) or in a star pattern (pl.
551). Most of these filling elements contain colored centers
which are based on the chromatic scheme of the strands of the
interlaces and are surrounded by small black crosslets and
stepped squares. The latter decorate the corners of the
concave-sided octagons which are filled with interlace patterns composed of a square (1 light greey/1 light bluish grey/
1 white) laced by a concave-sided square set on edge (red/1
white) both outlined in black. Along the margins of the
field, this pattern is replaced by single heart-shaped ivy
leaves with pointed tips and curving stems which are alternately light bluish grey and light purplish brown, outlined
in black. These colors, with the addition of ochre in the
center, decorate the single serrate-edged squares in the four
corners of the field (pls. 550, 552).

Additional color. Outlines: black. Alternating squares
and circles: squares have light bluish grey and red triangles with white centers and one small white square in the
corner; central circle, red and white hour glass motifs.
Alternating large and small circles: large circles, light
purplish brown and white hour glass motifs; small circles,
white centers; central square, red and light bluish grey triangles with black centers and a small white square in the
corner. Cruciform patterns: ochre and white hour glass
motifs and ochre peltae with white centers. Ellipses around
circles: red centers for those with 1 light green/1 grey/

l white strands; reverse coloration for the others; in circle, serrate-edged square set on edge (ochre/white/light
purplish brown outlined in red), with a black cross. Star
patterns: red ellipses and triangles with white centers.

Ic, west portico: extensive deterioration. No photographic or descriptive material available.[787]

End of the fifth century.

Illustrations. A. K. Orlandos, To Ergon, 1966, p. 176,
figs. 208-209 (pavement after restoration).

158   Room II (29.80 x 4.45). Narthex; on extreme south
side, pavement laid up to a diagonal drain (ca. 0.46
wide) and destroyed by later threshold blocks. Pls. 555-562.

Framing: to north, 0.74; to south, 0.57. Field: North
compartment, a: ca. 23.64 x 3.57.[788] South compartment, b:
4.45 x 3.57. Stone tesserae (ca. 0.01 sq) set 1-3mm apart.

Polychrome geometric mosaic composed of two compartments,
a-b, of unequal length, separated by a guilloche border and
surrounded by a continuous arcade. The color scheme is
identical to that in the south portico of the atrium (157).

Surround: destroyed.

---

[787]See preceding note.

[788]The length is only an approximation because the
central section of the room was covered with sand in 1969.

Framing (pl. 555): black fillet; white double fillet;
border,[789] black arcuated colonnade composed of narrow
columns supporting rectilinear capitals and resting on
stepped bases (for a similar pattern in Basilica Alpha at
Nikopolis, see 152, pls. 469-71). Suspended from the center
of each arch is a heart-shaped ivy leaf with a pointed tip
and a curving stem. These leaves, like the spandrels of
the arches, are alternately colored red and light bluish
grey; black fillet; middle border to north only (pl. 556),
imbrication pattern composed of alternating diagonal rows of
bichrome scales which are half white, and half red, light
green, light purplish brown, light bluish grey (for an
identical chromatic scheme in the atrium, see 150, and the
panels in this field); inner border to north only, two-
strand guilloche (light bluish grey/1 white; light purplish
brown/1 white, outlined in black with a white tessera at
each loop; identical to guilloche in field).

Field (pls. 556-557, 560-561): two compartments, a-b,
decorated with complex rectilinear and curvilinear designs.

IIa, north compartment (pl. 556), framed by a triple white
fillet which forms, at the same time, part of the design:
at least twenty row of three juxtaposed squares each

---

[789]There exists no inner border composed of alternating
squares and round shapes (cf. G. A. Soteriou, Praktika,
1938, p. 116; repeated by Sodini, Catalogue, p. 727). It
seems that G. A. Soteriou was describing the field in the
south compartment, IIb (pls. 560-562).

(1.00)[790] filled with geometric patterns and meanders. The
latter are disposed in alternating rows of two flanking
panels and one central panel in an a-b sequence along the
north-south axis.[791] In the rows with single meanders in
the center, identical decorative patterns occupy the outer
squares repeating, therefore, the symmetrical disposition of
the two identical meanders in the alternate rows. The alternating rhythm in the outer panels of two meanders and two
other patterns produces a completely unified design. This
cohesive element is reinforced by the action of the two-
strand guilloche (light bluish grey/1 white; light purplish
brown/1 white, outlined in black, with a white tessera at
each loop) which, although an integral part of the meander
pattern, spreads across the surface to envelop most of the
other squares.[792] The other component of the meanders comprises a wide rainbow cable (red/light bluish grey/light
purplish brown, outlined in black) which is shaped like a
double "T" with two vertical bars. The remaining patterns are
chromatically similar to the meanders and some are similar to
patterns in the south portico of the atrium. In the first
row on the north side, the central panel (pl. 558) is

---

[790]This is an approximation (vide supra, p. 478, n. 788.)

[791]The continuation of this sequence is predicated on
its appearance in the five rows on the north side and the
last row on the extreme south side.

[792]Since the central panels are not bordered by guilloches, the meander pattern is turned on its side so that the
guilloches can flow into the flanking east-west sectors.

decorated with patterns formed by four interlaced red ellipses around a square. The strands forming the ellipses are
light green/1 white while those around the circle are red/
1 white. A circle in the south portico (pl. 554) has the
same pattern and the same serrate-edged square set on edge
(white/red, outlined and crossed in black). There are some
differences in regard to the additional loops in the corners,
the use of black crosslets instead of stepped squares in the
interstices, and in the general color scheme. The multiple
chevron pattern (pl. 556) in the second row contains a
chromatic sequence similar to that in the south portico
with, however, the addition of an ochre/1 white chevron,
while the imbrication patterns in the north border, and in
the fourth (pls. 556-557) and extreme south rows are
identical.[793] Other squares are decorated with a black
straight grid inscribed with stepped squares (pl. 557) and a
close-knit interlace of circles forming concave-sided octagons which are inscribed with black stepped squares (pl.
559).[794] Beginning with the first panel on the northwest
side and moving eastward, the sequence of patterns in the
exposed segments of the north compartment is as follows.
First row: meander; interlace of four ellipses; meander.
Second row: multiple chevrons; meander; multiple chevrons.

---

[793]See color notes above, p. 476.

[794]This is a smaller version of the field design in the
south portico (pls. 550-551).

Third row: meander grid; meander. Fourth row: imbrication; meander; imbrication. Fifth row:[795] meander; interlace of circles; meander. Last row on extreme south side: only west panel with imbrication visible.

IIb, south compartment (pls. 560-562), separated from the north compartment by a two-strand guilloche (same colors as those in IIa).

Framing: triple white fillet; black fillet.

Field: two-strand interlace (red/1 white; light green/ 1 white, outlined in black) forming circles (0.21 diam) and squares (0.20)[796] which are set on a ground sprinkled with small black darts. The squares are bisected by red and light bluish grey triangles which are joined in the northeast corners by minute white squares, outlined in black (pl. 562). The circles, on the other hand, are inscribed with serrate-edged squares set on edge (white/ochre/red, outlined and crossed by single black fillets. The pavement was laid up to a diagonal drain which interrupts the field and the border (pls. 560-561). Traces of a framework composed of a black fillet and a white triple fillet survive in the northeast corner and along the major portion of the south side of the drain (pl. 561). This is substantiated by the crowding of

---

[795]It is not visible in the photographs.

[796]This field design is incorrectly described as an inner border (vide supra, p. 419, n. 789).

one serrate-edged square toward the extreme south side of a circle and by the diminution of another circle.[797]

Additional color. IIa. Stepped squares in grid: white/ red, outlined in black. IIb. Interlace: strands forming circles are red/1 white; ochre/1 white; strands forming squares are light bluish grey/1 white; light green/ 1 white.

End of the fifth century.

South Complex, West Side

159 Room XIIIa-b (south portico, 1.90 x 14.20;[798] west
     portico, 13.48 x 1.40). Atrium with south, a, and
west, b, porticoes. Pl. 549.

No published information on dimensions and material.

South and west porticoes, a-b, paved with well preserved mosaics decorated with interlaced circles, scales, and other kinds of geometric patterns.[799]

---

[797]This occurs along the south side; in the fourth circle from the right (west) side; beyond it, toward the left (east) side (pl. 561). This adjustment does not appear to have been necessary along the north side, but this section has undergone greater deterioration.

[798]A. Philadelpheus, DCAH, 4, 2 (1927), p. 47. In an earlier report, he lists the length as being 18.00 (Praktika, 1924, p. 109).

[799]For the south portico, see A. Philadelpheus, Praktika, 1924, p. 109; for the west portico, see idem, Praktika, 1926, p. 128.

484

Probably contemporary with the basilica and the chapel
(158, 160) and, therefore, end of the fifth century.

160   Room XV (4.00 x 9.50 including apse).   Chapel.   Pls.
     563-565.

   Apse: 2.00 radius.   Nave: 4.00 x 7.50.   Outer border:
0.60.[800]   No published information on material.

Polychrome geometric mosaics pave the nave and the apse.
   XVa, nave (pl. 563).
   Framing:[801]   outer border, imbrication pattern composed of
half white and half colored scales which, to the north at
least, were oriented in that direction (pl. 563, right);
white double or triple fillet; inner border, polychrome
overlapping lyre pattern.[802]
   Field: grid composed of juxtaposed circles which are united

-----

[800]There is no information on the width of the inner
border which appears to be between 20 to 25 centimeters
(pl. 563).

[801]This description is based on a published photograph
which is incorrectly attributed to Room I on the east side
of the complex (A. Philadelpheus, DCAH, 4, 2 [1927], p. 56,
fig. 8 = our pl. 563).

[802]It is possible that it also extended into the apse.
A. Philadelpheus notes that the border was 9.30 meters long
which is only 20 centimeters less than the entire length of
the room.   A comparable situation exists at Nikopolis Delta
where the inner border unites the nave and apse mosaics (165,
pls. 568, 575, 578).   On the other hand, A. Philadelpheus
states that the width of the border was 3.90 meters which is
incorrect since the room was only 4 meters wide and the outer
border would have occupied 1.20 meters of the width (cf.
DCAH, 4, 2 [1927], p. 52).

by short bars to form concave-sided octagons (for a similar
design in Basilica Delta at Nikopolis, see 164, pl. 576). In
a photograph (pl. 563), it appears that some of the octagons
are inscribed with plants and the circles with hour glass
motifs. The field is interrupted by two large rectilinear
panels inscribed with circles (ca. 2.00 diam) which extend
the full width of the field. The panel in front of the apse
(pl. 564), is decorated with a vase on a high base from which
issue spreading vines containing clusters of grapes and
leaves. Two brilliantly colored peacocks (ca. 60 high) with
occelate tail coverts decorated with three eyes stand on two
branches above the wide mouth of the vase.[803] The second
panel (pl. 565), perhaps set around one meter further
west,[804] contains a similar circle filled with various
"Byzantine" ornaments: interlace; fillets; knots. Unlike
the east circle, which is framed by a narrow undecorated
band, the west one appears to have been bordered by a two-
strand guilloche which separated the circle from the single

---

[803]A. Philadelpheus, Praktika, 1922-23, p. 41; idem,
DCAH, 4, 2 (1927), pp. 52-53. There is no description of the
motifs in the corners of the panel which appear to be plants
of some kind.

[804]Since the panels extended the width of the field, one
would expect the inner lyre border to enframe them on only
the north and south sides. At the bottom of pl. 565, however, two lyre borders are visible which are perpendicular to
each other. At the top is a third lyre border. The perpendicular arrangement of the two borders could only have
resulted if the panel were situated near the west border.
It is probable that this panel was situated near the west
door, which, unfortunately, is blurred in pl. 563.

dolphins in the four corners of the rectangular panel.[805]

XVb, apse, perhaps bordered by an overlapping lyre
pattern.[806]

Field: decorated with "rays emanating from the center."[807]

End of the fifth century.

PERIOD II

South Complex, East Side

No. 161

Room I is decorated with a mosaic pavement which con--
tains an inscription near the west entrance citing the name
of Alkison who was archbishop of Nikopolis between 491 and
516.[808] This chronology serves as a _terminus_ for the building and its decoration, and as an _ante quem_ for the other
buildings in the vicinity.

Bibliography. A. Philadelpheus, _Praktika_, 1922-23, pp. 8,
42; idem, _Praktika_, 1924, p. 110; idem, _DCAH_, 4, 2 (1927), p.

---

[805]A. Philadelpheus, _Praktika_, 1922-23, p. 41; idem,
DCAH, 4, 2 (1927), pp. 52-53. In an earlier description, he
states that the dolphins were in the four corners of a central cross (_Fouilles_, p. 16).

[806]_Vide supra_, p. 484, n. 802.

[807]A. Philadelpheus, _Praktika_, 1922-23, p. 41. This
description is rather vague. It is possible that the pattern
is related to the apsidal decoration in the south chapel at
Basilica Delta (164, pl. 577).

[808]_Vide supra_, p. 466 and n. 758.

55ff; Soteriou, Palaiochristianikai basilikai, p. 201, n. 1;
A. Philadelpheus, Fouilles de Nicopolis, 1913-1926, Athens,
1933, p. 16; Krautheimer, Tripartite Transept, p. 423;
Kitzinger, Mosaics at Nikopolis, pp. 88-90.

   Illustrations. A. Philadelpheus, DCAH, 4, 2 (1927), p. 48,
fig. 1 = our pl. 549, p. 55, fig. 7 (view looking east);
G. A. Soteriou and A. K. Orlandos, Praktika, 1929, p. 84, fig.
2 = our pl. 546; idem, Praktika, 1937, pl. opposite p. 78
= our pl. 547; G. A. Soteriou, Praktika, 1938, pl. 1 opposite
p. 116 = our pl. 548.

161 Room I (6.30 x 12.75 max). Large hall. Pls. 566-567.

   Outer border: 0.60. No other published information on

dimensions. Stone, marble, ceramic and glass (details)

tesserae.[809]

Polychrome rectilinear design with organic insets.

   Framing: outer border, imbrication pattern (for a similar

outer border on the west side of the complex, see 160, pl.

563); inner border, probably an undulating acanthus rinceau

forming circles.[810]

   Field (pl. 566): grid composed of striped bands forming

twenty-eight rows of ten squares each. The squares, which

vary in size (0.24 x 0.25; 0.24 x 0.27; 0.25 x 0.30) are

inscribed with organic and geometric motifs. Among the latter

motifs are interlaces and crosses while the former are

---

[809]A. Philadelpheus, DCAH, 4, 2 (1927), pp. 55-58.

   [810]This is described as many colored whirls inside a
large circle (ibid., p. 55). A small part of the border is
visible on the upper right side of the photograph (pl. 566)
and it appears that the circle is, in fact, formed by
serrated acanthus leaves.

represented by partridges, ducks, and animals and such flora
as pomegranates, cucumbers, eggplants, fig and ivy leaves,
and a vase filled with fruit (for similar designs in Basilica
Alpha at Nikopolis, see 152, pls. 466-468; 156, pls. 533-
536).[811] On the west side of the room, interrupting either
the border or field, or both, is a tabula ansata (1.39 x
0.39) with a four-line inscription (0.07-0.12 high).[812]
Oriented westward (pl. 567), it cites the donor, Archbishop
Alkison, who built the structure from its foundations:

[ ]ΟΥΚΥΡΙΟΥ ΗΜѠΝ/ΙΗC[ ]ΟΥΟ ΑΓΙѠΤΑΤΟ C/
ΑΡΧΙ[ ]ΑΓΟCΑΛΚΙCѠΝ/ЄΚΤΙCЄΝ[ ]ѲЄΜЄΛΙѠΝ
ΤΟΠΑΝЄΡΓΟΝ   813

Between 491 and 516.

Basilica Delta

At a place called Karaouli or Analepsis, east of the
city of Nikopolis, a large church, designated Delta (pl.
568), was discovered by chance in 1952. Three systematic
excavations between 1956 and 1961 brought to light the

---

[811]For a comparison of them, see Kitzinger, Mosaics at
Nikopolis, pp. 88-89.

[812]The location and orientation of the inscription are
indicated on a plan (pl. 549).

[813]A. Philadelpheus, Praktika, 1922-23, p. 42; idem,
Praktika, 1924, p. 110; idem, DCAH, 4, 2 (1927), pp. 57-58;
Soteriou, Palaiochristianikai basilikai, p. 201, n. 1.

narthex and most of the church proper (overall 22.75 x
37.50).[814] Fragments of mosaic pavements were discovered in
the atrium, I, narthex, II, and the south chapel, IV.[815]

Preceded by an atrium, I, and a shallow narthex, II
(22.75 x 5.00), with projecting wings, III, IV, the main body
of the church consists of a nave flanked by two aisles, V-
VII, and a transverse tripartite transept with projecting
wings and a raised semi-circular apse, VIII-X. The nave is
separated from the aisles and the bema from the north and
south transept wings by arcuated colonnades resting on bases
set on elevated stylobates.[816] A columnar division is als
used between the wings and the aisles while the bema, which
is raised one step above the nave and the wings, is enclosed
along the west side by a chancel screen with a prothuron
composed of four columns.[817] In the bema, traces were found

---

[814]The atrium and the north transept wing were not completely cleared.

[815]For a discussion of this room and its counterpart to
the south, see Orlandos, Hē metakinēsis tou diakonikou, p.
357, passim.

[816]The projection of the north wing is greater than that
of the south wing (A. K. Orlandos, Praktika, 1961, p. 98;
idem, To Ergon, 1961, p. 107. A similar tripartite transept
is represented in Basilica Alpha at Nikopolis (pl. 457).
There, however, no stylobates are used and simple projecting
piers divide the transepts. In a study of transepts, Krautheimer discusses this simpler form of separation but utilizes
a plan which erroneously shows stylobates (Tripartite
Transept, p. 418, fig. 16; idem, Architecture, p. 98, fig.
37). Cf. our pl. 568.

[817]A. K. Orlandos, Praktika, 1959, pp. 90, 94; idem,
To Ergon, 1959, pp. 67, 71; hereafter cited as Praktika, 1959,
and To Ergon, 1959, respectively. The columns are omitted
from the plan.

of the altar and two semi-independent clergy benches which
abutted the shoulders of the apse. Other liturgical furnishings have not survived in situ but a marble fragment belonging perhaps to the original ambon was found in the fill of
the north wing.[818] Mosaic pavements decorate the atrium,
narthex, and the small chapel to the south. The nave and
bema were paved in polychrome opus sectile, and the north
annex of the narthex and the south transept wing were covered
with irregular pieces of colored marble.[819]

Although no datable archaeological finds were unearthed
or reported, on the basis of the style of the capitals, the
church has been dated to the end of the fifth or the
beginning of the sixth century.[820]

Bibliography. A. K. Orlandos, Praktika, 1956, pp. 149-153;
idem, To Ergon, 1956, pp. 60-63; BCH, 81 (1957), pp. 581-583;
JHS, 77 (1957), Supplement, p. 17; A. K. Orlandos, Praktika,
1959, pp. 90-97; idem, To Ergon, 1959, pp. 67-75; D. I.
Pallas, RAC, 35 (1959), pp. 196-197; BCH, 84 (1960), p. 739;
JHS, 80 (1960), Supplement, p. 13; A. K. Orlandos, Praktika,
1961, pp. 98-101; idem, To Ergon, 1961, pp. 107-113; idem,

---

[818]Praktika, 1959, pp. 93-94, fig. 5 (misprinted as fig.
4). In the southeast corner of the south transept wing,
traces of a rectangular compartment (1.50 x 2.90; marked "K"
on our plan, pl. 568) were found. It is suggested that this
functioned as a sacristy or vestry (Praktika, 1959, p. 92).
In Room III, which communicates with the narthex as well as
with the outside, a low bench was found along the east wall.
The function of this room is problematic (vide supra, p. 489,
n. 815).

[819]Although not noted in the reports, a drawing of the
east side of the church shows irregular stone pieces in the
bema as well (Praktika, 1959, p. 92, fig. 2). The type of
pavements in the north and south aisles was not recorded.

[820]It is only in the first report that this chronology
is suggested (A. K. Orlandos, To Ergon, 1956, p. 63). Subsequent reports omit chronological discussions. D. I.

Deltion, 17 (1961-62), B: Chronika, pp. 199-201; BCH, 86
(1962), pp. 758-761; JHS, 82 (1962), Supplement, p. 13;
A. K. Orlandos, Praktika, 1966, p. 196; idem, To Ergon,
1966, p. 174; BCH, 91 (1967), p. 673; JHS, 87 (1967),
Supplement, p. 14; D. I. Pallas, "Epiros," RBK, cols. 221-
231.

   Illustrations. A. K. Orlandos, Praktika, 1956, p. 150,
fig. 1 (plan, with mosaics); idem, Praktika, 1959, p. 91,
fig. 1 (plan, after the excavations in 1959), p. 92, fig. 2
(plan of east side, with marble paving), pp. 94-95, figs.
4-5 (fragments of architectural and decorative sculpture),
pl. 87a (room in south transept wing), pl. 88a (north
stylobate); idem, Praktika, 1961, p. 99, fig. 1 = our pl.
568.

<h3 style="text-align:center">Nos. 162-164</h3>

   Fragments of polychrome geometric pavements with a few
figures are preserved in the atrium, I, narthex, II, and
the south chapel, IV. The mosaics were lifted in 1963,
consolidated, and reset in situ but, since then, they have
undergone further deterioration.

   On the basis of their style and technique the pavements
belong to the same workshop as those in three other Nikopolitan churches (150-156; 157-161; 165-167) and elsewhere (146-
147; 148). The same color scheme is employed (reds, grey,
purplish and reddish browns, brown and greens) the same kind
of unshaded, flat geometric configurations, composed of a
single color with one or two rows of white (pls. 575-578),
and the same type of wide borders. Although few figural

Pallas' argument for a date into the sixth century (RBK, col.
226) is correctly refuted by Sodini (Catalogue, p. 728,
n. 59).

elements are present, and these in poor condition (pls. 570-
571, 579), their two-dimensional rendering is apparent as is
their weightlessness which causes them to adhere to the
opaque surface of the floor. The aniconic grid in Room IV
(pl. 576) has an iconic counterpart in a more securely dated
Nikopolitan church, Beta (160, pl. 563), attributed to the
end of the fifth century, which may argue for a slightly
earlier date. The abstract style of the figures, however,
is closer to the sixth than to the fifth century. It is
probable, therefore, that the late fifth or early sixth century chronology proposed by the excavator on the basis of the
style of the capitals, obtains for the pavements as well.

Additional bibliography. Sodini, Catalogue, No. 45, pp.
727-728.

Illustration. A. K. Orlandos, Praktika, 1961, p. 99,
fig. = our pl. 568.

162   Room I (no dimensions published).   Atrium.

No published information on dimensions and material.

Brief mention of some mosaic fragments.[821]

Probably contemporary with the mosaics in the narthex and
south chapel (163-164) and, therefore, end of the fifth or
the beginning of the sixth century.

---

[821]A. K. Orlandos, Praktika, 1961, p. 101; hereafter
cited as Praktika, 1961.

163 Room II (22.75 x 4.50). Narthex. Pls. 568-574.

Fragment: ca. 6.00 x 3.10. Framing: 0.75[822] Field:
5.25 max x 1.60. Figure panels: ca. 0.75 x 0.60. Stone,
ceramic (red) and glass (dark blue, green, turquoise)
tesserae (ca. 0.01 sq) set 2-4mm apart.

Polychrome geometric pavement inscribed with a floral wreath
in the center and three small figural panels in front of the
entrance to the nave.

Surround: destroyed, but in a published photograph it is
dark in color.[823]

Framing (pls. 569, 572): traces of a white triple fillet;
black fillet; border, corregated ribbon pattern (or a wide
herringbone) composed or rows of white/pink/light purplish
brown/ red stripes which alternate with rows of dark grey
and white stripes. Along the preserved north side (pl. 572,
top), this pattern is rendered in perspective, placed on a
white ground, and articulated by small black diagonal crosslets.[824] The border is interrupted in the northwest and
southwest corners by small squares inscribed with interlaced

[822]This dimension is misprinted in the Praktika, 1961,
p. 101. Cf. A. K. Orlandos, Deltion, 17 (1961-62), B:
Chronika, p. 201; hereafter cited as Deltion, 17.

[823]A. K. Orlandos, Praktika, 1966, pl. 179a.

[824]This change is omitted from the drawing and it is
barely visible in the photograph.

circles[825] and by five rectangular panels at the entrance to
the nave (pls. 569-571). Three panels contain pairs of confronting birds, oriented westward, which flank or stand in
front of black or dark brown plants, some with red-tipped
white buds. The central panel contains two long-legged and
long-necked, dark blue and green birds, perhaps peahens, and
the two side panels have dark grey and white doves or
pigeons (pl. 570-571). These figural panels are flanked by
two complex meanders;[826] black fillet; white triple fillet.

   Field (pls. 569, 572), framed by a black fillet: red and
light green intersecting circles (0.32 diam), outlined by
black/white/black single fillets, forming white concave-
sided squares. The design is cut along the margins. The
squares are inscribed with crude, stepped squares, variously
red, light green, or dark blue, and the ovals, formed by the
intersection of the circles, have two to three short white
strokes in their centers.[827] In the center of the field,
near the entrance to the nave, is a large polychrome wreath
(2.33 or 2.53 diam),[828] now lost, which serves as the focal

---

[825]These squares, now lost, are visible in the drawing
(pl. 569).

[826]I was only able to see the right figural inset (pl.
571). Except for one distorted view of the meander (pl.
570), it has not been properly reproduced or described.

[827]These filling motifs are not as well executed as
they appear in the drawing (pls. 569, 573).

[828]For the former measurement, see Praktika, 1961, p.
101; for the second, see Deltion, 17, p. 201.

point of the all-over geometric design (pls. 569, 573-574).
The wreath is placed over the design and, apprently, encloses
intersecting circles which are smaller in diameter than
those in the rest of the field (see pl. 573). Fruit, flowers
and leaves executed in white, black, yellow, reddish brown,
and turquoise (glass) tesserae are bounded together by an
undulating ribbon.[829]

Additional color. Birds: dark blue outlines and red beaks
and legs. Field: stepped squares have black and red, or
white crosslets.

Late fifth or early sixth century.

Illustrations. A. K. Orlandos, Praktika, 1959, p. 96,
fig. 6 = our pl. 573; idem, Praktika, 1961, p. 102, fig. 3
= our pl. 569, pl. 57a (north corner), pl. 57b (detail of
east panel: peahens [?]), pl. 58a (detail of east panel:
pigeon or dove), pl. 58b (wreath); idem, Praktika, 1966,
pl. 178b = our pl. 574, pl. 179a (northeast corner).

164 Room IV (7.25 x 4.50, including apse). South chapel.
     Pls. 575-579.

Nave: 5.00 x 4.50. Framing: 0.50. Field: north compartment, a: ca. 3.14; length indeterminable. South compartment, b, apse: 2.39 diam. Materials identical to those
in Room II (163).

[829]Praktika, 1959, p. 96; To Ergon, 1959, p. 71;
Praktika, 1961, p. 101; A. K. Orlandos, To Ergon, 1961, p.
110.

Polychrome mosaic, united by a complex interlace, composed
of aniconic geometric panels in the nave and geometric and
organic patterns in the apse.

Surround: dark grey tesserae in rows parallel to the wall.

Framing (pl. 575): white double fillet; outer border in
nave only, single row of triangles set base-to-tip (alternately red, greyish green, pink, purplish brown, outlined in
white) on a black ground; white double fillet; inner border,
complex two-strand chain (1-3 light purplish brown/1-2 red;
1-2 light green; 1-3 greyish green, outlined by single white/
black fillets) forming circles (for similar chains, see 189,
pl. 620; 197, pl. 635).

Field (pl. 575).

IVa, north compartment: divided into two panels by black/
white/black single fillets and framed by a black fillet.

North panel (pls. 575, top, 576):[830] grid composed of juxtaposed circles (0.15 diam) which are united by short bars to
form concave-sided octagons (for a similar design in Basilica
Beta at Nikopolis, see 160, pl. 560). The white circles,
outlined in black, are decorated with alternating red and
white, light grey and white, or light grey and red hour glass
motifs. The light purplish brown octagons, outlined in red,
contain black and white crosslets, pink and red circles, and
a few red buds, all outlined in black.

South panel (pl. 575, bottom), framed by a double fillet:

---

[830]This panel is omitted from the plan (pl. 568).

imbrication composed of large scales, fanning eastward, formed
by wide strands (generally, light grey or light purplish
brown with red bases and white apeces). Rising from the base
of each scale is a long black bar supporting a small black
disk.[831] The scales are cut along the margins.

IVb, south compartment, apse (pls. 577-579), separated from
the north compartment by a two-strand guilloche (red/1 white;
greyish green/1 white; dark grey/1 white, outlined in black,
with a white tessera at each loop) and framed by a dark grey
triple fillet and, along the north side by additional white
and black double and single fillets, respectively.

Field (pl. 577): large medallion (2.00 diam) bordered by a
single row of chevrons (0.13 wide; brown, greyish green, red,
light and dark green) which follow no consistent chromatic
sequence. In the umbrella pattern which decorates the
medallion, the radiating ribs taper toward the center, now
lost, and are outlined on one side by a black fillet and, on
the other, by a white one. These ribs and the webbing between them, which also converge toward the center of the
design, are decorated with wide concentric rows of red, white,
pink, light and dark green tesserae which, also, do not follow
a consistent chromatic scheme. In the north spandrels,
toward the base of the apsidal panel (pls. 578-579), there

---

[831]No other preserved Greek pavement has this kind of
imbrication pattern.

are disposed single two-strand knots (red/1 white; dark green/
1 white, outlined in black) from which spring single dark
green laurel branches. Below this decoration and occupying
the east and west corners are two large peacocks whose curving bodies complement the shape of the medallion. They stand
with their backs to each other and their heads turned toward
the center of the composition. Of these peacocks, only the
heavily restored dark green (glass) head of the west one is
preserved. Scattered around these polychrome birds with
trailing tail coverts are a stepped square, a pinwheel motif,
two single ivy leaves or buds (pl. 579), and a pomegranate.

Additional color. Chevrons: outlined by white/black
single fillets. Umbrella pattern: outlined in black.
Peacock: outlined in dark blue glass.

Late fifth or early sixth century.

Illustrations. A. K. Orlandos, Praktika, 1956, p. 150,
fig. 1 (plan, with chapel pavement), pl. 52 = our pl. 579,
pl. 53 = our pl. 578, pl. 54 (IVa); idem, Praktika, 1966,
pl. 179a = our pl. 575.

Basilica Epsilon

The basilica, designated Epsilon (pl. 580), is located
about four kilometers from Nikopolis in the region of
Maragōna, near Preveza. During a short campaign in 1958, the
main outlines of the building were determined and mosaics
were discovered in the exonarthex, esonarthex, and in the

south wing of the transept. At the present time, the pavements are covered.

The church (39.30; width indeterminable) is preceded by
a large atrium and two narthexes (width, ca. 7.50 and 3.50,
respectively).[832] Like the other basilicas at Nikopolis
(pls. 457, 548, 568), the esonarthex has a south annex and
the nave and aisles are terminated by a tripartite transept
with projecting wings. The nave is separated from the aisles
by stylobates and the south wing of the transept contains a
narrow compartment (ca. 1.00 meter wide) along its east side.
Although no datable archaeological finds were unearthed or
reported, on the basis of this compartment which the excavator
believes functioned as a sacristy or vestry, the church was
attributed to the middle or third quarter of the sixth century.[833] In the modern period, a small church dedicated to
St. Menas was built over the bema.

Bibliography. D. I. Pallas, RAC, 35 (1959), pp. 199,
201-202; idem, "Epiros," RBK, col. 219; BCH, 83 (1959), pp.
664-665; JHS, 79 (1959), Supplement, p. 110.

Illustrations. D. I. Pallas, RAC, 35 (1959), p. 198, fig.
12 = our pl. 580, p. 201, fig. 15 = our pl. 582.

---

[832]Most of the measurements are taken from the plan
(pl. 580).

[833]D. I. Pallas, RAC, 35 (1959), pp. 199, 201-202. A
similar partition exists in the south transept wing of
Basilica Alpha at Nikopolis (pl. 548) but it is a later
addition. (D. I. Pallas, RBK, col. 219). The partition in
this basilica belongs to the original plan.

Nos. 165-167

Traces of polychrome geometric mosaics were discovered
in the narthexes and in the south wing of the transept.[834]
Since the site awaits a full-scale excavation, and the information on the pavements is inadequate, their chronology
is difficult to determine. It would appear, however, that
the pavements are not earlier than the second half of the
fifth century. The complexity of the patterns, the multi-
plicity of borders (pls. 581, 583) and the apparent polychromatic emphasis indicate an advanced date. Certainly,
they postdate the mosaics in a villa in neighboring Phtelia
(172-175) which are securely dated to the middle of the fifth
century. The half white, half colored imbrications, the
highlighting of the strand of the interlaces and the guilloche by means of one or two rows of white tesserae, and the
decoration of the circles in Room XI with hour glass motifs
are characteristics which are encountered in other Nikopolitan churches which have been attributed to the late fifth
and the early sixth centuries (157, pls. 550-551; 158, pl.
557; 160, pl. 563; 164, pl. 575, 578-579). It is necessary,
however, to await a systematic clearing of the site before
accepting the rather late date advanced by the excavator.[835]

---

[834]Sodini is incorrect in ascribing a mosaic to the
south aisle (Catalogue, p. 728).

[835]Vide supra, p. 499.

Additional bibliography. Sodini, Catalogue, No. 46, p. 728.

Illustration. D. I. Pallas, RAC, 35 (1959), p. 198, fig. 12 = our pl. 580.

165 Room II (7.50 wide; length indeterminate). Exonarthex.

Pl. 581.

No published information on dimensions and material.

In a published photograph, there is a framing unit composed of four borders (pl. 581).[836]

Framing: first border, meander pattern forming a single row of intersecting swastikas; narrow dark band; second border, row of squares which are inscribed with diagonal quatrefoils of lanceolate leaves. The corners of the squares are decorated with single peltae and the ground is colored; dark double fillet; third border, meander pattern forming a single row of intersecting swastikas; dark double fillet; white triple fillet; dark double fillet; fourth border, complex chain of interlacing circles.

No earlier than the late fifth century.

Illustration. D. I. Pallas, RAC, 35 (1959), p. 200, fig. 14 = our pl. 581.

---

[836]The relationship of the borders to the field is not discussed.

166 Room III (3.50; length indeterminate). Esonarthex.

No published information on dimensions and material.

Brief mention of a mosaic pavement.[837]

167 Room XI (ca. 7.00; width indeterminable). South wing

  of transept; pavement laid up to west wall of east

compartment. Pls. 582-583.

No published information on dimensions and material.

Two published photographs show the framing and part of the
field design of the pavement (pls. 582-583).

  Surround: dark tesserae.

  Framing (pl. 582): light band; dark band; border, two-
strand interlace (probably, one color per strand and 1 row
of white tesserae, outlined by a dark fillet) forming large
and small circles. The latter are decorated with a single
tessera and the former with alternating light and dark hour
glass motifs; dark fillet; triple light fillet.

  Field (pl. 583), framed by a dark fillet: checkerboard
pattern of small colored squares. Interrupting the field is
a circle or semi-circle surrounded by three borders and inscribed with an imbrication pattern of half white and half
colored scales. The triple border contains a two-strand
guilloche (probably like the interlace in the border), on a

---

[837]D. I. Pallas, RAC, 35 (1959), p. 199.

dark ground. This border is flanked by two bands decorated
with single (inner) and double (outer) rows of dark dentils.
The latter are separated from the guilloche by a dark fillet,
outlined in white.

No earlier than the late fifth century.

Illustrations. D. I. Pallas, RAC, 35 (1959), p. 199, fig.
13 - our pl. 583, p. 201, fig. 15 - our pl. 282.

Secular Building

In 1913, excavations were begun twenty-five meters west
of Basilica Alpha at Nikopolis (150-156). In four subsequent
campaigns, ending in 1926, the south part of a large secular
building was brought to light. The site was re-excavated in
1961 and a plan of the building was prepared (pl. 584).
Mosaic pavements were discovered in the porticoes, Ia-d,
Rooms V, VIII, and in "cells" for which no specific location
was given. The site is now completely overgrown and the
mosaics have disappeared.[838]

The paucity of descriptive and photographic material precludes a thorough survey of the architectural complex. The
excavated section contains a large atrium (18.15 x 23.40))
which is surrounded by a peristyle, Ia-d (12.78, north south;

[838]By 1926 the mosaics had been destroyed "through the
negligence of the authorities" (G. A. Soteriou, Praktika,
1926, p. 122; A. Philadelpheus, Praktika, 1926, p. 127).

15.68, east west), onto which various rooms open.[839]
Beneath the tessellated pavement in Room VIII (7.20 x 13.26)
is a hypocaust system for a bath,[840] and Room III contains a
staircase leading to the second storey.[841] A nymphaeum was
found somewhere to the south of the peristyle and in unspecified areas elsewhere there were "cells"[842] and two adjacent
rooms: one with hypocausts; the other with a hearth. The
rest of the rooms around the peristyle are not described in
the original publications or in the reports of the excavation
in 1961.

The building history of the complex has never been
clearly defined. The consensus is that it was built in the
Roman period and converted during the Early Christian
period.[843] Although the reasons for its Roman attribution
are never stated, it is clear that it was used by the
Christians. This is evident from the representations of
saints on the walls of the "cells" and the episcopal inscriptions in their pavements, another Christian inscription in

---

[839]A. Philadelpheus, Praktika, 1913, p. 105; idem,
Praktika, 1916, p. 60.

[840]A. Philadelpheus, Praktika, 1916, pp. 60, 64; hereafter cited as Praktika, 1916; A. K. Orlandos, Praktika, 1961,
p. 103.

[841]A. Philadelpheus, Praktika, 1914, p. 219; hereafter
cited as Praktika, 1914; A. K. Orlandos, op. cit., p. 105.

[842]A. Philadelpheus, Praktika, 1918, p. 16ff.

[843]Praktika, 1914, p. 220; A. Philadelpheus, Praktika,
1926, p. 127; G. A. Soteriou, Praktika, 1926, p. 125; A. K.
Orlandos, Praktika, 1961, p. 103.

the southwest part of the peristyle,[844] and from two large

crosses painted on a layer of plaster which covered a wall

mosaic in the nymphaeum.[845] Because of its proximity to

Basilica Alpha, its size, and the episcopal inscriptions in

the "cells," it is hypothesized that the building served as

the palace of the Bishop of Nikopolis[846] and that its conver-

sion was contemporaneous with the erection of Basilica Alpha,

because the mosaics are similar in style.[847] Although it is

possible that the building was an episcopal palace, it will

be shown below that not only are the mosaics different from

those in Nikopolis Alpha, datable to the second quarter of

the sixth century, but from those decorating other Nikopolitan

churches which belong to a slightly earlier period, that is,

to the late fifth and the early sixth centuries (157-161,

162-164). Given the dearth of illustrative material it is

only possible to ascribe some of them to the fourth or early

fifth century.

Bibliography. A. Philadelpheus, Praktika, 1913, pp. 103-

[844]A. Philadelpheus, Praktika, 1918, p. 17. Vide infra, p. 510.

[845]A. K. Orlandos is incorrect in ascribing crosses to the tessellated pavings in the porticoes (Praktika, 1961, p. 103). The only tessellated cross precedes the Christian inscription (pl. 586). The cross on the walls covered a mosaic which showed a Nereid riding on a sea monster. The replacement of this profane scene with Christian symbols may have been one of the reasons for ascribing the villa to the Roman period.

[846]Vide supra, p. 504, n. 843.

[847]Praktika, 1916, p. 33.

107; idem, Praktika, 1914, pp. 219-220; idem, Praktika, 1916, pp. 33, 60-64; idem, ArchEph, 1916, pp. 33, 122; idem, Praktika, 1918, pp. 16-18; idem, Praktika, 1919, p. 219; AA, 37 (1922), p. 249; A. Philadelpheus, Praktika, 1924, pp. 113-115; idem, Praktika, 1926, pp. 127-128; G. A. Soteriou, Praktika, 1926, pp. 122-123; A. K. Orlandos, Praktika, 1961, pp. 101-107; idem, To Ergon, 1961, pp. 107, 113-118; idem, Deltion, 17 (1961-1962), B: Chronika, pp. 201-203; BCH, 86 (1962), p. 758.

Illustrations. A. Philadelpheus, Praktika, 1913, p. 104, fig. 4 (peristyle, east side); A. K. Orlandos, Praktika, 1961, p. 104, fig. 4 = our pl. 584.

Nos. 168-171

The information on the mosaiv pavements in the porticoes of the atrium, Ia-d, Rooms V, VIII, and the "cells" is very inadequate. According to the reports all four porticoes were decorated with the same kind of interlace which paved the "southwest" portico (pl. 585) while somewhere in the "south portico" there was a "beautiful" polychrome panel with two borders (pl. 587), one an inhabited rinceau, and an "important composition".[848] The obvious location for this panel is Room V which is separated from the peristyle by narrow screen walls and from the atrium by two corner pillars (pl. 584). It served as an adjunct to Room IV which by its size and centralized position must have been a major, if not the major, room on the south side of the complex and, therefore, the most likely one to have been preceded by a

---

[848]Praktika, 1916, pp. 60, 64; idem, ArchEph, 1916, p. 122.

"beautiful" mosaic with an "important composition."[849]
Although a stylistic resemblance was noted between these
mosaics and those in Basilica Alpha (150-156),[850] this is
hardly the case. The mask in Room V (pl. 588) and the Triton
in Room VI (pl. 589) have no relationship to the figural
representations in Alpha (pls. 489, 506, 509, 512, 515, 526,
529, 531-532). The figures are more naturalistic and three-
dimensional, and the tesserae are much smaller and more carefully set. Moreover, the figure of the Triton, ostensibly,
an unrelieved dark or black form on white, with short white
strokes for anatomical details and features, is totally
different from similar full length or three-quarter length
figures in Alpha, and elsewhere for that matter. In regard
to the geometric design in the porticoes (pl. 585), again,
there are more differences than similarities. Generally, the
geometric designs in Alpha spread across the surface of each
compartment creating wide panels for representations of
flora, fauna, and multicolored geometric motifs (pls. 460-461;
466-472; 473-476). The peristyle pavement, on the other
hand, is aniconic, small in scale, and consists of compartmentalized sections of decorated and undecorated panels.[851]
Even earlier aniconic pavements in Nikopolis, datable to the

[849]These rooms were not discussed in the reports.

[850]Praktika, 1916, p. 33.

[851]In a similar compartmentalized surface at Alpha (pls.
473-474), the interstices between the panels are richly
decorated with complex interlaces.

late fifth century, contain continuous, all-over geometric
designs which clothe the surfaces with intersecting, interlocking or interlacing patterns (157-165). Nowhere are
plain and undecorated panels juxtaposed the way they are
here. It is unlikely, therefore, that this pavement was
executed in the sixth century much less the late fifth century. Does it belong to the Christian period at all? Part
of it certainly does and it is this part which creates a confusion in regard to the curious, uneven quadrupartite
division of the pavement. A careful study of this design
reveals that, contrary to the published description, the so-
called interlace does not spread all over the floor[852] but is
limited to a small section which is terminated on the east
side by a medallion. Beyond the medallion, the design dis-
appears and is succeeded by an undecorated white ground (pl.
585, top), the same kind of ground which covers the other
panels. Since the medallion contains a Christian inscription,
this section, at least, belongs to the Christian phase of the
building as does the central interlace border which continues
toward the east side. It is this border and the agglomerate
effect of the geometric design which create a discordant note.
They establish a fourth zone which has little relationship to
the flanking panels and to the white strip in the central
area. It is not unlikely, therefore, that they represent

---

[852]Praktika, 1914, p. 213; idem, Praktika, 1919, p. 219.

restorations and that the original decoration consisted of
the central white strip, which served as the tessellated
diadromos of the portico, and the two similar, flanking
panels. Thus, it is evident that two mosaic phases are
represented here and that the second, decorative one belongs
to the Christian period. To the latter period can be
ascribed the medallion in the lower left hand side of the
photograph (pl. 585) which also appears to be an isolated
intruder in an otherwise plain sector. The specific chronology of the original and restored parts of this pavement
cannot be determined because not enough is visible in the
photographs. It is certain, however, that neither phase reflects Nikopolitan workshop practices of the late fifth and
sixth centuries. Thus, the restored section with the
Christian inscription cannot be later than the second half of
the fourth or the first half of the fifth century. The
chronology of the figural pavements is more difficult to establish. The curious style of the monochrome Triton argues
for a date in the Roman period. As for the mask and the inhabited rinceau[853] of which it is a part, it could be Roman
or Early Christian. If it belongs to the latter period, then
it cannot be earlier than around the middle of the fifth century since it is at this time that figures are re-introduced
in Greek pavements. Earlier pavements in both secular and

---

[853]Since there is no clear photograph of the border (see
pl. 587), no comparison can be made with a similar one with
hunters in the south transept wing at Alpha (155).

religious structures are purely geometric and sober (1; 2-3; 4-5; 6-8; 21; 22; 44-49; 88-92; 130-138; 178-179; 196).

Illustration. A. K. Orlandos, Praktika, 1961, p. 104, fig. 4 = our pl. 584.

168   Room I (north to south, 12.78; east to west, 15.68;
       width, 4.50 to 5.00). Peristyle. Probable restoration
with geometric designs and an additional border moving east-
west. Pls. 585-586.

No published information on dimensions and material.

Described as being a very broad interlace developing without
interruption and forming various shapes over the whole floor:
squares; circles, parallelograms; other geometric designs.[854]
In a photograph, however (pl. 585), the pavement is not decorated with a continuous all-over design nor with an interlace.
The decorative designs are limited to two areas and show
small scale geometric units, outlined by light/dark double
fillets. The so-called interlace is really a grid composed
of a two-strand guilloche forming small squares. The guilloche bifurcates along the edges of the design and forms a
continuous border and, on the east side, a large medallion
(0.64). The medallion (pl. 586) contains a short inscription
in black letters (0.14 high) preceded by a cross: "ЄΠΙ/

[854]A. Philadelpheus, Praktika, 1919, p. 219. Vide
supra, pp. 507-508.

ΓЄѠΡΓΙ/ΟΥ ЄΚΔΙΚΟΥ .ⁿ[855] On the southwest side of the pavement (pl. 585, lower left), is another medallion with a geometric pattern composed of an alternating system of straight squares and squares set on edge which are disposed around an unidentifiable central motif. The rest of the pavement, which is earlier,[856] is composed of two long rectangular compartments with guilloche borders and a plain central strip.

Roman with a fourth or early fifth century restoration.

    Illustrations. A. Philadelpheus, Praktika, 1924, p. 113, fig. 1 = our pl. 585, p. 115, fig. 3 = our pl. 586.

169 Room V (ca. 5.00 x 7.50).[857] Vestibule? Pls. 587-588.

    Framing: at least 1.17. No other published information on dimensions and material.

Fragment of a polychrome panel decorated with geometric and figural borders and traces of an "important composition" in the center.[858]

    Framing (pl. 587): outer border, two rows of two wheel patterns each composed of four peltae around a Solomon's

---

    [855]A. Philadelpheus, Praktika, 1919, p. 219; idem, Praktika, 1926, p. 127.

    [856]Vide supra, pp. 507-508.

    [857]The measurements are taken from the plan (pl. 584).

    [858]Vide infra, p. 506 and n. 848.

knot; narrow light band; narrow dark band; wide light bands; inner border, inhabited rinceau forming circles which are filled with birds, animals, fruit allegorical heads, and a nude hunter aiming at a wild animal.[859] In the four corners, the rinceau is interrupted by single bearded masks (pl. 588) decorated with hoods of leaves (for similar masks, see pls. 120, 122-124).

Field: traces of an "important composition."[860]

Roman or Early Christian.

Illustrations. A. Philadelpheus, Praktika, 1916, p. 61, fig. 8 = our pl. 588; idem, Praktika, 1924, p. 115, fig. 4 = our pl. 587.

170 Room VIII (ca. 7.00 x 14.20). Bath? Pavement laid
     over a hypocaust system. Pl. 589.

No published information on dimensions and material.

Traces near the south wall of "life-size Tritons with sea serpents, dolphins, and similar sea demons."[861] In a photograph (pl. 589), there are traces of a frontal Triton with an outstretched right arm. His dark body and head are articulated by short light strokes.

---

[859]Praktika, 1916, pp. 60, 64; idem, ArchEph, 1916, p. 122.

[860]Praktika, 1916, p. 64.

[861]Praktika, 1916, pp. 63, 60; A. Philadelpheus, ArchEph, 1916, p. 122.

Roman.

Illustration. A. Philadelpheus, Praktika, 1924, p. 114, fig. 2 = our pl. 589.

171 "Cells" (no dimensions published).

No published information on dimensions and material.

Brief mention of mosaic pavemenes with inscriptions citing the names of bishops.[862]

Early Christian.

Villa at Phtelia

At a place called Phtelia, near Nikopolis, around five hundred meters east of Basilica Delta (162-164), the south side of a villa was cleared in 1959 (pl. 590) bringing to light traces of mosaic pavements in most of the rooms. The site is now overgrown and fragments of the mosaics are stored in the southwest chapel and the south transept wing of Basilica Alpha.

The narrow building (35.60 long),[863] oriented east-west,

[862]A. Philadelpheus, Praktika, 1918, p. 17. Vide supra, p. 504.

[863]A. K. Orlandos and D. I. Pallas, Praktika, 1959, p. 100, hereafter cited as Praktika, 1959. Elsewhere the length is listed as "over 37 meters" (A. K. Orlandos, To Ergon, 1959, p. 73, hereafter cited as To Ergon, 1959).

is divided into two sectors by Room V. In the east part,
Rooms II, III, IV served as the living quarters of the villa
and Room I to the north may have been a corridor or a sun
porch of some kind with colonnades along the north side.[864]
The west side is dominated by a large room, VI (ca. 10.00 x
ca. 8.30), which extends the full width of the building and
contains an inscribed apse (3.60 radius). This room and the
one preceding it, V (3.60 x ca. 100), belongs to the more
public area of the villa with V serving as a vestibule and
VI, perhaps, as a reception or audience hall.[865] The official character of Room VI and the general isolation of the
building on a hill overlooking the Gulf of Arta to the north
and the mountains of Epiros and Arcarnanias to the south suggest that the villa was the summer residence of a high
official from Nikopolis, perhaps the bishop of that city.[866]

On the basis of the masonry and the decorative treatment
of its plaster surface with incised lines, the building has
been attributed to a period not earlier than the middle of
the fifth century.[867] This date is supported by the style of

[864]Praktika, 1959, pp. 104-105; To Ergon, 1959, p. 73.

[865]Praktika, 1959, pp. 99, 105; To Ergon, 1959, p. 75.

[866]Praktika, 1959, p. 105; To Ergon, 1959, p. 75. For
his probable winter residence, see 168-171.

[867]Praktika, 1959, pp. 105, 112. Elsewhere, A. K.
Orlandos suggests the beginning or middle of the century
without corroborative evidence (To Ergon, 1959, p. 75).

the mosaic pavements.

Bibliography. A. K. Orlandos and D. I. Pallas, Praktika, 1959, pp. 98-113; A. K. Orlandos, To Ergon, 1959, pp. 72-75; BCH, 84 (1960), pp. 742-744; JHS, 80 (1960), Supplement, p. 13.

Illustration. A. K. Orlandos and D. I. Pallas, Praktika, 1959, p. 99, fig. 1 = our pl. 590.

Nos. 172-175

Simple in design and crude in execution, the preserved geometric mosaics in Rooms II, III, IV, VI contain homogeneous decorative schemes consisting of combinations of interlocking and intersecting circles, ellipses, and polygons (pls. 591-598). The austere geometricity of the field designs and borders is somewhat reduced by a bright color scheme which relies on purple, purplish brown, and red for its general effect with white and black serving primarily as delineative features.

On the basis of their style, they can be attributed to the middle of the fifth century, a date supported by architectural evidence as well. Although sharing with the late fourth and early fifth century pavements at Arkitsa, Demetrias, and Dion (88-92; 130-138; 178-179) a simplicity and austerity of design, the Phtelia pavements are richly colored, while the others are primarily black and white with color used only as a highlighting effect. On the other hand, since the Phtelia mosaics are not as coloristic and complex as those in Basilicas Beta, Delta, and Epsilon in the vicinity

(157-161; 162-164; 165-167), they clearly predate these late fifth century pavements. Indeed, the Phtelia pavements provide evidence that the Nikopolitan mosaic workshop which executed the mosaics in Basilicas Alpha, Beta, Delta and Epsilon, and elsewhere (146-147; 148) had not begun to function until the second half of the century.

Illustration. A. K. Orlandos, Praktika, 1959, p. 99, fig. 1 = our pl. 590.

172 Room II (5.75 x ca. 5.20). Kitchen?.

No published information on dimensions and material.

Brief mention of a mosaic pavement.[868]

Middle of the fifth century.

173 Room III (6.25 x ca. 6.35). Bedroom. Pl. 591.

No published information on dimensions and material.

Mosaic destroyed, except for a section of the border (pl. 591) decorated with an oblique grid of single serrate-edged fillets forming squares.[869] Each square is decorated with one tessera and the margins with very small stepped squares.

---

[868]Praktika, 1959, p. 105.

[869]Since both the published description and the drawing are unclear, this is my interpretation (cf. Praktika, 1959, pp. 110-111).

Middle of the fifth century.

   Illustration. A. K. Orlandos and D. I. Pallas, Praktika, 1959, p. 110, fig. 6 = our pl. 591.

174 Room IV (6.35 x 5.20). Bedroom.

   No published information on dimensions and material.

Mosaic destroyed, except for a section of the border which contains a double row of alternating white and purple triangles placed base-to-tip.[870]

Middle of the fifth century.

175 Room VI (10.00 x 11.90, including apse). Reception or audience hall. Pls. 592-598.

   No published information on dimensions. Stone tesserae (0.01 sq) set 1-3mm apart.

Fragment of a polychrome pavement composed of rectangular and apsidal compartments (a-b).

   VIa, rectangular compartment to east: two panels with geometric designs set within a double border (pls. 592-594).

   Framing (pl. 592): wide white band; outer border, interlocking pattern, on a purple ground, of two black opposed

---

   [870]No photograph or drawing accompanied the report. This is my interpretation of the pattern based on an inadequate description (ibid., p. 110).

"S-scrolls" forming white heart-shaped motifs; white triple
fillet; inner border, overlapping lyre pattern (no colors
published).

North panel (pl. 593): traces of an interlocking geometric
design composed of crosses of four ellipses around a small
circle separated by large red circles. The motifs are outlined by a black fillet and set on a light purplish brown
ground.[871] Red centers in the white ellipses and the small
circles complete the design.

South panel (pl. 594), framed by a white fillet: intersecting tetragons formed of small purple squares and red octagons.
The design is articulated by white/black/white single fillets,
and black crosses with white centers decorate the octagons.

VIb, apsidal compartment to west (pls. 595-598).

Framing (pls. 595-596): wide white band; outer border,
two-strand overlapping lyre pattern (1 to 2 red/2 white; 1 to
2 light purplish brown/2 white, outlined in black, with a
white tessera at each loop) on a black ground; double white
fillet; inner border, rainbow band (light purplish brown/
white/light purplish brown); double white fillet.

Field (pls. 597-598), framed by a black fillet: black
intersecting circles on a white ground forming white concave-
sided squares and opposed peltae. Each square and the tip of

---

[871]The ground is described as being strewn with small
crosslets, but this is omitted from the drawing and it is not
evident in a photograph (Praktika, 1959, pl. 97b).

each pelta are decorated with a small black crosslet.

Middle of the fifth century.

Illustrations. A. K. Orlandos and D. I. Pallas, Praktika, 1959, p. 106, fig. 3 = our pl. 597, p. 108, fig. 4 = our pl. 593, p. 109, fig. 5 (VIb, south panel: restored), pl. 97a = our pl. 595, pl. 97b (VIa, north panel), pl. 98a = our pl. 594, pl. 98b = our pl. 592.

STROUNI

Basilica

At Strouni, southwest of Doliana, a chance find brought to light traces of an Early Christian basilica with a mosaic pavement. The specific location of the site could not be determined and, therefore, the building was not examined.

Bibliography. D. I. Pallas, "Epiros," RBK, col. 241.

No. 176

176 Mosaic pavement (no dimensions published).

No published information on dimensions and material.

Brief mention of a mosaic pavement.

Early Christian.

Additional bibliography. Sodini, Catalogue, No. 47, pp. 728-729.

DOLIANA

Basilica

One hundred meters south of the road to Doliana and
around three kilometers north of the monastery of Vellas, the
ruins of an Early Christian basilica with traces of a mosaic
pavement were noted in 1964. The specific location of the
site could not be determined and, therefore, the building
was not examined.

Bibliography. S. I. Dakares, Deltion, 19 (1964), B3:
Chronika, p. 313.

No. 177

177 Mosaic fragments (no dimensions published).

No published information on dimensions and material.

Brief mention of fragments of a mosaic pavement.

Early Christian.

Additional bibliography. Sodini, Catalogue, No. 41,
p. 723.

PART VI. MACEDONIA AND THRACE

DION

Basilica Alpha

Basilica Alpha, located near the foot of Mount Olympus
in the ancient city of Dion, was discovered in 1927 during
the excavation of a later church (180-183) which lies
approximately two meters above it (pl. 600).[872] Between 1962
and 1965, the site was re-excavated and the greater portion
of the building was brought to light including well preserved
tessellated pavements in the narthex, I, and the nave, II.[873]
At the present time, the pavements are covered.

Since a plan of the building was published (pl.

---

[872]G. Soteriades, Praktika, 1928, pp. 59ff (history of
site), especially pp. 88-90; hereafter cited as Praktika,
1928; idem, Praktika, 1929, p. 72, p. 71, fig. 3; hereafter
cited as Praktika, 1929; Soteriou, Palaiochristianikai
basilikai, p. 180; G. Soteriades, Praktika, 1930, pp. 49-50;
idem, Actes du IIIme congrès international d'études byzantines, 1930, pp. 251-252; hereafter cited as Actes; Hoddinott,
Early Byzantine Churches, p. 124.

[873]St. Pelekanides, Deltion, 19 (1964), B3: Chronika, p.
384; hereafter cited as Deltion, 19; idem, Deltion, 20
(1965), B3: Chronika, pp. 477-478; hereafter cited as Deltion,
20; idem, Deltion, 21 (1966), B2: Chronika, p. 371. The
extent of the excavation is not clearly defined. Presumably,
the narthex and the church proper were cleared, since precise
data on their size and decoration is given. Although Sodini
notes that the north aisle was not cleared, this is not
stated in the reports (Catalogue, p. 734).

599)[874] and the reports contain little useful information,
only a summary description of its architectural plan will
follow. Preceded by a shallow, irregularly-shaped narthex
(18.10 long; width to north, 5.00; to south, 4.00), the
church proper comprises a nave flanked by two aisles and
terminated by a raised, semi-circular apse around which a
synthronon was placed. Except for this feature and a chancel
screen,[875] no other liturgical furnishing was found. The
narthex communicated with the church proper through three
doors, one for each aisle, and with the west through two
doors located on its north and south sides. Although no
trace of an atrium was found, it is possible that one existed
since evidence of rooms was found to the west of the narthex.[876] Traces of wall paintings were found in a room near

---

[874]This plan shows the location of Alpha in relation to
Beta after the first excavation.

[875]Deltion, 20, p. 478. The "ʊ-shape" of the east edge
of the mosaic reveals that the chancel screen had a projecting feature in the center of its west side. Although it is
described as a solea (ibid.), it is more probable that it was
a prothuron (pl. 605). In any case, the mosaic was laid up
to the screen and its opening. On the east side of the
screen, the bema floor is covered with long narrow bricks
arranged in geometric patterns. This floor is described as
the original pavement (ibid.; Praktika, 1928) and as a "replacement" of the mosaic (Sodini, Catalogue, p. 734). The
concave surfaces of some of the bricks and their arrangement
in wide and narrow bands suggest that they served as a bed
for marble slabs, perhaps in opus sectile. It is hardly
likely that this sacred and restricted area would have been
covered with a course, utilitarian brick pavement. I know of
no other church in Greece which has this type of crude paving
in the bema.

[876]Deltion, 20, p. 479; St. Pelekanides, Deltion, 21
(1966), B2: Chronika, p. 371.

the northwest side of the narthex, the narthex itself, and
in the aisles, and mosaic pavements in the narthex and
nave.[877]

With the absence of precise architectural and archaeological data, it is very difficult to date the building.
Although there are frequent references to fourth and some
fifth century coins, the latest belonging to Theodosius II
(408-450),[878] and to other portable finds, their stratigraphic provenance is not noted. It is possible, however, to
place the pavements within a secure chronological framework.
A comparison with the dated mosaics at Demetrias (130-138)
reveals such close stylistic similarities in regard to design
and color that they must belong to the same period.[879] The
dearth of sixth century coins suggests that the church was
destroyed in the fifth century during either the Hunnic (447)
or Gothic (480's) raids and that sometime after the cessation
of hostilities its successor, Basilica Beta (180-183) was

---

[877]Praktika, 1929, p. 72; Actes, p. 252; Deltion, 19,
p. 384; Deltion, 20, pp. 477-478. The paving in the other
sectors is not noted.

[878]Praktika, 1928, p. 87; Praktika, 1929, pp. 17, 73;
G. Soteriades, Praktika, 1930, p. 50; Actes, p. 252; St.
Pelekanides, Deltion, 21 (1966), B3: Chronika, p. 376. The
location of the coin of Theodosius II was never specified
(cf. Actes, p. 252 and Sodini, Catalogue, p. 734).

[879]G. Soteriades attributes the pavements to a very
early period. Because of the absence of crosses, he postu-
lates that the building was a private house which was converted into a chapel (Actes, p. 252; Praktika, 1930, p. 50).
St. Pelekanides (vide supra, p. 521, n. 873) is non-commital,
and Sodini tentatively assigns them to the first half of the
fifth century (Catalogue, p. 734).

erected. Since the basilicas differ so much in regard to the
quality of their decoration, one wonders if the results of
these raids had not permanently effected the economy of the
city. No other significant buildings, secular or ecclesiastical, have been found in the city.

Bibliography. G. Soteriades, Praktika, 1928, pp. 88-90;
idem, Praktika, 1929, pp. 69-82; Soteriou, Palaiochristianikai
basilikai, p. 180; G. Soteriades, Praktika, 1930, pp. 36-71;
idem, Actes du IIIᵐᵉ congrès international d'etudes byzantines,
1930, pp. 251-252; AA, 46 (1931), p. 272; Hoddinott, Early
Byzantine Churches, p. 124; M. Paraskevaides, Balkan Studies,
3, no. 2 (1962), pp. 447-448; St. Pelekanides, Deltion, 19
(1964), B3: Chronika, p. 384; idem, Deltion, 20 (1965), B3:
Chronika, pp. 477-478; JHS, 85 (1965), Supplement, p. 21;
St. Pelekanides, Deltion, 21 (1966), B2: Chronika, p. 371;
BCH, 90 (1966), p. 864; BCH, 92 (1968), p. 881; JHS, 88
(1968), Supplement, p. 14.

Illustrations. G. Soteriades, Praktika, 1929, p. 71, fig.
3 (section of the fresco of the west wall); Soteriou,
Palaiochristianikai basilikai, p. 180, fig. 11 = our pl. 599;
St. Pelekanides, Deltion, 19 (1964), B3: Chronika, pl. 449
gamma (northwest corner of south aisle), pl. 449d (pilaster
capital); idem, Deltion, 20 (1965), B3: Chronika, pl. 596b
(frescoes of narthex).

Nos. 178-179

The mosaics decorating the narthex, I, and the nave, II,
are composed of interlocking and tangent geometric forms
(pls. 601-605). The clarity and precision with which the
two-dimensional, ornamental patterns are arranged across the
surface result from light and dark contrasts and from uncomplicated filling motifs which are carefully inserted into
each unit. The austere geometricity of the pavements is
heightened by the simple color scheme which appears to be

bichrome, with grey for the leaves of one of the borders (pl. 601) and for the background of some of the geometric units (pl. 604).[880]

On the basis of a resemblance to the mosaics in Basilica Alpha at Demetrias, especially to those in the narthex and atrium (136-137), the Dion pavements can be dated to the early part of the fifth century.[881] A panel with lozenges, Ia (pl. 601), another with an octagon inscribed with a vase and surrounded by squares, Ib (pl. 602, bottom), and the types of borders are very similar to those in the narthex (pl. 436) and the north portico (pl. 437) at Demetrias. Even the nave design at Dion (pl. 604) appears to be a variation of one in the west portico at Demetrias (pl. 440). Moreover, in both basilicas the color scheme is subdued, primarily black and white, the configurations of the designs are flat and simple, and the filling motifs are either geometric or geometricized floral ones. The Dion pavements, therefore, belong to a group of early pavements in Greece which are distinguishable by their sober, austere designs, and their aniconic filling motifs (1; 2-3; 4-5; 6-9; 21-22; 44-49; 88-92; 196).

Additional bibliography. Sodini, Catalogue, No. 54, p. 734 and n. 70; idem, Compléments, p. 584.

---

[880]The tonal difference in some of the pavements appears to result from the use of grey as well.

[881]Vide supra, p. 523, and n. 879.

178   Room I (18.10 x 4.00-5.00). Narthex; pavement laid up
      to a square pit in northwest corner. Pls. 601-603.
   No published information on dimensions and material.

Quinquepartite pavement composed of square geometric panels
set within a guilloche framework and bordered by an ivy
rinceau. The mosaics are black and white with a middle tone,
probably grey, for additional contrast.[882]

   Framing (pl. 601-602): black fillet; outer border, undulating black rinceau (one fillet) forming rigidly arranged
narrow scrolls which are filled with single grey heart-
shaped ivy leaves. The pointed tips of the black-outlined
leaves touch the margins. Opposite the east entrance, the
border is interrupted by an oriented inscription containing
two large black letters, Alpha and Omega (A,ω) on a white
ground (pl. 603); wide white band; black double fillet;
narrow white band; inner border, two-strand guilloche (probably grey, outlined in black, with a white tessera at each
loop and four at the sides of each twist); narrow white band.

   Field (pls. 601-602): five geometric panels, of which
four, a-d, are visible in the published photographs.

   Ia (pl. 601), location indeterminable:[883] originally,

---

[882]For summary descriptions, see Praktika, 1929, p. 72;
G. Soteriades, Praktika, 1930, p. 50; Actes, p. 252; Deltion,
19, p. 384, Deltion, 20, p. 478.

[883]The location of this panel is not noted in the reports
and cannot be determined from the photograph (pl. 602).

probably similar to the narthex pavement in Basilica Alpha
at Demetrias (136, pl. 436) which can be read two ways:
interlocking stars composed of four pairs of black lozenges
forming a central four-pointed white star; white tangent
octagons filled with diagonal four-pointed stars inscribed
with small grey (?) squares set on edge. The design, which
is cut along the margins, is decorated with small grey (?)
squares inscribed with single letters of which two, "A, I ,"
are illustrated. Whether these formed part of an inscription
is not noted in the reports.

Ib (pl. 602, bottom), second panel from south: octagon
surrounded by a series of alternating lozenges and squares.
Every other lozenge has been bisected along the margins.
The octagon, delineated by a black fillet, is inscribed with
a long-necked ribbed vase with spiral handles, a narrow base,
and a wide mouth which is tipped forward. The vase is
flanked by two curving black branches with leaves which issue
from its mouth. The surrounding squares[884] are filled with
simple swastikas and quatrefoils with white lanceolate leaves
which alternate with white concave-sided squares in an
a-c-b-c sequence.

Ic (pls. 602, 603, right), third panel from south: geometric carpet composed of stars of eight lozenges and squares
forming interlocking cruciform patterns which are articulated
by black double fillets. Each star pattern comprises four

[884]The motifs in the lozenges are not visible.

pairs of lozenges terminated by squares set on edge which
alternate with a large straight square placed between each
arm. The large and small squares contain various types of
flat geometric motifs and the lozenges, simple grey (?)
lozenged fillers.

Id (pls. 602, 603, left), fourth panel from south: all
that is visible is part of a medallion and a corner motif
comprising a grey (?) pelta with trailing tendrils.

Early fifth century.

Illustrations. St. Pelekanides, Deltion, 19 (1964), B3:
Chronika, pl. 449b = our pl. 601; idem, Deltion, 20 (1965),
B3: Chronika, pl. 596a (narthex from south), pl. 596gamma =
our pl. 603; JHS, 88 (1968), Supplement, p. 15, fig. 20 =
our pl. 602.

179 Room II (22.40 x ca. 9.00). Nave; pavement laid up to
      the chancel screen of the bema which was probably paved
with marble slabs.[885] Pls. 604-605.

No published information on dimensions and material.

Predominently black and white mosaic decorated with tangent
crosses, octagons, and squares which are filled with simple
geometric and floral motifs.[886]

---

[885]Vide supra, p. 522, n. 875.

[886]In a photograph of the east side of the pavement (pl.
605), there appears to be a different design. Beneath the
dirt, it is possible to discern the outlines of two juxtaposed squares. Although the description of this pavement is
shorter than that of the narthex pavement, it is noted that

Field (pl. 604): straight grid, articulated by a black
double fillet, composed of octagons which in one row alternate with equilateral crosses and in the second row with
squares. The geometric shapes are tangent to each other and
form lozenges in the interstices. Schematized floral and
geometric motifs, outlined by a black fillet, fill the
octagons and squares: grey (?) heart-shaped ivy leaves, outlined in white, with black curving stems and pointed tips;
concave-sided black and grey (?) squares; interlaced squares;
simple swastika formed by single black fillets. The crosses
are decorated with single looped interlaces (grey?) and the
lozenges contain simple grey (?) lozenged fillers. To the
east (pl. 605), the mosaic is terminated by a white band
which bifurcates and encloses the two small panels on either
side of the prothuron of the chancel screen. Their designs
are not visible.

Early fifth century.

Illustrations. St. Pelekanides, _Deltion_, 20 (1965), B3:
Chronika, pl. 597a = our pl. 605, pl. 598a = our pl. 604.

---

both show the same "technique and diversity" (_Deltion_, 20,
p. 478). Presumably, "diversity" refers to the types of
designs. It is not impossible, therefore, that, like the
narthex, the nave was also compartmentalized, a common feature
of nave pavements (see 47; 64; 88; 95).

Basilica Beta

Basilica Beta at Dion, built over the ruins of a smaller
church (178-179, pl. 599), was discovered in 1927 and partially cleared in three subsequent campaigns.[887] Between
1962 and 1965, the site was re-excavated bringing to light
most of the design of the complex and fragments of coarse
tessellated pavements in the church proper and the atrium.[888]

As far as can be determined from the meager information
in the reports and the schematic plan (pl. 606), the church
complex comprises a colonnaded atrium, Ia-c (18.70 x 16.00),
flanked to the west by a three-room baptistery unit, II
(20.80 x 33.50), and to the east by a shallow narthex, III
(ca. 18.70 x 5.20), which precedes a three-aisled basilica,

---

[887]G. Soteriades, Praktika, 1928, pp. 86-90; hereafter
cited as Praktika, 1928; idem, Praktika, 1929, pp. 72-73;
Soteriou, Palaiochristianikai basilikai, p. 180; G. Soteriades, Praktika, 1930, pp. 49-50; idem, Actes du III^em congrès
international d'études byzantines, Athens, 1930, pp. 251-252;
hereafter cited as Actes; Hoddinott, Early Byzantine Churches,
pp. 124-125.

[888]St. Pelekanides, Deltion, 19 (1964), B3: Chronika,
p. 384; hereafter cited as Deltion, 19; idem, Deltion, 20
(1965), B3: Chronika, pp. 478-479; hereafter cited as Deltion,
20; idem, Deltion, 21 (1966), B2: Chronika, pp. 371-376;
hereafter cited as Deltion, 21. The results of these excavations were never correlated with the earlier findings. Consequently, some important differences between the two published plans cannot be explained (cf. pls. 599 and 606). The
bema and nave were decorated with stone plaques (Praktika,
1928, p. 89; G. Soteriades, Praktika, 1930, p. 50), and the
baptistery unit and atrium court with white (marble) and
colored (schist, limestone) plaques, respectively (Deltion,
21, pp. 372-373). An opus sectile panel published by G.
Soteriades (Praktika, 1931, p. 50, fig. 6) is attributed to
this basilica, but its provenance is not specified.

IV-VI (18.70 x 27.25).[889] The latter is divided by colonnades resting on bases set on elevated stylobates which, at
regular intervals along the nave, are doubled forming an
alternating 1-4-1 columnar sequence.[890] The nave is terminated by a semi-circular apse which is supported by three
external buttresses and inscribed with a synthronon.[891] The
atrium contains a court with a fountain and porticoes on the
north, a, west, b, and south, c, sides which are separated
from the court by arcuated colonnades resting on stylobates.[892] To the west of the atrium lies a large baptistery
unit which communicates with the porticoes through doors in
the east walls of the north and south rooms.[893] Ostensibly,

---

[889]The measurements are derived from Soteriou's plan (our
pl. 599) and from one report (Deltion, 21, pp. 371-376).

[890]On the disposition of the columns, cf. pls. 599 and
606.

[891]The synthronon is absent from a recent plan (pl. 606),
but it is described in one report (Praktika, 1928, pp. 87, 89)
and inserted in an early plan (pl. 599) which, however, omits
the buttresses.

[892]St. Pelekanides offers inconclusive evidence to support his argument that the south portico was closed off and
served as a diakonikon or skevophylakion. Besides creating
problems of communication between the east and west sectors,
no trace was found of a transverse wall in the south portico.
The dividing wall in one of the plans (pl. 606) belongs to a
later period and rests on the tessellated pavement (see St.
Pelekanides, Deltion, 20, p. 479). In an earlier report, he
identifies two rooms flanking the east side of the north and
south aisles as a prothesis and diakonikon (omitted from his
plan, our pl. 606; the north one is included in Soteriou's
plan, our pl. 599). Since they communicate with the bema and
aisles (not indicated in pl. 599), this would appear to be a
more plausible solution (Deltion, 19, p. 384).

[893]This is the only preserved example on the Greek mainland of a baptistery located on the opposite end of the longitudinal axis of the church proper. For additional comments,

these rooms offer the only means of entry into the baptistery proper.

Although no datable archaeological finds were unearthed or reported, a _terminus post quem_ of the second half of the fifth century is provided by the date of the destruction of Basilica Alpha during this period.[894]

Bibliography. G. Soteriades, _Praktika_, 1928, pp. 86-90; AA, 43 (1928), p. 602; G. Soteriades, _Praktika_, 1929, pp. 72-73; Soteriou, _Palaiochristianikai basilikai_, p. 180; G. Soteriades, _Praktika_, 1930, pp. 49-50; idem, _Actes du III^em congrès international d'études byzantines_, 1930, pp. 251-252; AA, 45 (1930), p. 126; G. Soteriades, _Praktika_, 1931, pp. 43-55; AA, 46 (1931), p. 272; AA, 48 (1933), p. 242; Hoddinott, _Early Byzantine Churches_, pp. 124-125; M. Paraskevaides, _Balkan Studies_, 3 no. 2 (1962), pp. 447-448; St. Pelekanides, _Deltion_, 19 (1964), B3: _Chronika_, p. 384; idem, _Deltion_, 20 (1965), B3: _Chronika_, pp. 478-479; idem, _Deltion_, 21 (1966), B2: _Chronika_, pp. 371-372; JHS, 85 (1965), _Supplement_, p. 21; BCH, 90 (1966), p. 864; BCH, 92 (1968), p. 881; JHS, 88 (1968), _Supplement_, p. 14.

Illustrations. G. Soteriades, _Praktika_, 1929, p. 71, fig. 3 (column base of south aisle, upper left); Soteriou, _Palaiochristianikai basilikai_, p. 180, fig. 11 = our pl. 599;

see _Deltion_, 21, p. 376; A. Khatchatrian, _Les baptistères paléochrétiennes_, Paris, 1962, pp. 19-25, figs. 150-193, especially, p. 19, fig. 156, showing a similar arrangement in a church complex at Argala, Lesbos, dated to the end of the fifth or the beginning of the sixth century. Although not discussed by St. Pelekanides, (vide supra, p. 530, n. 888), both G. Soteriades (_Actes_, p. 2) and Soteriou (_Palaiochristianikai basilikai_, p. 180) refer to a building on the south of the basilica (pl. 599). Soteriou describes it as being joined to the church and represents it by a textured line which differs from the solid line used for the design of the church proper. He also indicates that its north wall was cut off by the south wall of the basilica. Although he does not discuss its chronology, it appears that it belongs to an earlier period and was incorporated into the plan of the basilica. Indeed, G. Soteriades ascribes the building to Basilica Alpha (178-179), but does not note its relationship to Beta (ibid.).

[894]Vide supra, p. 523 and nn. 878-879.

St. Pelekanides, <u>Deltion</u>, 19 (1964), B3: <u>Chronika</u>, pl. 449a
(north facade of apse); idem, <u>Deltion</u>, 21 (1966), B2: <u>Chron-
ika</u>, p. 372, plan 1 = our pl. 606, p. 374, plan 3 (plan and
section of baptismal font), pl. 395a (atrium and baptistery,
from northeast), pl. 395b (atrium and south portico), pl.
396b (Ionic capital from south portico), pl. 396c (atrium,
from east), pl. 397c (baptistery, octagonal font).

Nos. 180-183

Traces of tessellated pavements (pls. 607-610) were
found in the south portico of the atrium, Ic, the narthex,
III, the north aisle, V, and in the annex on the northeast
side of the bema, VII.[895] Of these mosaics, two have decorative designs: south portico; north aisle. The others are
monochrome (narthex) or polychrome (northeast annex) and,
presumably, plain.[896]

An overall crudity of design and technique is evident
which contrasts sharply with the wall and floor decoration of
the earlier basilica, Alpha (178-179). The style and technique of the pavements substantiate the attribution of the
building to a period no earlier than the second half of the
fifth century. It is not until the turn of the fifth century
that this type of pavement composed of large, irregularly-cut
tesserae and simple flat geometric designs makes its appearance at Nea Anchialos and Longos (102-104, pls. 357-361;

---

[895]Sodini (<u>Catalogue</u>, p. 735) omits the pavements in the
narthex and the northeast annex. The latter room is only
shown on one plan (pl. 599).

[896]<u>Deltion</u>, 19, p. 384; <u>Deltion</u>, 20, p. 478.

197-202, pls. 633, 642). In these basilicas, however, the pavements are used either as repairs (Anchialos) or as late replacements (Longos), not as original floors which obtains at Dion. They are obviously a second-rate type of paving and may well represent an alternative to the more costly pavements with small tesserae, large stone slabs, or smaller slabs in opus sectile. In fact, the technique and form of the Dion mosaics closely resemble sectile pavements which are also defined by wide or narrow flat bands and simple rectilinear designs. This type of simulated opus sectile pavement has not, to my knowledge, been heretofore recognized (see also, 193, pls. 626-627; possibly, 210, pl. 647). It is possible, therefore, that earlier examples were discovered during the course of other excavations and not properly recorded. Their position in the development of tessellated pavings will be the subject of a study in the immediate future.

Additional bibliography. Sodini, Catalogue, No. 55, pp. 734-735.

Illustrations. Soteriou, Palaiochristianikai basilikai, p. 180, fig. 11 = our pl. 599; St. Pelekanides, Deltion, 21 (1966), B2: Chronika, p. 372, plan 1 = our pl. 606.

180   Room I (ca. 4.50 x 16.00). Atrium, south portico, c:

divided by later north-south wall which rests directly on the pavement. Pl. 607.

Fragment: 3.40 x ca. 6.90. Framing: ca. 0.50. East panel: 2.40 x 3.20. Second panel: ca. 2.45 x 2.75 max.[897]

---

[897]The measurements are taken from the drawing (pl. 607).

Irregularly-cut stone tesserae (0.015-0.025 long) set 5-7mm apart.

Originally, probably a series of juxtaposed panels, of which two are preserved on the east side, decorated with rectilinear designs and framed by wide plain bands.[898]

Framing: wide white band.

Field (pl. 607): two panels framed by single black bands.

East panel: black truncated lozenge, on a dark red ground, inscribed with an equilateral cross.

Second panel: white lozenge framed by a black strip and inscribed with a dark red square. Projecting from the center of each side of the square is a small dark red oval.

Around 500.

Illustrations. St. Pelekanides, Deltion, 21 (1966), B2: Chronika, p. 373, drawing 2 = our pl. 607, pl. 395b (south portico, looking west), pl. 395c (south portico, east panel).

181   Room II (ca. 18.70 x 5.20).   Narthex.

No published information on dimensions and material.

---

[898]St. Pelekanides suggests that there were only two panels (Deltion, 21, p. 371). This is hardly likely since the second panel which continues under the later wall would have been at least 11.30 meters long. It is probable that the floor was compartmentalized like those at Nea Anchialos (pl. 357) and at Longos (pls. 633, 642). The white circle between the narthex wall and the east panel is not discussed.

Fragment of a crude undecorated mosaic.[899]

Around 500; presumably contemporaneous with the other
mosaics (180, 182-183).

182   Room V (27.25; width indeterminate).   North aisle.
      Pls. 608-611.
   Fragment: 2.75 x 6.20.[900]   Material identical to that in
the south portico (180).

Originally, a series of rectangular compartments bordered by
triangles and set within a decorative framework.[901]
   Framing (pls. 608, 610): outer border, dark red and white
elongated triangles;[902] white band; narrow dark grey band;
inner border, except to west, two rows of red semi-circles
forming between them white concave-sided squares (pl. 610).
The semi-circles are inscribed with semi-circular or sometimes triangular motifs formed by white/dark red/white
fillets which enclose small truncated crosslets.   Each square
is also decorated with a small crosslet, but one which is
inscribed in a light grey circle.   At the northeast and southeast corners (pl. 609), these borders are terminated by black

---

[899]Deltion, 20, p. 478; Deltion, 21, p. 376.

[900]The measurements are taken from the drawing (pl. 609).

[901]See Deltion, 21, p. 376, where the pavement is
incorrectly assigned to the south aisle.

[902]The triangles are omitted from the drawing (pl. 609).

and white segmented squares; inner border to east, row of
irregular dark red, white, dark green zig zags.

Field: destroyed. In a published drawing (pl. 609),
there are two panels framed by a dark grey fillet.

East panel: large rectangle sub-divided into four rectangles and crossed by two diagonal lines. The chiastic
color scheme comprises dark red/dark grey angle pieces and
black and white ones.

Second panel: straight grid forming small squares (ca.
0.35). Generally, the chromatic sequence is arranged in rows
of red/black; dark grey/white; red/dark grey; white/black;
red/black.

Around 500.

Illustrations. St. Pelekanides, Deltion, 20 (1965), B3:
Chronika, p. 375, drawing 4 = our pl. 609, pl. 598b = our
pl. 608.

183 Room (no dimensions published). Northeast annex.[903]
No published information on dimensions and material.

Fragment of a crude undecorated mosaic.[904]

Around 500; presumably contemporaneous with the other
mosaics.

---

[903]Vide supra, p. 533, n. 895.

[904]Deltion, 21, p. 376.

ZIAKA

Mosaic Pavement

In the village of Ziaka, near Grevena, a mosaic floor
belonging to the Early Christian period was discovered by
chance in 1964. No systematic excavation of the site was
undertaken and the mosaic is covered.[905]

Bibliography. Ph. Petsas, Deltion, 20 (1965), B3:
Chronika, p. 438.

No. 184

184 Mosaic pavement (no dimensions reported).

No published information on dimensions and material.

Brief mention of an Early Christian mosaic pavement.

HAGHIA PARASKEVE

Basilica

In the town of Haghia Paraskeve, near Kozani, a section
of a mosaic pavement attributed to the south aisle of a
Christian basilica was brought to light. The pavement was

---

[905]At the time of its discovery, the pavement was exam-
ined by the Epimelitria of Byzantine Antiquities for Western
Macedonia, Mrs. Mavropoulou-Tsioumi, who confirmed the
Christian attribution.

covered with sand until a systematic excavation could be undertaken.

Because of the limited scope of the excavation, the plan and chronology of the building were not determined. On the basis of the style and iconography of the mosaic, however, a sixth century date is probable.

Bibliography. M. Michaelides, Deltion, 20 (1965), B3: Chronika, p. 475.

Illustration. M. Michaelides, Deltion, 20 (1965), B3: Chronika, pl. 590a-b (capitals from site).

No. 185

The south aisle contains traces of a polychrome geo-metric pavement with figural and ornamental inset panels. On the basis of the flat, two-dimensional and linear style of the animals (pl. 611), the pavement can be attributed to the sixth century. Iconographically, the rigid, heraldic pose of the deer and the equally rigid flora accompanying it are reminiscent of scenes at Hermione (60, pl. 165; 62, pl. 171), Longos (197, pls. 638-640), Stobi (pl. 641), and Amphipolis Alpha (213, pl. 667) which belong to the first half of the sixth century.

Additional bibliography. Sodini, Catalogue, No. 49, p. 731.

185 Room I (no dimensions published). South aisle. Pls. 611-612.

No published information on dimensions and material.

Partially excavated polychrome pavement composed of a rectilinear design with figural and ornamental insets.

Field: one part of the pavement (pl. 611) contains a
straight grid composed of octagons which in one row alternate with crosses and in the second row with squares. The
geometric units are tangent to each other and form lozenges
in the interstices (for a simplified version, see 179, pl.
604). Among the ornamental motifs in the octagons, there are
a rosette of five lanceolate leaves, an interlace forming an
isosceles cross, and a lozenge inscribed with a circle marked
by four small ovals on its cardinal axes. These inanimate
forms are accompanied by a large dark bird on a white ground
and a light deer on a dark ground which face in different
directions. The crosses appear to be decorated with a
single row of dark triangles placed base-to-tip on a light
ground.[906] Another part of the pavement is decorated with an
imbrication pattern (pl. 612) composed of polychrome scales
outlined by dark/light/light single fillets. This section
of the pavement is flanked by panels with indistinguishable
patterns.

Sixth century; probably first half of the century.

Illustrations. M. Michaelides, Deltion, 20 (1965), B3:
Chronika, pl. 589a = our pl. 61, pl. 589b = our pl. 612.

---

[906]The cross on the right side of pl. 611 appears to
contain a two-strand interlace.

VOSKOCHORI

Basilica

The basilica, located in the village of Voskochori near
Kozani; was discovered by chance in 1935. During one campaign the following year, the entire structure was cleared
(pl. 613) and mosaics were discovered in the narthex, I,
nave, II, and bema, III.[907] At the present time, the church
lies in the middle of a field and no trace of its foundations
is visible nor of the mosaic pavements which were covered
with sand after the excavation.

Preceded by a shallow narthex, I (10.60 x 2.50), the
church proper (10.60 x ca. 22.50, with apse) consists of a
nave, II, separated from single flanking aisles, IV-V, by
colonnades resting on bases and terminated by a bema, III,
with a semi-circular apse and a stepped synthronon which
reaches a height of one meter.[908] A chancel screen projects
from two lateral piers abutting the shoulders of the apse
and extends to the end of the third intercolumniation from
the east. Entrance to the bema is through a prothuron in the

---

[907]A. Xyngopoulos, Makedonika, I (1940), pp. 8-23;
hereafter cited as Xyngopoulos.

[908]Xyngopoulos, pp. 10-13, especially, p. 13; cf. p. 12,
fig. 3 (reconstruction of the synthronon and screen) and our
plan (pl. 613) which show some differences. The evidence for
his reconstruction is supplied by the preserved bottom step
and by similar tiered apses at Nea Anchialos (see G. A.
Soteriou, "Christianikai Thēvai," ArchEph, 1929, pl. B opposite p. 20 = our pl. 356; p. 120, fig. 164.

middle of the west side of the screen.[909] Traces of other
liturgical furnishings, altar and ambon, are not noted in the
report. Access to the narthex is through an off-axis door on
the west side and two doors on the north and south sides.
Thus, unlike most churches, an uninterrupted view of the
church proper is not possible until one approaches the three
doors leading from the narthex into the nave and side aisles.

Although preserved tessellated pavements were found in
three sectors of the church, severe damage caused by fire has
erased the colors and the designs in the narthex and in the
west half of the nave.[910] In the east half and in the bema
the floors are in good condition. Of the two mosaic inscriptions in the church (A and B on plan, pl. 613), the one in
front of the bema cites the names of two donors, Philippos
and Dometia.[911] Except, possibly, for the pavement in the
nave,[912] the mosaics reflect and accentuate the architectural

---

[909]The lateral piers contained no evidence of seats or
benches. Unlike many similar screens (88; 102; 105; 116), it
was a solid brick construction, not stone, which was stuccoed
and inscribed with schematic circles and crosses (Xyngopoulos,
pp. 12-13). The form of the prothuron is comparable to the
one at Tomba (Soteriou, Palaiochristianikai basilikai, p. 23,
fig. 9) and possibly to the one in Basilica Alpha at Dion
(vide supra, p. 522, n. 875, and pl. 606).

[910]Xyngopoulos, pp. 14-15. The aisles were paved with
cement.

[911]Ibid., pp. 17-20.

[912]By means of broken lines in the plan (pl. 613), the
tessellated pavements are represented as being aligned with
the edges of the chancel screen, not with the flanking colonnades. Whether the cement paving of the aisles continued
across the colonnades into the aisles, or some other paving
material was inserted between the colonnade and the mosaics
is problematic.

and internal divisions of their respective areas. Thus, a tessellated threshold panel with an inscription, A, serves as a transition between the mosaic pavement in the narthex and that in the nave. A second inscription, B, extending the width of the prothuron, bridges the space between the end of the nave mosaic proper and the bema, whose entry way contains its own threshold panel. With an imbrication pattern composed of scales fanning eastward, this panel leads to the major composition in the clergy-altar site.

Since no datable archaeological or sculptural finds were unearthed, and the photographs and descriptions of the mosaics are poor, it is difficult to establish the chronology of the church with any degree of certitude. A terminus post quem of the middle of the fifth century is indicated by the style of the stepped synthronon and the chancel screen,[913] and supported by the general style of the mosaics.[914]

Bibliography. A. Xyngopoulos, Makedonika, 1 (1940), pp. 8-23; Hoddinott, Early Byzantine Churches, pp. 183-184; Orlandos, Xylostegos basilikē, pp. 495, passim; idem, Actes du Vᵉ congrès international d'archéologie chrétienne, Aix-en-Provence, 1954 (1957), p. 109.

Illustrations. A. Xyngopoulos, Makedonika, 1 (1940), p. 9, fig. 1 = our pl. 613, p. 11, fig. 2 (chancel screen: actual state), p. 12, fig. 3 (chancel screen: reconstruction).

---

[913] I am less cautious than others in assigning a terminus for these two types of liturgical furnishings (cf. Soteriou, Palaiochristianikai basilikai, pp. 222-228, and Orlandos, Xylostegos basilikē, pp. 489-502, 509-512, 525-535, who place them within a general fifth century framework).

[914] Vide infra, p. 544

Nos. 186-188

Polychrome geometric mosaics with a few bird insets and
two inscriptions pave the narthex, nave, and bema, and cement
the side aisles. Since the pavements were severely damaged
by fire, only the general program of the nave and bema can,
for the most part, be reconstituted from the published
material.[915] The nave contains insets, some with birds, and
two tessellated inscriptions on its east and west sides, and
the bema has a panel with scales to the west and a small grid,
also with birds, to the east. In a description of the
mosaics, attention is drawn to the polychromy of the mosaics
and the "naturalism" of the birds.[916] In my judgment, the
birds (pls. 614-616) appear to be quite schematic and two-
dimensional, features which argue for a date in the early
part of the sixth century, or later.[917]

Additional bibliography. Hoddinott, Early Byzantine
Churches, p. 184; Sodini, Catalogue, No. 61, pp. 737, 739.

Illustration. A. Xyngopoulos, Makedonika, 1 (1940), p. 9,
fig. 1 = our pl. 613.

186   Room I (10.60 x 2.50). Narthex.

No published information on dimensions and material.

---

[915]The color and design in the narthex were erased by
fire.

[916]Xyngopoulos, p. 5 and n. 1.

[917]This is the conclusion drawn by A. Xyngopoulos (pp.
20-22) but his comparisons with other mosaics are, for the
most part, erroneous and misleading (see pp. 16-17, 20-22).

Brief mention of a mosaic pavement with its colors and design erased by fire.[918]

Probably contemporary with the other mosaics and, therefore, early sixth century.

187 Room II (10.60 x 19.50). Nave; pavement laid up to
     chancel screen. Pls. 614-615.
   Inscription A: overall, 1.87 x 0.70. Inscription B:
overall, 1.50 x 0.49. No other published information on
dimensions and material.

Polychrome geometric pavement with geometric and organic
filling motifs composed of two compartments, a-b. In the
west threshold and near the entrance to the bema are two
inscriptions.
   IIa, west compartment: three panels bordered by wave
crests.
   Framing: wave crests.
   Field.
   West panel: colors and design erased by fire.
   Central panel (pl. 614): small straight grid composed of a
two-strand guilloche (with a light tessera at each loop) on a
dark ground forming four squares which are alternately filled
with birds (partridges)[919] and rosettes with wide, curled

---

[918]Xyngopoulos, p. 14   [919]Ibid., p. 16.

leaves.

East panel (pl. 615): guilloche circle inscribed with a
bird and set on a field of intersecting circles forming
concave-sided squares set on edge.

West threshold panel: <u>tabula ansata</u> containing a four-line
black inscription separated by single fillets: "ΥΠΕΡΕΥΧΗC
ΕΠ/ΟΙΗCΑΝωΝ/ΟΙΔΕΝΟΘΕΟ/CΤΑΟΝΟΜΑΤΑ ."[920]

IIb, east compartment: composed of a narrow strip extending the width of the chancel screen and two small panels
flanking the prothuron.

Strip: decorated with a <u>tabula ansata</u> set on a field of
intersecting circles. A four-line white inscription records
the name of the two donors of the pavement, Philippos and
Dometia: "ΦΙΛΙΠΠΟCΚΑΙ/ΔΟΜΕΤΙΑΥΠ/ΕΡΕΥΧΗCΕΠΟΙ/ΗCΑΝ
ΜΝΗCΘΗΤΙ."[921]

Small panels: decorated with checkerboard patterns.[922]

Early sixth century.

---

[920]The color of the ground was erased by fire
(Xyngopoulos, p. 17, p. 18, fig. 8 (reproduction of inscription). For the following emendation, see ibid.: "ΥΠΕΡΕΥΧΗC
ΕΠ/ΟΙCΑΝ ωΝ/ ΟΙΔΕΝ Ο ΘΕΟ/C ΤΑ ΟΝΟΜΑΤΑ ." For a discussion
of this inscription and a similar one in a church at Ochrid,
see G. Babić, "North Chapel of the Quatrefoil Church at
Ochrid and its Mosaic Floor," <u>Recueil des travaux de
l'institut d'études byzantines</u>, 12 (1970), pp. 266-269.

[921]The color of the ground changes from red to blue in
the center (Xyngopoulos, pp. 17-18, p. 19, fig. 9 [inscrip-
tion]). For the following emendation, see ibid.: "ΦΙΛΙΠΠΟC
ΚΑΥ/ΔΟΜΕΤΙΑ ΥΠ/ΕΡ ΕΥΧΗC ΕΠΟΙ/ΗCΑΝ ΜΝΗCΘΗΤΙ."

[922]For similarly disposed panels, see 179, pl. 605.

188   Room III (ca. 3.50 x 5.80). Bema; pavement laid up to
      the synthronon to east and chancel screen to west.
Pls. 616-617.

No published information on dimensions and material.

Geometric pavement with two figural insets and a threshold
panel to west.

Framing: small circles enclosing circles and lozenges.

Field (pl. 616): two juxtaposed rectangular panels, outlined by a dark double fillet, each inscribed with a pair of
birds placed back-to-back.[923]

West threshold (pl. 617): imbrication pattern composed of
scales with light/dark/light outlines.

Color. Black, white, red, yellow, two shades of blue, and
three shades of green.[924]

Early sixth century.

AKRINI

Trefoil Church

At Akrini, thirty kilometers northwest of Kozani, a small

---

[923]The exact location and orientation of the panels cannot be determined. Presumably, they were situated in front
of the altar site.

[924]Xyngopoulos, p. 16.

trefoil church (overall, 12.15 x 12.40)[925] was excavated in 1959 which contained rich tessellated carpets in the narthex and nave. At the present time, the pavements are covered and the site overgrown.

Since the sole excavation report provides meager descriptive and photographic data, it is only possible to summarize the plan of this very important building (pl. 618). Preceded by a narrow narthex, I, with entrances on the short north and south sides only,[926] the church proper, II, comprises a triconch plan which is delineated by very thick walls. Unlike the semi-circular north and south conches, the east one has a curious, distorted shape. The reason for this irregularity is problematic at the present time, but it is clear that the east conch served as the bema of the church since a square enkainion was discovered at its chord.[927] No other liturgical furnishings are noted in the report nor the types of internal divisions between the north and south conches and the rectangular nave.

Pavements in opus tessellatum and opus sectile decorate the narthex, nave, and conches and clearly reflect and accentuate the formal arrangement and internal divisions of these areas. Surrounded by decorative borders or simple

---

[925]Only this dimension is published.

[926]It is curious that no entrance was found on the west side of the narthex.

[927]St. Pelekanides, Deltion, 16 (1960), B: Chronika, pp. 227-228; hereafter cited as Deltion, 16.

bands, each pavement extends the length and width of its respective area, but never exceeds the limits imposed by the walls, doors and thresholds. The most prominent liturgical area of the church, the east conch, is decorated with a panel in opus sectile, as are its north and south counterparts, while the remaining sectors are carpeted with polychrome mosaics.

On the basis of the style and technique of the mosaic paving, the excavator assigned the church to the second half of the fourth century and to the fifth century.[928] It will be shown below that the mosaics belong to a period no earlier than the second half of the fifth century.

Bibliography. St. Pelekanides, Deltion, 16 (1960), B: Chronika, pp. 227-228; BCH, 84 (1960), p. 767.

Illustration. St. Pelekanides, Deltion, 16 (1960), B: Chronika, plan on p. 227 = our pl. 618.

Nos. 189-190

Polychrome mosaic pavements with primarily large scale figural compositions and complex borders decorate the narthex and nave. Iconographically, the two panels in the narthex and nave (pl. 620)[929] containing confronting stags on either side of a ribbed fountain with water flowing from a

[928]For the first date, see BCH, 84 (1960), p. 767; for the second, Deltion, 16, p. 228.

[929]The nave mosaic is barely visible in the photograph.

decorative spout resemble those at Longos (197, pls. 638-640), Stobi (pl. 641), and Amphipolis (213, pl. 667) which are datable to the first half of the sixth century.[930] The panels at Akrini, however, appear to predate the others because the flora and fauna are less rigid and more active, less linear and more three-dimensional. The plethora of flora and fauna in the pavements at Akrini reflects a trend in the development of Greek pavements which can be assigned to the second half of the fifth century. In this period, the pavements are remarkable for their exuberant and rich figural insets and large scale compositions, complex designs, wide borders, which reduce the paths of the field designs, and for a figure style which still retains a degree of plasticity and three-dimensionality. The Akrini pavements represent the first preserved stage in the stylistic evolution of this scene with the pavements at Longos and Amphipolis occupying a middle point, and the mosaic at Hermione (67, pls. 190, 195, 195-196) a final one. In the last stage, the flora, fauna,

---

[930]Not only are there iconographic similarities, but their borders are identical. Each pavement has a complex chain pattern (at Akrini, it is barely visible at the top of the photograph) which does not predate the second half of the fifth century (see also Nikopolis Delta, 164, pls. 575, 578-579). The narthex pavement at Akrini and the nave panel at Longos also share a common stylized acanthus rinceau. I would like to thank the excavator, Professor Stelianos Pele-kanides for permitting me to view, albeit for a brief time, some of the unpublished photographs in his possession. The descriptions of the north and south panels in the narthex (Ia, c) and the panels in the nave are based on his photographs. The published descriptions are totally inadequate (see Deltion, 16, p. 228).

and vase become a means of filling the scene with attenuated
patterns and silhouettes of great linearity and variety,
creating thereby a kind of intricate and delicate polychromatic network across the surface.

Additional bibliography. Sodini, Catalogue, No. 49,
p. 731, 747-748.

Illustration. St. Pelekanides, Deltion, 16 (1960), B:
Chronika, plan on p. 227 = our pl. 618.

189   Room I (no dimensions published). Narthex. Pls.
      619-620.

No published information on dimensions and material.

Three large scenes, oriented westward, bordered by an
acanthus rinceau. The three thresholds leading into the
church proper are decorated with mosaic panels of which the
central one contains twelve birds with nimbi.

Framing: outer border to north only (pl. 619, bottom):
wave crests, inner border, wide undulating acanthus rinceau
with cornucopian ocreae enclosing fruit and spiral tendrils.
At the mouth of each ocrea are two spiral tendrils or three
dark flat leaves (for other acanthus rinceaux, see 55; 115-
197); dark fillet; light triple fillet.

Ia, north panel (pl. 619).

Framing: border, two-strand guilloche (with a white tessera at each loop) on a dark ground; light triple fillet.

Field, framed by a dark double fillet: in an unpublished

photograph,[931] there is a landscape filled with standing
figures of pecking and preening land birds and water fowl
disposed at various levels across the surface. They are
surrounded by stylized flora comprising tall stalks, possibly
of wheat, short tufts of grass,[932] and three trees. The
trees, which rest on the dark frame at the bottom of the
scene, create a measure of compositional stability by being
regularly spaced across the surface.

Ib, central panel (pl. 620), framed by a dark fillet.

Field: two registers with confronting animals and birds
amid flora identical to those in the north and south panels
(Ia, Ic). The lower register is filled with a stag and a doe
flanking a tall ribbed fountain filled with water flowing
from a decorative pine cone spout.[933] In front of each
animal, near the delicate, narrow base of the fountain, are
two land birds which also face each other. The upper register contains four small ducks disposed in groups of two each
above the deer.

Ic, south panel.

Framing: identical to that in the north panel (Ia, pl.
619).

Field, framed by a dark fillet: in an unpublished photo-

---

[931]The north side of this panel is visible in one published photograph (pl. 619); vide supra, p. 550, n. 930.

[932]The same type of flora is depicted in the two other
panels (pl. 620).

[933]For a similar device, see Longos and Amphipolis (pls.
639, 667).

graph,[934] there is a landscape comprising land birds and
water fowl amid flora identical to those in the two preceding
panels. Unlike the passive and idyllic themes of the first
two panels, this one also depicts a hunt in which a domesticated dog with a dark color chases a rabbit.

North and south threshold panels: in the plan (pl.
618), there are two large rectangles inscribed with a quincunxial pattern composed of a central lozenge[935] and corner
medallions (for a similar pattern in opus sectile, see north
and south conches).

Id, central threshold (pls. 620-621).

Framing: border, row of alternating light tangent diamonds
and circles on a dark ground; light double fillet.

Field (pl. 621), framed by a dark double fillet: twelve
birds with haloes, oriented westward, disposed in two rows
of two confronting groups each which are separated by single
flat flowers with dark-tipped light flowers.[936] Unlike the
fauna in the narthex, the birds are totally flat and two-
dimensional with sharply defined contours.

Second half of the fifth century.

Illustrations. St. Pelekanides, Deltion, 16 (1960), B:

---

[934]Vide supra, p. 550, n. 930.

[935]The type of filling motifs is not readily identifiable
in the drawings.

[936]St. Pelekanides suggests that they symbolize the
twelve apostles (Deltion, 16, p. 228).

Chronika, plan on p. 227 = our pl. 618; idem, Deltion, 16
(1960), Plates, pl. 200b = our pl. 619, pl. 201a = our pl.
621; BCH, 84 (1960), p. 768, fig. 9 = our pl. 620.

190   Room II (no dimensions published). Nave; pavement laid

up to the opus sectile panel on east.[937] Pl. 620.

No published information on dimensions and material.

In published and unpublished photographs (pl. 620),[938] there
are one large and two small figural panels, oriented westward, bordered by two complex interlaces.

IIa, west panel.

Framing: narrow light band; dark fillet; outer border,
chain forming circles which contain small crosses or stepped
squares with central crosses (for similar borders, see 164,
pls. 575, 578-579; 197, pl. 635); wide white band; inner
border, narrow braid, on a dark ground; narrow white band.

Field, framed by a dark double fillet: two confronting
stags walk toward a tall ribbed fountain filled with water
flowing from a decorative spout (for a similar scene in the
narthex, see pl. 620). These heraldic animals are followed
by two large peacocks with ocellate tail coverts and sinuous
elongated necks which look back at small birds perching precariously on the spreading branches of two tall palm trees in

[937]The type of paving or division between the nave and
the north and south conches is not recorded.

[938]In our photograph (pl. 620), only the west side of
the large panel is visible (vide supra, p. 550, n. 930).

the corners of the scene. Two small long-legged birds pecking at the base of the fountain complete the scene. The pavement continues toward the east and forms triangular soffits
for the opus sectile panel in the bema.

Framing: narrow black/white bands; border, two-strand
interlace; narrow black/white bands.

Field: identical compositions, each filled with two
opposing small birds which turn their heads to look at a
basket of fruit between them.

Second half of the fifth century.

Illustration. BCH, 84 (1960), p. 768, fig. 9 = our pl.
620.

ARGOS ORESTIKON

Mosaic Fragment

Outside the village of Argos Orestikon, near the city of
Kastoria, a fragment of a tessellated pavement was discovered
by chance in 1959. It was covered with plastic and sand
until a systematic excavation could be undertaken. Except
for one published photograph (pl. 622), no information is
available.[939]

Bibliography. St. Pelekanides, Deltion, 16 (1960), B:
Chronika, p. 229.

---

[939]St. Pelekanides, Deltion, 16 (1960), B: Chronika, p.
229. The function of the building cannot be determined. Cf.
Sodini, Catalogue, p. 731, n. 65, who suggests a secular
function with no corroborative evidence.

191 Mosaic fragment (no dimensions published). Pl. 622.

No published information on dimensions and material.

Mosaic fragment containing two superimposed birds and
stylized bushes.

Framing: border, probably a complex chain forming circles
(for similar borders, see 164, pls. 575, 578-579; 190; pl.
620; 197, pl. 635); dark fillet, light triple fillet.

Field (pl. 622), framed by a dark fillet: a duck and a
partridge stand in superimposed registers amid scattered
stylized bushes composed of three to four narrow branches.

Second half of the fifth century; probably related to the
pavements at Akrini (189, pls. 619-620).[940]

Additional bibliography. Sodini, Catalogue, p. 731, n. 65.

Illustration. St. Pelekanides, Deltion, 16 (1960), Plates,
pl. 202b = our pl. 622.

---

[940]The fragment shows close stylistic and iconographic
similarities with the pavements at Akrini. The interlace
borders at both sites are the same as are the types of plants
and birds and their disposition in superimposed registers.
Subsequent clearing of the pavement may very well reveal
that they are both products of a common workshop. Given
their geographic proximity, this would not be at all
impossible.

VEROIA

Mosaic Fragments

On property belonging to the Misyrlē-Mavridou family in
Veroia, a chance find in 1969 brought to light fragments of
three tessellated pavements.[941] They were covered with
plastic and sand until a systematic excavation of the site
could be undertaken.

Since the information on the pavements is very meager
and their architectural context was not established, their
relationship is problematic. According to the captions of
the published photographs (pls. 623, 626), each has been
assigned to an "Early Christian building" but it is not
specified if they belong to one building or to two separate
buildings on the same property. Obscuring the issue is the
presentation of two topographical plans of the same site:
one showing two tessellated pavements in close proximity to
each other (pl. 623); the other, a single fragment (pl. 626)
which apparently was in some other sector of the site. Given
these circumstances, the two groups of pavements will be presented in separate entries with the understanding that their

---

[941]Other chance finds in and around Veroia should be
noted in case systematic excavations establish their Christian provenance. Ph. Petsas, Deltion, 20 (1965), B3:
Chronika, p. 427, p. 425, plan 2, p. 426, plan 3, pls. 477a,
gamma, 478a-b (site north of Aristotle street), p. 438, pl.
497gamma (vicinity of Komanos Eordaia); idem, Deltion, 21
(1966), B2: Chronika, pp. 350-351, pl. 373a (Kouteri property, p. 351, plan 1 (Hippocratos Street).

architectural context and relationship is obscure. This, of
course, is subject to change upon the excavation of the site.

Evidently, the Early Christian attribution of the building or buildings is based on the style of the mosaics, since
no archaeological finds were unearthed or reported. This
attribution is manifestly correct with a probable date in
the second half of the fifth century.

Bibliography. A. Romiopoulou and J. Touratsoglou,
Deltion, 25 (1970), B2: Chronika, p. 381.

Illustrations. A. Romiopoulou and J. Touratsoglou,
Deltion, 25 (1970), B2: Chronika, p. 383, plan 5 = our pl.
623, p. 384, plan 6 = our pl. 626.

Nos. 192-193

The three fragments of mosaic pavements (pls. 623-627)
are decorated with primarily aniconic geometric designs which
are delineated and bordered by sharply defined, flat bands of
varying width. A limited color scheme is employed involving
combinations of black, white, ochre, and red and the filling
motifs are, for the most part, uncomplicated and two-
dimensional. The style, technique, and color of the pavements resemble those of mosaics in other parts of Macedonia
(192, pls. 607-610; 200, pl. 642) and in central Greece (103,
pls. 357-361) which have been assigned to the late fifth and
the sixth centuries. One mosaic (193, pl. 627) even has the
same kind of large, irregularly-cut tesserae which are common

features of the other pavements (193, pls. 626-627).[942]
Whether or not this establishes a chronological distance between it and the other pavements on the site is difficult to
postulate at the present time.

   Illustrations. A. Romiopoulou and J. Touratsoglou,
Deltion, 25 (1970), B2: Chronika, p. 383, plan 5 = our pl.
623, p. 384, plan 6 = our pl. 626

192 Two mosaic fragments. Pls. 623-625.

   Two fragments: to north, ca. 1.80 x 3.30; to south, ca.
5.70 x 3.00.[943] No published information on material.

Two fragments with polychrome geometric designs and part of
an inscription.

   North fragment (pl. 623, right).

   Framing to north: wide red band; narrow white band.

   Field: traces of three panels set within an undecorated
framework.

   Framework: wide ochre band.

   Field: traces of an ochre and red checkerboard pattern in
one panel. In the others, all that remain are some large and
small red triangles.[944]

---

   [942]For their probable relationship to pavements in opus
sectile, vide supra, p. 534.

   [943]The dimensions are taken from the plan (pl. 623).

   [944]The colors are indicated on the plan (pl. 623).

South fragment (pls. 623-625).

Framing: narrow red band; narrow white band which is interrupted by the first part of a two-line inscription, oriented
westward (pl. 624). It is preceded by a red ivy leaf and
contains the letters "ΑΓΑΘ[ ]/ΕΥ[ ]"; narrow red band.

Field (pls. 623, 625), framed by a white band: straight
grid composed of red bands, outlined in black, forming
squares and rectangles. The filling motifs comprise opposed
red and black peltae, red intersecting circles forming white
concave-sided squares, a black, white and red eight-pointed
lozenge star, and an oblique grid forming small squares which
are decorated with alternating red and white, and black and
white hour glass motifs. This segment of the mosaic appears
to have bordered a central design of which only some small
rectangles and squares, essentially red and white, survive.
The pavement continues toward the south and is connected by
multiple white/red/ochre bands to a panel decorated with an
oblique checkerboard pattern of red and white squares set on
a field of four juxtaposed ochre circles, with red centers,
set on a similarly colored ground.

Late fifth or sixth century.

    Illustrations. A. Romiopoulou and J. Touratsoglou,
Deltion, 25 (1970), B2: Chronika, p. 383, plan 5 = our pl.
623, pl. 318b = our pl. 625, pl. 319a = our pl. 624.

193 Mosaic fragment (4.00 x 3.10). Pls. 626-627.

No published information on dimensions and material.

Irregularly-cut tesserae.

Fragment with a grid design composed of flat black bands
forming squares and rectangles which are primarily inscribed
with ochre geometric motifs with black outlines and centers.[945]
Among the motifs are lozenges, quincunxes formed by single
circles flanked by four triangular darts, and straight or
concave-sided squares set on edge. Two small fish swim back-
to-back in the sole figural panel (pl. 627).

Late fifth or sixth century.

   Illustrations. A. Romiopoulou and J. Touratsoglou,
Deltion, 25 (1970), B2: Chronika, p. 384, plan 6 = our pl.
626, pl. 319b = our pl. 627.

BETWEEN VEROIA AND VERGINA

Mosaic Pavement

On the left bank of the Aliakmon river, somewhere between Veroia and Vergina, a chance find in 1961 brought to
light traces of an "Early Christian building" with a mosaic
pavement. The pavement was covered with plastic and sand
until a systematic excavation could be undertaken. The specific location of the site could not be determined and,
therefore, the building was not examined.

_____

   [945]The dimensions and the color notes are taken from the
plan (pl. 626).

Bibliography. St. Pelekanides, Deltion, 16 (1960),
B: Chronika, p. 225.

No. 194

194 Mosaic pavement (no dimensions published).

No published information on dimensions and material.

Brief mention of a mosaic pavement.

Early Christian.

NEOKASTRON

Basilica

In Neokastron, near Melikion and east of Veroia, an
Early Christian basilica with a mosaic pavement was found by
chance on property belonging to the Metropolitan church of
Veroia and Naoussa. No systematic excavation of the site was
undertaken and the pavement is covered.

Preceded by a narrow narthex (14.00 x 3.20), the church
proper (ca. 24.20 x 14.00) consists of a nave flanked by two
aisles. A polychrome pavement was found near the "Royal
Portal" but whether it was located on the east side of the
narthex or the west side of the nave is not noted in the very

brief report.[946]

It would appear that no datable archaeological finds were discovered because the archaeologist is silent on the chronology of the building and its pavement.

Bibliography. St. Pelekanides, Deltion, 17 (1961-62), B: Chronika, p. 257.

No. 195

195 Mosaic pavement (No dimensions published).

No published information on dimensions and material.

Polychrome mosaic pavement (dark green, white, yellow) composed of geometric motifs.[947]

Framing: border, simple bands interrupted at intervals by stepped or serrate-edged rectangles.

Field: squares inscribed in hexagons.

Early Christian.

---

[946]St. Pelekanides, Deltion, 17 (1961-62), B: Chronika, p. 257.

[947]Since no photograph accompanied the report, the description is drawn from the archaeological report (ibid.).

TSIPHLIKI

Building

In the village of Tsiphliki near Lefkadia, the west side
of a building comprising two rooms was cleared during a short
campaign in 1959.[948] Along the north side of the larger
room, I, fragments of a tessellated pavement were found.[949]
No subsequent excavation was undertaken and, at the present
time, the pavement is covered and the site overgrown.

The excavation brought to light a large, undivided room
or hall, I (13.90 x ca. 9.60),[950] and a small annex, II (6.10
x 4.60), which projected from its north side (pl. 628). Each
room contains an outside entrance but no trace was found of a
communicating door between them. In light of the size of
Room I, other entrances must have existed, perhaps in the unexcavated east sector, but it is clear from the tessellated
inscription in front of the west entrance (pl. 629)[951] that
this door represented a major ingress. Since only a small
portion of the building was cleared, its function cannot be
determined. Certain features, however, the single, off-axis

---

[948]E. G. Stikas, Praktika, 1959, pp. 85-87; hereafter
cited as Stikas; A. K. Orlandos, To Ergon, 1959, pp. 60-66;
Ph. Petsas, Makedonika, 7 (1966-67), p. 339.

[949]The type of pavement in Room II is not noted.

[950]The measurements are taken from the plan (pl. 628).

[951]Stikas, p. 85; vide infra, p. 567 and n. 955.

door on the north side of the west facade of Room I and its
undivided interior suggest a non-liturgical function.[952]

Although no datable archaeological evidence was uncovered
or reported, on the basis of the style of the mosaics, the
pavement can be attributed to the late fourth or the early
fifth century. In a later period, a bath comprising an
apsidal room (Δ , pl. 628) and a large hall with a hypocause
system (not on plan) was erected on the north side of Room II.
Whether the bath was an addition to the south building or was
built after its destruction cannot be determined from the
archaeological report.

Bibliography. E. G. Stikas, Praktika, 1959, pp. 85-87;
A. K. Orlandos, To Ergon, 1959, pp. 60-66; BCH, 84 (1960),
p. 770; JHS, 80 (1960), Supplement, p. 16; Ph. Petsas,
Makedonika, 7 (1966-67), p. 339.

Illustrations. E. G. Stikas, Praktika, 1959, p. 86, fig. 1
= our pl. 628, p. 87, fig. 2 (Early Christian plaque),
pl. 77 (general view of site), pl. 78a (Early Christian
plaque).

No. 196

A fragment of an aniconic geometric pavement (pls. 628-
632) is preserved on the north side of Room I. It is decorated with two large ornamental panels which are separated by
a wide white band. The simplicity and austerity of the
designs, their plain configurations, and the flat and

---

[952]No internal divisions are noted in the report or on
the plan (pl. 628). Moreover, it is quite clear that the two
mosaic compartments are tangent (pl. 632).

two-dimensional rendering of the filling motifs, which is
heightened by a light on dark and dark on light contrast, are
outstanding and consistent features of the decorative programs of pavements which belong to the late fourth and the
early fifth centuries (44-49; 88-92; 130-138; 178). For
stylistic and iconographic reasons, therefore, the pavement
can be assigned to an early phase in the development of Greek
pavements.

Additional bibliography. Sodini, Catalogue, No. 57, p. 735.

Illustration. E. G. Stikas, Praktika, 1959, p. 86, fig. 1
= our pl. 628.

196 Room I (13.90 x 9.60 max).[953] Hall? In front of the
northwest threshold, two narrow stone slabs were installed, destroying part of a tessellated inscription. Pls.
629-632.

No published information on dimensions and material.

Fragment of a polychrome pavement[954] decorated with two compartments, a-b, separated by a wide white band and enclosed
by different borders.

Ia, west compartment (pls. 630-631).

Framing (pl. 631): light double fillet; outer border,

---

[953]The measurements are taken from the plan (pl. 628).

[954]The color scheme is not noted, but judging from the
illustrations, it must have been quite limited. Certainly,
there was no shading or modeling.

alternating squares and beads, outlined by a single light
fillet, separated by two sets of two small light triangles or
darts placed tip-to-tip on a dark ground. In front of the
threshold, the border is interrupted by an inscription (pl.
629)[955] of which the first word "ΟΒΟΥΛΟΜΕΝΟ[C]" is pre-
served·in dark letters on a light ground; light double
fillet; inner border, single row of light triangles placed
base-to-tip on a dark ground; wide light band.

Field (pls. 630-631), framed by a dark fillet: two tangent
panels with predominently geometric filling motifs.

West panel: straight grid forming squares, each bisected
by two light and dark triangles. Set at regular intervals in
the field are small squares of which traces survive of three
along the west side (pl. 630). One is decorated with a
simple meander formed by two intersecting light double fillets set on a dark ground. A second contains traces of a
checkerboard composed of light and dark square tesserae and
the third has a quatrefoil formed of light heart-shaped ivy
leaves placed tip-to-tip on a dark ground.[956]

East panel (pls. 630-631): octagon inscribed with a

---

[955]The inscription is not placed in a "cartouche"
(Sodini, Catalogue, p. 736), a term which he uses elsewhere
to denote a tabula ansata (pp. 710, 711, 713). The inscription is placed on a light ground to distinguish it from the
dark ground of the outer border flanking it.

[956]There is no evidence in the plan that four squares
survived nor that each one contained a "labyrinth" (Stikas,
p. 85). Sodini repeats this error (Catalogue, p. 736
"meandres") but notes the quatrefoil.

medallion and surrounded by an alternating series of squares
and lozenges (for a similar design, see 137, pls. 437-438;
178, pl. 602). The preserved lozenges and squares along the
north and east sides of the octagon are inscribed with geometric and geometricized foliate motifs. The lozenges contain "eye motifs" consisting of a central medallion flanked
by single elongated beads. The filling motifs in the squares
are not identical, although the two along the west side
repeat the meander and grid patterns of the east panel (pl.
630). The other squares have a long-necked ribbed vase from
which issue two vines bearing stylized leaves, and a rosette
composed of six lanceolate leaves whose tips are united by
single lanceolate leaves. Peltae and single ivy leaves fill
the truncated interstices along the margins of the design.
All these motifs are schematic and two-dimensional and are
usually defined by plain white fillets on a dark ground. The
central medallion is bordered by a two-strand guilloche (with
a light tessera at each loop) on a dark ground, and is delineated by concentric light/dark bands. Its center is decorated with an unusual pattern composed of a square within a
square which are connected by short single bars in the center
of each of their four sides. Flanking these bars are smaller
ones which rise from the frame of the outer squares. In the
center of the smaller squares rests a simple, long-necked
vase with a narrow base facing westward.

    Ib, east compartment (pls. 628, 632).

Surround: light tesserae in rows at right angles to the north wall and to the mosaic on the west side. In the north-west corner there is a small panel decorated with a dark lozenge set on a light ground.

Framing: wide dark band; light band; border, large dark and light triangles; dark band; light band.

Field, framed by a dark triple fillet: oblique checker-board design composed of light and polychrome squares.[957]

Late fourth or early fifth century.

Illustrations. E. G. Stikas, _Praktika_, 1959, pl. 74gamma = our pl. 629, pl. 78d = our pl. 630, pl. 79b = our pl. 631, pl. 79a = our pl. 632.

LONGOS

Basilica

At Longos, on the main road leading to the foot of the cataracts of Edessa, a basilica, designated Alpha, was dis-covered by chance during the installation of a hydroelectric plant in 1962.[958] A systematic excavation was undertaken in 1964 which brought to light the main body of the church (pl. 633) and traces of two levels of floor decoration: in the

---

[957]Stikas, p. 87.

[958]At that time, the southwest side of the south aisle and the two narthexes were destroyed (M. Michaelides, _Deltion_, 23 [1968], _Meletai_, pp. 204-205; hereafter cited as _Deltion_, 23).

first phase, mosaics; in the second, mosaics, large marble
slabs, small schist and marble pieces in opus sectile. At
the present time, the pavements are covered and the church is
overgrown.

Since the information in the archaeological reports is
inadequate,[959] only a summary description of the building
will follow. Preceded by two narthexes, I-II,[960] the church
proper (14.85 x 13.20) comprises a nave flanked by two
aisles, II-V, and terminated by a bema with a raised semi-
circular apse, VI (0.85 high). The nave is separated from
the aisles by arcuated colonnades and parapets set on high
stylobates,[961] and from the bema by a low chancel screen.
This screen extends across the entire width of the nave and
is entered through a prothuron in the center of its west side.
Although the relationship between the screen and the pavements
is not clarified in the reports, the screen must have been
contemporaneous with the second decorative phase since the
marble pavements are laid up to it (pls. 633-634).[962] Moreover, the screen would have covered part of the mosaic pavement

[959]A. Drosoyianni, Deltion, 18 (1963), B2: Chronika,
pp. 251-252; hereafter cited as Deltion, 18; M. Michaelides,
Deltion, 20 (1965), B3: Chronika, pp. 475-476; Deltion, 23,
pp. 195-222.

[960]They are omitted from our plan (pl. 633), but see
Deltion, 23, p. 204, fig. 3.

[961]They are fifty-two centimeters above the mosaic level
and forty centimeters above the marble paving of the second
phase (Deltion, 23, p. 198).

[962]The opus sectile panels are also laid up to it.

beneath the marble paving because, according to the excavator, its three wide borders formed one continuous framework
for the fields in the nave and the bema.[963] This is substantiated to some degree by the evidence in a photograph which
shows that at least the middle and inner borders on the
south side of the east figural panel turned westward (pls.
634-635). Given this evidence, therefore, the present chancel screen belongs to the second phase of the building. Was
there one in the first architectural and decorative phase?
It would appear not, because it would have hidden part of
the mosaic pavement. Even if the borders had bifurcated
along the north-south axis and had formed separate frameworks
for the west side of the bema panel and the east side of the
nave panel, a part of the screen would have covered the borders near the north and south colonnades. In no church with
a chancel screen and a mosaic or stone pavement does the
screen rest directly on the pavement.[964] On the contrary,
the pavements are always laid up to it. If the nave and bema
formed one continuous architectural and decorative unit which
extended from the west wall up to the chord of the apse,
then the liturgical function of the original building is
problematic. Even the earliest churches had screens of some
kind to enclose and segregate the clergy-altar site.[965] For

---

[963]Deltion, 23, p. 217.

[964]See, for example, 49; 64; 83; 95; 130; 153; 178.

[965]Traces of the altar of the second phase were found
thirty centimeters beyond the chord of the apse (Deltion, 23,

the present, therefore, the function of the building during
the first phase is open to question and will remain so until
the later paving is removed. A liturgical function in its
second phase, however, is clearly established by the chancel
screen. It is at this time that, along with the marble
paving in the nave, the panels in opus sectile were installed
in the bema and apse, and the coarse tessellated mosaics were
placed in the narthexes (198; 199), in the north and south
aisles (200; 201) and in the curve of the apse (202).[966]

On the basis of the style of the capitals and the mosaic
pavement of the first phase, the basilica has been attributed
to the first half of the sixth century.[967]

Bibliography. Ph. A. Drosoyianni, Deltion, 18 (1963), B2:
Chronika, pp. 251-252; M. Michaelides, Deltion, 20 (1965), B3:
Chronika, pp. 475-476; BCH, 89 (1965), p. 799; JHS, 87 (1967),
Supplement, p. 15; M. Michaelides, Deltion, 23 (1968),
Meletai, pp. 195-222; BCH, 92 (1968), p. 898.

Illustrations. M. Michaelides, Deltion, 20 (1965), B3:
Chronika, pl. 591a = our pl. 634, pl. 591b = our pl. 636;
pl. 592b = our pl. 638; idem, Deltion, 23 (1968), Meletai,
p. 197, plan 1 = our pl. 633, p. 201, drawing 2 (reconstruction of chancel screen), p. 204, plan 3 (plan with southwest
side of south aisle and part of narthex), pl.gamma, between
pp. 216 and 217 (opus sectile designs: drawing), pl. 83d
(north stylobate), pl. 85b (steps of apse), pls. 90-94
(architectural and decorative sculpture), pl. 95a-b (opus
sectile panels, details).

---

p. 200). Needless to say, if an altar in the first phase had
been similarly positioned, it would have covered the borders
of the pavement (see pls. 634, 638).

[966]The original paving in these sectors is not noted.
For the panels in opus sectile, see Deltion, 23, p. 216, and
pl.gamma between pp. 216 and 217.

[967]Deltion, 23, p. 220. Sodini incorrectly notes that
the attribution was based solely on the capitals (Catalogue,
p. 735).

PERIOD I, PHASE 1

No. 197

Twelve centimeters below the present level a polychrome
pavement was found which extended from the west wall of the
nave to the chord of the apse. Three borders, two with complex geometric and floral patterns, enclose field designs of
which only the east one was cleared.[968] The other, or
others, remain hidden beneath large marble slabs which cover
the central and western half of the nave (pl. 636).

On the basis of its style, the pavement can be attributed to the early sixth century. The pronounced linearism
of the figures in the east panel (pls. 638-640), their rigid
poses, and two-dimensional, patternistic rendering clearly
reflect a somewhat late phase in Greek pavements. The
reduced plasticity, the thick black contour lines, the patternization of the belly of the stag by means of dark blue
lines[969] are characteristics which are encountered at Stobi
(pl. 641), ascribed to a period around 500 A. D.,[970] but
probably to be placed a decade or two later, and at Amphipolis
Alpha (213, pl. 667). The panels have similar scenes with

---

[968]Traces of at least one other design are visible on
the north side (pl. 634, left).

[969]They are not visible in the photographs (vide infra,
p. 577, n. 976.

[970]E. Kitzinger, "A Survey of the Christian Town of
Stobi," DOP, 3 (1946), p. 138.

confronting stags flanking a tall, ribbed fountain with water flowing from decorative spouts, aquatic birds in front of the animals, and flat black leaves. These iconographic and stylistic similarities, however, are accompanied by a contrast in execution, with the Longos panel clearly inferior and probably a provincial reflection. A comparison of these panels with a similar one at Akrini (189, pl. 620) reveals two successive stages in the stylistic evolution of this scene with the earlier one represented by the Akrini panel where the flora and fauna are less rigid, less abstract, and more three-dimensional. These differences are, admittedly, slight, but it is clear that the earlier panel reflects fifth century stylistic currents and those at Longos, Stobi, and Amphipolis sixth century ones.[971] A fourth panel at Hermione (67, pls. 193, 195-196), ascribed to the late sixth century, represents the final stage in the stylistic evolution of this scene and, in fact, of Greek mosaics, generally. All the objects become a means of filling the scene with attenuated patterns and silhouettes of great linearity and variety creating, thereby, a kind of intricate and delicate polychromatic network across the surface.

---

[971]The pavements at Akrini, Longos, and Stobi also have similar chain borders which do not predate the second half of the fifth century.

PERIOD I, PHASE 2

In this phase the church was repaved with three types
of stone floors. Large marble slabs were placed in the
nave, geometric panels in opus sectile in the bema and the
major part of the apse, and geometric panels composed of
large, irregularly-cut tesserae in the narthexes, the north
and south aisles, and in the curve of the apse.[972] The
tessellated pavements are simple in design and color (white,
brown, blue) and are similar to those in the basilicas at
Nea Anchialos and Dion (105, pls. 357-61; 182, pls. 607-610)
which belong to the sixth century.[973] Although an exact
chronology cannot be established for the Longos pavements, a
terminus post quem of the first decades of the sixth century
is provided by the figural pavement in the nave.

  Additional bibliography. Sodini, Catalogue, No. 56, pp.
735, 747-749, nn. 96-97.

  Illustration. M. Michaelides, Deltion, 23 (1968),
Meletai, p. 197, plan 1 = our pl. 633.

PERIOD I, PHASE 1

197 Room III (7.72 x 13.20). Nave-bema; pavement covered
     by marble slabs and geometric panels in opus sectile.

———————

[972]Vide supra, p. 572, n. 966.

[973]For their probable relationship to pavements in opus
sectile, vide supra, p. 534.

Pls. 634-642.

Framing: 2.21. Field: 3.30 x 8.78. No other dimensions published. Stone tesserae (0.01-0.015 sq).[974]

Traces of a polychrome pavement containing a large panel with animals and birds and three wide geometric and floral borders.

Surround, at least to east (pl. 635): in rows at right angles to the wall.

Framing (pls. 634-637): narrow white band; outer border, two rows of tangent, horizontal white lozenges, on a black ground, forming alternate rows of single black lozenges (pl. 635). The latter are inscribed with small white disks and the former with black ones; wide white band; middle border, two-strand chain (pink/yellow/blue; blue; blue/white, outlined in black) on a yellow ground forming circles which are inscribed with small black crosslets; black double fillet; white band; inner border (pls. 634, 636-637), undulating black acanthus rinceau with cornucopian ocreae enclosing red flowers and fruit (for other rinceau, see 55, 115, 189).

Field, exposed to east only (pls. 634, 638-640): originally, two confronting stags,[975] oriented eastward, flanking a

---

[974]For the size and color of the tesserae, see Deltion, 23, p. 217-218.

[975]Although only the stag on the left side has been entirely cleared, the snout of its counterpart to the right is visible (pls. 638-639).

large, ribbed fountain filled with water flowing from a
decorative spout. In front of each of the animals is a large
aquatic bird facing northward, while a third one, facing in
the opposite direction, stands above the back of the left stag
id y pecking at a black plant (pls. 638, 640). Traces of
other black plants are visible above the fountain and beneath
the stag. The forms are linear and two-dimensional and
rendered with pronounced black outlines which serve to emphasize their simple contours and the rigid poses of the
animals and birds. The fauna and the vase are executed in
blues, pinks, and reds, and the stag's body is striated with
dark blue rows of tesserae.[976]

Early sixth century.

Illustrations. M. Michaelides, Deltion, 20 (1965), B3:
Chronika, pl. 591a = our pl. 634, pl. 591b = our pl. 636,
pl. 592a = our pl. 638, pl. 592b = our pl. 635; idem, Deltion,
23 (1968), Meletai, p. 197, plan 1 = our pl. 633, pl. 96a
(east side, general view), pl. 96b (middle border), pl. 97a
= our pl. 637, pl. 97b (fountain), pl. 98b (east panel, south
side).

PERIOD I, PHASE 2

Nos. 198-202

198 Room I (dimensions indeterminable). Exonarthex;
     destroyed when hydroelectric plant built.

---

[976]This is not visible, but it must have been similar to
the striations decorating the hides of the stags at Amphipolis and Stobi (pls. 641; 667).

No published information on dimensions and material.
Large, irregularly-cut tesserae.

Traces of a pavement executed with large, irregularly-cut
tesserae were noted by the builders of the hydroelectric
plant. No other information was recorded, but the mosaic
was probably similar to the pavements in the esonarthex
(199), and the north and south aisles (200-201).[977]

Terminus post quem of the early sixth century.

199 Room II (dimensions indeterminable). Esonarthex;
     destroyed when hydroelectric plant installed. Pl.
641a, left.
  No published information on dimensions and material.
Large, irregularly-cut tesserae.[978]

Traces of a geometric pavement executed with large, irregularly-cut tesserae.
  Field: in a published photograph (pl. 641a, left), there
is a row of three dark juxtaposed rectangles inscribed with
quincunxes composed of a central lozenge and four corner
motifs. In two of the rectangles, the corner motifs consist

[977]Deltion, 23, p. 218. This pavement is omitted by
Sodini, Catalogue, p. 735.

[978]Deltion, 23, pp. 219-220. This pavement is omitted
by Sodini (ibid.)

of single dark leaves with pointed tips which are connected
to opposite angles of the lozenges by curving stalks. The
third rectangle is inscribed with four corner medallions
decorated with dark and light hour glass motifs.

Pavement destroyed.

Terminus post quem of the early sixth century.

Illustration. Ph. A. Drosoyianni, Deltion, 18 (1963), B2:
Chronika, pl. 282b = our pl. 641a (left).

200 Room IV (3.31 x 13.20). North aisle. Pls. 633, 642.

Fragment: 3.31; length indeterminable. Irregularly-cut
schist tesserae.

Fragment of a geometric pavement executed with large
irregularly-cut white, brown, and blue tesserae.

Framing: border, single row of light and dark hour glass
motifs.

Field (pl. 642): two juxtaposed rectangles inscribed with
quincunxes composed of a central lozenge and four corner
motifs. In the east panel the corners are decorated with
single curving leaves, while the adjacent panel has four
medallions which are formed by the bifurcation of the band
defining the lozenge. Like the border, they contain light
and dark hour glass motifs.

Threshold panel in southeast corner: rectangle inscribed
with a lozenge.

580

Terminus post quem of the early sixth century.

Illustrations. M. Michaelides, Deltion, 23 (1968), Meletai, p. 197, plan 1 = our pl. 633, p. 219, plan 11 = our pl. 642.

201 Room V (3.82 x ca. 12.50). South aisle; west side

destroyed when hydroelectric plant built. Pls. 633,

641a, right.

Two fragments: no dimensions published. Material identical to that in the north aisle (200).

Two fragments of a geometric pavement executed with large, irregularly-cut white, brown, and blue tesserae.

Framing: border to east, single row of light and dark hour glass motifs. In the west fragment, now lost (pl. 641a, right), the border on the north and south sides was decorated with straight squares inscribed with disks, and squares set on edge, placed in an alternating sequence. The borders on the west and east sides, on the other hand, were decorated with a simple undulating light ribbon on a dark ground, and light and dark hour glass motifs, respectively.

Field: traces of rectangles inscribed with quincunxes composed of a central lozenge and four corner disks.

Terminus post quem of the early sixth century.

Illustrations. Ph. A. Drosoyianni, Deltion, 18 (1963), B2: Chronika, pl. 282b = our pl. 641a (right); M. Michaelides, Deltion, 23 (1968), Meletai, p. 197, plan 1 = our pl. 633.

202 Room VI (4.10). Apse. Pl. 633.

No published information on dimensions. Material identical to that in the north and south aisles (200-201). Pl. 633.

Brief mention of the decoration of the curve of the apse with the same type of paving as those in the north and south aisles.[979] In the plan (pl. 633), traces are visible of a border with three rows of hour glass motifs like those in the aisles (pl. 642).

Terminus post quem of the early sixth century.

Illustration. M. Michaelides, Deltion, 23 (1968), Meletai, p. 197, plan 1 = our pl. 633.

EDESSA

Building

In 1963, a chance find in Edessa brought to light mosaic pavements belonging to a "fifth century" building. The mosaics were taken to the local museum but an investigation in 1970 failed to produce any trace of the building and its mosaics.

Bibliography. JHS, 83 (1963), Supplement, p. 24.

---

[979]Deltion, 23, pp. 218-219. This pavement is omitted by Sodini, Catalogue, p. 735.

No. 203

203   Mosaic Pavements (no dimensions published).

No published information on dimensions and material.

Brief mention of mosaic pavements with geometric designs,
and animals and birds (stags and storks).

Present location unknown.

"Fifth century;"[980] probably no earlier than the second half
of the fifth century (cf. 189-190; 197; 213).

SALONIKA

Mosaic Fragments

North of the University of Salonika, part of an Early
Christian building complex was discovered by chance in 1967.
During a brief campaign, six rooms were cleared, of which
two were decorated with tessellated pavements. At the present time, the pavements are covered and a systematic
excavation is planned.

No plan of the site is published and there is no information on the form and function of the complex. Many of the
rooms were destroyed by later graves which were dug into the

---

[980]JHS, 83 (1963), Supplement, p. 24, citing an announcement in a newspaper (Kathimerini, 8 May 1963).

pavements or set on them. Although only a fragment of one of the tessellated pavements is published (pl. 643), its style and iconography substantiate the attribution of the complex to the Early Christian period.[981]

  Bibliography. M. Michaelides, Deltion, 22 (1967), B2: Chronika, pp. 437-438.

No. 204

204 Mosaic pavements (no dimensions published). Extensive
     damage by later graves. Pl. 643.

  No published information on dimensions and material.

In a published photograph, there is part of an interlace of large and small circles forming octagons (pl. 643). Beyond, there is another design which, except for a rectangular panel, is still covered. The large circles and octagons were filled with birds[982] of which one is visible in the photograph standing amid two plants. The cords of the design are decorated with a two-strand guilloche (with single light tesserae in each loop and at each twist) which is set on a dark ground and outlined in white/black.

Probably middle or second half of the fifth century; on the

---

     [981]M. Michaelides, Deltion, 22 (1967), B2: Chronika, p. 438.
     [982]Ibid.

basis of the type of the design and the plasticity and three-
dimensionality of the bird (see for example, 14, pls. 42-43;
16, pls. 47-48; 106, pls. 363-365; 107, pl. 367; 108, pls.
369-374).

Additional bibliography. Sodini, Catalogue, pp. 737, n.
78, 747, n. 95.

Illustration. M. Michaelides, Deltion, 22 (1967), B2:
Chronika, pl. 324gamma = our pl. 643.

LAKE DOÏRANIS

Building

A brief campaign in 1936 brought to light an apsidal
building (pl. 644) near the south shore of Lake Doïranis
in northern Macedonia. Traces of mosaic pavements were
found in the rectangular hall and the apse. At the present
time, the mosaics are covered and the site overgrown.[983]

Since the excavation lasted a few days, it was only
possible to determine the general outlines of the building.
It comprises a rectangular hall (10.44 x 7.30) which is terminated on the northwest side by a semi-circular apse (ca.
4.00 diam). Access to the building was through a door on
each side of the hall. Given the limited scope of the investigation, the function of the building was not determined.

---

[983]This information was given to me by the excavator,
Ch. I. Makaronas, whose article is the sole source for this
entry (Makedonika, 1 [1940], pp. 227-235); hereafter cited
as Makaronas.

It was attributed to the Roman period,[984] but the design of
the pavement in the apse indicates that it belongs to the
Early Christian period.

  Bibliography. Ch. I. Makaronas, Makedonika, 1 (1940),
pp. 227-235.

  Illustrations. Ch. I. Makaronas, Makedonika, 1 (1940),
p. 228, fig. 1 (map of area), p. 229, fig. 2 = our pl. 644.

                              No. 205

     Traces of polychrome pavements were found in the rec-
tangular hall and the apse. In the only published photograph (pl. 645), the apse is shown with an imbrication pattern composed of scales delineated by a single white fillet
and then a single or double dark fillet. Although the
drawing is somewhat confusing in this respect, a clearer
version of this pattern can be seen in a photograph of a
pavement at Lavreotikon (35, pl. 89), where, however, the
color of the outlines is reversed. In both pavements,
strong outlines define the contours of the scales, a feature
which is absent from all the examples of this pattern which
are reliably dated to the late fourth and the early fifth
centuries. At Athens (2, pl. 8; 6, pl. 18; 21, pl. 61; 23,
pl. 65) and Epidauros (46, pl. 108), for example, the scales
are outlined by single fillets, not multiple ones. It is
not until around the middle of the fifth century and later

---

[984]Makaronas, p. 232.

that this type of delineation appears for the first time in
such places as Lavreotikon (35, pl. 89) and Voskochori (188,
pl. 617). The addition of stepped triangles in the center
of the scales may also argue for a later date, although they
are absent from the others. For this reason, the pavement
at Lake Doïranis can be assigned to the middle of the fifth
century.

Illustration. Ch. I. Makaronas, Makedonika, 1 (1940),
p. 229, fig. 2 = our pl. 644.

205   Room I (14.45 x 7.30, including apse).   Pl. 645.

No published information on dimensions. Marble, stone,
and ceramic tesserae.[985]

Fragments in the hall and apse of well executed polychrome
pavements in white, brown, dark blue, and red.

Ia, rectangular hall: destroyed, except for traces of a
geometric rectilinear design which extends up to the chord
of the apse.[986]

Ib, apse (pl. 645).

Framing: wide white band; narrow dark band; border, narrow
undulating dark rinceau forming rigidly arranged and widely
spaced scrolls filled with single ivy leaves; narrow dark

---

[985]Makaronas, p. 228.

[986]Makaronas, p. 230.

band; white band.[987]

Field, framed by a single or dark double fillet: imbrication pattern, oriented northward, composed of scales which are outlined by white/dark single and double fillets, respectively, and decorated with small stepped triangles.

Around the middle of the fifth century.

Illustration. Ch. I. Makaronas, Makedonika, 1 (1940), p. 231, fig. 3 (general view of apse), p. 233, fig. 4 = our pl. 645.

AMPHIPOLIS

Basilica Alpha

In the course of seven campaigns between 1920 and 1972, the first of four Christian basilicas, designated Alpha (overall, ca. 35.00 max x ca. 60.00)[988] was cleared on the acropolis of Amphipolis (pl. 646). Ten rooms were carpeted with mosaic pavements (II, V, VI, VII, VIII-IX, XIII, XIV,

[987]Mr. Makaronas told me that this band is narrower than it is in the drawing.

[988]This measurement is taken from the plan (pl. 647). Unless otherwise noted, the measurements are published. Basilicas Beta and Gamma (215-216; 217-223) are also paved with mosaics. For Delta which has marble paving, see D. I. Lazarides, Praktika, 1964, p. 36; A. K. Orlandos, To Ergon, 1964, pp. 21-23; E. G. Stikas, Praktika, 1966, pp. 45-46, fig. 6 (plan); A. K. Orlandos, To Ergon, 1966, pp. 37-42, p. 39, fig. 44 (plan). Excavations were halted in 1966 and resumed in 1972 at which time a new plan of the basilica was published (A. K. Orlandos, To Ergon, 1972, p. 21, fig. 14).

XV) and others were paved with marble slabs (I, III, IV, X).[989] At the present time, all the tessellated pavements are covered.

Since the archaeological and architectural data are insufficient, only a general survey of its plan (pl. 647) will follow. Preceded by a large atrium, I (21.10 x 13.70),[990] and two narthexes, II, III (21.19 x 3.91; 20.50 x 3.65, respectively), with flanking rooms, IV-IX, the church proper comprises a nave and a bema, X, XI (overall, 10.50 x 29.40), terminated by a semi-circular apse, XII. The nave is separated from single lateral aisles, XIII, XIV-XV (overall, ca. 4.00 x 29.50),[991] by elevated stylobates with colonnades running from the east to the west walls and from the bema by an independent "⊔-shaped" chancel screen containing a prothuron in the center of its west side. An additional partition on the east side of the south aisle divides this sector into two separate rooms, XIV, XV. Unlike a similar compartmentalization in Basilica Gamma to the northwest, however, there appears to have been a doorway between the two

---

[989]The type of paving in Rooms XI and XII is not recorded.

[990]The division of the northeast side of the ambulatory by a curious zig-zag wall, which forms a sector marked "P" on the plan (pl. 647), is not satisfactorily discussed in the reports (E. G. Stikas, Praktika, 1970, p. 50; hereafter cited as Praktika, 1970; A. K. Orlandos, To Ergon, 1970, p. 33; hereafter cited as To Ergon, 1970).

[991]The measurement is taken from the plan.

rooms.[992] In the bema, traces were found of an altar surmounted by a canopy and the foundations of a stepped, semi-
circular synthronon on the chord of the apse. Beyond this
clergy-altar site, lies a double-stepped ambon which rises
from a hexagonal base.[993] Stone benches are located along
the outer walls of the south compartments (XIV, XV), an
arrangement comparable to the one in the south aisle of
Basilica Gamma (pl. 676). Unlike the latter, however, the
north side of the east room (XV) also contains a bench and
this poses problems concerning the accessibility of this
room from the bema. Until a complete publication of this
church appears, one must accept the isolation of this room
from the bema and regard the southwest door leading into the
aisle as the sole means of communication with the rest of the
church.[994] Additional rooms are situated to the northwest
and southwest. Room V with its apse and chancel screen[995]
is clearly a chapel and the adjacent room, IV, probably the
mytatorion where the bishop or priest changed his garments.[996] The function of the two other north rooms, VI-VII,

[992]Pl. 676. There is no discussion of this doorway.

[993]E. G. Stikas, Praktika, 1967, p. 86, pl. 61b.

[994]There is no discussion of the benches, but it is
clear that the pavements were laid up to them (pls. 668-669).

[995]The latter is not indicated on the plan (pl. 647).
See E. G. Stikas, Praktika, 1971, p. 43, pl. 55b; hereafter
cited as Praktika, 1971.

[996]Ibid.; A. K. Orlandos, To Ergon, 1971, p. 37; hereafter cited as To Ergon, 1971.

is problematic at the present time,[997] as are the two south annexes, VIII-IX. Judging from the opposing orientation of the two figural panels in the large room to the west, it is possible that it was used as a reception or audience hall, with Room VIII serving as its vestibule. This may explain the technical and decorative poverty of the pavement in the latter room in contrast to the rich, exuberant figural compositions in Room IX where the priest or bishop held court.

On the basis of the style of the architectural sculpture and the mosaics, the church has been assigned to the first half or the middle of the sixth century.[998] In a subsequent period, during the rebuilding of sections of the outer walls of the acropolis, the west side of Rooms III and VIII and almost all of Room VI were destroyed.[999]

Bibliography. E. Pelekides, Praktika, 1920, pp. 85-89; AA, 37 (1923), p. 245; E. G. Stikas, Praktika, 1966, pp. 39-46; A. K. Orlandos, To Ergon, 1966, pp. 29-37; BCH, 91

[997]For a general discussion of annexes in Christian churches, see A. K. Orlandos, Hē metakinēsis tou diakonikou, pp. 353-372.

[998]E. G. Stikas, Praktika, 1966, p. 42. In an analysis of the capitals, Sodini attributes them to the late fifth or the early sixth century (Catalogue, p. 732, n. 68). Since, however, his comparisons are based on material which is not securely dated, they could just as easily be placed into the sixth century. Certainly, one piece of evidence which the excavator uses (ibid.) must be rejected out of hand. He found two coins of Justin II and Sophia (571-572) in the south aisle. Since, however, they were found in the fill and not in a sealed layer, their value for chronological purposes is limited. Moreover, according to A. K. Orlandos, much of the fill from an excavation in 1920 was dumped in the basilica (To Ergon, 1967, p. 54).

[999]E. Stikas, Praktika, 1969, p. 55; hereafter cited as Praktika, 1969; Praktika, 1970, p. 52.

(1967), pp. 718-721; JHS, 87 (1967), Supplement, p. 16;
E. G. Stikas, Praktika, 1967, pp. 83-88; A. K. Orlandos, To
Ergon, 1967, pp. 54-65; BCH, 92 (1968), pp. 908-911; JHS, 88
(1968), Supplement, pp. 15-16; E. G. Stikas, Praktika, 1969,
pp. 54-57; A. K. Orlandos, To Ergon, 1969, pp. 49-65; E. G.
Stikas, Praktika, 1970, pp. 50-53; A. K. Orlandos, To Ergon,
1970, pp. 33-42; BCH, 94 (1970), p. 1071; E. G. Stikas,
Praktika, 1971, pp. 43-45; A. K. Orlandos, To Ergon, 1971,
pp. 37-40; BCH, 95 (1971), p. 976; A. K. Orlandos, To Ergon,
1972, pp. 18-20; BCH, 96 (1972), p. 736.

Illustrations. E. G. Stikas, Praktika, 1966, p. 41, fig.
2 = our pl. 646, pl. 24b (south stylobate with columns and
imposts), pl. 26a-b (sculptural fragments); idem, Praktika,
1967, p. 84, fig. 1 (plan with mosaics), pls. 60-61a (architectural sculpture), pl. 61b (base of ambon), pl. 62a (apse
with synthronon); idem, Praktika, 1969, pl. A after p. 56
(plan, with mosaic), pl. 57 (south aisle, XIV, before clearing), pl. 60a (narthex from south, with later wall); idem,
Praktika, 1970, pl. A after p. 50 (plan with mosaics), pls.
77-79 (architectural sculpture); idem, Praktika, 1971,pl.
A after p. 48 = our pl. 647, pl. 55b (Room V), p. 44, fig. 1
= our pl. 649.

Nos. 206-214

Polychrome pavements with multiple ornamental borders
and figural insets and scenes decorate many sectors of the
church. The mosaics spread across the surface of each room
and form dense, all-over carpets of rectilinear and curvilinear designs which serve as frameworks for heraldic scenes
and lively denizens of the land and sea. In the former, confronting bulls, deer, and peacocks are shown in rectangular
or circular panels drinking from decorative fountains with
running water (pls. 652, 667, 670, 672), while in another
scene two fishermen are depicted landing their catch (pls.
659-660). The scenes are accompanied by delicate and
complex grids which are primarily filled with birds and

fish.[1000] The exuberance and richness of the pavements, the
plethora of organic elements and the strongly defined borders reflect a stylistic and iconographic trend in Greek
pavements which begins to appear in the second half of the
fifth century and continues into the sixth century. The
pavements at Amphipolis Alpha are to be assigned to the
latter century and, therefore, postdate the pavements in
Basilica Gamma (217-223, pl. 646) which were probably executed by the same workshop. The chronological difference is
only a matter of a few decades since both share common figure types, among them birds and fish, and in one example
identical designs (pls. 648; 683-684). Gamma, however,
possesses aniconic as well as iconic pavements and all its
figures are contained within clearly defined geometric
frameworks and designs. There are no large scale figural
compositions, only figural insets. In addition, there are
stylistic differences. In Alpha, the figures appear more
stylized and two-dimensional and their poses are stiffer and
less fluid. They resemble the figures at Nikopolis Alpha
(150, pls. 460-464; 152, pl. 470; 154, pl. 493; 155, pls.
506-507) and Longos (197, pls. 638-640), which are securely
dated to the first half of the sixth century.

Although one must await the final publication of the
church, including color notations and better photographs of

[1000]Only the grid in Room IX (pl. 652) contains some
animals.

the pavements, it is very probable that the decorative program belongs to the sixth century and that it was the
product of the same workshop which executed the earlier
pavements in Gamma, and possibly the ones in Beta (215-216).

Additional bibliography. Sodini, Catalogue, No. 51, p.
732.

Illustration. E. G. Stikas, Praktika, 1971, pl. A after
p. 48 = our pl. 647.

206   Room II (21.10 x 3.91).   Exonarthex.   Pl. 648.

Framing: 0.37.   Field: 20.36 x 3.19.   No other published
information on dimensions and material.

Straight grid with multiple figural insets enclosed by a
double border (for a similar pavement at Basilica Gamma, see
217, pl. 684).

Framing (pl. 648): outer border, undulating vine rinceau
(two fillets) forming widely spaced scrolls, each filled
with a leaf and a cluster of grapes (for a similar border in
the northwest chapel, see 207, pl. 650); dark fillet; inner
border, dark meander (double fillet) forming swastikas.

Field (pl. 648), framed by a dark fillet which forms, at
the same time, part of the design: straight grid, formed by
a dark fillet, composed of single juxtaposed squares (0.28)
which are axially connected by single bars flanking small
squares set on edge. The squares formed by the grid enclose
land birds and water fowl while the interstitial registers
are decorated with confronting fish which, usually, alternate

with juxtaposed sepia in an a-b sequence. At regular intervals, the marine representations are replaced by a series of
broad wicker baskets. Unlike the homogeneous disposition of
the figures in an identical design in Basilica Gamma (217,
pl. 684), a complex axial disposition is achieved in this
pavement by the east-west orientation of the birds and the
south-north and north-south directions of the fish and
baskets, respectively.

First half of the sixth century.
    Illustrations. E. G. Stikas, Praktika, 1970, pl. 68a
(northeast corner), pl. 68b = our pl. 648, pl. 69a (west
side), pl. 69b (central section).

207 Room V (2.38 x 4.35). Chapel.[1001] Pls. 649-651.
    Framing: 0.28. Field: 1.82 x 3.79.[1002] No other pub-
lished information on dimensions and material.

Polychrome geometric mosaic composed of seventeen rows of
small tangent octagons with figural insets and a rinceau
border.
    Framing (pl. 650): border, undulating vine rinceau (two
fillets) forming loosely arranged and widely spaced scrolls

    [1001]The relationship between the pavement and the
chancel screen cannot be determined (vide supra, p. 589,
n. 995).

    [1002]The field dimensions are incorrectly cited as being
1.62 x 2.63 in one report (A. K. Orlandos, To Ergon, 1972,
pp. 18-19; hereafter cited as To Ergon, 1972).

which are alternately filled with a single serrated grape leaf and a cluster of grapes (for a similar border in the exonarthex, see 207, pl. 648); dark double fillet.

Field (pls. 650-651): alternate rows of five and six juxtaposed octagons which form between them small straight squares. The design is cut along the margins and along the north side, at least, the squares are replaced by wide double bars (pl. 650). The octagons, framed by an inner checkerboard fillet[1003] and an outer dark double fillet, are inscribed with various denizens of the land and sea, oriented westward, which are arranged in rows according to species. Thus, rows of land birds and water fowl alternate with rows of sepiae, dolphins, and other types of fish.

First half of the sixth century.

Illustrations. E. G. Stikas, *Praktika*, 1971, p. 44, fig. 1 = our pl. 649, pl. 56a = our pl. 651; A. K. Orlandos, *To Ergon*, 1972, p. 19, fig. 12 = our pl. 650.

208 Room VI (5.30 x 3.70).[1004] Annex; pavement almost completely destroyed by later walls of the acropolis.

No published information on dimensions and material.

[1003]This type of fillet is also used in Basilica Gamma (pl. 678).

[1004]In one report, a typographical error caused the north-south dimension to be printed as 3.30 (*Praktika*, 1970, p. 52).

Brief mention of traces of a mosaic pavement.[1005]

Probably contemporary with the other pavements and, therefore, first half of the sixth century.

209 Room VII (5.30 x 3.84).[1006] Annex.
   No published information on dimensions and material.

Brief mention of traces of a mosaic pavement.[1007]
   Mosaic destroyed.

Probably contemporary with the other pavements and, therefore, first half of the sixth century.

210 Room VIII (5.35 sq). Vestibule? West side of pavement
       destroyed by later wall of the acropolis. Pl. 647.
   Framing: ca. 0.60. Field: 4.70 sq.[1008] Irregularly-cut
stone tesserae (0.05-0.08 long).

[1005]Praktika, 1970, pp. 51-52. On the plan (pl. 647),
the letter should be read as a Zeta not a Nu.

[1006]The dimensions are taken from the plan (pl. 647).

[1007]This pavement is omitted by Sodini (Catalogue, p.
732).

[1008]The published dimensions of the pavement are completely erroneous. The framing is recorded as being 0.12 and
the circle as 1.40 diam (see Praktika, 1970, p. 51 and To
Ergon, 1970, p. 41, respectively).

In the plan (pl. 647), there is a simple geometric pavement
(blue and white) composed of large tesserae forming a square
inscribed with a medallion.[1009]

Framing: wide blue band.

Field: square inscribed with a medallion (ca. 260)
decorated with a wheel pattern composed of blue and white
curvilinear ribs (for similar pavements with large tesserae,
see 102-104; 180-183; 198-202).

First half of the sixth century.

211 Room IX (5.21 x 9.15). Audience or reception hall?[1010]
      Pla. 652-660.

Fragment: 5.21 x ca. 4.20 max. Framing: ca. 1.40.[1011]
Field: east panel, a, including border, 2.70 x 1.40; west
panel, b, including border, 2.70 x 1.20 max.

Polychrome figural pavement composed of two long rectangular
panels facing in opposite directions which are enclosed by
ornamental and figural borders and separated by a luxuriant
acanthus rinceau.

[1009]Praktika, 1970, p. 51. No photograph of this pavement is published.

[1010]Vide supra, p. 590.

[1011]This dimension is taken from the plan (pl. 647) and
the succeeding ones from a report (To Ergon, 1970, p. 37).

Framing:[1012] outer border, undulating vine rinceau (two
fillets) forming widely spaced scrolls which are filled with
single, agitated heart-shaped ivy leaves; dark single fillet;
light triple fillet; middle border, narrow band with dark
and light wave crests; dark fillet, narrow white band; dark
fillet; light double fillet; inner border (pls. 652-658),
grid composed of a row of bars with semi-circular termini
forming juxtaposed squares (0.60) with concave-sided
corners.[1013] The latter enclose land and marine creatures
which, in the preserved sections, are disposed on two axes:
north-south (north and south sides); east-west (east side).
Starting at the northwest side and moving eastward, the
sequence of figural insets is as follows. North side:
small bull; bees (pl. 654); erect deer (pl. 655); eagle with
a bird in its talons; boar (pl. 652, right). South side (pl.
652, left): water fowl; dolphin; land bird or water fowl;
long-legged bird pecking at the ground; bird. East side (pl.
652): octopus, two crossed fish (pl. 656); dog amid bushes
(pl. 657) chasing a leaping rabbit in the next inset (pl.
657) which looks back toward its pursuer (pl. 653).[1014]

[1012]The outer and middle borders are not visible in the
photographs. For the best reproduction of this sector, see
Praktika, 1970, pl. 70b.

[1013]This pattern is a truncated version of a field
design (160, pl. 563; 164, pl. 576).

[1014]For summary descriptions, see Praktika, 1969, p. 56;
A. K. Orlandos, To Ergon, 1969, pp. 57-61; hereafter cited
as To Ergon, 1969.

Field.

IXa, east panel (pls. 652-653), bordered by an undulating
ribbon with a floret at each wave: heraldic composition
composed of two confronting bulls, oriented eastward, drinking from a cross-shaped fountain overflowing with water
which cascades from a decorative spout (for a similar scene
in Room XIV, see 213, pl. 667). Behind each bull is a large
tree flanked by small bushes.[1015]

IXb, west panel (pls. 652, 659-660), bordered by an undulating acanthus rinceau with cornucopian ocreae:[1016] fragment containing a fishing scene, oriented westward, composed
of two men set against a mountainous landscape. As the
youthful man to the left spears a fish (pl. 659), his
bearded counterpart on the right (pl. 660) rushes forward
with a net to bring it to shore.

First half of the sixth century.

[1015]Since the background is not too clear and it is not
described in the reports, it is impossible to say if other
animals are present in the scene as in Room XIV (214, pls.
670-672) and in other similar scenes at Akrini and Longos
(189-190); 197). For descriptions of this panel, see
Praktika, 1969, p. 56; Praktika, 1970, p. 51; To Ergon, 1969,
pp. 57-61; To Ergon, 1970, pp. 36-37.

[1016]For a more detailed reproduction, see Praktika,
1970, pl. 74a.

[1017]Unfortunately, the published photographs and descriptions are inadequate for stylistic and iconographic
purposes. Similar fishing scenes occupy the borders in the
north and south wings of Basilica Alpha at Nikopolis (153,
154), but this is the only preserved field composition.

Illustrations. E. Stikas, 1969, pl. 58 = our pl. 667, pl.
62a (IXa, north side), pl. 62b (IXa), pl. 63a = our pl. 656,
pl. 63b = our pl. 657, pl. 64a = our pl. 658, pl. 64b (IXa,
north border: boar), pl. 65a (IXa, north border: eagle), pl.
65b = our pl. 655, pl. 66a = our pl. 654, pl. 66b = our pl.
653; idem, Praktika, 1970, pl. 70a = our pl. 652, pl. 70b
(IXa, northeast side), pl. 71a (IXa, south side), pl. 71b
(IXa, southeast side), pls. 72-73 (figural insets), pl. 74a
(IXb, acanthus border), pl. 74b (IXb, general view), pl. 75a
= our pl. 659, pl. 75b = our pl. 660.

212 Room XIII (ca. 4.00 x 29.50). North aisle.

No published information on dimensions and material.

Brief mention of traces of a mosaic pavement on the east

side containing birds, fish, and ornamental motifs.[1018]

    Mosaic destroyed.

First half of the sixth century.

213 Room XIV (ca. 4.00 x 19.80).[1019] South aisle. Pavement

    laid up to a narrow screen wall to east and stone

benches to west and along south wall; covered in northwest

corner by a block (pls. 663, 666) and destroyed to southwest

by a sunken feature (pls. 662-663). Pls. 661-667.

    Framing: ca. 0.65. Field: 2.70 x 19.15 max. Central

[1018]E. G. Stikas, Praktika, 1966, p. 46. Mr. Stikas
informed me that the pavement was identical to the one in
the south aisle (213, pls. 661-662). This pavement is
omitted by Sodini (Catalogue, p. 732).

[1019]Except for the threshold panel, the dimensions for
this entry are taken from the plan (pl. 647).

panel: 2.30 sq. Threshold: 1.50 x 0.50. No published
information on material.

Complex geometric pavement composed of a central square with
a heraldic animal composition, b, and two lateral panels, a,
c, decorated with straight grids embellished with interlacing elements and figural insets.

Framing (pls. 663, 666): outer border, light and dark
wave crests which are inverted in the south east corner.
The center of the west side is marked by a dart pointing
toward the threshold panel (pl. 666); middle border, overlapping lyre pattern highlighted by small circles at each
loop; inner border, light and dark wave crests which on the
west side change to tear drops in the corners and the center
(pl. 666). At the latter point the waves change direction;
narrow light band.

Field: three panels, a-c, oriented westward, with complex
figural and geometric designs.

XIVa, west panel (pls. 661-665), framed by a dark fillet
which forms, at the same time, part of the design: straight
grid formed by wide bands containing single rows of concave-
sided triangles placed base-to-tip. The intersections of
the bands are decorated with small medallions inscribed with
diagonal crosses (one fillet) which accent the corners of
the squares (ca. 0.80) formed by the grid (for a similar
grid, see 152, pls. 466-468; 156, pls. 533-536; 161, pl. 566).
The remaining sections of the squares are entwined by two

sinuous interlacing bands decorated with a two-strand guilloche and an undulating ribbon pattern which form circles
on the main axis of the squares (pls. 664-665).[1020] These
bands serve as framing devices for the insets containing
birds and marine creatures arranged chiastically and
oriented westward in ten rows on the east-west axis. Thus,
each row contains a marine creature, either an octopus or a
pair of crossed or superimposed fish, and a land bird
accompanied by sparse flora.[1021]

XIVb, central panel (pl. 667), framed by a black fillet
which forms, at the same time, part of the design.

Field: square decorated with a quincunxial design composed of a central medallion with a heraldic figural composition, oriented westward, and interlaced circles in the
four spandrels. The medallion, bordered by a two-strand
guilloche (with a light tessera at each loop) on a dark
ground,[1022] contains two large confronting stags drinking
from a two-tiered, ribbed fountain filled with water flowing from a decorative spout. Below them are two swans or
geese who stretch their undulating necks to peck at the
bushes flanking the rectangular base of the fountain between

[1020]The design is cut along the margins and accented by
tangent light/dark bands along the north and south sides.

[1021]No water fowl are visible in the reproductions.

[1022]For summary descriptions, see Praktika, 1969, p.
55; To Ergon, 1969, p. 51.

them. The top register of the composition is occupied by
two other confronting water fowl who stand above the backs
of the stags, and by a seated rabbit nibbling on a cluster
of grapes (for similar scenes, see 189, pl. 620; 197, pls.
638-640). Although clearer and more detailed photographs
and color descriptions of this panel are needed, some general observations on the style of the figures can be made.
Each figure appears to be executed with strong dark contours
which, in the bodies of the stags and the rabbit, reach a
width of between three and five fillets. This sharp delineation is accompanied by a loss of plasticity and modeling,
and by a patternization of the hides of the stags in the
form of networks of variecolored straight lines. The spandrels between the edge of the medallion and the corners of
the square are decorated with short branches and simple
interlaces comprising a large circle flanked by two smaller
ones. The former encloses a bird and the latter disks with
diagonal crosses.

XIVc, east panel.

Field: identical to that in the west panel, XIVa.[1023]

West threshold panel (pls. 663, 666), framed by a light
triple fillet: quincunxial pattern composed of a large
lozenge and four slender stalks in the corners. The lozenges, truncated by the margins, contain a dark central

---

[1023]For the east panel, see _Praktika_, 1969, pl. 59a-b;
To Ergon, 1969, p. 51, fig. 46.

medallion inscribed with a circular knot of six loops, on a
dark ground, which is framed by concentric light/dark/light
fillets. Completing the decoration are two opposed fish
with open mouths which face the medallion and, like all the
organic filling motifs in the pavement, are oriented westward.

First half of the sixth century.

Illustrations. E. G. Stikas, Praktika, 1966, p. 44, fig.
5 = our pl. 663, pl. 27a (west side with threshold panel),
pl. 27b = our pl. 665, pl. 28a (bird), pl. 28b (XIVa, fish),
pl. 29a (XIVa, bird), pl. 29b (XIVa, fish), pl. 30 = our pl.
661; idem, Praktika, 1969, pl. 58 = our pl. 667, pl. 59a-b
(XIVc); A. K. Orlandos, To Ergon, 1969, p. 51, fig. 46 =
our pl. 664.

214 Room XV (ca. 3.75 x 7.50).[1024] Southeast chamber; pavement laid up to stone benches along north, south, and
east sides, and to a screen wall with a doorway to west.
Pls. 668-674.

Framing: ca. 0.45. Field: ca. 2.35 x 6.90. Central
panel, b: ca. 2.35. No published information on dimensions
and material.

Complex polychrome pavement composed of a central square
with a heraldic composition, b, flanked by two identical
panels with interlaces and tangent geometric shapes

[1024]The measurements for this entry are taken from the
plan (pl. 647).

enclosing land and marine creatures, a, c (pls. 668-669).

Framing (pls. 668, 671): light narrow band; outer border,
light and dark wave crests; middle border, braid (with a
white tessera at each loop); inner border, light and dark
wave crests; narrow band.[1025]

Field (pls. 668-669): three panels (a-c) oriented westward, with figural and geometric designs set within a light
narrow band (three fillets).

XVa, west panel, framed by a dark single fillet: field
design and filling motifs identical to those of its counterpart to the east (XVc).[1026]

XVb, central panel (pls. 670-672), framed by a two-tone
double fillet: square decorated with a quincunxial design
composed of corner birds facing a central decorative wreath
with a heraldic figural composition which is oriented westward. Within the flower and fruit laden wreath, which is
bound on each side by a decorative clasp (pl. 671), five
birds amid bushes surround a large cantharus set on a rectangular base and filled with flowing water (pls. 670-672).
The scene is dominated by a pyramidal composition comprising
three peacocks and two other birds. One of the peacocks is
shown standing de face on the rim of the fountain, its

[1025]Although this border is similar to the one in Room
XIV (213, pls. 663, 666), their middle borders differ (cf.
Sodini, Catalogue, p. 732).

[1026]No photograph of this panel is published, but from
the plan (pl. 647) it appears to be a mirror image of the
east panel (pls. 669, 673-674).

displaying occelate tail covert serving as a decorative
mandorla for its slender body (for similar peacocks, see 85;
127, pl. 417; 152, pls. 469-471). Near its thin legs, two
unidentifiable birds rush toward each other while below two
other peacocks drink from the fountain between them, their
graceful bodies and trailing tail coverts repeating and reflecting the curves of the fountain and the wreath. In the
spandrels between the edge of the medallion and the corners
of the square, stand single pecking birds amid slender
branches (pl. 671).

XVc, east panel (pls. 669, 673-674), framed by a single
dark fillet: all-over geometric design of alternating rows
of interlaces and tangent lozenges and circles[1027] set
against a dark sea stocked with marine creatures. The lozenges and circles are cut along the north and south margins.
The interlaces form large and small circles and are bordered
by two-strand guilloches which serve as decorative frameworks for the organic and geometric filling elements. Single
birds accompanied by sparse foliage and simple star-crossed
disks decorate the large and small circles, respectively,
and, also the lozenges and circles between them which produces an alternating system of geometric and organic motifs
along the east-west axis.[1028] The regularity and harmony of

---

[1027]Sodini is incorrect in describing the rows with
lozenges as interlaces (ibid.).

[1028]One circle on the east side is decorated with an
interlace forming six loops (pl. 673).

this disposition are somewhat contradicted by the freedom of
movement and orientation of the fish and sepiae which swim
in the choppy, striated sea in the interstices.

First half of the sixth century.

    Illustrations. E. G. Stikas, _Praktika_, 1967, p. 87, fig.
2 = our pl. 670, pl. 63a = our pl. 673, pl. 63b = our pl. 674,
pl. 64a = our pl. 668, pl. 64b = our pl. 672, pl. 66a (XVb,
right spandrels).

Basilica Beta

    At Amphipolis, a brief excavation in 1959 brought to
light the east and south sides of an Early Christian
basilica, designated Beta, and a mosaic pavement in its
south aisle (pls. 646, 675). Systematic excavations were
begun in 1972 at which time the north wall of the church
proper and the south wall of the narthex and atrium were
cleared, and fragments of a second mosaic were discovered in
the north aisle. By 1969, the mosaic in the south aisle had
disappeared.[1029]

    In the course of the second excavation, it was deter-
mined that the three-aisled basilica (16.32 x 23.25) is
preceded by an atrium, I, and a narthex, II, and that the
nave, III, is separated from the aisles, IV-V, by stylobates
running from the east to the west walls. Except for traces

    [1029]This was communicated to me by the present excava-
tor, Mr. E. G. Stikas.

of a room on the north side of the church proper, no annexes
have been uncovered, to date. The limited scope of the
excavations and the dearth of datable archaeological finds
preclude a determination of the chronology of the building
with any degree of certitude. Since, however, Amphipolis
served as an important ecclesiastical center between the
second half of the fifth and the first half of the sixth
centuries, as witnessed by the other basilicas (206-214;
217-223) and the episcopal megaron on the west side of the
acropolis (pl. 646), the basilica can be placed within this
chronological framework.[1030]

Bibliography. D. I. Lazarides, Praktika, 1959, p. 44; A.
K. Orlandos, To Ergon,1959, pp. 40-41; BCH, 84 (1960), pp.
796-797; A. K. Orlandos, To Ergon, 1972, pp. 24-26.

Illustrations. D. I. Lazarides, Praktika, 1959, pl. 46a
(section of south aisle), pl. 47a (apse); E. G. Stikas,
Praktika, 1966, p. 41, fig. 2 = our pl. 646; A. K. Orlandos,
To Ergon, 1972, p. 25, fig. 18 (plan).

Nos. 215-216

Two mosaic pavements containing geometric field designs
with figural and geometric insets decorate the north and
south aisles, IV, V. Although the archaeological reports
contain meager descriptive and illustrative data, the presence of birds in the south aisle and a bull in the north

---

[1030]For Basilica Delta, vide supra, p. 587, n. 988.

aisle[1031] are features which are not found in mosaics in Greece or, for that matter, in Macedonia until the second half of the fifth century. Early Macedonian pavements such as those at Dion (178-179) and Tsiphliki (196) and those in other parts of Greece (1; 2-3; 4-5; 6-9, 21; 22; 44-49; 88-92; 130-138) are notable for their aniconic and austere designs which are delineated by simple multiple fillets or bands. Although one must await the results of the excavations of the church, it would not be surprising if its decorative program reflected in varying degrees those of two other Amphipolitan churches in the vicinity, Alpha and Gamma, which are filled with rich and complex designs and a plethora of organic filling motifs. A terminus post quem of the middle of the fifth century, therefore, is tentatively ascribed to the pavements until the completion of the excavations.

Additional bibliography. Sodini, Catalogue, No. 52, p. 732.

Illustration. A. K. Orlandos, To Ergon, 1972, p. 25, fig. 18 (plan).

215 Room IV (ca. 3.00 x 16.48 max). North aisle.

No published information on dimensions and material.

Fragment of a mosaic pavement decorated with geometric

[1031]For the former, see D. I. Lazarides, Praktika, 1959, p. 44; A. K. Orlandos, To Ergon, 1959, p. 40; for the latter, A. K. Orlandos, To Ergon, 1972, p. 26.

designs and an animal inscribed in a large circle. Although
only its legs are preserved, the animal is identified as a
bull.[1032] (For a scene with bulls at Amphipolis Alpha, see
211, pls. 653-654).

No earlier than the middle of the fifth century.
  Illustration. A. K. Orlandos, To Ergon, 1972, p. 24, fig.
17 (general view).

216 Room V (ca. 3.00 wide; length indeterminable). South
     aisle. Pl. 675.
  No published information on dimensions and material.

Pavement decorated with circles inscribed with birds and
geometric motifs.[1033] In a bad published photograph (pl.
675), there are traces of a circle decorated with a wave
crest border and an indistinguishable central motif. This
nucleus is surrounded by what may have been an outer border
of which some undulating lines are visible.
  Pavement destroyed.

No earlier than the middle of the fifth century.
  Illustration. D. Lazarides, Praktika, 1959, pl. 466 =
our pl. 675.

[1032]A. K. Orlandos, To Ergon, 1972, p. 26.

[1033]D. I. Lazarides, Praktika, 1959, p. 44; A. K.
Orlandos, To Ergon, 1959, pp. 40-41.

Basilica Gamma

In the course of eight campaigns between 1959 and 1971 a third Christian basilica, designated Gamma[1034] (overall, 18.20 x 28.10, including apse),[1035] was cleared on the acropolis at Amphipolis (pl. 646). With the exception of the bema and apse, the former paved with marble chips, mosaic pavements decorated each sector of the building. At the present time, only a few traces of the mosaic in the north aisle survive; the rest are in good condition and protected by plastic sheets and sand.

The main entrance to the complex (pls. 676-677) is situated on the south side and is distinguished by a large atrium, I,[1036] flanked by a wall on the east side[1037] and an "L"-shaped corridor, II, III, on the west and south sides. The latter communicates with a large room, IV (10.10 x 5.75), to the southwest and with the narthex, V (16.64 x

---

[1034]For Alpha and Beta, see 206-214; 215-216; for Delta, vide supra, p. 590, n. 998.

[1035]The measurement of the narthex is cited as being 16.64 long (E. G. Stikas, Praktika, 1962, p. 42; hereafter cited as Praktika, 1962). Although this would make the narthex one and one half meters shorter than the church proper, this difference is not indicated on the plan (pl. 676).

[1036]The traditional location of an atrium in a Greek church is the west side (Orlandos, Xylostegos basilikē, pp. 94-110, pp. 100-101, pls. A and B).

[1037]The east wall is not indicated on the plan (pl. 676). See E. G. Stikas, Praktika, 1971, pl. B after p. 48; hereafter cited as Praktika, 1971.

3.78), to the north through wide doors with marble
thresholds. The only other entrance to the narthex is situated in the northeast corner.[1038] The church proper comprises a nave, V (8.50 x ca. 13.50), which is separated from
single lateral aisles (overall, 3.50 x 18.36) by elevated
stylobates with colonnades running from the east to the west
walls and from the bema by a chancel screen with a prothuron
in the center of its west side. Additional partitions divide
the north and south aisles but, apparently, only those to
the north contain doorways.[1039] In the south aisle, the
east compartment, XII, is completely closed off by a screen
wall (0.39 thick) and it is clear, therefore, that, since it
is accessible only to the bema, the room was restricted to
members of the clergy.[1040] The destruction of the church
and the erection of a small, one-aisled chapel on the east
side destroyed all traces of the synthronon and altar.
Fragments of a polygonal ambon were found somewhere in the
church,[1041] marble foundations of a basin on the northwest

[1038]It appears that at a later date its threshold was
widened by a second block which covered part of the pavement.

[1039]The kind of triple compartmentalization of the
north aisle is unusual and one questions its purpose and
chronology. Since these walls are not discussed in the reports, an on site examination of their fabric and bonding is
necessary.

[1040]A similar division is employed in Alpha, but the
west wall has a doorway. On the other hand, the north side
is blocked by benches (vide supra, pp. 588, 589).

[1041]A. K. Orlandos, To Ergon, 1964, pp. 36-37, figs.
35, 37.

side of the narthex,[1042] and stone benches along the outer walls of the north and south aisles.[1043]

Although no datable internal evidence was uncovered or reported, nor even a chronology advanced, on the basis of the style of the capitals and the mosaics, the basilica can be assigned to the end of the fifth or the beginning of the sixth century.[1044]

Bibliography. D. I. Lazarides, Praktika, 1959, pp. 44-45; idem, Deltion, 16 (1960), B: Chronika, p. 218; A. K. Orlandos, To Ergon, 1959, pp. 41-42; BCH, 84 (1960), p. 798; BCH, 85 (1961), p. 823; E. G. Stikas, Praktika, 1962, pp. 42-46; A. K. Orlandos, To Ergon, 1962, pp. 55-65; BCH, 87 (1963), pp. 802-810; JHS, 83 (1963), Supplement, p. 24; E. G. Stikas, Praktika, 1964, pp. 41-43; A. K. Orlandos, To Ergon, 1964, pp. 30-45; BCH, 89 (1965), pp. 816-823; JHS, 85 (1965), p. 22; E. G. Stikas, Praktika, 1966, p. 39; A. K. Orlandos, To Ergon, 1966, pp. 25-29; BCH, 91 (1967), p. 717; JHS, 87 (1967), Supplement, p. 16; E. G. Stikas, Praktika, 1969, pp. 57-58; A. K. Orlandos, To Ergon, 1969, pp. 65-68; BCH, 94 (1970), p. 1071; JHS, 90 (1970), p. 159; E. G. Stikas, Praktika, 1970, pp. 53-54; A. K. Orlandos, To Ergon, 1970, pp. 42-47; BCH, 95 (1971), p. 976; E. G. Stikas, Praktika, 1971, pp. 45-46; A. K. Orlandos, To Ergon, 1971, pp. 41-47; BCH, 96 (1972), pp. 736-738.

Illustrations. D. I. Lazarides, Praktika, 1959, pl. 49 a-b (capitals); E. G. Stikas, Praktika, 1962, pls. 24-25 (capitals); idem, Praktika, 1964, pl. A after p. 44 (plan, with mosaics), pl. 30a-b (views, looking east), pl. 32a,b,d (fragments of ambon), pl. 34b (general view of south aisle, from west); idem, Praktika, 1966, p. 41, fig. 2 = our pl. 646; idem, Praktika, 1969, pl. B opposite p. 57 = our pl. 676; idem, Praktika, 1971, pl. B after p. 48 = our pl. 677.

[1042]Praktika, 1962, p. 44; A. K. Orlandos, To Ergon, 1962, p. 58.

[1043]The curious niches on the east side of the north aisle are not described or illustrated.

[1044]For the capitals, see Sodini, Catalogue, p. 733, n. 69.

Polychrome geometric pavements with multiple ornamental
borders and many figure insets decorate the major sectors.
The mosaics spread across the surface of each compartment
forming dense all-over carpets of complex designs which
serve as frameworks for various land and sea animals (pls.
678-686, 697-705) or purely geometric motifs (687-696). The
exuberance and richness of the designs, the plethora of
organic filling motifs, and the strongly defined borders
reflect a stylistic and iconographic trend in Greek pavements
which begins to appear in the second half of the fifth century and continues into the sixth century. Unlike the
securely dated mid-sixth century pavements at Klapsi (94-
100) and Nikopolis Alpha (150-155) and the ones in Basilica
Alpha to the southeast (206-214),[1045] the flora and fauna in
this church are more three-dimensional and their contour
lines and poses more fluid and natural. They are more closely related to those at Delphi (82-83), Akrini (189-190), and
Philippi (224) and elsewhere which have been attributed to
the late fifth or early sixth century. Although one must
await the final publication of the architectural and decorative programs of this church, including clearer photographs

[1045]For a comparison of their programs, vide supra,
p. 592.

and color notations, it is certain that its mosaics postdate
by many decades the earliest preserved Greek pavements in
the late fourth and early fifth century buildings at Demetrias (130-138), Dion (178-179) and Tsiphliki (196) which are
aniconic, simple in design, and contain a limited chromatic
scheme. Thus, it is quite possible that the seventh indication cited in an inscription in the west border of Room III
(217, pl. 683) refers to the period between 484 and 514.[1046]

Additional bibliography. Sodini, Catalogue, No. 53,
p. 733.

Illustrations. E. G. Stikas, Praktika, 1969, pl. B
opposite p. 57 = our pl. 676; idem, Praktika, 1971, pl. B
opposite p. 48 = our pl. 677.

217   Room III (4.33 wide; north-south, 20.05; east-west,

11.30). "L-shaped" corridor; pavement terminates
approximately 1.90 meters from the east entrance;[1047] some
lacunae on the south side of IIIa and in the middle of IIIb.
Pls. 677-684.

No published information on dimensions and material.[1048]

"L-shaped" pavement composed of two straight grids, a-b,
with figural insets, enclosed by different borders.

[1046]V. Grumel, Traité d'études byzantines, Vol. 1. La
chronologie, Paris, 1958, p. 314.

[1047]The type of pavement between the end of the mosaic
and the door sill is not noted. To some extent the excavator has restored the damaged section on the plans.

[1048]Only the material in the nave (220) is noted.

IIIa, north panel (pls. 678-682).

Framing: outer border except to north, two undulating
vine rinceaux issue from a ribbed vase with spiral handles
and a small triangular base located in the middle of the
south side (pl. 682). For similar borders in Amphipolis
Alpha, see 206, pl. 648; 207, pls. 649-650. The rinceaux
form widely spaced scrolls which are filled with large
single clusters of grapes.[1049] To the north the pattern is
replaced by "polychrome" fish scales;[1050] dark fillet; light
double fillet; inner border, light and dark wave crests.[1051]

Field (pls. 678-682), framed by a dark single or double
fillet: straight grid composed of a two-strand guilloche
(with a white tessera at each loop) forming seven rows of
three squares each. The squares (0.58), framed by dark
single fillets and single checkerboard fillets, are inscribed
primarily with figures oriented southward and facing westward. Starting with the square in the northwest corner and
moving eastward, the sequence of filling elements is as
follows. First row (pls. 678-679): destroyed, except for
the base of a basket; rabbit flanked above and below by
stylized bushes; wicker basket with a broad base and mouth

[1049]Although the ground is speckled in the plan (pl.
677), it is, in fact, composed of regularly-set rows of
tesserae.

[1050]E. G. Stikas, Praktika, 1966, p. 38, p. 40, fig. 1;
hereafter cited as Praktika, 1966.

[1051]Contrary to the drawing (pl. 676), there is no
light band framing the field.

filled with fruit and decorated with a checkerboard pattern.
Second row: land bird;[1052] long-legged bird (pl. 681);[1053]
land bird (pl. 680).[1054] Third row: quatrefoil of four ivy
leaves placed tip-to-tip inscribed in a medallion outlined
by dark/light/dark fillets; Solomon's knot; quatrefoil
identical to the first one. Fourth row: duck; dolphin and
a small cuttlefish or sepia; speckled fish flanked above and
below by worms or waves. Fifth row: basket similar to the
ones in the first row; bird; basket (see first row). Sixth
row (pl. 682): bird, bird; destroyed. Seventh row:
Solomon's knot; quatrefoil (see third row); destroyed.

IIIb, southeast panel (pls. 677, 682-684).

Framing (pl. 682): dark fillet; outer border, dark undulating vine rinceau (two fillets) forming widely spaced
scrolls which are filled with single agitated heart-shaped
ivy leaves. The border is interrupted in the center of the
west wall by a two-line inscription (4.09 long) containing
the seventh indic⁄tion (pl. 683):"ΥΠΕΡΕΥΧΗϹΟΥΟΙΔΕΝΟΘΕΟϹ
ΤΑΟΝΟΜΑΤΑΚΑΛΙΕΡΓΗϹΑΝ/ΙΝΔ ΕΒΔΟΜΗΝ ";[1055] dark fillet;

[1052]The text incorrectly refers to the bird as a water
fowl (Praktika, 1966, p. 38).

[1053]Surely, it is not a peacock (cf. ibid.).

[1054]Vide supra, p. 617, n. 1052.

[1055]In its transcription in block form in the reports,
it is incorrectly presented as a three-line inscription (see
E. G. Stikas, Praktika, 1969, p. 58; hereafter cited as
Praktika, 1969; A. K. Orlandos, To Ergon, 1969, p. 67; hereafter cited as To Ergon, 1969). For the following transcription, see ibid.: "ΥΠΕΡ ΕΥΧΗϹ ΟΥ ΟΙΔΕΝ Ο ΘΕΟϹ ΤΑ
ΟΝΟΜΑΤΑ ΚΑΛΙΕΡΓΗϹΑΝ/ ΙΝΔ ΕΒΔΟΜΗΝ."

inner border, dark meander patterns (double fillet) forming swastikas.

Field (pls. 682-684), framed by a dark double fillet which forms, at the same time, part of the design: straight grid, formed by a dark fillet, composed of juxtaposed squares joined by single bars flanking a small square set on edge (for an identical design in Amphipolis Alpha, see 206, pl. 648). The squares formed by the grid enclose land birds and water fowl[1056] while the interstitial registers are primarily decorated with pairs of confronting fish, and with single fish along the margins.[1057] In conformance with the "L-shape" design of the corridor, the figures along the north-south axis are oriented southward and those in the east extension of the room are placed on that axis.

Late fifth or early sixth century.

Illustrations. E. Stikas, Praktika, 1966, p. 40, fig. 1 (plan with drawing of north part of IIIa), pl. 20a (rabbit), pl. 20b (bird), pl. 21a = our pl. 681; pl. 21b = our pl. 680, pl. 22a = our pl. 678; idem, Praktika, 1969, pl. 68b = our pl. 679, pl. 69a = our pl. 682, pl. 70a = our pl. 684, pl. 70b = our pl. 683; idem, Praktika, 1971, pl. 57b (IIIb, detail).

[1056]The reports only note water fowl (Praktika, 1969, p. 57; Praktika, 1971, p. 45.)

[1057]In addition to the marine creatures, there are two rows of wicker baskets with fruit and a row of confronting peacocks near the southwest side. It is not possible to determine from the text and illustrations if the marine and land creatures are arranged according to species (Praktika, 1969, p. 57; To Ergon, 1969, p. 67).

218 Room IV (10.10 x 5.75). Southwest annex; outer border
covered by later threshold block; lacunae in center of
pavement.[1058] Pls. 677, 685-686.

Framing: 0.50. Field: 8.92 x 4.57.[1059] No published
information on material.

Polychrome geometric mosaic composed of meanders and
squares, many with figures, enclosed by a double border (for
an identical design in Room XI, see 222, pls. 697-701).

Framing: outer border, row of single, light intersecting
circles on a dark ground; narrow light band; dark triple
fillet; inner border, dark and light wave crests.[1060]

Field (pl. 685), framed by a light triple fillet which
forms, at the same time, part of the design: continuous
meander composed of two intersecting two-strand guilloches,
outlined in white on a dark ground, forming swastikas.
Alternating with the swastikas are dark-framed squares (0.52)
inscribed with flora, fauna and geometric motifs which follow
no specific direction. Starting with the square in the northwest corner and moving eastward, the sequence of filling

---

[1058]This section is restored in the plan (pl. 676); cf.
E. G. Stikas, Praktika, 1970, pl. 81a: hereafter cited as
Praktika, 1970; A. K. Orlandos, To Ergon, 1970, p. 45, fig.
48; hereafter cited as To Ergon, 1970.

[1059]Praktika, 1971, p. 46; A. K. Orlandos, To Ergon,
1971, p. 43; hereafter cited as To Ergon, 1971.

[1060]Although the ground is speckled in the plan (pl.
677), it is, in fact, composed of regularly-set rows of
tesserae.

elements is as follows.[1061]   First row: medallion with an
interlaced straight and concave-sided square; wheel of peltae
inscribed with a small Solomon's knot. Second row: medallion with an eight-pointed star; long-legged bird flanked
above and below by thin bushes; medallion with two interlaced straight squares inscribed with an equilateral cross
composed of four small squares around a central one. Third
row: parrot (pl. 686, bottom left); dolphin (pl. 686, top
left). Fourth row: long-legged bird flanked above and
below by thin bushes; destroyed; bird (pl. 686, center
right). Fifth row: vase with a small base and long spiral
handles and two birds perched on the rim of its mouth (pl.
686, center left); destroyed. Sixth row: small bird
flanked above and below by thin bushes (pl. 686, center
right); destroyed; destroyed. Seventh row: both squares
destroyed. Eighth row: long-legged bird (pl. 686, bottom
right); dolphin (see third row); rooster (pl. 686, top
right). Ninth row: destroyed; small bird (see sixth row).
Tenth row: dolphin (see third and eighth rows); vase (see
fifth row); long-legged bird (see fourth and eighth rows).[1062]

Late fifth or early sixth century.

[1061]For a drawing of this floor, see _Praktika_, 1971,
pl.gamma after p. 48.

[1062]The description of the filling motifs in the reports
does not correspond, in some instances, with the drawings
(see _Praktika_, 1971, p. 46; _To Ergon_, 1971, pp. 43-44).

Illustrations. E. G. Stikas, Praktika, 1971, pl. B after
p. 48 = our pl. 677, pl. 59a (general view), pl. 59b = our
pl. 685, pl. 60a = our pl. 685, pl. 60b (north side); A. K.
Orlandos, To Ergon, 1971, p. 48, fig. 54 = our pl. 686.

219 Room V (16.64 x 3.78). Narthex; pavement laid up to a

marble plaque to northwest and interrupted by a later

threshold block.[1063] South side of pavement destroyed or

damaged.[1064] Pls. 676, 687-690.

No published information on dimensions and material.

Polychrome geometric carpet composed of three panels, a-c,

set within a guilloche framework and bordered by a rinceau.

Framing (pl. 688): border, dark undulating vine rinceau

(two-three fillets) forming rigidly arranged wide scrolls

filled with single heart-shaped ivy leaves. The narrow tips

of the leaves touch the margins;[1065] double fillet.

Field: square panel, b, flanked by two rectangular panels,

a, c, each outlined in white.

Framework: two strand guilloche (pl. 689).

Va (pls. 687-688), north panel, framed by a dark double

fillet which forms, at the same time, part of the design.

[1063]Vide supra, p. 612, n. 1038.

[1064]The extent of the damage is not noted in the
reports, but it is clear that IIIb and IIIc contain lacunae
(see pls. 689-690).

[1065]Only the rinceau is represented in the plan (pl.
676). The descriptive and illustrative data on this pavement are inadequate (see Praktika, pp. 42-44).

The design, articulated by dark double fillets and cut along the margins, can be read two ways: interlocking stars composed of four pairs of light lozenges forming a central four-pointed dark star, outlined in white, which is inscribed with straight concentric squares; white tangent octagons, set on edge, filled with diagonal four-pointed dark stars inscribed with squares set on edge (for simpler versions, see 136, pl. 436; 178, pl. 601). The center of each lozenge is accented by a small quatrefoil composed of heart-shaped leaves placed base-to-tip. Unlike the rinceau and guilloche in the border and framework, which are laid up to the edge of a marble plaque (pl. 688), a white surround, framed in black, separates the plaque from the field design.

Vb, central panel (pl. 688), framed by a dark double fillet: tilted square inscribed with a shield pattern composed of spiral rows of small squares radiating from a circle. In each of the four spandrels between the edge of the dark/light/dark-outlined shield and the square frame, stands a single, ribbed vase with two long spiral handles and a triangular base. Single rigid vines issue symmetrically from its wide mouth and cover the surface with clusters of grapes, spiral tendrils, and leaves (for a similar panel in Room VI, see 220, pls. 694-696).

Vc, south panel (pl. 690), framed by a dark double fillet: stars of eight lozenges, outlined by a dark double fillet, forming large straight squares and small squares set on edge (for a similar design, see 20, pls. 56-57). The large

squares are cut along the north and west margins. The lozenges and small squares have dark centers, outlined in white,
and, except for the small diagonal crosslets accenting the
squares, are plain. The large squares, on the other hand,
contain decorative motifs, of which three are preserved on
the east side: checkerboard; meander; quatrefoil composed
of four lanceolate leaves set on a diagonal square.

Late fifth or early sixth century.

   Illustrations. E. G. Stikas, Praktika, 1959, pl. 47 (Vc,
detail), pl. 48a = our pl. 687, pl. 48b = our pl. 689; idem,
Praktika, 1962, pl. 26a = our pl. 690, pl. 26b (Vc, detail),
pl. 28a = our pl. 688, pl. 28b (Vc, detail).

220 Room VI (8.50 x ca. 13.50). Nave; pavement laid up to
      the prothuron;[1066] east side destroyed by the founda-
tions of a later chapel. Pls. 676, 691-696.
   Fragment: 8.50 x 10.70 max. Stone tesserae.[1067] No
other published information on dimensions and material.

_____

   [1066]The exact disposition of the east side of the pavement is problematic. Since traces of the fifth, inner border were found on the east side, it is clear that the borders
or at least four of them, turned in front of the prothuron
(pl. 676). Since there is no room for the first rinceau
border, it must have continued beyond this point and up to
the north and south sides of the screen and perhaps served
as a framework for the paving in the rectangular sectors
between the prothuron and the north and south stylobates. It
is not unusual to find separate panels in these two sectors
(see 182; 188).

   [1067]Praktika, 1962, p. 45.

Polychrome geometric pavement, enclosed by five borders,
composed of a central square set on a ground of interlaced
lozenges.

Framing (pls. 691-692): first border, undulating dark
rinceau (one fillet) forming widely spaced scrolls which are
filled with single agitated heart-shaped ivy leaves. The
width of the border is increased at the west entrance (cf.
pls. 691 and 692); dark double fillet; light triple fillet;
second border, dark and light wave crests; dark fillet;
light triple fillet; third border, overlapping lyre pattern
(with clusters of small tesserae at each loop) on a dark
ground; light triple fillet; dark fillet; fourth border,
light and dark wave crests; light triple fillet; fifth
border, undulating ribbon pattern with single lotiform
flowers at each wave, set on a dark ground.

Ground (pls. 693, 695), framed by a light triple fillet
which forms, at the same time, part of the design: interlocking design of diagonal stars, separated by lozenges, each
composed of two interlaced lozenges with truncated semi-
circular ends. The latter are decorated with small disks and
the overall design is cut along the margins. Each star comprises a lozenge bordered by a two-strand guilloche and by
either a rainbow cable or an undulating ribbon. The complexity of the design is heightened by the inner white bands,
outlined in black, defining each segment of the lozenges and
by the abstract filling motifs. Among the latter there are
concentric stepped squares set on edge, "eye motifs," groups

of four tangent perspectivized lozenges, polyfoils composed
of lanceolate leaves, and straight or diagonal four-pointed
stars.

Central panel (pls. 694-696): square (ca. 2.80 diam)
inscribed with a shield pattern, framed by a white band with
black outlines, comprising spiral rows of small squares
radiating from a small circle. The latter also contains a
shield motif and a light frame, outlined in black. In each
of the four spandrels between the edge of the large shield
and the square frame, stands a single ribbed vase with two
spiral handles and a triangular base. Single undulating
vines issue symmetrically from the wide mouth of the vase
and fill the surface with clusters of grapes, leaves, and
spiral tendrils (for a similar panel in Room V, see 219,
pl. 688). The chromatic scheme of the pavement is based on
various combinations of white, black, red, rose, yellow,
green, and purple.[1068]

Late fifth or early sixth century.

Illustrations. E. G. Stikas, Praktika, 1962, p. 43, fig.
1 (plan with west side of pavement), p. 45, fig. 2 (west
side, drawing), pl. 30a (borders), pl. 30b (west side), pl.
31b = our pl. 691; idem, Praktika, 1964, pl. A after p. 42
(plan, with mosaics), pl. 28a = our pl. 695, pl. 28b (north
side), pl. 29a (south side), pl. 29b = our pl. 696, pl. 31a
(detail of vase); A. K. Orlandos, To Ergon, 1964, p. 34,
fig. 33 = our pl. 693.

[1068]Ibid.

221 Room (s) VIII-X (3.50 x 18.36). North aisle.

No published information on dimensions and material.

Brief mention of a polychrome mosaic pavement.[1069]

Probably contemporary with the other pavements and, therefore, late fifth or early sixth century.

222 Room XI (3.50 x 13.34). South aisle; pavement laid up
     to stone benches along south and west sides and to
screen wall to east. Pls. 676, 697-701.

No published information on dimensions and material.

Polychrome geometric mosaic composed of meanders and squares
enclosed by a double border (for an identical design in Room
IV, see 218, pls. 677, 685).

  Framing: outer border, undulating vine rinceau forming
rigidly arranged narrow scrolls which are filled with single
agitated heart-shaped ivy leaves;[1070] dark double fillet;
light triple fillet; inner border, undulating ribbon with

[1069]E. G. Stikas, Praktika, 1964, p. 42; hereafter cited
as Praktika, 1964; A. K. Orlandos, To Ergon, 1964, p. 37. On
the problematic division of this sector, vide supra, p. 612
n. 1039.

[1070]Since only the inner border is visible in a photograph (pl. 698), this description is based on the drawing
in the plan (pl. 676).

four dots at each wave (pl. 698).[1071]

Field, framed by a light double or triple fillet which forms, at the same time, part of the design: continuous meander design composed of two intersecting two-strand guilloches, outlined in white on a dark ground, forming swastikas. Alternating with the swastikas are dark-framed squares inscribed with birds and domesticated and wild animals[1072] amid trees and bushes with spatulate leaves (for similar flora in Room XII, see 223, pls. 702-704). On the east side (pl. 697), there are a leaping panther (pl. 698), a running rabbit, a long-legged bird pecking at its feet (pl. 699), a walking bull and a leaping dog. Toward the west, other animals and birds are depicted, including a leaping stag (pl. 700), land birds and water fowl, a horse, a hippopotamus (pl. 701), a boar, and a lamb.[1073]

Late fifth or early sixth century.

Illustrations. E. G. Stikas, Praktika, 1964, pl. 34a (west side, lamb), pl. 34b (general view, looking east), pl. 35a (beribboned bird), pl. 35b = our pl. 698, pl. 36a = our pl. 700, pl. 37a (boar), pl. 37b = our pl. 701, pl. 38a = our pl. 699, pl. 38b (dog).

[1071]A report incorrectly lists three borders (Praktika, 1964, p. 41).

[1072]Because of the meager descriptive and illustrative data, the sequence and orientation of the figures cannot be determined.

[1073]See Praktika, 1964, pp. 42-43. The other figural pavements in the building do not contain animals (217, 218, 223).

223 Room XII (3.50 x 4.62). Southeast annex; pavement
laid up to west screen wall and to stone benches along
east and south walls; south bench interrupted in the middle
by a narrow figural panel. Pls. 676, 702-704.

No published information on dimensions and material.

Polychrome pavement comprising ellipses with birds surrounded
by geometric and marine motifs and bordered by a vine rinceau.

Framing (pl. 705): border, undulating vine rinceau (one
fillet) forming widely spaced scrolls which are filled with
single agitated heart-shaped ivy leaves (for a similar border in Room VI, see 220, pls. 691-692); dark fillet; light
band.

Field (pls. 702-704), framed by a dark fillet: on the east-
west axis, two groups of diagonal stars composed of four
ellipses each which radiate from a concave-sided, two-strand
guilloche square set on edge.[1074] The ellipses, bordered by
undulating ribbons, enclose single water fowl (pls. 702-703)
and land birds (pls. 702, 704) amid stalks articulated by
spatulate leaves (for similar flora in Room XI, see 222, pls.

[1074]Although it is true that this grouping of the
ellipses can also be read from the north-south axis, that is
to say from the north entrance, the chiastic relationship of
the birds and their westward orientation establish their disposition on the minor axis. On the other hand, the figures
in the small south panel (pl. 705) are oriented northward.
This dual orientation is also present in Room III where the
figures and the inscription face in different directions
(pl. 677).

697-701).[1075] Completing the design are various "decorative
motifs and fish"[1076] which encircle each ellipse and fill
the intervening spaces with complex surface patterns.

A narrow rectangular panel (0.36 x 1.68) interrupts the
stone bench to the south (pl. 705). It contains three groups
of two opposed birds, oriented northward, which turn toward
each other and hold single garlands of flowers in their
beaks.

Late fifth or early sixth century.

Illustrations. E. G. Stikas, _Praktika_, 1964, pl. 39a =
our pl. 705, pl. 39b = our pl. 702, pl. 40a = our pl. 704,
pl. 40b = our pl. 703.

PHILIPPI

Basilica beneath the Octagonal Church

East of the forum and agora at Philippi, excavations
were begun in 1962 on a building which lay beneath an octagonal Early Christian church. In two subsequent campaigns,
1963 and 1966, parts of its east and north sides were brought
to light along with a large segment of a well preserved tessellated pavement. At the present time, the mosaics are

---

[1075]Although the birds and leaves are identified as
"aquatic," this is not substantiated by the photographs (cf.
pl. 703 and 704). See _Praktika_, 1964, p. 43.

[1076]Ibid.

covered.

Since the major portion of the earlier building remains covered by the octagonal church, it was only possible to determine its overall shape and probable function. It is a rectangular building comprising an apse to the east and an interior subdivided at least to the south by a stylobate. The shape and internal division suggest a Christian basilica with the exposed stylobate (0.80 wide)[1077] serving as a probable separator between the nave and the south aisle. Part of the central aisle was cleared bringing to light a mosaic decorated with four figural panels which are enclosed by two wide decorative borders (pls. 706-713). Given the complexities and difficulties associated with excavating a building which is far less important than its successor,[1078] it is probable that its overall plan and decorative program will never be determined.

A terminus ante quem of around 500 A.D. is supplied by the date of the octagonal church[1079] and it is substantiated by the style of the pavement. The chronological distance between the first and second churches is not a great one

[1077]Surely, the published height (1.42) is a misprint (see St. Pelekanides, Praktika, 1962, p. 177); hereafter cited as Praktika, 1962.

[1078]See Krautheimer, Architecture, pp. 97-98.

[1079]Ibid., p. 97. The date is, of course, tentative because the building had only been partially cleared at the time of the publication of his book. One awaits final word on the matter in the forth-coming second edition.

because the pavement can be attributed to the second half of
the fifth century.

Bibliography. St. Pelekanides, Praktika, 1962, pp. 177-178;
A. K. Orlandos, To Ergon, 1962, p. 74; St. Pelekanides,
Praktika, 1963, pp. 87-88; A. K. Orlandos, To Ergon, 1963,
pp. 56-57; BCH, 87 (1963), p. 814; JHS, 83 (1963), Supplement,
p. 24; St. Pelekanides, Deltion, 19 (1964), B3: Chronika, p.
385; BCH, 88 (1964), p. 791; JHS, 84 (1964), Supplement, pp.
19-20; St. Pelekanides, Praktika, 1966, pp. 56-58; A. K.
Orlandos, To Ergon, 1966, pp. 53-54; St. Pelekanides,
Praktika, 1967, p. 82; idem, Balkan Studies, 8, no. 1 (1967),
pp. 123-126; A. K. Orlandos, To Ergon, 1967, pp. 53-54;
BCH, 92 (1968), p. 916; JHS, 88 (1968), p. 16.

Illustrations. St. Pelekanides, Praktika, 1961, p. 70,
fig. 1 (plan of octagon and adjacent buildings); idem,
Praktika, 1966, p. 48, fig. 1 (plan of east side of octagon,
showing apse of earlier church).

No. 224

A segment of a pavement is decorated with four figural

panels and multiple ornamental borders of varying width. The

square panels are filled with large and small birds shown

pecking at leaves suspended from attenuated branches which

spread across the surface. In two scenes (pls. 711, 713), a

tree with a wide bulbous crown of branches and leaves rises

in the center and is surrounded by branches and birds which

are disposed in multiple registers and in various directions.

Another scene contains peacocks and other birds which are

scattered among a sinuous, spreading grape-bearing vine

issuing from a vase.[1080] In light of the essentially aniconic

———————————

[1080]Parts of this scene are visible in two photographs
(pls. 712, top and 713, top).

and less decorative pavements in the Extra Muros church at
Philippi (225-226, pls. 716-719), in other areas of northern
Greece (178-179; 196), and in central Greece (88-92; 130-
138) which can be dated to a period no later than the first
half of the fifth century, the Philippi pavement can be
assigned to the second half of the century. At this time
and continuing into the sixth century, multiple figural
compositions enclosed by wide and complex geometric and
floral borders become popular in Macedonia (189-190; 197;
206-214; 217-223).

Additional bibliography. Sodini, Catalogue, No. 58, p.
736.

224 Room I (dimensions indeterminable). Nave; pavement
continues under the foundations of a later church and
up to a stylobate to the south (pl. 712). Pls. 706-713.
No published information on dimensions and material.

Segment of a mosaic pavement containing four tangent figural
panels with decorative bands enclosed by geometric and interlace borders.

Framing (pls. 706-707): outer border, two rows of intersecting octagons forming small squares and elongated hexagons. The pattern is articulated by light double fillets
and set on a dark ground (for a similar pattern in a field,
see 90, pls. 311-312); white triple fillet; second border,
narrow row of light and dark crowsteps; third border, double

overlapping lyre pattern on a dark ground with clusters of
white tesserae between each loop and a single one along its
sides; fourth border, narrow row of light and dark crowsteps.

Field (pls. 708-713): traces of four panels, a-d, set
within a narrow white framework and surrounded by different
borders. Beginning with the west panel, the sequence of
scenes is as follows.

Ia, west panel (pls. 708-709), framed by a dark fillet:
large medallion bordered by a two-strand guilloche (with
a white tessera at each loop and along its sides) on a dark
ground and inscribed with a wheel pattern containing eight
small radiating compartments. These wedge-shaped units are
filled with an alternating series of single pecking land
birds, surrounded by leaf-bearing branches,[1081] and flower
laden baskets or fruit bearing branches. Since the birds
are too large for their compartments (pls. 709-710), they
are represented in a seated position with their legs thrust
awkwardly in front of them (pls. 709-710). This obtains as
well for the flora whose spreading branches and leaves are
constricted by the size of the panels. In the spandrels between the edge of the medallion and the corners of the
square, there are single ornamental motifs composed of pairs
of peltae placed tip-to-tip which are bisected by single
leaf-bearing branches.

[1081]Sodini incorrectly identifies the birds as water
fowl and omits the baskets (Catalogue, p. 736); for the
excavator's description, see Praktika, 1962, p. 178.

Ib, second panel (pl. 711).

Framework: border, wide dark band which is striated at
regular intervals by single, serrate-edged rows of light
tesserae.

Field, framed by a light double fillet: truncated octagon
decorated with a large tree with a gnarled trunk and a
bulbous crown of leaves and branches. Oriented westward,
it rises from a rocky terrain inhabited by three pecking
birds amid leaf-bearing branches which spring from the
ground and the tree trunk. Above, to the right, an isolated
bird is shown suspended in space as it pecks at the leaves
of the tree. Of the decoration in the spandrels between
the angles of the square and the edge of the octagon, only
a small white wheel motif is visible. Whether it represents
a restoration or an isolated mark cannot be determined.

Ic, third panel: in two partial views (pl. 712, top and
713, top) it appears that, unlike the scenes which flank it,
it is oriented southward.

Framing: light and dark wave crests.

Field: visible are the ocellate tail coverts of two large
peacocks and traces of vines with leaves and clusters of
grapes. The birds presumably occupied the east and west
sides of the panels and by their size must have dominated
the scene. A published description states that it ". . . was
filled with various scenes . . . a tree with birds pecking at
fruit and buds (and) confronting peacocks on a crator from
which issues a fruit bearing vine which climbs and spreads

across the entire surface."[1082] Until a complete photograph
of this scene is reproduced, its precise composition remains
problematic.

Id, east panel (pl. 713).

Border: crude white on dark meander forming swastikas and
squares.[1083]

Field, framed by a dark fillet: like the second panel
(Ib, pl. 711), it is dominated by a central tree with a
bulbous crown of leaves and branches. Around it are arrayed
two large peacocks and three land birds which are asymetri-
cally disposed in unrelated registers. The total absence of
organization, coupled with the curious half-seated, half-
standing poses of the birds[1084] reflect an attempt to unite
figures from disparate sources. Although the other panels
also appear to be conflations of one sort or another, this
is by far the least imaginative and successful one among
them.

Late fifth century.

Illustrations. St. Pelekanides, Praktika, 1962, pl. 173a
= our pl. 708, pl. 173b = our pl. 709, pl. 174a = our pl.

[1082]St. Pelekanides, Praktika, 1963, pp. 87-88; see
also A. K. Orlandos, To Ergon, 1963, pp. 56-57. Since Sodini
omits the crator, it is obvious that he bases his description
on the published photographs (Catalogue, p. 736).

[1083]This is a curious meander pattern because one of
the vertical bars of the swastika is not joined to the horizontal framing along the top.

[1084]See also the west panel (Ia, pls. 709-710).

710, pl. 174b = our pl. 707; idem, Praktika, 1963, pl. 62b
= our pl. 712; idem, Deltion, 19 (1964), B3: Chronika, pl.
450gamma = our pl. 711; A. K. Orlandos, To Ergon, 1967, p.
53, fig. 49 (Id); St. Pelekanides, Praktika, 1967, pl. 55 =
our pl. 713, pl. 56b = our pl. 706.

Basilica Extra Muros

In the town of Krenis, about one kilometer beyond the
Roman and Christian walls of the city of Philippi, an Early
Christian basilica with many annexes (overall, 43.00 x
22.00) was excavated in 1956 and 1957.[1085] Traces of tessellated pavements were found in the esonarthex and nave and
stone and brick slabs in the other rooms.[1086] At the present
time, the mosaics have disappeared and the site is overgrown.

Although the building history of this Extra Muros complex appears to be clearly defined, the sole archaeological
report raises more questions than it answers, especially in
regard to the chronology of two of the three building phases
and, ultimately, of the mosaic pavements. In the first
phase (pl. 714), the basilica was preceded by an atrium, I,
and two narthexes, III-IV, with north and south annexes V-
VIII. The church proper consisted of a nave, IX (9.20 x

[1085]For churches within the walls, see 224, and P.
Lemerle, Philippes et la Macédoine orientale, Paris, 1945.

[1086]Stone slabs were found in Rooms III, XII, dark blue
shist in the aisles, X-XI, and ceramic slabs in VII and VIII.
The paving in the other rooms is not noted (St. Pelekanides,
ArchEph, 1955, pp. 130ff; hereafter cited as Pelekanides).

27.50), separated from two lateral aisles, X-XI (3.20 wide),
by colonnades resting on bases and terminated by a raised
semi-circular apse with an inscribed, stepped synthronon.
In front of the synthronon and approximately fifty centimeters from the chord of the apse, an enkainion was found and
in the center of the nave a section of the base of an ambon.
No trace is preserved of a chancel screen or an altar above
the enkainion, although presumably they formed part of the
liturgical furnishings. The annexes along the north side of
the church are assigned pre-liturgical functions, with Rooms
VI and VII serving as the diakonikon and Room XIII as the
prothesis.[1087] The tessellated pavements have been assigned
to the first building phase which the excavator assigns to
the Constantinian period.[1088] Sodini has correctly pointed
out that the numismativ evidence used to substantiate this
chronology is inconclusive, since the coins were not found
in a sealed layer but in the fill between the top of the
tombs (B and H, pl. 714) and the slabs.[1089] In addition, in
my judgment, the presence of Latin inscriptions on two tomb

[1087]Pelekanides, pp. 132-135; Hoddinott, Early Byzantine
Churches, pp. 100-101. For studies on protheses and diakonika, see Orlandos, Hē metakinēsis tou diakonikou, pp. 353-
372; G. Babić, Les chapelles annexes des églises byzantines:
fonction liturgique et programmes iconographiques, Paris,
1969. The function of the room on the south side (VIII) is
not discussed.

[1088]Pelekanides, pp. 172-179, especially pp. 175-176.

[1089]Catalogue, p. 737 and n. 77; cf. Pelekanides, pp.
153, 161.

slabs (Θ; other not identified)[1090] does not militate
against a later date, as the excavator argues, because Latin
continued to be used well into the fifth and sixth centuries.[1091] The absence of a baptistery and the presence of
an enkainion are also cited as arguments for an early date.
Since enkainia are found in later churches (102-115) and
baptisteries are frequently absent from later churches (150-
161; 206-223), this evidence is also inconclusive. A pur-
suasive counter-argument is supplied by the style and iconography of the narthex mosaic. The published photographs of
the mosaic (pls. 716-719) refute the claim that the organic
forms are subtly modeled and three-dimensional. They are,
in fact, somewhat schematic and two-dimensional and not,
therefore, "reminiscent of mosaic work of the Late Antique
period,"[1092] whatever is implied by that general attribution.
This is substantiated by the presence of figural insets of
birds and dolphins which are absent from the earliest preserved Greek pavements at Epidaurus (44-49), Arkitsa (88-92),
Demetrias (130-138), Dion (178-179) and Tsiphliki (196) and

[1090]Pelekanides, pp. 171-172, figs. 59-60, p. 175.

[1091]For important epigraphical studies, see H. Zilliacus,
Zum Kampf der Weltsprachen im östromischen Reich, Helsingfors, 1935, pp. 20 and passim; H. Mihaescu, Revue des études
sud-est européennes, 6 (1968), pp. 481-498; idem, Revue des
études sud-est européennes, 7 (1969), pp. 267-280. I am
grateful to Mr. John Wiita of Dumbarton Oaks for these
references.

[1092]Pelekanides, pp. 140-141. An accompanying note (1)
on page 141 refers to Doro Levi's study, Antioch Mosaic Pavements, Princeton, 1947, without citing specific illustrations.

which, on internal and external evidence, are reliably dated
to the late fourth or early fifth century. For these
reasons, therefore, if one is to accept the contemporaneity
of the building and the mosaics, then a fifth century date,
not an early fourth century date, is certain.

The basilica was partially destroyed by fire and rebuilt and remodeled during the period of Justinian I (527-
565).[1093] At this time (pl. 715), elevated stylobates
with piers were installed between the nave and the aisles
and benches were placed along the north and south walls of
the church proper and the south wall of the narthex.[1094] The
east side was converted into a tripartite transept and was
separated from the rest of the church by a chancel screen extending from the north to the south walls of the aisles.[1095]
Evidently, except for the entrance to Room VII, which was
blocked by a bench, the other annexes continued in use. The
third and last phase of the site is represented by a small
one-aisled apsidal basilica (6.00 x 2.90) which was

[1093]Pelekanides, pp. 125-127; coins of Justinian I were
found beneath the north stylobate (p. 174, fig. 61, 7-8).

[1094]The north bench closed off Room VII. Since the
tombs scattered throughout the church do not belong to a
specific building phase, they will not be discussed here (see
Pelekanides, pp. 150-172; Hoddinott, Early Byzantine
Churches, pp. 103-106. It should be noted, however, that
the arguments for the installation of the majority of them
between the first and second building phases are not convincing.

[1095]Pelekanides, pp. 125-126. The south side of the
screen was covered by a later wall which is visible in the
plan (pl. 715). This wall is not assigned to any specific
phase.

constructed with material from the earlier church.

Bibliography. St. Pelekanides, ArchEph, 1955, pp. 114-179; Hoddinott, Early Byzantine Churches, pp. 98-106; D. I. Pallas, RAC, 35 (1959), p. 194.

Illustrations. St. Pelekanides, ArchEph, 1955, p. 114, fig. 1 (general view, from west), p. 117, fig. 2 = our pl. 714, p. 118, fig. 3 (apse, showing synthronon), p. 119, fig. 4 (enkainion), p. 123, fig. 7 = our pl. 715, p. 125, fig. 8 (south stylobate), p. 134, fig. 13 (bases of table in room VII), p. 144-153, figs. 23-35 (decorative sculpture), pp. 154-172, figs. 36-60 (plans, decoration, and inscriptions of tombs).

Nos. 225-226

Red, white and blue mosaics pave the narthex and nave. Of these pavements only the one in the narthex can, for the most part, be reconstituted from the published material (pls. 716-717). It comprises a central panel with intersecting circles which is flanked to the north and south by identical grids inscribed with ornamental and organic motifs. The presence of birds and dolphins in rather simple geometric designs argues for a date in the fifth century when figural insets begin to become popular in Greek pavements. The pavement and the others are to be placed between the aniconic geometric pavements of the late fourth or early fifth centuries[1096] and the late fifth century pavement at Philippi (224, pls. 706-713) which contains large figural compositions

[1096]Vide supra, p. 638.

set within complex borders.[1097] They can be assigned, therefore, to around the middle of the fifth century.

Additional bibliography. Sodini, Catalogue, No. 59, pp. 736-737.

Illustration. St. Pelekanides, ArchEph, 1955, p. 117, fig. 2 = our pl. 714.

225 Room IV (15.60 x 5.30). Esonarthex; two tombs installed
along the north wall and before the entrance to the
nave, destroying the pavement; benches installed along the
south wall (pl. 715). Pls. 716-717.

No published information on dimensions. White (stone),
red (ceramic), and blue (glass and stone) tesserae.[1098]

Tripartite pavement composed of a central panel with intersecting circles, b, and flanking panels, a,c, with identical
grids.

IVa (pls. 716-717).

Framing: blue fillet; white double fillet; blue fillet;
outer border, white bead-and-reel on a variegated red and
ochre ground; blue fillet; inner border, blue and white wave
crests.

Field, framed by a blue fillet which forms, at the same

[1097]See also Basilica Gamma at Amphipolis, 217-227
which is datable to the late fifth or early sixth century.

[1098]No information on the color and material of the tesserae is contained in the report but a colored reproduction
in Hoddinott's study (Early Byzantine Churches, pl. II)
clearly shows that these materials were used.

time, part of the design: straight grid, outlined in blue, forming red and white squares which are inscribed with an alternating series of diagonal quatrefoils and circles. The lanceolate leaves of the white quatrefoils are usually accented by single red or red and white elliptical filling motifs and the circles contain red or red and blue umbrella motifs and single birds or dolphins which follow no compositional sequence.[1099]

IVb, central panel (pl. 717): traces of white intersecting circles forming red concave-sided squares.[1100]

IVc, south panel: framing and field identical to those in north panel (IVa, pls. 716-717).

Around the middle of the fifth century.

Illustrations. St. Pelekanides, ArchEph, 1955, p. 140, fig. 18 = our pl. 717, p. 141, fig. 19 (general view); Hoddinott, Early Byzantine Churches, pl. 12a = our pl. 716, pl. 12b (border, north side), pl. II (colored reproduction).

226 Room IX (15.50 x 27.50). Nave. Pls. 718-719.

Fragment along north and northeast sides. No published information on dimensions. Materials identical to those in Room IV (225).

[1099]For somewhat different descriptions, see Pelekanides, pp. 140-141; Sodini, Catalogue, p. 737. The dolphins are not visible in the illustrations.

[1100]It cannot be determined if the borders around the north and south panels (IVa, c) surround this panel.

Traces of a triple border with geometric and floral patterns.

Framing (pls. 718-719): red double fillet; outer border, "continuous floral pattern;"[1101] red double fillet; middle border, row of intersecting semi-circles forming alternating red and blue ogive arches; red double fillet; inner border, undulating rinceau (double fillet) forming rigidly arranged and widely spaced scrolls filled with single heart-shaped ivy leaves. The pointed tips of the alternating blue and red leaves touch the margins; red double fillet.

Field: destroyed.

Around the middle of the fifth century.

Illustrations. St. Pelekanides, ArchEph, 1955, p. 139, fig. 16 = our pl. 719, p. 140, fig. 17 = our pl. 718.

MARONEIA

Two Mosaic Fragments

In 1917, a mosaic pavement was noted in the ancient town of Maroneia, northwest of Alexandroupolis. It was described as containing an interlace, and scrolls and fish scale patterns. Accompanying the report was a photograph of a fragment decorated with a scale and scroll pattern (pl.

[1101]St. Pelekanides, p. 139; Hoddinott, Early Byzantine Churches, p. 102. This is not visible in the photographs and it is omitted by Sodini, Catalogue, p. 737.

720),[1102] but not the interlace. In 1971, an excavation in
the same city brought to light a mosaic decorated with an
interlace design (pl. 721)[1103] which may or may not be part
of the pavement recorded in 1917. Since no subsequent report
on this site has appeared, and the style of the two designs
are different, they will be presented as separate entries
until their architectural provenance can be determined.

   Bibliography. AA, 1-2 (1918), cols. 34-36; A. K. Orlandos,
To Ergon, 1971, pp. 97-98.

227 Mosaic fragment (no dimensions published). Pl. 720.
   No published information on dimensions and material.

In a photograph (pl. 720), there are four vertical bands
separated by dark single fillets. The first two on the left
side appear to be plain while the third contains an undulating rinceau (one fillet) forming regularly disposed spirals
which are filled with single volutes. This band flanks an
imbrication pattern composed of scales with colored tips
which fan in the same direction. The pavement was described
as being composed of white, red, and dark blue tesserae and
it was assigned to the Christian period.[1104] Since so
little of the design is visible, it is impossible to accept

[1102]AA, 1-2 (1918), col. 34-36.

[1103]A. K. Orlandos, To Ergon, 1971, pp. 97-98.

[1104]AA, 1-2 (1918), col. 35.

or reject this attribution.

Early Christian?

Illustration. AA, 1-2 (1918), col. 36, fig. 39 = our pl. 720.

No. 228

A fragment of a mosaic (pl. 721) was discovered in the course of an excavation in 1971 which may be part of the preceding pavement (227) or belong to the same building.[1105] On the basis of its design and style, it can be assigned to a period no earlier than the second half of the fifth century when complex interlaces with organic filling elements begin to appear as field designs (14, pls. 42-43; 18, pls. 51-52; 19, pls. 53-54).[1106]

Bibliography. A. K. Orlandos, To Ergon, 1971, pp. 97-98; BCH, 96 (1972), p. 746.

228 Mosaic fragment (no dimensions published). Pl. 721.

No published information on dimensions and material.

In a photograph (pl. 721), there are two compartments with

[1105]Vide supra, p. 644.

[1106]It is curious that this interlace does not appear elsewhere in Greece. The more common design is composed of a less intricate interlace of circles forming straight or curvilinear octagons (see, for example, 150, pls. 460-461).

identical designs separated by a wide horizontal border.

Border: wide light band; light and dark stepped triangles; dark band; light band; dark band; light and dark stepped triangles; light band.

Field: complex interlace of "knots of Herakles"[1107] forming large and small curvilinear octagons. The latter are decorated with buds in various combinations and the former with a variety of figural elements which face in various directions. Among them are birds, a dolphin with a trident, an oenochoë, and two wicker baskets flanked by curving branches.

No earlier than the second half of the fifth century.

[1107]For the nomenclature and other examples of this interlace, see H. Stern et al., Répertoire graphique du décor géométrique dans la mosaïque antique. Bulletin de l'association internationale pour l'etude de la mosaïque antique, 4th fascicule, May (1973), Paris, p. 45, nos. 211-213.

APPENDIX I

CHRONOLOGICAL TABLE OF THE PAVEMENTS[1108]

Fourth Century

*Kenchreae. Building (38-41)

Anchialos Gamma (110-111) ?

Tanagra. Basilica (74) ?

Late Fourth or Early
Fifth Century

Nikopolis. Secular Building
  (168). Restoration

*Demetrias Beta (139-140)

Arkitsa. Basilica (88-92)

*Demetrias Alpha. PERIOD I
  (130-132)

Epidauros. Basilica (44-49)

Tsiphliki. Building (196)

Hermione. Mosaic Fragment (66)

*Athens. Private House South of
  the Acropolis (2-3)

*Athens. Metroon (1)

*Athens. Tetraconch (6-9)

Athens. Fragment in Byzantine
  Museum (24)

Athens. Villa or Gymnaseion (21)

_____

    [1108]Asterisks denote pavements which are securely dated
by external evidence.

*Demetrias Alpha. PERIOD II
  (133-135)

Dion Alpha (178-179)

Astros. Christian Chapel (58) ?

Middle or Second Half of
the Fifth Century

Demetrias Alpha. PERIOD III,
  PHASE 1 (136-138)

Epidauros. Secular Building
  (50-51)

Aixone. Hall (28)

Athens. Ilissos Basilica (10-13)

Philippi. Basilica Extra Muros
  (225-226)

Anchialos Gamma. PERIOD I
  (105-109)

Lavreotic Olympus. Basilica
  (34-35)

Lake Doïranis. Building (205)

Saint Constantine. Basilica
  (93)

Phtelia. Villa (172-175)

Anthedon. Basilica (77-78)

Trikkala. Basilica (142)

Anchialos Gamma. PERIOD I or II
  (112-113)

Mariolata. Basilica (87)

Salonika. Mosaic Fragments (204)

Kalambaka. Basilica (143-145)

Demetrias Alpha. PERIOD III,
  PHASE 2 (138)

Post Middle of the
Fifth Century

Athens. Building South of the
  Acropolis (4-5)

<u>Possibly up to the
  Sixth Century</u>

<u>Second Half of the
  Fifth Century</u>

Hermione. Basilica (61, 64-65)

Anchialos Delta. PERIOD I,
  PHASE 1 (116-120)

Athens. Villa in National Garden
  (14-20)

Athens. Thermae near Zappeion
  (22)

Athens. Villa on Nikē and
  Apollo Streets (23)

Akrini. Trefoil Church
  (189-190)

Argos Orestikon. Mosaic
  Fragment (191)

Amphissa. Mosaic Fragments
  (85)

Philippi. Basilica under
  Octagonal Church (224)

Elis. Mosaic Pavement (43)

Tegea. Christian Building
  (69-70)

Tegea. Basin (71) ?

Old Corinth. Building (42)

Edessa. Building (203

Amphipolis Beta (215-216)

Maroneia. Mosaic Fragment (228)

Late Fifth or Early
Sixth Century

*Nikopolis Beta. PERIOD I
(157-160)

Thebes. Christian Building
(75-76)

Delphi. Basilica (82-83)

Hypati. Mosaic Fragment (101)

Amphipolis Gamma (217-223)

Nikopolis Delta (162-164)

Paleopyrga. Building. PERIOD I,
PHASE 1 (152)

Nikopolis Epsilon (165-167)

*Nikopolis Beta. PERIOD II
(161)

Philiatra. Basilica (73)   Possibly up to the First Half
                                       of the Sixth Century

Kephalos Beta (148)   Perhaps only Sixth Century

Veroia. Three Mosaic
Fragments (192-193   Perhaps only Sixth Century

Paleopyrga. Building (54).   Possibly up to the Middle of
PERIOD I, PHASE 1 or 2   the Sixth Century

Sixth Century

Dion Beta (180-183)

Hermione. Basilica (59-60,
62-63)

Voskochori. Basilica
(186-188)

Kephalos Alpha (146-147)

Theotokou. Basilica (123-128)

Longos. Basilica Alpha.
PERIOD I, PHASE 1 (197)

Sixth Century
(Cont.)

Kerameikos. Mosaic Fragments
(25-27)

Aigosthena. Basilica (29-33)

*Nikopolis Alpha. PERIOD I,
PHASE 1 (150-155)

Argos. Villa (55-57)

Klapsi. Basilica (94-100)

Amphipolis Alpha (206-214)

Haghia Paraskeve (185)

*Anchialos Gamma. PERIOD II
(114-115)

Anchialos Delta. PERIOD I,
PHASE 2 (121-122)

Paleopyrga. Building. PERIOD
I, PHASE 2 (53)

*Nikopolis Alpha. PERIOD I,
PHASE 2 (156)

Pallandion. Basilica (72)

Hermione. Mosaic Fragment.
Restoration (66)

Hermione. Villa (67-68)

Mbozika. Basilica (37)

Longos. Basilica Alpha. PERIOD
I, PHASE 2 (198-202)

Anchialos Alpha (102-104)

Delphi. Mosaic Fragment (84)

ADDENDUM

Mosaic pavements for which only a general attribution
to the Roman, Roman or Early Christian, and Early Christian
periods is possible.

<u>Roman</u>

Nikopolis. Secular Building
  (168, 170)

<u>Roman or Early Christian</u>

Dentra. Mosaic Fragment (81)

Maroneia. Mosaic Fragment
  (227)

Nikopolis. Secular Building
  (169)

Saint George. Mosaic Pavement
  (149)

<u>Early Christian</u>

Ano Tithoria-Velitsa. Mosaic
  Fragment (86)

Maladrino. Mosaic Fragment
  (80)

Neokastron. Basilica (195)

Nikopolis. Secular Building
  (171)

Patras. Mosaic Fragment (36)

Philia. Basilica (141)

Platanidia. Christian Building
  (129)

Skripou. Basilica (79)

Strouni. Basilica (176)

<u>Early Christian</u>
<u>(Cont.)</u>

Veroia-Vergina. Mosaic
  Pavement (194)

Ziaka. Mosaic Pavement (184)

APPENDIX II

TABLE OF INSCRIPTIONS WITH TRANSLATIONS[1109]

Lavreotic Olympus: Basilica.

No. 35

For a vow, one whose name God knows has
beautified the (ΑΡΙΦΝΟΝ?)   p. 85

Patras: Mosaic Fragment.

No. 36

Reference to a deaconess Appiana.   p. 86

Old Corinth: Building.

No. 42

The Beautiful Seasons.   p. 100

Argos: Villa.

No. 55

January and February; March and April;
May and June; July and August; September
and October; November and December.   pp. 140-142

Hermione: Basilica.

No. 60

In the time of our most God-loving bishop,
Epiphanios, the building was restored.   p. 158

[1109]The location and catalogue number of fragments of
inscriptions which could not be translated are also cited.
I am indebted to Dr. Dennis Sullivan of the Dumbarton Oaks
Library for his invaluable assistance with the translations
which approximate the syntax and structure of the Greek.

c) Polygeros the most reverent reader
and Andromache the most God-loving
deaconess for their vow have done this
beautiful work.   pp. 296-297

No. 99

In the time of Didymos the mosaic was made.   p. 299

Nea Anchialos: Basilica Gamma.

No. 115

The teacher of Melissa, the wise and
spiritual Archbishop Paul, a well-known
man, fittingly offered this holy work,
suitable for God's church.   p. 349

Nea Anchialos: Basilica Delta.

No. 121

Demetrios, help (me).   p. 365

Demetrias: Basilica Alpha.

No. 130

Damokratia the illustrious.   p. 390

No. 136

Damokratia the illustrious.   p. 397

Trikkala: Basilica.

No. 142

For a vow, the archpriest Pardalas paved
the narthex.   p. 412

Nikopolis: Basilica Alpha.

No. 152

A house flashing forth God's grace hither
and thither he built and adorned and gave
all splendor, Dometios, widely known archpriest of faultless priests, best of all,
great light of all the fatherland.   pp. 439-440

No. 153

A stone flashing forth God's grace hither and
thither from the foundations he finished and
all splendor gave Dometios widely known archpriest of faultless priests, great light of
all the fatherland; the very gate of the Lord.
Let just men enter.   p. 444

No. 154

Here you see the famous and boundless ocean
Containing in its midst the earth
Bearing round about in the skillful images of
   art everything that breathes and creeps
The foundation of Dometios, the greathearted
   archpriest.[1112]   p. 453

No. 155

a) Ophellyras; Hermes   p. 455

b)   p. 459

No. 156

Dometios the first built the revered church,
the present Dometios of Nikopolis, being
successor of the former and of his episcopate,
by the power of Christ beautified all the
atrium. Happy, indeed, in youth as a pupil of
the former (shepherd [?]) each giving thanks
for the protection of the martyr Demetrios.   p. 464

Nikopolis: Basilica Beta.

No. 161

. . . the most holy archbishop Alkison
constructed the entire building from the
foundations.   p. 488

Nikopolis: Secular Building.

No. 168

In the time of Georgios, the advocate.   pp. 510-511

[1112]Translation by Kitzinger, Mosaics at Nikopolis,
p. 101.

INDEX OF SITES

LIST OF PRINCIPAL ABBREVIATIONS

AA	Archäologischer Anzeiger
AAA	Archaiologika Analekta ex Athēnōn
AB	The Art Bulletin
ABME	Archeion tōn Byzantinōn Mnēmeiōn tēs Hellados
ArchEph	Archaiologikē Ephēmeris
AJA	American Journal of Archaeology
BCH	Bulletin de Correspondence Hellénique: Chronique des Fouilles
BSA	British School at Athens. Annual
BSR	British School of Archaeology at Rome. Papers
CA	Cahiers Archéologiques
CIG	Corpus Inscriptionum Graecarum
DCAH	Deltion tēs Christianikēs Archaiologikēs Hetaireias
Deltion	Archaiologikon Deltion
DOP	Dumbarton Oaks Papers
EEBS	Epetēris Hetaireias Byzantinōn Spoudōn
Hoddinott, Early Byzantine Churches	R. F. Hoddinott, Early Byzantine Churches in Macedonia and Southern Serbia, London, 1963
JHS, Supplement	Journal of Hellenic Studies. Supplement
JOAI, Beiblatt	Jahreshefte des oesterreichischen archäologischen Instituts, Beiblatt
JRS	Journal of Roman Studies
Judeich, Topographie	W. Judeich, Topographie von Athens, München, 1931
Kautzsch, Kapitellstudien	R. Kautzsch, Kapitellstudien, Berlin, 1936

Kitzinger, Mosaic Pavements in the Greek East — E. Kitzinger, "Mosaic Pavements in the Greek East and the Question of a 'Renaissance' under Justinian," Actes du VIe congrès internationale d'etudes byzantines, 2, 1948 (Paris, 1951), pp. 209-223

————, Mosaics at Nikopolis — ————, "Studies on Late Antique and Early Byzantine Floor Mosaics, I: Mosaics at Nikopolis," DOP, 6 (1951), pp. 83-125

————, Mosaics in the Greek East — ————, "Mosaics in the Greek East from Constantine to Justinian," La mosaïque Gréco-Romaine, Paris, 1965

Krautheimer, Tripartite Transept — R. Krautheimer, "S. Pietro in Vincoli and the Tripartite Transept in the Early Christian Basilica," Proceedings of the American Philosophical Society, 84 (1941), pp. 353-429

————, Architecture — ————, Early Christian and Byzantine Architecture, Baltimore, 1965

————, Studies — ————, Studies in Early Christian, Medieval, and Renaissance Art. The Transept in the Early Christian Basilica, pp. 59-69, trans. by Alfred Frazer, New York, 1969

MAAR — Memoires of the American Academy in Rome

Orlandos, Xylostegos basilike — A. K. Orlandos, Hē xylostegos palaiochristianikē basilikē tēs mesogeianikēs lekanēs, Athens, 1952-1957

————, Hē metakinēsis tou diakonikou — ————, "Hē apo tou narthēkos pros to hieron metakinēsis tou diakonikou eis tas hellenistikas basilikas," DCAH, 4 (1964-65), pp. 353-372

PraktAkAth — Praktika tēs Akademias Athēnōn

Praktika — Praktika tēs en Athēnais Archaiologikēs Hetaireias

RA — Revue Archéologique

RAC — Rivista di Archeologia Cristiana

RBK   Reallexikon für Byzantinischen Kunst

Soteriou, Evretērion   G. A. Soteriou, Evretērion tōn mnēmeiōn tēs Hellados, I, 1. Mesaiōnika mnēmia Attikēs, Athens, 1927

_____, Palaio-christianikai basilikai   _____, "Hai palaiochristianikai basilikai tēs Hellados, ArchEph, 1929, pp. 21-254

Sodini, Catalogue   J-P. Sodini, "Mosaïques paléo-chrétiennes de Grèce," BCH, 94 (1970), pp. 699-755

_____, Compléments   _____, "Mosaïques paléochrétiennes de Grèce: Compléments," BCH, 95 (1971), pp. 581-584

To Ergon   To Ergon tēs Archaiologikēs Hetaireias

SELECTED BIBLIOGRAPHY

Åkerström-Hougen, G. "The Calendar and Hunting Mosaics of the Villa of the Falconer in Argos. A Study in Early Byzantine Iconography." Acta Instituti Atheniensis Regni Sueciae, Series in 4°, 23, 1974.

Alexander, M. A., M. Ennaifer, J. Gretzinger, G. P. R. Metraux, and M. Spiro. Corpus des mosaïques de Tunisie. Utique: Fascicule 1, Insulae I-II-III. Tunis: n.p., 1973.

Arvanitopoulos, A. "Ekthesis tōn pepragmenōn," Praktika, 1916, p. 31.

_____. "Anaskaphai kai erevnai en thessalea," Praktika, 1916, p. 166.

Babić, G. Les chapelles annexes des égleses byzantines: fonction liturgique et programmes iconographiques. Paris: Bibliotheque des Cahiers Archeologiques, III, 1969.

_____. "North Chapel of the Quatrefoil Church at Ockred and its Mosaic Floor." Recueil des travaux de l'institut d'études byzantines, 12 (1970), pp. 263-275.

Barnsley, S. H. The Architectural Association Sketchbook, New Series, 9, 5. London: n.p., 1889.

Becatti, G, E. Fabbricotti, A. Gallina, P. Saronio, F. R. Serra, and M. P. Tambella. Mosaici Antichi in Italia. Regione settima. Baccano: Villa Romana. Rome: Instituto poligrafico dello stato, Libreria, 1970.

Bérard, V. "Tégée et la Tégéatide. Géographie et topographie," BCH, 16 (1892), pp. 528-549.

_____. "Tégée et la Tégéatide. Les quatre tribus-la ville." BCH, 17 (1893), pp. 1-24.

The main archaeological reports are listed but secondary notices appearing in the Archäologischer Anzeiger, Bulletin de Correspondance Hellénique, and the Journal of Hellenic Studies are only cited in the text.

Bettini, S. _La pittura bizantina_. Parte II: I mosaici.
Florence: Novissima enciclopedia monografica illustrata,
1939.

Bianchi Bandinelli, R. _Rome: The Late Empire_. Trans. by
Peter Green. New York: George Braziller, 1971.

Blake, M. E. "The Pavements of the Roman Buildings of the
Republic and Early Empire," _MAAR_, 8 (1930, pp. 7-159.

Blanchard, M., J. Christophe, J. P. Darmon, H. Lavagne,
R. Prudhomme, and H. Stern. _Répertoire graphique du_
décor géométrique dans la mosaïque graphique. Bulletin
de l'association internationale pour l'etude de la
mosaïque antique, fourth fascicule. Paris, 1973.

Boëthius, A. and J. B. Ward Perkins. _Etruscan and Roman_
Architecture, The Pelican History of Art, England,
1970.

Brown, B. R. _Ptolemaic Painting and Mosaics and the_
Alexandrian Style. Cambridge, Mass.: Archaeological
Institute of America, 1957.

Bulletin d'information de l'association internationale pour
l'etude de la mosaïque antique. Fascicules 1-3, 5,
1968-1973.

Chatzē, A. Ch. "Eis Nikopoleōs epigraphas," _ArchEph_, 1918,
pp. 28-33.

Chatzidakis, E. "Anaskaphē en Athēnais kata tēn basilikēn
tou Ilissou," _Praktika_, 1948, pp. 69-80.

_____. "Remarques sur la basilique de l'Ilissos," _CA_,
5 (1951), pp. 61-74.

_____. "Note sur la basilique de l'Ilissos," _CA_, 6
(1952), p. 192.

_____. "Anaskaphē basilikēs Klavseiou Evrytanias,"
Praktika, 1958, pp. 58-63.

_____. "Anaskaphē basilikēs Klavseiou Evrytanias,"
Praktika, 1959, pp. 34-36.

_____. "Byzantinon kai christianikon mouseion. Basilikē
Klavseion Evrytanias," _Deltion_, 21 (1966), B1:
Chronika, p. 19.

_____. "Byzantinon kai Christianikon mouseion. Psiphidoton Byzantinou mouseion," Deltion, 22 (1967), B1: Chronika, p. 18.

Dakares, S. I. "Nomos Prevezēs: Haghios Georgios," Deltion, 19 (1964), B3: Chronika, p. 309.

_____. "Nomos Iōanninōn," Deltion, 19 (1964), B3: Chronika, p. 313.

Dontas, G. "Eideseis ek tēs A' archaiologikēs periphereias," AAA, 3, 2(1970), pp. 169-170.

_____. "Bibliothēkē Hadrianou," Deltion, 25 (1970), B1: Chronika, pp. 28-29.

Drosoyianni, Ph. A. "Basilike Longou," Deltion, 18 (1963), B2: Chronika, pp. 251-252.

_____. "Archaia Corinthos," Deltion, 22 (1967), B1: Chronika, p. 222.

Duliére, C. Corpus des mosaïques de Tunisie. Fascicule 2. Les mosaïques in situ en dehors des Insulae I-II-III. Tunis: n.p., 1974.

Dyggve, E. "Les traditions cultuelles de Delphes et l'église Chrétienne: quelques notes sur ΔΕΛΦΟΙ ΧΡΙCΤΙΑΝΙΚΟΙ," CA, 3 (1948), pp. 9-28.

Foucart, M. P. "Mémoire sur les ruins et l'histoire de Delphes," Archives des missions scientifiques, second series, 10 (1865), pp. 1-230.

Frantz, A. "Herculius in Athens: Pagan or Christian?" Acts of the VIIth International Congress of Christian Archaeology, Trier, 1965, pp. 527-530.

_____. "From Paganism to Christianity in the Temples of Athens," DOP, 19 (1965), pp. 187-205.

_____. "Honors to a Librarian," Hesperia, 35 (1966), pp. 377-380.

Ginouvés, R. "Mosaïques de la maison Kolivinou," BCH, 80 (1956), pp. 396-398.

_____. "La mosaïque des mois à Argos," BCH, 81 (1957), pp. 216-268.

Goffinet, E. "L'église Saint-Georges à Delphes," BCH, 86 (1962), pp. 242-260.

Gonzenbach, V. von. Die römischen Mosaiken der Schweiz. Basel: Birkhäuser, 1961.

Grabar, A. "Recherche sur les sources Juivres de l'art paléochrétien," CA, 12 (1962), pp. 115-152.

Grossi-Gondi, F. "Una basilica cristiana a Nicopolis in Epiro," Nuovo bullettino di archeologia cristiana, 23 (1917), pp. 121-127.

Grumel, V. Traité d'études byzantines. Vol. 1: La chronologie. Paris: Presses universitaires de France, 1958.

Les guides bleus-Grèce. Paris: Librarie Hachette, 1953.

Hanfmann, G. M. A. The Seasons Sarcophagus at Dumbarton Oaks. Cambridge, Mass.: Harvard University Press, 1957.

Hawthorne, J. "Cenchreai, Port of Corinth," Archaeology, 18 (1965), pp. 191-200.

Hinks, R. P. Catalogue of the Greek, Etruscan and Roman Paintings and Mosaics in the British Museum. London: British Museum, 1933.

Hoddinott, R. F. Early Byzantine Churches in Macedonia and Southern Serbia. London: MacMillan and Co., 1963.

Jameson, V. B. and M. H. "An Archaeological and Topographical Survey of the Hermionid," Papers of the American School of Classical Studies at Athens, June, 1950.

Jerphanion, G. de. "L'ambon de Salonique, l'arc de Galère et l'ambon de Thèbes," Atti della Pontificia Accademia Romana di archeologia, serie 3, memorie 3 (1932-33), pp. 107-132.

Judeich, W. Topographie von Athens. München: C. H. Beck, 1931.

Karageorghis, V. "Chronique des fouilles à Chypre en 1970,"
BCH, 95 (1971), pp. 335-432.

Karusos, C. "Eine Kirche bei Maladrino in W. Lokris,"
Praktika tēs Christianikēs archaeologikēs hetaireias,
4 (1936-38), pp. 50-52.

Kautzsch, R. Kapitellstudien. Berlin: W. deGruyter, 1936.

Kavvadias, P. "Peri tōn kata to etos 1888 anaskaphōn,"
Praktika, 1889, pp. 8-18.

_____. "Anaskaphē Epidaurou," Praktika, 1916, pp. 39-41.

_____. "Anaskaphai en Epidaurō," ArchEph, 1918, pp. 172-195.

Keramopoulos, A. D. "Anaskaphē en Aixōnē Attikēs,"
Praktika, 1919, pp. 32-46.

Khatchatrian, A. Les baptistères paléochrétiennes.
Paris: Imprimerie nationale, 1962.

Kitzinger, E. "A Survey of the Christian Town of Stobi,"
DOP, 3 (1946), pp. 79-162.

_____. "Mosaic Pavements in the Greek East and the
Question of a 'Renaissance' under Justinian," Actes du
VIe congrès internationale d'études byzantines, 2,
1948 (Paris, 1951), pp. 209-223.

_____. "Studies on Late Antique and Early Byzantine
Floor Mosaics, I: Mosaics at Nikopolis," DOP, 6 (1951),
pp. 83-125.

_____. "Mosaics in the Greek East from Constantine to
Justinian," La mosaïque Gréco-Romaine. Paris: Centre
national de la recherche scientifique, 1965.

_____. "World Map and Fortune's Wheel: A Medieval Mosaic
Floor in Turin," Proceedings of the American Philosophical Society, 117, No. 5 (1973), pp. 344-373.

Kotzia, N. Ch. "Anaskaphai tēs basilikēs tou Lavreōtikou
Olympou," Praktika, 1952, pp. 92-128.

Koumanoudes, J. A. "Secretary's Report," Praktika, 1873-74,
pp. 33-77.

_____. "Oikodomēma romaikōn chronōn en Athēnais kai
epigraphai ex avtou," ArchEph, 1888, cols. 199-200.

Kounoupiotou, E. "Anaskaphē agrou Stathopoulou eis
    Paleōpyrga Argous," Deltion, 24 (1969), B1: Chronika,
    pp. 164-165.

Kourkoutidou, E. "Basilikē Platanidiōn Volou," Deltion,
    22 (1967), B2: Chronika, p. 317.

_____. "Mesaiōnika mnēmeia Thessalias: Basilikē Theotokou,"
    Deltion, 23 (1968), B2: Chronika, p. 275.

Kraus, T. "Autour d'un corpus international des mosaïques
    Gréco-Romaines," La mosaïque Gréco-Romaine. Paris:
    Centre national de la recherche scientifique, 1965.

Krautheimer, R. "S. Pietro in Vincoli and the Tripartite
    Transept in the Early Christian Basilika," Proceedings
    of the American Philosophical Society, 84 (1941),
    pp. 353-429.

_____. Early Christian and Byzantine Architecture.
    Pelican History of Art, Baltimore, 1965.

_____. Studies in Early Christian, Medieval, and
    Renaissance Art. New York: New York University
    Press, 1969.

Lavin, I. "Field Notes: Hermione," Dumbarton Oaks, Center
    for Byzantine Studies.

_____. "Field Notes: Late Roman Villa at Athens,"
    Dumbarton Oaks, Center for Byzantine Studies.

_____. "Field Notes: Nea Anchialos, Basilicas Alpha,
    Gamma, Delta," Dumbarton Oaks, Center for Byzantine
    Studies.

_____. "Field Notes: Pallandion," Dumbarton Oaks, Center
    for Byzantine Studies.

_____. "The Hunting Mosaics of Antioch and their Sources,"
    DOP, 17 (1963), pp. 181-286.

Lazarides, D. I. "Anaskaphai kai erevnai eis Amphipolin,"
    Praktika, 1959, pp. 42-46.

_____. "Anaskaphai kai allai ergasiae eis A. Makedonian,"
    Deltion, 16 (1960), B: Chronika, pp. 217-221.

_____. "Anaskaphai kai erevnai eis Amphipolin," Praktika,
    1964, pp. 35-40.

Lazarides, P. "Ano Tithorēa-Velitsa," Deltion, 16 (1960),
    B: Chronika, pp. 164-165.

_____. "Mesaiōnika mnēmeia: Hypati; Delphoi," Deltion,
    16 (1960), B: Chronika, pp. 165-167.

_____. "Mesaiōnika Phōkidos: Mariolata," Deltion,
    18 (1963), B1: Chronika, p. 132.

_____. "Dōris Parnassidos: Palaiochristianikē basilikē
    Mariolatas," Deltion, 19 (1964), B2: Chronika, pp.
    237-238.

_____. "Anaskaphikai erevnai entos tēs poleōs tōn Thērōn:
    Oikopedon Stamatiou Stamatē, Hodos Ploutarchou,
    arith. 6," Deltion, 20 (1965), B2: Chronika, p. 237.

_____. "Thevai: Oikopedon St. Stamatē," Deltion, 20
    (1965), B2: Chronika, pp. 253-255.

_____. "Klavseion," Deltion, 21 (1966), B2: Chronika,
    pp. 238, 274-275.

_____. "Mesaiōnika Phōkidos-Phthiōtidos: Daphnousia-
    Haghios Konstantinos," Deltion, 21 (1966), B1:
    Chronika, p. 246.

_____. "Mesaiōnika mnēmeia Phthiōtidos kai Phōkidos,"
    Deltion, 22 (1967), B1: Chronika, pp. 292-293.

_____. "Anaskaphai Neas Anchialou," Praktika, 1969,
    pp. 16-25.

_____. "Byzantina kai mesaiōnika mnēmeia Thessalias,"
    Deltion, 25 (1970), B2: Chronika, pp. 286-288.

_____. "Anaskaphai Neas Anchialou," Praktika, 1970,
    pp. 37-49.

_____. "Anaskaphai Neas Anchialou," Praktika, 1971,
    pp. 20-42.

Leake, W. M. Travels in Northern Greece. London:
    J. Rodwell, 1835.

Lemerle, P. Philippes et la Macédoine orientale à l'époque
    chrétienne et byzantine: recherches d'histoire et
    d'archéologie. Paris: Boccard, 1945.

_____. "Bulletin archéologique, 4 (1952-1954)," Revue
    des études byzantines, 13 (1955), pp. 224-225.

672

Leon, V. "Funfter vorläufiger Bericht über die Grabungen in Alt-Elis," JOAI, 47 (1964-1965), Beiblatt, pp. 74-102.

Levi, D. "The Allegories of the Months in Classical Art," AB, 23 (1941), pp. 251-291.

_____. Antioch Mosaic Pavements, 2 vols. Princeton University Press, 1947.

Libertini, G. "Scani in Arcadia," Annuario della regia scuolo archeologica di Atene della Missioni Italiane in orienta, n.s., 1-2 (1939-40), pp. 225-230.

_____. "Chiese bizantine nell'area dell'antica Pallanzio," Actes du IXe congrès international d'études byzantines, 1953, Hellenika, 9 (1955), pp. 250-254.

Makaronas, Ch. I. "Anaskaphē para tēn limnēn tēs Doïranēs," Makedonika, 1 (1940), pp. 227-235.

Marinos. Vita Procli. Edited by J. Boissonade. Leipsig, 1814; reprint ed., Amsterdam: Hakkert, 1966.

Marricone Matini, M. L. Mosaici Antichi in Italia. Regione prima. Roma: Reg. X Palatium. Rome: Instituto poligrafico dello stato, Libreria, 1967.

_____. Mosaici Antichi in Italia. Studi monografico, 1. Pavimenti di signino repubblicani di Roma e dintorni. Rome: Instituto poligrafico dello stato, Libreria, 1971.

Matton, L and R. Athènes et ses monuments. Athens: Institut français d'Athènes, 1963.

Mbarla, C. N. "Anaskaphē Kephalou Ambrakikou," Praktika, 1965, pp. 78-84.

_____. "Anaskaphē Kephalou Ambrakikou," Praktika, 1966, pp. 95-102.

_____. "Anaskaphē Kephalou Ambrakikou," Praktika, 1967, pp. 28-32.

_____. "Anaskaphē Kephalou Ambrakikou," Praktika, 1968, pp. 16-23.

_____. "Anaskaphē Kephalou Ambrakikou," Praktika, 1970, pp. 90-95.

Meer, F. van der and C. Mohrmann. Atlas of the Early
Christian World. Translated by Mary F. Hedlund and
H. H. Rowley. London: Thomas Nelson and Sons, 1958.

Megaw, A. H. S. "The Skripou Screen," BSA, 61 (1966),
pp. 1-32.

Meliades, J. "Anaskaphai notiōs tēs Akropoleōs," Praktika,
1955, pp. 36-52.

Michaelides, M. "Haghia Paraskevē Kozanēs," Deltion, 20
(1965), B3: Chronika, p. 475.

_____. "Palaiochristianikē basilikē Longou Edessēs,"
Deltion, 20 (1965), B3: Chronika, pp. 475-476.

_____. "Anaskaphikai erevnai: Thessalonikē," Deltion,
22 (1967), B2: Chronika, pp. 437-438.

_____. "Palaiochristianikē Edessa: Anaskaphē basilikēs A,"
Deltion, 23 (1968), Meletai, pp. 195-222.

_____. "Byzantinon kai christianikon mouseion: Amphessa,"
Deltion, 25 (1970), B1: Chronika, p. 18.

Mihăescu, H. "Les éléments latins des 'Tactica-strategica'
de Maurice-Urbicius et leur écho en néo-grec, I,"
Revue des études sud-est européennes, 6 (1968), pp.
481-498.

_____. "Les éléments latins des 'Tactica-strategica'
de Maurice-Urbicus et leur écho en néo-grec, II, III,"
Revue des études sud-est européennes, 7 (1969),
pp. 155-166, 267-280.

Mustakidos, B. A. "Episcopoi katalogoi," EEBS, 12 (1936),
pp. 139-238.

Nikolaides, G. "Hē ex ekatōn eikosi kionōn Phrygiou lithou
oikodomē en Hadrianos Athēnois kataskevasato," ArchEph,
3 (1888), pp. 58-66.

Nikonanos, N. "Kalambaka: Naos Koimēseōs Theotokou,"
Deltion, 25 (1970), B2: Chronika, pp. 290-291.

"Nouvelles archéologiques," RA, 2 (1873), pp. 50-54.

Orlandos, A. K. "Hē palaiochristianikē basilikē tōn Daphnousiōn tēs Lokridos," PraktAkAth, 4 (1929), pp. 226-231.

_____. "Une basilique paléochrétienne en Locride," Byzantion, 5 (1929/30), pp. 207-228.

_____. "Hē basilikē tēs Anthēdonos," ABME, 3 (1937), pp. 172-174.

_____. "Haghios Athanasios tēs Lokridos," ABME, 3 (1937), pp. 185-186.

_____ and G. A. Soteriou. "Anaskaphai Nikopoleōs," Praktika, 1937, pp. 78-83.

_____. Hē xylostegos palaiochristianikē basilikē tēs mesoyeianikēs lekanēs. 3 vols. Athens: Archaeologikēs Hetaireias, 1952-1957.

_____. "Les monuments paléochrétiennes découverts ou étud_es en Grèce de 1938 à 1954," Actes du Ve congrès d'archéologie chrétienne, Aix-en-Provence, 1954 (Vatican, 1957), pp. 109-116.

_____. "Anaskaphē tēs basilikēs tōn Aigosthēnōn," Praktika, 1954, pp. 129-142.

_____. "Aigosthēna," To Ergon, 1954, pp. 16-18.

_____. "Christianikai thēvai tēs Thessalias (N. Anchialos)," To Ergon, 1954, pp. 19-21.

_____. "Athēnai. Notiōs tēs Akropoleōs," To Ergon, 1955, pp. 5-11.

_____. "Hermione," To Ergon, 1955, pp. 76-83.

_____. "Psēphidoton dapedon ek basilikēs tōn Trikkalōn," ABME, 8 (1955-56), pp. 117-125.

_____. "Anaskaphē Nikopoleōs," Praktika, 1956, pp. 149-153.

_____. "Nikopolis," To Ergon, 1956, pp. 60-63.

_____. "Hermionē," To Ergon, 1956, pp. 76-80.

_____. "Evrytania. Klavseion," To Ergon, 1958, pp. 63-68.

_____. "Anaskaphē basilikēs delta Nikopoleōs," Praktika, 1959, pp. 90-97.

675

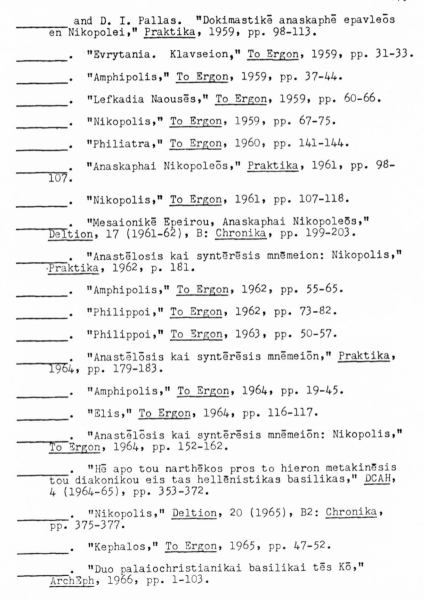

_____ and D. I. Pallas. "Dokimastikē anaskaphē epavleōs en Nikopolei," Praktika, 1959, pp. 98-113.

_____. "Evrytania. Klavseion," To Ergon, 1959, pp. 31-33.

_____. "Amphipolis," To Ergon, 1959, pp. 37-44.

_____. "Lefkadia Naousēs," To Ergon, 1959, pp. 60-66.

_____. "Nikopolis," To Ergon, 1959, pp. 67-75.

_____. "Philiatra," To Ergon, 1960, pp. 141-144.

_____. "Anaskaphai Nikopoleōs," Praktika, 1961, pp. 98-107.

_____. "Nikopolis," To Ergon, 1961, pp. 107-118.

_____. "Mesaionikē Epeirou, Anaskaphai Nikopoleōs," Deltion, 17 (1961-62), B: Chronika, pp. 199-203.

_____. "Anastēlosis kai syntērēsis mnēmeion: Nikopolis," ·Praktika, 1962, p. 181.

_____. "Amphipolis," To Ergon, 1962, pp. 55-65.

_____. "Philippoi," To Ergon, 1962, pp. 73-82.

_____. "Philippoi," To Ergon, 1963, pp. 50-57.

_____. "Anastēlōsis kai syntērēsis mnēmeiōn," Praktika, 1964, pp. 179-183.

_____. "Amphipolis," To Ergon, 1964, pp. 19-45.

_____. "Elis," To Ergon, 1964, pp. 116-117.

_____. "Anastēlōsis kai syntērēsis mnēmeiōn: Nikopolis," To Ergon, 1964, pp. 152-162.

_____. "Hē apo tou narthēkos pros to hieron metakinēsis tou diakonikou eis tas hellēnistikas basilikas," DCAH, 4 (1964-65), pp. 353-372.

_____. "Nikopolis," Deltion, 20 (1965), B2: Chronika, pp. 375-377.

_____. "Kephalos," To Ergon, 1965, pp. 47-52.

_____. "Duo palaiochristianikai basilikai tēs Kō," ArchЭph, 1966, pp. 1-103.

_____. "Anastēlosis kai syntērēsis mnēmeiōn," Praktika, 1966, pp. 194-199.

_____. "Amphipolis," To Ergon, 1966, pp. 25-42.

_____. "Philippoi," To Ergon, 1966, pp. 42-54.

_____. "Kephalos," To Ergon, 1966, pp. 87-92.

_____. "Anastēlōsis kai syntērēsis mnēmeiōn," To Ergon, 1966, pp. 171-178.

_____. "Ēlis," To Ergon, 1967, pp. 17-18.

_____. "Kephalos," To Ergon, 1967, pp. 24-27.

_____. "Philippoi," To Ergon, 1967, pp. 43-54.

_____. "Amphipolis," To Ergon, 1967, pp. 54-65.

_____. "Kephalos," To Ergon, 1968, pp. 21-27.

_____. "Nikopolis," To Ergon, 1968, p. 148.

_____. "Phthiōtides Thēvai. Nea Anchialos," To Ergon, 1969, pp. 11-19.

_____. "Amphipolis," To Ergon, 1969, pp. 49-68.

_____. "Phthiōtides Thēvai. Nea Anchialos," To Ergon, 1970, pp. 22-33.

_____. "Amphipolis," To Ergon, 1970, pp. 33-48.

_____. "Kephalos," To Ergon, 1970, pp. 82-87.

_____. "Anastēlōsis, stereōsis, kai syntērēsis Archaiōn," To Ergon, 1970, pp. 192-203.

_____. "Phthiōtides Thēvai. Nea Anchialos," To Ergon, 1971, pp. 27-36.

_____. "Amphipolis," To Ergon, 1971, pp. 36-53.

_____. "Maroneia," To Ergon, 1971, pp. 97-98.

_____. "Phthiōtides Thēvai. Nea Anchialos," To Ergon, 1972, pp. 13-18, 131.

_____. "Amphipolis," To Ergon, 1972, pp. 18-26.

_____. "Palaiochristianika kai byzantina mnēmeia Tegeas-Nykliou: Hē basilikē tou Thyrsou," ABME, 12 (1973), pp. 12-81.

Pallas, D. I. "Scoperte archeologiche in Grecia degli anni 1956-1958," RAC, 35 (1959), pp. 187-223.

_____. "Anaskaphē para ta Philiatra," Deltion, 16 (1960), B: Chronika, pp. 122-125.

_____. "Anaskaphē eis Philiatra tēs triphylias," Praktika, 1960, pp. 177-194.

Paraskevaides, M. "Archaeological Research in Greek Macedonia and Thrace, 1912-1962," Balkan Studies, 3, 2 (1962), pp. 443-458.

Parlasca, K. Die römischen Mosaiken in Deutschland. Berlin: Wide Gruyter, 1959.

Pelekanides, St. "Die Symbolik der frühchristlichen Fussbodenmosaiken Greichenlands," Zeitschrift für Kirchengeschichte, 3, 10, 59 (1940), pp. 114-124.

_____. "Hē exō tōn teichōn palaiochristianikē basilikē tōn Philippōn," ArchEph, 1955, pp. 114-179.

_____. "Veroia," Deltion, 16 (1960), B: Chronika, p. 225.

_____. "Dytikē Makedonia: Periphereia Kozanēs," Deltion, 16 (1960), B: Chronika, pp. 226-229.

_____. "Veroia," Deltion, 17 (1961-62), B: Chronika, p. 257.

_____. "Anaskaphē oktagōnou Philippōn," Praktika, 1962, pp. 169-178.

_____. "Anaskaphē oktagōnou Philippōn," Praktika, 1963, pp. 87-88.

_____. "Anaskaphikai erevnai eis tēn christianikēn basilikēn Diou Pierias," Deltion, 19 (1964), B3: Chronika, p. 384.

_____. "Philippoi," Deltion, 19 (1964), B3: Chronika, p. 385.

_____. "Anaskaphikai erevnai eis Dion Pierias," Deltion, 20 (1965), B3: Chronika, pp. 477-479.

_____. "Anaskaphē basilikēs Diou," Deltion, 21 (1966), B2: Chronika, pp. 371-376.

_____. "Anaskaphai oktagōnou Philippōn," Praktika, 1966, pp. 47-58.

_____. "Excavations at Philippi," Balkan Studies, 8, No. 1 (1967), pp. 123-126.

_____. "Anaskaphai oktagōnou Philippōn," Praktika, 1967, pp. 70-82.

Pelekides, E. "Anaskaphai en Amphipolei," Praktika, 1920, pp. 80-94.

"Peri tōn en tē Akropolei anaskaphōn," Praktika, 1885, pp. 13-35.

Petsas, Ph. "Anaskaphē oikopedōn en Veroia," Deltion, 20 (1965), B3: Chronika, pp. 423-433.

_____. "Makedonia: Ziaka Grevenōn," Deltion, 20 (1965), B3: Chronika, p. 438.

_____. "Anaskaphai en Veroia," Deltion, 21 (1966), B2: Chronika, pp. 350-352.

_____. "Chronika archaiologika: Tsiphliki," Makedonika, 7 (1966-67), p. 339.

Pharaklas, N, B. Philippake, and S. Symeonoglou. "Phthiōtis: Ag. Kōnstantinos," Deltion, 22 (1967), B1: Chronika, p. 246.

Philadelpheus, A. "Anaskaphai en Nikopolei," Praktika, 1913, pp. 83-112.

_____. "Anaskaphai Nikopoleōs," Praktika, 1914, pp. 219-220.

_____. "Hai en Nikopolei anaskaphai," Praktika, 1915, pp. 31-33.

_____. "Anaskaphai Nikopoleōs," ArchEph, 1916, pp. 33-54, 65-73, 121-122.

_____. "Anaskaphai Nikopoleōs," Praktika, 1916, pp. 32-33, 49-54.

_____. "Anaskaphai Nikopoleōs," ArchEph, 1917, pp. 48-72.

_____. "Nikopoleōs anaskaphai," ArchEph, 1918, pp. 34-41.

_____. "Hai en Nikopolei anaskaphai en etei 1918," Praktika, 1918, pp. 16-18.

_____. "Mouseion Prevezēs," ArchEph, 1922, pp. 69-79.

_____. "Anaskaphai Nikopoleōs," Praktika, 1922-23, pp. 8, 40-44.

_____. "Anaskaphai Nikopoleōs, Christianika mnēmeia," DCAH, 4, 2 (1924), pp. 121-127.

_____. "Anaskaphai Nikopoleōs," Praktika, 1924, pp. 72-74, 108-115.

_____. "Anaskaphai Nikopoleōs," Praktika, 1926, pp. 127-130.

_____. "Anaskaphai Nikopoleōs: Christianika mnēmeia," DCAH, 4, 2 (1927), pp. 46-61.

_____. "Anaskaphai Nikopoleōs," Praktika, 1929, pp. 11-12, 42-44.

_____. Les fouilles de Nicopolis, 1913-26. Athens: Imprimerie Vidori, 1933.

Platon, N. "Christianikē epigraphē ek Tanagras," ArchEph, 2 (1937), pp. 665-667.

Protonotariou-Deïlakē, E. "Anaskaphē eis thesin Paleōpyrga Argous," Deltion, 19 (1964), B1: Chronika, pp. 126-127.

Ramage, E. S. "Excavations at Kenchreai, 1963," AJA, 68 (1964), pp. 198-199.

_____. "Excavations at Kenchreai," AJA, 69 (1965), pp. 173-174.

Reallexikon für bizantinischen kunst. s.v. "Epiros," by D. I. Pallas.

Robinson, D. M. Excavations at Olynthus, II. Baltimore: Johns Hopkins University Press, 1930.

Robinson, H. S. "Notebook 346: 22-23 August, 1966, pp. 165-167 and 26 August, 1966, pp. 178-179," Archives of the Corinth Excavations.

Rolfe, J. C. "Discoveries at Anthedon in 1889," AJA, 6 (1890), pp. 96-107.

Romiopoulou, A., and S. Touratsoglou. "Veroia," Deltion 25 (1970), B2: Chronika, pp. 379-385.

Rousopoulos, A. S. "Athēnai," ArchEph, 2 (1862), cols. 150-155.

Scranton, R. L. and E. S. Ramage. "Investigations at Kenchreai, 1963," Hesperia, 33 (1964), pp. 134-146.

_____. "Investigations at Corinthian Kenchreai," Hesperia, 36 (1967), pp. 124-186.

Sisson, M. A. "The Stoa of Hadrian," BSR, 11 (1929), pp. 50-72.

Skias, A. N. "Peri tēs en tē koitē toys Ilisou anaskaphēs, Praktika, 1893, pp. 124-125.

Smith, C. "Panathenaic Amphorae," BSA, 3 (1896-7), pp. 182-200.

Sodini, J-P. "Mosaïques paléochrétiennes de Grèce," BCH, 94 (1970), pp. 699-755.

_____. "Mosaïques paléochrétiennes de Grèce: Compléments," BCH, 95 (1971), pp. 581-584.

Soteriou, G. A. To psēphidoton dapedon tou en anevrethentos naou en Nikopolei tēs epeirou. Reprint from Hieros syndesmos, December, 1-15, 1915, nos. 255-256.

_____. "Palaia christianikē basilikē tou Illisou," ArchEph, 1917, p. 106.

_____. "Palaia christianikē basilikē tou Ilissou," ArchEph, 1919, pp. 1-31.

_____. "Anaskaphai Nikopoleōs," Praktika, 1926, pp. 122-127.

_____. Evretērion tōn mnēmeiōn tēs Hellados, I, 1. Mesaiōnika mnēmeia Attikēs. Athens: Archaiologiko tmēma tou ypourgeiou paideias kai thrēskevmatōn, 1927.

_____. "Hai Christianikai Thēvai tēs Thessalias," ArchEph, 1929, pp. 6-247.

_____. "Hai palaiochristianikai basilikai tēs Hellados," ArchEph, 1929, pp. 21-254.

_____. "Byzantina mnēmeia tēs Thessaleas, 13 kai 14 aiōnas," EEBS, 6 (1929), pp. 291-315.

_____. "Hē basilikē tēs Epidavrou," PraktAkAth, 4 (1929), pp. 91-95.

_____ and A. K. Orlandos. "Anaskaphai Nikopoleōs," Praktika, 1929, pp. 22-24, 83-86.

_____ and A. K. Orlandos. "Anaskaphai Nikopoleōs," Praktika, 1930, pp. 21-23, 79-80.

_____. "Anaskaphai Neas Anchialou," Praktika, 1930, pp. 30-35.

_____. "Anaskaphai Neas Anchialou," Praktika, 1931, pp. 37-43.

_____. "Peri tōn en N. Anchialō anaskaphōn," Praktika, 1933, pp. 46-57.

_____. "Anaskaphai Neas Anchialou," Praktika, 1934, pp. 58-66.

_____. "Anaskaphai Neas Anchialou," Praktika, 1935, pp. 52-69.

_____. "Anaskaphai Neas Anchialou," Praktika, 1936, pp. 57-67.

_____ and A. K. Orlandos. "Anaskaphai Nikopolēos," Praktika, 1937, pp. 15, 78-81.

_____. "Die altchristlichen Basiliken Griechenlands," Atti del IV congresso internazionale di archeologia Cristiana, 1, 1930 (Vatican, 1940), pp. 355-380.

_____. "Anaskaphai Nikopoleōs," Praktika, 1938, pp. 16-18, 112-117.

_____. "Anaskaphai en Nea Anchialō," Praktika, 1940, pp. 18-22.

_____. "Anaskaphai en Nea Anchialō," Praktika, 1954, pp. 143-152.

Soteriades, G. "Anaskaphē Diou Makedonias," Praktika, 1928, pp. 59-97.

_____. Anaskaphē Diou Makedonias," Praktika, 1929, pp. 69-82.

_____. "Hē basilikē tou Diou," Actes du IIIne congrès international d'études byzantines, 1930, pp. 251-252.

_____. "Anaskaphai Diou Makedonias," Praktika, 1930, pp. 36-51.

_____. "Anaskaphai Diou Makedonias," Praktika, 1931, pp. 43-55.

Stählen, F., E. Meyer and A. Heidner. Pegasai und Demetrias. Berlin-Leipzig: W. deGruyter, 1934.

Stassinopoulos, E. "Scoperte archeologiche in Grecia," RAC, 32 (1956), pp. 94-99.

Stern, H. Le calendrier de 354. Paris: Librarie orientaliste Paul Geuthner, 1953.

_____. Recueilgénéral des mosaïques de la Gaule. Xe Supplément à Gallia. 2 vols. 1957-1967.

Stikas, E. G. "Anaskaphē paleochristianikēs basilikēs Hermionēs," Praktika, 1955, pp. 236-240.

_____. "Synechisis anaskaphēs tēs basilikēs Hermionēs," Praktika, 1956, pp. 179-184.

_____. "Anaskaphai Lefkadiōn Naousēs," Praktika, 1959, pp. 85-89.

_____. "Anaskaphē basilikēs Gamma Amphipoleōs," Praktika, 1962, pp. 42-46.

_____. "Anaskaphē palaiochristianikēs basilikēs Gamma Amphipoleōs," Praktika, 1964, pp. 41-43.

_____. "Anaskaphai Amphipoleōs," Praktika, 1966, pp. 39-46.

_____. "Anaskaphē palaiochristianikōn basilikōn Amphipoleōs," Praktika, 1967, pp. 83-88.

_____. "Anaskaphē palaiochristianikōn basilikōn Amphipoleōs," Praktika, 1969, pp. 54-58.

_____. "Anaskaphē palaiochristianikōn basilikōn Amphipoleōs," Praktika, 1970, pp. 50-54.

_____. "Anaskaphē palaiochristianikōn basilikōn Amphipoleōs," Praktika, 1971, pp. 43-49.

Theoharis, D. R. "Anaskaphai kai erevnai en Trikkē," Praktika, 1958, pp. 64-80.

_____. "Thessalia: Demetrias," Deltion, 18 (1963), B1: Chronika, pp. 139-140.

_____. "Hieron Athēnas en Philia Karditsēs," Deltion, 19 (1964), B2: Chronika, pp. 244-245.

_____. "Platanidia Magnēsias," Deltion, 21 (1966), B2: Chronika, pp. 254-255.

Thompson, H. A. "Buildings on the West Side of the Agora," Hesperia, 6 (1937), pp. 172-217.

_____. "Activities in the Athenian Agora," Hesperia, 28 (1959), pp. 91-108.

_____. "Athenian Twilight: A.D. 267-600," JRS, 49 (1959), pp. 66-67.

_____ and R. E. Wycherly. The Athenian Agora. Vol. 14: The Agora of Athens. New Jersey: Princeton University Press, 1972.

Threpsiades, I. C. "Romaikē epavlis en Athēnais," Polemōn, 5, part 3 (1954), pp. 126-141.

Thrēskevtikē kai ēthikē enkyklopaideia. S.v. "Aimilianos," by P. I. Basileiou.

Thrēskevtikē kai ēthikē enkyklopaideia. S.v. "Christianikai Athēnai," by J. Travlos.

Tomasevic. "Mosaic Pavements in the Narthex of the Large Basilica," Herachea-3 (1967), pp. 9-62.

Travlos, J. Poleodomikē exelixis tōn Athēnōn. Athens, 1950.

_____. "Anaskaphai en tē bibliothēkē tou Hadrianou," Praktika, 1950, pp. 41-63.

Tsimas, G. and P. Papahadjidakis, ed. Monuments de Nikopolis. 3 vols. Monuments de l'art byzantin en Grèce series. Athens: n.p., n.d.

Ussing, L. "Bulletino dell'instituto di correspondenza archaeologica per l'anno 1846," Archäologische institut des Deutschen Reichs, 1846, p. 178.

Volgraff, W. "Nieuwe Opgravingen te Argos," Mededelingen der Koninklijke Akademie van Wetenschappen, 72, B, 3 (1931), pp. 71-124.

Wace, A. J. B. and J. B. Droop. "Excavations in Thessaly: The Byzantine Church," BSA, 13 (1906-07), pp. 309-327.

Webster, J. C. The Labors of the Months in Antique and Medieval Art. Princeton: Monographs in Art and Archaeology, 21, 1938.

Williams, C. K. "Excavations at Corinth," Deltion, 22 (1967), B1: Chronika, pp. 184-185.

Xyngopoulos, A. "Palaiochristianikē basilikē tou Voskochoriou," Makedonika, 1 (1940), pp. 8-23.

_____. "Hai duo psēphidotai prosōgraphiae tēs Nikopoleōs," Deltion, 22 (1967), Meletai, pp. 14-20.

Yialouris, N. Ph. "Anaskaphai Ēlidos," Praktika, 1964, pp. 136-139.

_____. "Anaskaphai archaias Ēlidos," Deltion, 20 (1965), B2: Chronika, p. 211.

_____. "Anaskaphai Ēlidos," Praktika, 1967, pp. 20-21.

Zilliacus, H. Zum Kampf der Weltsprachen im östromischen Reich. Helsingfors: Mercators Tryckeri Antiebolag, 1935.